T0298020

THE QUEST FOR ARTIFICIAL INTELLIGENCE

Artificial intelligence (AI) is a field within computer science that is attempting to build enhanced intelligence into computer systems. This book traces the history of the subject, from the early dreams of eighteenth-century (and earlier) pioneers to the more successful work of today's AI engineers. AI is becoming more and more a part of everyone's life. The technology is already embedded in face-recognizing cameras, speech-recognition software, Internet search engines, and health-care robots, among other applications. The book's many diagrams and easy-to-understand descriptions of AI programs will help the casual reader gain an understanding of how these and other AI systems actually work. Its thorough (but unobtrusive) end-of-chapter notes containing citations to important source materials will be of great use to AI scholars and researchers. This book promises to be the definitive history of a field that has captivated the imaginations of scientists, philosophers, and writers for centuries.

Nils J. Nilsson, Kumagai Professor of Engineering (Emeritus) in the Department of Computer Science at Stanford University, received his doctorate in electrical engineering from Stanford in 1958. He then spent twenty-three years at the Artificial Intelligence Center of SRI International working on statistical and neural-network approaches to pattern recognition, co-inventing the A^* heuristic search algorithm and the STRIPS automatic planning system, directing work on the integrated mobile robot Shakey, and collaborating in the development of the PROSPECTOR expert system. Professor Nilsson returned to Stanford in 1985 and served as Chairman of the Department of Computer Science, taught courses in artificial intelligence and machine learning, and conducted research on flexible robots. He has served on the editorial boards of *Artificial Intelligence* and the *Journal of Artificial Intelligence Research*. He was also an area editor for the *Journal of the Association for Computing Machinery*. He is a past president and Fellow of the Association for the Advancement of Artificial Intelligence and a Fellow of the American Association for the Advancement of Science. Professor Nilsson has also published five textbooks on artificial intelligence.

The Quest for
Artificial Intelligence

A History of Ideas and Achievements

Nils J. Nilsson
Stanford University

CAMBRIDGE
UNIVERSITY PRESS

CAMBRIDGE
UNIVERSITY PRESS

32 Avenue of the Americas, New York NY 10013-2473, USA

Cambridge University Press is part of the University of Cambridge.

It furthers the University's mission by disseminating knowledge in the pursuit of
education, learning and research at the highest international levels of excellence.

www.cambridge.org
Information on this title: www.cambridge.org/9780521122931

First published 2010

A catalogue record for this publication is available from the British Library

Library of Congress Cataloguing in Publication data

Nilsson, Nils J., 1933–
The quest for artificial intelligence : a history of ideas and achievements / Nils J. Nilsson.
    p.   cm.
Includes bibliographical references and index.
ISBN 978-0-521-11639-8 (hardback) – ISBN 978-0-521-12293-1 (pbk.)
1. Artificial intelligence – History.   2. Artificial intelligence – Philosophy.   I. Title.
Q335.N55   2010
006.3 – dc22   2009022604

ISBN 978-0-521-11639-8 Hardback
ISBN 978-0-521-12293-1 Paperback

For Grace McConnell Abbott,
my wife and best friend

Contents

vii

Preface

Artificial intelligence (AI) may lack an agreed-upon definition, but someone writing about its history must have some kind of definition in mind. For me, artificial intelligence is that activity devoted to making machines intelligent, and intelligence is that quality that enables an entity to function appropriately and with foresight in its environment. According to that definition, lots of things – humans, animals, and some machines – are intelligent. Machines, such as "smart cameras," and many animals are at the primitive end of the extended continuum along which entities with various degrees of intelligence are arrayed. At the other end are humans, who are able to reason, achieve goals, understand and generate language, perceive and respond to sensory inputs, prove mathematical theorems, play challenging games, synthesize and summarize information, create art and music, and even write histories. Because "functioning appropriately and with foresight" requires so many different capabilities, depending on the environment, we actually have several continua of intelligences with no particularly sharp discontinuities in any of them. For these reasons, I take a rather generous view of what constitutes AI. That means that my history of the subject will, at times, include some control engineering, some electrical engineering, some statistics, some linguistics, some logic, and some computer science.

There have been other histories of AI, but time marches on, as has AI, so a new history needs to be written. I have participated in the quest for artificial intelligence for fifty years – all of my professional life and nearly all of the life of the field. I thought it would be a good idea for an "insider" to try to tell the story of this quest from its beginnings up to the present time.

I have three kinds of readers in mind. One is the intelligent lay reader interested in scientific topics who might be curious about what AI is all about. Another group, perhaps overlapping the first, consists of those in technical or professional fields who, for one reason or another, need to know about AI and would benefit from a complete picture of the field – where it has been, where it is now, and where it might be going. To both of these groups, I promise no complicated mathematics or computer jargon, lots of diagrams, and my best efforts to provide clear explanations of how AI programs and techniques work. (I also include several photographs of AI people. The selection of these is somewhat random and doesn't necessarily indicate prominence in the field.)

A third group consists of AI researchers, students, and teachers who would benefit from knowing more about the things AI has tried, what has and hasn't worked, and good sources for historical and other information. Knowing the history of a field is important for those engaged in it. For one thing, many ideas that were explored and then abandoned might now be viable because of improved technological capabilities. For that group, I include extensive end-of-chapter notes citing source material. The general reader will miss nothing by ignoring these notes. The main text itself mentions Web sites where interesting films, demonstrations, and background can be found. (If links to these sites become broken, readers may still be able to access them using the "Wayback Machine" at http://www.archive.org.)

The book follows a roughly chronological approach, with some backing and filling. My story may have left out some actors and events, but I hope it is reasonably representative of AI's main ideas, controversies, successes, and limitations. I focus more on the ideas and their realizations than on the personalities involved. I believe that to appreciate AI's history, one has to understand, at least in lay terms, something about how AI programs actually work.

If AI is about endowing machines with intelligence, what counts as a machine? To many people, a machine is a rather stolid thing. The word evokes images of gears grinding, steam hissing, and steel parts clanking. Nowadays, however, the computer has greatly expanded our notion of what a machine can be. A functioning computer system contains both hardware and software, and we frequently think of the software itself as a "machine." For example, we refer to "chess-playing machines" and "machines that learn," when we actually mean the programs that are doing those things. The distinction between hardware and software has become somewhat blurred because most modern computers have some of their programs built right into their hardware circuitry.

Whatever abilities and knowledge I bring to the writing of this book stem from the support of many people, institutions, and funding agencies. First, my parents, Walter Alfred Nilsson (1907–1991) and Pauline Glerum Nilsson (1910–1998), launched me into life. They provided the right mixture of disdain for mediocrity and excuses (Walter), kind care (Pauline), and praise and encouragement (both). Stanford University is literally and figuratively my *alma mater* (Latin for "nourishing mother"). First as a student and later as a faculty member (now emeritus), I have continued to learn and to benefit from colleagues throughout the university and especially from students. SRI International (once called the Stanford Research Institute) provided a home with colleagues who helped me to learn about and to "do" AI. I make special acknowledgment to the late Charles A. Rosen, who persuaded me in 1961 to join his Learning Machines Group there. The Defense Advanced Research Projects Agency (DARPA), the Office of Naval Research (ONR), the Air Force Office of Scientific Research (AFOSR), the U.S. Geological Survey (USGS), the National Science Foundation (NSF), and the National Aeronautics and Space Administration (NASA) all supported various research efforts I was part of during the last fifty years. I owe thanks to all.

To the many people who have helped me with the actual research and writing for this book, including anonymous and not-so-anonymous reviewers, please accept my sincere appreciation together with my apologies for not naming all of you personally in this preface. There are too many of you to list, and I am afraid I might forget to mention someone who might have made some brief but important suggestions. Anyway, you know who you are. You are many of the people whom I mention in the book itself. However, I do want to mention Heather Bergman of Cambridge University Press; Mykel Kochenderfer, a former student; and Wolfgang Bibel of the Darmstadt University of Technology. They all read carefully early versions of the entire manuscript and made many helpful suggestions. (Mykel also provided invaluable advice about the LaTeX typesetting program.)

I also want to thank the people who invented, developed, and now manage the Internet, the World Wide Web, and the search engines that helped me in writing this book. Using Stanford's various site licenses, I could locate and access journal articles, archives, and other material without leaving my desk. (I did have to visit libraries to find books. Publishers, please allow copyrighted books, especially those whose sales have now diminished, to be scanned and made available online. Join the twenty-first century!)

Finally, and most importantly, I thank my wife, Grace, who cheerfully and patiently urged me on.

In 1982, the late Allen Newell, one of the founders of AI, wrote, "Ultimately, we will get real histories of Artificial Intelligence . . . , written with as much objectivity as the historians of science can muster. That time is certainly not yet."

Perhaps it is now.

Part I

Beginnings

1

Dreams and Dreamers

T HE QUEST FOR ARTIFICIAL INTELLIGENCE (AI) BEGINS WITH DREAMS – AS ALL quests do. People have long imagined machines with human abilities – automata that move and devices that reason. Human-like machines are described in many stories and are pictured in sculptures, paintings, and drawings.

You may be familiar with many of these, but let me mention a few. The *Iliad of Homer* talks about self-propelled chairs called "tripods" and golden "attendants" constructed by Hephaistos, the lame blacksmith god, to help him get around.[1][*] And, in the ancient Greek myth as retold by Ovid in his *Metamorphoses*, Pygmalian sculpts an ivory statue of a beautiful maiden, Galatea, which Venus brings to life:[2]

The girl felt the kisses he gave, blushed, and, raising her bashful eyes to the light, saw both her lover and the sky.

The ancient Greek philosopher Aristotle (384–322 BCE) dreamed of automation also, but apparently he thought it an impossible fantasy – thus making slavery necessary if people were to enjoy leisure. In his *The Politics*, he wrote[3]

For suppose that every tool we had could perform its task, either at our bidding or itself perceiving the need, and if – like . . . the tripods of Hephaestus, of which the poet [that is, Homer] says that "self-moved they enter the assembly of gods" – shuttles in a loom could fly to and fro and a plucker [the tool used to pluck the strings] play a lyre of their own accord, then master craftsmen would have no need of servants nor masters of slaves.

Aristotle might have been surprised to see a Jacquard loom weave of itself or a player piano doing its own playing.

Pursuing his own visionary dreams, Ramon Llull (circa 1235–1316), a Catalan mystic and poet, produced a set of paper discs called the *Ars Magna* (Great Art), which was intended, among other things, as a debating tool for winning Muslims to the Christian faith through logic and reason. (See Fig. 1.1.) One of his disc assemblies was inscribed with some of the attributes of God, namely goodness, greatness, eternity, power, wisdom, will, virtue, truth, and glory. Rotating the discs appropriately was supposed to produce answers to various theological questions.[4]

Ahead of his time with inventions (as usual), Leonardo Da Vinci sketched designs for a humanoid robot in the form of a medieval knight around the year 1495. (See Fig. 1.2.) No one knows whether Leonardo or contemporaries tried to build his

---

[*] So as not to distract the general reader unnecessarily, numbered notes containing citations to source materials appear at the end of each chapter. Each of these is followed by the number of the page where the reference to the note occurred.

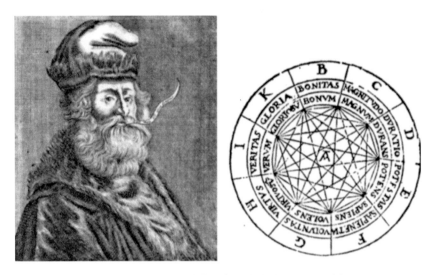

Figure 1.1. Ramon Llull (left) and his *Ars Magna* (right).

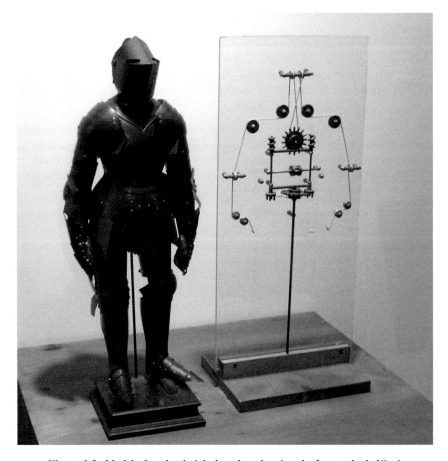

Figure 1.2. Model of a robot knight based on drawings by Leonardo da Vinci.

design. Leonardo's knight was supposed to be able to sit up, move its arms and head, and open its jaw.[5]

The Talmud talks about holy persons creating artificial creatures called "golems." These, like Adam, were usually created from earth. There are stories about rabbis using golems as servants. Like the Sorcerer's Apprentice, golems were sometimes difficult to control.

In 1651, Thomas Hobbes (1588–1679) published his book *Leviathan* about the social contract and the ideal state. In the introduction, Hobbes seems to say that it might be possible to build an "artificial animal."[6]

For seeing life is but a motion of limbs, the beginning whereof is in some principal part within, why may we not say that all automata (engines that move themselves by springs and wheels as doth a watch) have an artificial life? For what is the heart, but a spring; and the nerves, but so many strings; and the joints, but so many wheels, giving motion to the whole body . . .

Perhaps for this reason, the science historian George Dyson refers to Hobbes as the "patriarch of artificial intelligence."[7]

In addition to fictional artifices, several people constructed actual automata that moved in startlingly lifelike ways.[8] The most sophisticated of these was the mechanical duck designed and built by the French inventor and engineer, Jacques de Vaucanson (1709–1782). In 1738, Vaucanson displayed his masterpiece, which could quack, flap its wings, paddle, drink water, and eat and "digest" grain.

As Vaucanson himself put it,[9]

My second Machine, or *Automaton*, is a *Duck*, in which I represent the Mechanism of the Intestines which are employed in the Operations of Eating, Drinking, and Digestion: Wherein the Working of all the Parts necessary for those Actions is exactly imitated. The Duck stretches out its Neck to take Corn out of your Hand; it swallows it, digests it, and discharges it digested by the usual Passage.

There is controversy about whether or not the material "excreted" by the duck came from the corn it swallowed. One of the automates-anciens Web sites[10] claims that "In restoring Vaucanson's duck in 1844, the magician Robert-Houdin discovered that 'The discharge was prepared in advance: a sort of gruel composed of green-coloured bread crumb . . . '."

Leaving digestion aside, Vaucanson's duck was a remarkable piece of engineering. He was quite aware of that himself. He wrote[11]

I believe that Persons of Skill and Attention, will see how difficult it has been to make so many different moving Parts in this small *Automaton*; as for Example, to make it rise upon its Legs, and throw its Neck to the Right and Left. They will find the different Changes of the *Fulchrum's* or Centers of Motion: they will also see that what sometimes is a Center of Motion for a moveable Part, another Time becomes moveable on that Part, which Part then becomes fix'd. In a Word, they will be sensible of a prodigious Number of Mechanical Combinations.

This Machine, when once wound up, performs all its different Operations without being touch'd any more.

I forgot to tell you, that the *Duck* drinks, plays in the Water with his Bill, and makes a gurgling Noise like a real living *Duck*. In short, I have endeavor'd to make it imitate all the Actions of the living Animal, which I have consider'd very attentively.

Figure 1.3. Frédéric Vidoni's ANAS, inspired by Vaucanson's duck. (Photograph courtesy of Frédéric Vidoni.)

Unfortunately, only copies of the duck exist. The original was burned in a museum in Nijninovgorod, Russia around 1879. You can watch, ANAS, a modern version, performing at http://www.automates-anciens.com/video_1/duck_automaton_vaucanson_500.wmv.[12] It is on exhibit in the Museum of Automatons in Grenoble and was designed and built in 1998 by Frédéric Vidoni, a creator in mechanical arts. (See Fig. 1.3.)

Figure 1.4. A scene from a New York production of *R.U.R.*

Returning now to fictional automata, I'll first mention the mechanical, life-sized doll, Olympia, which sings and dances in Act I of *Les Contes d'Hoffmann* (*The Tales of Hoffmann*) by Jacques Offenbach (1819–1880). In the opera, Hoffmann, a poet, falls in love with Olympia, only to be crestfallen (and embarrassed) when she is smashed to pieces by the disgruntled Coppélius.

A play called *R.U.R.* (*Rossum's Universal Robots*) was published by Karel Čapek (pronounced CHAH pek), a Czech author and playwright, in 1920. (See Fig. 1.4.) Čapek is credited with coining the word "robot," which in Czech means "forced labor" or "drudgery." (A "robotnik" is a peasant or serf.)

The play opened in Prague in January 1921. The Robots (always capitalized in the play) are mass-produced at the island factory of Rossum's Universal Robots using a chemical substitute for protoplasm. According to a Web site describing the play,[13] "Robots remember everything, and think of nothing new. According to Domin [the factory director] 'They'd make fine university professors.' . . . once in a while, a Robot will throw down his work and start gnashing his teeth. The human managers treat such an event as evidence of a product defect, but Helena [who wants to liberate the Robots] prefers to interpret it as a sign of the emerging soul."

I won't reveal the ending except to say that Čapek did not look eagerly on technology. He believed that work is an essential element of human life. Writing in a 1935 newspaper column (in the third person, which was his habit) he said: "With outright horror, he refuses any responsibility for the thought that machines could take the place of people, or that anything like life, love, or rebellion could ever awaken in their cogwheels. He would regard this somber vision as an unforgivable overvaluation of mechanics or as a severe insult to life."[14]

There is an interesting story, written by Čapek himself, about how he came to use the word robot in his play. While the idea for the play "was still warm he rushed immediately to his brother Josef, the painter, who was standing before an easel and painting away. . . . 'I don't know what to call these artificial workers,' he said. 'I could call them Labori, but that strikes me as a bit bookish.' 'Then call them Robots,' the painter muttered, brush in mouth, and went on painting."[15]

The science fiction (and science fact) writer Isaac Asimov wrote many stories about robots. His first collection, *I, Robot*, consists of nine stories about "positronic" robots.[16] Because he was tired of science fiction stories in which robots (such as Frankenstein's creation) were destructive, Asimov's robots had "Three Laws of Robotics" hard-wired into their positronic brains. The three laws were the following:

FIRST LAW: A robot may not injure a human being, or, through inaction, allow a human being to come to harm.

SECOND LAW: A robot must obey the orders given it by human beings except where such orders would conflict with the First Law.

THIRD LAW: A robot must protect its own existence as long as such protection does not conflict with the First or Second Law.

Asimov later added a "zeroth" law, designed to protect humanity's interest:[17]

ZEROTH LAW: A robot may not injure humanity, or, through inaction, allow humanity to come to harm.

The quest for artificial intelligence, quixotic or not, begins with dreams like these. But to turn dreams into reality requires usable clues about how to proceed. Fortunately, there were many such clues, as we shall see.

Notes

1. *The Iliad of Homer*, translated by Richmond Lattimore, p. 386, Chicago: The University of Chicago Press, 1951. (Paperback edition, 1961.) [3]
2. Ovid, *Metamorphoses*, Book X, pp. 243–297, from an English translation, circa 1850. See http://www.pygmalion.ws/stories/ovid2.htm. [3]
3. Aristotle, *The Politics*, p. 65, translated by T. A. Sinclair, London: Penguin Books, 1981. [3]
4. See E. Allison Peers, *Fool of Love: The Life of Ramon Lull*, London: S. C. M. Press, Ltd., 1946. [3]
5. See http://en.wikipedia.org/wiki/Leonardo's_robot. [5]
6. Thomas Hobbes, *The Leviathon*, paperback edition, Kessinger Publishing, 2004. [5]
7. George B. Dyson, *Darwin Among the Machines: The Evolution of Global Intelligence*, p. 7, Helix Books, 1997. [5]
8. For a Web site devoted to automata and music boxes, see http://www.automates-anciens.com/english_version/frames/english_frames.htm. [5]
9. From Jacques de Vaucanson, "An account of the mechanism of an automaton, or image playing on the German-flute: as it was presented in a memoire, to the gentlemen of the Royal-Academy of Sciences at Paris. By M. Vaucanson . . . Together with a description of an artificial duck. . . . " Translated out of the French original, by J. T. Desaguliers, London, 1742. Available at http://e3.uci.edu/clients/bjbecker/NatureandArtifice/week5d.html. [5]
10. http://www.automates-anciens.com/english_version/automatons-music-boxes/vaucanson-automatons-androids.php. [5]
11. de Vaucanson, Jacques, *op. cit.* [5]

12. I thank Prof. Barbara Becker of the University of California at Irvine for telling me about the automates-anciens.com Web sites. [6]

13. http://jerz.setonhill.edu/resources/RUR/index.html. [7]

14. For a translation of the column entitled "The Author of Robots Defends Himself," see http://www.depauw.edu/sfs/documents/capek68.htm. [7]

15. From one of a group of Web sites about Čapek, http://Capek.misto.cz/english/robot.html. See also http://Capek.misto.cz/english/. [8]

16. The Isaac Asimov Web site, http://www.asimovonline.com/, claims that "Asimov did not come up with the title, but rather his publisher 'appropriated' the title from a short story by Eando Binder that was published in 1939." [8]

17. See http://www.asimovonline.com/asimov_FAQ.html#series13 for information about the history of these four laws. [8]

2

Clues

CLUES ABOUT WHAT MIGHT BE NEEDED TO MAKE MACHINES INTELLIGENT ARE scattered abundantly throughout philosophy, logic, biology, psychology, statistics, and engineering. With gradually increasing intensity, people set about to exploit clues from these areas in their separate quests to automate some aspects of intelligence. I begin my story by describing some of these clues and how they inspired some of the first achievements in artificial intelligence.

2.1 From Philosophy and Logic

Although people had reasoned logically for millennia, it was the Greek philosopher Aristotle who first tried to analyze and codify the process. Aristotle identified a type of reasoning he called the *syllogism* "... in which, certain things being stated, something other than what is stated follows of necessity from their being so."[1]

Here is a famous example of one kind of syllogism:[2]

1. *All humans are mortal.* (stated)
2. *All Greeks are humans.* (stated)
3. *All Greeks are mortal.* (result)

The beauty (and importance for AI) of Aristotle's contribution has to do with the *form* of the syllogism. We aren't restricted to talking about humans, Greeks, or mortality. We could just as well be talking about something else – a result made obvious if we rewrite the syllogism using arbitrary symbols in the place of *humans*, *Greeks*, and *mortal*. Rewriting in this way would produce

1. *All B's are A.* (stated)
2. *All C's are B's.* (stated)
3. *All C's are A.* (result)

One can substitute anything one likes for *A*, *B*, and *C*. For example, *all athletes are healthy* and *all soccer players are athletes*, and therefore *all soccer players are healthy*, and so on. (Of course, the "result" won't necessarily be true unless the things "stated" are. Garbage in, garbage out!)

Aristotle's logic provides two clues to how one might automate reasoning. First, patterns of reasoning, such as syllogisms, can be economically represented as *forms* or *templates*. These use generic symbols, which can stand for many different concrete instances. Because they can stand for anything, the symbols themselves are unimportant.

Figure 2.1. Gottfried Leibniz.

Second, after the general symbols are replaced by ones pertaining to a specific problem, one only has to "turn the crank" to get an answer. The use of general symbols and similar kinds of crank-turning are at the heart of all modern AI reasoning programs.

In more modern times, Gottfried Wilhelm Leibniz (1646–1716; Fig. 2.1) was among the first to think about logical reasoning. Leibniz was a German philosopher, mathematician, and logician who, among other things, co-invented the calculus. (He had lots of arguments with Isaac Newton about that.) But more importantly for our story, he wanted to mechanize reasoning. Leibniz wrote[3]

It is unworthy of excellent men to lose hours like slaves in the labor of calculation which could safely be regulated to anyone else if machines were used.

and

For if praise is given to the men who have determined the number of regular solids . . . how much better will it be to bring under mathematical laws human reasoning, which is the most excellent and useful thing we have.

Leibniz conceived of and attempted to design a language in which all human knowledge could be formulated – even philosophical and metaphysical knowledge. He speculated that the propositions that constitute knowledge could be built from a smaller number of primitive ones – just as all words can be built from letters in an alphabetic language. His *lingua characteristica* or universal language would consist of these primitive propositions, which would comprise an *alphabet for human thoughts*.

The alphabet would serve as the basis for automatic reasoning. His idea was that if the items in the alphabet were represented by numbers, then a complex proposition could be obtained from its primitive constituents by multiplying the corresponding numbers together. Further arithmetic operations could then be used to determine whether or not the complex proposition was true or false. This whole process was to be accomplished by a *calculus ratiocinator* (calculus of reasoning). Then, when

Figure 2.2. The Stanhope Square Demonstrator, 1805. (Photograph courtesy of Science Museum/SSPL.)

philosophers disagreed over some problem they could say, "*calculemus*" ("let us calculate"). They would first pose the problem in the *lingua characteristica* and then solve it by "turning the crank" on the *calculus ratiocinator*.

The main problem in applying this idea was discovering the components of the primitive "alphabet." However, Leibniz's work provided important additional clues to how reasoning might be mechanized: Invent an alphabet of simple symbols and the means for combining them into more complex expressions.

Toward the end of the eighteenth century and the beginning of the nineteenth, a British scientist and politician, Charles Stanhope (Third Earl of Stanhope), built and experimented with devices for solving simple problems in logic and probability. (See Fig. 2.2.) One version of his "box" had slots on the sides into which a person could push colored slides. From a window on the top, one could view slides that were appropriately positioned to represent a specific problem. Today, we would say that Stanhope's box was a kind of analog computer.

The book *Computing Before Computers* gives an example of its operation:[4]

To solve a numerical syllogism, for example:

> *Eight of ten A's are B's; Four of ten A's are C's;*
> *Therefore, at least two B's are C's.*

Stanhope would push the red slide (representing B) eight units across the window (representing A) and the gray slide (representing C) four units from the opposite direction. The two units that the slides overlapped represented the minimum number of B's that were also C's.
. . .

In a similar way, the Demonstrator could be used to solve a traditional syllogism like:

> *No M is A; All B is M; Therefore, No B is A.*

Stanhope was rather secretive about his device and didn't want anyone to know what he was up to. As mentioned in *Computing Before Computers*, "The few friends and relatives who received his privately distributed account of the Demonstrator, *The Science of Reasoning Clearly Explained Upon New Principles* (1800), were advised

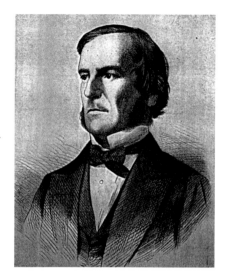

Figure 2.3. George Boole.

to remain silent lest 'some bastard imitation' precede his intended publication on the subject."

But no publication appeared until sixty years after Stanhope's death. Then, the Reverend Robert Harley gained access to Stanhope's notes and one of his boxes and published an article on what he called "The Stanhope Demonstrator."[5]

Contrasted with Llull's schemes and Leibniz's hopes, Stanhope built the first logic machine that actually worked – albeit on small problems. Perhaps his work raised confidence that logical reasoning could indeed be mechanized.

In 1854, the Englishman George Boole (1815–1864; Fig. 2.3) published a book with the title *An Investigation of the Laws of Thought on Which Are Founded the Mathematical Theories of Logic and Probabilities.*[6] Boole's purpose was (among other things) "to collect . . . some probable intimations concerning the nature and constitution of the human mind." Boole considered various logical principles of human reasoning and represented them in mathematical form. For example, his "Proposition IV" states ". . . *the principle of contradiction . . . affirms that it is impossible for any being to possess a quality, and at the same time not to possess it. . . .*" Boole then wrote this principle as an algebraic equation,

$$x(1 - x) = 0,$$

in which x represents "any class of objects," $(1 - x)$ represents the "contrary or supplementary class of objects," and 0 represents a class that "does not exist."

In Boolean algebra, an outgrowth of Boole's work, we would say that 0 represents *falsehood*, and 1 represents *truth*. Two of the fundamental operations in logic, namely OR and AND, are represented in Boolean algebra by the operations $+$ and $\times$, respectively. Thus, for example, to represent the statement "either p or q or both," we would write $p + q$. To represent the statement "p and q," we would write $p \times q$. Each of p and q could be true or false, so we would evaluate the value (truth or falsity) of $p + q$ and $p \times q$ by using definitions for how $+$ and $\times$ are used, namely,

$$1 + 0 = 1,$$
$$1 \times 0 = 0,$$
$$1 + 1 = 1,$$
$$1 \times 1 = 1,$$
$$0 + 0 = 0,$$

and

$$0 \times 0 = 0.$$

Boolean algebra plays an important role in the design of telephone switching circuits and computers. Although Boole probably could not have envisioned computers, he did realize the importance of his work. In a letter dated January 2, 1851, to George Thomson (later Lord Kelvin) he wrote[7]

I am now about to set seriously to work upon preparing for the press an account of my theory of Logic and Probabilities which in its present state I look upon as the most valuable if not the only valuable contribution that I have made or am likely to make to Science and the thing by which I would desire if at all to be remembered hereafter . . .

Boole's work showed that some kinds of logical reasoning could be performed by manipulating equations representing logical propositions – a very important clue about the mechanization of reasoning. An essentially equivalent, but not algebraic, system for manipulating and evaluating propositions is called the "propositional calculus" (often called "propositional logic"), which, as we shall see, plays a very important role in artificial intelligence. [Some claim that the Greek Stoic philospher Chrysippus (280–209 BCE) invented an early form of the propositional calculus.[8]]

One shortcoming of Boole's logical system, however, was that his propositions p, q, and so on were "atomic." They don't reveal any entities *internal* to propositions. For example, if we expressed the proposition "Jack is human" by p, and "Jack is mortal" by q, there is nothing in p or q to indicate that the Jack who is human is the very same Jack who is mortal. For that, we need, so to speak, "molecular expressions" that have internal elements.

Toward the end of the nineteenth century, the German mathematician, logician, and philosopher Friedrich Ludwig Gottlob Frege (1848–1925) invented a system in which propositions, along with their internal components, could be written down in a kind of graphical form. He called his language *Begriffsschrift*, which can be translated as "concept writing." For example, the statement "All persons are mortal" would have been written in *Begriffsschrift* something like the diagram in Fig. 2.4.[9]

Note that the illustration explicitly represents the x who is predicated to be a person and that it is the same x who is then claimed to be mortal. It's more convenient nowadays for us to represent this statement in the linear form $(\forall x)P(x) \supset M(x)$, whose English equivalent is "for all x, if x is a person, then x is mortal."

Frege's system was the forerunner of what we now call the "predicate calculus," another important system in artificial intelligence. It also foreshadows another

Figure 2.4. Expressing "All persons are mortal" in *Begriffsschrift*.

$$\overbrace{}^{x}\!\!\!\!\!\!\!\Big\lbrace\begin{matrix} M(x) \\ P(x) \end{matrix}$$

representational form used in present-day artificial intelligence: semantic networks. Frege's work provided yet more clues about how to mechanize reasoning processes. At last, sentences expressing information to be reasoned about could be written in unambiguous, symbolic form.

2.2 From Life Itself

In Proverbs 6:6–8, King Solomon says "Go to the ant, thou sluggard; consider her ways and be wise." Although his advice was meant to warn against slothfulness, it can just as appropriately enjoin us to seek clues from biology about how to build or improve artifacts.

Several aspects of "life" have, in fact, provided important clues about intelligence. Because it is the *brain* of an animal that is responsible for converting sensory information into action, it is to be expected that several good ideas can be found in the work of neurophysiologists and neuroanatomists who study brains and their fundamental components, neurons. Other ideas are provided by the work of psychologists who study (in various ways) intelligent behavior as it is actually happening. And because, after all, it is evolutionary processes that have produced intelligent life, those processes too provide important hints about how to proceed.

2.2.1 *Neurons and the Brain*

In the late nineteenth and early twentieth centuries, the "neuron doctrine" specified that living cells called "neurons" together with their interconnections were fundamental to what the brain does. One of the people responsible for this suggestion was the Spanish neuroanatomist Santiago Ramón y Cajal (1852–1934). Cajal (Fig. 2.5) and Camillo Golgi won the Nobel Prize in Physiology or Medicine in 1906 for their work on the structure of the nervous system.

A neuron is a living cell, and the human brain has about ten billion (10^{10}) of them. Although they come in different forms, typically they consist of a central part called a *soma* or *cell body*, incoming fibers called *dendrites*, and one or more outgoing fibers called *axons*. The axon of one neuron has projections called *terminal buttons* that come very close to one or more of the dendrites of other neurons. The gap between the terminal button of one neuron and a dendrite of another is called a *synapse*. The size of the gap is about 20 nanometers. Two neurons are illustrated schematically in Fig. 2.6.

Through electrochemical action, a neuron may send out a stream of pulses down its axon. When a pulse arrives at the synapse adjacent to a dendrite of another neuron, it may act to excite or to inhibit electrochemical activity of the other neuron across

Figure 2.5. Ramón y Cajal.

the synapse. Whether or not this second neuron then "fires" and sends out pulses of its own depends on how many and what kinds of pulses (excitatory or inhibitory) arrive at the synapses of its various incoming dendrites and on the efficiency of those synapses in transmitting electrochemical activity. It is estimated that there are over half a trillion synapses in the human brain. The neuron doctrine claims that the

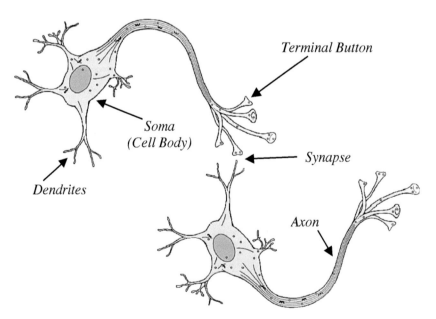

Figure 2.6. Two neurons. (Adapted from *Science*, Vol. 316, p. 1416, 8 June 2007. Used with permission.)

Figure 2.7. Warren McCulloch.

various activities of the brain, including perception and thinking, are the result of all of this neural activity.

In 1943, the American neurophysiologist Warren McCulloch (1899–1969; Fig. 2.7) and logician Walter Pitts (1923–1969) claimed that the neuron was, in essence, a "logic unit." In a famous and important paper they proposed simple models of neurons and showed that networks of these models could perform all possible computational operations.[10] The McCulloch–Pitts "neuron" was a mathematical abstraction with inputs and outputs (corresponding, roughly, to dendrites and axons, respectively). Each output can have the value 1 or 0. (To avoid confusing a McCulloch–Pitts neuron with a real neuron, I'll call the McCulloch–Pitts version, and others like it, a "neural element.") The neural elements can be connected together into networks such that the output of one neural element is an input to others and so on. Some neural elements are excitatory – their outputs contribute to "firing" any neural elements to which they are connected. Others are inhibitory – their outputs contribute to inhibiting the firing of neural elements to which they are connected. If the sum of the excitatory inputs less the sum of the inhibitory inputs impinging on a neural element is greater than a certain "threshold," that neural element fires, sending its output of 1 to all of the neural elements to which it is connected.

Some examples of networks proposed by McCullough and Pitts are shown in Fig. 2.8.

The Canadian neuropsychologist Donald O. Hebb (1904–1985) also believed that neurons in the brain were the basic units of thought. In an influential book,[11] Hebb suggested that "when an axon of cell A is near enough to excite B and repeatedly or persistently takes part in firing it, some growth process or metabolic change takes place in one or both cells such that A's efficiency, as one of the

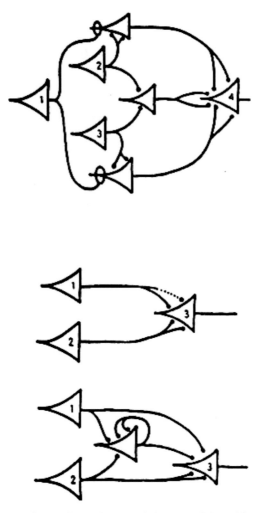

Figure 2.8. Networks of McCulloch–Pitts neural elements. (Adapted from Fig. 1 of Warren S. McCulloch and Walter Pitts, "A Logical Calculus of Ideas Immanent in Nervous Activity," *Bulletin of Mathematical Biophysics*, Vol. 5, pp. 115–133, 1943.)

cells firing B, is increased." Later, this so-called Hebb rule of change in neural "synaptic strength" was actually observed in experiments with living animals. (In 1965, the neurophysiologist Eric Kandel published results showing that simple forms of learning were associated with synaptic changes in the marine mollusk *Aplysia californica*. In 2000, Kandel shared the Nobel Prize in Physiology or Medicine "for their discoveries concerning signal transduction in the nervous system.")

Hebb also postulated that groups of neurons that tend to fire together formed what he called *cell assemblies*. Hebb thought that the phenomenon of "firing together" tended to persist in the brain and was the brain's way of representing the perceptual event that led to a cell-assembly's formation. Hebb said that "thinking" was the sequential activation of sets of cell assemblies.[12]

Figure 2.9. B. F. Skinner. (Courtesy of the B. F. Skinner Foundation.)

2.2.2 *Psychology and Cognitive Science*

Psychology is the science that studies mental processes and behavior. The word is derived from the Greek words *psyche*, meaning breath, spirit, or soul, and *logos*, meaning word. One might expect that such a science would have much to say of interest to those wanting to create intelligent artifacts. However, until the late nineteenth century, most psychological theorizing depended on the insights of philosophers, writers, and other astute observers of the human scene. (Shakespeare, Tolstoy, and other authors were no slouches when it came to understanding human behavior.)

Most people regard serious scientific study to have begun with the German Wilhelm Wundt (1832–1920) and the American William James (1842–1910).[13] Both established psychology labs in 1875 – Wundt in Leipzig and James at Harvard. According to C. George Boeree, who teaches the history of psychology at Shippens-burg University in Pennsylvania, "The method that Wundt developed is a sort of experimental introspection: The researcher was to carefully observe some simple event – one that could be measured as to quality, intensity, or duration – and record his responses to variations of those events." Although James is now regarded mainly as a philosopher, he is famous for his two-volume book *The Principles of Psychology*, published in 1873 and 1874.

Both Wundt and James attempted to say something about *how* the brain worked instead of merely cataloging its input–output behavior. The psychiatrist Sigmund Freud (1856–1939) went further, postulating internal components of the brain, namely, the *id*, the *ego*, and the *superego*, and how they interacted to affect behavior. He thought one could learn about these components through his unique style of guided introspection called *psychoanalysis*.

Attempting to make psychology more scientific and less dependent on subjective introspection, a number of psychologists, most famously B. F. Skinner (1904–1990; Fig. 2.9), began to concentrate solely on what could be objectively measured, namely, specific behavior in reaction to specific stimuli. The *behaviorists* argued that psychology should be a science of behavior, not of the mind. They rejected the idea

Figure 2.10. Noam Chomsky. (Photograph by Don J. Usner.)

of trying to identify internal mental states such as beliefs, intentions, desires, and goals.

This development might at first be regarded as a step backward for people wanting to get useful clues about the internal workings of the brain. In criticizing the statistically oriented theories arising from "behaviorism," Marvin Minsky wrote "Originally intended to avoid the need for 'meaning,' [these theories] manage finally only to avoid the possibility of explaining it."[14] Skinner's work did, however, provide the idea of a *reinforcing* stimulus – one that rewards recent behavior and tends to make it more likely to occur (under similar circumstances) in the future.

Reinforcement learning has become a popular strategy among AI researchers, although it does depend on internal states. Russell Kirsch (circa 1930–), a computer scientist at the U.S. National Bureau of Standards (now the National Institute for Standards and Technology, NIST), was one of the first to use it. He proposed how an "artificial animal" might use reinforcement to learn good moves in a game. In some 1954 seminar notes he wrote the following:[15] "The animal model notes, for each stimulus, what move the opponent next makes, . . . Then, the next time that same stimulus occurs, the animal duplicates the move of the opponent that followed the same stimulus previously. The more the opponent repeats the same move after any given stimulus, the more the animal model becomes 'conditioned' to that move."

Skinner believed that reinforcement learning could even be used to explain verbal behavior in humans. He set forth these ideas in his 1957 book *Verbal Behavior*,[16] claiming that the laboratory-based principles of selection by consequences can be extended to account for what people say, write, gesture, and think.

Arguing against Skinner's ideas about language the linguist Noam Chomsky (1928– ; Fig. 2.10), in a review[17] of Skinner's book, wrote that

careful study of this book (and of the research on which it draws) reveals, however, that [Skinner's] astonishing claims are far from justified . . . the insights that have been achieved in the laboratories of the reinforcement theorist, though quite genuine, can be applied to complex human behavior only in the most gross and superficial way, and that speculative attempts to discuss linguistic behavior in these terms alone omit from consideration factors of fundamental importance . . .

How, Chomsky seems to ask, can a person produce a potentially infinite variety of previously unheard and unspoken sentences having arbitrarily complex structure (as indeed they can do) through experience alone? These "factors of fundamental importance" that Skinner omits are, according to Chomsky, linguistic abilities that must be innate – not learned. He suggested that "human beings are somehow specially created to do this, with data-handling or 'hypothesis-formulating' ability of [as yet] unknown character and complexity." Chomsky claimed that all humans have at birth a "universal grammar" (or developmental mechanisms for creating one) that accounts for much of their ability to learn and use languages.[18]

Continuing the focus on internal mental processes and their limitations, the psychologist George A. Miller (1920–) analyzed the work of several experimenters and concluded that the "immediate memory" capacity of humans was approximately seven "chunks" of information.[19] In the introduction to his paper about this "magical number," Miller humorously notes "My problem is that I have been persecuted by an integer. For seven years this number has followed me around, has intruded in my most private data, and has assaulted me from the pages of our most public journals. This number assumes a variety of disguises, being sometimes a little larger and sometimes a little smaller than usual, but never changing so much as to be unrecognizable. The persistence with which this number plagues me is far more than a random accident." Importantly, he also claimed that "the span of immediate memory seems to be almost independent of the number of bits per chunk." That is, it doesn't matter what a chunk represents, be it a single digit in a phone number, a name of a person just mentioned, or a song title; we can apparently only hold seven of them (plus or minus two) in our immediate memory.

Miller's paper on "The Magical Number Seven," was given at a Symposium on Information Theory held from September 10 to 12, 1956, at MIT.[20] Chomsky presented an important paper there too. It was entitled "Three Models for the Description of Language," and in it he proposed a family of rules of syntax he called *phrase-structure grammars*.[21] It happens that two pioneers in AI research (of whom we'll hear a lot more later), Allen Newell (1927–1992), then a scientist at the Rand Corporation, and Herbert Simon (1916–2001), a professor at the Carnegie Institute of Technology (now Carnegie Mellon University), gave a paper there also on a computer program that could prove theorems in propositional logic. This symposium, bringing together as it did scientists with these sorts of overlapping interests, is thought to have contributed to the birth of *cognitive science*, a new discipline devoted to the study of the mind. Indeed, George Miller wrote[22]

I went away from the Symposium with a strong conviction, more intuitive than rational, that human experimental psychology, theoretical linguistics, and computer simulation of cognitive processes were all pieces of a larger whole, and that the future would see progressive elaboration and coordination of their shared concerns . . .

In 1960, Miller and colleagues wrote a book proposing a specific internal mechanism responsible for behavior, which they called the TOTE unit (Test–Operate–Test–Exit).[23] There is a TOTE unit corresponding to every goal that an agent might have. Using its perceptual abilities, the unit first tests whether or not its goal is satisfied. If so, the unit rests (exits). If not, some operation specific to achieving that goal is performed, the test for goal achievement is performed again, and so on repetitively until the goal finally is achieved. As a simple example, consider the TOTE unit for driving a nail with a hammer. So long as the nail is not completely driven in (the goal), the hammer is used to strike it (the operation). Pounding stops (the exit) when the goal is finally achieved. It's difficult to say whether or not this book inspired similar work by artificial intelligence researchers. The idea was apparently "in the air," because at about the same time, as we shall see later, some early work in AI used very similar ideas. [I can say that my work at SRI with behavior (intermediate-level) programs for the robot, Shakey, and my later work on what I called "teleo-reactive" programs were influenced by Miller's ideas.]

Cognitive science attempted to explicate internal mental processes using ideas such as goals, memory, task queues, and strategies without (at least during its beginning years) necessarily trying to ground these processes in neurophysiology.[24] Cognitive science and artificial intelligence have been closely related ever since their beginnings. Cognitive science has provided clues for AI researchers, and AI has helped cognitive science with newly invented concepts useful for understanding the workings of the mind.

2.2.3 *Evolution*

That living things evolve gives us two more clues about how to build intelligent artifacts. First, and most ambitiously, the processes of evolution itself – namely, random generation and selective survival – might be simulated on computers to produce the machines we dream about. Second, those paths that evolution followed in producing increasingly intelligent animals can be used as a guide for creating increasingly intelligent artifacts. Start by simulating animals with simple tropisms and proceed along these paths to simulating more complex ones. Both of these strategies have been followed with zest by AI researchers, as we shall see in the following chapters. Here, it will suffice to name just a few initial efforts.

Early attempts to simulate evolution on a computer were undertaken at Princeton's Institute for Advanced Study by the viral geneticist Nils Aall Barricelli (1912–1993). His 1954 paper described experiments in which numbers migrated and reproduced in a grid.[25]

Motivated by the success of biological evolution in producing complex organisms, some researchers began thinking about how programs could be evolved rather than written. R. N. Friedberg and his IBM colleagues[26] conducted experiments in which, beginning with a population of random computer programs, they attempted to evolve ones that were more successful at performing a simple logical task. In the summary of his 1958 paper, Friedberg wrote that "[m]achines would be more useful if they could learn to perform tasks for which they were not given precise methods. . . . It is proposed that the program of a stored-program computer be gradually improved by a learning procedure which tries many programs and chooses, from the instructions that may occupy a given location, the one most often associated with a successful result." That is, Friedberg installed instructions from "successful" programs into the programs of the next "generation," much as how the genes of individuals successful enough to have descendants are installed in those descendants.

Unfortunately, Friedberg's attempts to evolve programs were not very successful. As Marvin Minsky pointed out,[27]

The machine [described in the first paper] did learn to solve some extremely simple problems. But it took of the order of 1000 times longer than pure chance would expect. . . .

The second paper goes on to discuss a sequence of modifications . . . With these, and with some 'priming' (starting the machine off on the right track with some useful instructions), the system came to be only a little worse than chance.

Minsky attributes the poor performance of Friedberg's methods to the fact that each descendant machine differed very little from its parent, whereas any helpful improvement would require a much larger step in the "space" of possible machines.

Other early work on artificial evolution was more successful. Lawrence Fogel (1928–2007) and colleagues were able to evolve machines that could make predictions of the next element in a sequence.[28] Woodrow W. Bledsoe (1921–1995) at Panoramic Research and Hans J. Bremermann (1926–1969) at the University of California, Berkeley, used simulated evolution to solve optimization and mathematical problems, respectively.[29] And Ingo Rechenberg (according to one AI researcher) "pioneered the method of artificial evolution to solve complex optimization tasks, such as the design of optimal airplane wings or combustion chambers of rocket nozzles."[30]

The first prominent work inspired by biological evolution was John Holland's development of "genetic algorithms" beginning in the early 1960s. Holland (1929–), a professor at the University of Michigan, used strings of binary symbols (0's and 1's), which he called "chromosomes" in analogy with the genetic material of biological organisms. (Holland says he first came up with the notion while browsing through the Michigan math library's open stacks in the early 1950s.)[31] The encoding of 0's and 1's in a chromosome could be interpreted as a solution to some given problem. The idea was to evolve chromosomes that were better and better at solving the problem. Populations of chromosomes were subjected to an evolutionary process in which individual chromosomes underwent "mutations" (changing a component 1 to a 0 and vice versa), and pairs of the most successful chromosomes at each stage of evolution were combined to make a new chromosome. Ultimately, the process would produce a population containing a chromosome (or chromosomes) that solved the problem.[32]

Researchers would ultimately come to recognize that all of these evolutionary methods were elaborations of a very useful mathematical search strategy called "gradient ascent" or "hill climbing." In these methods, one searches for a local maximum of some function by taking the steepest possible uphill steps. (When searching for a local minimum, the analogous method is called "gradient descent.")

Rather than attempt to duplicate evolution itself, some researchers preferred to build machines that followed along evolution's paths toward intelligent life. In the late 1940s and early 1950s, W. Grey Walter (1910–1977), a British neurophysiologist (born in Kansas City, Missouri), built some machines that behaved like some of life's most primitive creatures. They were wheeled vehicles to which he gave the

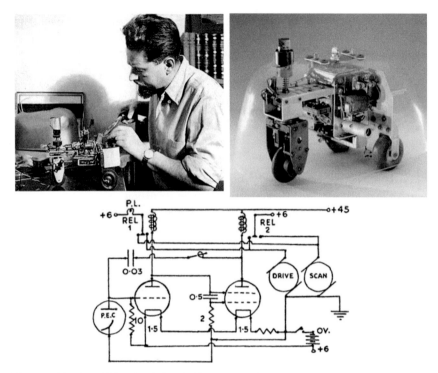

Figure 2.11. Grey Walter (top left), his *Machina speculatrix* (top right), and its circuit diagram (bottom). (Grey Walter photograph from Hans Moravec, *ROBOT*, Chapter 2: Caution! Robot Vehicle!, p. 18, Oxford: Oxford University Press, 1998; "Turtle" photograph courtesy of National Museum of American History, Smithsonian Institution; the circuit diagram is from W. Grey Walter, *The Living Brain*, p. 200, London: Gerald Duckworth & Co., Ltd., 1953.)

taxonomic name *Machina speculatrix* (machine that looks; see Fig. 2.11).[33] These tortoise-like machines were controlled by "brains" consisting of very simple vacuum-tube circuits that sensed their environments with photocells and that controlled their wheel motors. The circuits could be arranged so that a machine either moved toward or away from a light mounted on a sister machine. Their behaviors seemed purposive and often complex and unpredictable, so much so that Walter said they "might be accepted as evidence of some degree of self-awareness." *Machina speculatrix* was the beginning of a long line of increasingly sophisticated "behaving machines" developed by subsequent researchers.

2.2.4 *Development and Maturation*

Perhaps there are alternatives to rerunning evolution itself or to following its paths toward increasing complexity from the most primitive animals. By careful study of the behavior of young children, the Swiss psychologist Jean Piaget proposed a set of stages in the maturation of their thinking abilities from infancy to adolescence.[34] Might these stages provide a set of steps that could guide designers of intelligent artifacts? Start with a machine that is able to do what an infant can do, and then design machines that can mimic the abilities of children at each rung of the ladder. This strategy might be called "ontogenetic" to contrast it with the "phylogenetic" strategy of using simlulated evolution.

Of course, it may be that an infant mind is far too complicated to simulate and the processes of its maturation too difficult to follow. In any case, this particular clue remains to be exploited.

2.2.5 *Bionics*

At a symposium in 1960, Major Jack E. Steele, of the Aerospace Division of the United States Air Force, used the term "bionics" to describe the field that learns lessons from nature to apply to technology.[35]

Several bionics and bionics-related meetings were held during the 1960s. At the 1963 Bionics Symposium, Leonard Butsch and Hans Oestreicher wrote "Bionics aims to take advantage of millions of years of evolution of living systems during which they adapted themselves for optimum survival. One of the outstanding successes of evolution is the information processing capability of living systems [the study of which is] one of the principal areas of Bionics research."[36]

Today, the word "bionics" is concerned mainly with orthotic and prosthetic devices, such as artificial cochleas, retinas, and limbs. Nevertheless, as AI researchers continue their quest, the study of living things, their evolution, and their development may continue to provide useful clues for building intelligent artifacts.

2.3 From Engineering

2.3.1 *Automata, Sensing, and Feedback*

Machines that move by themselves and even do useful things by themselves have been around for centuries. Perhaps the most common early examples are the "verge-and-foliot" weight-driven clocks. (See Fig. 2.12.) These first appeared in the late Middle Ages in the towers of large Italian cities. The verge-and-foliot mechanism converted the energy of a falling weight into stepped rotational motion, which could be used to move the clock hands. Similar mechanisms were elaborated to control the actions of automata, such as those of the Munich Glockenspiel.

One of the first automatic machines for producing goods was Joseph-Marie Jacquard's weaving loom, built in 1804. (See Fig. 2.13.) It followed a long history of looms and improved on the "punched card" design of Jacques de Vaucanson's loom of 1745. (Vaucanson did more than build mechanical ducks.) The punched cards of the Jacquard loom controlled the actions of the shuttles, allowing automatic production of fabric designs. Just a few years after its invention, there were some 10,000 Jacquard looms weaving away in France. The idea of using holes in paper or cards was later adopted by Herman Hollerith for tabulating the 1890 American census data and in player pianos (using perforated rolls instead of cards). The very first factory "robots" of the so-called pick-and-place variety used only modest elaborations of this idea.

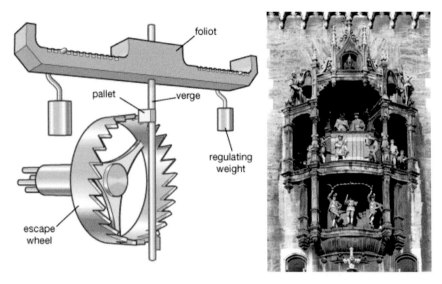

Figure 2.12. A verge-and-foliot mechanism (left) and automata at the Munich Glockenspiel (right).

It was only necessary to provide these early machines with an external source of energy (a falling weight, a wound-up spring, or humans pumping pedals). Their behavior was otherwise fully automatic, requiring no human guidance. But, they had an important limitation – they did not perceive anything about their environments. (The punched cards that were "read" by the Jacquard loom are considered part of the machine – not part of the environment.) Sensing the environment and then letting what is sensed influence what a machine does is critical to intelligent behavior. Grey Walters's "tortoises," for example, had photocells that could detect the presence or

Figure 2.13. Reconstruction of a Jacquard loom.

absence of light in their environments and act accordingly. Thus, they seem more intelligent than a Jacquard loom or clockwork automata.

One of the simplest ways to allow what is sensed to influence behavior involves what is called "feedback control." The word derives from feeding some aspect of a machine's behavior, say its speed of operation, back into the internals of the machine. If the aspect of behavior that is fed back acts to diminish or reverse that aspect, the process is called "negative feedback." If, on the other hand, it acts to increase or accentuate that aspect of behavior, it is called "positive feedback." Both types of feedback play extremely important roles in engineering.

Negative feedback techniques have been used for centuries in mechanical devices. In 270 BCE, a Greek inventor and barber, Ktesibios of Alexandria, invented a float regulator to keep the water level in a tank feeding a water clock at a constant depth by controlling the water flow into the tank.[37] The feedback device was a float valve consisting of a cork at the end of a rod. The cork floated on the water in the tank. When the water level in the tank rose, the cork would rise, causing the rod to turn off the water coming in. When the water level fell, the cork would fall, causing the rod to turn on the water. The water level in modern flush toilets is regulated in much the same way. In 250 BCE, Philon of Byzantium used a similar float regulator to keep a constant level of oil in a lamp.[38]

The English clockmaker John Harrison (1693–1776) used a type of negative feedback control in his clocks. The ambient temperature of a clock affects the length of its balance spring and thus its time-keeping accuracy. Harrison used a bimetallic strip (sometimes a rod), whose curvature depends on temperature. The strip was connected to the balance spring in such a way that it produced offsetting changes in the length of the spring, thus making the clock more independent of its temperature. The strip senses the temperature and causes the clock to behave differently, and more accurately, than it otherwise would. Today, such bimetallic strips see many uses, notably in thermostats. (Dava Sobel's 1995 book, *Longitude: The True Story of a Lone Genius Who Solved the Greatest Scientific Problem of His Time*, recounts the history of Harrison's efforts to build a prize-winning clock for accurate time-keeping at sea.)

Perhaps the most graphic use of feedback control is the centrifugal flyball governor perfected in 1788 by James Watt for regulating the speed of his steam engine. (See Fig. 2.14.) As the speed of the engine increases, the balls fly outward, which causes a linking mechanism to decrease air flow, which causes the speed to decrease, which causes the balls to fall back inward, which causes the speed to increase, and so on, resulting in an equilibrium speed.

In the early 1940s, Norbert Wiener (1894–1964) and other scientists noted similarities between the properties of feedback control systems in machines and in animals. In particular, inappropriately applied feedback in control circuits led to jerky movements of the system being controlled that were similar to pathological "tremor" in human patients. Arturo Rosenblueth, Norbert Wiener, and Julian Bigelow coined the term "cybernetics" in a 1943 paper. Wiener's book by that name was published in 1948. The word is related to the word "governor." (In Latin *gubernaculum* means helm, and *gubernator* means helmsman. The Latin derives from the Greek *kybernetike*, which means the art of steersmanship.[39])

Figure 2.14. Watt's flyball governor.

Today, the prefix "cyber" is used to describe almost anything that deals with computers, robots, the Internet, and advanced simulation. For example, the author William Gibson coined the term "cyberspace" in his 1984 science fiction novel *Neuromancer*. Technically, however, cybernetics continues to describe activities related to feedback and control.[40]

The English psychiatrist W. Ross Ashby (1903–1972; Fig. 2.15) contributed to the field of cybernetics by his study of "ultrastability" and "homeostasis." According to Ashby, ultrastability is the capacity of a system to reach a stable state under a wide variety of environmental conditions. To illustrate the idea, he built an electromechanical device called the "homeostat." It consisted of four pivoted magnets whose positions were rendered interdependent through feedback mechanisms. If the position of any was disturbed, the effects on the others and then back on itself would result in all of them returning to an equilibrium condition. Ashby described this device in Chapter 8 of his influential 1952 book *Design For a Brain*. His ideas had an influence on several AI researchers. My "teleo–reactive programs," to be described later, were motivated in part by the idea of homeostasis.

Another source of ideas, loosely associated with cybernetics and bionics, came from studies of "self-organizing systems." Many unorganized combinations of simple parts, including combinations of atoms and molecules, respond to energetic "jostling" by falling into stable states in which the parts are organized in more complex assemblies. An online dictionary devoted to cybernetics and systems theory has a nice example: "A chain made out of paper clips suggests that someone has taken the trouble to link paper clips together to make a chain. It is not in the nature of paper clips to make themselves up into a chain. But, if you take a number of paper clips, open them up slightly and then shake them all together in a cocktail shaker, you will find at the end that the clips have organized themselves into short or long chains. The chains are not so neat as chains put together by hand but, nevertheless, they are chains."[41]

Figure 2.15. W. Ross Ashby, Warren McCulloch, Grey Walter, and Norbert Wiener at a meeting in Paris. (From P. de Latil, *Thinking by Machine*, 1956.)

The term "self-organizing" seems to have been first introduced by Ashby in 1947.[42] Ashby emphasized that self-organization is not a property of an organism itself, in response to its environment and experience, but a property of the organism and its environment *taken together*. Although self-organization appears to be important in ideas about how life originated, it is unclear whether or not it provides clues for building intelligent machines.

2.3.2 *Statistics and Probability*

Because nearly all reasoning and decision making take place in the presence of uncertainty, dealing with uncertainty plays an important role in the automation of intelligence. Attempts to quantify uncertainty and "the laws of chance" gave rise to statistics and probability theory. What would turn out to be one of the most important results in probability theory, at least for artificial intelligence, is Bayes's rule, which I'll define presently in the context of an example. The rule is named for Reverend Thomas Bayes (1702–1761), an English clergyman.[43]

One of the important applications of Bayes's rule is in signal detection. Let's suppose a radio receiver is tuned to a station that after midnight broadcasts (randomly) one of two tones, either tone A or tone B, and on a particular night we want to decide which one is being broadcast. On any given day, we do not know ahead of time which tone is to be broadcast that night, but suppose we do know their probabilities. (For example, it might be that both tones are equally probable.) Can we find out which tone is being broadcast by listening to the signal coming into the receiver? Well, listening can't completely resolve the matter because the station is far away, and random noise partially obscures the tone. However, depending on the nature of the obscuring noise, we can often calculate the probability that the actual tone that night is A (or that it is B). Let's call the signal y and the actual tone x (which can be either A or B). The probability that $x = A$, given the evidence for it contained in the incoming signal, y, is written as $p(x = A \mid y)$ and read as "the probability that x is A, given that the signal is y." The probability that $x = B$, given the same evidence is $p(x = B \mid y)$.

A reasonable "decision rule" would be to decide in favor of tone A if $p(x = A \mid y)$ is larger than $p(x = B \mid y)$. Otherwise, decide in favor of tone B. (There is a straightforward adjustment to this rule that takes into account differences in the "costs" of the two possible errors.) The problem in applying this rule is that these two probabilities are not readily calculable, and that is where Bayes's rule comes in. It allows us to calculate these probabilities in terms of other probabilities that are more easily guessed or otherwise obtainable. Specifically, Bayes's rule is

$$p(x \mid y) = p(y \mid x)p(x)/p(y).$$

Using Bayes's rule, our decision rule can now be reformulated as

Decide in favor of tone A if $p(y \mid x = A)p(x = A)/p(y)$ is greater than $p(y \mid x = B)p(x = B)/p(y)$. Otherwise, decide in favor of tone B.

Because $p(y)$ occurs in both expressions and therefore does not affect which one is larger, the rule simplifies to

Decide in favor of tone A if $p(y \mid x = A)p(x = A)$ is greater than $p(y \mid x = B)p(x = B)$. Otherwise, decide in favor of tone B.

We assume that we know the *a priori* probabilities of the tones, namely, $p(x = A)$ and $p(x = B)$, so it remains only for us to calculate $p(y \mid x)$ for $x = A$ and $x = B$. This expression is called the *likelihood* of y given x. When the two probabilities, $p(x = A)$ and $p(x = B)$, are equal (that is, when both tones are equally probable *a priori*), then we can decide in favor of which likelihood is greater. Many decisions that are made in the presence of uncertainty use this "maximum–likelihood" method. The calculation for these likelihoods depends on how we represent the received signal, y, and on the statistics of the interfering noise.

In my example, y is a radio signal, that is, a voltage varying in time. For computational purposes, this time-varying voltage can be represented by a sequence of samples of its values at appropriately chosen, uniformly spaced time points, say $y(t_1)$, $y(t_2), \ldots y(t_i), \ldots, y(t_N)$. When noise alters these values from what they would have been without noise, the probability of the sequence of them (given the cases when the tone is A and when the tone is B) can be calculated by using the known statistical properties of the noise. I won't go into the details here except to say that, for many types of noise statistics, these calculations are quite straightforward.

In the twentieth century, scientists and statisticians such as Karl Pearson (1857–1936), Sir Ronald A. Fisher (1890–1962), Abraham Wald (1902–1950), and Jerzey Neyman (1894–1981) were among those who made important contributions to the use of statistical and probabilistic methods in estimating parameters and in making decisions. Their work set the foundation for some of the first engineering applications of Bayes's rule, such as the one I just illustrated, namely, deciding which, if any, of two or more electrical signals is present in situations where noise acts to obscure the signals. A paper by the American engineers David Van Meter and David Middleton, which I read as a beginning graduate student in 1955, was my own introduction to these applications.[44] For artificial intelligence, these uses of Bayes's rule provided clues about how to mechanize the perception of both speech sounds and visual images. Beyond perception, Bayes's rule lies at the center of much other modern work in artificial intelligence.

2.3.3 *The Computer*

A. Early Computational Devices

Proposals such as those of Leibniz, Boole, and Frege can be thought of as early attempts to provide foundations for what would become the "software" of artificial intelligence. But reasoning and all the other aspects of intelligent behavior require, besides software, some sort of *physical* engine. In humans and other animals, that engine is the brain. The simple devices of Grey Walter and Ross Ashby were, of course, physical manifestations of their ideas. And, as we shall see, early networks of neuron-like units were realized in physical form. However, to explore the ideas inherent in most of the clues from logic, from neurophysiology, and from cognitive science, more powerful engines would be required. While McCulloch, Wiener, Walter, Ashby, and others were speculating about the machinery of intelligence, a very powerful and essential machine bloomed into existence – the general-purpose digital computer. This single machine provided the engine for all of these ideas and more. It is by far the dominant hardware engine for automating intelligence.

Building devices to compute has a long history. William Aspray has edited an excellent book, *Computing Before Computers*, about computing's early days.[45] The first machines were able to do arithmetic calculations, but these were not programmable. Wilhelm Schickard (1592–1635; Fig. 2.16) built one of the first of these in 1623. It is said to have been able to add and subtract six-digit numbers for use in calculating astronomical tables. The machine could "carry" from one digit to the next.

In 1642 Blaise Pascal (1623–1662; Fig. 2.16) created the first of about fifty of his computing machines. It was an adding machine that could perform automatic carries from one position to the next. "The device was contained in a box that was small enough to fit easily on top of a desk or small table. The upper surface of the box . . . consisted of a number of toothed wheels, above which were a series of small windows to show the results. In order to add a number, say 3, to the result register, it was only necessary to insert a small stylus into the toothed wheel at the position marked 3 and rotate the wheel clockwise until the stylus encountered the fixed stop . . ."[46]

Inspired by Pascal's machines, Gottfried Leibniz built a mechanical multiplier called the "Step Reckoner" in 1674. It could add, subtract, and do multiplication

Figure 2.16. Wilhelm Schickard (left) and Blaise Pascal (right).

(by repeated additions). "To multiply a number by 5, one simply turned the crank five times."[47]

Several other calculators were built in the ensuing centuries. A particularly interesting one, which was too complicated to build in its day, was designed in 1822 by Charles Babbage (1791–1871), an English mathematician and inventor. (See Fig. 2.17.) Called the "Difference Engine," it was to have calculated mathematical tables (of the kind used in navigation at sea, for example) using the method of finite differences. Babbage's Difference Engine No. 2 was actually constructed in 1991 (using Babbage's designs and nineteenth-century mechanical tolerances) and is now on display at the London Science Museum. The Museum arranged for another copy

Figure 2.17. Charles Babbage (left) and a model of his Analytical Engine (right).

to be built for Nathan Myhrvold, a former Microsoft Chief Technology Officer. (A description of the machine and a movie is available from a Computer History Museum Web page at http://www.computerhistory.org/babbage/.)

Adding machines, however, can only add and subtract (and, by repetition of these operations, also multiply and divide). These are important operations but not the only ones needed. Between 1834 and 1837 Babbage worked on the design of a machine called the "Analytical Engine," which embodied most of the ideas needed for general computation. It could store intermediate results in a "mill," and it could be programmed. However, its proposed realization as a collection of steam-driven, interacting brass gears and cams ran into funding difficulties and was never constructed.

Ada Lovelace (1815–1852), the daughter of Lord Byron, has been called the "world's first programmer" for her alleged role in devising programs for the Analytical Engine. However, in the book *Computing Before Computers* the following claim is made:[48]

This romantically appealing image is without foundation. All but one of the programs cited in her notes [to her translation of an account of a lecture Babbage gave in Turin, Italy] had been prepared by Babbage from three to seven years earlier. The exception was prepared by Babbage for her, although she did detect a "bug" in it. Not only is there no evidence that Ada Lovelace ever prepared a program for the Analytical Engine but her correspondence with Babbage shows that she did not have the knowledge to do so.

For more information about the Analytical Engine and an emulator and programs for it, see http://www.fourmilab.ch/babbage/.

Practical computers had to await the invention of electrical, rather than brass, devices. The first computers in the early 1940s used electromechanical relays. Vacuum tubes (thermionic valves, as they say in Britain) soon won out because they permitted faster and more reliable computation. Nowadays, computers use billions of tiny transistors arrayed on silicon wafers. Who knows what might someday replace them?

B. Computation Theory

Even before people actually started building computers, several logicians and mathematicians in the 1930s pondered the problem of just what could be computed. Alonzo Church came up with a class of functions that could be computed, ones he called "recursive."[49] The English logician and mathematician, Alan Turing (1912–1954; Fig. 2.18), proposed what is now understood to be an equivalent class – ones that could be computed by an imagined machine he called a "logical computing machine (LCM)," nowadays called a "Turing machine."[50] (See Fig. 2.19.) The claim that these two notions are equivalent is called the "Church–Turing Thesis." (The claim has not been proven, but it is strongly supported by logicians and no counterexample has ever been found.)[51]

The Turing machine is a hypothetical computational device that is quite simple to understand. It consists of just a few parts. There is an infinite tape (which is one reason the device is just imagined and not actually built) divided into cells and a tape drive. Each cell has printed on it either a 1 or a 0. The machine also has a

Figure 2.18. Alan Turing. (Alan Mathison Turing by Elliott & Fry © National Portrait Gallery, London)

read–write head positioned over one cell of the tape. The read function reads what is on the tape. There is also a logic unit that can decide, depending on what is read and the state of the logic machine, to change its own state, to command the write function to write either a 1 or a 0 on the cell being read (possibly replacing what is already there), to move the tape one cell to the left or to the right (at which time the new cell is read and so on), or to terminate operation altogether. The input (the "problem" to be computed) is written on the tape initially. (It turns out that any such input can be coded into 1's and 0's.) When, and if, the machine terminates, the output (the coded "answer" to the input problem) ends up being printed on the tape.

Turing proved that one could always specify a particular logic unit (the part that decides on the machine's actions) for his machine such that the machine would

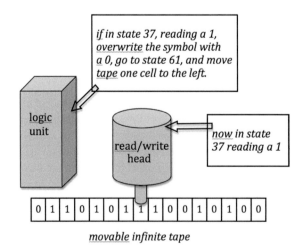

Figure 2.19. A Turing machine.

Figure 2.20. Claude Shannon. (Photograph courtesy of MIT Museum.)

compute any computable function. More importantly, he showed that one could encode on the tape itself a prescription for any logic unit specialized for a particular problem and then use a general-purpose logic unit for *all* problems. The encoding for the special-purpose logic unit can be thought of as the "program" for the machine, which is stored on the tape (and thus subject to change by the very operation of the machine!) along with the description of the problem to be solved. In Turing's words, "It can be shown that a single special machine of that type can be made to do the work of all. It could in fact be made to work as a model of any other machine. The special machine may be called the universal machine."[52]

C. Digital Computers

Somewhat independently of Turing, engineers began thinking about how to build actual computing devices consisting of programs and logical circuitry for performing the instructions contained in the programs. Some of the key ideas for designing the logic circuits of computers were developed by the American mathematician and inventor Claude Shannon (1916–2001; Fig. 2.20).[53] In his 1937 Yale University master's thesis[54] Shannon showed that Boolean algebra and binary arithmetic could be used to simplify telephone switching circuits. He also showed that switching circuits (which can be realized either by combinations of relays, vacuum tubes, or whatever) could be used to implement operations in Boolean logic, thus explaining their importance in computer design.

It's hard to know who first thought of the idea of storing a computer's program along with its data in the computer's memory banks. Storing the program allows changes in the program to be made easily, but more importantly it allows the program to change itself by changing appropriate parts of the memory where the program is stored. Among those who might have thought of this idea first are the German engineer Konrad Zuse (1910–1995) and the American computer pioneers J. Presper Eckert (1919–1995) and John W. Mauchly (1907–1980). (Of course Turing had already proposed storing what amounted to a program on the tape of a universal Turing machine.)

For an interesting history of Konrad Zuse's contributions, see the family of sites available from http://irb.cs.tu-berlin.de/~zuse/Konrad_Zuse/en/index.html. One of these mentions that "it is undisputed that Konrad Zuse's Z3 was the first fully functional, program controlled (freely programmable) computer of the world.... The Z3 was presented on May 12, 1941, to an audience of scientists in Berlin." Instead of vacuum tubes, it used 2,400 electromechanical relays. The original Z3 was destroyed by an Allied air raid on December 21, 1943.[55] A reconstructed version was built in the early 1960s and is now on display at the Deutsche Museum in Munich. Zuse also is said to have created the first programming language, called the Plankalkül.

The American mathematician John von Neumann (1903–1957) wrote a "draft report" about the EDVAC, an early stored-program computer.[56] Perhaps because of this report, we now say that these kinds of computers use a "von Neumann architecture." The ideal von Neumann architecture separates the (task-specific) stored program from the (general-purpose) hardware circuitry, which can execute (sequentially) the instructions of any program whatsoever. (We usually call the program "software" to distinguish it from the "hardware" part of a computer. However, the distinction is blurred in most modern computers because they often have some of their programs built right into their circuitry.)

Other computers with stored programs were designed and built in the 1940s in Germany, Great Britain, and the United States. They were large, bulky machines. In Great Britain and the United States, they were mainly used for military purposes. Figure 2.21 shows one such machine.

We call computers "machines" even though today they can be made completely electrical with no moving parts whatsoever. Furthermore, when we speak of computing machines we usually mean the combination of the computer and the program it is running. Sometimes we even call just the program a machine. (As an example of this usage, I'll talk later about a "checker-playing machine" and mean a program that plays checkers.)

The commanding importance of the stored-program digital computer derives from the fact that it can be used for any purpose whatsoever – that is, of course, any computational purpose. The modern digital computer is, for all practical purposes, such a universal machine. The "all-practical-purposes" qualifier is needed because not even modern computers have the infinite storage capacity implied by Turing's infinite tape. However, they do have prodigious amounts of storage, and that makes them practically universal.

D. "Thinking" Computers

After some of the first computers were built, Turing reasoned that if they were practically universal, they should be able to do anything. In 1948 he wrote, "The importance of the universal machine is clear. We do not need to have an infinity of different machines doing different jobs. A single one will suffice. The engineering problem of producing various machines for various jobs is replaced by the office work of 'programming' the universal machine to do these jobs."[57]

Figure 2.21. The Cambridge University EDSAC computer (circa 1949). (Copyright Computer Laboratory, University of Cambridge. Reproduced by permission.)

Among the things that Turing thought could be done by computers was mimicking human intelligence. One of Turing's biographers, Andrew Hodges, claims, "he decided the scope of the computable encompassed far more than could be captured by explicit instruction notes, and quite enough to include all that human brains did, however creative or original. Machines of sufficient complexity would have the capacity for evolving into behaviour that had never been explicitly programmed."[58]

The first modern article dealing with the possibility of mechanizing *all* of human-style intelligence was published by Turing in 1950.[59] This paper is famous for several reasons. First, Turing thought that the question "Can a machine think?" was too ambiguous. Instead, he proposed that the matter of machine intelligence be settled by what has come to be called "the Turing test."

Although there have been several reformulations (mostly simplifications) of the test, here is how Turing himself described it:

The new form of the problem [Can machines think?] can be described in terms of a game which we call the "imitation game." It is played with three people, a man (A), a woman (B), and an interrogator (C) who may be of either sex. The interrogator stays in a room apart from the other two. The object of the game for the interrogator is to determine which of the other two is the man and which is the woman. He knows them by labels X and Y, and at the end of the game he says either "X is A and Y is B" or "X is B and Y is A." The interrogator is allowed to put questions to A and B thus:

C: Will X please tell me the length of his or her hair?

Now suppose X is actually A, then A must answer. It is A's object in the game to try and cause C to make the wrong identification. His answer might therefore be

"My hair is shingled, and the longest strands are about nine inches long."

In order that tones of voice may not help the interrogator the answers should be written, or better still, typewritten. The ideal arrangement is to have a teleprinter communicating between the two rooms. Alternatively the question and answers can be repeated by an intermediary. The object of the game for the third player (B) is to help the interrogator. The best strategy for her is probably to give truthful answers. She can add such things as "I am the woman, don't listen to him!" to her answers, but it will avail nothing as the man can make similar remarks.

We now ask the question, "What will happen when a machine takes the part of A in this game?" Will the interrogator decide wrongly as often when the game is played like this as he does when the game is played between a man and a woman? These questions replace our original, "Can machines think?"

Most of the simplifications of Turing's test involve attempting to have a computer "in the other room" fool an interrogator into believing the computer is a human. To stimulate progress toward that goal, a prize has been established – annual prizes in fact. In the words of the Web site announcing the prizes, "In 1990 Hugh Loebner agreed with The Cambridge Center for Behavioral Studies to underwrite a contest designed to implement the Turing Test. Dr. Loebner pledged a Grand Prize of $100,000 and a Gold Medal for the first computer whose responses were indistinguishable from a human's. Such a computer can be said 'to think.' Each year an annual prize of $2000 and a bronze medal is awarded to the most human-like computer. The winner of the annual contest is the best entry relative to other entries that year, irrespective of how good it is in an absolute sense."[60]

However, several people have pointed to inadequacies of both the simplifications and even of the original test.[61] In fact, it has been alleged that even Joseph Weizenbaum's patently unintelligent 1966 conversational program, ELIZA, has fooled people into thinking it is human.[62]

For example, here is part of a transcript of a conversation with ELIZA:

ELIZA: How do you do. Please state your problem.
 > I spend too much time with computers.
ELIZA: Why do you mention computers?
 > You are one.
ELIZA: Does it please you to believe I am one?
 > Yes.
ELIZA: You seem to be quite positive.
 > I suppose I am.
ELIZA: How long have you been?
 > 31 years.
ELIZA: I'm not sure I understand you fully.
 > Join the club.
ELIZA: Please go on.
 > You don't make too much sense yourself.
ELIZA: We were discussing you – not me.

The first part of the conversation seems reasonable, but ELIZA bogs down in the middle because the program was expecting "I suppose I am" to be followed by some word like "happy." (There are several ELIZA simulations on the Web. One that claims to reproduce faithfully the original ELIZA program is at http://www.chayden.net/eliza/Eliza.html. Try one out!)

A second important feature of Turing's 1950 paper was his handling of arguments that people might raise against the possibility of achieving intelligent computers. I'll quote the ones Turing mentions:

(1) The Theological Objection: Thinking is a function of man's immortal soul. God has given an immortal soul to every man and woman, but not to any other animal or to machines. Hence no animal or machine can think.

(2) The 'Heads in the Sand' Objection: "The consequences of machines thinking would be too dreadful. Let us hope and believe that they cannot do so."

(3) The Mathematical Objection: There are a number of results of mathematical logic that can be used to show that there are limitations to the powers of discrete-state machines.

(4) The Argument from Consciousness: This argument is very well expressed in Professor Jefferson's Lister Oration for 1949, from which I quote:
"Not until a machine can write a sonnet or compose a concerto because of thoughts and emotions felt, and not by the chance fall of symbols, could we agree that machine equals brain – that is, not only write it but know that it had written it. No mechanism could feel (and not merely artificially signal, an easy contrivance) pleasure at its successes, grief when its valves fuse, be warmed by flattery, be made miserable by its mistakes, be charmed by sex, be angry or depressed when it cannot get what it wants."

(5) Arguments from Various Disabilities: These arguments take the form, "I grant you that you can make machines do all the things you have mentioned but you will never be able to make one to do X."

(6) Lady Lovelace's Objection: Our most detailed information of Babbage's Analytical Engine comes from a memoir by Lady Lovelace. In it she states, "The Analytical Engine has no pretensions to originate anything. It can do *whatever we know* how *to order it* to perform" (her italics).

(7) Argument from Continuity in the Nervous System: The nervous system is certainly not a discrete-state machine. A small error in the information about the size of a nervous impulse impinging on a neuron may make a large difference to the size of the outgoing impulse. It may be argued that, this being so, one cannot expect to be able to mimic the behavior of the nervous system with a discrete-state system.

(8) The Argument from Informality of Behavior: It is not possible to produce a set of rules purporting to describe what a man should do in every conceivable set of circumstances.

(9) The Argument from Extra-Sensory Perception.

In his paper, Turing nicely (in my opinion) handles all of these points, with the possible exception of the last one (because he apparently thought that extra-sensory perception was plausible). I'll leave it to you to read Turing's 1950 paper to see his counterarguments.

Figure 2.22. Herbert Simon (seated) and Allen Newell (standing). (Courtesy of Carnegie Mellon University Archives.)

The third important feature of Turing's 1950 paper is his suggestion about how we might go about producing programs with human-level intellectual abilities. Toward the end of his paper, he suggests, "Instead of trying to produce a programme to simulate the adult mind, why not rather try to produce one which simulates the child's? If this were then subjected to an appropriate course of education one would obtain the adult brain." This suggestion is really the source for the idea mentioned earlier about using an ontogenetic strategy to develop intelligent machines.

Allen Newell and Herb Simon (see Fig. 2.22) were among those who had no trouble believing that the digital computer's universality meant that it could be used to mechanize intelligence in all its manifestations – provided it had the right soft-ware. In their 1975 ACM Turing Award lecture,[63] they described a hypothesis that they had undoubtedly come to believe much earlier, the "Physical Symbol System Hypothesis." It states that "a physical symbol system has the necessary and sufficient means for intelligent action." Therefore, according to the hypothesis, appropriately programmed digital computers would be capable of intelligent action. Conversely, because humans are capable of intelligent action, they must be, according to the hypothesis, physical symbol systems. These are very strong claims that continue to be debated.

Both the imagined Turing machine and the very real digital computer are symbol systems in the sense Newell and Simon meant the phrase. How can a Turing machine, which uses a tape with 0's and 1's printed on it, be a "symbol system"? Well, the 0's and 1's printed on the tape can be thought of as symbols standing for their associated numbers. Other symbols, such as "A" and "M," can be encoded as sequences of primitive symbols, such as 0's and 1's. Words can be encoded as sequences of letters, and so on. The fact that one commonly thinks of a digital computer as a machine operating on 0's and 1's need not prevent us from thinking of it also as operating on more complex symbols. After all, we are all used to using computers to do "word processing" and to send e-mail.

Newell and Simon admitted that their hypothesis could indeed be false: "Intelligent behavior is not so easy to produce that any system will exhibit it willy-nilly. Indeed, there are people whose analyses lead them to conclude either on philosophical or on scientific grounds that the hypothesis is false. Scientifically, one can attack or defend it only by bringing forth empirical evidence about the natural world." They conclude the following:

The symbol system hypothesis implies that the symbolic behavior of man arises because he has the characteristics of a physical symbol system. Hence, the results of efforts to model human behavior with symbol systems become an important part of the evidence for the hypothesis, and research in artificial intelligence goes on in close collaboration with research in information processing psychology, as it is usually called.

Although the hypothesis was not formally described until it appeared in the 1976 article, it was certainly implicit in what Turing and other researchers believed in the 1950s. After Allen Newell's death, Herb Simon wrote, "From the very beginning something like the physical symbol system hypothesis was embedded in the research."[64]

Inspired by the clues we have mentioned and armed with the general-purpose digital computer, researchers began, during the 1950s, to explore various paths toward mechanizing intelligence. With a firm belief in the symbol system hypothesis, some people began programming computers to attempt to get them to perform some of the intellectual tasks that humans could perform. Around the same time, other researchers began exploring approaches that did not depend explicitly on symbol processing. They took their inspiration mainly from the work of McCulloch and Pitts on networks of neuron-like units and from statistical approaches to decision making. A split between symbol-processing methods and what has come to be called "brain-style" and "nonsymbolic" methods still survives today.

Notes

1. Aristotle, *Prior Analytics, Book 1*, written circa 350 BCE, translated by A. J. Jenkinson, Web addition published by eBooks@Adelaide, available online at http://etext.library.adelaide.edu.au/a/aristotle/a8pra/. [10]
2. Medieval students of logic gave names to the different syllogisms they studied. They used the mnemonic *Barbara* for this one because each of the three statements begins with "All," whose first letter is "A." The vowels in "Barbara" are three "a"s. [10]
3. From Martin Davis, *The Universal Computer: The Road from Leibniz to Turing*, New York: W.W. Norton & Co., 2000. For an excerpt from the paperback version containing this quotation, see http://www.wwnorton.com/catalog/fall01/032229EXCERPT.htm. [11]

4. Quotation from William Aspray (ed.), *Computing Before Computers*, Chapter 3, "Logic Machines," pp. 107–8, Ames, Iowa: Iowa State Press, 1990. (Also available from http://ed-thelen.org/comp-hist/CBC.html.) [12]

5. Robert Harley, "The Stanhope Demonstrator," *Mind*, Vol. IV, pp. 192–210, 1879. [13]

6. George Boole, *An Investigation of the Laws of Thought on Which are Founded the Mathematical Theories of Logic and Probabilities*, Dover Publications, 1854. [13]

7. See D. McHale, *George Boole: His Life and Work*, Dublin, 1985. This excerpt was taken from http://www-groups.dcs.st-and.ac.uk/~history/Mathematicians/Boole.html. [14]

8. See, for example, Gerard O'Regan, *A Brief History of Computing*, p. 17, London: Springer-Verlag, 2008. [14]

9. I follow the pictorial version used in the online Stanford Encyclopedia of Philosophy (http://plato.stanford.edu/entries/frege/), which states that "... we are modifying Frege's notation a bit so as to simplify the presentation; we shall not use the special typeface (Gothic) that Frege used for variables in general statements, or observe some of the special conventions that he adopted. . . . " [14]

10. Warren S. McCulloch and Walter Pitts, "A Logical Calculus of Ideas Immanent in Nervous Activity," *Bulletin of Mathematical Biophysics*, Vol. 5, pp. 115–133, Chicago: University of Chicago Press, 1943. (See Marvin Minsky, *Computation: Finite and Infinite Machines*, Englewood Cliffs, NJ: Prentice-Hall, 1967, for a very readable treatment of the computational aspects of "McCulloch–Pitts neurons.") [17]

11. Donald O. Hebb, *The Organization of Behavior: A Neuropsychological Theory*, New York: John Wiley, Inc., 1949. [17]

12. For more about Hebb, see http://www.cpa.ca/Psynopsis/special_eng.html. [18]

13. For a summary of the lives and work of both men, see a Web page entitled "Wilhelm Wundt and William James" by Dr. C. George Boeree at http://www.ship.edu/~cgboeree/wundtjames.html. [19]

14. M. Minsky (ed.), "Introduction," *Semantic Information Processing*, p. 2, Cambridge, MA: MIT Press, 1968. [20]

15. Russell A. Kirsch, "Experiments with a Computer Learning Routine," Computer Seminar Notes, July 30, 1954. Available online at http://www.nist.gov/msidlibrary/doc/kirsch_1954_artificial.pdf. [20]

16. B. F. Skinner, *Verbal Behavior*, Engelwood Cliffs, NJ: Prentice Hall, 1957. [20]

17. Noam Chomsky, "A Review of B. F. Skinner's *Verbal Behavior*," in Leon A. Jakobovits and Murray S. Miron (eds.), *Readings in the Psychology of Language*, Engelwood Cliffs, NJ: Prentice-Hall, 1967. Available online at http://www.chomsky.info/articles/1967—.htm. [20]

18. See, for example, N. Chomsky, *Aspects of the Theory of Syntax*, Cambridge: MIT Press, 1965. [21]

19. George A. Miller, "The Magical Number Seven, Plus or Minus Two: Some Limits on Our Capacity for Processing Information," *The Psychological Review*, Vol. 63, pp. 81–97, 1956. [21]

20. *IRE Transactions on Information Theory*, Vol IT-2, 1956. [21]

21. For a copy of his paper, see http://www.chomsky.info/articles/195609–.pdf. [21]

22. George A. Miller, "A Very Personal History," MIT Center for Cognitive Science Occasional Paper No. 1, 1979. [21]

23. George A. Miller, E. Galanter, and K. H. Pribram, *Plans and the Structure of Behavior*, New York: Holt, Rinehart & Winston, 1960. [21]

24. For a thorough history of cognitive science, see Margaret A. Boden, *Mind As Machine: A History of Cognitive Science*, vols. 1 and 2, Oxford: Clarendon Press, 2006. For an earlier,

one-volume treatment, see Howard E. Gardner, *The Mind's New Science: A History of the Cognitive Revolution*, New York: Basic Books, 1985. [22]

25. An English translation appeared later: N.A. Barricelli, "Symbiogenetic Evolution Processes Realized by Artificial Methods," *Methodos*, Vol. 9, Nos. 35–36, pp. 143–182, 1957. For a summary of Barricelli's experiments, see David B. Fogel, "Nils Barricelli – Artificial Life, Coevolution, Self-Adaptation," *IEEE Computational Intelligence Magazine*, Vol. 1, No. 1, pp. 41–45, February 2006. [22]

26. R. M. Friedberg, "A Learning Machine: Part I," *IBM Journal of Research and Development*, Vol. 2, No. 1, pp. 2–13, 1958, and R. M. Friedberg, B. Dunham, and J. H. North, "A Learning Machine: Part II," *IBM Journal of Research and Development*, Vol. 3, No. 3, pp. 282–287, 1959. The papers are available (for a fee) at http://www.research.ibm.com/journal/rd/021/ibmrd0201B.pdf and http://www.research.ibm.com/journal/rd/033/ibmrd0303H.pdf. [22]

27. Marvin L. Minsky, "Steps Toward Artificial Intelligence," *Proceedings of the Institute of Radio Engineers*, Vol. 49, pp. 8–30, 1961. Paper available at http://web.media.mit.edu/~minsky/papers/steps.html. [23]

28. Lawrence J. Fogel, A. J. Owens, and M. J. Walsh, *Artificial Intelligence through Simulated Evolution*, New York: Wiley, 1966. [23]

29. Woodrow W. Bledsoe, "The Evolutionary Method in Hill Climbing: Convergence Rates," Technical Report, Panoramic Research, Inc., Palo Alto, CA, 1962.; Hans J. Bremermann, "Optimization through Evolution and Recombination," M. C. Yovits, G. T. Jacobi, and G. D. Goldstein (eds.), *Self-Organizing Systems*, pp. 93–106, Washington, DC: Spartan Books, 1962. [23]

30. Jürgen Schmidhuber, "2006: Celebrating 75 Years of AI – History and Outlook: The Next 25 Years," in Max Lungarella et al. (eds.), *50 Years of Artificial Intelligence: Essays Dedicated to the 50th Anniversary of Artificial Intelligence*, Berlin: Springer-Verlag, 2007. Schmiduber cites Ingo Rechenberg, "Evolutionsstrategie – Optimierung Technischer Systeme Nach Prinzipien der Biologischen Evolution," Ph.D. dissertation, 1971 (reprinted by Frommann-Holzboog Verlag, Stuttgart, 1973). [23]

31. See http://www.aaai.org/AITopics/html/genalg.html. [23]

32. John H. Holland, *Adaptation in Natural and Artificial Systems*, Ann Arbor: The University of Michigan Press, 1975. Second edition, MIT Press, 1992. [23]

33. W. Grey Walter, "An Imitation of Life," *Scientific American*, pp. 42–45, May 1950. See also W. Grey Walter, *The Living Brain*, London: Gerald Duckworth & Co. Ltd., 1953. [24]

34. B. Inhelder and J. Piaget, *The Growth of Logical Thinking from Childhood to Adolescence*, New York: Basic Books, 1958. For a summary of these stages, see the following Web pages: http://www.childdevelopmentinfo.com/development/piaget.shtml and http://www.ship.edu/~cgboeree/piaget.html. [24]

35. *Proceedings of the Bionics Symposium: Living Prototypes – the Key to new Technology*, Technical Report 60-600, Wright Air Development Division, Dayton, Ohio, 1960. [25]

36. *Proceedings of the Third Bionics Symposium*, Aerospace Medical Division, Air Force Systems Command, United States Air Force, Wright-Patterson AFB, Ohio, 1963. [25]

37. http://www.mlahanas.de/Greeks/Ctesibius1.htm. [27]

38. http://www.asc-cybernetics.org/foundations/timeline.htm. [27]

39. From http://www.nickgreen.pwp.blueyonder.co.uk/control.htm. [27]

40. For a history of cybernetics, see a Web page of the American Society for Cybernetics at http://www.asc-cybernetics.org/foundations/history.htm. [28]

41. From http://pespmc1.vub.ac.be/ASC/SELF-ORGANI.html. [28]

42. W. Ross Ashby, "Principles of the Self-Organizing Dynamic System," *Journal of General Psychology*, Vol. 37, pp. 125–128, 1947. See also the Web pages at http://en.wikipedia.org/wiki/Self_organization. **[29]**

43. Bayes wrote an essay that is said to have contained a version of the rule. Later, the Marquis de Laplace (1749–1827) generalized (some say independently) what Bayes had done. For a version of Bayes's essay (posthumously written up by Richard Price), see http://www.stat.ucla.edu/history/essay.pdf. **[29]**

44. David Van Meter and David Middleton, "Modern Statistical Approaches to Reception in Communication Theory," Symposium on Information Theory, *IRE Transactions on Information Theory*, PGIT-4, pp. 119–145, September 1954. **[31]**

45. William Aspray (ed.), *Computing Before Computers*, Ames, Iowa: Iowa State University Press, 1990. Available online at http://ed-thelen.org/comp-hist/CBC.html. **[31]**

46. *Ibid*, Chapter 1. **[31]**

47. *Ibid*. **[32]**

48. *Ibid*, Chapter 2. **[33]**

49. Alonzo Church, "An Unsolvable Problem of Elementary Number Theory," *American Journal of Mathematics*, Vol. 58, pp. 345–363, 1936. **[33]**

50. Alan M. Turing, "On Computable Numbers, with an Application to the Entscheidungsproblem," *Proceedings of the London Mathematical Society*, Series 2, Vol. 42, pp. 230–265, 1936–1937. **[33]**

51. For more information about Turing, his life and works, see the Web pages maintained by the Turing biographer, Andrew Hodges, at http://www.turing.org.uk/turing/. **[33]**

52. The quotation is from Alan M. Turing, "Lecture to the London Mathematical Society," p. 112, typescript in King's College, Cambridge, published in Alan M. Turing's *ACE Report of 1946 and Other Papers* (edited by B. E. Carpenter and R. W. Doran, Cambridge, MA: MIT Press, 1986), and in Volume 3 of *The Collected Works of A. M. Turing* (edited D. C. Ince, Amsterdam: North-Holland 1992). **[35]**

53. For a biographical sketch, see http://www.research.att.com/~njas/doc/shannonbio.html. **[35]**

54. In his book *The Mind's New Science*, Howard Gardner called this thesis "possibly the most important, and also the most famous, master's thesis of the century." **[35]**

55. Various sources give different dates for the air raid, but a letter in the possession of Zuse's son, Horst Zuse, gives the 1943 date (according to an e-mail sent me on February 10, 2009, by Wolfgang Bibel, who has communicated with Horst Zuse). **[36]**

56. A copy of the report, plus introductory commentary, can be found from http://qss.stanford.edu/~godfrey/. **[36]**

57. Alan M. Turing, "Intelligent Machinery," National Physical Laboratory Report, 1948. Reprinted in B. Meltzer and D. Michie (eds), *Machine Intelligence 5*, Edinburgh: Edinburgh University Press, 1969. A facsimile of the report is available online at http://www.AlanTuring.net/intelligent_machinery. **[36]**

58. Andrew Hodges, *Turing*, London: Phoenix, 1997. **[37]**

59. Alan M. Turing, "Computing Machinery and Intelligence," *Mind*, Vol. LIX, No. 236, pp. 433–460, October 1950. (Available at http://www.abelard.org/turpap/turpap.htm.) **[37]**

60. See the "Home Page of the Loebner Prize in Artificial Intelligence" at http://www.loebner.net/Prizef/loebner-prize.html. **[38]**

61. For discussion, see the Wikipedia article at http://en.wikipedia.org/wiki/Turing_test. **[38]**

62. Joseph Weizenbaum, "ELIZA—A Computer Program for the Study of Natural Language Communication between Man and Machine," *Communications of the ACM*,

Vol. 9, No. 1, pp. 36–35, January 1966. Available online at http://i5.nyu.edu/~mm64/x52.9265/january1966.html. [38]

63. Allen Newell and Herbert A. Simon, "Computer Science as Empirical Inquiry: Symbols and Search," *Communications of the ACM*, Vol. 19, No. 3, pp. 113–126, March 1976. [40]

64. National Academy of Sciences, *Biographical Memoirs*, Vol. 71, 1997. Available online at http://www.nap.edu/catalog.php?record_id=5737. [41]

Part II

Early Explorations:
1950s and 1960s

I F MACHINES ARE TO BECOME INTELLIGENT, THEY MUST, AT THE VERY LEAST, BE able to do the thinking-related things that humans can do. The first steps then in the quest for artificial intelligence involved identifying some specific tasks thought to require intelligence and figuring out how to get machines to do them. Solving puzzles, playing games such as chess and checkers, proving theorems, answering simple questions, and classifying visual images were among some of the problems tackled by the early pioneers during the 1950s and early 1960s. Although most of these were laboratory-style, sometimes called "toy," problems, some real-world problems of commercial importance, such as automatic reading of highly stylized magnetic characters on bank checks and language translation, were also being attacked. (As far as I know, Seymour Papert was the first to use the phrase "toy problem." At a 1967 AI workshop I attended in Athens, Georgia, he distinguished among *tau* or "toy" problems, *rho* or real-world problems, and *theta* or "theory" problems in artificial intelligence. This distinction still serves us well today.)

In this part, I'll describe some of the first real efforts to build intelligent machines. Some of these were discussed or reported on at conferences and symposia – making these meetings important milestones in the birth of AI. I'll also do my best to explain the underlying workings of some of these early AI programs. The rather dramatic successes during this period helped to establish a solid base for subsequent artificial intelligence research.

Some researchers became intrigued (one might even say captured) by the methods they were using, devoting themselves more to improving the power and generality of their chosen techniques than to applying them to the tasks thought to require them. Moreover, because some researchers were just as interested in explaining how human brains solved problems as they were in getting machines to do so, the methods being developed were often proposed as contributions to theories about human mental processes. Thus, research in cognitive psychology and research in artificial intelligence became highly intertwined.

3

Gatherings

IN SEPTEMBER 1948, AN INTERDISCIPLINARY CONFERENCE WAS HELD AT THE California Institute of Technology (Caltech) in Pasadena, California, on the topics of how the nervous system controls behavior and how the brain might be compared to a computer. It was called the Hixon Symposium on Cerebral Mechanisms in Behavior. Several luminaries attended and gave papers, among them Warren McCulloch, John von Neumann, and Karl Lashley (1890–1958), a prominent psychologist. Lashley gave what some thought was the most important talk at the symposium. He faulted behaviorism for its static view of brain function and claimed that to explain human abilities for planning and language, psychologists would have to begin considering dynamic, hierarchical structures. Lashley's talk laid out the foundations for what would become cognitive science.[1]

The emergence of artificial intelligence as a full-fledged field of research coincided with (and was launched by) three important meetings – one in 1955, one in 1956, and one in 1958. In 1955, a "Session on Learning Machines" was held in conjunction with the 1955 Western Joint Computer Conference in Los Angeles. In 1956, a "Summer Research Project on Artificial Intelligence" was convened at Dartmouth College. And in 1958, a symposium on the "Mechanization of Thought Processes," was sponsored by the National Physical Laboratory in the United Kingdom.

3.1 Session on Learning Machines

Four important papers were presented in Los Angeles in 1955. In his chairman's introduction to this session, Willis Ware wrote

These papers do not suggest that future learning machines should be built in the pattern of the general-purpose digital computing device; it is rather that the digital computing system offers a convenient and highly flexible tool to probe the behavior of the models. . . . This group of papers suggests directions of improvement for future machine builders whose intent is to utilize digital computing machinery for this particular model technique. Speed of operation must be increased manyfold; simultaneous operation in many parallel modes is strongly indicated; the size of random access storage must jump several orders of magnitude; new types of input–output equipment are needed. With such advancements and the techniques discussed in these papers, there is considerable promise that systems can be built in the relatively near future which will imitate considerable portions of the activity of the brain and nervous system.

Fortunately, we have made substantial progress on the items on Ware's list of "directions for improvement." Speed of operation has increased manyfold, parallel

Figure 3.1. Oliver Selfridge. (Photograph courtesy of Oliver Selfridge.)

operation is utilized in many AI systems, random access storage has jumped several orders of magnitude, and many new types of input–output equipment are available. Perhaps even further improvements will be necessary.

The session's first paper, by Wesley Clark and Belmont Farley of MIT's Lincoln Laboratory, described some pattern-recognition experiments on networks of neuron-like elements.[2] Motivated by Hebb's proposal that assemblies of neurons could learn and adapt by adjusting the strengths of their interconnections, experimenters had been trying various schemes for adjusting the strengths of connections within their networks, which were usually simulated on computers. Some just wanted to see what these networks might do whereas others, such as Clark and Farley, were interested in specific applications, such as pattern recognition. To the dismay of neurophysiologists, who complained about oversimplification, these networks came to be called *neural networks*. Clark and Farley concluded that "crude but useful generalization properties are possessed even by randomly connected nets of the type described."[3]

The next pair of papers, one by Gerald P. Dinneen (1924–) and one by Oliver Selfridge (1926–2008; Fig. 3.1), both from MIT's Lincoln Laboratory, presented a different approach to pattern recognition. Dinneen's paper[4] described computational techniques for processing images. The images were presented to the computer as a rectangular array of intensity values corresponding to the various shades of gray in the image. Dinneen pioneered the use of filtering methods to remove random bits of noise, thicken lines, and find edges. He began his paper with the following:

Over the past months in a series of after-hour and luncheon meetings, a group of us at the laboratory have speculated on problems in this area. Our feeling, pretty much unanimously, was that there is a real *need* to get practical, to pick a real live problem and go after it.

Selfridge's paper[5] was a companion piece to that of Dinneen. Operating on "cleaned-up" images (as might be produced by Dinneen's program, for example), Selfridge described techniques for highlighting "features" in these images and then classifying them based on the features. For example, corners of an image known to be either a square or a triangle are highlighted, and then the number of corners is counted to determine whether the image is of a square or of a triangle. Selfridge said that "eventually, we hope to be able to recognize other kinds of features, such as curvature, juxtaposition of singular points (that is, their relative bearings and distances), and so forth."

The methods pioneered by Selfridge and Dinneen are fundamental to most of the later work in enabling machines to "see." Their work is all the more remarkable when one considers that it was done on a computer, the Lincoln Laboratory "Memory Test Computer," that today would be regarded as extremely primitive. [The Memory Test Computer (MTC) was the first to use the ferrite core random-access memory modules developed by Jay Forrester. It was designed and built by Ken Olsen in 1953 at the Digital Equipment Corporation (DEC). The MTC was the first computer to simulate the operation of neural networks – those of Clark and Farley.]

The next paper[6] was about programming a computer to play chess. It was written by Allen Newell, then a researcher at the Rand Corporation in Santa Monica. Thanks to a biographical sketch of Newell written by his colleague, Herb Simon of Carnegie Mellon University, we know something about Newell's motivation and how he came to be interested in this problem:[7]

In September 1954 Allen attended a seminar at RAND in which Oliver Selfridge of Lincoln Laboratory described a running computer program that learned to recognize letters and other patterns. While listening to Selfridge characterizing his rather primitive but operative system, Allen experienced what he always referred to as his "conversion experience." It became instantly clear to him "that intelligent adaptive systems could be built that were far more complex than anything yet done." To the knowledge Allen already had about computers (including their symbolic capabilities), about heuristics, about information processing in organizations, about cybernetics, and proposals for chess programs was now added a concrete demonstration of the feasibility of computer simulation of complex processes. Right then he committed himself to understanding human learning and thinking by simulating it.

Simon goes on to summarize Newell's paper on chess:

[It] outlined an imaginative design for a computer program to play chess in humanoid fashion, incorporating notions of goals, aspiration levels for terminating search, satisfying with "good enough" moves, multidimensional evaluation functions, the generation of subgoals to implement goals, and something like best first search. Information about the board was to be expressed symbolically in a language resembling the predicate calculus. The design was never implemented, but ideas were later borrowed from it for use in the NSS [Newell, Shaw, and Simon] chess program in 1958.[8]

Newell hinted that his aims extended beyond chess. In his paper, he wrote "The aim of this effort, then, is to program a current computer to learn to play good chess. This is the means to understanding more about the kinds of computers, mechanisms, and programs that are necessary to handle ultracomplicated problems." Newell's

Figure 3.2. John McCarthy (left) and Marvin Minsky (right). (McCarthy photograph courtesy of John McCarthy. Minsky photograph courtesy MIT Museum.)

proposed techniques can be regarded as his first attempt to produce evidence for what he and Simon later called the Physical Symbol System Hypothesis.

Walter Pitts, a commentator for this session, concluded it by saying, "But, whereas Messrs. Farley, Clark, Selfridge, and Dinneen are imitating the nervous system, Mr. Newell prefers to imitate the hierarchy of final causes traditionally called the mind. It will come to the same thing in the end, no doubt. . . . " To "come to the same thing," these two approaches, neural modeling and symbol processing, must be recognized simply as different levels of description of what goes on in the brain. Different levels are appropriate for describing different kinds of mental phenomena. I'll have more to say about description levels later in the book.

3.2 The Dartmouth Summer Project

In 1954, John McCarthy (1927– ; Fig 3.2) joined Dartmouth College in Hanover, New Hampshire, as an Assistant Professor of Mathematics. McCarthy had been developing a continuing interest in what would come to be called artificial intelligence. It was "triggered," he says, "by attending the September 1948 Hixon Symposium on Cerebral Mechanisms in Behavior held at Caltech where I was starting graduate work in mathematics."[9] While at Dartmouth he was invited by Nathaniel Rochester (1919–2001) to spend the summer of 1955 in Rochester's Information Research Department at IBM in Poughkeepsie, New York. Rochester had been the designer of the IBM 701 computer and had also participated in research on neural networks.[10]

At IBM that summer, McCarthy and Rochester persuaded Claude Shannon and Marvin Minsky (1927– ; Fig. 3.2), then a Harvard junior fellow in mathematics and neurology, to join them in proposing a workshop to be held at Dartmouth during the following summer. Shannon, whom I have previously mentioned, was a mathematician at Bell Telephone Laboratories and already famous for his work on switching theory and statistical information theory. McCarthy took the lead in writing the proposal and in organizing what was to be called a "Summer Research Project on Artificial Intelligence." The proposal was submitted to the Rockefeller Foundation in August 1955.

Extracts from the proposal read as follows:[11]

We propose that a 2 month, 10 man study of artificial intelligence be carried out during the summer of 1956 at Dartmouth College in Hanover, New Hampshire. The study is to proceed on the basis of the conjecture that every aspect of learning or any other feature of intelligence can in principle be so precisely described that a machine can be made to simulate it. An attempt will be made to find how to make machines use language, form abstractions and concepts, solve kinds of problems now reserved for humans, and improve themselves. We think that a significant advance can be made in one or more of these problems if a carefully selected group of scientists work on it together for a summer.

. . .

For the present purpose the artificial intelligence problem is taken to be that of making a machine behave in ways that would be called intelligent if a human were so behaving.

The Rockefeller Foundation did provide funding for the event, which took place during six weeks of the summer of 1956. It turned out, however, to be more of a rolling six-week workshop than a summer "study." Among the people attending the workshop that summer, in addition to McCarthy, Minsky, Rochester, and Shannon were Arthur Samuel (1901–1990), an engineer at the IBM corporation who had already written a program to play checkers, Oliver Selfridge, Ray Solomonoff of MIT, who was interested in automating induction, Allen Newell, and Herbert Simon. Newell and Simon (together with another Rand scientist, Cliff Shaw) had produced a program for proving theorems in symbolic logic. Another attending IBM scientist was Alex Bernstein, who was working on a chess-playing program.

McCarthy has given a couple of reasons for using the term "artificial intelligence." The first was to distinguish the subject matter proposed for the Dartmouth workshop from that of a prior volume of solicited papers, titled *Automata Studies*, co-edited by McCarthy and Shannon, which (to McCarthy's disappointment) largely concerned the esoteric and rather narrow mathematical subject called "automata theory." The second, according to McCarthy, was "to escape association with 'cybernetics.' Its concentration on analog feedback seemed misguided, and I wished to avoid having either to accept Norbert Wiener as a guru or having to argue with him."[12]

There was (and still is) controversy surrounding the name. According to Pamela McCorduck's excellent history of the early days of artificial intelligence, Art Samuel remarked, "The word artificial makes you think there's something kind of phony about this, or else it sounds like it's all artificial and there's nothing real about this work at all."[13] McCorduck goes on to say that "[n]either Newell or Simon liked the phrase, and called their own work complex information processing for years thereafter." But most of the people who signed on to do work in this new field (including myself) used the name "artificial intelligence," and that is what the field is called today. (Later, Newell became reconciled to the name. In commenting about the content of the field, he concluded, "So cherish the name *artificial intelligence*. It is a good name. Like all names of scientific fields, it will grow to become exactly what its field comes to mean.")[14]

The approaches and motivations of the people at the workshop differed. Rochester came to the conference with a background in networks of neuron-like elements. Newell and Simon had been pursuing (indeed had helped originate) the symbol-processing approach. Among the topics Shannon wanted to think about (according to the proposal) was the "application of information theory concepts to computing machines and brain models." (After the workshop, however, Shannon turned his attention away from artificial intelligence.)

McCarthy wrote that he was interested in constructing "an artificial language which a computer can be programmed to use on problems requiring conjecture and self-reference. It should correspond to English in the sense that short English statements about the given subject matter should have short correspondents in the language and so should short arguments or conjectural arguments. I hope to try to formulate a language having these properties . . . " Although McCarthy later said that his ideas on this topic were still too "ill formed" for presentation at the conference, it was not long before he made specific proposals for using a logical language and its inference mechanisms for representing and reasoning about knowledge.

Although Minsky's Ph.D. dissertation[15] and some of his subsequent work concentrated on neural nets, around the time of the Dartmouth workshop he was beginning to change direction. Now, he wrote, he wanted to consider a machine that "would tend to build up within itself an abstract model of the environment in which it is placed. If it were given a problem, it could first explore solutions within the internal abstract model of the environment and then attempt external experiments." At the workshop, Minsky continued work on a draft that was later to be published as a foundational paper, "Steps Toward Artificial Intelligence."[16]

One of the most important technical contributions of the 1956 meeting was work presented by Newell and Simon on their program, the "Logic Theorist (LT)," for proving theorems in symbolic logic. LT was concrete evidence that processing "symbol structures" and the use of what Newell and Simon called "heuristics" were fundamental to intelligent problem solving. I'll describe some of these ideas in more detail in a subsequent chapter.

Newell and Simon had been working on ideas for LT for some months and became convinced in late 1955 that they could be embodied in a working program. According to Edward Feigenbaum (1936–), who was taking a course from Herb Simon at Carnegie in early 1956, "It was just after Christmas vacation – January 1956 – when Herb Simon came into the classroom and said, 'Over Christmas Allen Newell and I invented a thinking machine.'"[17] What was soon to be programmed as LT was the "thinking machine" Simon was talking about. He called it such, no doubt, because he thought it used some of the same methods for solving problems that humans use. Simon later wrote[18] "On Thursday, Dec. 15 . . . I succeeded in simulating by hand the first proof . . . I have always celebrated Dec. 15, 1955, as the birthday of heuristic

Figure 3.3. Some of AI's founders at the July 2006 Dartmouth fiftieth anniversary meeting. From the left are Trenchard More, John McCarthy, Marvin Minsky, Oliver Selfridge, and Ray Solomonoff. (Photograph courtesy of photographer Joe Mehling and the Dartmouth College Artificial Intelligence Conference: The Next Fifty Years.)

problem solving by computer." According to Simon's autobiography *Models of My Life*,[19] LT began by hand simulation, using his children as the computing elements, while writing on and holding up note cards as the registers that contained the state variables of the program.[20]

Another topic discussed at Dartmouth was the problem of proving theorems in geometry. (Perhaps some readers will recall their struggles with geometry proofs in high school.) Minsky had already been thinking about a program to prove geometry theorems. McCorduck quotes him as saying the following:[21]

[P]robably the important event in my own development – and the explanation of my perhaps surprisingly casual acceptance of the Newell–Shaw–Simon work – was that I had sketched out the heuristic search procedure for [a] geometry machine and then been able to hand-simulate it on paper in the course of an hour or so. Under my hand the new proof of the isosceles-triangle theorem came to life, a proof that was new and elegant to the participants – later, we found that proof was well-known . . .

In July 2006, another conference was held at Dartmouth celebrating the fiftieth anniversary of the original conference. (See Fig. 3.3.) Several of the founders and other prominent AI researchers attended and surveyed what had been achieved since 1956. McCarthy reminisced that the "main reason the 1956 Dartmouth workshop did not live up to my expectations is that AI is harder than we thought." In any case, the 1956 workshop is considered to be the official beginning of serious work in artificial intelligence, and Minsky, McCarthy, Newell, and Simon came to be regarded as the "fathers" of AI. A plaque was dedicated and installed at the Baker Library at Dartmouth commemorating the beginning of artificial intelligence as a scientific discipline.

3.3 Mechanization of Thought Processes

In November 1958, a symposium on the "Mechanisation of Thought Processes" was held at the National Physical Laboratory in Teddington, Middlesex, England. According to the preface of the conference proceedings, the symposium was held "to bring together scientists studying artificial thinking, character and pattern recognition, learning, mechanical language translation, biology, automatic programming, industrial planning and clerical mechanization."

Among the people who presented papers at this symposium were many whom I have already mentioned in this story. They include Minsky (by then a staff member at Lincoln Laboratory and on his way to becoming an assistant professor of Mathematics at MIT), McCarthy (by then an assistant professor of Communication Sciences at MIT), Ashby, Selfridge, and McCulloch. (John Backus, one of the developers of the computer programming language FORTRAN, and Grace Murray Hopper, a pioneer in "automatic programming," also gave papers.)

The proceedings of this conference[22] contains some papers that became quite influential in the history of artificial intelligence. Among these, I'll mention ones by Minsky, McCarthy, and Selfridge.

Minsky's paper, "Some Methods of Artificial Intelligence and Heuristic Programming," was the latest version of a piece he had been working on since just before the Dartmouth workshop. The paper described various methods that were (and could be) used in heuristic programming. It also covered methods for pattern recognition, learning, and planning. The final version, which was soon to be published as "Steps Toward Artificial Intelligence," was to become required reading for new recruits to the field (including me).

I have already mentioned McCarthy's hope to develop an artificial language for AI. He summarized his conference paper, "Programs with Common Sense," as follows:

This paper will discuss programs to manipulate in a suitable formal language (most likely a part of the predicate calculus) common instrumental statements. The basic program will draw immediate conclusions from a list of premises. These conclusions will be either declarative or imperative sentences. When an imperative sentence is deduced, the program takes a corresponding action.

In his paper, McCarthy suggested that facts needed by an AI program, which he called the "advice taker," might be represented as expressions in a mathematical (and computer-friendly) language called "first-order logic." For example, the facts "I am at my desk" and "My desk is at home" would be represented as the expressions at(I, desk) and at(desk, home). These, together with similarly represented information about how to achieve a change in location (by walking and driving for example), could then be used by the proposed (but not yet programmed) advice taker to figure out how to achieve some goal, such as being at the airport. The advice taker's reasoning process would produce imperative logical expressions involving walking to the car and driving to the airport.

Representing facts in a logical language has several advantages. As McCarthy later put it,[23]

Expressing information in declarative sentences is far more modular than expressing it in segments of computer program or in tables. Sentences can be true in much wider contexts than specific programs can be useful. The supplier of a fact does not have to understand much about how the receiver functions, or how or whether the receiver will use it. The same fact can be used for many purposes, because the logical consequences of collections of facts can be available.

McCarthy later expanded on these ideas in a companion memorandum.[24] As I'll mention later, some of McCarthy's advice-taker proposals were finally implemented by a Stanford graduate student, C. Cordell Green.

I have already mentioned the 1955 pattern-recognition work of Oliver Selfridge. At the 1958 Teddington Symposium, Selfridge presented a paper on a new model for pattern recognition (and possibly for other cognitive tasks also).[25] He called it "Pandemonium," meaning the place of all the demons. His model is especially interesting because its components, which Selfridge called "demons," can either be instantiated as performing lower level nerve-cell-type functions or higher level cognitive functions (of the symbol-processing variety). Thus, Pandemonium can take the form of a neural network, a hierarchically organized set of symbol processors – all working in parallel, or some combination of these forms. If the latter, the model is a provocative proposal for joining these two disparate approaches to AI.

In the introduction to his paper, Selfridge emphasized the importance of computations performed in parallel:

The basic motif behind our model is the notion of parallel processing. This is suggested on two grounds: first, it is often easier to handle data in a parallel manner, and, indeed, it is usually the more "natural" manner to handle it in; and, secondly, it is easier to modify an assembly of quasi-independent modules than a machine all of whose parts interact immediately and in a complex way.

Selfridge made several suggestions about how Pandemonium could learn. It's worth describing some of these because they foreshadow later work in machine learning. But first I must say a bit more about the structure of Pandemonium.

Pandemonium's structure is something like that of a business organization chart. At the bottom level are workers, whom Selfridge called the "data demons." These are computational processes that "look at" the input data, say an image of a printed letter or number. Each demon looks for something specific in the image, perhaps a horizontal bar; another might look for a vertical bar; another for an arc of a circle; and so on. Each demon "shouts" its findings to a set of demons higher in the organization. (Think of these higher level demons as middle-level managers.) The loudness of a demon's shout depends on how certain it is that it is seeing what it is looking for. Of course, Selfridge is speaking metaphorically when he uses terms such as "looking for" and "shouting." Suffice it to say that it is not too difficult to program computers to "look for" certain features in an image. (Selfridge had already shown how that could be done in his 1955 paper that I mentioned earlier.) And a "shout" is really the strength of the output of a computational process.

Each of the next level of demons specializes in listening for a particular combination of shouts from the data demons. For example, one of the demons at this level might be tuned to listen for shouts from data demon 3, data demon 11, and data demon 22. If it finds that these particular demons are shouting loudly, it responds with a shout of its own to the demons one level up in the hierarchy, and so on.

Just below the top level of the organization are what Selfridge called the "cognitive demons." As at the other levels, these listen for particular combinations of shouts from the demons at the level below, and they respond with shouts of their own to a final "decision demon" at the top – the overall boss. Depending on what it hears from its "staff," the decision demon finally announces what it thinks is the identity of the image – perhaps the letter "A" or the letter "R" or whatever.

Actual demon design depends on what task Pandemonium is supposed to be doing. But even without specifying what each demon was to do, Selfridge made very interesting proposals about how Pandemonium could learn to perform better at whatever it was supposed to be doing. One of his proposals involved equipping each demon with what amounted to a "megaphone" through which it delivered its shout. The volume level of the megaphone could be adjusted. (Selfridge's Pandemonium is just a bit more complicated than the version I am describing. His version has each demon using different channels for communicating with each of the different demons above it. The volume of the shout going up each channel is individually adjusted by the learning mechanism.) The demons were not allowed to set their own volume levels, however. All volume levels were to be set through an outside learning process attempting to improve the performance of the whole assembly. Imagine that the volume levels are initially set either at random or at whatever a designer thinks would be appropriate. The device is then tested on some sample of input data and its performance score is noted. Say, it gets a score of 81%. Then, small adjustments are made to the volume levels in all possible ways until a set of adjustments is found that improves the score the most, say to 83%. This particular set of small adjustments is then made and the process is repeated over and over (possibly on additional data) until no further improvement can be made.

(Because there might be a lot of megaphones in the organization, it might seem impractical to make adjustments in all possible ways and to test each of these ways to find its score. The process might indeed take some time, but computers are fast – even more so today. Later in the book, I'll show how one can calculate, rather than find by experiment, the best adjustments to make in neural networks organized like Pandemonium.)

If we think of the score as the height of some landscape and the adjustments as movements over the landscape, the process can be likened to climbing a hill by always taking steps in the direction of steepest ascent. Gradient ascent (or hill-climbing methods, as they are sometimes called) are well known in mathematics. Selfridge had this to say about some of the pitfalls of their use:

This may be described as one of the problems of training, namely, to encourage the machine or organism to get enough on the foot-hills so that small changes . . . will produce noticeable improvement in his altitude or score. One can describe learning situations where most of the difficulty of the task lies in finding any way of improving one's score, such as learning to ride a unicycle, where it takes longer to stay on for a second than it does to improve that one second to a minute; and others where it is easy to do a little well and very hard to do very well, such as learning to play chess. It's also true that often the main peak is a plateau rather than an isolated spike.

Selfridge described another method for learning in Pandemonium. This method might be likened to replacing managers in an organization who do not perform well. As Selfridge puts it,

At the conception of our demoniac assembly we collected somewhat arbitrarily a large number of subdemons which we guessed would be useful... but we have no assurance at all that the particular subdemons we selected are good ones. Subdemon selection generates new subdemons for trial and eliminates inefficient ones, that is, ones that do not much help improve the score.

The demon selection process begins after the volume-adjusting learning mechanism has run for a while with no further improvements in the score. Then the "worth" of each demon is evaluated by using, as Selfridge suggests, a method based on the learned volume levels of their shouting. Demons having high volume levels have a large effect on the final score, and so they can be thought to have high worth. First, the demons with low volume levels are eliminated entirely. (That step can't hurt the score very much.) Next, some of the demons undergo random "mutations" and are put back in service. Next, some pairs of worthy demons are selected and, as Selfridge says, "conjugated" into offspring demons. The precise method Selfridge proposed for conjugation need not concern us here, but the spirit of the process is to produce offspring that share, one hopes, useful properties of the parents. The offspring are then put into service. Now the whole process of adjusting volume levels of the surviving and "evolved" demons can begin again to see whether the score of the new assembly can be further improved.

Notes

1. The proceedings of the symposium were published in L. A. Jeffries (ed.), *Cerebral Mechanisms in Behavior: The Hixon Symposium*, New York: Wiley, 1951. An excellent review of Lashley's points are contained in Chapter 2 of *The Mind's New Science: A History of the Cognitive Revolution*, by Howard E Gardner, New York: Basic Books, 1985. [49]
2. W. A. Clark and B. G. Farley, "Generalization of Pattern Recognition in a Self-Organizing System," *Proceedings of the 1955 Western Joint Computer Conference*, Institute of Radio Engineers, New York, pp. 86–91, 1955. Clark and Farley's experiments continued some work they had reported on earlier in B. G. Farley and W. A. Clark, "Simulation of Self-Organizing Systems by Digital Computer, *IRE Transactions on Information Theory*, Vol. 4, pp. 76–84, 1954. (In 1962, Clark built the first personal computer, the LINC.) [50]
3. Alan Wilkes and Nicholas Wade credit Scottish psychologist Alexander Bain (1818–1903) with the invention of the first neural network, which Bain described in his 1873 book *Mind and Body: The Theories of Their Relation."* (See Alan L. Wilkes and Nicholas J.

Wade, "Bain on Neural Networks," *Brain and Cognition*, Vol. 33, pp. 295–305, 1997.) **[50]**

4. Gerald P. Dinneen, "Programming Pattern Recognition," *Proceedings of the 1955 Western Joint Computer Conference*, Institute of Radio Engineers, New York, pp. 94–100, 1955. **[50]**

5. Oliver Selfridge, "Pattern Recognition and Modern Computers," *Proceedings of the 1955 Western Joint Computer Conference*, Institute of Radio Engineers, New York, pp. 91–93, 1955. **[51]**

6. Allen Newell, "The Chess Machine: An Example of Dealing with a Complex Task by Adaptation," *Proceedings of the 1955 Western Joint Computer Conference*, Institute of Radio Engineers, New York, pp. 101–108, 1955. (Also issued as RAND Technical Report P-620.) **[51]**

7. National Academy of Sciences, *Biographical Memoirs*, Vol. 71, 1997. Available online at http://www.nap.edu/catalog.php?record_id=5737. **[51]**

8. Allen Newell, J. C. Shaw, and Herbert A. Simon, "Chess-Playing Programs and the Problem of Complexity," *IBM Journal of Research and Development*, Vol. 2, pp. 320–335, 1958. The paper is available online at http://domino.watson.ibm.com/tchjr/journalindex.nsf/0/237cfeded3be103585256bfa00683d4d?OpenDocument. **[51]**

9. From John McCarthy's informal comments at the 2006 Dartmouth celebration. **[52]**

10. Nathan Rochester *et al.*, "Tests on a Cell Assembly Theory of the Action of the Brain Using a Large Digital Computer," *IRE Transaction of Information Theory*, Vol. IT-2, pp. 80–93, 1956. **[52]**

11. From http://www-formal.stanford.edu/jmc/history/dartmouth/dartmouth.html. Portions of the proposal have been reprinted in John McCarthy, Marvin L. Minsky, Nathaniel Rochester, and Claude E. Shannon, "A Proposal for the Dartmouth Summer Research Project on Artificial Intelligence," *AI Magazine*, Vol. 27, No. 4, p. 12, Winter 2006. **[53]**

12. From http://www-formal.stanford.edu/jmc/reviews/bloomfield/bloomfield.html. **[53]**

13. Pamela McCorduck, *Machines Who Think: A Personal Inquiry into the History and Prospects of Artificial Intelligence*, p. 97, San Francisco: W. H. Freeman and Co., 1979. **[53]**

14. See Allen Newell, "The First AAAI President's Message," *AI Magazine*, Vol. 26, No. 4, pp. 24–29, Winter 2005. **[54]**

15. M. L. Minsky, *Theory of Neural-Analog Reinforcement Systems and Its Application to the Brain-Model Problem*, Ph.D. thesis, Princeton University, 1954. **[54]**

16. Marvin L. Minsky, "Steps Toward Artificial Intelligence," *Proceedings of the IRE*, Vol. 49, No. 1, pp. 8–30, January 1961. Also appears in Edward A. Feigenbaum, and Julian Feldman (eds.), *Computers and Thought*, New York: McGraw Hill, 1963. (Available online at http://web.media.mit.edu/~minsky/papers/steps.html.) **[54]**

17. Pamela McCorduck, *op. cit.*, p. 116. **[54]**

18. Herbert A. Simon, *Models of My Life*, Cambridge, MA: MIT Press, 1996. The quote is from http://www.post-gazette.com/pg/06002/631149.stm. **[54]**

19. *Ibid.* **[55]**

20. http://www.post-gazette.com/downloads/20060102simon_notes.pdf contains sketches of Simon's simulation of an LT proof. **[55]**

21. Pamela McCorduck, *op. cit.*, p. 106. **[55]**

22. D. V. Blake and A. M. Uttley (eds.), *Proceedings of the Symposium on Mechanisation of Thought Processes*, Vols. 1 and 2, London: Her Majesty's Stationary Office, 1959. **[56]**

23. John McCarthy, "Artificial Intelligence, Logic and Formalizing Common Sense," in *Philosophical Logic and Artificial Intelligence*, Richmond Thomason (ed.), Dordrecht: Kluwer Academic, 1989. **[57]**

24. J. McCarthy, "Situations, Actions and Causal Laws, Stanford Artificial Intelligence Project," Memo 2, 1963. The two pieces are reprinted together in M. Minsky (ed.), *Semantic Information Processing*, pp. 410–417, Cambridge, MA: MIT Press, 1968. Related topics are explored in J. McCarthy and Patrick Hayes, "Some Philosophical Ideas From the Standpoint of Artificial Intelligence," MI-4, 1969. [57]

25. Oliver G. Selfridge, "Pandemonium: A Paradigm for Learning," in D. V. Blake and A. M. Uttley (eds.), *Proceedings of the Symposium on Mechanisation of Thought Processes*, pp. 511–529, London: Her Majesty's Stationary Office, 1959. [57]

4

Pattern Recognition

M OST OF THE ATTENDEES OF THE DARTMOUTH SUMMER PROJECT WERE INTER-
ested in mimicking the higher levels of human thought. Their work benefitted
from a certain amount of introspection about how humans solve problems. Yet, many
of our mental abilities are beyond our power of introspection. We don't know how
we recognize speech sounds, read cursive script, distinguish a cup from a plate, or
identify faces. We just do these things automatically without thinking about them.
Lacking clues from introspection, early researchers interested in automating some
of our perceptual abilities based their work instead on intuitive ideas about how to
proceed, on networks of simple models of neurons, and on statistical techniques.
Later, workers gained additional insights from neurophysiological studies of animal
vision.

In this chapter, I'll describe work during the 1950s and 1960s on what is called
"pattern recognition." This phrase refers to the process of analyzing an input image,
a segment of speech, an electronic signal, or any other sample of data and classifying it
into one of several categories. For character recognition, for example, the categories
would correspond to the several dozen or so alphanumeric characters.

Most of the pattern-recognition work in this period dealt with two-dimensional
material, such as printed pages or photographs. It was already possible to scan
images to convert them into arrays of numbers (later called "pixels"), which could
then be processed by computer programs such as those of Dinneen and Selfridge.
Russell Kirsch and colleagues at the National Bureau of Standards (now the National
Institute for Standards and Technology) were also among the early pioneers in image
processing. In 1957, Kirsch built and used a drum scanner to scan a photograph of his
three-month-old son, Walden. Said to be the first scanned photograph, it measured
176 pixels on a side and is depicted in Fig. 4.1.[1] Using his scanner, he and colleagues
experimented with picture-procesing programs running on their SEAC (Standards
Eastern Automatic Computer) computer.[2]

4.1 Character Recognition

Early efforts at the perception of visual images concentrated on recognizing alphanumeric characters on documents. This field came to be known as "optical character
recognition." A symposium devoted to reporting on progress on this topic was held
in Washington, DC, in January 1962.[3] In summary, devices existed at that time for
reasonably accurate recognition of fixed-font (typewritten or printed) characters on
paper. Perhaps the state of things then was best expressed by one of the participants

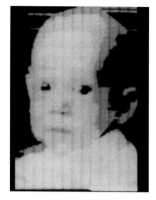

Figure 4.1. An early scanned photograph. (Photograph used with permission of NIST.)

of the symposium, J. Rabinow of Rabinow Engineering, who said "We think, in our company, that we can read anything that is printed, and we can even read some things that are written. The only catch is, 'how many bucks do you have to spend?'"[4]

A notable success during the 1950s was the magnetic ink character recognition (MICR) system developed by researchers at SRI International (then called the Stanford Research Institute) for reading stylized magnetic ink characters at the bottom of checks. (See Fig. 4.2.) MICR was part of SRI's ERMA (Electronic Recording Method of Accounting) system for automating check processing and checking account management and posting.

According to an SRI Web site, "In April 1956, the Bank of America announced that General Electric Corporation had been selected to manufacture production models. . . . In 1959, General Electric delivered the first 32 ERMA computing systems to the Bank of America. ERMA served as the Bank's accounting computer and check handling system until 1970."[5]

Most of the recognition methods at that time depended on matching a character (after it was isolated on the page and converted to an array of 0's and 1's) against prototypical versions of the character called "templates" (also stored as arrays in the computer). If a character matched the template for an "A," say, sufficiently better than it matched any other templates, the input was declared to be an "A." Recognition accuracy degraded if the input characters were not presented in standard orientation, were not of the same font as the template, or had imperfections.

The 1955 papers by Selfridge and Dinneen (which I have already mentioned on p. 50) proposed some ideas for moving beyond template matching. A 1960 paper by Oliver Selfridge and Ulrich Neisser carried this work further.[6] That paper is

Figure 4.2. The MICR font set.

important because it was a successful, early attempt to use image processing, feature extraction, and learned probability values in hand-printed character recognition. The characters were scanned and represented on a 32×32 "retina" or array of 0's and 1's. They were then processed by various refining operations (similar to those I mentioned in connection with the 1955 Dinneen paper) for removing random bits of noise, filling gaps, thickening lines, and enhancing edges. The "cleaned-up" images were then inspected for the occurrence of "features" (similar to the features I mentioned in connection with the 1955 Selfridge paper.) In all, 28 features were used – features such as the maximum number of times a horizontal line intersected the image, the relative lengths of different edges, and whether or not the image had a "concavity facing south."

Recalling Selfridge's Pandemonium system, we can think of the feature-detection process as being performed by "demons." At one level higher in the hierarchy than the feature demons were the "recognition demons" – one for each letter. (The version of this system tested by Worthie Doyle of Lincoln Laboratory was designed to recognize ten different hand-printed characters, namely, A, E, I, L, M, N, O, R, S, and T.) Each recognition demon received inputs from each of the feature-detecting demons. But first, the inputs to each recognition demon were multiplied by a weight that took into account the importance of the contribution of the corresponding feature to the decision. For example, if feature 17 were more important than feature 22 in deciding that the input character was an "A," then the input to the "A" recognizer from feature 17 would be weighted more heavily than would be the input from feature 22. After each recognition demon added up the total of its weighted inputs, a final "decision demon" decided in favor of that character having the largest sum.

The values of the weights were determined by a learning process during which 330 "training" images were analyzed. Counts were tabulated for how many times each feature was detected for each different letter in the training set. These statistical data were used to make estimates of the probabilities that a given feature would be detected for each of the letters. These probability estimates were then used to weight the features summed by the recognizing demons.

After training, the system was tested on samples of hand-printed characters that it had not yet seen. According to Selfridge and Neisser, "This program makes only about 10 percent fewer correct identifications than human readers make – a respectable performance, to be sure."

4.2 Neural Networks

4.2.1 *Perceptrons*

In 1957, Frank Rosenblatt (1928–1969; Fig. 4.3), a psychologist at the Cornell Aeronautical Laboratory in Buffalo, New York, began work on neural networks under a project called PARA (Perceiving and Recognizing Automaton). He was motivated by the earlier work of McCulloch and Pitts and of Hebb and was interested in these networks, which he called *perceptrons*, as potential models of human learning, cognition, and memory.[7]

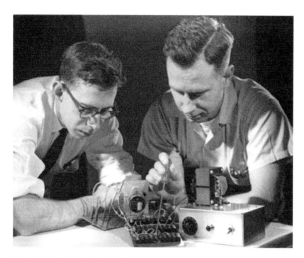

Figure 4.3. Frank Rosenblatt (left) working (with Charles Wrightman) on a prototype A–unit. (Courtesy of the Division of Rare and Manuscript Collections, Cornell University Library.)

Continuing during the early 1960s as a professor at Cornell University in Ithaca, New York, he experimented with a number of different kinds of perceptrons. His work, more than that of Clark and Farley and of the other neural network pioneers, was responsible for initiating one of the principal alternatives to symbol-processing methods in AI, namely, neural networks.

Rosenblatt's perceptrons consisted of McCulloch–Pitts-style neural elements, like the one shown in Fig. 4.4. Each element had inputs (coming in from the left in the figure), "weights" (shown by bulges on the input lines), and one output (going out to the right). The inputs had values of either 1 or 0, and each input was multiplied by its associated weight value. The neural element computed the sum of these weighted values. So, for example, if all of the inputs to the neural element in Fig. 4.4 were equal to 1, the sum would be 13. If the sum were greater than (or just equal to) a "threshold value," say 7, associated with the element, then the output of the neural element would be 1, which it would be in this example. Otherwise the output would be 0.

A perceptron consists of a network of these neural elements, in which the outputs of one element are inputs to others. (There is an analogy here with Selfridge's

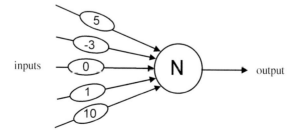

Figure 4.4. Rosenblatt's neural element with weights.

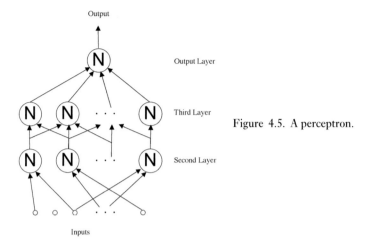

Figure 4.5. A perceptron.

Pandemonium in which mid-level demons receive "shouts" from lower level demons. The weights on a neural element's input lines can be thought of as analogous to the strength-enhancing or strength-diminishing "volume controls" in Pandemonium.) A sample perceptron is illustrated in Fig. 4.5. [Rosenblatt drew his perceptron diagrams in a horizontal format (the electrical engineering style), with inputs to the left and output to the right. Here I use the vertical style generally preferred by computer scientists for hierarchies, with the lowest level at the bottom and the highest at the top. To simplify the diagram, weight bulges are not shown.] Although the perceptron illustrated, with only one output unit, is capable of only two different outputs (1 or 0), multiple outputs (sets of 1's and 0's) could be achieved by arranging for several output units.

The input layer, shown at the bottom of Fig. 4.5, was typically a rectangular array of 1's and 0's corresponding to cells called "pixels" of a black-and-white image. One of the applications Rosenblatt was interested in was, like Selfridge, character recognition.

I'll use some simple algebra and geometry to show how the neural elements in perceptron networks can be "trained" to produce desired outputs. Let's consider, for example, a single neural element whose inputs are the values x_1, x_2, and x_3 and whose associated weight values are w_1, w_2, and w_3. When the sum computed by this element is exactly equal to its threshold value, say t, we have the equation

$$w_1 x_1 + w_2 x_2 + w_3 x_3 = t.$$

In algebra, such an equation is called a "linear equation." It defines a linear boundary, that is, a plane, in a three-dimensional space. The plane separates those input values that would cause the neural element to have an output of 1 from those that would cause it to have an output of 0. I show a typical planar boundary in Fig. 4.6.

An input to the neural element can be depicted as a point (that is, a vector) in this three-dimensional space. Its coordinates are the values of x_1, x_2, and x_3, each of which can be either 1 or 0. The figure shows six such points, three of them (the small circles, say) causing the element to have an output of 1 and three (the small squares,

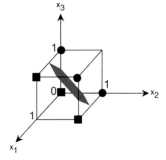

Figure 4.6. A separating plane in a three-dimensional space.

say) causing it to have an output of 0. Changing the value of the threshold causes the plane to move sideways in a direction parallel to itself. Changing the values of the weights causes the plane to rotate. Thus, by changing the weight values, points that used to be on one side of the plane might end up on the other side. "Training" takes place by performing such changes. I'll have more to say about training procedures presently.

In dimensions higher than three (which is usually the case), a linear boundary is called a "hyperplane." Although it is not possible to visualize what is going on in spaces of high dimensions, mathematicians still speak of input points in these spaces and rotations and movements of hyperplanes in response to changes in the values of weights and thresholds.

Rosenblatt defined several types of perceptrons. He called the one shown in the diagram a "series-coupled, four-layer perceptron." (Rosenblatt counted the inputs as the first layer.) It was termed "series-coupled" because the output of each neural element fed forward to neural elements in a subsequent layer. In more recent terminology, the phrase "feed-forward" is used instead of "series-coupled." In contrast, a "cross-coupled" perceptron could have the outputs of neural elements in one layer be inputs to neural elements in the same layer. A "back-coupled" perceptron could have the outputs of neural elements in one layer be inputs to neural elements in lower numbered layers.

Rosenblatt thought of his perceptrons as being models of the wiring of parts of the brain. For this reason, he called the neural elements in all layers but the output layer "association units" ("A–units") because he intended them to model associations performed by networks of neurons in the brain.

Of particular interest in Rosenblatt's research was what he called an "alpha–perceptron." It consisted of a three-layer, feed-forward network with an input layer, an association layer, and one or more output units. In most of his experiments, the inputs had values of 0 or 1, corresponding to black or white pixels in a visual image presented on what he called a "retina." Each A-unit received inputs (which were not multiplied by weight values) from some randomly selected subset of the pixels and sent its output, through sets of adjustable weights, to the final output units, whose binary values could be interpreted as a code for the category of the input image.

Various "training procedures" were tried for adjusting the weights of the output units of an alpha–perceptron. In the most successful of these (for pattern-recognition purposes), the weights leading in to the output units were adjusted only when those units made an error in classifying an input. The adjustments were such as to force the output to make the correct classification for that particular input. This technique, which soon became a standard, was called the "error-correction procedure." Rosenblatt used it successfully in a number of experiments for training perceptrons to classify visual inputs, such as alphanumeric characters, or acoustic inputs, such as speech sounds. Professor H. David Block, a Cornell mathematician working with Rosenblatt, was able to prove that the error-correction procedure was guaranteed to find a hyperplane that perfectly separated a set of training inputs when such a hyperplane existed.[8] (Other mathematicians, such as Albert B. Novikoff at SRI, later developed more elegant proofs.[9] I give a version of this proof in my book *Learning Machines*.[10])

Although some feasibility and design work was done using computer simulations, Rosenblatt preferred building hardware versions of his perceptrons. (Simulations were slow on early computers, thus explaining the interest in building special-purpose perceptron hardware.) The MARK I was an alpha-perceptron built at the Cornell Aeronautical Laboratory under the sponsorship of the Information Systems Branch of the Office of Naval Research and the Rome Air Development Center. It was first publicly demonstrated on 23 June 1960. The MARK I used volume controls (called "potentiometers" by electrical engineers) for weights. These had small motors attached to them for making adjustments to increase or decrease the weight values.

In 1959, Frank Rosenblatt moved his perceptron work from the Cornell Aeronautical Laboratory in Buffalo, New York, to Cornell University, where he became a professor of psychology. Together with Block and several students, Rosenblatt continued experimental and theoretical work on perceptrons. His book *Principles of Neurodynamics* provides a detailed treatment of his theoretical ideas and experimental results.[11] Rosenblatt's last system, called Tobermory, was built as a speech-recognition device.[12] [Tobermory was the name of a cat that learned to speak in *The Chronicles of Clovis*, a group of short stories by Saki (H. H. Munro).] Several Ph.D. students, including George Nagy, Carl Kessler, R. D. Joseph, and others, completed perceptron projects under Rosenblatt at Cornell.

In his last years at Cornell, Rosenblatt moved on to study chemical memory transfer in flatworms and other animals – a topic quite removed from his perceptron work. Tragically, Rosenblatt perished in a sailing accident in Chesapeake Bay in 1969.

Around the same time as Rosenblatt's alpha-perceptron, Woodrow W. (Woody) Bledsoe (1921–1995) and Iben Browning (1918–1991), two mathematicians at Sandia Laboratories in Albuquerque, New Mexico, were also pursuing research on character recognition that used random samplings of input images. They experimented with a system that projected images of alphanumeric characters on a 10×15 mosaic of photocells and sampled the states of 75 randomly chosen pairs of photocells. Pointing out that the idea could be extended to sampling larger groups of pixels, say N of them, they called their method the "N-tuple" method. They used the results of this sampling to make a decision about the category of an input letter.[13]

4.2.2 *ADALINES and MADALINES*

Independently of Rosenblatt, a group headed by Stanford Electrical Engineering Professor Bernard Widrow (1929–) was also working on neural-network systems during the late 1950s and early 1960s. Widrow had recently joined Stanford after completing a Ph.D. in control theory at MIT. He wanted to use neural-net systems for what he called "adaptive control." One of the devices Widrow built was called an "ADALINE" (for adaptive linear network). It was a single neural element whose adjustable weights were implemented by switchable (thus adjustable) circuits of resistors. Widrow and one of his students, Marcian E. "Ted" Hoff Jr. (who later invented the first microprocessor at Intel), developed an adjustable weight they called a "memistor." It consisted of a graphite rod on which a layer of copper could be plated and unplated – thus varying its electrical resistance. Widrow and Hoff developed a training procedure for their ADALINE neural element that came to be called the Widrow–Hoff least-mean-squares adaptive algorithm. Most of Widrow's experimental work was done using simulations on an IBM1620 computer. Their most complex network design was called a "MADALINE" (for many ADALINEs). A training procedure was developed for it by Stanford Ph.D. student William Ridgway.[14]

4.2.3 *The MINOS Systems at SRI*

Rosenblatt's success with perceptrons on pattern-recognition problems led to a flurry of research efforts by others to duplicate and extend his results. During the 1960s, perhaps the most significant pattern-recognition work using neural networks was done at the Stanford Research Institute in Menlo Park, California. There, Charles A. Rosen (1917–2002) headed a laboratory that was attempting to etch microscopic vacuum tubes onto a solid-state substrate. Rosen speculated that circuits containing these tubes might ultimately be "wired-up" to perform useful tasks using some of the training procedures being explored by Frank Rosenblatt. SRI employed Rosenblatt as a consultant to help in the design of an exploratory neural network.

When I interviewed for a position at SRI in 1960, a team in Rosen's lab, under the leadership of Alfred E. (Ted) Brain (1923–2004), had just about completed the construction of a small neural network called MINOS (Fig. 4.7). (In Greek mythology, Minos was a king of Crete and the son of Zeus and Europa. After his death, Minos was one of the three judges in the underworld.) Brain felt that computer simulations of neural networks were too slow for practical applications, thus leading to his decision to build rather than to program. (The IBM 1620 computer being used at the same time by Widrow's group at Stanford for simulating neural networks had a basic machine cycle of 21 microseconds and a maximum of 60,000 "digits" of random-access memory.) For adjustable weights, MINOS used magnetic devices designed by Brain. Rosenblatt stayed in close contact with SRI because he was interested in using these magnetic devices as replacements for his motor-driven potentiometers.

Rosen's enthusiasm and optimism about the potential for neural networks helped convince me to join SRI. Upon my arrival in July 1961, I was given a draft of

Figure 4.7. MINOS. Note the input switches and corresponding indicator lights in the second-from-the-left rack of equipment. The magnetic weights are at the top of the third rack. (Photograph used with permission of SRI International.)

Rosenblatt's book to read. Brain's team was just beginning work on the construction of a large neural network, called MINOS II, a follow-on system to the smaller MINOS. (See Fig. 4.8.)

Work on the MINOS systems was supported primarily by the U.S. Army Signal Corps during the period 1958 to 1967. The objective of the MINOS work was "to conduct a research study and experimental investigation of techniques and equipment characteristics suitable for practical application to graphical data processing for military requirements." The main focus of the project was the automatic recognition of symbols on military maps. Other applications – such as the recognition of military vehicles, such as tanks, on aerial photographs and the recognition of hand-printed characters – were also attempted.[15]

In the first stage of processing by MINOS II, the input image was replicated 100 times by a 10×10 array of plastic lenses. Each of these identical images was then sent through its own optical feature-detecting mask, and the light through the mask was detected by a photocell and compared with a threshold. The result was a set of 100 binary (off–on) values. These values were the inputs to a set of 63 neural elements ("A-units" in Rosenblatt's terminology), each with 100 variable magnetic weights.

Figure 4.8. MINOS II: operator's display board (left), an individual weight frame (middle), and weight frames with logic circuitry (right). (Photographs used with permission of SRI International.)

The 63 binary outputs from these neural elements were then translated into one of 64 decisions about the category of the original input image. (We constructed 64 equally distant "points" in the sixty-three-dimensional space and trained the neural network so that each input image produced a point closer to its own prototype point than to any other. Each of these prototype points was one of the 64 "maximal-length shift-register sequences" of 63 dimensions.)[16]

During the 1960s, the SRI neural network group, by then called the Learning Machines Group, explored many different network organizations and training procedures. As computers became both more available and more powerful, we increasingly used simulations (at various computer centers) on the Burroughs 220 and 5000 and on the IBM 709 and 7090. In the mid-1960s, we obtained our own dedicated computer, an SDS 910. (The SDS 910, developed at Scientific Data Systems, was the first computer to use silicon transistors.) We used that computer in conjunction with the latest version of our neural network hardware (now using an array of 1,024 preprocessing lenses), a combination we called MINOS III.

One of the most successful results with the MINOS III system was the automatic recognition of hand-printed characters on FORTRAN coding sheets. (In the 1960s, computer programs were typically written by hand and then converted to punched cards by key-punch operators.) This work was led by John Munson (1939–1972; Fig. 4.9), Peter Hart (1941– ; Fig. 4.9), and Richard Duda (1936– ; Fig. 4.9). The neural net part of MINOS III was used to produce a ranking of the possible classifications for each character with a confidence measure for each. For example, the first character encountered in a string of characters might be recognized by the neural net as a "D" with a confidence of 90 and as an "O" with a confidence of 10. But accepting the most confident decision for each character might not result in a string that is a legal statement in the FORTRAN language – indicating that one or more of the decisions was erroneous (where it is assumed that whoever wrote statements on the coding

Figure 4.9. John Munson (left), Peter Hart (middle), and Richard Duda (right). (Photographs courtesy of Faith Munson, of Peter Hart, and of Richard Duda.)

sheet wrote legal statements). Accepting the second or third most confident choices for some of the characters might be required to produce a legal string.

The overall confidence of a complete string of characters was calculated by adding the confidences of the individual characters in the string. Then, what was needed was a way of ranking these overall confidence numbers for each of the possible strings resulting from all of the different choices for each character. Among this ranking of all possible strings, the system then selected the most confident *legal* string.

As Richard Duda wrote, however, "The problem of finding the 1st, 2nd, 3rd, ... most confident string of characters is by no means a trivial problem." The key to computing the ranking in an efficient manner was to use a method called *dynamic programming*.[17] (In a later chapter, we'll see dynamic programming used again in speech recognition systems.)

An illustration of a sample of the original source and the final output is shown in Fig. 4.10.

After the neural net part of the system was trained, the overall system (which decided on the most confident legal string) was able to achieve a recognition accuracy of just over 98% on a large sample of material that was not part of what the system

```
        DIMENSION IMACM[2]
20      ACCEPT 31,I,J
31      FORMAT[215]
        IF[I]79,99,40
40      IF[I-IMACHL]50,50,60
50      IMACH[I]=J
60      GO TO 20
99      RETURN
```

Figure 4.10. Recognition of FORTRAN characters. Input is above and output (with only two errors) is below. (Illustration used with permission of SRI International.)

was trained on. Recognizing handwritten characters with this level of accuracy was a significant achievement in the 1960s.[18]

Expanding its interests beyond neural networks, the Learning Machines Group ultimately became the SRI Artificial Intelligence Center, which continues today as a leading AI research enterprise.

4.3 Statistical Methods

During the 1950s and 1960s there were several applications of statistical methods to pattern-recognition problems. Many of these methods bore a close resemblance to some of the neural network techniques. Recall that earlier I explained how to decide which of two tones was present in a noisy radio signal. A similar technique could be used for pattern recognition. For classifying images (or other perceptual inputs), it was usual to represent the input by a list of distinguishing "features," such as those used by Selfridge and his colleagues. In alphanumeric character recognition for example, one first extracted features from the image of the character to be classified. Usually the features had numerical values, such as the number of times lines of different angles intersected the character or the length of the perimeter of the smallest circle that completely enclosed the character. Selecting appropriate features was often more art than science, but it was critical to good performance.

We'll need a bit of elementary mathematical notation to help describe these statistically oriented pattern-recognition methods. Suppose the list of features extracted from a character is $\{f_1, f_2, \ldots, f_i, \ldots, f_N\}$. I'll abbreviate this list by the boldface symbol X. Suppose there are k categories, $C_1, C_2, \ldots, C_i, \ldots, C_k$ to which the character described by X might belong. Using Bayes's rule in a manner similar to that described earlier, the decision rule is the following:

Decide in favor of that category for which $p(X \mid C_i)p(C_i)$ is largest, where $p(C_i)$ is the *a priori* probability of category C_i and $p(X \mid C_i)$ is the likelihood of X given C_i. These likelihoods can be inferred by collecting statistical data from a large sample of characters.

As I mentioned earlier, researchers in pattern recognition often describe the decision process in terms of geometry. They imagine that the values of the features obtained from an image sample can be represented as a point in a multidimensional space. If we have several samples for each of, say, two known categories of data, we can represent these samples as scatterings of points in the space. In character recognition, scattering can occur not only because the image of the character might be noisy but also because characters in the same category might be drawn slightly differently. I show a two-dimensional example, with features f_1 and f_2, in Fig. 4.11. From the scattering of points in each category we can compute an estimate of the probabilities needed for computing likelihoods. Then, we can use the likelihoods and the prior probabilities to make decisions.

I show in this figure the boundary, computed from the likelihoods and the prior probabilities, that divides the space into two regions. In one region, we decide in favor of category 1; in the other, we decide in favor of category 2. I also show a new feature point, X, to be classified. In this case, the position of X relative to the boundary dictates that we classify X as a member of category 1.

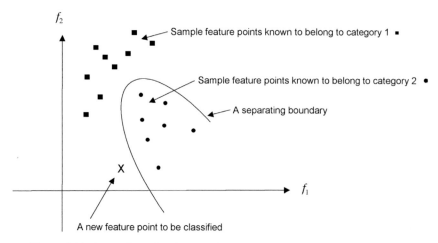

Figure 4.11. A two-dimensional space of feature points and a separating boundary.

There are other methods also for classifying feature points. An interesting example is the "nearest-neighbor" method. In that scheme, invented by E. Fix and J. L. Hodges in 1951,[19] a new feature point is assigned to the same category as that sample feature point to which it is closest. In Fig. 4.11, the new point X would be classified as belonging to category 2 using the nearest-neighbor method.

An important elaboration of the nearest-neighbor method assigns a new point to the same category as the majority of the k closest points. Such a decision rule seems plausible (in the case in which there are many, many sample points of each category) because there being more sample points of category C_i closer to an unknown point, X, than sample points of category C_j is evidence that $p(\mathbf{X} \mid C_i)p(C_i)$ is greater than $p(\mathbf{X} \mid C_j)p(C_j)$. Expanding on that general observation, Thomas Cover and Peter Hart rigorously analyzed the performance of nearest-neighbor methods.[20]

Any technique for pattern recognition, even those using neural networks or nearest neighbors, can be thought of as constructing separating boundaries in a multi-dimensional space of features. Another method for constructing boundaries using "potential functions" was suggested by the Russian scientists M. A. Aizerman, E. M. Braverman, and L. I. Rozonoer in the 1960s.[21]

Some important early books on the use of statistical methods in pattern recognition are ones by George Sebestyen,[22] myself,[23] and Richard Duda and Peter Hart.[24] My book also describes some of the relationships between statistical methods and those based on neural networks. The technology of pattern recognition as of the late 1960s is nicely reviewed by George Nagy (who had earlier been one of Frank Rosenblatt's graduate students).[25]

4.4 Applications of Pattern Recognition to Aerial Reconnaissance

The neural network and statistical methods for pattern recognition attracted much attention in many aerospace and avionics companies during the late 1950s and early 1960s. These companies had ample research and development budgets stemming

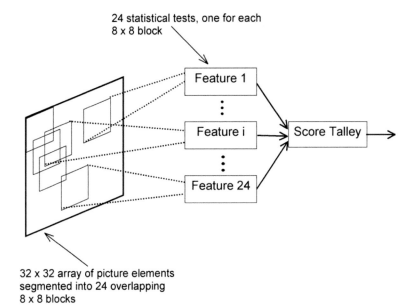

24 statistical tests, one for each
8 x 8 block

Feature 1

⋮

Feature i   Score Talley

⋮

Feature 24

32 x 32 array of picture elements
segmented into 24 overlapping
8 x 8 blocks

Figure 4.12. A Philco tank-recognition system. (Adapted from Laveen N. Kanal and Neal C. Randall, "Target Detection in Aerial Photography," paper 8.3, *Proceedings of the 1964 Western Electronics Show and Convention (WESCON)*, Los Angeles, CA, Institute of Radio Engineers (now IEEE), August 25–28, 1964.)

from their contracts with the U.S. Department of Defense. Many of them were particularly interested in the problem of aerial reconnaissance, that is, locating and identifying "targets" in aerial photographs. Among the companies having substantial research programs devoted to this and related problems were the Aeronutronic Division of the Ford Motor Co.,[26] Douglas Aircraft Company (as it was known at that time), General Dynamics, Lockheed Missiles and Space Division, and the Philco Corporation. (Philco was later acquired by Ford in late 1961.)

I'll mention some of the work at Philco as representative. There, Laveen N. Kanal (1931–), Neil C. Randall (1930–), and Thomas Harley (1929–) worked on both the theory and applications of statistical pattern-recognition methods. The systems they developed were for screening aerial photographs for interesting military targets such as tanks. A schematic illustration of one of their systems is shown in Fig. 4.12.[27]

Philco's apparatus scanned material from 9-inch film negatives gathered by a U2 reconnaissance airplane during U.S. Army tank maneuvers at Fort Drum, New York. A small section of the scanned photograph, possibly containing an M-48 tank (in standard position and size), was first processed to enhance edges, and the result was presented to the target detection system as an array of 1's and 0's. The first of their systems used a 22×12 array; later ones used a 32×32 array as shown in Fig. 4.12. The array was then segmented into 24 overlapping 8×8 "feature blocks." The data in each feature block were then subjected to a statistical test to decide whether or not the small area of the picture represented by this block contained part of a tank.

The statistical tests were based on a "training sample" of 50 images containing tanks and 50 samples of terrain not containing tanks. For each 8 × 8 feature block, statistical parameters were compiled from these samples to determine a (linear) boundary in the sixty-four-dimensional space that best discriminated the tank samples from the nontank samples.

Using these boundaries, the system was then tested on a different set of 50 images containing tanks and 50 images not containing tanks. For each test image, the number of feature blocks deciding "tank present" was tallied to produce a final numerical "score" (such as 21 out of the 24 blocks decided a tank was present). This score could then be used to decide whether or not the image contained a tank.

The authors stated that "the experimental performance of the statistical classification procedure exceeded all expectations." Almost half of the test samples had perfect scores (that is, all 24 feature blocks correctly discriminated between tank and nontank). Furthermore, all of the test samples containing tanks had a score greater than or equal to 11, and all of the test samples not containing tanks had a score less than or equal to 7.

An early tank-detecting system at Philco was built with analog circuitry – not programmed on a computer. As Thomas Harley, the project leader for this system, later elaborated,[28]

It is important to remember the technological context of the era in which this work was done. The system we implemented had no built-in computational capabilities. The weights in the linear discriminant function were resistors that controlled the current coming from the (binary) voltage source in the shift register elements. Those currents were added together, and each feature was recognized or not depending whether on the sum of those currents exceeded a threshold value. Those binary feature decisions were then summed, again in an analog electrical circuit, not in a computer, and again a decision [tank or no tank] was made depending on whether the sum exceeded a threshold value.

In another system, the statistical classification was implemented by a program, called MULTINORM, running on the Philco 2000 computer.[29] In other experiments, Philco used additional statistical tests to weight some of the feature blocks more heavily than others in computing the final score. Kanal told me that these experiments with weighting the outputs of the feature blocks "anticipated the support vector machine (SVM) classification idea . . . [by] using the first layer to identify the training samples close to the boundary between tanks and non-tanks."[30] (I'll describe the important SVM method in a later chapter.)

Of course, these systems had a rather easy task. All of the tanks were in standard position and were already isolated in the photograph. (The authors mention, however, how the system could be adapted to deal with tanks occurring in any position or orientation in the image.) The photograph in Fig. 4.13 shows a typical tank image. (The nontank images are similar, except without the tank.)

I find the system interesting not only because of its performance but also because it is a layered system (similar to Pandemonium and to the alpha-perceptron) and because it is an example in which the original image is divided into overlapping subimages, each of which is independently processed. As I'll mention later,

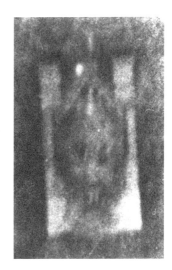

Figure 4.13. A typical tank image. (Photograph courtesy of Thomas Harley.)

overlapping subimages play a prominent role in some computational models of the neocortex.

Unfortunately, the Philco reports giving details of this work aren't readily available.[31] Furthermore, Philco and some of the other groups engaged in this work have disappeared. Here is what Tom Harley wrote me about the Philco reports and about Philco itself:[32]

Most of the pattern recognition work done at Philco in the 1960s was sponsored by the DoD [Department of Defense], and the reports were not available for public distribution. Since then, the company itself has really vanished into thin air. Philco was bought by Ford Motor Company in 1961, and by 1966, they had eliminated the Philco research labs where Laveen [Kanal] and I were working. Ford tried to move our small pattern recognition group to Newport Beach, CA [the location of Ford's Aeronutronic Division, whose pattern recognition group folded later also], and when we all decided not to go, they transferred us to their Communications Division, and told us to close out our pattern recognition projects. Laveen eventually went off to the University of Maryland, and in 1975, I transferred to the Ford Aerospace Western Development Labs (WDL) in Palo Alto, where I worked on large systems for the intelligence community. In later years, what had been Philco was sold to Loral, and most of that was later sold to Lockheed Martin. I retired from Lockheed in 2001.

Approaches to AI problems involving neural networks and statistical techniques came to be called "nonsymbolic" to contrast them with the "symbol-processing" work being pursued by those interested in proving theorems, playing games, and problem solving. These nonsymbolic approaches found application mainly in pattern recognition, speech processing, and computer vision. Workshops and conferences devoted especially to those topics began to be held in the 1960s. A subgroup of the IEEE Computer Society (the Pattern Recognition Subcommittee of the Data Acquisition and Transformation Committee) organized the first "Pattern Recognition Workshop," which was held in Puerto Rico in October 1966.[33] A second one (which I attended) was held in Delft, The Netherlands, in August 1968. In 1966, this subgroup became the IEEE Computer Society Pattern Analysis and Machine

Intelligence (PAMI) Technical Committee, which continued to organize conferences and workshops.[34]

Meanwhile, during the late 1950s and early 1960s, the symbol-processing people did their work mainly at MIT, at Carnegie Mellon University, at IBM, and at Stanford University. I'll turn next to describing some of what they did.

Notes

1. See http://www.nist.gov/public_affairs/techbeat/tb2007_0524.htm. [62]
2. Russell A. Kirsch *et al.*, "Experiments in Processing Pictorial Information with a Digital Computer," *Proceedings of the Eastern Joint Computer Conference*, pp. 221–229, Institute of Radio Engineering and Association for Computing Machinery, December 1957. [62]
3. The proceedings of the conference were published in George L. Fischer Jr. *et al.*, *Optical Character Recognition*, Washington, DC: Spartan Books, 1962. [62]
4. From J. Rabinow, "Developments in Character Recognition Machines at Rabinow Engineering Company," in George L. Fischer Jr. *et al.*, *op. cit.*, p. 27. [63]
5. From http://www.sri.com/about/timeline/erma-micr.html. [63]
6. Oliver G. Selfridge and Ulrich Neisser, "Pattern Recognition by Machine," *Scientific American*, Vol. 203, pp. 60–68, 1960. (Reprinted in Edward A. Feigenbaum and Julian Feldman (eds.), *Computers and Thought*, pp. 237ff, New York: McGraw Hill, 1963.) [63]
7. An early reference is Frank Rosenblatt, "The Perceptron: A Probabilistic Model for Information Storage and Organization in the Brain," *Psychological Review*, Vol. 65, pp. 386ff, 1958. [64]
8. H. David Block, "The Perceptron: A Model for Brain Functioning," *Reviews of Modern Physics*, Vol. 34, No. 1, pp. 123–135, January 1962. [68]
9. Albert B. J. Novikoff, "On Convergence Proofs for Perceptrons," in *Proceedings of the Symposium on Mathematical Theory of Automata*, pp. 615–622, Brooklyn, NY: Polytechnic Press of Polytechnic Inst. of Brooklyn, 1963. [68]
10. Nils J. Nilsson, *Learning Machines: Foundations of Trainable Pattern-Classifying Systems*, New York: McGraw-Hill Book Co., 1965; republished as *The Mathematical Foundations of Learning Machines*, San Francisco: Morgan Kaufmann Publishers, 1990. [68]
11. Frank Rosenblatt, *Principles of Neurodynamics*, Washington, DC: Spartan Books, 1962. [68]
12. Frank Rosenblatt, "A Description of the Tobermory Perceptron," *Collected Technical Papers*, Vol. 2, Cognitive Systems Research Program, Cornell University, 1963. [68]
13. Woodrow W. Bledsoe and Iben Browning, "Pattern Recognition and Reading by Machine," *Proceedings of the Eastern Joint Computer Conference*, pp. 225–232, New York: Association for Computing Machinery, 1959. [68]
14. William C. Ridgway, "An Adaptive Logic System with Generalizing Properties," *Stanford Electronics Laboratories Technical Report 1556-1*, Stanford University, Stanford, CA, 1962. [69]
15. For a description of MINOS II, see Alfred E. Brain, George Forsen, David Hall, and Charles Rosen, "A Large, Self-Contained Learning Machine," *Proceedings of the Western Electronic Show and Convention*, 1963. The paper was reprinted as Appendix C of an SRI proposal and is available online at http://www.ai.sri.com/pubs/files/rosen65-esu65-1tech.pdf. [70]
16. For a discussion of shift-register codes and other codes, see W. Peterson, *Error-Correcting Codes*, New York: John Wiley & Sons, 1961. Our technique was reported in A. E. Brain and N. J. Nilsson, "Graphical Data Processing Research Study and Experimental

Investigation," Quarterly Progress Report No. 8, p. 11, SRI Report, June 1962; available online at http://www.ai.sri.com/pubs/files/1329.pdf. [71]

17. Robert E. Larsen of SRI suggested using this method. The online encyclopedia Wikipedia has a clear description of dynamic programming. See http://en.wikipedia.org/wiki/Dynamic_programming. [72]

18. The technical details of the complete system are described in two papers: John Munson, "Experiments in the Recognition of Hand-Printed Text: Part I – Character Recognition," and Richard O. Duda and Peter E. Hart, "Experiments in the Recognition of Hand-Printed Text: Part II – Context Analysis," *AFIPS Conference Proceedings*, (of the 1968 Fall Joint Computer Conference), Vol. 33, pp. 1125–1149, Washington, DC: Thompson Book Co., 1968. Additional information can be found in SRI AI Center Technical reports, available online at http://www.ai.sri.com/pubs/files/1343.pdf and http://www.ai.sri.com/pubs/files/1344.pdf. [73]

19. E. Fix and J. L. Hodges Jr., "Discriminatory analysis, nonparametric discrimination," USAF School of Aviation Medicine, Randolph Field, Texas, Project 21-49-004, Report 4, Contract AF41(128)-31, February 1951. See also B. V. Dasarathy (ed.), *Nearest Neighbor (NN) Norms: NN Pattern Classification Techniques*, Los Alamitos, CA: IEEE Computer Society Press, which is a reprint of 1951 unpublished work of Fix and Hodges. [74]

20. Thomas M. Cover and Peter E. Hart, "Nearest Neighbor Pattern Classification," *IEEE Transactions on Information Theory*, pp. 21–27, January 1967. Available online at http://ieeexplore.ieee.org/iel5/18/22633/01053964.pdf. [74]

21. See M. A. Aizerman, E. M. Braverman, and L. I. Rozonoer, "Theoretical Foundations of the Potential Function Method in Pattern Recognition Learning," *Automation and Remote Control*, Vol. 25, pp. 917–936, 1964, and A. G. Arkadev and E. M. Braverman, *Computers and Pattern Recognition*, (translated from the Russian by W. Turski and J. D. Cowan), Washington, DC: Thompson Book Co., Inc., 1967. [74]

22. George S. Sebestyen, *Decision-Making Processes in Pattern Recognition*, Indianapolis, IN: Macmillan Publishing Co., Inc., 1962. [74]

23. Nils J. Nilsson, *op. cit.* [74]

24. Richard O. Duda and Peter E. Hart, *Pattern Classification and Scene Analysis*, New York: John Wiley & Sons, 1973; updated version: Richard O. Duda, Peter E. Hart, and David G. Stork, *Pattern Classification*, 2nd Edition, New York: John Wiley & Sons, 2000. [74]

25. George Nagy, "State of the Art in Pattern Recognition," *Proceedings of the IEEE*, Vol. 56, No. 5, pp. 836–857, May 1968. [74]

26. See, for example, Joseph K. Hawkins and C. J. Munsey, "An Adaptive System with Direct Optical Input," *Proceedings of the IEEE*, Vol. 55, No. 6, pp. 1084–1085, June 1967. Available online for IEEE members at http://ieeexplore.ieee.org/iel5/5/31078/01446273.pdf?tp=&arnumber=1446273&isnumber=31078. [75]

27. Laveen N. Kanal and Neal C. Randall, "Target Detection in Aerial Photography," paper 8.3, *Proceedings of the 1964 Western Electronics Show and Convention (WESCON)*, Los Angeles, CA, Institute of Radio Engineers (now IEEE), August 25–28, 1964. (Several other papers on pattern recognition were presented at this conference and are contained in the proceedings.) [75]

28. Thomas Harley, personal e-mail communication, July 15, 2007. [76]

29. Laveen N. Kanal and Neal C. Randall, *op. cit.* [76]

30. Laveen Kanal, personal e-mail communication, July 13, 2007. [76]

31. Laveen N. Kanal, "Statistical Methods for Pattern Classification," Philco Report, 1963; originally appeared in T. Harley *et al.*, "Semi-Automatic Imagery Screening Research Study and Experimental Investigation," Philco Reports VO43-2 and VO43-3, Vol. I,

Sec. 6, and Appendix H, prepared for U.S. Army Electronics Research and Development Laboratory under Contract DA-36-039-SC-90742, March 29, 1963. [77]

32. Thomas Harley, personal e-mail communication, July 11, 2007. [77]

33. Laveen N. Kanal (ed.), *Pattern Recognition, Proceedings of the IEEE Workshop on Pattern Recognition*, held at Dorado, Puerto Rico, Washington, DC: Thompson Book Co., 1968. [77]

34. See the Web page at http://tab.computer.org/pamitc/. [78]

5

Early Heuristic Programs

5.1 The Logic Theorist and Heuristic Search

Just prior to the Dartmouth workshop, Newell, Shaw, and Simon had programmed a version of LT on a computer at the RAND Corporation called the JOHNNIAC (named in honor of John von Neumann). Later papers[1] described how it proved some of the theorems in symbolic logic that were proved by Russell and Whitehead in Volume I of their classic work, *Principia Mathematica*.[2] LT worked by performing transformations on Russell and Whitehead's five axioms of propositional logic, represented for the computer by "symbol structures," until a structure was produced that corresponded to the theorem to be proved. Because there are so many different transformations that could be performed, finding the appropriate ones for proving the given theorem involves what computer science people call a "search process."

To describe how LT and other symbolic AI programs work, I need to explain first what is meant by a "symbol structure" and what is meant by "transforming" them. In a computer, symbols can be combined in lists, such as (A, 7, Q). Symbols and lists of symbols are the simplest kinds of symbol structures. More complex structures are composed of lists of lists of symbols, such as ((B, 3), (A, 7, Q)), and lists of lists of lists of symbols, and so on. Because such lists of lists can be quite complex, they are called "structures." Computer programs can be written that transform symbol structures into other symbol structures. For example, with a suitable program the structure "(the sum of seven and five)" could be transformed into the structure "(7 + 5)," which could further be transformed into the symbol "12."

Transforming structures of symbols and searching for an appropriate problem-solving sequence of transformations lies at the heart of Newell and Simon's ideas about mechanizing intelligence. In a later paper (the one they gave on the occasion of their receiving the prestigious Turing Award), they summarized the process as follows:[3]

The solutions to problems are represented as symbol structures. A physical symbol system exercises its intelligence in problem solving by search – that is, by generating and progressively modifying symbol structures until it produces a solution structure.

. . .

To state a problem is to designate (1) a test for a class of symbol structures (solutions of the problem), and (2) a generator of symbol structures (potential solutions). To solve a problem is to generate a structure, using (2), that satisfies the test of (1).

Figure 5.1. Start (left) and goal (right) configurations of a fifteen-puzzle problem.

Understanding in detail how LT itself used symbol structures and their transformations to prove theorems would require some mathematical and logical background. The process is easier to explain by using one of AI's favorite "toy problems" – the "fifteen-puzzle." (See Fig. 5.1.) The fifteen-puzzle is one of several types of sliding-block puzzles. The problem is to transform an array of tiles from an initial configuration into a "goal" configuration by a succession of moves of a tile into an adjacent empty cell.

I'll use a simpler version of the puzzle – one that uses a 3 × 3 array of eight sliding tiles instead of the 4 × 4 array. (AI researchers have experimented with programs for solving larger versions of the puzzle also, such as 5 × 5 and 6 × 6.)

Suppose we wanted to move the tiles from their configuration on the left to the one on the right as illustrated in Fig. 5.2.

Following the Newell and Simon approach, we must first represent tile positions for the computer by symbol structures that the computer can deal with. I will represent the starting position by the following structure, which is a list of three sublists:

$$((2, 8, 3), (1, 6, 4), (7, B, 5)).$$

The first sublist, namely, (2, 8, 3), names the occupants of the first row of the puzzle array, and so on. B stands for the empty cell in the middle of the third row.

In the same fashion, the goal configuration is represented by the following structure:

$$((1, 2, 3), (8, B, 4), (7, 6, 5)).$$

Next, we have to show how a computer can transform structures of the kind we have set up in a way that corresponds to the allowed moves of the puzzle. Note that when a tile is moved, it swaps places with the blank cell; that is, the blank cell moves too. The blank cell can either move within its row or can change rows.

Corresponding to these moves of the blank cell, when a tile moves within its row, B swaps places with the number either to its left in its list (if there is one) or to its

Figure 5.2. The eight-puzzle.

right (if there is one). A computer can easily make either of these transformations. When the blank cell moves up or down, B swaps places with the number in the corresponding position in the list to the left (if there is one) or in the list to the right (if there is one). These transformations can also be made quite easily by a computer program.

Using the Newell and Simon approach, we start with the symbol structure representing the starting configuration of the eight-puzzle and apply allowed transformations until a goal is reached. There are three transformations of the starting symbol structure. These produce the following structures:

$$((2, 8, 3), (1, 6, 4), (B, 7, 5)),$$

$$((2, 8, 3), (1, 6, 4), (7, 5, B)),$$

and

$$((2, 8, 3), (1, B, 4), (7, 6, 5)).$$

None of these represents the goal configuration, so we continue to apply transformations to each of these and so on until a structure representing the goal is reached. We (and the computer) can keep track of the transformations made by arranging them in a treelike structure such as the one shown in Fig. 5.3. (The arrowheads on both ends of the lines representing the transformations indicate that each transformation is reversible.)

This version of the eight-puzzle is relatively simple, so not many transformations have to be tried before the goal is reached. Typically though (especially in larger versions of the puzzle), the computer would be swamped by all of the possible transformations – so much so that it would never generate a goal expression. To constrain what was later called "the combinatorial explosion" of transformations, Newell and Simon suggested using "heuristics" to generate only those transformations guessed as likely to be on the path to a solution.

In one of their papers about LT, they wrote "A process that *may* solve a problem, but offers no guarantees of doing so, is called a *heuristic* for that problem." Rather than blindly striking out in all directions in a search for a proof, LT used search guided by heuristics, or "heuristic search." Usually, as was the case with LT, there is no guarantee that heuristic search will be successful, but when it is successful (and that is quite often) it eliminates much otherwise fruitless search effort.

The search for a solution to an eight-puzzle problem involves growing the tree of symbol structures by applying transformations to the "leaves" of the tree and thus extending it. To limit the growth of the tree, we should use heuristics to apply transformations only to those leaves thought to be on the way to a solution. One such heuristic might be to apply a transformation to that leaf with the smallest number of tiles out of position compared to the goal configuration. Because sliding tile problems have been thoroughly studied, there are a number of heuristics that have proved useful – ones much better than the simple number-of-tiles-out-of-position one I have just suggested.

Using heuristics keyed to the problem being solved became a major theme in artificial intelligence, giving rise to what is called "heuristic programming." Perhaps

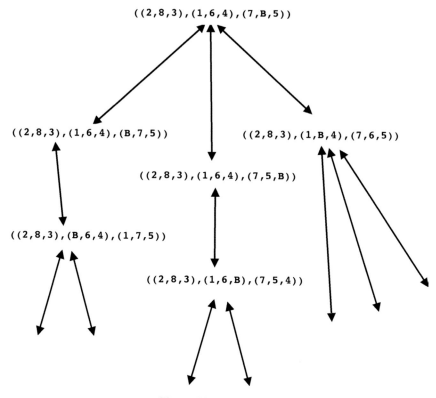

Figure 5.3. A search tree.

the idea of heuristic search was already "in the air" around the time of the Dartmouth workshop. It was implicit in earlier work by Claude Shannon. In March 1950, Shannon, an avid chess player, published a paper proposing ideas for programming a computer to play chess.[4] In his paper, Shannon distinguished between what he called "type A" and "type B" strategies. Type A strategies examine every possible combination of moves, whereas type B strategies use specialized knowledge of chess to focus on lines of play thought to be the most productive. The type B strategies depended on what Newell and Simon later called heuristics. And Minsky is quoted as saying "...I had already considered the idea of heuristic search obvious and natural, so that the Logic Theorist was not impressive to me."[5]

It was recognized quite early in AI that the way a problem is set up, its "representation," is critical to its solution. One example of how a representation affects problem solving is due to John McCarthy and is called the "mutilated checkerboard" problem.[6] Here's the problem: "Two diagonally opposite corner squares are removed from a checkerboard. Is it possible to cover the remaining squares with dominoes?" (A domino is a rectangular tile that covers two adjacent squares.) A naive way of searching for a solution would be to try to place dominoes in all possible ways over the checkerboard. But, if one uses the information that a checkerboard consists of 32 squares of one color and 32 of another color, and that the opposite corner squares are of the same color, then one realizes that the mutilated board consists of 30 squares of one color and 32 of another. Because a domino covers two squares of opposite colors, there is no way that a set of them can cover the remaining colors. McCarthy was interested in whether or not people could come up with "creative" ways to formulate the puzzle so that it could be solved by computers using methods based on logical deduction.

Another classic puzzle that has been used to study the effects of different representations is the "missionary and cannibals" problem: Three cannibals and three missionaries must cross a river. Their boat can only hold two people. If the cannibals outnumber the missionaries, on either side of the river, the missionaries on that side perish. Each missionary and each cannibal can row the boat. How can all six get across the river safely? Most people have no trouble formulating this puzzle as a search problem, and the solution is relatively easy. But it does require making one rather nonintuitive step. The computer scientist and AI researcher Saul Amarel (1928–2002) wrote a much-referenced paper analyzing this puzzle and various extended versions of it in which there can be various numbers of missionaries and cannibals.[7] (The extended versions don't appear to be so easy.) After moving from one representation to another, Amarel finally developed a representation for a generalized version of the problem whose solution required virtually no search. AI researchers are still studying how best to represent problems and, most importantly, how to get AI systems to come up with their own representations.

5.2 Proving Theorems in Geometry

Nathan Rochester returned to IBM after the Dartmouth workshop excited about discussions he had had with Marvin Minsky about Minsky's ideas for a possible computer program for proving theorems in geometry. He described these ideas to a new IBM employee, Herb Gelernter (1929–). Gelernter soon began a research project to develop a geometry-theorem-proving machine. He presented a paper on the first version of his program at a conference in Paris in June 1959,[8] acknowledging that

[t]he research project itself is a consequence of the Dartmouth Summer Research Project on Artificial Intelligence held in 1956, during which M. L. Minsky pointed out the potential utility of the diagram to a geometry theorem-proving machine.

Gelernter's program exploited two important ideas. One was the explicit use of subgoals (sometimes called "reasoning backward" or "divide and conquer"), and the other was the use of a diagram to close off futile search paths.

The strategy taught in high school for proving a theorem in geometry involves finding some subsidiary geometric facts from which, if true, the theorem would follow immediately. For example, to prove that two angles are equal, it suffices to show that they are corresponding angles of two "congruent" triangles. (A triangle is congruent to another if it can be translated and rotated, possibly even flipped over, in such a way that it matches the other exactly.) So now, the original problem is transformed into the problem of showing that two triangles are congruent. One way (among others) to show that two triangles are congruent is to show that two

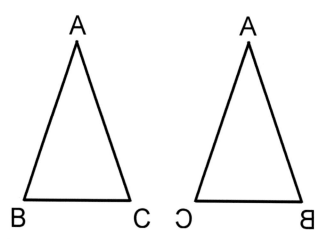

Figure 5.4. A triangle with two equal sides (left) and its flipped-over version (right).

corresponding sides and the enclosed angle of the two triangles all have the same sizes. This backward reasoning process ends when what remains to be shown is among the premises of the theorem.

Readers familiar with geometry will be able to follow the illustrative example shown in Fig. 5.4. There, on the left-hand side, we are given triangle ABC with side AB equal to side AC and must prove that angle ABC is equal to angle ACB. The triangle on the right side is a flipped-over version of triangle ABC.

Here is how the proof goes: If we could prove that triangle ABC is congruent to triangle ACB, then the theorem would follow because the two angles are corresponding angles of the two triangles. These two triangles can be proved congruent if we could establish that side AB (of triangle ABC) is equal to side AC (of triangle ACB) and that side AC (of triangle ABC) is equal to side AB (of triangle ACB) and that angle A (of triangle ABC) is equal to angle A (of triangle ACB). But the premises state that side AB is equal to side AC, and these lengths don't change in the flipped-over triangle. Similarly, angle A is equal to its flipped-over version – so we have our proof.

Before continuing my description of Gelernter's program, a short historical digression is in order. The geometry theorem just proved is famous – being the fifth proposition in Book I of Euclid's *Elements*. Because Euclid's proof of the proposition was a difficult problem for beginners it became known as the *pons asinorum* or "fools bridge." The proof given here is simpler than Euclid's – a version of it was given by Pappus of Alexandria (circa 290–350 CE).

Minsky's "hand simulation" of a program for proving theorems in geometry, discussed at Dartmouth, came up with this very proof (omitting what I think is the helpful step of flipping the triangle over). Minsky wrote[9]

In 1956 I wrote two memos about a hand-simulated program for proving theorems in geometry. In the first memo, the procedure found the simple proof that if a triangle has two equal sides then the corresponding angles are equal. It did this by noticing that triangle ABC was congruent to triangle CBA because of "side-angle-side." What was interesting is that this was found after a very short search – because, after all, there weren't many things to do. You might say the program was too stupid to do what a person might do, that is, think, "Oh, those are both the same triangle. Surely no good could come from giving it two different names." (The program has a collection of heuristic methods for proving Euclid-Like theorems, and one was that "if you want to prove two angles are equal, show that they're corresponding parts of congruent triangles." Then it also had several ways to demonstrate congruence. There wasn't much more in that first simulation.) But I can't find that memo anywhere.

As Minsky said, this is a very easy problem for a computer. Gelernter's program proved much more difficult theorems, and for these his use of a diagram was essential. The program did not literally draw and look at a diagram. Instead, as Gelernter wrote,

[The program is] supplied with the diagram in the form of a list of possible coordinates for the points named in the theorem. This point list is accompanied by another list specifying the points joined by segments. Coordinates are chosen to reflect the greatest possible generality in the figures.

So, for example, the points named in the problem about proving two angles equal are the vertices of the triangle ABC, namely, points A and B and C. Coordinates for each of these points are chosen, and care is taken to make sure that these coordinates do not happen to satisfy any special unnamed properties.

Gelernter's program worked by setting up subgoals and subsubgoals such as those I used in the example just given. It then searched for a chain of these ending in subgoals that could be established directly from the premises. Before any subgoal was selected by the program to be worked on however, it was first tested to see whether it held in the diagram. If it did hold, it might possibly be provable and could therefore be considered as a possible route to a proof. But, if it did not hold in the diagram, it could not possibly be true. Thus, it could be eliminated from further consideration, thereby "pruning" the search tree and saving what would certainly be fruitless effort. Later work in AI would also exploit "semantic" information of this sort.

We can see similarities between the strategies used in the geometry program and those used by humans when we solve problems. It is common for us to work backward – transforming a hard problem into subproblems and those into subsub-problems and so on until finally the problems are trivial. When a subproblem has many parts, we know that we must solve all of them. We also recognize when a proposed subproblem is patently impossible and thus can reject it. The next program I describe was based explicitly on what its authors thought were human problem-solving strategies.

5.3 The General Problem Solver

At the same 1959 Paris conference where Gelernter presented his program, Allen Newell, J. C. Shaw, and Herb Simon gave a paper describing their recent work on mechanizing problem solving.[10] Their program, which they called the "General Problem Solver (GPS)," was an embodiment of their ideas about how humans solve problems. Indeed, they claimed that the program itself was a theory of human problem-solving behavior. Newell and Simon were among those who were just as interested (perhaps even more interested) in explaining the intelligent behavior of humans as they were in building intelligent machines. They wrote "It is often argued that a careful line must be drawn between the attempt to *accomplish* with machines the same tasks that humans perform, and the attempt to *simulate* the processes humans actually use to accomplish these tasks. . . . GPS maximally confuses the two approaches – with mutual benefit."[11]

GPS was an outgrowth of their earlier work on the Logic Theorist in that it was based on manipulating symbol structures (which they believed humans did also). But GPS had an important additional mechanism among its symbol-manipulating strategies. Like Gelernter's geometry program, GPS transformed problems into subproblems, and so on. GPS's innovation was to compute a "difference" between a problem to be solved (represented as a symbol structure) and what was already known or given (also represented as a symbol structure). The program then attempted to reduce this difference by applying some symbol-manipulating "operator" (known to be relevant to this difference) to the initial symbol structure. Newell and Simon called this strategy "means–ends analysis." (Note the similarity to feedback control systems, which continuously attempt to reduce the difference between a current setting and a desired setting.) To do so, it would have to show that the operator's applicability condition was satisfied – a subproblem. The program then started up another version of itself to work on this subproblem, looking for a difference and so on.

For example, suppose the goal is to have Sammy at school when Sammy is known to be at home.[12] GPS computes a "difference," namely, Sammy is in the wrong place, and it finds an operator relevant to reducing this difference, namely, driving Sammy to school. To drive Sammy to school requires that the car be in working order. To make the problem interesting, we'll suppose that the car's battery is dead, so GPS can't apply the drive-car operator because that operator requires a working battery. Getting a working battery is a subproblem to which GPS can apply a version of itself. This "lower" version of GPS computes a difference, namely, the need for a working battery, and it finds an operator, namely, calling a mechanic to come and install a new battery. To call a mechanic requires having a phone number (and let us suppose we have it), so GPS applies the call-mechanic operator, resulting in the mechanic coming to install a new battery. The lower version of GPS has successfully solved its problem, so the superordinate GPS can now resume – noting that the condition for drive-car, namely, having a working battery, is satisfied. So GPS applies this operator, Sammy gets to school, and the original problem is solved. (This example illustrates the general workings of GPS. A real one using actual symbol structures, differences, and operators with their conditions and so on would be cumbersome but not more revealing.)

When GPS works on subproblems by starting up a new version of itself, it uses a very important idea in computer science (and in mathematics) called "recursion." You might be familiar with the idea that computer programmers organize complex programs hierarchically. That is, main programs fire up subprograms, which might fire-up subsubprograms, and so on. When a main program "calls" a subprogram, the main program suspends itself until the subprogram completes what it is supposed to do (possibly handing back data to the main program), and then the main program resumes work. In AI (and in other applications also), it is common to have a main program call a version of itself – taking care that the new version works on a simpler problem so as to avoid endless repetition and "looping." Having a program call itself is called "recursion."

Do people use subprograms and recursion in their own thinking? Quite possibly, but their ability to recall how to resume what some higher level thought process was doing when that process starts up a chain of lower level processes is certainly limited. I don't believe that GPS attempted to mimic this limitation of human thinking.

Newell and Simon believed that the methods used by GPS could be used to solve a wide variety of different problems, thus giving rise to the term "general." To apply it to a specific problem, a "table of differences" for that problem would have to be supplied. The table would list all the possible differences that might arise and match them to operators, which, for that problem, would reduce the corresponding differences. GPS was, in fact, applied to a number of different logical problems and puzzles[13] and inspired later work in both artificial intelligence and in cognitive science. Its longevity as a problem-solving program itself and as a theory of human problem solving was short, however, and lives on only through its various descendants (about which more will be discussed later).

Heuristic search procedures were used in a number of AI programs developed in the early 1960s. For example, another one of Minsky's Ph.D. students, James Slagle, programmed a system called SAINT that could solve calculus problems, suitably represented as symbol structures. It solved 52 of 54 problems taken from MIT freshman calculus final examinations.[14] Much use of heuristics was used in programs that could play board games, a subject to which I now turn.

5.4 Game-Playing Programs

I have already mentioned some of the early work of Shannon and of Newell, Shaw, and Simon on programs for playing chess. Playing excellent chess requires intelligence. In fact, Newell, Shaw, and Simon wrote that if "one could devise a successful chess machine, one would seem to have penetrated to the core of human intellectual endeavor."[15]

Thinking about programs to play chess goes back at least to Babbage. According to Murray Campbell, an IBM researcher who helped design a world-champion chess-playing program (which I'll mention later), Babbage's 1845 book, *The Life of a Philosopher*, contains the first documented discussion of programming a computer to play chess.[16] Konrad Zuse, the German designer and builder of the Z1 and Z3 computers, used his programming language called Plankalkül to design a chess-playing program in the early 1940s.

In 1946 Turing mentioned the idea of a computer showing "intelligence," with chess-playing as a paradigm.[17] In 1948, Turing and his former undergraduate colleague, D. G. Champernowne, began writing a chess program. In 1952, lacking a computer powerful enough to execute the program, Turing played a game in which he simulated the computer, taking about half an hour per move. (The game was recorded. You can see it at http://www.chessgames.com/perl/chessgame?gid= 1356927.) The program lost to a colleague of Turing, Alick Glennie; however, it is said that the program won a game against Champernowne's wife.[18]

After these early programs, work on computer chess programs continued, with off-again–on-again effort, throughout the next several decades. According to John McCarthy, Alexander Kronrod, a Russian AI researcher, said "Chess is the

Figure 5.5. Arthur Samuel. (Photograph courtesy of Donna Hussain, Samuel's daughter.)

Drosophila of AI" – meaning that it serves, better than more open-ended intellectual tasks do, as a useful laboratory specimen for research. As Minsky said, "It is not that the games and mathematical problems are chosen because they are clear and simple; rather it is that they give us, for the smallest initial structures, the greatest complexity, so that one can engage some really formidable situations after a relatively minimal diversion into programming."[19] Chess presents very difficult problems for AI, and it was not until the mid-1960s that the first competent chess programs appeared. I'll return to discuss these in a subsequent chapter.

More dramatic early success, however, was achieved on the simpler game of checkers (or draughts as the game is known in British English). Arthur Samuel (Fig. 5.5) began thinking about programming a computer to play checkers in the late 1940s at the University of Illinois where he was a Professor of Electrical Engineering. In 1949, he joined IBM's Poughkeepsie Laboratory and completed his first operating checkers program in 1952 on IBM's 701 computer. The program was recoded for the IBM 704 in 1954. According to John McCarthy,[20] "Thomas J. Watson Sr., the founder and President of IBM, remarked that the demonstration [of Samuel's program] would raise the price of IBM stock 15 points. It did."

[Apparently, Samuel was not the first to write a checkers-playing program. According to the *Encyclopedia Brittanica, Online*, "The earliest successful AI program was written in 1951 by Christopher Strachey, later director of the Programming Research Group at the University of Oxford. Strachey's checkers (draughts) program ran on the Ferranti Mark I computer at the University of Manchester, England. By the summer of 1952 this program could play a complete game of checkers at a reasonable speed."][21]

Samuel's main interest in programming a computer to play checkers was to explore how to get a computer to learn. Recognizing the "time consuming and costly procedure[s]" involved in programming, Samuel wrote "Programming computers to learn from experience should eventually eliminate the need for much of this detailed programming effort."[22] Samuel's efforts were among the first in what was to become a very important part of artificial intelligence, namely, "machine learning." His first program that incorporated learning was completed in 1955 and demonstrated on television on February 24, 1956.

Before describing his learning methods, I'll describe in general how Samuel's program chose moves. The technique is quite similar to how moves were chosen in the eight-puzzle I described earlier. Except now, provision must be made for the fact that the opponent chooses moves also. Again, a tree of symbolic expressions, representing board positions, is constructed. Starting with the initial configuration, all possible moves by the program (under the assumption that the program moves first) are considered. The result is all the possible resulting board configurations branching out from the starting configuration. Then, from each of these, all possible moves of the opponent are considered – resulting in more branches, and so on.

If such a tree could be constructed for an entire game, a winning move could be computed by examination of the tree. Unfortunately, it has been estimated that there are about 5×10^{20} possible checkers positions. A leading expert in programming computers to play games, Jonathan Schaeffer, was able to "solve" checkers (showing that optimal play by both players results in a draw) by time-consuming analysis of around 10^{14} positions. He wrote me that "This was the result of numerous enhancements aimed at focussing the search at the parts of the search space where we were most likely to find what we needed."[23] I'll describe his work in more detail later.

Samuel's program then could necessarily construct only a part of the tree – that is, it could look only a few moves ahead. How far ahead it looked, along various of its branches, depended on a number of factors that need not concern us here. (They involved such matters as whether or not an immediate capture was possible.) Looking ahead about three moves was typical, although some branches might be explored (sparsely) to a depth of as many as ten moves. A diagram from Samuel's paper, shown in Fig. 5.6, gives the general idea. Samuel said that the "actual branchings are much more numerous."

So, how is the program to choose a move from such an incomplete tree? This problem is faced by all game-playing programs, and they all use methods that involve computing a score for the positions at the tips, or "leaves," of the tree (that is, the leaves of the incomplete tree generated by the program) and then "migrating" this score back up to the positions resulting from moves from the current position. First, I will describe how to compute the score, then how to migrate it back, and then how Samuel used learning methods to improve performance.

Samuel's program first computed the points to be awarded to positions at the leaves of the tree based on their overall "goodness" from the point of view of the program. Among the features contributing points were the relative piece advantage (with kings being worth more than ordinary pieces), the overall "mobility" (freedom to move) of the program's pieces, and center control. (The program had access to 38 such features but only used the 16 best of these at any one time.) The points contributed by each feature were then multiplied by a "weight" (reflecting the relative importance of its corresponding feature), and the result was summed to give an overall score for a position.

Initial board position ⟶

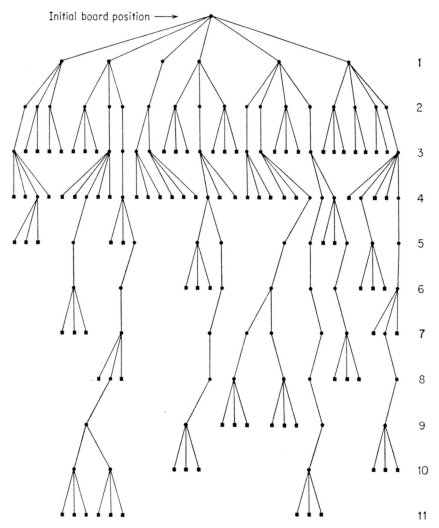

Figure 5.6. An illustrative checkers game tree. (From p. 74 of Edward A. Feigenbaum and Julian Feldman (eds.), *Computers and Thought*, New York: McGraw Hill, 1963.)

Starting with a position immediately above those at the tip of the tree, if it is a position for which it is the program's turn to move, we can assume that the program would want to move to that position with the highest score, so that highest score is migrated back to this "immediately above" position. If, however, it is a position from which it is the opponent's turn to move, we assume that the opponent would want to move to that position with the lowest score. In that case, the lowest score is migrated back to this immediately above position. This alternately "highest–lowest" migration strategy is continued back all the way up the tree and is called the "minimax" strategy.

[A simple modification of this strategy, called the "alpha–beta" procedure, is used to infer (correctly) from already-migrated scores that certain branches need not be examined at all – thus allowing other branches to be explored more deeply. Opinions differ about who first thought of this important modification. McCarthy and Newell and Simon all claim credit. Samuel told me he used it but that it was too obvious to write about.]

If one assumes that it is the program's turn to move from the current position, and that scores have already been migrated back to the positions just below it, the program would make its move to that position with the highest score. And then the game would continue with the opponent making a move, another stage of tree growth, score computation and migration, and so on until one side wins or loses.

One of the learning methods in Samuel's program adjusted the values of the weights used by the scoring system. (Recall that weight adjustments in Pandemonium and in neural networks were ways in which those systems learned.) The weights were adjusted so that the score of a board position (as computed by the sum of the weighted feature scores) moved closer to the value of its migrated score after finishing a search. For example, if the score of an initial position was computed (using the weights before adjustment) to be 22, and the migrated score of that position after search was 30, then the weights used to compute the score of the initial position were adjusted in a manner so that the new score (using the adjusted value of the weights) was made closer to 30, say 27. (This technique foreshadowed a very important learning method later articulated by Richard Sutton called "temporal-difference learning.") The idea here was that the migrated score, depending as it did on looking ahead in the game, was presumed to be a better estimate than the original score. The estimating procedure was thereby improved so that it produced values more consistent with the "look-ahead" score.

Samuel also used another method called "rote learning" in which the program saved various board positions and their migrated scores encountered during actual play. Then, at the end of a search, if a leaf position encountered was the same as one of these stored positions, its score was already known (and would not have to be computed using the weights and features). The known score, based as it was on a previous search, would presumably be a better indicator of position value than would be the computed score.

Samuel's program also benefitted from the use of "book games," which are re- cords of the games of master checkers players. In commenting about Samuel's work, John McCarthy wrote that "checker players have many volumes of annotated games with the good moves distinguished from the bad ones. Samuel's learning program used *Lee's Guide to Checkers*[24] to adjust its criteria for choosing moves so that the program would choose those thought good by checker experts as often as possible."

Samuel's program played very good checkers and, in the summer of 1962, beat Robert Nealey, a blind checkers master from Connecticut. (You can see a game played between Mr. Nealey and Samuel's program at http://www.fierz.ch/samuel.htm.) But, according to Jonathan Schaeffer and Robert Lake, "In 1965, the program played four games each against Walter Hellman and Derek Oldbury (then playing a match for the World Championship), and lost all eight games."[25]

Notes

1. A. Newell and H. A. Simon, "The Logic Theory Machine: A Complex Information Processing System," *Proceedings IRE Transactions on Information Theory*, Vol. IT-2, pp. 61–79, September 1956, and A. Newell, J. C. Shaw, and H. A. Simon, "Empirical Explorations of the Logic Theory Machine: A Case Study in Heuristics," *Proceedings of the 1957 Western Joint Computer Conference*, Institute of Radio Engineers, pp. 218–230, 1957. [81]
2. Alfred North Whitehead and Bertrand Russell, *Principia Mathematica*, Vol. 1, Cambridge: Cambridge University Press, 1910. [81]
3. Allen Newell and Herbert A. Simon, "Computer Science as Empirical Inquiry: Symbols and Search," *Communications of the ACM*, Vol. 19, No. 3, pp. 113–126, March 1976. [81]
4. Claude E. Shannon, "Programming a Computer for Playing Chess," *Philosophical Magazine*, Ser. 7, Vol. 41, No. 314, March 1950. Text available online at http://www.pi .infn.it/~carosi/chess/shannon.txt. (The paper was first presented in March 1950 at the National Institute for Radio Engineers Convention in New York.) [84]
5. Pamela McCorduck, *Machines Who Think: A Personal Inquiry into the History and Prospects of Artificial Intelligence*, p. 106, San Francisco: W. H. Freeman and Co., 1979. [84]
6. John McCarthy, "A Tough Nut for Theorem Provers," Stanford Artificial Intelligence Project Memo No. 16, July 17, 1964; available online at http://www-formal.stanford .edu/jmc/toughnut.pdf. [84]
7. Saul Amarel, "On Representations of Problems of Reasoning About Actions," in Donald Michie (ed.), *Machine Intelligence 3*, pp. 131–171, Edinburgh: Edinburgh University Press, 1968. [85]
8. Herbert Gelernter, "Realization of a Geometry-Theorem Proving Machine," *Proceedings of the International Conference on Information Processing*", pp. 273–282, Paris: UNESCO House, Munich: R. Oldenbourg, and London: Butterworths, 1960. Also in Edward A. Feigenbaum and Julian Feldman (eds.), *Computers and Thought*, pp. 134–152, New York: McGraw Hill, 1963. [85]
9. From http://www.math.niu.edu/~rusin/known-math/99/minsky. [86]
10. Allen Newell, J. C. Shaw, and Herbert A. Simon, "Report on a General Problem-Solving Program," *Proceedings of the International Conference on Information Processing*, pp. 256–264, Paris: UNESCO House, Munich: R. Oldenbourg, and London: Butterworths, 1960. [87]
11. For more about GPS as a theory and explanation for human problem solving, see Allen Newell and Herbert Simon, "GPS, a Program That Simulates Human Thought," in H. Billings (ed.), *Lernende Automaten*, pp. 109–124, Munich: R. Oldenbourg KG, 1961. Reprinted in *Computers and Thought*, pp. 279–293. [88]
12. I adapt an example from http://www.math.grinnell.edu/~stone/events/scheme-workshop/gps.html. [88]
13. See George Ernst and Allen Newell, *GPS: A Case Study in Generality and Problem Solving*, New York: Academic Press, 1969. [89]
14. James R. Slagle, "A Heuristic Program That Solves Symbolic Integration Problems in Freshman Calculus," Ph.D. dissertation, MIT, May 1961. For an article about SAINT, see James R. Slagle, "A Heuristic Program That Solves Symbolic Integration Problems in Freshman Calculus," *Journal of the ACM*, Vol. 10, No. 4, pp. 507–520, October 1963. [89]
15. Allen Newell, J. Shaw, and Herbert Simon, "Chess-Playing Programs and the Problem of Complexity," *IBM Journal of Research and Development*, Vol. 2, pp. 320–335, October 1958. [89]

16. Chapter 5 of *Hal's Legacy: 2001's Computer as Dream and Reality*, David G. Stork (ed.), Cambridge, MA: MIT Press, 1996. See the Web site at http://mitpress.mit.edu/e-books/Hal/chap5/five3.html. **[89]**

17. Andrew Hodges, "Alan Turing and the Turing Test," in *Parsing the Turing Test: Philosophical and Methodological Issues in the Quest for the Thinking Computer*, Robert Epstein, Gary Roberts, and Grace Beber (ed.), Dordrecht, The Netherlands: Kluwer, 2009. See A. M. Turing, "Proposed Electronic Calculator," report for National Physical Laboratory, 1946, in *A. M. Turing's ACE Report of 1946 and Other Papers*, B. E. Carpenter and R. W. Doran (eds.), Cambridge, MA: MIT Press, 1986. **[89]**

18. http://en.wikipedia.org/wiki/Alan_Turing. **[89]**

19. Marvin Minsky (ed.), "Introduction," *Semantic Information Processing*, p. 12, Cambridge, MA: MIT Press, 1968. **[90]**

20. From a Web retrospective at http://www-db.stanford.edu/pub/voy/museum/samuel.html. **[90]**

21. See Christopher Strachey, "Logical or Non-mathematical Programmes," *Proceedings of the 1952 ACM National Meeting (Toronto)*, pp. 46–49, 1952. **[90]**

22. Arthur L. Samuel, "Some Studies in Machine Learning Using the Game of Checkers," *IBM Journal of Research and Development*, Vol. 3, No. 3, pp. 210–229, 1959. Reprinted in Edward A. Feigenbaum and Julian Feldman (eds.), *Computers and Thought*, p. 71, New York: McGraw Hill, 1963. **[91]**

23. E-mail of February 14, 2009. **[91]**

24. John W. Dawson, *Lee's Guide to the Game of Draughts*, Revised Edition, London: E. Marlborough, 1947. **[93]**

25. Jonathan Schaeffer and Robert Lake, "Solving the Game of Checkers," *Games of No Chance*, pp. 119–133, MSRI Publications, Vol. 29, 1996. (Available online at http://www.msri.org/communications/books/Book29/files/schaeffer.pdf.) **[93]**

6

Semantic Representations

T HE COMPUTER PROGRAMS I HAVE DESCRIBED SO FAR PERFORMED TRANSFORMA-
tions on relatively simple symbol structures, which were all that were required
for the mathematical problems, puzzles, and games that these programs dealt with.
The main effort was in coming up with and using problem-specific heuristics (such
as features to be used in computing the value of a checkers position, for example)
to limit the number of transformations of these structures in searches for solutions.
As Minsky put it, "The most central idea of the pre-1962 period was that of finding
heuristic devices to control the breadth of a *trial-and-error search*."[1] In the early
1960s, several Ph.D. research projects, some performed under Minsky's direction at
MIT, began to employ more complex symbol structures in programs for performing
various intellectual tasks. Because of their rich, articulated content of information
about their problem topic, these structures were called *semantic representations*.[2]
As Minsky wrote, "Within the small domain in which each program operates,
the performance [of these programs] is not too bad compared with some human
activities.... But much more important than what these particular experiments
achieve are the methods they use to achieve what they do, *for each is a first trial of
previously untested ideas*."[3] I'll describe some examples of these sorts of projects and
the new methods that they employed.

6.1 Solving Geometric Analogy Problems

Thomas G. Evans (1934–) programmed a system that was able to perform well on
some standard geometric analogy tests. It was apparently the largest program written
up to that time in John McCarthy's new programming language, LISP (which I'll
describe later). I quote from an article based on Evans's 1963 dissertation, which
presented this work:[4]

We shall be considering the solution by machine of so-called "geometric-analogy" intelligence-
test questions. Each member of this class of problems consists of a set of labeled line drawings.
The task to be performed can be described by the question: "Figure A is to Figure B as
Figure C is to which of the following figures?" For example [in Fig. 6.1] it seems safe to say that
most people would agree with the program we are about to describe, in choosing [number 4]
as the desired answer.

He further noted that "problems of this type are widely regarded as requiring a
high degree of intelligence for their solution and in fact are used as a touchstone of
intelligence in some general intelligence tests used for college admission and other

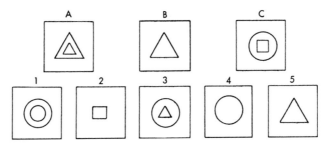

Figure 6.1. An analogy problem.

purposes." So, again, AI research concentrated on mechanizing tasks requiring human intelligence.

Evans's program first transformed the diagrams presented to it so that they revealed how they were composed out of parts. He called these "articular" representations. Of the possibly several decompositions possible, the one chosen by the program depended on its "context." (This choice is one example of a heuristic used by the program.) For example, the diagram

could either be decomposed into

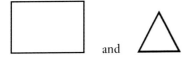 and

or into

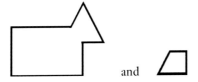 and

But if the analogy problem contained another diagram (part of the context):

then the first decomposition would be chosen.

Evans represented diagrams and their parts as complex symbol structures consisting of rather elaborate combinations of lists and lists of lists whose elements indicated which parts were inside or outside (or above or below) which other parts, and so on. Those details need not concern us here, but they did allow Evans to specify "rules" for his program that could be used to show how one diagram could be transformed into another. The program was able to infer which combinations of these rules transformed Figure A of a given problem into Figure B. Then it could apply this transformation to Figure C. If one of the multiple-choice answers resulted, it would give that one as its answer. Otherwise, the program "weakened" the transformation just enough so that one of the answers was produced, and that would be the program's answer.

Evans summarized his results as follows:

Allowing ourselves only [the parts of the program actually implemented], our estimate would be that of the 30 geometric-analogy problems on a typical edition of the ACE tests, [the program] can successfully solve at least 15 and possibly as many as 20 problems.

He notes that this level of performance compares favorably with the average high school student.

6.2 Storing Information and Answering Questions

Another of Minsky's Ph.D. students during the early 1960s, Bertram Raphael (1936–), focused on the problem of "machine understanding." In his dissertation,[5] Raphael explained that

a computer should be considered able to "understand" if it can converse intelligently, i.e., if it can remember what it is told, answer questions, and make responses which a human observer considers reasonable.

Raphael wanted to be able to tell things to a computer and then ask it questions whose answers could be deduced from the things it had been told. (The telling and asking were to be accomplished by typing sentences and queries.) Here are some examples of the kinds of things he wanted to tell it:

Every boy is a person.
A finger is part of a hand.
There are two hands on each person.
John is a boy.
Every hand has five fingers.

Given this information, Raphael would want his system to be able to deduce the answer to the question "How many fingers does John have?"

Because Raphael wanted his system to communicate with people, he wanted its input and output languages to be "reasonably close to natural English." He recognized that "the linguistic problem of transforming natural language input into a usable form will have to be solved before we obtain a general semantic information retrieval system." This "linguistic problem" is quite difficult and still not "solved" even though much progress has been made since the 1960s. Raphael used various "devices" (as he called them and which are not germane to our present discussion) to "bypass [the general problem of dealing with natural language] while still utilizing understandable English-like input and output."

The main problem that Raphael attacked was how to organize facts in the computer's memory so that the relevant deductions could be made. As Raphael put it, "The most important prerequisite for the ability to 'understand' is a suitable internal representation, or model, for stored information. The model should be structured so that information relevant for question-answering is easily accessible."[6]

Raphael called his system SIR, for Semantic Information Retrieval, (which he programmed in LISP). He used the word "semantic" because SIR modeled sentences in a way dependent on their meanings. The sentences that SIR could deal with involved "entities" (such as John, boy, hand, finger, and so on) and relations among these entities (such as "set-membership," "part–whole," "ownership," "above," "beside," and other spatial relationships). The model, then, had to have ways for representing entities and the relationships among them.

Entities such as John and boy were represented by the LISP computer words JOHN and BOY, respectively. (Of course, the computer had no way of knowing that the computer word JOHN had anything to do with the person John. Raphael could have just as well represented John in the computer by X13F27 so long as he used that representation consistently for John. Using the computer word JOHN was a mnemonic convenience for the programmer – not for the computer!) When representing the fact that John is a boy, SIR would "link" a computer expression (SUPER-SET JOHN BOY) to the expression JOHN and link a computer expression (SUB-SET BOY JOHN) to the expression BOY. Thus, if SIR were asked to name a boy, it could reply "JOHN" by referring to BOY in its model, looking at its SUB-SET link and retrieving JOHN. (I have simplified the representations somewhat to get the main ideas across; SIR's actual representations were a bit more complicated.)

SIR could deal with dozens of different entities and relations among them. Every time it was told new information, it would add new entities and links as needed. It also had several mechanisms for making logical deductions and for doing simple arithmetic. The very structure of the model facilitated many of its deductions because, as Minsky pointed out in his discussion of Raphael's thesis, "the direct predicate-links . . . almost physically chain together the immediate logical consequences of the given information."[7]

SIR was also the first AI system to use the "exception principle" in reasoning. This principle is best explained by quoting directly from Raphael's thesis:

General information about "all the elements" of a set is considered to apply to particular elements only in the absence of more specific information about those elements. Thus it is not necessarily contradictory to learn that "mammals are land animals" and yet "a whale is a mammal which always lives in water." In the program, this idea is implemented by always referring for desired information to the property-list [that is, links] of the individual concerned *before* looking at the descriptions of sets to which the individual belongs.

The justification for this departure from the no-exception principles of Aristotelian logic is that this precedence of specific facts over background knowledge seems to be the way people operate, and I wish the computer to communicate with people as naturally as possible.

The present program does not experience the uncomfortable feeling people frequently get when they must face facts like "a whale is a mammal which lives in water although mammals as a rule live on land."

The exception principle was studied by AI researchers in much more detail later and led to what is called default reasoning and nonmonotonic logics, as we shall see.

6.3 Semantic Networks

It is instructive to think of SIR's representational scheme in terms of a network. The entities (such as JOHN and BOY) are the "nodes" of the network, and the relational links (such as SUB-SET) are the connections between nodes. SIR was an early version of what would become an important representational idea in artificial intelligence, namely, *semantic networks*. It was not the first, however. John Sowa, who has written extensively about semantic networks, claims that the "oldest known semantic network was drawn in the 3rd century AD by the Greek philosopher Porphyry in his commentary on Aristotle's categories."[8] In 1961 Margaret Masterman (1910–1986), Director of the Cambridge Language Research Unit, used a semantic network in a translation system in which concepts were ordered in a hierarchy.[9]

M. Ross Quillian, a student of Herb Simon's at the Carnegie Institute of Technology, was interested, along with Newell and Simon, in computational models of human mental processes, specifically memory organization. He developed a memory model consisting of a semantic network of nodes representing English words. The nodes were interconnected by what he called "associative links." In Quillian's words, "In the memory model, ingredients used to build up a concept are represented by the token nodes naming other concepts, while the configurational meaning of the concept is represented by the particular structure of interlinkages connecting those token nodes to each other."

Quillian goes on to write that "[t]he central question asked in this research has been: What constitutes a reasonable view of how semantic information is organized within a person's memory? In other words: What sort of representational format can permit the 'meanings' of words to be stored, so that humanlike use of these meanings is possible?"[10]

I can illustrate how Quillian's network format represents meaning by using one of his examples. Consider the different meanings of the word "plant." One such meaning is given by linking the node PLANT to other nodes, such as LIVE, LEAF, FOOD, AIR, WATER, and EARTH, through connections that represent that a plant (according to this meaning of the word) is alive, has leaves, and gets its food from air, water, and earth. Another meaning of "plant" links PLANT to other nodes, such as PEOPLE, PROCESS, and INDUSTRY, through connections that represent that a plant (according to this other meaning of the word) is an apparatus that uses people for engaging in a process used in industry.

According to Quillian, the meaning of a term is represented by its place in the network and how it is connected to other terms. This same idea is used in dictionaries where the meaning of a word is given by mentioning the relationship of this word to other words. The meanings of those other words are, in turn, given by their relationships to yet other words. So we can think of a dictionary as being like a large semantic network of words linked to other words.

By using this view, the *full* meaning of a concept can be quite extensive. As Quillian puts it,

Suppose that a person were asked to state everything he knows about the concept "machine." ... This information will start off with the more "compelling" facts about machines, such as that they are usually man-made, involve moving parts, and so on, and will proceed "down" to less and less inclusive facts, such as the fact that typewriters are machines, and then eventually will get to much more remote information about machines, such as the fact that a typewriter has a stop which prevents its carriage from flying off each time it is returned. We are suggesting that this information can all usefully be viewed as part of the subject's concept of "machine."

In what way is Quillian's network a model of human memory organization? Quillian explored two capabilities of human memory modeled by his network. One was comparing and contrasting two different words. Quillian proposed that this be done by a process that came to be called "spreading activation." Conceptually, one starts at the nodes representing the two words and gradually traverses the links emanating from them, "activating" the nodes along the way. This process continues until the two "waves" of activation intersect, thus producing a "path" between the two original nodes. Quillian proposed that the total "distance" along this path between the two words could be used as a measure of their similarity. The path can be used to produce an account comparing the two words. (Quillian's program had mechanisms for expressing this account in simple English.)

To use one of Quillian's examples, suppose we wanted to compare the words "cry" and "comfort." The spreading activations would intersect at the word "sad," and the English account would express something like "to cry is to make a sad sound, and to comfort is to make something less sad."

Quillian was also interested in how the network could be used to "disambiguate" two possible uses of the same word. Consider, for example, the sentence "After the strike, the president sent him away." The network can encode different meanings of the word "strike." One such might involve a labor dispute, another might involve baseball, and yet another involve a raid by military aircraft. Which of these meanings is intended by the sentence? Presumably, activation proceeding outward from the word "president" would eventually reach concepts having to do with labor disputes before reaching concepts having to do with baseball or the military. Thus, the "labor dispute" meaning would be preferred because it is "closer," given that the word "president" is in the sentence. In contrast, a different conclusion would be reached for the sentence "After the strike, the umpire sent him away."

Quillian's model differs from some later semantic networks in that it does not have a predetermined hierarchy of superclasses and subclasses. As Quillian puts it, "every word is the patriarch of its own separate hierarchy *when some search process starts with it*. Similarly, every word lies at various places down within the hierarchies of (i.e., is an ingredient in) a great many other word concepts, when processing starts with them."

Notes

1. Marvin Minsky (ed.), "Introduction," *Semantic Information Processing*, p. 9, Cambridge, MA: MIT Press, 1968. **[96]**
2. It might be argued that the diagram used by Gelernter's geometry program was an earlier use of a semantic representation. **[96]**
3. Marvin Minsky, *op. cit.*, p. 1. **[96]**
4. Thomas G. Evans, "A Program for the Solution of a Class of Geometric-Analogy Intelligence-Test Questions," in Marvin L. Minsky, *op. cit.*, p. 271. **[96]**
5. Bertram Raphael, "SIR: Semantic Information Retrieval," in Marvin Minsky, *op. cit.*, pp. 33–145. (This is a partial reprint of his 1964 Ph.D. dissertation.) **[98]**
6. Marvin Minsky, *op. cit.*, p. 35. **[99]**
7. Marvin Minsky, *op. cit.*, p. 17. **[99]**
8. From an article by John F. Sowa at http://www.jfsowa.com/pubs/semnet.htm. (This is a revised and extended version of one that was originally written for the *Encyclopedia of Artificial Intelligence*, edited by Stuart C. Shapiro, Wiley, 1987, second edition, 1992.) **[100]**
9. Margaret Masterman, "Semantic Message Detection for Machine Translation, Using an Interlingua," in *Proceedings of the 1961 International Conference on Machine Translation of Languages and Applied Language Analysis*, pp. 438–475, London: Her Majesty's Stationery Office, 1962. **[100]**
10. M. Ross Quillian, "Semantic Memory," Ph.D. dissertation, Carnegie Institute of Technology (now Carnegie Mellon University), October 1966. (This work also appears as Report AFCRL-66-189 and is partially reprinted in M. Minsky (ed.), *Semantic Information Processing*, pp. 216–270, Cambridge, MA: MIT Press, 1968.) **[100]**

7

Natural Language Processing

B EYOND PATTERN RECOGNITION OF INDIVIDUAL ALPHANUMERIC CHARACTERS, whether they be of fixed font or handwritten, lies the problem of understanding strings of characters that form words, sentences, or larger assemblages of text in a "natural" language, such as English. To distinguish languages such as English from the languages used by computers, the former are usually called "natural languages." In artificial intelligence, "understanding" natural language input usually means either converting it to some kind of memory model (such as the one used by Raphael in his SIR system or the semantic network used by Quillian) or the evocation of some action appropriate to the input.

Natural languages are spoken as well as written. And, because speech sounds are not as well segmented as are the characters printed on a page, speech understanding presents additional difficulties, which I'll describe in a later chapter.

The inverse of understanding natural language input is generating natural language output – both written and spoken. Translating from one language to another involves both understanding and generation. So does carrying on a conversation. All of these problems – understanding, generation, translation, and conversing – fall under the general heading of "natural language processing" (sometimes abbreviated as NLP).

7.1 Linguistic Levels

Linguists and others who study language recognize several levels at which language can be analyzed. These levels can be arranged in a sort of hierarchy, starting with those dealing with the most basic components of language (sounds and word parts) and proceeding upward to levels dealing with sequences of sentences. If speech is being dealt with, there are the levels of *phonetics* (language sounds) and *phonology* (organization of sounds into words). For both speech and text, *morphology* deals with how whole words are put together from smaller parts. For example, "walking" consists of "walk" plus "-ing."

Next, *syntax* is concerned with sentence structure and grammar. It attempts to describe rules by which a string of words in a certain language can be labeled either grammatical or not. For example, the string "John hit the ball" is grammatical but the string "ball the hit John" is not. Together with the dictionary definitions of words, syntax comes next in importance for understanding the meaning of a sentence. For example, the sentence "John saw the man with a telescope" has two different

103

meanings depending on its syntactic structure (that is, depending on whether "with a telescope" refers to "the man" who had a telescope or to "saw").

But grammaticality alone is insufficient for determining meaning. For example, the sentence "Colorless green ideas sleep furiously" might be considered grammatical, but it is nonsensical. The *semantics* level helps to determine the meaning (or the meaninglessness) of a sentence by employing logical analyses. For example, through semantic analysis, an "idea" can't be both "colorless" and "green."

Next comes the *pragmatics* level, which considers the context of a sentence to pin down meaning. For example, "John went to the bank" would have a different meaning in a sentence about stream fishing than it would in a sentence about commerce. Pragmatics deals with meanings in the context of specific situations.

One of these levels in particular, namely, syntax, was the subject of much early study and continues to be an important aspect of NLP. In 1957, the American linguist Noam Chomsky published a ground-breaking book titled *Syntactic Structures* in which he proposed sets of grammatical rules that could be used for generating the "legal" sentences of a language.[1] The same rules could also be used to analyze a string of words to determine whether or not they formed a legal sentence of the language. I'll illustrate how this analysis is done using what Chomsky called a *phrase-structure grammar* (PSG).[2] The process is very similar to how we all "diagrammed" sentences back in grade school.

Grammars are defined by stating rules for replacing words in the string by symbols corresponding to syntactic categories, such as noun or verb or adjective. Grammars also have rules for replacing strings of these syntactic symbols by additional symbols. To illustrate these ideas, I'll use a very simple grammar adapted from one of Chomsky's examples. This grammar has only three syntactic categories: determiner, noun, and verb. Those three are sufficient for analysing strings such as "the man hit the ball."

One of the rules in this illustrative grammar states that we can replace either of the words "the" or "a" by the symbol "DET" (for determiner). Linguists write this rule as follows:

the | a → DET
(The symbol | is used to indicate that *either* of the words that surround it can be replaced by the syntactic symbol to the right of the arrow.)

Here are some other rules, written in the same format:

man | ball | john → N
(The words "man," "ball," and "john" can be replaced by the symbol "N" for noun.)

hit | took | threw → V
(The words "hit," "took," and "threw" can be replaced by the symbol "V" for verb.)

DET N → NP
(The string of symbols "DET" and "N" can be replaced by the symbol "NP" for noun phrase.)

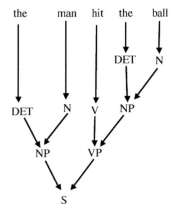

Figure 7.1. A parse tree for analyzing a sentence.

V NP → VP
(The string of symbols "V" and "NP" can be replaced by the symbol
"VP" for verb phrase.)

NP VP → S
(The string of symbols "NP" and "VP" can be replaced by the symbol
"S" for sentence.)

Symbols such as "S," "DET," "NP," and so on are called the "nonterminal" symbols
of the language defined by the grammar, whereas vocabulary words such as "ball,"
"john," and "threw" are the "terminal" symbols of the language.

We can apply these rules to the string "the man hit the ball" to transform it into
"S." Any string that can be changed into "S" in this way is said to be grammatical –
a legal sentence in the language defined by this very simple grammar. One way to
illustrate the rule applications, called a *parse tree*, is shown in Fig. 7.1.[3]

This example was based on a small set of syntactic categories and replacement
rules just to illustrate the main ideas about syntactic analysis. To make the grammar
slightly more realistic, we would need to include symbols and replacement rules
for adjectives, adverbs, prepositions, and so on. And, of course, we would have to
include many more vocabulary words.

Grammars are called *context-free grammars* (CFGs) if all of their rules have just a
single nonterminal symbol on the right side of the arrow. They are called that because
when the rules are used in reverse (to generate rather than to analyze grammatical
sentences), the way in which a nonterminal symbol is replaced does not depend on
the presence of any other symbols. PSGs are context free.

The diagram in Fig. 7.2 shows how the rules of our simple grammar can be used
to generate sentences. In this case, it starts with the symbol for sentence, namely,
"S," and generates the sentence "John threw the ball."

This simple grammar certainly can't generate all of the sentences we would claim
to be legal or acceptable. It also generates sentences that we would not ordinarily
want to accept, such as "the john threw the ball." Chomsky's book presents much
more complex grammars, and later work has produced quite elaborate ones. By
the early 1960s, several grammars had been encoded in computer programs that

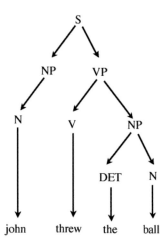

Figure 7.2. A parse tree for generating a sentence.

could parse samples of English text.[4] I'll be mentioning several different grammars, some more complex than CFGs in succeeding chapters. Nevertheless, even the most complex grammars can't cleanly distinguish between sentences we would accept as grammatically correct and those we would not. I will return to this difficulty and one way to deal with it in a later chapter.

The way a sentence is parsed by a grammar can determine its meaning, so an important part of natural language processing involves using the grammar rules to find acceptable parse trees for sentences. Finding a parse tree involves search – either for the several different ways that the nonterminal symbols, beginning with "S," can be replaced using grammar rules in an attempt to match a target sentence or for the several different ways the words in a target sentence can be replaced by nonterminal symbols in an attempt to produce the symbol "S." The first of these kinds of searches is called "top-down" (from "S" to a sentence); the second is called "bottom-up" (from a sentence to "S").

It is often (if not usually) the case that, given a grammar, sentences can have more than one parse tree, each with a different meaning. For example, "the man hit the ball in the park" could have a parse tree in which "in the park" is part of a verb phrase along with "hit" or a parse tree in which "in the park" is part of a noun phrase along with "ball." Moreover, as I have already mentioned, some parsings of sentences might be meaningless. For example, according to my simple grammar, "the ball threw the man" is a legal but probably meaningless sentence. Deciding which parse tree is appropriate is part of the process of deciding on meaning and is a job for the semantics (and possibly even the pragmatics) level. During the late 1950s and throughout most of the 1960s and beyond, syntactic analysis was more highly developed than was semantics.

Semantic analysis usually involves using the parse tree to guide the transformation of the input sentence into an expression in some well-defined "meaning representation language" or into a program that responds in the appropriate way to the input sentence. For example, "the man threw the ball" might be transformed into a logical expression such as

$(\exists x, y, z)[\text{Past}(z) \land \text{Man}(x, z) \land \text{Ball}(y, z) \land \text{Event}(z) \land \text{Throws}(x, y, z)],$

which can be interpreted as "there are x, y, and z, such that z is an event that occurred in the past, x is a man in that event, y is a ball in that event, and x throws y in that event."

Semantic analysis might also transform the sentence "the man threw the ball" into a program that, in some way, simulates a man throwing the ball in the past.

7.2 Machine Translation

Some of the first attempts to use computers for more than the usual numerical calculations were in automatic translation of sentences in one language into sentences of another. Word dictionaries could be stored in computer memory (either on tapes or on punched cards), and these could be used to find English equivalents for foreign words. It was thought that selecting an appropriate equivalent for each foreign word in a sentence, together with a modest amount of syntactic analysis, could be used to translate a sentence in a foreign language (Russian, for example) into English.

Reporting about a new computer[5] being developed by a team led by Harry D. Huskey at the National Bureau of Standards (now called the National Institute of Standards and Technology), the *New York Times* reported the following on May 31, 1949:[6]

A new type of "electric brain" calculating machine capable not only of performing complex mathematical problems but even of translating foreign languages, is under construction here at the United States Bureau of Standards Laboratory at the University of California's Institute of Numerical Analysis. While the exact scope the machine will have in the translating field has not been decided, the scientists working on it say it would be quite possible to make it encompass the 60,000 words of the Webster Collegiate Dictionary with equivalents for each word in as many as three foreign languages.

Explaining how the machine might do translation, the *Times* reporter wrote

When a foreign word for translation is fed into the machine, in the form of an electro-mathematical symbol on a tape or card, the machine will run through its "memory" and if it finds that symbol as record, will automatically emit a predetermined equivalent – the English word.
. . .
This admittedly will amount to a crude word-for-word translation, lacking syntax, but will nevertheless be extremely valuable, the designers say, for such purposes as scientists' translations of foreign technical papers in which vocabulary is far more of a problem than syntax.

The machine had not actually performed any translations – the idea of doing so was still just a possibility envisioned by Huskey. But even nonscientists could imagine the difficulties. An editorial in the *New York Times* the next day put the problem well:

We have our misgivings about the accuracy of every translation. How is the machine to decide if the French word "pont" is to be translated as "bridge" or "deck" or to know that "operation" in German means a surgical operation? All the machine can do is to simplify the task of looking up words in a dictionary and setting down their English equivalents on a tape, so that the translator still has to frame the proper sentences and give the words their contextual meaning.

In a 1947 letter to Norbert Wiener, Warren Weaver, a mathematician and science administrator, mentioned the possibility of using digital computers to translate documents between natural human languages. Wiener was doubtful about this possibility. In his reply to Weaver, Wiener wrote "I frankly am afraid the boundaries of words in different languages are too vague and the emotional and international connotations are too extensive to make any quasi-mechanical translation scheme very hopeful." Nevertheless, by July 1949, Weaver had elaborated his ideas into a memorandum, titled "Translation" that he sent to several colleagues.

Weaver began his memorandum by stating the following:

There is no need to do more than mention the obvious fact that a multiplicity of languages impedes cultural interchange between the peoples of the earth, and is a serious deterrent to international understanding. The present memorandum, assuming the validity and importance of this fact, contains some comments and suggestions bearing on the possibility of contributing at least something to the solution of the world-wide translation problem through the use of electronic computers of great capacity, flexibility, and speed.

According to the editors of the published volume[7] in which the memorandum was reprinted, "When he sent it to some 200 of his acquaintances in various fields, it was literally the first suggestion that most had ever seen that language translation by computer techniques might be possible." Weaver's document is often credited with initiating the field of machine translation (often abbreviated as MT).[8]

In June 1952 at MIT, Yehoshua Bar-Hillel (1915–1975), an Israeli logician who was then at MIT's Research Laboratory for Electronics, organized the first conference devoted to machine translation.[9] Originally optimistic about the possibilities, Bar-Hillel was later to conclude that full automatic translation was impossible.

In January 1954, automatic translation of samples of Russian text to English was demonstrated at IBM World Headquarters, 57th Street and Madison Avenue, New York City. The demonstration, using a small vocabulary and limited grammar, was the result of a collaboration between IBM and Georgetown University. The project was headed by Cuthbert Hurd, director of the Applied Sciences Division at IBM, and Léon Dostert of Georgetown. According to an IBM press release[10] on January 8, 1954,

Russian was translated into English by an electronic "brain" today for the first time.

Brief statements about politics, law, mathematics, chemistry, metallurgy, communications and military affairs were submitted in Russian by linguists of the Georgetown University Institute of Languages and Linguistics to the famous 701 computer of the International Business Machines Corporation. And the giant computer, within a few seconds, turned the sentences into easily readable English.

A girl who didn't understand a word of the language of the Soviets punched out the Russian messages on IBM cards. The "brain" dashed off its English translations on an automatic printer at the breakneck speed of two and a half lines per second.

"Mi pyeryedayem mislyi posryedstvom ryechyi," the girl punched. And the 701 responded: "We transmit thoughts by means of speech."

"Vyelyichyina ugla opryedyelyayetsya otnoshyenyiyem dlyini dugi k radyiusu," the punch rattled. The "brain" came back: "Magnitude of angle is determined by the relation of length of arc to radius."

Although the demonstration caused a great deal of excitement and led to increased funding for translation research, subsequent work in the field was disappointing.[11] Evaluating MT work in a 1959 report circulated among researchers, Bar-Hillel had become convinced that fully automatic, high-quality translation (which he dubbed FAHQT) was not feasible "not only in the near future but altogether." His expanded report appeared in a 1960 paper that enjoyed wide distribution.[12]

One of the factors leading Bar-Hillel to his negative conclusions was the apparent difficulty of giving computers the "world knowledge" they would need for high-quality translation. He illustrated the problem with the following story:

Little John was looking for his toy box. Finally he found it. The box was in the pen. John was very happy.

How should one translate "The box was in the pen"? Bar-Hillel argued that even if there were only two definitions of "pen" (a writing utensil and an enclosure where small children play), a computer knowing only those definitions would have no way of deciding which meaning was intended. In addition to its knowledge of vocabulary and syntax, a translating computer would need to know "the relative sizes of pens, in the sense of writing implements, toy boxes, and pens, in the sense of playpens." Such knowledge, Bar-Hillel claimed, was not at the disposal of the electronic computer. He said that giving a computer such encyclopedic knowledge was "utterly chimerical and hardly deserves any further discussion."

As later researchers would finally concede, Bar-Hillel was right about his claim that highly competent natural language processing systems (indeed, broadly competent AI systems in general) would need to have encyclopedic knowledge. However, most AI researchers would disagree with him about the futility of attempting to give computers the required encyclopedic knowledge. Bar-Hillel was well known for being a bit of a nay-sayer regarding artificial intelligence. (Commenting on John McCarthy's "Programs with Common Sense" paper at the 1958 Teddington Conference, Bar-Hillel said "Dr. McCarthy's paper belongs in the Journal of Half-Baked Ideas, the creation of which was recently proposed by Dr. I. J. Good.")[13]

In April 1964, the National Academy of Sciences formed the Automatic Language Processing Advisory Committee (ALPAC), with John R. Pierce (1910–2002) of Bell Laboratories as chair, to "advise the Department of Defense, the Central Intelligence Agency, and the National Science Foundation on research and development in the general field of mechanical translation of foreign languages." The committee issued its report in August 1965 and concluded, among other things, that ". . . there is no immediate or predictable prospect of useful machine translation."[14] They recommended support for basic linguistics science and for "aids" to translation, but not for further support of fully automatic translation. This report caused a dramatic reduction of large-scale funding of research on machine translation. Nonetheless, machine translation survived and eventually thrived, as we shall see in later chapters.

The Association for Machine Translation and Computational Linguistics (AMTCL) held its first meeting in 1962. In 1968, it changed its name to the Association for Computational Linguistics (ACL) and has become an international scientific and professional society for people working on problems involving natural language

and computation. It publishes the quarterly journal *Computational Linguistics* and
sponsors conferences and workshops.[15]

7.3 Question Answering

In addition to work on machine translation, researchers began exploring how sentences in a natural language, such as English, could be used to communicate with
computers. You will recall Weizenbaum's ELIZA program that was able to engage
a person in a conversation even though the program "understood" nothing about
what was being said. And, I have already mentioned Raphael's SIR system that could
represent information given to it and then answer questions.

I'll mention a few other projects to give a flavor of natural language processing
work during this period. A program called BASEBALL (written in IPL-V, a special
list-processing programming language developed by Newell, Shaw, and Simon to
be described later) was developed at the Lincoln Laboratory under the direction of
Bert Green, a professor of Psychology at the Carnegie Institute of Technology.[16] It
could answer simple English questions about baseball using a database about baseball
games played in the American League during a single year. For example, it could
answer a question such as "Where did the Red Sox play on July 7?" The questions
had to be of a particularly simple form and restricted to words in the program's
vocabulary. In the authors' words,[17]

Questions are limited to a single clause; by prohibiting structures with dependent clauses the
syntactic analysis is considerably simplified. Logical connectives, such as *and*, *or*, and *not*, are
prohibited, as are constructions implying relations like *most* and *highest*. Finally, questions
involving sequential facts, such as "Did the Red Sox ever win six games *in a row*?" are
prohibited.

The program worked by converting a question into a special form called a "specification list" using both special-purpose syntactic and semantic analyses. This list
would then be used to access the program's database to find an answer to the question. For example, the question "Where did the Red Sox play on July 7?" would first
be converted to the list:

Place = ?
Team = Red Sox
Month = July
Day = 7

The authors claimed that their "restrictions were temporary expedients that will
be removed in later versions of the program." As far as I know, there were no later
versions of the program. (As we will see as my history of AI unfolds, there are several
instances in which it proved very difficult to remove "temporary" restrictions.)

Another natural language program, SAD SAM, was written in IPL-V in 1962–1963 by
Robert Lindsay at the Carnegie Institute of Technology.[18] It could analyze English
sentences about family relationships and encode these relationships in a family tree.
Using the tree, it could then answer English questions about relationships.

For example, if SAD SAM received the sentence "Joe and Jane are Tom's off-spring," it would construct a treelike list structure for a certain "family unit" in which Tom is the father and Joe and Jane are the children. Then, if it received the sentence "Mary is Jane's mother," it would add Mary to this structure as Tom's wife. It would then be able to answer the question "Who is Joe's mother?"

SAD SAM is an acronym for Sentence Appraiser and Diagrammer and Semantic Analyzing Machine. The SAD part parsed the input sentences and passed them to SAM, which extracted the semantic information needed for building family trees and for finding answers to questions. The program could accept a wide variety of sentences in Basic English – a system of grammar and a vocabulary of about 850 words defined by Charles K. Ogden.[19]

Robert F. Simmons (1925–1994), a psychologist and linguist at the Systems Development Corporation (SDC) in Santa Monica, California, had grander goals for his own work in natural language processing. According to an "In Memoriam" page written by Gordon Novak, one of his Ph.D. students at the University of Texas in Austin where Simmons took up a position as Professor of Computer Sciences and Psychology,[20]

Simmons' dream was that one could have "a conversation with a book;" the computer would read the book, and then the user could have a conversation with the computer, asking questions to be answered from the computer's understanding of the book.

Accomplishing this "dream" would turn out to be as hard as AI itself. In a 1961 note about his proposed "Synthex" project, Simmons described how he would begin:[21]

The objective of this project is to develop a research methodology and a vehicle for the design and construction of a general purpose computerized system for synthesizing complex human cognitive functions. The initial vehicle, proto-synthex, will be an elementary language-processing device which reads simple printed material and answers simple questions phrased in elementary English.

By 1965, Simmons and Lauren Doyle had conducted some experiments with their Protosynthex system. According to a report by Trudi Bellardo Hahn,[22] "A small prototype full-text database of chapters from a child's encyclopedia (*Golden Book*) was loaded on the system. Protosynthex could respond to simple questions in English with an 'answer.' . . . it was a pioneering effort in the use of natural language for text retrieval."

In the meantime, Daniel G. Bobrow (1935–), a Ph.D. student of Marvin Minsky's at MIT, wrote a set of programs, called the STUDENT system, that could solve algebra "story problems" given to it in a restricted subset of English. Here is an example of a problem STUDENT could solve:

The distance from New York to Los Angeles is 3000 miles. If the average speed of a jet plane is 600 miles per hour, find the time it takes to travel from New York to Los Angeles by jet.

STUDENT solved the problem by using some known relationships about speed and distance to set up and solve the appropriate equations. Bobrow's dissertation gave several other examples of problems STUDENT could solve and the methods used.[23]

Notes

1. Noam Chomsky, *Syntactic Structures,* 's-Gravenhage: Mouton & Co., 1957. **[104]**

2. The basic structure of PSGs was independently invented by computer scientist John Backus to describe the syntax of the ALGOL programming language. See John Backus, "The Syntax and Semantics of the Proposed International Algebraic Language of the Zürich ACM-GAMM Conference," *Proceedings on the International Conference on Information Processing,* pp. 125–132, UNESCO, 1959. **[104]**

3. According to C. George Boeree (see http://www.ship.edu/~cgboeree/wundtjames.html), Wilhelm Wundt "invented the tree diagram of syntax we are all familiar with in linguistics texts." **[105]**

4. For a survey of work during this period, see Daniel Bobrow, "Syntactic Analysis of English by Computer: A Survey," *Proceedings of the 1963 Fall Joint Computer Conference,* Vol. 24, pp. 365–387, Baltimore: Spartan Books, 1963. **[106]**

5. The Standards Western Automatic Computer (later abbreviated to SWAC) **[107]**

6. The quotation appears in John Hutchins, "From First Conception to First Demonstration: The Nascent Years of Machine Translation, 1947–1954. A chronology," *Machine Translation,* Vol. 12 No. 3, pp. 195–252, 1997. (A corrected 2005 version, with minor additions, appears at http://www.hutchinsweb.me.uk/MTJ-1997-corr.pdf.) **[107]**

7. W. N. Locke and A. D. Booth (eds.), *Machine Translation of Languages: Fourteen Essays,* pp. 15–23, Cambridge, MA: MIT Press, 1955. **[108]**

8. For a history of MT, see W. John Hutchins, "Machine Translation: A Brief History," in E. F. K. Koerner and R. E. Asher (eds.), *Concise History of the Language Sciences: From the Sumerians to the Cognitivists,* pp. 431–445, Oxford: Pergamon Press, 1995. (Also available online at http://www.hutchinsweb.me.uk/ConcHistoryLangSci-1995.pdf.) Hutchins also has a Web page devoted to his publications at http://www.hutchinsweb.me.uk/. **[108]**

9. For reports about this conference see, E. Reifler, "The First Conference on Mechanical Translation," *Mechanical Translation,* Vol. 1 No. 2, pp. 23–32, 1954, and A. C. Reynolds, "The Conference on Mechanical Translation Held at MIT, June 17–20, 1952," *Mechanical Translation,* Vol. 1, No. 3, pp. 47–55, 1954. **[108]**

10. http://www-03.ibm.com/ibm/history/exhibits/701/701_translator.html. **[108]**

11. For a summary of the IBM–Georgetown work, see W. John Hutchins, "The Georgetown–IBM Experiment Demonstrated in January 1954," in Robert E. Frederking and Kathryn B. Taylor (eds.), *Proceedings of Machine Translation: From Real Users to Research,* 6th Conference of the Association for Machine Translation in the Americas, AMTA-2004, pp. 102–114, Washington DC, USA, September 28–October 2, 2004, Berlin: Springer, 2004. An online version is available at http://www.hutchinsweb.me.uk/ATMA-2004.pdf. **[109]**

12. Yehoshua Bar-Hillel, "The Present Status of Automatic Translation of Languages," *Advances in Computers,* Vol. 1, No. 1, pp. 91–163, 1960. **[109]**

13. In D. V. Blake and A. M. Uttley (eds.), *Proceedings of the Symposium on Mechanisation of Thought Processes,* p. 85, London: Her Majesty's Stationary Office, 1959. **[109]**

14. John R. Pierce *et al., Language and Machines: Computers in Translation and Linguistics,* ALPAC Report, National Academy of Sciences Publication 416, National Research Council, Washington, DC, 1966. **[109]**

15. See http://www.aclweb.org/. **[110]**

16. Bert F. Green Jr., Alice K. Wolf, Carol Chomsky, and Kenneth Laughery, "BASEBALL: An Automatic Question Answerer," pp. 219–224, *Proceedings of the Western Joint Computer Conference,* May 1961. Reprinted in Edward A. Feigenbaum and Julian Feldman (eds.),

Computers and Thought, pp. 207–216, New York: McGraw Hill, 1963, and in B. Grosz, K. Spark Jones, and B. Lynn Webber (eds.), *Readings in Natural Language Processing*, Morgan Kaufman, Los Altos, CA, 1986. [110]

17. *Ibid*. [110]

18. See Robert K. Lindsay, "Inferential Memory as the Basis of Machines Which Understand Natural Language," in Edward A. Feigenbaum, and Julian Feldman, *op. cit.*, pp. 217–233. [110]

19. Charles K. Ogden, *Basic English: A General Introduction with Rules and Grammar*, 4th edition, London: Kegan, Paul, Trench, Trubner & Co., Ltd., 1933. (Lindsay says 1,700 words; other sources say 850.) [111]

20. From http://www.cs.utexas.edu/users/ai-lab/simmons.html. [111]

21. Robert F. Simmons, "Synthex," *Communications of the ACM*, Vol. 4 , No. 3, p. 140, March 1961. [111]

22. From "Text Retrieval Online: Historical Perspective on Web Search Engines," by Trudi Bellardo Hahn, *ASIS Bulletin*, April/May 1998. Available online at http://www.asis.org/Bulletin/Apr-98/hahn.html. [111]

23. Daniel G. Bobrow, "Natural Language Input for a Computer Problem Solving System," MIT Artificial Intelligence Project Memo 66, Memorandum MAC-M-148, March 30, 1964. Available online at http://dspace.mit.edu/bitstream/handle/1721.1/5922/AIM-066.pdf?sequence=2. An article based on the dissertation is Chapter 3 of Marvin Minsky (ed.), *Semantic Information Processing*, Cambridge, MA: MIT Press, 1968. [111]

8

1960s' Infrastructure

T HE TECHNICAL DEVELOPMENTS DURING THE 1960s WERE AIDED (INDEED, ONE might say made possible) by several systems support and societal factors. New computer languages made it much easier to build AI systems. Researchers from mathematics, from cognitive science, from linguistics, and from what soon would be called "computer science" came together in meetings and in newly formed laboratories to attack the problem of mechanizing intelligent behavior. In addition, government agencies and companies, concluding that they had an important stake in this new enterprise, provided needed research support.

8.1 Programming Languages

Newell and Simon were among the first to realize that a specialized computer language would be useful for manipulating the symbolic expressions that were at the heart of their approach to mechanizing intelligence. The most elementary kind of symbolic expression is a list of symbols, such as (7, B, 5). More complex structures can be composed by creating lists of lists of symbols and lists of lists of lists, and so on.

In my description of symbol structures for the eight-puzzle, I mentioned the kinds of manipulations that are needed. Recall that the starting position of the eight-puzzle was represented by the expression

$$((2, 8, 3), (1, 6, 4), (7, B, 5)).$$

What was needed was a language for writing programs that could produce expressions representing the positions corresponding to moves of the puzzle. For example, one of the moves that can be made from the starting position is represented by the expression

$$((2, 8, 3), (1, 6, 4), (B, 7, 5)).$$

To produce this expression, the program must copy the starting position expression and then interchange the first and second elements of the third list in that expression.

Newell, Shaw, and Simon set about to develop a language in which these kinds of manipulations could be programmed. Starting around 1954 at the RAND Corporation, they created a series of languages all called IPL (for information-processing language). Several versions of the language were developed. IPL-I was not actually implemented but served as a design specification. IPL-II was implemented in 1955 for the RAND Corporation's JOHNNIAC computer. Later versions (through IPL-VI) were implemented at Carnegie Tech.

The IPL languages were used to program several early AI programs, including LT, GPS, NSS (the Newell, Shaw, Simon chess-playing program), and the programs written by Newell's and Simon's students, such as Quillian and George Ernst. After the Dartmouth summer project, John McCarthy also began thinking about using list-processing languages. He was aware of the use of FLPL (FORTRAN fortified by some list-processing operations) in Gelernter's geometry theorem-proving machine. Ultimately, however, McCarthy concluded a new language was needed that was easier to use than IPL and more powerful than FLPL.

Starting in the fall of 1958 at MIT, McCarthy began the implementation of a programming language he called LISP (for list processing). He based it (loosely) on a branch of mathematics of special interest in computation called recursive function theory. LISP had several elementary operations for copying a list, stripping off elements of a list, adding an element to a list, and checking to see whether something were an element of a list. From these, arbitrarily complex manipulations of lists could be composed. An important feature of LISP was that programs for manipulating lists were themselves represented as lists. Such programs could thus be elements of other lists and could have subprograms embedded in them. A program could even have a version of itself embedded in it. As I have already mentioned, programs that can activate versions of themselves as part of their operation are called "recursive" and are very useful (if used with the care needed to avoid endless circularity).[1]

Because it was easier to use, LISP soon replaced IPL as the primary language of artificial intelligence research and applications. The programs produced by Minsky's students, Evans, Raphael, Bobrow, Slagle, and others, were all written in LISP. (Interestingly, Arthur Samuel did not use a list-processing language for writing his checkers-playing programs. Rather heroically, he programmed them in the base language of elementary machine operations to make them run efficiently and use memory sparingly.)

Besides developing LISP, McCarthy proposed a method, called "time-sharing," by which a single computer could be made to serve several users simultaneously – acting as if each user had his or her own private machine.[2] Working initially with Ed Fredkin at Bolt, Beranek, and Newman (BBN) and later with others, McCarthy developed an early time-sharing system at MIT using a DEC PDP-1 computer.[3]

8.2 Early AI Laboratories

In 1955, Newell moved from the RAND Corporation to Carnegie Tech (which became Carnegie Mellon University, CMU, in 1967) to work on a Ph.D. degree in industrial management under Herb Simon. After completing his degree, Newell stayed on as a professor at Carnegie, and he and Simon began advising a number of Ph.D. students – using the phrase "complex information processing (CIP)" to describe their work. (For several years they avoided the AI sobriquet.) In the fall of 1956, Herb Simon took delivery of an IBM 650, which was the first computer used for CIP work. Later, they used an IBM 704, followed by a series of DEC machines.

Figure 8.1. Site of the Stanford AI Lab from 1966 until 1980. (Photograph courtesy of Lester Earnest.)

John McCarthy moved from Dartmouth to MIT in the fall of 1958. Minsky joined MIT a year later. As Minsky puts it,[4]

[McCarthy and I] were walking down the hall and we met Jerry Wiesner or Zimmerman or someone and he said how's it going and we said well, we're working on these artificial intelligence ideas but we need a little more room and support for some graduate students. So then a room appeared a few days later . . .

The "room" soon developed into the MIT Artificial Intelligence Project. Initially, the group used MIT's IBM 704 computer, which proved not to have sufficient memory for the programs being written. So it began to use a DEC PDP-1 belonging to BBN. With funding from another project at MIT, it bought its own PDP-1, which was followed by the PDP-6 and PDP-10. Several of the group's Ph.D. students did their work at BBN and at the nearby Lincoln Laboratory where Oliver Selfridge continued his AI research – mainly on pattern recognition and machine learning. In 1962, McCarthy moved to Stanford where he began an AI project. Seymour Papert (1928–), a mathematician who had worked with Jean Piaget, joined Minsky as co-director of the AI Lab in 1963.

By 1965 at Stanford, McCarthy and colleagues had created a time-sharing system, called Thor, on a PDP-1 computer. It included twelve Philco display terminals, which made it the first display-oriented time-sharing system anywhere in the world.

With the help of Lester Earnest (1930–), who had moved to Stanford from Lincoln Laboratory, McCarthy set up the Stanford AI Laboratory (SAIL) in 1965. Outgrowing its on-campus facilities, SAIL moved to a building in the Stanford foothills during the summer of 1966. (See Fig. 8.1.) With additional support from

Figure 8.2. Donald Michie. (Photograph courtesy of the Michie Family.)

ARPA, the Lab took delivery of a DEC PDP-6 computer and, later, a PDP-10 computer. In addition to its work in AI (which I'll describe in subsequent chapters), SAIL was involved in many other computer-related projects including the development of a precursor to computer "windows" and the early installation of terminals in everyone's offices.[5]

Since their early days, the groups at CMU, MIT, and Stanford have been among the leaders of research in AI. Often graduates of one of these institutions became faculty members of one of the other ones.

Around 1965, another world-class AI center emerged at the University of Edinburgh in Scotland. Its founder was Donald Michie (1923–2007; Fig. 8.2), who had worked with Alan Turing and I. J. (Jack) Good at Bletchley Park during the Second World War. Discussions there with Turing and Good about intelligent machines captivated Michie. As he reported in an October 2002 interview, "I resolved to make machine intelligence my life as soon as such an enterprise became feasible."[6] Because computer facilities in the mid- to late 1940s were primitive and scarce, Michie became a geneticist and molecular biologist.

Pursuing his interest in machine intelligence, from the sidelines as it were, in 1960 he put together a "contraption of matchboxes and glass beads" that could learn to play tic-tac-toe (noughts and crosses). He named his "machine" MENACE, an acronym for Matchbox Educable Noughts and Crosses Engine.[7] (See Fig. 8.3.) (As I'll explain later, MENACE foreshadowed work in what is now called "reinforcement learning.") During a year-long visit to Stanford (sponsored by the Office of Naval Research) in the early 1960s, Michie met John McCarthy, Bernard Widrow, and others working in AI (including me). While there, he worked on a learning program for balancing a pole on a motor-driven cart.

In January 1965, Michie became the Director of the UK's first AI laboratory, the Experimental Programming Unit, at the University of Edinburgh. This group was to become the Department of Machine Intelligence and Perception in October 1966. Michie recruited some top-flight computer talent, including Rod Burstall, Robin Popplestone, and John Collins. Those three developed a list-processing language called POP-2, which was the language used for AI program-writing by members of the Unit. (I'll describe some of these programs later.) For many years, Michie's group worked collaboratively with a nearby University of Edinburgh group, the Metamathematics Unit under Bernard Meltzer (circa 1916–2008). The Metamathematics Unit is famous for the work of Robert Boyer and J Strother Moore in mechanized theorem proving and of Robert Kowalski in developing some of the principles of logic programming.[8]

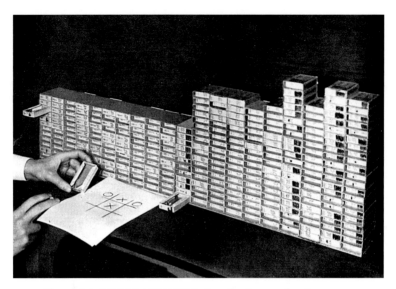

Figure 8.3. Michie's MENACE for learning how to play tic-tac-toe.

At IBM in Poughkeepsie, Nathan Rochester and Herb Gelernter continued AI research for a short time after the Dartmouth workshop. This research resulted in the geometry-theorem-proving machine. However, soon after, according to a book about government support for computing research, "in spite of the early activity of Rochester and other IBM researchers, the corporation's interest in AI cooled. Although work continued on computer-based checkers and chess, an internal report prepared about 1960 took a strong position against broad support for AI."[9] Perhaps IBM wanted to emphasize how computers *helped* people perform tasks rather than how they might *replace* people. McCarthy's view about all of this is that "IBM thought that artificial intelligence [that machines were as smart as people] was bad for IBM's image... This may have been associated with one of their other image slogans, which was 'data processing, not computing.'"[10]

8.3 Research Support

As the computing systems needed for AI research became larger and more expensive, and as AI laboratories formed, it became necessary to secure more financial support than was needed in the days when individual investigators began work in the field. Two of the major sources of funding during the late 1950s and early 1960s were the Office of Naval Research (ONR) and the Advanced Research Projects Agency (ARPA), each a part of the U.S. defense establishment.

ONR was formed shortly after the end of the Second World War. Its mission was "to plan, foster, and encourage scientific research in recognition of its paramount importance as related to the maintenance of future naval power and the preservation of national security." Its Information Systems Branch was set up in the mid-1950s under the direction of Marshall Yovits. The branch supported AI work at several

Figure 8.4. J. C. R. Licklider. [Photograph by Koby-Antupit from MIT Collection (JCL.8).]

institutions and also sponsored conferences and workshops on self-organizing systems, cybernetics, optical character recognition, and artificial intelligence. All of this was done in anticipation that these technologies would be generally useful to the U.S. Navy. (A later director, Marvin Denicoff, supported some of my research and my AI textbook writing.)

The formation of ARPA was, in part, a response to the successful launch of the Soviet satellite *Sputnik* in 1957. ARPA's mission was to provide significant amounts of research funds to attack problem areas important to U.S. defense. One of its most important projects in the late 1950s was the development of ablative nose cones to absorb and dissipate heat during ballistic missile reentry. Its Information Processing Techniques Office (IPTO) was set up in 1962 under the direction of J. C. R. (Lick) Licklider (1915–1990; Fig. 8.4).

"Lick" (as he was called by all who knew him) was a psychoacoustician who worked first at Lincoln Laboratory and MIT and later at BBN. Lick's 1960 paper, "Man-Computer Symbiosis," proposed that men and computers should "cooperate in making decisions and controlling complex situations without inflexible dependence on predetermined programs."[11]

Lick was persuaded that computers would play a very important role in defense – especially in those applications in which people and computers worked together. At ARPA, he provided funds to MIT for the formation of Project MAC (an acronym for Machine-Aided Cognition and perhaps for Multi-Access Computing or Man And Computers). [Project MAC, initially founded in July 1963, was later to become the Laboratory for Computer Science (LCS), and still later to evolve into the Computer Science and Artificial Intelligence Laboratory (CSAIL).] Project MAC took Minsky and McCarthy's Artificial Intelligence Project under its wing and also supported the development of MIT's Compatible Time-Sharing System (CTSS) under Fernando Corbató. (CTSS work was separate from McCarthy's time-sharing project.)

ARPA funds helped to establish "centers of excellence" in computer science. Besides MIT, these centers included Stanford, Carnegie Mellon, and SRI. ARPA also supported computer science work at the RAND Corporation, the Systems Development Corporation, and BBN, among others. AI was just one of ARPA's interests. IPTO also supported research that led to graphical user interfaces (and the mouse), supercomputing, computer hardware and very-large-scale integrated circuits (VLSI), and, perhaps most famously, research that led to the Internet. According to Licklider, "ARPA budgets did not even include AI as a separate line item until 1968."[12]

But as far as AI was concerned, Lick believed that Newell and Simon, Minsky, and McCarthy ought to be provided with research funds adequate to support big AI projects. With regard to the situation at Stanford (and probably to that at MIT and CMU also), Paul Edwards explained that[13]

[F]unding from ARPA was virtually automatic; Licklider simply asked McCarthy what he wanted and then gave it to him, a procedure unthinkable for most other government agencies. Licklider remembered that "it seemed obvious to me that he should have a laboratory supported by ARPA. . . . So I wrote him a contract at that time."

McCarthy remembers all of this somewhat differently. Soon after arriving at Stanford in 1962, he sent a proposal to Licklider "to do AI." McCarthy claims that Licklider demurred at first – citing their close relationship when McCarthy was at MIT and Licklider at BBN – but then gave him "a small contract."[14] But perhaps it was not so "small" compared with how research was usually supported (say by the National Science Foundation) at the time. Les Earnest claims that McCarthy "obtained financial support for a small activity (6 persons) from the Advanced Research Projects Agency (ARPA) beginning June 15, 1963."[15]

Later, ARPA was renamed DARPA (for Defense Advanced Research Projects Agency) to emphasize its role in defense-related research. DARPA projects and grants were typically much larger than those of ONR and allowed the purchase of computers and other equipment as well as support for personnel. It's hardly an exaggeration to say that a good part of today's computer-based infrastructure is the result of DARPA research support.

8.4 All Dressed Up and Places to Go

By the mid-1960s AI was well prepared for further advances. Flushed with early successes it was poised to make rapid progress during the rest of the 1960s and 1970s. Indeed, many people made enthusiastic predictions. For example, in a 1957 talk[16] Herb Simon predicted that within ten years "a digital computer will be the world's chess champion unless the rules bar it from competition." He made three other predictions too. Within ten years computers would compose music, prove a mathematical theorem, and embody a psychological theory as a program. He said "it is not my aim to surprise or shock you . . . but the simplest way I can summarize is to say that there are now in the world machines that think, that learn and that create. Moreover, their ability to do these things is going to increase rapidly until – in a visible future – the range of problems they can handle will be coextensive with the range to which the human mind has been applied."[17] Later Simon said that his predictions were part of an attempt "to give some feeling for what computers would mean" to society.

One could argue that Simon's predictions about computers composing music and proving a mathematical theorem were realized soon after he made them, but a computer chess champion was not to emerge until forty years later. And, we are still far, I think, from achieving things "coextensive" with what the human mind can achieve.

Simon was not alone in being optimistic. According to Hubert Dreyfus, "Marvin Minsky, head of MITs Artificial Intelligence Laboratory, declared in a 1968 press release for Stanley Kubrick's movie, *2001: A Space Odyssey*, that 'in 30 years we should have machines whose intelligence is comparable to man's.'"[18] The difficulty in assessing these sorts of predictions is that "human–level intelligence" is multi-faceted. By the year 2000, AI programs *did* outperform humans in many intellectual feats while still having a long way to go in most others.

Even so, what had already been accomplished was an impressive start. More important perhaps than the specific demonstrations of intelligent behavior by machines was the technical base developed during the 1950s and early 1960s. AI researchers now had the means to represent knowledge by encoding it in networks, as logical formulas, or in other symbol structures tailored to specific problem areas. Furthermore, they had accumulated experience with heuristic search and other tech-niques for manipulating and using that knowledge. Also, researchers now had new programming languages, IPL, LISP, and POP-2, that made it easier to write symbol-processing programs. Complementing all of this symbol-processing technology were neural networks and related statistical approaches to pattern recognition. These tech-nical assets, along with the organizational and financial ones, provided a solid base for the next stage of AI's development.

Notes

1. For McCarthy's own history of the development of LISP, see http://www-formal. stanford.edu/jmc/history/lisp.html. Also see Herbert Stoyan's history of LISP at http://www8.informatik.uni-erlangen.de/html/lisp-enter.html. [115]
2. See McCarthy's memo proposing how to build a time-sharing system at http://www-formal.stanford.edu/jmc/history/timesharing-memo.html. [115]
3. For more about these early days of computing at MIT and of time-sharing work there (among other things), see the interview with John McCarthy conducted by William Aspray of the Charles Babbage Institute on March 2, 1989. It is available online at http://www.cbi.umn.edu/oh/display.phtml?id=92. [115]
4. From an interview conducted by Arthur L. Norberg on November 1, 1989, for the Charles Babbage Institute. Available online at http://www.cbi.umn.edu/oh/display. phtml?id=107. [116]
5. For a history of AI work in the lab up to 1973, see Lester Earnest (ed.), "Final Report: The First Ten Years of Artificial Intelligence Research at Stanford," Stanford Artifi-cial Intelligence Laboratory Memo AIM-228 and Stanford Computer Science Depart-ment Report No. STAN-CS-74-409, July 1973. (Available online at http://www-db. stanford.edu/pub/cstr/reports/cs/tr/74/409/CS-TR-74-409.pdf.) For other SAIL

history, see "SAIL Away" by Les Earnest at http://www.stanford.edu/~learnest/sailaway.htm. [117]

6. A textscript of the interview can be found online at http://www.aiai.ed.ac.uk/events/ccs2002/CCS-early-british-ai-dmichie.pdf. [117]

7. Donald Michie, "Experiments on the Mechanisation of Game Learning: 1. Characterization of the Model and its Parameters," *Computer Journal*, Vol. 1, pp. 232–263, 1963. [117]

8. For a history of these Edinburgh groups, see Jim Howe's online 1994 article "Artificial Intelligence at Edinburgh University: A Perspective" at http://www.dai.ed.ac.uk/AI_at_Edinburgh_perspective.html. [117]

9. National Research Council, *Funding a Revolution: Government Support for Computing Research*, Washington, DC: National Academy Press, 1999. (An html version of this book, which contains a rather conservative account of AI history, is available from http://www.nap.edu/catalog.php?record_id=6323#toc.) [118]

10. From "An Interview with John McCarthy," conducted by William Aspray on 2 March 1989, Palo Alto, CA, Charles Babbage Institute, The Center for the History of Information Processing, University of Minnesota, Minneapolis. [118]

11. J. C. R. Licklider, "Man–Computer Symbiosis," *IRE Transactions on Human Factors in Electronics*, HFE-1, pp. 4–11, 1960. Available online at http://memex.org/licklider.html. [119]

12. J. C. R. Licklider, "The Early Years: Founding IPTO," p. 220 in Thomas C. Bartee (ed.), *Expert Systems and Artificial Intelligence: Applications And Management*, Indianapolis: Howard W. Sams, 1988. [120]

13. Paul Edwards, *The Closed World: Computers and the Politics of Discourse in Cold War America*, p. 270, Cambridge, MA: MIT Press, 1996. [120]

14. From "An Interview with John McCarthy," *op. cit.* [120]

15. Lester Earnest (ed.), "Final Report: The First Ten Years of Artificial Intelligence Research at Stanford," Stanford Artificial Intelligence Laboratory Memo AIM-228 and Stanford Computer Science Department Report No. STAN-CS-74-409, July 1973. (Available online at http://www-db.stanford.edu/pub/cstr/reports/cs/tr/74/409/CS-TR-74-409.pdf.) [120]

16. 12th National Meeting of the Operations Research Society (ORSA) in Pittsburgh. [120]

17. The published version of this talk is in Herbert Simon and Allen Newell, "Heuristic Problem Solving: The Next Advance in Operations Research," *Operations Research*, Vol. 6, January–February 1958. [121]

18. Hubert L. Dreyfus, "Overcoming the Myth of the Mental," *Topoi*, Vol. 25, pp. 43–49, 2006. [121]

Part III

Efflorescence: Mid-1960s to Mid-1970s

D URING THE 1960s AND WELL INTO THE 1970s, AI RESEARCH BLOSSOMED AND progress seemed rapid. The laboratories established at MIT, Carnegie Mellon, Stanford, SRI, and Edinburgh expanded, and several new groups got started at other universities and companies. Achievements during the preceding years, even though modest in retrospect, were exciting and full of promise, which enticed several new people into the field, myself included. Many of us were just as optimistic about success as Herb Simon and Marvin Minsky were when they made their predictions about rapid progress.

AI entered a period of flowering that led to many new and important inventions. Several ideas originated in the context of Ph.D. dissertation research projects. Others emerged from research laboratories and from individual investigators wrestling with theoretical problems. In this part, I'll highlight some of the important projects and research results. Although not a complete account, they typify much of what was going on in AI during the period. I'll begin with work in computer vision.

9

Computer Vision

S IGHTED HUMANS GET MUCH OF THEIR INFORMATION THROUGH VISION. THAT PART of AI called "computer vision" (or, sometimes, "machine vision") deals with giving computers this ability. Most computer vision work is based on processing two-dimensional images gathered from a three-dimensional world – images gathered by one or more television cameras, for example. Because the images are two-dimensional projections of a three-dimensional scene, the imaging process loses information. That is, different three-dimensional scenes might produce the same two-dimensional image. Thus, the problem of reconstructing the scene faithfully from an image is impossible in principle.

Yet, people and other animals manage very well in a three-dimensional world. They seem to be able to interpret the two-dimensional images formed on their retinas in a way that gives them reasonably accurate and useful information about their environments.

Stereo vision, using two eyes, helps provide depth information. Computer vision too can use "stereopsis" by employing two or more differently located cameras look-ing at the same scene. (The same effect can be achieved by having one camera move to different positions.) When two cameras are used, for example, the images formed by them are slightly displaced with respect to each other, and this displacement can be used to calculate distances to various parts of the scene. The computation involves comparing the relative locations in the images that correspond to the objects in the scene for which depth measurements are desired. This "correspondence problem" has been solved in various ways, one of which is to seek high correlations between small areas in one image with small areas in the other. Once the "disparity" of the location of an image feature in the two images is known, the distance to that part of the scene giving rise to this image feature can be calculated by using trigonometric calculations (which I won't go into here.)[1]

Perhaps surprisingly, a lot of depth information can be obtained from other cues besides stereo vision. Some of these cues are inherent in a single image, and I'll be describing these in later chapters. Even more importantly, background knowledge about the kinds of objects one is likely to see accounts for much of our ability to interpret images. Consider the image shown in Fig. 9.1 for example.

Most people would describe this image as being of two tables, one long and narrow and the other more-or-less square. Yet, if you measure the actual table tops in the image itself, you might be surprised to find that they are exactly the same size and shape! (The illustration is based on an illusion called "turning the tables" by the psychologist Roger Shepherd and is adapted from Michael Bach's version

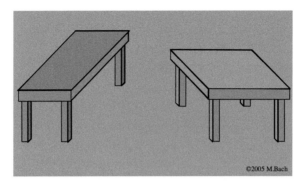

Figure 9.1. Two tables. (Illustration courtesy of Michael Bach.)

of Shepherd's diagram. If you visit Bach's Web site, http://www.michaelbach.de/
ot/sze_shepardTables/, you can watch while one table top moves over to the other
without changing shape.)

Something apart from the image provides us with information that induces us to
make inferences about the shapes of the three-dimensional tables captured in the
two-dimensional image shown in Fig. 9.1. As we shall see, that extra information
consists of two things: knowledge about the image-forming process under various
lighting conditions and knowledge about the kinds of things and their surfaces that
occur in our three-dimensional world. If we could endow computers with this sort
of knowledge, perhaps they too would be able to see.

9.1 Hints from Biology

There has been a steady flow of information back and forth between scientists
attempting to understand how vision works in animals and engineers working on
computer vision. An early example of work at the intersection of these two interests
was described in an article titled "What the Frog's Eye Tells the Frog's Brain"[2]
by four scientists at MIT. Guided by previous biological work, the four, Jerome
Lettvin, H. R. Maturana, Warren McCulloch, and Walter Pitts, probed the parts
of the frog's brain that processed images. They found that the frog's visual system
consisted of "detectors" that responded only to certain kinds of things in its visual
field. It had detectors for small, moving convex objects (such as flies) and for a
sudden darkening of illumination (such as might be caused by a looming predator).
These, together with a couple of other simple detectors, gave the frog information
about food and danger. In particular, the frog's visual system did not, apparently,
construct a complete three-dimensional model of its visual scene. As the authors
wrote,

The frog does not seem to see or, at any rate, is not concerned with the detail of stationary
parts of the world around him. He will starve to death surrounded by food if it is not moving.
His choice of food is determined only by size and movement. He will leap to capture any
object the size of an insect or worm, providing it moves like one. He can be fooled easily not
only by a bit of dangled meat but by any moving small object. His sex life is conducted by

sound and touch. His choice of paths in escaping enemies does not seem to be governed by anything more devious than leaping to where it is darker. Since he is equally at home in water and on land, why should it matter where he lights after jumping or what particular direction he takes?

Other experiments produced further information about how the brain processes visual images. Neurophysiologists David Hubel (1926–) and Torsten Wiesel (1924–) performed a series of experiments, beginning around 1958, which showed that certain neurons in the mammalian visual cortex responded selectively to images and parts of images of specific shapes. In 1959, they implanted microelectrodes in the primary visual cortex of an anesthetized cat. They found that certain neurons fired rapidly when the cat was shown images of small lines at one angle and that other neurons fired rapidly in response to small lines at another angle. In fact, they could make a "map" of this area of the cat's brain, relating neuron location to line angle. They called these neurons "simple cells" – to be distinguished from other cells, called "complex cells," that responded selectively to lines moving in a certain direction. Later work revealed that other neurons were specialized to respond to images containing more complex shapes such as corners, longer lines, and large edges.[3] They found that similar specialized neurons also existed in the brains of monkeys.[4] Hubel and Wiesel were awarded the Nobel Prize in Physiology or Medicine in 1981 (jointly with Roger Sperry for other work).[5]

As I'll describe in later sections, computer vision researchers were developing methods for extracting lines (both large and small) from images. Hubel and Wiesel's work helped to confirm their view that finding lines in images was an important part of the visual process. Yet, straight lines seldom occur in the natural environments in which cats (and humans) evolved, so why do they (and we) have neurons specialized for detecting them? In fact, in 1992 the neuroscientists Horace B. Barlow and David J. Tolhurst wrote a paper titled "Why Do You Have Edge Detectors?"[6] As a possible answer to this question, Anthony J. Bell and Terrence J. Sejnowski later showed mathematically that natural scenes can be analyzed as a weighted summation of small edges even though the scenes themselves do not have obvious edges.[7]

9.2 Recognizing Faces

In the early 1960s at his Palo Alto company, Panoramic Research, Woodrow (Woody) W. Bledsoe (who later did work on automatic theorem proving at the University of Texas), along with Charles Bisson and Helen Chan (later Helen Chan Wolf), developed techniques for face recognition supported by projects from the CIA.[8] Here is a description of their approach taken from a memorial article:[9]

This [face-recognition] project was labeled man-machine because the human extracted the coordinates of a set of features from the photographs, which were then used by the computer for recognition. Using a GRAFACON, or RAND TABLET, the operator would extract the coordinates of features such as the center of pupils, the inside corner of eyes, the outside corner of eyes, point of widows peak, and so on. From these coordinates, a list of 20 distances, such as width of mouth and width of eyes, pupil to pupil, were computed. These operators could process about 40 pictures an hour. When building the database, the name of the person in the photograph was associated with the list of computed distances and stored in the computer. In the recognition phase, the set of distances was compared with the corresponding distance for each photograph, yielding a distance between the photograph and the database record. The closest records are returned.

Bledsoe continued this work with Peter Hart at SRI after leaving Panoramic in 1966.[10]

Then, in 1970, a Stanford Ph.D. student, Michael D. Kelly, wrote a computer program that was able automatically to detect facial features in pictures and use them to identify people.[11] The task for his program was, as he put it,

to choose, from a collection of pictures of people taken by a TV camera, those pictures that depict the same person....

In brief, the program works by finding the location of features such as eyes, nose, or shoulders in the pictures.... The interesting and difficult part of the work reported in this thesis is the detection of these features in digital pictures. The nearest-neighbor method is used for identification of individuals once a set of measurements has been obtained.

Another person who did pioneering work in face recognition was vision researcher Takeo Kanade, now a professor at Carnegie Mellon University. In a 2007 speech at the Eleventh IEEE International Conference on Computer Vision, he reflected on his early work in this field:[12] "I wrote my face recognition program in an assembler language, and ran it on a machine with 10 microsecond cycle time and 20 kB of main memory. It was with pride that I tested the program with 1000 face images, a rare case at the time when testing with 10 images was called a 'large-scale' experiment." (By the way, Kanade has continued his face recognition work up to the present time. His face-recognition Web page is at http://www.ri.cmu.edu/labs/lab_51.html.)

Face recognition programs of the 1960s and 1970s had several limitations. They usually required that images be of faces of standard scale, pose, expression, and illumination. Toward the end of the book, I'll describe research leading to much more robust automatic face recognition.

9.3 Computer Vision of Three-Dimensional Solid Objects

9.3.1 *An Early Vision System*

Lawrence G. Roberts (1937–), an MIT Ph.D. student working at Lincoln Laboratory, was perhaps the first person to write a program that could identify objects in black-and-white (gray-scale) photographs and determine their orientation and position in space. (His program was also the first to use a "hidden-line" algorithm, so important in subsequent work in computer graphics. As chief scientist and later director of ARPA's Information Processing Techniques Office, Roberts later played an important role in the creation of the Arpanet, the forerunner of the Internet.)

In the introduction to his 1963 MIT Ph.D. dissertation,[13] Roberts wrote

The problem of machine recognition of pictorial data has long been a challenging goal, but has seldom been attempted with anything more complex than alphabetic characters. Many people have felt that research on character recognition would be a first step, leading the way to

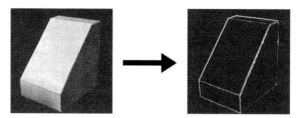

Figure 9.2. Detecting changes in intensity. (Photographs used with permission of Lawrence Roberts.)

a more general pattern recognition system. However, the multitudinous attempts at character recognition, including my own, have not led very far. The reason, I feel, is that the study of abstract, two-dimensional forms leads us away from, not toward, the techniques necessary for the recognition of three-dimensional objects. The perception of solid objects is a process which can be based on the properties of three-dimensional transformations and the laws of nature. By carefully utilizing these properties, a procedure has been developed which not only identifies objects, but also determines their orientation and position in space.

Roberts's system first processed a photograph of a scene to produce a representation of a line drawing. It then transformed the line drawing into a three-dimensional representation. Matching this representation against a stored list of representations of solid objects allowed it to classify the object it was viewing. It could also produce a computer-graphics image of the object as it might be seen from any point of view.

Our main interest here is in how Roberts processed the photographic image. After scanning the photograph and representing it as an array of numbers (pixels) representing intensity values, Roberts used a special calculation, later called the "Roberts Cross," to determine whether or not each small 2×2 square in the array corresponded to a part of the image having an abrupt change in image intensity. (The Roberts Cross was the first example of what were later called "gradient operators.") He then rerepresented the image "lighting up" only those parts of the image where the intensity changed abruptly and leaving "dark" those parts of the image with more-or-less uniform intensity. The result of this process is illustrated in Fig. 9.2 for a typical image used in Roberts's dissertation. As can be seen in that figure, large changes in image intensity are usually associated with the edges of objects. Thus, gradient operators, such as the Roberts Cross, are often called "edge detectors."

Further processing of the image on the right attempted to connect the dots representing abrupt intensity changes by small straight-line segments, then by longer line segments. Finally, a line drawing of the image was produced. This final step is shown in Fig. 9.3.

Roberts's program was able to analyze many different photographs of solid objects. He commented that "The entire picture-to-line-drawing process is not optimal but works for simple pictures." Roberts's success stimulated further work on programs for finding lines in images and for assembling these lines into representations of objects. Perhaps primed by Roberts's choice of solid objects, much of the subsequent work dealt with toy blocks (or "bricks" as they are called in Britain).

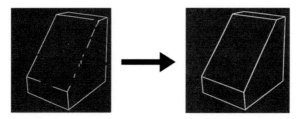

Figure 9.3. Producing the final line drawing. (Photographs used with permission of Lawrence Roberts.)

9.3.2 *The "Summer Vision Project"*

Interestingly, Larry Roberts was a student of MIT information theory professor Peter Elias, not of Marvin Minsky. But Minsky's group soon began to work on computer vision also. In the summer of 1966, the mathematician and psychologist Seymour Papert, a recent arrival at MIT's Artificial Intelligence Group, launched a "summer vision project." Its goal was to develop a suite of programs that would analyze a picture from a "videsector" (a kind of scanner) to "actually name objects [such as balls, cylinders, and blocks] by matching them with a vocabulary of known objects." One motivation for the project was "to use our summer workers effectively in the construction of a significant part of a visual system."[14]

Of course, the problem of constructing "a significant part of a visual system" was much more difficult than Papert expected. Nevertheless, the project was successful in that it began a sustained effort in computer vision research at MIT, which continues to this day.

After these early forays at MIT (and similar ones at Stanford and SRI to be described shortly), computer vision research focused on two areas. The first was what might be called "low-level" vision – those first stages of image processing that were aimed at constructing a representation of the image as a line drawing, given an image that was of a scene containing rather simple objects. The second area was concerned with how to analyze the line drawing as an assemblage of separate objects that could be located and identified. An important part of low-level vision was "image filtering," to be described next.

9.3.3 *Image Filtering*

The idea of filtering an image to simplify it, to correct for noise, and to enhance certain image features had been around for a decade or more. I have already mentioned, for example, that in 1955 Gerald P. Dinneen processed images to remove noise and enhance edges. Russell Kirsch and colleagues had also experimented with image processing.[15] (Readers who have manipulated their digital photography pictures on a computer have used some of these image filters.) Filtering two-dimensional images is not so very different from filtering one-dimensional electronic signals – a commonplace operation. Perhaps the simplest operation to describe is "averaging," which blurs fine detail and removes random noise specks. As in all averaging operations, image averaging takes into account adjacent values and combines them. Consider,

0	0	0	0	0	10	10	10	10	10
0	0	0	0	0	10	10	10	10	10
0	0	0	0	0	10	10	10	10	10
0	0	0	0	0	10	10	10	10	10
0	0	0	0	0	10	10	10	10	10
0	0	0	0	0	10	10	10	10	10
0	0	0	0	0	10	10	10	10	10
0	0	0	0	0	10	10	10	10	10
0	0	0	0	0	10	10	10	10	10
0	0	0	0	0	10	10	10	10	10

Figure 9.4. An array of image intensity values and an averaging window.

for example, the image array of intensity values shown in Fig. 9.4 containing a 3 × 3 "averaging window" outlined in bold. These intensity values correspond to an image whose right side is bright and whose left side is dark with a sharp edge between. (I adopt the convention that large numbers, such as 10 correspond to brightly illuminated parts of the image, and the number 0 corresponds to black.)

The averaging operation moves the averaging window over the entire image so that its center lies over each pixel in turn. For each placement of the window, the value of the intensity at its center is replaced (in the filtered version) by the average intensity of the values within the window. (The process of moving a window around the image and doing calculations based on the numbers in the window is called *convolution*.) In this example, the 0 at the center of the window would be replaced by 3.33 (perhaps rounded down to 3). One can see that averaging blurs the sharp edge – with the 10 fading to (a rounded) 7 fading to 3 fading to 0 as one moves from right to left. However, intensities well within evenly illuminated regions are not changed.

I have already mentioned another important filtering operation, the Roberts Cross, for detecting abrupt brightness changes in an image. Another one was developed in 1968 by a Ph.D. student at Stanford, Irwin Sobel. It was dubbed the "Sobel Operator" by Raj Reddy who described it in a Computer Vision course at Stanford.[16] The operator uses two filtering windows – one sensitive to large gradients (intensity changes) in the vertical direction and one to large gradients in the horizontal direction. These are shown in Fig. 9.5.

Each of the Sobel filters works the same way as the averaging filter, except that the image intensity at each point is multiplied by the number in the corresponding cell of the filtering window before adding all of the numbers. The sum would be 0

Figure 9.5. Sobel's vertical (left) and horizontal (right) filters.

-1	0	+1
-2	0	+2
-1	0	+1

+1	+2	+1
0	0	0
-1	-2	-1

Figure 9.6. Finding abrupt changes in image brightness with the Sobel Operator. (Photographs taken by George Miller. Used under the terms of the GNU Free Documentation License.)

inside regions of uniform illumination. If the vertical filter is centered over a vertical edge (with the right side brighter than the left), the sum would be positive. (I'll let you think about the other possibilities.) Results from the two filtering windows are combined mathematically to detect abrupt changes in any direction.

The images in Fig. 9.6 illustrate the Sobel Operator. The image on the right is the result of applying the Sobel Operator to the image on the left.

A number of other more complex and robust image processing operations have been proposed and used for finding edges, lines, and vertices of objects in images.[17] A particularly interesting one for finding edges was proposed by the British neuroscientist and psychologist David Marr (1945–1980) and Ellen Hildreth.[18] The Marr–Hildreth edge detector uses a filtering window called a "Laplacian of Gaussian (LoG)." (The name arises because a mathematical operator called a "Laplacian" is used on a bell-shaped curve called a "Gaussian," commemorating two famous mathematicians, namely, Pierre-Simon Laplace and Carl Friedrich Gauss.) In Fig. 9.7, I show an example of LoG numbers in a 9×9 filtering window. This window is moved around an image, multiplying image numbers and adding them up, in the same way as the other filtering windows I have already mentioned.

If LoG numbers are plotted as "heights" above (and below) a plane, an interesting-looking surface results. An example is shown in Fig. 9.8. This LoG function is often called, not surprisingly, a Mexican hat or sombrero function.

0	0	3	2	2	2	3	0	0
0	2	3	5	5	5	3	2	0
3	3	5	3	0	3	5	3	3
2	5	3	−12	−23	−12	3	5	2
2	5	0	−23	−40	−23	0	5	2
2	5	3	−12	−23	−12	3	5	2
3	3	5	3	0	3	5	3	3
0	2	3	5	5	5	3	2	0
0	0	3	2	2	2	3	0	0

Figure 9.7. A Laplacian of Gaussian filtering window.

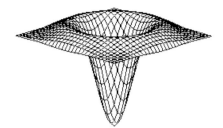

Figure 9.8. A Laplacian of Gaussian surface.

Marr and Hildreth used the LoG filtering window on several example images. One example, taken from their paper, is shown in Fig 9.9. Notice that the image on the right has whitish bands surrounding darker parts of the image. The Marr–Hildreth edge detector employs a second image-processing operation that looks for the transitions from light to dark (and vice versa) in the LoG-processed image to produce a final "line drawing," as shown in Fig. 9.10.

Further advances have been made in edge detection since Marr and Hildreth's work. Among the currently best detectors are those related to one proposed by John Canny called the Canny edge detector.[19]

As a neurophysiologist, Marr was particularly interested in how the human brain processes images. In a 1976 paper,[20] he proposed that the first stage of processing produces what he called a "primal sketch." As he puts it in his summary of that paper,

It is argued that the first step of consequence is to compute a primitive but rich description of the grey-level changes present in an image. The description is expressed in a vocabulary of kinds of intensity change (EDGE, SHADING-EDGE, EXTENDED-EDGE, LINE, BLOB etc.). . . . This description is obtained from the intensity array by fixed techniques, and it is called the primal sketch.

Marr and Hildreth put forward their edge detector as one of the operations the brain uses in producing a primal sketch. They stated that their theory "explains

Figure 9.9. An image (left) and its LoG-processed version (right). (Images taken from David Marr and E. Hildreth, "Theory of Edge Detection," *Proceedings of the Royal Society of London*, Series B, Biological Sciences, Vol. 207, No. 1167, p. 198, February 1980.)

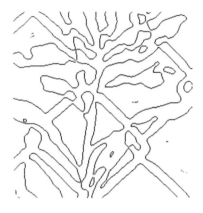

Figure 9.10. The final result of a Marr–Hildreth edge-detecting operation. (From David Marr and E. Hildreth, "Theory of Edge Detection," *Proceedings of the Royal Society of London*, Series B, Biological Sciences, Vol. 207, No. 1167, p. 198, February 1980.)

several basic psychophysical findings, and . . . forms the basis for a physiological model of simple [nerve] cells."

Marr's promising career in vision research ended when he succumbed to cancer in 1980. During the last years of his life he completed an important book detailing his theories of human vision.[21] I'll describe some of Marr's ideas about other visual processing steps in a subsequent chapter.

9.3.4 *Processing Line Drawings*

Assuming, maybe somewhat prematurely, that low-level vision routines could produce a line-drawing version of an image, many investigators moved on to develop methods for analyzing line drawings to find objects in images.

Adolfo Guzman-Arenas (1943–), a student in Minsky's AI Group, focused on how to segment a line drawing of a scene containing blocks into its constituents, which Guzman called "bodies." His LISP program for accomplishing this separation was called SEE and ran on the MIT AI Group's PDP-6 computer.[22] The input to SEE was a line-drawing representation of a scene in terms of its surfaces, lines (where two surfaces came together), and vertices (where lines came together).

SEE's analysis of a scene began by sorting its vertices into a number of different types. For each vertex, depending on its type, SEE connected adjacent planar surfaces with "links." The links between surfaces provide evidence that those surfaces belong to the same body. For example, some links for a scene analyzed by SEE are shown in Fig. 9.11.

SEE performed rather well on a wide variety of line drawings. For example, it correctly found all of the bodies in the scene shown in Fig. 9.12.

For most of his work, Guzman assumed that somehow other programs would produce his needed line drawings from actual images. As he wrote in a paper describing his research,[23]

The scene itself is not obtained from a visual input device, or from an array of intensities of brightness. Rather, it is assumed that a preprocessing of some sort has taken place, and the scene to be analyzed is available in a symbolic format . . . in terms of points (vertices), lines (edges), and surfaces (regions)."

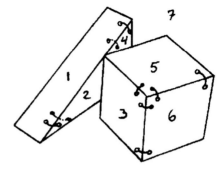

Figure 9.11. Links established by SEE for a sample scene. (Illustration used with permission of Adolpho Guzman.)

Additionally, Guzman did not concern himself with what might be done after the scene had been separated into bodies:

. . . it cannot find "cubes" or "houses" in a scene, since it does not know what a "house" is. Once SEE has partitioned a scene into bodies, some other program will work on them and decide which of those bodies are "houses."

Later extensions to SEE, reported in the final version of his thesis, involved some procedures for image capture. But the images were of specially prepared scenes, as he recently elaborated:[24]

Originally SEE worked on hand-drawn scenes, "perfect scenes" (drawings of lines). . .

Later, I constructed a bunch of wooden polyhedra (mostly irregular), painted them black, carefully painted their edges white, piled several of them together, and took pictures of the scenes. The pictures were scanned, edges found, and given to SEE. It worked quite well on them.

Although SEE was capable of finding bodies in rather complex scenes, it also could make mistakes, and it could not identify blocks that had holes in them.

The next person to work on the problem of scene articulation was David Huffman (1925–1999), a professor of Electrical Engineering at MIT. (Huffman was famous for

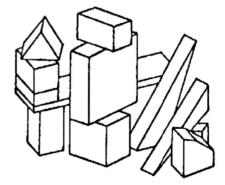

Figure 9.12. A scene analyzed by SEE. (Illustration used with permission of Adolpho Guzman.)

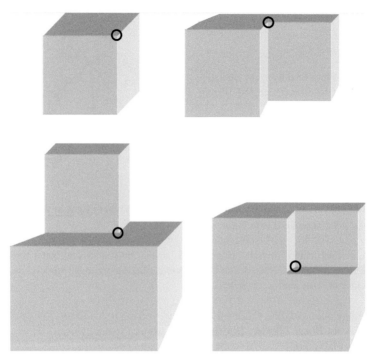

Figure 9.13. The four different kinds of vertices that can occur in trihedral solids.

his invention, while a graduate student at MIT, of what came to be called "Huffman coding," an efficient scheme that is used today in many applications involving the compression and transmission of digital data.) Huffman was bothered by what he considered Guzman's incomplete analysis of what kinds of objects could correspond to what kinds of line drawings. After leaving MIT in 1967 to become a professor of Information and Computer Science at the University of California at Santa Cruz, he completed a theory for assigning labels to the lines in drawings of trihedral solids – objects in which exactly three planar surfaces join at each vertex of the object. The labels depended on the ways in which planes could come together at a vertex. (I got to know Huffman well at that time because he consulted frequently at the Stanford Research Institute.)

Huffman pointed out that there are only four ways in which three plane surfaces can come together at a vertex.[25] These are shown in Fig. 9.13. In addition to these four kinds of vertices, a scene might contain what Huffman called "T-nodes" – line intersection types caused by one object in a scene occluding another. These all give rise to a number of different kinds of labels for the lines in the scene; these labels specify whether the lines correspond to convex, concave, or occluding edges.

Huffman noted that the labels of the lines in a drawing might be locally consistent (around some vertices) but still be globally inconsistent (around all of the vertices). Consider, for example, Roger Penrose's famous line drawing of an "impossible

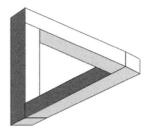

Figure 9.14. An impossible object.

object" shown in Fig. 9.14.[26] (It is impossible because no three-dimensional object, viewed in "general position," could produce this image.) No "real scene" can have a line with two different labels.

Max Clowes (circa 1944–1981) of Sussex University in Britain developed similar ideas independently,[27] and the labeling scheme is now generally known as Huffman–Clowes labeling.

Next comes David Waltz (1943–). In his 1972 MIT Ph.D. thesis, he extended the Huffman–Clowes line-labeling scheme to allow for line drawings of scenes with shadows and possible "cracks" between two adjoining objects.[28] Waltz's important contribution was to propose and implement an efficient computational method for satisfying the constraint that all of the lines must be assigned one and only one label. (For example, an edge can't be concave at one end and convex at the other.) In Fig. 9.15, I show an example of a line drawing that Waltz's program could correctly segment into its constituents.

Summarizing some of the work on processing line drawings at MIT, Patrick Winston says that "Guzman was the experimentalist, Huffman the theoretician, and Waltz the encyclopedist (because Waltz had to catalog thousands of junctions, in order to deal with cracks and shadows)."[29]

Meanwhile, similar work for finding, identifying, and describing objects in three-dimensional scenes was being done at Stanford. By 1972 Electrical Engineering Ph.D. student Gilbert Falk could segment scenes of line drawings into separate objects using techniques that were extensions of those of Guzman.[30] And by 1973, Computer Science Ph.D. student Gunnar Grape performed segmentation of scenes containing parallelepipeds and wedges using models of those objects.[31]

Other work on analysis of scenes containing polyhedra was done by Yoshiaki Shirai while he was visiting MIT's AI Lab[32] and by Alan Mackworth at the Laboratory of Experimental Psychology of the University of Sussex.[33]

Figure 9.15. A scene with shadows analyzed by Waltz's program. (Illustration used with permission of David Waltz.)

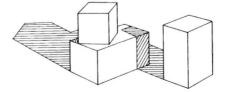

Notes

1. For a thorough treatment, see David Forsyth and Jean Ponce, *Computer Vision: A Modern Approach*, Chapter 13, Upper Saddle River, NJ: Prentice Hall, 2003. **[125]**

2. Lettvin *et al.*, "What the Frog's Eye Tells the Frog's Brain," *Proceedings of the IRE*, Vol. 47, No. 11, pp. 1940–1951, 1959. [Reprinted as Chapter 7 in William C. Corning and Martin Balaban (eds.), *The Mind: Biological Approaches to Its Functions*, pp. 233–258, 1968.] **[126]**

3. David H. Hubel and Torsten N. Wiesel, "Receptive Fields, Binocular Interaction and Functional Architecture in the Cat's Visual Cortex," *Journal of Physiology*, Vol. 160, pp. 106–154, 1962. **[127]**

4. David H. Hubel and Torsten N. Wiesel, "Receptive Fields and Functional Architecture of Monkey Striate Cortex," *Journal of Physiology*, Vol. 195, pp. 215–243, 1968. **[127]**

5. An interesting account of Hubel's and Wiesel's work and descriptions about how the brain processes visual images can be found in Hubel's online book *Eye, Brain, and Vision* at http://neuro.med.harvard.edu/site/dh/index.html. **[127]**

6. Horace B. Barlow and D. J. Tolhurst, "Why Do You Have Edge Detectors?," in *Proceedings of the 1992 Optical Society of America Annual Meeting*, Technical Digest Series, Vol. 23, pp. 172, Albuquerque, NM, Washington: Optical Society of America, 1992. **[127]**

7. Anthony J. Bell and Terrence J. Sejnowski, "Edges Are the 'Independent Components' of Natural Scenes," *Advances in Neural Information Processing Systems*, Vol. 9, Cambridge, MA: MIT Press, 1996. Available online at ftp://ftp.cnl.salk.edu/pub/tony/edge.ps.Z. **[127]**

8. Woodrow W. Bledsoe and Helen Chan, "A Man–Machine Facial Recognition System: Some Preliminary Results," Technical Report PRI 19A, Panoramic Research, Inc., Palo Alto, CA, 1965. **[127]**

9. Michael Ballantyne, Robert S. Boyer, and Larry Hines, "Woody Bledsoe: His Life and Legacy," *AI Magazine*, Vol. 17, No. 1, pp. 7–20, 1996. Also available online at http://www.utexas.edu/faculty/council/1998-1999/memorials/Bledsoe/bledsoe.html. **[127]**

10. Woodrow W. Bledsoe, "Semiautomatic Facial Recognition," Technical Report SRI Project 6693, Stanford Research Institute, Menlo Park, CA, 1968. **[128]**

11. Michael D. Kelly, "Visual Identification of People by Computer," Stanford AI Project, Stanford, CA, Technical Report AI-130, 1970. **[128]**

12. http://iccv2007.rutgers.edu/TakeoKanadeResponse.htm. **[128]**

13. Lawrence G. Roberts, "Machine Perception of Three-Dimensional Solids," MIT Ph.D. thesis, 1963; published as Lincoln Laboratory Technical Report #315, May 22, 1963; appears in J. T. Tippett *et al.* (eds.), *Optical and Electro-Optical Information Processing*, pp. 159–197, Cambridge, MA: MIT Press, 1965. Available online at http://www.packet.cc/files/mach-per-3D-solids.html. **[128]**

14. The project is described in MIT's Artificial Intelligence Group Vision Memo No. 100 available at ftp://publications.ai.mit.edu/ai-publications/pdf/AIM-100.pdf. **[130]**

15. Russell A. Kirsch *et al.*, "Experiments in Processing Pictorial Information with a Digital Computer," *Proceedings of the Eastern Joint Computer Conference*, pp. 221–229, Institute of Radio Engineers and Association Association for Computing Machinery, December 1957. **[130]**

16. According to Sobel, he and a fellow student, Gary Feldman, first presented the operator in a Stanford AI seminar in 1968. It was later described in Karl K. Pingle, "Visual Perception by a Computer," in A. Grasselli (ed.), *Automatic Interpretation and Classification of Images*,

pp. 277–284, New York: Academic Press, 1969. It was also mentioned in Richard O. Duda and Peter E. Hart, *Pattern Classification and Scene Analysis*, pp. 271–272, New York: John Wiley & Sons, 1973. [131]

17. See, for example, M. H. Hueckel, "An Operator Which Locates Edges in Digitized Pictures," *Journal of the ACM*, Vol. 18, No. 1, pp. 113–125, January 1971, and Berthold K. P. Horn, "The Binford–Horn Line Finder," MIT AI Memo 285, MIT, July 1971 (revised December 1973 and available online at http://people.csail.mit.edu/bkph/AIM/AIM-285-OPT.pdf). [132]

18. David Marr and Ellen Hildreth, "Theory of Edge Detection," *Proceedings of the Royal Society of London*, Series B, Biological Sciences, Vol. 207, No. 1167, pp. 187–217, February 1980. [132]

19. John E. Canny, "A Computational Approach to Edge Detection," *IEEE Transactions Pattern Analysis and Machine Intelligence*, Vol. 8, pp. 679–714, 1986. [133]

20. David Marr, "Early Processing of Visual Information," *Philosophical Transactions of the Royal Society of London*, Series B, Biological Sciences, Vol. 275, No. 942, pp. 483–519, October 1976. [133]

21. David Marr, *Vision: A Computational Investigation into the Human Representation and Processing of Visual Information*, San Francisco: W.H. Freeman and Co., 1982. [134]

22. Guzman's 1968 Ph.D. thesis is titled "Computer Recognition of Three Dimensional Objects in a Visual Scene" and is available online at http://www.lcs.mit.edu/publications/pubs/pdf/MIT-LCS-TR-059.pdf. [134]

23. Adolfo Guzman, "Decomposition of a Visual Scene into Three-Dimensional Bodies," *AFIPS*, Vol. 33, pp. 291–304, Washington, DC: Thompson Book Co., 1968. Available online as an MIT AI Group memo at ftp://publications.ai.mit.edu/ai-publications/pdf/AIM-171.pdf. [134]

24. Personal communication, September 14, 2006. [135]

25. David A. Huffman, "Impossible Objects as Nonsense Sentences," in B. Meltzer and D. Michie (eds.), *Machine Intelligence 6*, pp. 195–234, Edinburgh: Edinburgh University Press, 1971, and David A. Huffman, "Realizable Configurations of Lines in Pictures of Polyhedra," in E. W. Elcock and D. Michie (eds.), *Machine Intelligence 8*, pp. 493–509, Chicester: Ellis Horwood, 1977. [136]

26. According to Wikipedia, this impossible object was first drawn by the Swedish artist Oscar Reutersvärd in 1934. [137]

27. Max B. Clowes, "On Seeing Things," *Artificial Intelligence*, Vol. 2, pp. 79–116, 1971. [137]

28. David L. Waltz, "Generating Semantic Descriptions from Drawings of Scenes with Shadows," MIT AI Lab Technical Report No. AITR-271, November 1, 1972. Available online at https://dspace.mit.edu/handle/1721.1/6911. A condensed version appears in Patrick Winston (ed.), *The Psychology of Computer Vision*, pp. 19–91, New York: McGraw-Hill, 1975. [137]

29. Personal communication, September 20, 2006. [137]

30. Gilbert Falk, "Computer Interpretation of Imperfect Line Data as a Three-Dimensional Scene," Ph.D. thesis in Electrical Engineering, Stanford University, Artificial Intelligence Memo AIM-132, and Computer Science Report No. CS180, August 1970. Also see Gilbert Falk, "Interpretation of Imperfect Line Data as a Three-Dimensional Scene," *Artificial Intelligence*, Vol. 3, pp. 101–144, 1972. [137]

31. Gunnar Rutger Grape, "Model Based (Intermediate Level) Computer Vision," Stanford Computer Science Ph.D. thesis, Artificial Intelligence Memo AIM-204, and Computer Science Report No. 266, May 1973. [137]

32. Yoshiaki Shirai, "A Heterarchical Program for Recognition of Polyhedra," MIT AI Memo No. 263, June 1972. Available online at ftp://publications.ai.mit.edu/ai-publications/pdf/AIM-263.pdf. [137]

33. Alan K. Mackworth, "Interpreting Pictures of Polyhedral Scenes," *Artificial Intelligence*, Vol. 4, No. 2, pp. 121–137, June 1973. [137]

10

"Hand–Eye" Research

T HE MOTIVATION FOR MUCH OF THE COMPUTER VISION RESEARCH THAT I HAVE
described during this period was to provide information to guide a robot arm.
Because the images that could be analyzed best were of simple objects such as toy
blocks, work was concentrated on getting a robot arm to stack and unstack blocks.
I'll describe some typical examples of this "hand–eye" research, beginning with a
project that did not actually involve an "eye."

10.1 At MIT

A computer-guided mechanical "hand" was developed by Heinrich A. Ernst in
1961 as part of his Electrical Engineering Sc.D. work at MIT.[1] (His advisor was
Claude Shannon.) The hand, named MH-1, was a "mechanical servomanipulator
[an American Machine and Foundry model 8] adapted for operation by the TX-0
computer." It used tactile sensors mounted on the hand to guide it because, as Ernst
wrote, "organs for vision are too difficult to build at the present time." The abstract
of Ernst's thesis describes some of what the system could do:

[O]ne program consisting of nine statements will make the hand do the following: Search the
table for a box, remember its position, search the table for blocks, take them and put them into
the box. The position of the objects is irrelevant as long as they are on the table. If as a test
for the built-in mechanical intelligence, the box should be taken away and placed somewhere
else while the hand searches for blocks, MH-1 will remember the new position of the box
and continue to work with it as soon as it has realized the change in the situation, that is, has
bumped into the box while looking for blocks. This will be done automatically, without any
need to mention it in the specific program for this block-and-box performance.

Actually, MH-1 was not the first computer-guided hand, although it was the first
to employ touch sensors to guide its motion. One was developed and patented in 1954
by George Devol, an American engineer. Based on this invention, he and another
engineer, Joseph F. Engelberger, founded Unimation, Inc. Soon after, they installed
a prototype of their first industrial robot, called a "Unimate," in the General Motors
Corporation Ternstedt Division plant near Trenton, New Jersey.

Back at MIT, Ph.D. students Patrick Winston (later an MIT professor and director
of its AI Laboratory), Thomas O. Binford (later a Stanford professor), Berthold
K. P. Horn (later an MIT professor), and Eugene Freuder (later a University of
New Hampshire professor) developed a system that used an AMF Versatran robot

Figure 10.1. A block arrangement for the MIT copy demo. (Used with permission of Berthold Horn.)

arm to "copy" a configuration of blocks. The scene consisting of the blocks was first scanned, and lines were extracted from the image using a "line-finder," which was under development by Binford and Horn.[2] Using these lines, objects in the image were identified, and a plan was made for the robot arm to disassemble the blocks in the scene. The robot arm then carried out this plan and reassembled the blocks in their original configuration. The system was demonstrated in December 1970 for various configurations of blocks. An example block configuration successfully handled by their "copy demo" is shown in Fig. 10.1. (A film, called *Eye of the Robot*, showing the copy demo in action is available at http://projects.csail.mit.edu/films/aifilms/digitalFilms/9mpeg/88-eye.mpg.)

The system depended on precise illumination and carefully constructed blocks. Attempts to extend the range of computer vision to less constrained scenes led to further concentration at MIT and elsewhere on the early stages of vision processing. I'll describe some of the ensuing work on these problems in more detail later.[3]

10.2 At Stanford

Meanwhile at John McCarthy's SAIL, a team led by Professor Jerome Feldman (1938–) pursued work on hand–eye projects using the PDP-1 and later the PDP-6 and PDP-10 computers.[4] McCarthy later told me that he got interested in robots because of his interest in computer vision. He was not very excited about the work in pattern recognition – it was "discrimination" rather than "description." "If you want to pick something up, you have to describe it not merely recognize it."[5]

In 1966, SAIL had acquired a Rancho Los Amigos Hospital electromechanical prosthetic arm. By the spring of 1967, a hand–eye system was developed by Karl Pingle, Jonathan Singer, and Bill Wichman that could use a TV camera and primitive vision routines to locate blocks scattered on a table. Using the information thus obtained, it could control the arm to sort the blocks.[6] According to the authors,

One section of the system scans the TV image to find the outer edge of an object, then traces around the outside edges of the object using a gradient operator [an edge detector] to find the location and direction of the edge. Curve fitting routines fit straight lines to a list of points found on the edges and calculate the position of the corners. . . . A second section of the

Figure 10.2. Raj Reddy. (Photograph courtesy of Raj Reddy.)

system is devoted to control of the arm. . . . The sections which control it consist of a solution program which calculates the angular position required at each actuator and a servo program which drives the arm to the desired positions . . .

Les Earnest wrote that this was "the first robotics visual feedback system," although "only the outer edges of the blocks were observed, [and] the hand had to be removed from view when visual checking was done. . . ."[7]

Several versions of this block–sorting and stacking system were demonstrated. In one, the system located colored blocks on a table and placed them in separate stacks of red and blue blocks.[8]

By 1971, a vision–guided block stacking system solved the "instant insanity" puzzle.[9] In that puzzle, four cubes, each face of which has one of four different colors, must be arranged in a tower such that each side of the tower shows four different colors. The system, running on SAIL's PDP-10 computer, used a TV camera equipped with a turret of four lenses and a color wheel to locate four cubes on a table top. The arm picked up and turned each cube to expose all faces to the camera. Then, knowing the color of each face and having found a solution to the puzzle, the arm stacked the cubes in a tower exhibiting the solution. [A silent, 16-mm color six-minute film, titled *Instant Insanity*, was made by Richard Paul and Karl Pingle in August 1971 and shown at the second International Joint Conference on Artificial Intelligence (IJCAI) in London. The film can be seen at http://www.youtube.com/watch?v=O1oJzUSITeY.]

Dabblal Rajagopal "Raj" Reddy (1937– ; Fig. 10.2) was the first Ph.D. student of Stanford's new Department of Computer Science. His thesis research was on speech recognition. After obtaining his Ph D. in 1966, Reddy joined Stanford's faculty and continued research on speech recognition at SAIL. While there he participated in a project to control a hand–eye system by voice commands.[10] As stated in a project review, "Commands as complicated as 'Pick up the small block in the lower lefthand corner,' are recognized and the tasks are carried out by the computer controlled arm." (The system was demonstrated in a 1969 fifteen–minute, 16-mm color, sound film showing some of Reddy's results on speech recognition. It is titled *Hear Here*

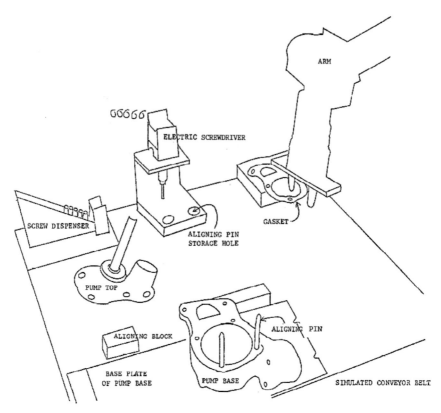

Figure 10.3. Diagram of a water pump assembly workspace. (Illustration used with permission of Robert Bolles.)

and was produced by Raj Reddy, Dave Espar, and Art Eisensen. The film is available at http://www.archive.org/details/sailfilm_hear.) In 1969, Reddy moved to CMU where he pursued research in speech recognition and later became Dean of CMU's School of Computer Science.

In the early 1970s, the Stanford team used a vision system and a new electromechanical hand designed by mechanical engineering student Vic Scheinman[11] to assemble a model "T" Ford racing water pump.[12] An industrial-style setup was used with tools in fixed places, screws in a feeder, and the pump body and cover on a pallet. A diagram of the workspace is shown in Fig. 10.3.

The hand–eye system executed the following complex set of steps that was computed previously:

locate the pump base, move it into standard position, determine the final grasping position by touch, place the pump base in its standard position, insert two pins to guide the alignment of the gasket and cover, put on the gasket, visually check the position of the gasket, locate the cover by touch, put on the cover over the guide pins, pick up a hex head power screw driver, pick up a screw from the feeder, screw in the first two screws, remove the aligning pins, screw in the last four screws, and finally check the force required to turn the rotor.

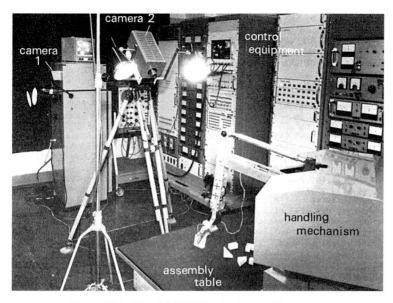

Figure 10.4. Hitachi's HIVIP robotic assembly system.

A film of the water pump assembly can be seen at http://www.archive.org/details/sailfilm_pump. It is also available at http://www.saildart.org/films/, along with several other Stanford AI Lab films.

10.3 In Japan

Hand–eye work was also being pursued at Hitachi's Central Research Laboratory in Tokyo. There, Masakazu Ejiri and colleagues developed a robot system called HIVIP consisting of three subsystems called EYE, BRAIN, and HAND. (See Fig. 10.4.) One of EYE's two television cameras looked at a plan drawing depicting an assembly of blocks. The other camera looked at some blocks on a table. Then, BRAIN figured out how to pick up and assemble the blocks as specified in the drawing, and HAND did the assembly.[13]

10.4 Edinburgh's "FREDDY"

During the late 1960s and into the 1970s, researchers under the direction of Professor Donald Michie in the Department of Machine Intelligence and Perception at the University of Edinburgh developed robot systems generally called "FREDDY."[14] The best known of these was the hand–eye system FREDDY II, which had a large robot arm and two TV cameras suspended over a moving table. Even though the arm did not move relative to the room, it did relative to its "world," the table. The setup is shown in Fig. 10.5.

A demonstration task for FREDDY II was to construct complete assemblies, such as a toy car or boat, from a kit of parts dumped onto the table. The aim was to develop AI techniques that could provide the basis for better industrial assembly robots, that

Figure 10.5. FREDDY II, the University of Edinburgh robot. (Photograph courtesy of University of Edinburgh.)

is, robots that were more versatile, more reliable, and more easily programmed than those in operation at that time.

At the beginning, the component parts were in an unorganized jumble. FREDDY had to find and identify them and then lay them out neatly. Once it had found all the parts needed, FREDDY could then perform the assembly sequence, using a small workstation with a vice.

Isolated parts were recognized from features of their outline (corners, curves, etc.), their holes, and their general properties. These were taught to FREDDY by showing it different views of each of the parts in a prior training phase.

To deal with heaps of parts, FREDDY applied several tactics: It could try to find something protruding from the heap, which it could grasp and pull out; it could attempt to lift something (unknown) off the top; or it could simply plough the hand through the heap to try to split it into two smaller ones.

Constructing the assembly was performed by following a sequence of instructions that had been programmed interactively during the training phase. Some instructions were simple movements, but others were much more sophisticated and used the force sensors in the hand. For example, in a "constrained move," the hand would slide the part it held along a surface until it hit resistance; in "hole fitting," the hand would fit one part (such as an axle) into a hole in another (such as a wheel) by feel, as humans do.

FREDDY could assemble both the car and the boat when the two kits were mixed together and dumped on the table. It took about four hours to do so, primarily because of the limited power of FREDDY's two computers.[15] The main computer was an Elliot 4130 with 64k 24-bit words (later upgraded to 128k) and with a clock speed of 0.5 MHz. It was programmed in the POP-2 language. The robot motors and cameras were controlled by a Honeywell H316, with 4k 16-bit words (later upgraded to 8k words, at a cost of about $8,000 for the additional 8k bytes!).

Harry Barrow (1943–), a key person involved in the work, later gave this account of FREDDY's operation:[16]

[A]cquiring an image from the TV camera took quite a few seconds and processing took even longer, and in a single run FREDDY took between 100 and 150 pictures! It took a picture every time it picked up an object to check it has successfully lifted it and not dropped it, and it took a picture every time it put an object down to verify the space was empty. It also scanned the entire world (which required multiple pictures) several times to make a map, and it looked at each object from two different cameras to do some stereo-style estimation of position and size. In fact, the system made the most intensive use of image data of any robot system in the world. The Stanford and MIT systems only took a very small number of pictures to perform their tasks, and relied heavily on dead reckoning and things not going wrong. We, on the other hand, assumed that things were likely to go wrong (objects dropped, rolling, etc.) and made our system highly robust. I really believe that in many ways it was probably the most advanced hand–eye system in existence at the time.

FREDDY is now on permanent exhibition in the Royal Scottish Museum in Edinburgh, with a continuous-loop movie of FREDDY assembling the mixed model car and boat kits.

Hand–eye research at Edinburgh was suspended during the mid-1970s in part owing to an unfavorable assessment of its prospects in a study commissioned by the British Science Research Council. (I'll have more to say about that assessment later.)

Notes

1. Heinrich A. Ernst, "MH-1, A Computer-Operated Mechanical Hand," Sc.D. thesis, Massachusetts Institute of Technology, Department of Electrical Engineering, 1962. Available online at http://dspace.mit.edu/bitstream/handle/1721.1/15735/09275630.pdf?sequence=1. [141]
2. Reported in Berthold K. P. Horn, "The Binford–Horn Line Finder," MIT AI Memo 285, MIT, July 1971 (revised December 1973). Available online at http://people.csail.mit.edu/bkph/AIM/AIM-285-OPT.pdf. [142]
3. Patrick Winston gives a nice description of the MIT programs just mentioned (including the copy demo and Winston's own thesis work on learning structural descriptions of object configurations) in Patrick H. Winston, "The MIT Robot," *Machine Intelligence 7*, Bernard Meltzer and Donald Michie (eds.), pp. 431–463, New York: John Wiley and Sons, 1972. [142]
4. For a brief review, see Lester Earnest (ed.), "Final Report: The First Ten Years of Artificial Intelligence Research at Stanford," Stanford Artificial Intelligence Laboratory Memo AIM-228 and Stanford Computer Science Department Report No. STAN-CS-74-409, July 1973. (Available online at http://www-db.stanford.edu/pub/cstr/reports/cs/tr/74/409/CS-TR-74-409.pdf.) For more details see Jerome A. Feldman *et al.*, "The Stanford Hand–Eye Project," *Proceedings of the IJCAI*, pp. 521–526, Washington, DC, 1969, and Jerome A. Feldman *et al.*, "The Stanford Hand-Eye Project – Recent Results," presented at IFIP Congress, Stockholm, 1974. [142]
5. John McCarthy, private communication, August 11, 2007. [142]

6. The system is described in Karl K. Pingle, Jonathan A. Singer, and William M. Wichman, "Computer Control of a Mechanical Arm through Visual Input," *Proceedings of the IFIP Congress (2)*, pp. 1563–1569, 1968. The vision part of the system is described in William Wichman, "Use of Optical Feedback in the Computer Control of an Arm," Stanford Electrical Engineering Department Engineers thesis, August 1967 (and also appears as Stanford Artificial Intelligence Memo AIM-56, 1967.) [142]

7. Lester Earnest, *op. cit.* [143]

8. *Butterfinger*, an 8-minute, 16-mm color film showing a version of this sorting system in operation was produced and directed by Gary Feldman in 1968. The film is available at http://projects.csail.mit.edu/films/aifilms/digitalFilms/1mp4/09-robot.mp4. [143]

9. The system is described in Jerome Feldman *et al.*, "The Use of Vision and Manipulation to Solve the 'Instant Insanity' Puzzle," *Proceedings of the IJCAI*, pp. 359–364, London: British Computer Society, September 1971. [143]

10. The system is described in Les Earnest *et al.*, "A Computer with Hands, Eyes, and Ears," *Proceedings of the 1968 Fall Joint Computer Conference*, Washington, DC: Thompson, 1968. [143]

11. Victor D. Scheinman, "Design of a Computer Manipulator," Stanford AI Memo AIM-92, June 1, 1969. [144]

12. This task is described in Robert Bolles and Richard Paul, "The Use of Sensory Feedback in a Programmable Assembly System," Stanford AI Laboratory Memo AIM-220, Stanford Computer Science Department Report STAN-CS-396, October 1973, which is available online at ftp://reports.stanford.edu/pub/cstr/reports/cs/tr/73/396/CS-TR-73-396.pdf. [144]

13. See Masakazu Ejiri *et al.*, "An Intelligent Robot with Cognition and Decision-Making Ability," *Proceedings of the IJCAI*, pp. 350–358, London: British Computer Society, September 1971, and Masakazu Ejiri *et al.*, "A Prototype Intelligent Robot That Assembles Objects from Plan Drawings," *IEEE Transactions on Computers*, Vol. 21, No. 2, pp. 161–170, February 1972. [145]

14. This is an abbreviation, according to Donald Michie, of Frederick, an acronym of Friendly Robot for Education, Discussion and Entertainment, the Retrieval of Information, and the Collation of Knowledge. [145]

15. http://www.aiai.ed.ac.uk/project/freddy/. The key reference is A. P. Ambler, H. G. Barrow, C. M. Brown, R. M. Burstall, and R. J. Popplestone, "A Versatile Computer-Controlled Assembly System," *Artificial Intelligence*, Vol. 6, pp. 129–156, 1975. [146]

16. E-mail note from Harry Barrow of January 3, 2009. [147]

11

Knowledge Representation and Reasoning

F OR A SYSTEM TO BE INTELLIGENT, IT MUST HAVE KNOWLEDGE ABOUT ITS WORLD and the means to draw conclusions from, or at least act on, that knowledge. Humans and machines alike therefore must have ways to represent this needed knowledge in internal structures, whether encoded in protein or silicon. Cognitive scientists and AI researchers distinguish between two main ways in which knowledge is represented: procedural and declarative. In animals, the knowledge needed to perform a skilled action, such as hitting a tennis ball, is called procedural because it is encoded directly in the neural circuits that coordinate and control that specific action. Analogously, automatic landing systems in aircraft contain within their control programs procedural knowledge about flight paths, landing speeds, aircraft dynamics, and so on. In contrast, when we respond to a question, such as "How old are you?," we answer with a declarative sentence, such as "I am twenty-four years old." Any knowledge that is most naturally represented by a declarative sentence is called declarative.

In AI research (and in computer science generally), procedural knowledge is represented directly in the programs that use that knowledge, whereas declarative knowledge is represented in symbolic structures that are more-or-less separate from the many different programs that might use the information in those structures. Examples of declarative-knowledge symbol structures are those that encode logical statements (such as those McCarthy advocated for representing world knowledge) and those that encode semantic networks (such as those of Raphael or Quillian). Typically, procedural representations, specialized as they are to particular tasks, are more efficient (when performing those tasks), whereas declarative ones, which can be used by a variety of different programs, are more generally useful. In this chapter, I'll describe some of the ideas put forward during this period for reasoning with and for representing declarative knowledge.

11.1 Deductions in Symbolic Logic

Aristotle got things started in logic with his analysis of syllogisms. In the nineteenth century, George Boole developed the foundations of propositional logic, and Gottlob Frege improved the expressive power of logic by proposing a language that could include internal components (called "terms") as part of propositions. Later developments by various logicians gave us what we call today the predicate calculus – the very language in which McCarthy proposed to represent the knowledge needed by an intelligent system.

Here is an instance of one of Aristotle's syllogisms, stated in the language of the predicate calculus:

1. $(\forall x)[Man(x) \supset Mortal(x)]$
   (The expression "$(\forall x)$" is a way of writing "for all x"; and the expression "$\supset$" is a way of writing "implies that." "Man(x)" is a way of writing "x is a man"; and "Mortal(x)" is a way of writing "x is mortal." Thus, the entire expression is a way of writing "for all x, x is a man implies that x is mortal" or, equivalently, "all men are mortal.")
2. Man(Socrates)
   (Socrates is a man.)
3. Therefore, Mortal(Socrates)
   (Socrates is mortal.)

Statement 3, following "Therefore," is an example of a *deduction* in logic. McCarthy proposed that the knowledge that an intelligent agent might need in a specific situation could be deduced from the general knowledge given to it earlier. Thus, for McCarthy-style AI, not only do we need a language (perhaps that of the predicate calculus) but a way to make the necessary deductions from statements in the language.

Logicians have worked out a variety of deduction methods based on what they call "rules of inference." For example, one important inference rule is called *modus ponens* (Latin for "mode that affirms"). It states that if we have the two logical statements P and P $\supset$ Q, then we are justified in deducing the statement Q.

By the 1960s programs had been written that could use inference rules to prove theorems in the predicate calculus. Chief among these were those of Paul Gilmore at IBM,[1] Hao Wang at IBM,[2] and Dag Prawitz,[3] now at Stockholm University. Although their programs could prove simple theorems, proving more complex ones would have required too much search.[4]

A Harvard Ph.D. student, Fisher Black (1938–1995), later a co-inventor of the Black–Scholes equation for pricing options,[5] had done early work implementing some of McCarthy's ideas.[6] But it was a Stanford Ph.D. student and SRI researcher, C. Cordell Green, who programmed a system, QA3, that more fully realized McCarthy's recommendation. Although it was not difficult to represent world knowledge as logical statements, what was lacking at the time of Black's work was an efficient mechanical method to deduce conclusions from these statements. Green was able to employ a new method for efficient reasoning developed by John Alan Robinson.

During the early 1960s, the English (and American) mathematician and logician John Alan Robinson (1930–) developed a deduction method particularly well suited to computer implementation. It was based on an inference rule he called "resolution."[7] Although a full description of resolution would involve too much technical detail, it is a rule (as *modus ponens* is) whose application produces a new statement from two other statements. For example, resolution applied to the two statements ¬P ∨ Q and P produces Q. (The symbol "¬" is a way of writing "not," and the symbol "∨" is a way of writing "or.") Resolution can be thought of as canceling out the P and the ¬P in the two statements. (Resolution is a kind of generalized *modus ponens* as can be seen from the fact that ¬P ∨ Q is logically equivalent to P ⊃ Q.) This example was particularly simple because the statements had no internal terms. Robinson's key contribution was to show how resolution could be applied to general expressions in the predicate calculus, expressions such as ¬P(x) ∨ Q(x) with internal terms.

The advantage of resolution is that it can be readily implemented in programs to make deductions from a set of logical statements. To do so, the statements must first be converted to a special form consisting of what logicians call "clauses." (Loosely speaking, a clause is a formula that uses only ∨'s and ¬'s.) Any logical statement can be converted to clause form (although some, such as John McCarthy, complain that conversion might eliminate clues about how statements might best be used in logical deductions).

The first use of resolution was in computer programs to prove mathematical theorems. (Technically, a "theorem" is any logical statement obtained by successively applying a rule of inference, such as resolution, to members of a base set of logical statements, called "axioms," and to statements deduced from the axioms.) Groups at Argonne National Laboratories (under Lawrence Wos), at the University of Texas at Austin (under Woody Bledsoe), and at the University of Edinburgh (under Bernard Meltzer) soon began work developing theorem-proving programs based on resolution. These programs were able to prove theorems that had previously been proved "by hand" and even some new, never-before-proved, mathematical theorems.[8] One of these latter concerned a conjecture by Herbert Robbins that a Robbins algebra was Boolean. The conjecture was proved in 1996 by William McCune, using an automated theorem prover.[9]

Our concern here, though, is with using deduction methods to automate the reasoning needed by intelligent systems. Around 1968, Green (aided by another Stanford student, Robert Yates) programmed, in LISP, a resolution-based deduction system called QA3, which ran on SRI's time-shared SDS 940 computer. (QA1, Green's first effort, guided by Bertram Raphael at SRI, was an attempt to improve on Raphael's earlier SIR system. QA2 was Green's first system based on resolution, and QA3 was a more sophisticated and practical descendant.) "QA" stood for "question answering," one of the motivating applications.

I'll present a short illustrative example of QA3's question-answering ability taken from Green's Stanford Ph.D. thesis.[10] First, two statements are given to the system, namely,

1. ROBOT(Rob)
   (Rob is a robot.)
2. (∀x)[MACHINE(x) ⊃ ¬ANIMAL(x)]
   (x is a machine implies that it is not an animal.)

The system is then asked "Is everything an animal?" by having it attempt to deduce the statement

3. (∀x)ANIMAL(x)

QA3 not only answers "NO," finding that such a deduction is impossible, but it also gives a "counterexample" as an answer to the question:

4. x = Rob

(This indicates that ¬ANIMAL(Rob) contradicts what was to be deduced.)

The use of resolution, like that of any inference rule, to deduce some specific conclusion from a large body of logical statements involves the need to decide to which two statements, among the many possibilities, the rule should be applied. Then a similar decision must be made again and again until, one hopes, finally the desired conclusion is obtained. So just as with programs for playing checkers, solving puzzles, and proving geometry theorems, deduction programs are faced with the need to try many possibilities in their search for a solution. As with those other programs, various heuristic search methods have been developed for deduction programs.

11.2 The Situation Calculus

Green realized that "question answering" was quite a broad topic. One could ask questions about almost anything. For example, one could ask "What is a program for rearranging a list of numbers so that they are in increasing numerical order?" Or one could ask, "What is the sequence of steps a robot should take to assemble a tower of toy blocks?" The key to applying QA3 to answer questions of this sort lay in using McCarthy's "situation calculus."

McCarthy proposed a version of logic he called the "situation calculus" in which one could write logical statements that explicitly named the situation in which something or other was true. For example, one toy block may be on top of another in one situation but not in another. Green developed a version of McCarthy's logic in which the situation, in which something was true, appeared as one of the terms in an expression stating that something was true. For example, to say that block A is on top of block B in some situation S (allowing for the fact that this might not be the case in other situations), Green would write

On(A, B, S),

to say that block A is blue in all situations, Green would write

(∀s)Blue(A, s),

and to say that there exists *some* situation in which block A is on block B, Green would write

(∃s)On(A, B, s).

Here "(∃s)" is a way of writing "there exists some *s* such that . . . "

Not only was QA3 able to deduce statements, but when it deduced a so-called existential statement (such as the one just mentioned), it was able to compute an instance of what was alleged to "exist." Thus, when it deduced the statement (∃s)On(A, B, s), it also computed for which situation the deduction was valid. Green devised a way in which this value could be expressed in terms of a list of actions for a robot that would change some initial situation into the situation for which the

Figure 11.1. Robert Kowalski (left) and Alain Colmerauer (right). (Photographs courtesy of Robert Kowalski and of Alain Colmerauer.)

deduced statement was true. Thus, for example, QA3 could be used to plan courses of action for a robot. Later, we'll see how it was used for this purpose.

11.3 Logic Programming

In the same way that QA3 could be used to make robot plans, it could also construct simple computer programs. In his 1969 paper, Green wrote

The formalization given here [can] be used to precisely state and solve the problem of automatic generation of programs, including recursive programs, along with concurrent generation of proofs of the correctness of these programs. Thus any programs automatically written by this method have no errors.

Green's work on automatic programming was the first attempt to write programs using logical statements. Around this time, Robert A. Kowalski (1941– ; Fig. 11.1), an American who had just earned a Ph.D. at the University of Edinburgh, and Donald Kuehner developed a more efficient version of Robinson's resolution method, which they called "SL-resolution."[11] In the summer of 1972, Kowalski visited Alain Colmerauer (1941– ; Fig. 11.1), the head of Groupe d'Intelligence Artificielle (GIA), Centre National de la Recherche Scientifique and Université II of Aix-Marseille in Marseille. Kowalski wrote "It was during that second visit that logic programming, as we commonly understand it, was born."[12]

Colmerauer and his Ph.D. student, Philippe Roussel, were the ones who developed, in 1972, the new programming language, PROLOG. (Roussel chose the name as an abbreviation for "PROgrammation en LOGique.") In PROLOG, programs consist of an ordered sequence of logical statements. The exact order in which these statements are written, along with some other constructs, is the key to efficient program execution. PROLOG uses an ordering based on the ordering of deductions in SL-resolution. Kowalski, Colmerauer, and Roussel all share credit for PROLOG, but Kowalski admits ". . . it is probably fair to say that my own contributions were mainly philosophical and Alain's were more practical."[13]

The PROLOG language gradually grew in importance to rival LISP, although it is used mainly by AI people outside of the United States. Some American researchers, especially those at MIT, argued against PROLOG (and other resolution-based deduction systems), claiming (with some justification) that computation based on deduction was not efficient. They advocated computation controlled by embedding knowledge about the problem being solved and how best to solve it directly into programs to reduce search. This "procedural embedding of knowledge" was a feature of the PLANNER languages developed by Carl Hewitt and colleagues at MIT. (Hewitt coined the phrase "procedural embedding of knowledge" in a 1971 paper.)[14]

11.4 Semantic Networks

Semantic networks were (and still are) another important format for representing declarative knowledge. I have already mentioned their use by Ross Quillian as a model of human long-term memory. In the 1970s, Stanford cognitive psychologist Gordon Bower (1932–) and his student John Anderson (1947–) presented a network-based theory of human memory in their book *Human Associative Memory*.[15] According to a biographical sketch of Anderson, the book "immediately attracted the attention of everyone then working in the field. The book played a major role in establishing propositional semantic networks as the basis for representation in memory and spreading activation through the links in such networks as the basis for retrieval of information from memory."[16]

The theory was partially implemented in a computer simulation called HAM (an acronym for Human Associative Memory). HAM could parse simple propositional sentences and store them in a semantic network structure. Using its accumulated memory, HAM could answer simple questions.

Several other network-based representations were explored during the late 1960s and early 1970s. Robert F. Simmons, after moving from SDC to the University of Texas in Austin, began using semantic networks as a computational linguistic theory of structures and processing operations required for computer understanding of natural language. He wrote "Semantic nets are simple – even elegant – structures for representing aspects of meaning of English strings in a convenient computational form that supports useful language-processing operations on computers."[17]

In 1971, Stuart C. Shapiro (1944–), then at the University of Wisconsin in Madison, introduced a network structure called MENS (MEmory Net Structure) for storing semantic information.[18] An auxiliary system called MENTAL (MEmory Net That Answers and Learns) interacted with a user and with MEMS. MENTAL aided MEMS in deducing new information from that already stored. Shapiro envisioned that MENTAL would be able to answer users' questions using information stored in MEMS.

Shapiro later moved to the State University of New York at Buffalo where he and colleagues are continuing to develop a series of systems called SNePS (Semantic NEtwork Processing System).[19] SNePS combines features of logical representations

Figure 11.2. Roger Schank. (Photograph courtesy of Roger Schank.)

with those of network representations and has been used for natural language understanding and generation and other applications.[20]

In his Ph.D. research in linguistics at the University of Texas at Austin, Roger C. Schank (1946– ; Fig. 11.2) began developing what he called "conceptual dependency representations for natural language sentences."[21] Subsequently, as a Professor at Stanford and at Yale, he and colleagues continued to develop these ideas. The basis of Schank's work was his belief that people transform natural language sentences into "conceptual structures" that are independent of the particular language in which the sentences were originally expressed. These conceptual structures, he claimed, were how the information in sentences is understood and remembered. So, for example, when one translates a sentence from one language into another, one first represents its information content as a conceptual structure and then uses that structure to reason about what was said or to regenerate the information as a sentence in another language. As he put it in one of his papers, ". . . any two utterances that can be said to mean the same thing, whether they are in the same or different languages, should be characterized in only one way by the conceptual structures."[22]

The notation Schank used for his conceptual structures (sometimes called "conceptual dependency graphs") evolved somewhat during the 1970s.[23] As an example, Fig. 11.3, taken from one of his papers, shows how he would represent the sentence "John threw the pencil to Sam." This structure uses three of the "primitive actions" Schank has defined for these representations. These are ATRANS, which means a transfer of possession; PTRANS, which means a transfer of physical location; and PROPEL, which means an application of force to an object. Schank defined several other primitive actions to represent movement, attending to, speaking, transferring of ideas, and so on.

An expanded literal reading of what this structure represents would be "John applied physical force to a pencil, which caused it to go through the air from John's location to Sam's location, which caused Sam to possess it" or something like that. Schank, like many others who are interested in meaning representation languages, notes that these representations can be used directly to perform deductions and answer questions. For example, answers to questions such as "How did Sam get the pencil?" and "Who owned the pencil after John threw it?" are easily extracted.

Although network structures are illustrated graphically in papers about them, they were encoded using LISP for computer processing.

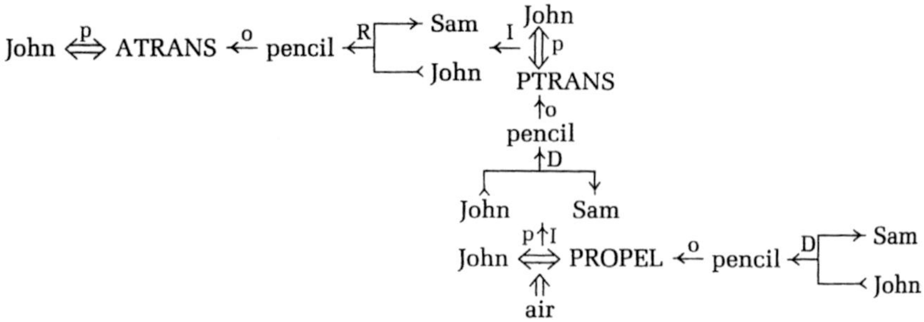

John $\overset{p}{\Longleftrightarrow}$ ATRANS $\overset{o}{\longleftarrow}$ pencil $\overset{R}{\longleftarrow}$ ⎡→ Sam $\overset{I}{\longleftarrow}$ John
                                                              ⎣→ John $\Updownarrow$ p
                                                                        PTRANS
                                                                        ↑o
                                                                        pencil
                                                                        ↑D
                                                              ⎡   ⎤
                                                            John   Sam
                                                              p↑I
                                                    John $\overset{o}{\Longleftrightarrow}$ PROPEL $\overset{o}{\longleftarrow}$ pencil $\overset{D}{\longleftarrow}$ ⎡→ Sam
                                                              ⇑   ⎣→ John
                                                             air

Figure 11.3. Conceptual structure for "John threw the pencil to Sam." (From Roger C. Schank, "Identification of Conceptualizations Underlying Natural Langauge," in Roger Schank and Kenneth Colby (eds.), *Computer Models of Thought and Language*, p. 226, San Francisco: W. H. Freeman and Co., 1973.)

11.5 Scripts and Frames

Graphical knowledge representations, such as semantic networks and conceptual structures, connect related entities together in groups. Such groupings are efficient computationally because things that are related often participate in the same chain of reasoning. When accessing one such entity it is easy to access close-by ones also. Roger Schank and Robert Abelson expanded on this idea by introducing the concept of "scripts."[24] A script is a way of representing what they call "specific knowledge," that is, detailed knowledge about a situation or event that "we have been through many times." They contrast specific knowledge with "general knowledge," the latter of which is the large body of background or commonsense knowledge that is useful in many situations.

Their "restaurant" script ("Coffee Shop version") became their most famous illustrative example. The script consists of four "scenes," namely, Entering, Ordering, Eating, and Exiting. Its "Props" are Tables, Menu, F-Food, Check, and Money. Its "Roles" are S-Customer, W-Waiter, C-Cook, M-Cashier, and O-Owner. Its "Entry conditions" are S is hungry and S has money. Its "Results" are S has less money, O has more money, S is not hungry, and S is pleased (optional). Figures 11.4 shows their script for the "Ordering" scene.

Besides the actions PTRANS (transfer of location) and ATRANS (transfer of possession), this script uses two more of their primitive actions, namely, MTRANS (transfer of information) and MBUILD (creating or combining thoughts). CP(S) stands for S's "conceptual processor" where thought takes place, and DO stands for a "dummy action" defined by what follows. The lines in the diagram show possible alternative paths through the script. So, for example, if the menu is already on the table, the script begins at the upper left-hand corner; otherwise it begins at the upper right-hand corner. I believe most of the script is self-explanatory, but I'll help out by explaining what goes on in the middle. S brings the "food list" into its central processor where it is able to mentally decide (build) a choice of food. S then transfers information to the waiter to come to the table, which the waiter does. Then, S transfers the information about his or her choice of food to the waiter. This continues

Scene 2: Ordering

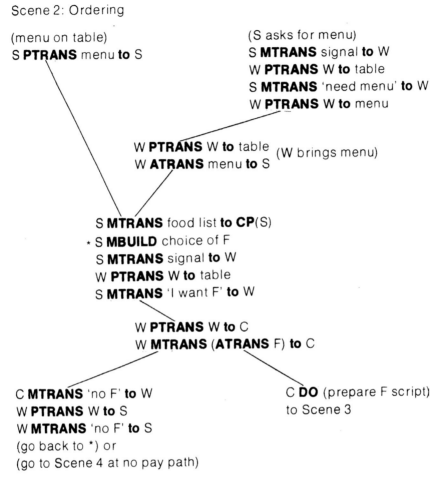

(menu on table)
S **PTRANS** menu **to** S

(S asks for menu)
S **MTRANS** signal **to** W
W **PTRANS** W **to** table
S **MTRANS** 'need menu' **to** W
W **PTRANS** W **to** menu

W **PTRANS** W **to** table
W **ATRANS** menu **to** S   (W brings menu)

S **MTRANS** food list **to** **CP**(S)
⋆ S **MBUILD** choice of F
S **MTRANS** signal **to** W
W **PTRANS** W **to** table
S **MTRANS** 'I want F' **to** W

W **PTRANS** W **to** C
W **MTRANS** (**ATRANS** F) **to** C

C **MTRANS** 'no F' **to** W
W **PTRANS** W **to** S
W **MTRANS** 'no F' **to** S
(go back to ⋆) or
(go to Scene 4 at no pay path)

C **DO** (prepare F script)
to Scene 3

Figure 11.4. A scene in the restaurant script. (From Roger C. Schank and Robert P. Abelson, *Scripts, Plans, Goals, and Understanding: An Inquiry into Human Knowledge Structures*, p. 43, Hillsdale, NJ: Lawrence Erlbaum Associates, 1977.)

until either the cook tells the waiter that he does not have the food that is ordered or the cook prepares the food. The three other scenes in the restaurant script are similarly illustrated in Schank and Abelson's book.[25] Several other variations of the restaurant script (for different kinds of restaurants, and so on) are possible.

Scripts help explain some of the reasoning we do automatically when we hear a story. For example, if we hear that John went to a coffee shop and ordered lasagne, we can reasonably assume that lasagne was on the menu. If we later learn that John had to order something else instead, we can assume that the coffee shop was out of lasagne. Schank and Abelson give anecdotal evidence that even small children build such scripts and that people must have a great number of them to enable them to navigate through and reason about situations they encounter.

Schank later expanded on scripts and related ideas in another book, in which he introduced the idea of "memory organization packets" (MOPS) that describe situations in a more distributed and dynamic way than scripts do.[26] He later "revisited" some of these ideas in a book about their application to education, a field to which he has made significant contributions.[27]

Schank and his claims generated a good deal of controversy among AI researchers. For example, I remember arguing with him in 1983 in a restaurant somewhere (while waiting for the menu?) about the comparative performance of his programs for natural language understanding and that of our programs at SRI. As I recall, he was eager to make more grandiose claims about what his programs could do than I was prepared to believe or to claim about ours. Tufts University philosopher Daniel Dennett is quoted as having said "I've always relished Schank's role as a gadfly and as a naysayer, a guerrilla in the realm of cognitive science, always asking big questions, always willing to discard his own earlier efforts and say they were radically incomplete for interesting reasons. He's a gadfly and a good one."[28] I think his basic idea about scripts was prescient. Also, he has produced a great bunch of students. The "AI Genealogy" Web site[29] lists almost four dozen Schank students, many of whom have gone on to distinguished careers.

Around the time of Schank's work, Marvin Minsky proposed that knowledge about situations be represented in structures he called "frames."[30] He mentioned Schank's ideas (among others) as exemplary of a movement away from "trying to represent knowledge as collections of separate, simple fragments" such as sentences in a logical language. As he defined them,

A *frame* is a data-structure for representing a stereotyped situation, like being in a certain kind of living room, or going to a child's birthday party. Attached to each frame are several kinds of information. Some of this information is about how to use the frame. Some is about what one can expect to happen next. Some is about what to do if these expectations are not confirmed.
. . .
Collections of related frames are linked together into *frame-systems*. The effects of important actions are mirrored by transformations between the frames of a system. These are used to make certain kinds of calculations economical, to represent changes of emphasis and attention, and to account for the effectiveness of "imagery."

Minsky's paper described how frame systems could be applied to vision and imagery, linguistic and other kinds of understanding, memory acquisition, retrieval of knowledge, and control. Although his paper was rich in ideas, Minsky did not actually implement any frame systems. A couple of years later, some of his students and former students did implement some framelike systems. One, called FRL (for Frame Representation Language), was developed by R. Bruce Roberts and Ira P. Goldstein.[31] Daniel Bobrow and Terry Winograd (the latter being one of Papert's students), implemented a more ambitious system called KRL (for Knowledge Representation Language).[32]

Frame systems accommodated a style of reasoning in which details "not specifically warranted" could be assumed, thus "bypassing "logic," as Minsky would have it. This style was already used earlier in Raphael's SIR system (see p. 98), and researchers advocating the use of logical languages for knowledge representation would later extend logic in various ways to accommodate this style also. Even so, the last section (titled "Criticism of the Logistic Approach") of Minsky's paper about frames gives many reasons why one might doubt (along with Minsky) "the feasibility of representing ordinary knowledge effectively in the form of many small, independently 'true' propositions."

Notes

1. Paul C. Gilmore, "A Proof Method for Quantification Theory: Its Justification and Realization," *IBM Journal of Research and Development*, Vol. 4, pp. 28–35, 1960. [150]
2. Hao Wang, "Proving Theorems by Pattern Recognition," *Communications of the ACM*, Vol. 4, No. 3, pp. 229–243, 1960, and Hao Wang, "Toward Mechanical Mathematics," *IBM Journal of Research and Development*, Vol. 4, pp. 2–21, 1960. [150]
3. D. Prawitz, H. Prawitz, and N. Voghera, "A Mechanical Proof Procedure and Its Realization in an Electronic Computer," *Journal of the Association for Computing Machinery*, Vol. 7, pp. 102–128, 1960. [150]
4. For additional background and history about automated deduction, see Wolfgang Bibel, "Early History and Perspectives of Automated Deduction," in J. Hertzberg, M. Beetz, and R. Englert (eds.), *Proceedings of the 30th Annual German Conference on Artificial Intelligence (KI-2007)*, Lecture Notes on Artificial Intelligence, pp. 2–18, Berlin: Springer-Verlag, 2007. [150]
5. In 1997, Myron Scholes and Robert C. Merton were awarded a Nobel Prize in economics for their option-pricing work. Black died of cancer in 1995. The Nobel Prize is not given posthumously; however, in its announcement of the award, the Nobel committee prominently mentioned Black's key role. [150]
6. Fischer Black, "A Deductive Question-Answering System," Ph.D. dissertation, Harvard University, June 1964. Reprinted in Marvin Minsky (ed.), *Semantic Information Processing*, pp. 354–402, Cambridge, MA: MIT Press, 1968. [150]
7. John Alan Robinson, "A Machine-Oriented Logic Based on the Resolution Principle," *Journal of the ACM*, Vol. 12, No. 1, pp. 23–41, 1965. [150]
8. For a description of some of this work, see Larry Wos, Ross Overbeek, Ewing Lusk, and Jim Boyle, *Automated Reasoning: Introduction and Applications*, second edition, New York: McGraw-Hill, 1992. For more recent work, visit Larry Wos's Web page at http://www.mcs.anl.gov/~wos/ [151]
9. William McCune, "Solution of the Robbins Problem," *Journal of Automated Reasoning*, Vol. 19, No. 3, pp. 263–276, 1997. [151]
10. Available as an SRI Technical Note: C. Green, "Application of Theorem Proving to Problem Solving," Technical Note 4, AI Center, SRI International, 333 Ravenswood Ave, Menlo Park, CA 94025, March 1969. Online version available at http://www.ai.sri.com/pubs/files/tn004-green69.pdf. See also C. Green, "Theorem Proving by Resolution as a Basis for Question-Answering Systems," in B. Meltzer and D. Michie, *Machine Intelligence 4*, pp. 183ff, Edinburgh: Edinburgh University Press, 1969, and C. Green, "Applications of Theorem Proving to Problem Solving," reprinted from a 1969 IJCAI conference article in B. L. Webber and N. J. Nilsson (eds.), *Readings in Artificial Intelligence*, pp. 202–222, San Francisco: Morgan Kaufmann, 1981. [151]
11. Robert A. Kowalski and Donald Kuehner, "Linear Resolution with Selection Function," *Artificial Intelligence*, Vol. 2, Nos. 3–4, pp. 227–260, 1971. [153]
12. From one of Kowalski's Web pages: http://www.doc.ic.ac.uk/~rak/history.html. [153]

13. http://www.doc.ic.ac.uk/~rak/history.html. For Colmerauer and Roussel's account of the birth of PROLOG see Alain Colmerauer and Philippe Roussel, "The Birth of PROLOG, in Thomas J. Bergin and Richard G. Gibson (eds.), *Programming Languages*, New York: ACM Press, Addison-Wesley, 1996. Available online at http://alain .colmerauer.free.fr/ArchivesPublications/HistoireProlog/19november92.pdf. [154]

14. See Carl Hewitt, "Procedural Embedding of Knowledge in PLANNER," *Proceedings of the Second International Joint Conference on Artificial Intelligence*, pp. 167–182, Los Altos, CA: Morgan Kaufmann Publishing Co., 1971. [154]

15. John R. Anderson and Gordon H. Bower, *Human Associative Memory*, Washington, DC: Winston and Sons, 1973. [154]

16. From the Web site http://rumelhartprize.org/john.htm. [154]

17. Robert F. Simmons, "Semantic Networks: Computation and Use for Understanding English Sentences," in Roger Schank and Kenneth Colby (eds.), *Computer Models of Thought and Language*, pp. 63–113, San Francisco: W. H. Freeman and Co., 1973. [154]

18. Stuart C. Shapiro, "A Net Structure for Semantic Information Storage, Deduction and Retrieval," *Proceedings of the Second International Joint Conference on Artificial Intelligence*, pp. 512–523, Los Altos, CA: Morgan Kaufmann Publishing Co., 1971. [154]

19. An early paper is Stuart C. Shapiro, "The SNePS Semantic Network Processing System," in Nicholas V. Findler (ed.), *Associative Networks: The Representation and Use of Knowledge by Computers*, pp. 179–203, New York: Academic Press, 1979. [154]

20. The SNePS Web page is at http://www.cse.buffalo.edu/sneps/. [155]

21. Roger C. Schank, "A Conceptual Dependency Representation for a Computer-Oriented Semantics," Ph.D. thesis, University of Texas at Austin, 1969. Available as Stanford AI Memo 83 or Computer Science Technical Note 130, Computer Science Department, Stanford University, Stanford, CA, 1969. [155]

22. Roger C. Schank, "Identification of Conceptualizations Underlying Natural Language," in Roger Schank and Kenneth Colby (eds.), *Computer Models of Thought and Language*, pp. 187–247, San Francisco: W. H. Freeman and Co., 1973. [155]

23. Interested readers might refer to various of his books and papers – for example, Roger C. Schank, "Conceptual Dependency: A Theory of Natural Language Understanding" *Cognitive Psychology*, Vol. 3, pp. 552–631, 1972, and Roger C. Schank, *Conceptual Information Processing*, New York: Elsevier, 1975. [155]

24. Roger C. Schank and Robert P. Abelson, *Scripts, Plans, Goals, and Understanding: An Inquiry into Human Knowledge Structures*, Hillsdale, NJ: Lawrence Erlbaum Associates, 1977. [156]

25. *Ibid.* [157]

26. Roger C. Schank, *Dynamic Memory: A Theory of Reminding and Learning in Computers and People*, Cambridge: Cambridge University Press, 1982. [158]

27. Roger C. Schank, *Dynamic Memory Revisited*, Cambridge: Cambridge University Press, 1999. [158]

28. See http://www.edge.org/3rd_culture/bios/schank.html. [158]

29. See http://aigp.csres.utexas.edu/~aigp/researcher/show/192. [158]

30. Marvin Minsky, "A Framework for Representing Knowledge," MIT AI Laboratory Memo 306, June 1974. Reprinted in Patrick Winston (ed.), *The Psychology of Computer Vision*, New York: McGraw-Hill, 1975. Available online at http://web.media.mit. edu/~minsky/papers/Frames/frames.html. [158]

31. R. Bruce Roberts and Ira P. Goldstein, *The FRL Primer*, Massachusetts Institute of Technology AI Laboratory Technical Report AIM-408, July 1977; available online at ftp://publications.ai.mit.edu/ai-publications/pdf/AIM-408.pdf. [158]

32. Daniel G. Bobrow and Terry A. Winograd, "An overview of KRL, a Knowledge Representation Language," Report Number CS-TR-76-581, Department of Computer Science, Stanford University, November 1976. Available online at ftp://reports.stanford.edu/pub/cstr/reports/cs/tr/76/581/CS-TR-76-581.pdf. Appeared later as Daniel Bobrow and Terry Winograd, "An Overview of KRL, a Knowledge Representation Language," Cognitive Science, Vol. 1, No. 1, pp. 3–46, January 1977. [158]

12

Mobile Robots

T HE HAND–EYE SYSTEMS DESCRIBED EARLIER MIGHT BE THOUGHT OF AS "ROBOTS," but they could not move about from their fixed base. Up to this time, very little work had been done on mobile robots even though they figured prominently in science fiction. I have already mentioned Grey Walter's "tortoises," which were early versions of autonomous mobile robots. In the early 1960s researchers at the Johns Hopkins University Applied Physics Laboratory built a mobile robot they called "The Beast." (See Fig. 12.1.) Controlled by on-board electronics and guided by sonar sensors, photocells, and a "wallplate-feeling" arm, it could wander the white-walled corridors looking for dark-colored power plugs. Upon finding one, and if its batteries were low, it would plug itself in and recharge its batteries. The system is described in a book by Hans Moravec.[1]

Beginning in the mid-1960s, several groups began working on mobile robots. These included the AI Labs at SRI and at Stanford. I'll begin with an extended description of the SRI robot project for it provided the stimulus for the invention and integration of several important AI technologies.

12.1 Shakey, the SRI Robot

In November 1963, Charles Rosen, the leader of neural-network research at SRI, wrote a memo in which he proposed development of a mobile "automaton" that would combine the pattern-recognition and memory capabilities of neural networks with higher level AI programs – such as were being developed at MIT, Stanford, CMU, and elsewhere. Rosen had previously attended a summer course at UCLA on LISP given by Bertram Raphael, who was finishing his Ph.D. (on SIR) at MIT.

Rosen and I and others in his group immediately began thinking about mobile robots. We also enlisted Marvin Minsky as a consultant to help us. Minsky spent two weeks at SRI during August 1964. We made the first of many trips to the ARPA office (in the Pentagon at that time) to generate interest in supporting mobile robot research at SRI. We also talked with Ruth Davis, the director of the Department of Defense Research and Engineering (DDR&E) – the office in charge of all Defense Department research. We wrote a proposal in April 1964 to DDR&E for "Research in Intelligent Automata (Phase I)" that would, we claimed, "ultimately lead to the development of machines that will perform tasks that are presently considered to require human intelligence."[2] The proposal, along with several trips and discussions culminated, in November 1964, in a "work statement" issued by the then-director of

Figure 12.1. The Johns Hopkins "Beast." (Courtesy of Johns Hopkins University Applied Physics Laboratory.)

ARPA's Information Processing Techniques Office, Ivan Sutherland. The excerpt in Fig. 12.2 describes the goals of the program.[3]

In the meantime, Bertram Raphael completed his MIT Ph.D. degree in 1964 and took up a position at UC Berkeley for an academic year. In April 1965, he accepted our offer to join SRI to provide our group with needed AI expertise. After several research proposal drafts and discussions with people in the relevant offices in the Defense Department (complicated by the fact that Ivan Sutherland left ARPA during this time), SRI was finally awarded a rather large (for the time) contract based essentially on Sutherland's work statement. The "start-work" date on the project, which was administered for ARPA by the Rome Air Development Center (RADC) in Rome, New York, was March 17, 1966. (Coincidentally, just before joining SRI in 1961, I had just finished a three-year stint of duty as an Air Force Lieutenant at RADC working on statistical signal-processing techniques for radar systems.) Ruth Davis played a prominent role in getting ARPA and RADC to move forward on getting the project started. The "knitting together" of several disparate AI technologies was one of the primary challenges and one of the major contributions of SRI's automaton project.[4]

A RESEARCH AND DEVELOPMENT PROGRAM IN APPLICATIONS OF INTELLIGENT

AUTOMATA TO RECONNAISSANCE

Goals

The long-range goal of this program will be to develop automatons capable of gathering processing and transmitting information in a hostile environment. The time period involved is 1970-1980.

The first short-range goal of the program will be to design and develop a mobile automaton to accomplish non-trivial missions in a real environment. External control will be exercised over the automaton from a computer. The automaton will have at least visual and tactile sensor capability.

The second short-range goal will be to design and develop a mobile automaton to accomplish non-trivial missions in a real environment in a self-contained mode, e.g., with little or no external control.

. . . .

Such a long-range goal attained by stepping through a number of intermediary ones is believed essential to knit together as many of the constituent subject areas of "artificial intelligence" as possible. It has been so stated as to require the successful application of many techniques with all the attendant problems of interaction and feed-back. It is difficult of realization but by the same token it will provide solutions to existing pressing military problems.

Figure 12.2. Excerpt from the typescript of the automaton work statement.

One of the tasks was the actual construction of a robot vehicle whose activities would be controlled by a suite of programs. Because of various engineering idiosyncrasies, the vehicle shook when it came to an abrupt stop. We soon called it "Shakey," even though one of the researchers thought that sobriquet too disrespectful. [Shakey was inducted into the "Robot Hall of Fame" (along with C-3PO among others) in 2004.[5] It was also named as the fifth-best robot ever (out of 50) by *Wired Magazine* in January 2006. *Wired*'s numbers 2 and 4 were fictional, "Spirit" and "Opportunity" (the Mars robots) were number 3, and "Stanley" (winner of the 2005 DARPA "Grand Challenge") was named "the #1 Robot of All Time." Shakey is now exhibited at the Computer History Museum in Mountain View, California.][6]

Shakey had an on-board television camera for capturing images of its environment, a laser range finder (triangulating, not time-of-flight) for sensing its distance from walls and other objects, and cat-whisker-like bump detectors. Shakey's environment was a collection of "rooms" connected by doorways but otherwise separated by low walls that we could conveniently see over but Shakey could not. Some of the rooms contained large objects, as shown in Fig. 12.3. The size of Shakey can be discerned from inspection of Fig. 12.4.

Most of the programs that we developed to control Shakey were run on a DEC PDP-10 computer. Between the PDP-10 and the mobile vehicle itself were a PDP-15 peripheral computer (for handling the lower level communications and commands to on-board hardware) and a two-way radio and video link. The PDP-10 programs were organized in what we called a "three-layer" hierarchy. Programs in the lowest level drove all of the motors and captured sensory information. Programs in the

Figure 12.3. Shakey as it existed in November 1968 (with some of its components labeled). (Photograph courtesy of SRI International.)

intermediate level supervised primitive actions, such as moving to a designated position, and also processed visual images from Shakey's TV camera. Planning more complex actions, requiring the execution of a sequence of intermediate-level actions, was done by programs in the highest level of the hierarchy. The Shakey project involved the integration of several new inventions in search techniques, in robust control of actions, in planning and learning, and in vision. Many of these ideas are widely used today. The next few subsections describe them.

12.1.1 *A*: A New Heuristic Search Method*

One of the first problems we considered was how to plan a sequence of "way points" that Shakey could use in navigating from place to place. In getting around a single obstacle lying between its initial position and a goal position, Shakey should first head toward a point near an occluding boundary of the obstacle and then head straight for the unobstructed final goal point. However, the situation becomes more complicated if the environment is littered with several obstacles, and we sought a general solution to this more difficult problem.

Figure 12.4. Charles A. Rosen with Shakey. (Photograph courtesy of SRI International.)

Shakey kept information about the location of obstacles and about its own position in a "grid model," such as the one shown in Fig. 12.5. (To obtain the required accuracy, grid cells were decomposed into smaller cells near the objects. I think this was one of the first applications of adaptive cell decomposition in robot motion planning and is now a commonly used technique.) Consider, for example, the navigation problem in which Shakey is at position R and needs to travel to G (where R and G are indicated by the shaded squares). It can use a computer representation of the grid model to plan a route before beginning its journey – but how? The map shows the positions of three objects that must be avoided. It is not too difficult to compute the locations of some candidate way points near the corners of the objects. (These way points must be sufficiently far from the corners so that Shakey wouldn't bump into the objects.) The way points are indicated by shaded stars and labeled "A," "B," and so on through "K." Using techniques now familiar in computer graphics, it also is not difficult to compute which way points are reachable using an obstacle-free, straight-line path from any other way point and from R and G.

Looked at in this way, Shakey's navigation problem is a search problem, similar to ones I have mentioned earlier. Here is how a search tree can be constructed and then searched for a shortest path from R to G. First, because A and F are directly

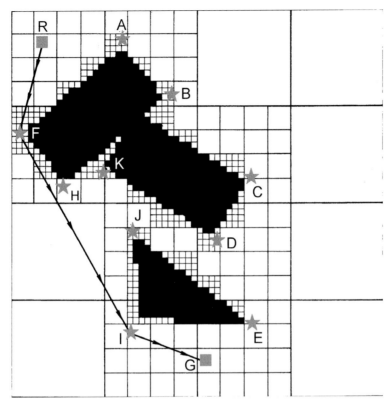

Figure 12.5. A navigation problem for Shakey. (Illustration used with permission of SRI International.)

reachable by obstacle-free, straight-line paths from R, these are set up as direct-descendant "nodes" of R in the search tree. We continue the process of computing descendant nodes (along obstacle-free, straight-line paths) from each of A and F and so on until G is added to the tree. Then, it is a simple matter to identify the shortest path from R to G.

Several methods for searching trees (and their more general cousins, graphs) were already in use by the mid-1960s. One point in favor of these known methods was that they were guaranteed to find shortest paths when used to solve Shakey's navigation problems. However, they could be computationally inefficient for difficult problems. Of course, solving simple navigation problems (such as the one in the diagram) does not involve much search, so any search method would solve such problems quickly. But we were interested in general methods that would work efficiently on larger, more difficult problems. I was familiar with the heuristic search method proposed by J. Doran and Donald Michie for solving the eight-piece, sliding-tile puzzle. They assigned a numerical value to each node in the search tree, based on the estimated difficulty of reaching the goal from that node. The node with the lowest score was the one that was selected next to have its descendants generated.[7]

I reasoned that a good "heuristic" estimate for the difficulty of getting from a way point position to the goal (before actually searching further) would be the "airline distance," ignoring any intervening obstacles, from that position to the goal. I suggested that we use that estimate as the score of the corresponding node in the search tree. Bertram Raphael, who was directing work on Shakey at that time, observed that a better value for the score would be the sum of the distance traveled so far from the initial position plus my heuristic estimate of how far the robot had to go.[8]

Raphael and I described this idea to Peter Hart, who had recently obtained a Ph.D. from Stanford and joined our group at SRI. Hart recalls[9] "going home that day, sitting in a particular chair and staring at the wall for more than an hour, and concluding" that if the estimate of remaining distance (whatever it might be) was never larger than the actual remaining distance, then the use of such an estimate in our new scoring scheme would *always* find a path having the shortest distance to the goal. (Of course, my heuristic airline distance satisfied Hart's more–general condition.) Furthermore, he thought such a procedure would generate search trees no larger than any other procedures that were also guaranteed to find shortest paths and that used heuristic estimates no better than ours.

Together, Hart, Raphael, and I were able to construct proofs for these claims, and we named the resulting search process "A*." (The "A" was for algorithm and the "*" denoted its special property of finding shortest paths. I think Hart and Raphael did most of the heavy lifting in devising the proofs.) When paths have costs associated with them that depend on more than just distance, and when such costs (rather than distances) are taken into account in computing scores, A* is guaranteed to find lowest cost paths.[10]

The inclusion of the estimate of remaining distance (or cost) to the goal contributes to searching in the general direction of the goal. The inclusion of the actual distance (or cost) incurred so far ensures that the search process will not forever be led down promising but perhaps futile paths and will be able to "leak around" obstacles.

A* has been extended in many ways – especially by Richard Korf to make it more practical when computer memory is limited.[11] Today, A* is used in many applications including natural language parsing,[12] the computation of driving directions,[13] and interactive computer games.[14]

12.1.2 *Robust Action Execution*

The A* algorithm was embedded in Shakey's programs for navigating from one place to another within a room containing obstacles and for pushing an object from one place to another. Navigation programs, along with others, occupied the middle level of the hierarchy of Shakey's programs. These intermediate–level programs were all designed to achieve certain goals, such as getting an object in front of a doorway for example. They were also quite robust in that they "kept trying" even in the face of unforeseen difficulties. For example, if an object being pushed happened accidentally to slip off the front "pushing bar," the push program noticed this problem (through built–in contact sensors in the pushing bar) and repositioned Shakey so that it could reengage the object and continue pushing.

In thinking about how to achieve this robustness, I was inspired both by Miller, Galanter, and Pribram's TOTE units and by the idea of homeostasis. (Recall that a TOTE unit for driving in a nail keeps pounding until the nail is completely driven in and that homeostatic systems take actions to return them to stability in the face of perceived environmental disturbances.) I wanted the mid-level programs to seek and execute that action that was both "closest" to achieving their goals and that could actually be executed in the current situation. If execution of that action produced a situation in which, as anticipated, an action even closer to achieving the goal could be executed, fine; the mid-level program was at least making progress. If not, or something unexpected caused a setback, some other action would be executed next to get back on track. Richard Duda and I developed a format, called "Markov tables," for writing these intermediate-level programs having this "keep-trying" property.[15]

12.1.3 *STRIPS: A New Planning Method*

The mid-level programs could accomplish a number of simple tasks, such as getting Shakey from one place to another in the same room, pushing objects, and getting Shakey through a doorway into an adjoining room. However, to go to some distant room and push an object there into some designated position would require joining together a sequence of perhaps several of these mid-level programs. Just as humans sometimes make and then execute plans for accomplishing their tasks, we wanted Shakey to be able to assemble a plan of actions and then to execute the plan. The plan would consist of a list of the programs to be executed.

Information needed for planning was stored in what was called an "axiom model." This model contained logical statements in the language of the predicate calculus (which I talked about earlier.) For example, Shakey's location was represented by a statement such as AT(ROBOT, 7,5), the fact that Box1 was pushable was represented by the statement PUSHABLE(BOX1), and the fact that there was a doorway named D1 between rooms R1 and R2 was represented by the statement JOINSROOMS(D1, R1,R2). The axiom model had close to two-hundred statements such as these and was the basis of Shakey's reasoning and planning abilities.

Our first attempt at constructing plans for Shakey used the QA3 deduction system and the situation calculus. We would ask QA3 to prove (using a version of the axiom model) that there existed a situation in which Shakey's goal (for example, being in some distant room) was true. The result of the deduction (if successful) would name that situation in terms of a list of mid-level actions to be executed.[16]

The use of the situation calculus for planning how to assemble mid-level actions involved using logical statements to describe the effects of these actions on situations. Not only did we have to describe how a mid-level action changed certain things about the world, but we also had to state that it left many things unaffected. For example, when Shakey pushed an object, the position of that object in the resulting situation was changed, but the positions of all other objects were not. That most things in Shakey's world did not change had to be explicitly represented as logical statements and, worse, reasoned about by QA3. This difficulty, called the "frame problem," has been the subject of a great deal of research in AI, and there have been many attempts to mitigate it, if not solve it.[17] Because of the frame problem, QA3 could be used only for putting together the simplest two- or three-step plans. Any attempt to generate plans very much longer would exhaust the computer's memory.

The problem with the situation calculus (as it was used then) was that it assumed that all things might change unless it was explicitly stated that they did not change. I reasoned that a better convention would be to assume that all things remained unchanged unless it was explicitly stated that they did change. To employ a convention like that, I proposed a different way of updating the collection of logical statements describing a situation. The idea was that certain facts, specifically those that held before executing the action but might not hold after, should be deleted and certain new facts, namely, those caused by executing the action, should be added. All other facts (those not slated for deletion) should simply be copied over into the collection describing the new situation. Besides describing the *effects* of an action in this way, each action description would have a *precondition*, that is, a statement of what had to be true of a situation to be able to execute the action in that situation. (A year or so earlier, Carl Hewitt, a Ph.D. student at MIT, was developing a robot programming language called PLANNER that had mechanisms for similar kinds of updates.)[18]

For example, to describe the effects of the program goto((X1,Y1),(X2,Y2)) for moving Shakey from some position (X1,Y1) to some position (X2,Y2), one should delete the logical statement AT(ROBOT, X1,Y1), add the statement AT(ROBOT, X2,Y2), and keep all of the other statements. Of course, to execute goto((X1,Y1), (X2,Y2)), Shakey would already have to be at position (X1,Y1); that is, the axiom model had to contain the precondition statement AT(ROBOT,X1,Y1), or at least contain statements from which AT(ROBOT,X1,Y1) could be proved.

Around this time (1969), Richard Fikes (1942–) had just completed his Ph.D. work under Allen Newell at Carnegie and joined our group at SRI. Fikes's dissertation explored some new ways to solve problems using procedures rather than using logic as in QA3. Fikes and I worked together on designing a planning system that used preconditions, delete lists, and add lists (all expressed as logical statements) to describe actions. Fikes suggested that in performing a search for a goal-satisfying sequence of actions, the system should use the "means–ends" analysis heuristic central to Newell, Shaw, and Simon's General Problem Solver (GPS). Using means–ends analysis, search would begin by identifying those actions whose add lists contained statements that helped to establish the goal condition. The preconditions of those actions would be set up as subgoals, and this backward reasoning process would continue until a sequence of actions was finally found that transformed the initial situation into one satisfying the goal.

By 1970 or so, Fikes had finished programming (in LISP) our new planning system. We called it STRIPS, an acronym for Stanford Research Institute Problem Solver.[19] After its completion, STRIPS replaced QA3 as Shakey's system for generating plans of action. Typical plans consisting of six or so mid-level actions could be generated on the PDP-10 in around two minutes.

The STRIPS planning system itself has given way to more efficient AI planners, but many of them still describe actions in terms of what are called "STRIPS operators" (sometimes "STRIPS rules") consisting of preconditions, delete lists, and add lists.

12.1.4 *Learning and Executing Plans*

It's one thing to make a plan and quite another to execute it properly. Also, we wanted to be able to save the plans already made by STRIPS for possible future use. We were able to come up with a structure, called a "triangle table," for representing plans that was useful not only for executing plans but also for saving them. (John Munson originally suggested grouping the conditions and effects of robot actions in a triangular table. Around 1970, Munson, Richard Fikes, Peter Hart, and I developed the triangle table formalism to represent plans consisting of STRIPS operators.) The triangle table tabulated the preconditions and effects of each action in the plan so that it could keep track of whether or not the plan was being executed properly.

Actions in the plans generated by STRIPS had specific values for their parameters. For example, if some goto action was part of a plan, actual place coordinates were used to name the place that Shakey was to go from and the place it was to go to, perhaps goto((3,7),(8,14)). Although we might want to save a plan that had that specific goto as a component, a more generally applicable plan would have a goto component with nonspecific parameters that could be replaced by specific ones depending on the specific goal. That is, we would want to generalize something like goto((3,7),(8,14)), for example, to goto((x1,y1),(x2,y2)). One can't willy-nilly replace constants by variables, but one must make sure that any such generalizations result in viable and executable plans for all values of the variables. We were able to come up with a procedure that produced correct generalizations, and it was these generalized plans that were represented in the triangle table.

After a plan was generated, generalized, and represented in the triangle table, Shakey's overall executive program, called "PLANEX," supervised its execution.[20] In the environment in which Shakey operated, plan execution would sometimes falter, but PLANEX, using the triangle table, could decide how to get Shakey back on the track toward the original goal. PLANEX gave the same sort of "keep-trying" robustness to plan execution that the Markov tables gave to executing mid-level actions.

12.1.5 *Shakey's Vision Routines*

Shakey's environment consisted of the floor it moved about on, the walls bounding its rooms, doorways between the rooms, and large rectilinear objects on the floor in some of the rooms. We made every effort to make "seeing" easy for Shakey. A dark baseboard separated the light-colored floor from the light-colored walls. The objects were painted various shades of red, which appeared dark to the vidicon camera and light to the infrared laser range finder. Even so, visual processing still presented challenging problems.

Rather than attempt complete analyses of visual scenes, our work concentrated on using vision to acquire specific information that Shakey needed to perform its tasks. This information included Shakey's location and the presence and locations of objects – the sort of information that was required by the mid-level actions. The visual routines designed to gather that information were embedded in the programs

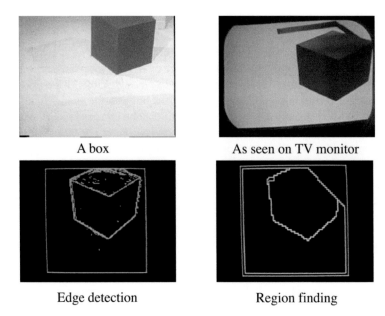

A box   As seen on TV monitor

Edge detection   Region finding

Figure 12.6. Using vision to locate an object. (From the film *Shakey: An Experiment in Robot Planning and Learning*. Used with permission of SRI International.)

for performing those actions. Known properties of Shakey's environment were exploited in these routines.

Exploiting the fact that the objects, the floor, and the wall contained planes of rather constant illumination, Claude Brice and Claude Fennema in our group developed image-processing routines that identified regions of uniform intensity in an image.[21] Because the illumination on a single plane, say the face of an object, might change gradually over the region, the region-finding routine first identified rather small regions. These were then merged across region boundaries in the image if the intensity change across the boundary was not too great. Eventually, the image would be partitioned into a number of large regions that did a reasonable job of representing the planes in the scene. The boundaries of these regions could then be fitted with straight-line segments.

Another vision routine was able to identify straight-line segments in the image directly. Richard Duda and Peter Hart developed a method for doing this based on a modern form of the "Hough transform."[22] After edge-detection processing had identified the locations and directions of small line segments, the Hough transform was used to construct those longer lines that were statistically the most likely, given the small line segments as evidence.

Both region finding and line detection were used in various of the vision routines for the mid-level actions. One of these routines, called obloc, was used to refine the location of an object whose location was known only roughly. The pictures in Fig. 12.6 show a box, how it appears as a TV image from Shakey's camera, and two of the stages of obloc's processing. From the regions corresponding to the box and the

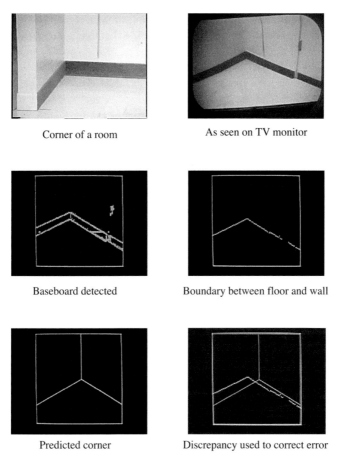

Corner of a room   As seen on TV monitor

Baseboard detected   Boundary between floor and wall

Predicted corner   Discrepancy used to correct error

Figure 12.7. Using vision to update position. (From the film *Shakey: An Experiment in Robot Planning and Learning*. Used with permission of SRI International.)

floor (and using the fact that Shakey is on the same floor as the box), straightforward geometric computations could add the box and its location to Shakey's models.

Shakey ordinarily kept track of its location by dead-reckoning (counting wheel revolutions), but this estimate gradually accumulated errors. When Shakey determined that it should update its location, it used another vision routine, called `picloc`. A nearby "landmark," such as the corner of a room, was used to update Shakey's position with respect to the landmark. The pictures in Fig. 12.7 show how `obloc` traces out the baseboard and finds the regions corresponding to the walls and the floor. The final picture shows the discrepancy between Shakey's predicted location of the corner (based on Shakey's estimate of its own location) and the actual location based on `picloc`. This discrepancy was used to correct Shakey's estimate of its position.

Before Shakey began a straight-line motion in a room where the presence of obstacles might not be known, it used a routine called `clearpath` to determine whether its path was clear. This routine checked the image of its path on the floor (a trapezoidal-shaped region) for changes in brightness that might indicate the presence of an obstacle.

In appraising Shakey's visual performance, it is important to point out that it was really quite primitive and subject to many errors – even in Shakey's specially designed environment. As one report acknowledges, "Regions that we wish to keep distinct – such as two walls meeting at a corner – are frequently merged, and fragments of meaningful regions that should be merged are too often kept distinct." Regarding clearpath, for example, this same report notes that ". . . shadows and reflections can still cause false alarms, and the only solution to some of these problems is to do more thorough scene analysis."[23] Nevertheless, vision played an important part in Shakey's overall performance, and many of the visual processing techniques developed during the Shakey project are still used (with subsequent improvements) today.[24]

12.1.6 *Some Experiments with Shakey*

To illustrate Shakey's planning and plan-execution and learning methods in action, we set up a task in which Shakey was to push a specified box in front of a specified doorway in a nonadjacent room. To do so, Shakey had to use STRIPS to make a plan to travel to that room and then to push the box. Before beginning its execution of the plan, Shakey saved it in the generalized form described earlier. In the process of executing the plan, we arranged for Shakey to encounter an unexpected obstacle. Illustrating its robust plan execution procedure, Shakey was able to find a different version of the generalized plan that would take it on a somewhat different route to the target room where it could carry on.[25]

One of the researchers working on the Shakey project was L. Stephen Coles (1941–), who had recently obtained a Ph.D. degree under Herb Simon at Carnegie Mellon University working on natural language processing. Coles wanted to give Shakey tasks stated in English. He developed a parser and semantic analysis system that translated simple English commands into logical statements for STRIPS. For example, the task of box pushing just mentioned was posed for Shakey in English as follows:

Use BOX2 to block door DPDPCLK from room RCLK.

(BOX2, DPDPCLK, and RCLK were the names Shakey used to identify the box, door, and room in question. We were obliging enough to use Shakey's names for things when giving it tasks to perform.)

Coles's program, called ENGROB,[26] translated this English command into the following condition to be made true (expressed in the language of the predicate calculus):

BLOCKED(DPDPCLK, RCLK, BOX2)

This condition was then given to STRIPS to make a plan for achieving it.

Coles was also interested in getting Shakey to solve problems requiring indirect reasoning. He set up an experiment in which Shakey was to push a box off an elevated platform. To do so, it would have to figure out that it would need to push a ramp to the platform, roll up the ramp, and then push the box. This task was given to Shakey in English as "Push the box that is on the platform onto the floor." The task was successfully executed and described in one of the Shakey technical reports.[27]

The "push-the-box-off-the-platform" task was Coles's way of showing that Shakey could solve problems like the "monkey-and-bananas" problem. That problem, made famous by John McCarthy as an example for deductive reasoning, involved a monkey, a box, and some bananas hanging out of reach. The monkey was supposed to be able to reason that to get the bananas, it would have to push the box under the bananas, climb up on the box, and then grab the bananas.[28] McCarthy is said to have heard Karl Lashley at the 1948 Caltech Hixon symposium describe a similar problem for demonstrating intelligent problem solving by chimpanzees.

One of the persons who was impressed with Shakey was Bill Gates, who later co-founded Microsoft. He saw the 1972 Shakey film as a junior in high school and drove down from Seattle to SRI (with Paul Allen, who would be the other co-founder of Microsoft) to have a look. According to one source, he was "particularly excited about Shakey moving things around so it could go up a ramp."[29]

12.1.7 *Shakey Runs into Funding Troubles*

Shakey was the first robot system having the abilities to plan, reason, and learn; to perceive its environment using vision, range-finding, and touch sensors; and to monitor the execution of its plans. It was, perhaps, a bit ahead of its time. Much more research (and progress in computer technology generally) would be needed before practical applications of robots with abilities such as these would be feasible. We mentioned some of the limiting assumptions that were being made by robot research projects at that time in one of our reports about Shakey:

Typically, the problem environment [for the robot] is a dull sort of place in which a single robot is the only agent of change – even time stands still until the robot moves. The robot itself is easily confused; it cannot be given a second problem until it finishes the first, even though the two problems may be related in some intimate way. Finally, most robot systems cannot yet generate plans containing explicit conditional statements or loops.

Even though the SRI researchers had grand plans for continuing work on Shakey, DARPA demurred, and the project ended in 1972. This termination was unfortunate, because work on planning, vision, learning, and their integration in robot systems had achieved a great deal of momentum and enthusiasm among SRI researchers. Furthermore, several new ideas for planning and visual perception were being investigated. Many of these were described in detail in a final report for the Shakey project.[30]

Among these ideas, a particularly important one involved techniques for constructing plans in a hierarchical fashion. To do so, an overall plan consisting of just "high-level" actions must be composed first. Such a plan can be found with much less searching than one consisting of all of the lowest level actions needed. For example, one's plan for getting to work might involve only the decision either to take the subway or to drive one's car. Then, gradually, the high-level plan must be refined in more and more detail until actions at the lowest level (such as which set of car keys should be used) would eventually be filled in.

A Stanford computer science graduate student working at SRI, Earl Sacerdoti (1948–), proposed two novel methods for hierarchical planning. First (as part of his master's degree work), he programmed a system he called ABSTRIPS.[31] It consisted of a series of applications of STRIPS – beginning with an easy-to-compose plan that ignored all but the most important operator preconditions. Subsequent applications of STRIPS, guided by the higher level plans already produced, would then gradually take the more detailed preconditions into account. The result was a series of evermore-detailed plans, culminating in one that could actually be executed.

For his Ph.D. work, Sacerdoti went on to develop a more powerful hierarchical planning system he called NOAH (for Nets of Action Hierarchies).[32] Unlike ABSTRIPS, whose action operators were all at the same level of detail (albeit with preconditions that could be selectively ignored), NOAH employed action operators at several levels of detail. Each operator came equipped with specifications for how it could be elaborated by operators at a lower level of detail. Furthermore, NOAH's representation of a plan, in a form Sacerdoti called a "procedural network," allowed indeterminacy about the order in which plan steps at one level might be carried out. This "delayed commitment" about ordering permitted the more detailed steps of the elaborations of nonordered plans at one level to be interleaved at the level below, often with a consequent improvement in overall efficiency.

Sacerdoti was hoping to use his hierarchical planning ideas in the Shakey project, so he and the rest of us at SRI were quite disappointed that DARPA was not going to support a follow-on project. (Basic research on robots was one of the casualties of the DARPA emphasis on applications work that began in the early 1970s.) However, we were able to talk DARPA into a project that had obvious military relevance but still allowed us to continue work on automatic planning, vision, and plan execution. Interestingly, the project was pretty much a continuation of our research work on Shakey but with a human carrying out the planned tasks instead of a robot. We called it the "computer-based consultant (CBC) project." I'll describe it in a subsequent chapter.

Sacerdoti and the SRI researchers were not alone in recognizing the importance of hierarchical planning. As part of his Ph.D. work at the University of Edinburgh, Austin Tate (1951–) was developing a network-based planning system called INTERPLAN.[33] In 1975 and 1976, supported by the British Science Research Council, Tate and colleagues from operations research produced a hierarchical planner called NONLIN.[34] The planner took its name from the fact that, like NOAH, some of the plan steps were left unordered until they were elaborated at lower levels of the hierarchy.

Other planning systems grew out of the NOAH and NONLIN tradition. One was the interactive plan-generation and plan-execution system SIPE-2 developed by David E. Wilkins at SRI International.[35] Another was O-PLAN developed by Tate and colleagues at the Artificial Intelligence Applications Institute (AIAI) at the University of Edinburgh.[36] These systems have been widely used, extended, and applied.[37]

12.2 The Stanford Cart

In the early 1960s, James Adams, a Mechanical Engineering graduate student at Stanford (and later a Stanford professor), began experimenting with a four-wheeled, mobile cart with a TV camera and a radio control link. Lester Earnest wrote (in his

Figure 12.8. The Stanford cart. (Photograph courtesy of Lester Earnest.)

history of the several projects using this cart) "Among other things, Adams showed in his dissertation that with a communication delay corresponding to the round trip to the Moon (about $2\frac{1}{2}$ seconds) the vehicle could not be reliably controlled if traveling faster than about 0.2 mph (0.3 kph)."[38]

After Earnest joined the Stanford AI Laboratory, he and Rodney Schmidt, an Electrical Engineering Ph.D. student, got an upgraded version of the cart to "follow a high contrast white line [on the road around the Lab] under controlled lighting conditions at a speed of about 0.8 mph (1.3 kph)." Other AI graduate students also experimented with the cart from time to time during the early 1970s. A picture of the cart (as it then appeared) is shown in Fig. 12.8.

When Hans Moravec came to Stanford to pursue Ph.D. studies on visual navigation, he began work with the cart, "but suffered a setback in October 1973 when the cart toppled off an exit ramp while under manual control and ended up with battery acid throughout its electronics." By 1979 Moravec got the refurbished cart, now equipped with stereo vision, to cross a cluttered room without human intervention. But it did this very slowly. According to Moravec,[39]

The system was reliable for short runs, but slow. The Cart moved 1 m every 10 to 15 min, in lurches. After rolling a meter it stopped, took some pictures, and thought about them for a long time. Then it planned a new path, executed a little of it, and paused again. It successfully drove the Cart through several 20-m courses (each taking about 5 h) complex enough to necessitate three or four avoiding swerves; it failed in other trials in revealing ways.

A short video of the cart in action can be seen at http://www.frc.ri.cmu.edu/ users/hpm/talks/Cart.1979/Cart.final.mov. Along with Shakey, the Stanford Cart resides in the Computer History Museum in Mountain View, California. They were the progenitors of a long line of robot vehicles, which will be described in subsequent chapters.

Notes

1. Hans P. Moravec, *Robot: Mere Machine to Transcendent Mind*, pp. 18–19, Oxford: Oxford University Press, 1999. **[162]**
2. A copy of the proposal is available online at http://www.ai.sri.com/pubs/files/1320.pdf. Its cover page says "Prepared by Nils J. Nilsson," but it was really a team effort, and many of the ideas were elaborations of those put forward in Rosen's 1963 memo. **[162]**
3. A copy of the complete statement can be found at http://ai.stanford.edu/~nilsson/automaton-work-statement.pdf. **[163]**
4. Online copies of SRI's proposals for the automaton project, subsequent progress reports, and related papers can be found at http://www.ai.sri.com/shakey/. **[163]**
5. See http://www.robothalloffame.org/. **[164]**
6. See http://www.computerhistory.org/timeline/?category=rai. **[164]**
7. J. Doran and Donald Michie, "Experiments with the Graph Traverser Program," *Proceedings of the Royal Society of London*, Series A, Vol. 294, pp. 235–259, 1966. **[167]**
8. The first written account of this idea was in Charles A. Rosen and Nils Nilsson, "Application of Intelligent Automata to Reconnaissance," pp. 21–22, SRI Report, December 1967. Available online at http://www.ai.sri.com/pubs/files/rosen67-p5953-interim3.pdf. **[168]**
9. Personal communication, October 24, 2006. **[168]**
10. See Peter Hart, Nils Nilsson, and Bertram Raphael, "A Formal Basis for the Heuristic Determination of Minimum Cost Paths," *IEEE Transactions System Science and Cybernetics*, Vol. 4, No. 2, pp. 100–107, 1968, and Peter Hart, Nils Nilsson, and Bertram Raphael, "Correction to 'A Formal Basis for the Heuristic Determination of Minimum-Cost Paths,'" *SIGART Newsletter*, No. 37, pp. 28–29, December 1972. **[168]**
11. See, for example, Korf's publications at http://www.cs.ucla.edu/~korf/publications.html. **[168]**
12. In a 2003 paper titled "A* Parsing: Fast Exact Viterbi Parse Selection," Dan Klein and Christopher Manning wrote "The use of A* search can dramatically reduce the time required to find a best parse by conservatively estimating the probabilities of parse completions." **[168]**
13. In an e-mail to Peter Hart dated March 27, 2002, Brian Smart, the chief technical officer of a vehicle-navigation company, wrote "Like most of the 'location based services' and 'vehicle navigation' industry, we use a variant of A* for computing routes for vehicle and pedestrian navigation applications." **[168]**
14. In an e-mail to me dated June 14, 2003, Steven Woodcock, a consultant on the use of AI in computer games, wrote "A* is far and away the most used . . . and most useful . . . algorithm for pathfinding in games today. At GDC roundtables since 1999, developers have noted that they make more use of A* than any other tool for pathfinding." **[168]**
15. See Bertram Raphael *et al.*, "Research and Applications – Artificial Intelligence," pp. 27–32, SRI Report, April 1971. Available online at http://www.ai.sri.com/pubs/files/raphael71-p8973-semi.pdf. **[169]**
16. For a description of how QA3 developed a plan for Shakey to push three objects to the same place, for example, see Nils J. Nilsson, "Research on Intelligent Automata," Stanford Research Institute Report 7494, pp. 10ff, February 1969; available online at http://www.ai.sri.com/pubs/files/nilsson69-p7494-interim1.pdf. **[169]**
17. McCarthy and Hayes first described this problem in John McCarthy and Patrick Hayes, "Some Philosophical Problems from the Standpoint of Artificial Intelligence," in Donald Michie and Bernard Meltzer (eds.), *Machine Intelligence*, Vol. 4, pp. 463–502, 1969. Reprinted in Matthew Ginsberg (ed.), *Readings in Nonmonotonic Reasoning*, pp. 26–45,

San Francisco: Morgan Kaufmann Publishers, Inc., 1987. Preprint available online at http://www-formal.stanford.edu/jmc/mcchay69/mcchay69.html. [169]

18. See Carl Hewitt, "PLANNER: A Language for Proving Theorems in Robots," *Proceedings of the First International Joint Conference on Artificial Intelligence*, pp. 295–301, 1969. [170]

19. See Richard Fikes and Nils Nilsson, "STRIPS: A New Approach to the Application of Theorem Proving to Problem Solving," *Artificial Intelligence*, Vol. 2, Nos. 3–4, pp. 189–208, 1971. Available online at http://ai.stanford.edu/users/nilsson/OnlinePubs-Nils/PublishedPapers/strips.pdf. [170]

20. The generalization and execution mechanisms are described in Richard Fikes, Peter Hart, and Nils Nilsson, "Learning and Executing Generalized Robot Plans," *Artificial Intelligence*, Vol. 3, No. 4, pp. 251–288, 1972. Available online (as an SRI report) at http://www.ai.sri.com/pubs/files/tn070-fikes72.pdf. [171]

21. See Claude Brice and Claude Fennema, "Scene Analysis Using Regions," *Artificial Intelligence*, Vol. 1, No. 3, pp. 205–226, 1970. [172]

22. Richard O. Duda and Peter E. Hart, "Use of the Hough Transformation to Detect Lines and Curves in Pictures," *Communications of the ACM*, Vol. 15, pp. 11–15, January 1972. See also, Peter E. Hart, "How the Hough Transform Was Invented," *IEEE Signal Processing Magazine*, November, 2009. [172]

23. Bertram Raphael *et al.*, "Research and Applications – Artificial Intelligence," Part V, SRI Final Report, December 1971; available online at http://www.ai.sri.com/pubs/files/raphael71-p8973-final.pdf. [174]

24. For more information about Shakey's visual routines, in addition to the final report just cited, see Richard O. Duda, "Some Current Techniques for Scene Analysis," SRI Artificial Intelligence Group Technical Note 46, October 1970, available online at http://www.ai.sri.com/pubs/files/tn046-duda70.pdf. [174]

25. This experiment, as well as other information about Shakey, is described in Bertram Raphael *et al.*, "Research and Applications – Artificial Intelligence," SRI Final Report, December 1971, available online at http://www.ai.sri.com/pubs/files/raphael71-p8973-final.pdf; in Nils Nilsson (ed.), "Shakey The Robot," SRI Technical Note 323, April 1984, available online at http://www.ai.sri.com/pubs/files/629.pdf; and in a 1972 film, *Shakey: An Experiment in Robot Planning and Learning*, available online at http://www.ai.sri.com/movies/Shakey.ram. [174]

26. L. Stephen Coles, "Talking with a Robot in English," *Proceedings of the International Joint Conference on Artificial Intelligence*, Washington, DC, May 7–9, Bedford, MA: The MITRE Corporation, 1969. [174]

27. See L. Stephen Coles *et al.*, "Application of Intelligent Automata to Reconnaissance," SRI Final Report, November 1969, available online at http://www.ai.sri.com/pubs/files/coles69-p7494-final.pdf. [175]

28. The problem was introduced by McCarthy in his July 1963 memo "Situations, Actions, and Causal Laws," reprinted as Section 7.2 of his paper "Program with Commonsense," which appeared in Marvin Minsky (ed.), *Semantic Information Processing*, pp. 403–418, Cambridge, MA: MIT Press, 1968. [175]

29. E-mail from Eric Horvitz of May 12, 2003. [175]

30. Peter E. Hart *et al.*, "Artificial Intelligence – Research and Applications," Technical Report, Stanford Research Institute, December 1972. (Available online at http://www.ai.sri.com/pubs/files/hart72-p1530-annual.pdf.) See also Richard E. Fikes, Peter E. Hart, and Nils J. Nilsson, "Some New Directions in Robot Problem Solving," in *Machine Intelligence 7*, Bernard Meltzer and Donald Michie (eds.), pp. 405–430, Edinburgh:

Edinburgh University Press, 1972. (The SRI Technical Note 68 version is available online at http://www.ai.sri.com/pubs/files/1484.pdf.) [175]

31. Earl D. Sacerdoti, "Planning in a Hierarchy of Abstraction Spaces," pp. 412–422, *Proceedings of the Third International Joint Conference on Artificial Intelligence*, 1973. (The SRI AI Center Technical Note 78 version is available online at http://www.ai.sri .com/pubs/files/1501.pdf.) [176]

32. Earl D. Sacerdoti, "The Non-Linear Nature of Plans," *Proceedings of the International Joint Conference on Artificial Intelligence*, 1975. (The SRI AI Center Technical Note 101 version is available online at http://www.ai.sri.com/pubs/files/1385.pdf.) Also see Earl D. Sacerdoti, *A Structure for Plans and Behavior*, New York: Elsevier North-Holland, 1977. (The SRI AI Center Technical Note No. 109 version is available online at http://www.ai.sri.com/pubs/files/762.pdf.) [176]

33. Austin Tate, "Interacting Goals and Their Use," *Proceedings of the Fourth International Joint Conference on Artificial Intelligence (IJCAI-75)*, pp. 215–218, Tbilisi, USSR, September 1975; available online at http://www.aiai.ed.ac.uk/project/oplan/ documents/1990-PRE/1975-ijcai-tate-interacting-goals.pdf. Austin Tate, "Using Goal Structure to Direct Search in a Problem Solver," Ph.D. thesis, University of Edinburgh, September 1975 available online at http://www.aiai.ed.ac.uk/project/oplan/ documents/1990-PRE/. [176]

34. Austin Tate, "Generating Project Networks," *Proceedings of the Fifth International Joint Conference on Artificial Intelligence (IJCAI-77)*, pp. 888–893, Boston, MA, August 1977; available online at http://www.aiai.ed.ac.uk/project/oplan/documents/1990- PRE/1977-ijcai-tate-generating-project-networks.pdf. [176]

35. See the SIPE-2 Web page at http://www.ai.sri.com/~sipe/. [176]

36. Ken Currie and Austin Tate, "O-PLAN: The Open Planning Architecture," *Artificial Intelligence*, Vol. 52, pp. 49–86, 1991. Available online at http://www.aiai.ed.ac.uk/ project/oplan/documents/1991/91-aij-oplan-as-published.pdf. [176]

37. See, for example, AIAI's "Planning and Activity Management" Web page at http://www .aiai.ed.ac.uk/project/plan/. [176]

38. Lester Earnest, "Stanford Cart," August 2005; available online at http://www.stanford .edu/~learnest/cart.htm. [177]

39. Hans P. Moravec, "The Stanford Cart and the CMU Rover," *Proceedings of the IEEE*, Vol. 71, No. 7, pp. 872–884, July 1983. [177]

13

Progress in Natural Language Processing

$\mathbf{A}$S MENTIONED PREVIOUSLY, THE PROBLEMS OF UNDERSTANDING, GENERATING, and translating material in ordinary human (rather than computer) languages fall under the heading of natural language processing. During the "early explorations" phase of AI research, some good beginnings were made on NLP problems. In the subsequent phase, the late 1960s to early 1970s, new work built on these foundations, as I'll describe in this part of the book.

13.1 Machine Translation

W. John Hutchins, who has written extensively about the history of machine translation (MT), has called the period 1967 to 1976, "the quiet decade."[1] Inactivity in the field during this period is due in part to the ALPAC report, which, as I have already said, was pessimistic about the prospects for machine translation. Hutchins claimed "The influence of the ALPAC report was profound. It brought a virtual end to MT research in the USA for over a decade and MT was for many years perceived as a complete failure. . . . The focus of MT activity switched from the United States to Canada and to Europe."[2]

One exception to this decade-long lull in the United States was the development of the Systran (System Translator) translating program by Petr Toma, a Hungarian-born computer scientist and linguistics researcher who had worked on the Georgetown Russian-to-English translation system. In 1968, Toma set up a company called Latsec, Inc., in La Jolla, California, to continue the Systran development work he had begun earlier in Germany. The U.S. Air Force gave the company a contract to develop a Russian-to-English translation system. It was tested in early 1969 at the Wright-Patterson Air Force Base in Dayton, Ohio, "where it continues to provide Russian–English translations for the USAF's Foreign Technology Division to this day."[3] Systran has evolved to be one of the main automatic translation systems. It is marketed by the Imageforce Corporation in Tampa, Florida.[4]

How well does Systran translate? It all depends on how one wants to measure performance. Margaret Boden mentions two measures, namely, "intelligibility" and "correctness." Both of these measures depend on human judgement. For the first, one asks "Can the translation be generally understood?" For the second, one asks "Do human 'post-editors' need to modify the translation?" Boden states that "in the two-year period from 1976 to 1978, the intelligibility of translations generated by Systran rose from 45 to 78 percent for [raw text input] . . . " She also notes that human translations score only 98 to 99 percent, not 100 percent. Regarding correctness,

Figure 13.1. Terry Winograd. (Photograph courtesy of Terry Winograd.)

Boden states that in 1978 "only 64 percent of the words were left untouched by human post-editors. Even so, human post-editing of a page of Systran output took only twenty minutes in the mid-1980s, whereas normal (fully human) translation would have taken an hour."[5]

13.2 Understanding

Although the late 1960s and early 1970s might have been a "quiet decade" for machine translation, it was a very active period for other NLP work. Researchers during these years applied much more powerful syntactic, semantic, and inference abilities to the problem of understanding natural language. Typical of the new attitude was the following observation by Terry Winograd, an MIT Ph.D. student during the late 1960s:[6]

If we really want computers to understand us, we need to give them ability to use more knowledge. In addition to a grammar of the language, they need to have all sorts of knowledge about the subject they are discussing, and they have to use reasoning to combine facts in the right way to understand a sentence and to respond to it. The process of understanding a sentence has to combine grammar, semantics, and reasoning in a very intimate way, calling on each part to help with the others.

13.2.1 *SHRDLU*

Perhaps the NLP achievement that caused the greatest excitement was the SHRDLU natural language dialog system programmed by Terry Winograd (1946– ; Fig. 13.1) for his Ph.D. dissertation (under Seymour Papert) at MIT.[7]

SHRDLU was able to carry on a dialog about what Winograd called a "micro-world," a world consisting of toy blocks and a "gripper" for moving them about. Unlike the the world of real blocks used in previous MIT and Stanford hand–eye research, Winograd's blocks world was simulated on a DEC PDP-10 computer and viewed on a DEC 340 black-and-white graphics display such as that shown in

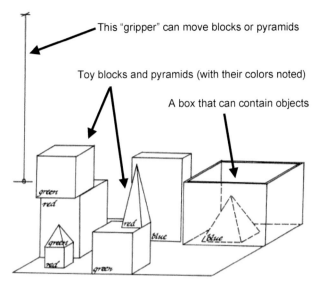

This "gripper" can move blocks or pyramids

Toy blocks and pyramids (with their colors noted)

A box that can contain objects

Figure 13.2. SHRDLU's world. (Illustration used with permission of Terry Winograd.)

Fig. 13.2. SHRDLU could be given commands, typed in ordinary English, to manipulate the blocks using its gripper. It could also be asked questions about the state of its
world. It could "understand" those commands and questions, carry out requested
manipulations, and ask the user clarifying questions in English about questions or
commands it did not understand.

Before describing something about SHRDLU's design, let us look at an example
of part of a dialog.[8] In the following, the user's input is numbered and shown in
lowercase letters, and SHRDLU's response is in all caps, Winograd's commentary
follows in the same typeface, and mine is in parentheses in normal type:

1. pick up a big red block.

In order to pick up the red block, it had to clear it off by
finding a space for the green one and moving the green one away.

OK.

The system answers "OK" when it carries out a command.

(I won't bother to show what the block configuration looks like as the dialog proceeds,
assuming you can use your own mental "model" to keep track of things. The gripper
is now holding the red block.)

2. grasp the pyramid.

There are three pyramids in the scene, so the program does
nothing.

I DON'T UNDERSTAND WHICH PYRAMID YOU MEAN.

3. find a block which is taller than the one you are holding and
put it into the box.

(The user has now apparently changed his mind about pyramid grasping.)

```
The system has to figure out what is meant by "one" and "it,"
as well as using deduction to decide which block it is holding.

BY "IT," I ASSUME YOU MEAN THE BLOCK WHICH IS TALLER THAN THE
ONE I AM HOLDING.

Printed out to keep us informed.

The hand has to set down the red block to pick up the taller blue
one.

OK.

4. what does the box contain?

THE BLUE PYRAMID AND THE BLUE BLOCK.

5. what is the pyramid supported by?

Earlier the system responded to "the pyramid" by saying
"I don't understand which pyramid you mean." now, it knows
that we must mean the one which was just mentioned.

THE BOX
```

This dialog illustrating SHRDLU's capabilities goes on for forty-two more user inputs and system responses.[9]

To engage in dialogs like this, SHRDLU needed "knowledge." It needed to know about the syntax of that part of English it used, and it needed to know what various words and word combinations mean in the context of their use. It also needed to know about its blocks world – how blocks can be manipulated and what it means for an object to be inside of the "box." It needed to keep track of the dialog so that it could decide to which object mentioned previously a word such as "it" referred.

All of this needed knowledge was represented in LISP programs, or "procedures," as Winograd called them. Knowledge about syntax was represented as a collection of procedures based on the principles of "systemic grammar."[10]Knowledge about the meanings of words in context was represented in procedures that could refer to a dictionary of word meanings, to other parts of the sentence in which the word was used, and to the discourse. Knowledge about the blocks world was represented in two ways: There was a model that gave the locations of all of the objects and there were procedures that could infer the predicted effects (in the model) of manipulations by the gripper on the various objects. The object-moving procedures had information both about the preconditions and about the effects of these manipulations. These procedures were encoded in a version of Hewitt's PLANNER language, which, as mentioned previously, bore some resemblance to STRIPS operators. Additional procedures in the PLANNER language were used for other types of inference needed by the system. Logical rules were expressed as programs, which were capable of making both forward and backward deductions.

SHRDLU's processes for language understanding can be divided into three parts, namely, syntax, semantics, and inference, but doing so is somewhat misleading because the interplay among these parts was a key feature of the system. As Winograd stated, "Since each piece of knowledge can be a procedure, it can call on any other piece of knowledge of any type." For example, Winograd wrote, "As it finds each piece of the syntactic structure, it checks its semantic interpretation, first to see if it is plausible, then (if possible) to see if it is in accord with the system's knowledge of the world, both specific and general."

Winograd's procedural representation of knowledge (together with Hewitt's PLANNER language for encoding such representations) can be contrasted with McCarthy's use of logical formulas to represent knowledge declaratively. The success of SHRDLU fueled a debate among AI researchers about the pros and cons of these two knowledge representation strategies – procedural versus declarative. Actually, the use of LISP to represent procedures blurs this distinction to some extent because, as Winograd pointed out, "LISP allows us to treat programs as data and data as programs." So, even though SHRDLU's knowledge was represented procedurally, it was able to incorporate some declarative new knowledge (presented to it as English sentences) into its procedures.

SHRDLU's performance was indeed quite impressive and made some natural language researchers optimistic about future success.[11] However, Winograd soon abandoned this line of research in favor of pursuing work devoted to the interaction of computers and people. Perhaps because he had first-hand experience of how much knowledge was required for successful language understanding in something so simple as the blocks world, he despaired of ever giving computers enough knowledge to duplicate the full range of human verbal competence. In a 2004 e-mail, Winograd put SHRDLU's abilities in context with those of humans:[12]

There are fundamental gulfs between the way that SHRDLU and its kin operate, and whatever it is that goes on in our brains. I don't think that current research has made much progress in crossing that gulf, and the relevant science may take decades or more to get to the point where the initial ambitions become realistic. In the meantime AI took on much more doable goals of working in less ambitious niches, or accepting less-than-human results (as in translation).

13.2.2 *LUNAR*

On their return from the first manned moon landing, the Apollo 11 astronauts brought back several pounds of moon rocks for scientific study. Various data about these rocks were stored in databases that could be accessed by geologists and other scientists. To make retrieval of this information easier for lunar geologists, NASA asked William A. Woods, a young computer scientist at BBN, about the possibility of designing some sort of natural-language "front end" so that the databases could be queried in English instead of in arcane computer code. Woods had just completed his Ph.D. research at Harvard on question-answering systems.[13]

Sponsored by NASA's Manned Spacecraft Center, Woods and BBN colleagues Ron Kaplan and Bonnie Webber developed a system they called "LUNAR" for answering questions about the moon rocks.[14] LUNAR used both syntactic and semantic processes to transform English questions into moon rock database queries. Syntactic analysis was performed by using "augmented transition networks" (ATNs), a methodology developed by Woods during his Harvard Ph.D. research. (I'll describe what ATNs are all about shortly.) The semantic component, guided by the ATN-derived parse trees, transformed English sentences into what Woods called a "meaning representation language" (MRL). This language was a logical language (like that of the predicate calculus) but extended with procedures that could be executed. MRL was originally conceived by Woods at Harvard and further developed at BBN.

LUNAR was able to "understand" and answer a wide variety of questions, including, for example,

"What is the average concentration of aluminum in high alkali rocks?"
"How many breccias contain olivine?"
"What are they?" (LUNAR recognized that "they" referred to the breccias named as answers to the last question.)

LUNAR was the first question-answering system to publish performance data. It was able to answer successfully 78% of the questions put to it by geologists at the Second Annual Lunar Science Conference held in Houston in January 1971. Reportedly, 90% would have been answerable with "minor fixes" to the system.

In a June 2006 talk[15] about LUNAR, Woods mentioned some of its limitations. The following dialog illustrates one shortcoming:

User: What is a breccia?
LUNAR: S10018.
User: What is S10018?
LUNAR: S10018.

Woods said, "LUNAR simply finds referents of referring expressions and gives their names. There is no model of the purpose behind the user's question or of different kinds of answers for different purposes."

Although LUNAR could recognize several different ways of phrasing essentially the same question, Woods claimed that "there are other requests which (due to limitations in the current grammar) must be stated in a specific way in order for the grammar to parse them and there are others which are only understood by the semantic interpreter when they are stated in certain ways."[16]

13.2.3 *Augmented Transition Networks*

Many people realized that context-free grammars (like the ones I discussed earlier) were too weak for most practical natural language processing applications. For example, if we were to expand the illustrative grammar I described in Section 7.1 so that it included (in addition to "threw" and "hit" and "man") the present-tense verbs "throw," "throws," and "hits" and the plural noun "men," then the strings "the men hits the ball" and "the man throw the ball" would be inappropriately accepted as grammatical sentences. To expand a context-free grammar to require that nouns and verbs must agree as to number would involve an impractically large collection of rules. Also, allowing for passive sentences, such as "the ball was hit by the men," would require even further elaboration. Clearly, the sorts of sentences that geologists might ask about moon rocks required more powerful grammars – such as the augmented transition networks that Woods and others had been developing.

In Chomsky's 1957 book[17] he had proposed a hierarchy of grammatical systems of which context-free grammars were just one example. His more powerful grammars had a "transformational component" and were able, for example, to parse a sentence such as "the ball was hit by the man" and give it the same "deep structure" as it would give the sentence "the man hit the ball." Augmented transition network grammars could also perform these kinds of transformations but in a more computationally satisfying way.

An augmented transition network is a maplike graphical structure in which the nodes represent points of progress in the parsing process, and the paths connecting two nodes represent syntactic categories. We can think of parsing a sentence as traversing a path through the network from the start node (no progress at all yet) to an end node (where the sentence has been successfully parsed). Traversing the path builds the syntactic structure of the sentence in the form of a parse tree. Analysis of a sentence involves peeling off the words in left-to-right fashion and using them to indicate which path in the network to take.

Syntactic analysis could begin by peeling off a single word and finding out from a lexicon whether it was a noun, a determiner, an auxiliary (such as "does"), an adjective, or some other "terminal" syntactic category. Or it could begin by peeling off a group of words and checking to see whether this group was a noun phrase, a verb phrase, a prepositional phrase, or what have you. In the first case, depending on the category of the single word, we would take a path corresponding to that category leading out from the start node. To accommodate the second case, there would be possible paths corresponding to a noun phrase and the other possible higher level syntactic categories.

But how would we decide whether or not we could take the noun-phrase path, for example? The answer proposed by Woods and others was that there would be additional transition networks corresponding to these higher level categories. We would be permitted to take the noun-phrase path in the main transition network only if we could successfully traverse the noun-phrase network. And because one path in the noun-phrase network might start with a prepositional phrase, we would have to check to see whether we could take that path (in the noun-phrase network) by successfully traversing a prepositional-phrase network. This process would continue with one network "calling" other networks in a manner similar to the way in which a program can fire up (or "call") other programs, possibly *recursively*. (You will recall my discussion of recursive programs: programs that can call versions of themselves.) For this reason, assemblages of networks like these are called recursive transition networks.

The first networks of this kind were developed at the University of Edinburgh in Scotland by James Thorne, Paul Bratley, and Hamish Dewar.[18] Later, Dan Bobrow and Bruce Fraser proposed a transition network system that elaborated on the Scottish one.[19] Both of these systems also performed auxiliary computations while traversing their networks. These "augmentations" allowed the construction of a "deep structure" representation of the sentence being analyzed. Woods's work

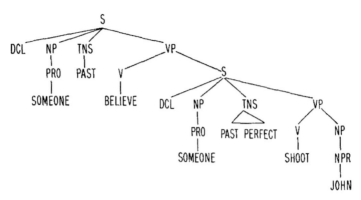

Figure 13.3. A parse tree obtained for the sentence "John was believed to have been shot." (From William A. Woods, "Transition Network Grammars for Natural Language Analysis," *Communications of the ACM*, Vol. 13, No. 10, pp. 591–606, 1970.)

on "augmented, recursive transition networks" built on and refined these ideas and introduced an elegant network definition language.[20]

As an example, Woods described how one of his networks analyzed the sentence "John was believed to have been shot."[21] After all of the calls to subsidiary networks and all of the auxiliary computations were performed the parse tree shown in Fig. 13.3 was obtained. We can observe two things about this parse tree. First, note the occurrence of "PAST" and "PAST PERFECT" as tense markers. Second, note that the form of the original passive-voice sentence has been transformed to an active-voice sentence using a presumed pronoun "SOMEONE." As Woods notes, the structure can be paraphrased as "Someone believed that someone had shot John." Network grammars get at the "deep structure" of sentences by transforming them into a standard form.

13.2.4 *GUS*

Dan Bobrow and Ronald Kaplan, two of the researchers doing NLP work at BBN, moved to the newly formed Palo Alto Research Center (PARC) of Xerox in the mid-1970s. One of the projects that they and other researchers worked on there was GUS (an acronym for Genial Understander System), which was "intended to engage a sympathetic and highly cooperative human in an English dialog, directed towards a specific goal within a very restricted domain of discourse."[22] The restricted domain was that of a travel agent engaged in "a conversation with a client who wants to make a simple return trip to a single city in California." The following transcript of an actual dialog shows off some of its abilities:

GUS: Hello. My name is GUS. I can help you plan a simple trip by air. Where do you want to go?
(1) *Client*: I want to go to San Diego on May 28.
GUS: What time do you want to leave?

(2) *Client*: I must be in San Diego before 10 am.
GUS: Would you like P.S.A. flight 102 that arrives at 9.15 am?
(3) *Client*: What is the next flight?
GUS: Air California flight 310 that leaves at 8.30 am and arrives at 10.00 am.
(4) *Client*: I'll take the first one.
GUS: In what name should I make a reservation, please?
(5) *Client*: Dan Bobrow.
GUS: I have confirmed the following flight: P.SA. flight 102 on Wednesday May 28 from San Jose to San Diego that leaves at 7.30 am and arrives at 9.15 am. What date do you want to return on?
(6) *Client*: On Friday in the evening.
GUS: Would you like the flight that leaves at 7.45 pm?
(7) *Client*: That's fine.
GUS: I have confirmed the following flight: P.S.A. flight 307 on Friday May 30 from San Diego to San Jose that leaves at 7.45 pm and arrives at 9.30 pm. Thank you for calling. Goodbye.

Although the abilities of the system were certainly limited, GUS was able to deal with a number of problems. One of these involves what NLP researchers call "resolving anaphora," by which they mean deciding on the objects or events to which various words or phrases in a dialog refer. Several examples, keyed to the numbered sentences in the dialog above, are mentioned in the paper about GUS:

At line (3), for example, the client's query refers to the flight mentioned in GUS's immediately preceding utterance. In (4) there is a reference to the flight mentioned earlier in the conversation, [following line (2)]. Note that "next flight" in (3) was to be interpreted relative to the order of flights in the airline guide whereas "first one" in (4) refers to the order in which the flights were mentioned. Another implicit referent underlies the use of "Friday" to specify a date in (6). Resolution of this reference requires some complicated reasoning involving both the content and the context of the conversation. Since May 28 has been given as the departure date, it must presumably be the following Friday that the client has in mind. On the other hand, suppose that the specifications were reversed and Friday had been given as the departure date at line (1). It would then be most readily interpretable as referring to the Friday immediately following the conversation.

GUS was a combination of several communicating subsystems, a morphological analyzer for dealing with word components, a syntactic analyzer for generating parse trees, a "reasoner" for figuring out a user's meanings and intentions, and a language generator for responding. Controlling these components was done by using an "agenda" mechanism. As the authors explain,

GUS operates in a cycle in which it examines this agenda, chooses the next job to be done, and does it. In general, the execution of the selected task causes entries for new tasks to be created and placed on the agenda. Output text generation can be prompted by reasoning processes at any time, and inputs from the client are handled whenever they come in. There are places at which information from a later stage (such as one involving semantics) are fed back to an earlier stage (such as the parser). A supervisory process can reorder the agenda at any time.

The syntactic component of GUS had "access to a main dictionary of more than 3,000 stems and simple idioms." The syntactic analyzer was based on a system developed earlier by Ronald Kaplan, which used a transition–network grammar and was called a "General Syntactic Processor."[23] Client sentences were encoded in "frames" (which are related to Minsky's frames but closer in form to semantic networks). Some frames described the sequence of a normal dialog, whereas others represented the attributes of a date, a trip plan, or a traveler. GUS's reasoning component used the content and structure of the frames to deduce how best to interpret client sentences.

Besides anaphora, the paper mentioned several other problems that GUS was able to deal with. However, it also cautioned that "it is much too easy to extrapolate from [the sample dialog] a mistaken notion that GUS contained solutions to far more problems than it did." Sample dialogs recorded between human clients and humans playing the role of a GUS revealed numerous instances in which the computer GUS would fail. The authors concluded that if users of systems like GUS departed "from the behavior expected of them in the minutest detail, or if apparently insignificant adjustments are made in their structure," the systems would act as if they had "gross aphasia" or had just simply died. The authors conceded that "GUS itself is not very intelligent, but it does illustrate what we believe to be essential components of [an intelligent language understanding] system. . . . [It] must have a high quality parser, a reasoning component, and a well structured data base of knowledge." Subsequent work on NLP at PARC and many other places sought to improve all of these components.

The systems developed by researchers such as Winograd, Woods, Bobrow, and their colleagues were very impressive steps toward conversing with computers in English. Yet, there was still a long way to go before natural language understanding systems could perform in a way envisioned by Winograd in the preface to his Ph.D. dissertation:

Let us envision a new way of using computers so they can take instructions in a way suited to their jobs. We will talk to them just as we talk to a research assistant, librarian, or secretary, and they will carry out our commands and provide us with the information we ask for. If our instructions aren't clear enough, they will ask for more information before they do what we want, and this dialog will all be in English.

Notes

1. W. John Hutchins, "Machine Translation: A Brief History," in E. F. K. Koerner and R. E. Asher (eds.), *Concise History of the Language Sciences: From the Sumerians to the Cognitivists*, pp. 431–445, Oxford: Pergamon Press, 1995. (Also available online at http://www.hutchinsweb.me.uk/ConcHistoryLangSci-1995.pdf.) [181]

2. *Ibid.* [181]

3. W. John Hutchins, *Machine Translation: Past, Present, Future*, Chichester: Ellis Horwood, 1986. An updated (2003) version is available online at http://www.hutchinsweb.me.uk/PPF-TOC.htm. Some of the technical details of Systran's operation are described in the book. [181]

4. http://www.translationsoftware4u.com/. [181]

5. Margaret A. Boden, *Mind as Machine: A History of Cognitive Science*, p. 683, Oxford: Oxford University Press, 2006. **[182]**

6. This quote is from the preface of Winograd's Ph.D. dissertation. **[182]**

7. SHRDLU is described in Winograd's dissertation "Procedures as a Representation for Data in a Computer Program for Understanding Natural Language." It was issued as an MIT AI Technical Report No. 235, February 1971, and is available online at https://dspace.mit.edu/bitstream/1721.1/7095/2/AITR-235.pdf. The thesis was also published as a full issue of *Cognitive Psychology*, Vol. 3, No. 1, 1972, and as a book *Understanding Natural Language*, New York: Academic Press, 1972. The letters in SHRDLU comprise the second column of keys in linotype machines, which were used to set type before computers were used for that. This nonsense word was often used in *MAD* magazine, which Winograd read in his youth. Failing to think of an acceptable acronym to use to name his system, Winograd used SHRDLU. For Winograd's account, see http://hci.stanford.edu/~winograd/shrdlu/name.html. **[182]**

8. Taken from Section 1.3 of Winograd's thesis. **[183]**

9. Readers interested in the entire dialog can see it either in Winograd's thesis or on one of his Web sites at http://hci.stanford.edu/~winograd/shrdlu/. **[184]**

10. Winograd cites, among others, M. A. K. Halliday, "Categories of the Theory of Grammar," *Word*, Vol. 17, No. 3, pp. 241–292, 1961. **[184]**

11. For a short film of SHRDLU in action, see http://projects.csail.mit.edu/films/aifilms/digitalFilms/3mpeg/26-robot.mpg. **[185]**

12. From http://www.semaphorecorp.com/misc/shrdlu.html. **[185]**

13. William A. Woods, "Semantics for a Question-Answering System," Ph.D. dissertation, Harvard University, August 1967. Reprinted as a volume in the series *Outstanding Dissertations in the Computer Sciences*, New York: Garland Publishing, 1979. **[185]**

14. William A. Woods, Ron M. Kaplan, and Bonnie Nash-Webber, "The Lunar Sciences Natural Language Information System: Final Report," BBN, Cambridge, MA, June 1, 1972. See also William A. Woods, "Progress in Natural Language Understanding – An Application to Lunar Geology," *AFIPS Conference Proceedings*, Vol. 42, pp. 441–450, Montvale, New Jersey: AFIPS Press, 1973. **[185]**

15. See http://www.ils.albany.edu/IQA06/Files/Bill_Woods_IQA06.pdf. **[186]**

16. William A. Woods, "Progress in Natural Language Understanding – An Application to Lunar Geology," *AFIPS Conference Proceedings*, Vol. 42, pp. 441–450, Montvale, New Jersey: AFIPS Press, 1973. **[186]**

17. Noam Chomsky, *Syntactic Structures*, 's-Gravenhage: Mouton & Co., 1957. **[187]**

18. James Thorne, Paul Bratley, and Hamish Dewar, "The Syntactic Analysis of English by Machine," in D. Michie (ed.), *Machine Intelligence 3*, pp. 281–309, New York: American Elsevier Publishing Co., 1968; Hamish Dewar, Paul Bratley, and James Thorne, "A Program for the Syntactic Analysis of English Sentences," *Communications of the ACM*, Vol. 12, No. 8, pp. 476–479, August 1969. **[187]**

19. Daniel Bobrow and Bruce Fraser, "An Augmented State Transition Network Analysis Procedure," *Proceedings of the International Joint Conferenece on Artificial Intelligence*, pp. 557–567, Washington, DC, 1969. **[187]**

20. William A. Woods, "Augmented Transition Networks for Natural Language Analysis," Report CS-1, Aiken Computation Laboratory, Harvard University, Cambridge, MA, December 1969; William A. Woods, "Transition Network Grammars for Natural Language Analysis," *Communications of the ACM*, Vol. 13, No. 10, pp. 591–606, 1970. The ACM article has been reprinted in Yoh-Han Pao and George W. Ernest (eds.), *Tutorial: Context-Directed Pattern Recognition and Machine Intelligence Techniques for Information Processing*, Silver Spring, MD: IEEE Computer Society Press, 1982, and in Barbara

Grosz, Karen Sparck Jones, and Bonnie Webber (eds.), *Readings in Natural Language Processing*, San Mateo, CA: Morgan Kaufmann, 1986. [188]

21. William A. Woods, *op. cit.*, pp. 602ff. [188]

22. Daniel G. Bobrow *et al.*, "GUS, A Frame-Driven Dialog System," *Artificial Intelligence*, Vol. 8, pp. 155–173, 1977. [188]

23. Ronald Kaplan, "A General Syntactic Processor," in R. Rustin (ed.), *Natural Language Processing*, New York: Algorithmics Press, 1973. [190]

14

Game Playing

I HAVE ALREADY MENTIONED ATTEMPTS TO PROGRAM COMPUTERS TO PLAY BOARD games, such as chess and checkers. The most successful of these was Arthur Samuel's checker-playing program. In 1967, Samuel published a paper describing an improved version of his program.[1] He had refined the program's search procedure and incorporated better "book-learning" capabilities, and instead of calculating the estimated value of a position by adding up weighted feature values, he used hierarchically organized tables. According to Richard Sutton, "This version learned to play much better than the 1959 program, though still not at a master level."[2]

Between 1959 and 1962, a group of MIT students, advised by John McCarthy, developed a chess-playing program. It was based on earlier programs for the IBM 704 written by McCarthy. One of the group members, Alan Kotok (1941–2006) described the program in his MIT bachelor's thesis.[3] The program was written in a combination of FORTRAN and machine (assembly) code and ran on the IBM 7090 computer at MIT. It used the alpha–beta procedure (as discussed earlier) to avoid generating branches of the search tree that could be eliminated without altering the final result. Kotok claimed that his program did not complete any games but "played four long game fragments in which it played chess comparable to an amateur with about 100 games experience. . . . Most of the machine's moves are neither brilliant nor stupid. It must be admitted that it occasionally blunders."[4] When McCarthy moved to Stanford, he took the program along with him and continued to work on it.

In the meantime, a computer chess program was being developed by Georgi Adelson-Velskiy and colleagues in Alexander Kronrod's laboratory at the Institute for Theoretical and Experimental Physics (ITEP) in Moscow.[5] During a visit to the Soviet Union in 1965, McCarthy accepted a challenge to have the Kotok–McCarthy program play the Soviet program. Beginning on November 22, 1967, and continuing for about nine months, the Kotok–McCarthy program (running on a DEC PDP-6 at Stanford) played the Russian program (running on the Russian M-20 computer at ITEP) – the first match to be played by a computer against a computer. In each of the first two games, the Stanford program eked out a draw (by surviving until the agreed-upon limit of 40 moves) against a weak version of the Russian program. However, it lost the last two games against a stronger version of the ITEP program. McCarthy later claimed that, although Stanford had the better computer, ITEP had the better programs.[6] The ITEP program was the forerunner of the much improved Kaissa program developed later by Misha Donskoy, Vladimir Arlazarov, and Alexander Ushkov at the Institute of Control Science in Moscow.

Richard Greenblatt, an expert programmer at the AI Lab at MIT, thought he could improve on Kotok's chess program. His work on computer chess eventually led to a program he called MAC HACK VI.[7] Being an expert chess player himself, he was able to incorporate a number of excellent heuristics for choosing moves and for evaluating moves in his program. Running on the AI Lab's DEC PDP-6 and written in efficient machine code, MAC HACK VI was the first program to play in tournaments against human chess players. In an April 1967 tournament, it won two games and drew two, achieving a rating of 1450 on the U.S. Chess Federation rating scale, about the level of an amateur human player. (According to the international rating system for human chess players, the highest level is that of Grand Masters. Then come International Masters, National Masters, Experts, Class A, Class B, and so on. MAC HACK VI played at the high Class C to low Class B level, which is still quite far from master play.) It became an honorary member of the U.S. Chess Federation and of the Massachusetts Chess Association. In a famous match at MIT in 1967,[8] Greenblatt's program beat Hubert Dreyfus (1929–), an AI critic who had earlier observed that "no chess program could play even amateur chess."[9] Although Dreyfus's observation was probably true in 1965, Greenblatt's MAC HACK VI was playing at the amateur level two years later.

Perhaps encouraged by MAC HACK's ability, in 1968 Donald Michie and John McCarthy made a bet of £250 each with David Levy (1945–), a Scottish International Master, that a computer would be able to beat him within ten years. (The following year Seymour Papert joined in, and in 1971 Ed Kozdrowicki of the University of California at Davis did also, bringing the total bet to £1000. In 1974, Donald Michie raised the total to £1250.) In 1978, Levy collected on his bet – as we shall see later.[10]

Around 1970, three students at Northwestern University in Illinois, David Slate, Larry Atkin, and Keith Gorlen, began writing a series of chess programs. The first of these, CHESS 3.0, running on a CDC 6400 computer, won the first Association for Computing Machinery's computer chess tournament (computers against computers) in New York in 1970. There were six entries – MAC HACK VI not among them. According to David Levy, "CHESS 3.0 evaluated approximately 100 positions per second and played at the 1400 level on the U.S. Chess Federation rating scale." Subsequent Northwestern programs, up through CHESS 4.6, achieved strings of wins at this annual event. Meanwhile, however, CHESS 4.2 was beaten in an early round of the first World Computer Chess Championship tournament held at the International Federation of Information Processing Societies (IFIPS) meeting in Stockholm in 1974. The Russian program, Kaissa, won all four games in that tournament, thereby becoming the world computer chess champion.[11]

These years, the late 1960s through the mid-1970s, saw computer chess programs gradually improving from beginner-level play to middle-level play. Work on computer chess during the next two decades would ultimately achieve expert-level play, as we shall see in a subsequent chapter. Despite this rapid progress, it was already becoming apparent that there was a great difference between how computers played chess and how humans played chess. As Hans Berliner, a chess expert and a chess programming expert, put it in an article in *Nature*,[12]

[A human] uses prodigious amounts of knowledge in the pattern-recognition process [to decide on a good maneuver] and a small amount of calculation to verify the fact that the proposed solution is good in the present instance. . . . However, the computer would make the same maneuver because it found at the end of a very large search that it was the most advantageous way to proceed out of the hundreds of thousands of possibilities it looked at. CHESS 4.6 has to date made several well known maneuvers without having the slightest knowledge of the maneuver, the conditions for its applications, and so on; but only knowing that the end result of the maneuver was good.

Berliner summed up the difference by saying that "The basis of human chess strength, by contrast [with computers], is *accumulated knowledge*" (my italics). Specific knowledge about the problem being solved, as opposed to the use of massive search in solving the problem, came to be a major theme of artificial intelligence research during this period. (Later, however, massive search regained some of its importance.) Perhaps the most influential proponents of the use of knowledge in problem solving were Edward Feigenbaum and his colleagues at Stanford. I'll turn next to their seminal work.

Notes

1. Arthur L. Samuel, "Some Studies in Machine Learning Using the Game of Checkers II – Recent Progress," *IBM Journal of Research and Development*, Vol. 11, No. 6, pp. 601– 617, 1967. [193]
2. http://www.cs.ualberta.ca/~sutton/book/11/node3.html. [193]
3. Alan Kotok, "A Chess Playing Program for the IBM 7090 Computer" MIT bachelor's thesis in Electrical Engineering, June 1962. Online versions of the thesis are available at http://www.kotok.org/AK-Thesis-1962.pdf and http://www.kotok.org/AI_Memo_41.html. (The latter is an MIT memo in which Kotok pointed out that " . . . this report, while written by me, represents joint work of 'the chess group,' which consisted of me, Elwyn R. Berlekamp (for the first year), Michael Lieberman, Charles Niessen, and Robert A. Wagner (for the third year). We are all members of the MIT [undergraduate] Class of 1962.) [193]
4. The Computer History Museum has a video "oral history" of Kotok available at http://www.computerhistory.org/chess/alan_kotok.oral_history_highlight.102645440/index.php?iid=orl-433444ecc827d. [193]
5. G. M. Adelson-Velskiy, V. L. Arlazarov, A. R. Bitman, A. A. Zhivotovskii and A. V. Uskov, "Programming a Computer to Play Chess," *Russian Mathematical Surveys* 25, March–April 1970, pp. 221–262, London: Cleaver-Hume Press. (Translation of *Proceedings of the 1st Summer School on Mathematical Programming*, Vol. 2, pp. 216–252, 1969.) [193]
6. See the oral presentation about the history of computer chess at http://video.google.com/videoplay?docid=-1583888480148765375. [193]
7. Richard D. Greenblatt, Donald E. Eastlake III, and Stephen D. Crocker, "The Greenblatt Chess Program," AI Memo 174, April 1969. Available online at https://dspace.mit.edu/bitstream/1721.1/6176/2/AIM-174.pdf. [194]
8. See an account in the *SIGART Newsletter*, December 1968. [194]
9. Hubert L. Dreyfus, "Alchemy and Artificial Intelligence," RAND paper P-3244, p. 10, The RAND Corporation, Santa Monica, CA, December 1965. Available online at http://www.rand.org/pubs/papers/2006/P3244.pdf. [194]

10. For first-hand details about the bet, see David Levy, *Robots Unlimited: Life in a Virtual Age*, p. 83, Wellesley, MA: A K Peters, Ltd., 2006. **[194]**
11. See the Computer History Museum's exhibits on the history of computer chess at http://www.computerhistory.org/chess/index.php. For a concise timeline of computer chess history compiled by Bill Wall, visit http://www.geocities.com/SiliconValley/Lab/7378/comphis.htm. **[194]**
12. Hans J. Berliner, "Computer Chess," *Nature*, Vol. 274, p. 747, August 1978. **[194]**

15

The Dendral Project

A FTER ED FEIGENBAUM MOVED FROM UC BERKELEY TO STANFORD IN 1965, HE became interested in "creating models of the thinking processes of scientists, especially the processes of empirical induction by which hypotheses and theories were inferred from data." As he put it, "What I needed was a specific task environment in which to study these issues concretely."[1] Feigenbaum recalls attending a Behavioral Sciences workshop at Stanford and hearing a talk by Joshua Lederberg (1925–2008; Fig. 15.1), a Nobel Prize–winning geneticist and founder of the Stanford Department of Genetics. Lederberg talked about the problem of discerning the structure of a chemical compound from knowledge of its atomic constituents and from its mass spectrogram. This sounded like the kind of problem Feigenbaum was looking for, and he and Lederberg soon agreed to collaborate on it.[2]

Chemical molecules are described by formulas that give their atomic constituents. For example, the formula for propane is C_3H_8, indicating that it consists of three carbon atoms and eight hydrogen atoms. But there is more to know about a compound than what atoms it is made of. The atoms composing a molecule are arranged in a geometric structure, and chemists want to know what that structure is. The three carbon atoms in propane, for example, are attached together in a chain. The two carbon atoms at the ends of the chain each have three hydrogen atoms attached to them, and the single carbon atom in the middle of the chain has two hydrogen atoms attached to it. Chemists represent this structure by the diagram shown in Fig. 15.2.

Chemists have found that it is not too difficult to discern the structure of simple compounds like propane. However, it is more difficult for more complex compounds, such as 2-methyl-hexan-3-one, a ketone with chemical formula C_7H_{140}. One method that chemists have used to infer the structure of a compound is to bombard it with high-energy electrons in a mass spectrometer. The electron beam of a mass spectrometer breaks the compound into fragments, and the resulting fragments are sorted according to their masses by a magnetic field within the spectrometer. A sample mass spectrogram is shown in Fig. 15.3.

The fragments produced by the mass spectrometer tend to be composed of robust substructures of the compound, and the masses of these reveal hints about the main structure. An experienced chemist uses "accumulated knowledge" (to use Berliner's phrase) about how compounds tend to break up in the mass spectrometer to make good guesses about a compound's structure.

Figure 15.1. Edward Feigenbaum (left), Joshua Lederberg (middle), and Bruce Buchanan (right). (Photographs courtesy of Edward Feigenbaum.)

Feigenbaum and Lederberg, together with their colleague Bruce Buchanan (1940–), who had joined Stanford in 1966 after obtaining a Ph.D. in Philosophy at the University of Michigan, set about attempting to construct computer programs that could use mass spectrogram data, together with the chemical formula of a compound, to "elucidate" (as they put it) the structure of the compound.

Lederberg had already developed a computer procedure called Dendral (an acronym for Dendritic Algorithm) that could generate all topologically possible acyclic structures given the chemical formula and other basic chemical information about how atoms attach to other atoms. (An acyclic structure is one that does not contain any rings. You might recall, for example, that benzene contains six carbon atoms arranged in a hexagon, which chemists call a ring. Each of the carbon atoms has a hydrogen atom attached to it.) Lederberg's algorithm proceeded incrementally by generating partial structures from the main formula, then generating more articulated partial structures from these and so on in a treelike fashion. The tips or leaves of the tree would contain the final, fully articulated topologically possible structures. Finding the actual structure of a compound (or at least the most plausible actual structures) can be likened to a search down the tree to the appropriate tip or tips.

Feigenbaum and colleagues proposed using the knowledge that skilled chemists used when interpreting mass-spectral data. The chemists knew that certain features of the spectrograms implied that the molecule under study would contain certain substructures and would not contain other ones. This knowledge could be used to limit the possible structures generated by Lederberg's Dendral algorithm.

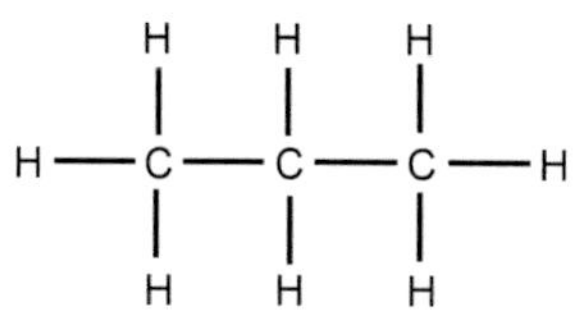

Figure 15.2. The structure of the propane molecule.

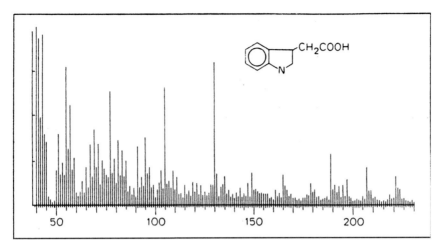

Figure 15.3. A mass spectrogram. (Illustration used with permission of Edward Feigen-baum.)

Knowledge of this sort was represented as "rules." Here is one example of a Dendral rule:

```
Rule 74:
    IF   The spectrum for the molecule has two peaks
         at masses X1 and X2 such that:
            X1 + X2 = M + 28
                and
            X1 - 28 is a high peak
                and
            X2 - 28 is a high peak
                and
            at least one of X1 or X2 is high
    THEN The molecule contains a ketone group
```

The first program to employ this kind of knowledge was called HEURISTIC DENDRAL. (The adjective "heuristic" was used because knowledge from the chemists was used to control search down the Dendral tree.) It used as input the chemical formula and mass-spectrometer data (and sometimes nuclear-magnetic-resonance data) and produced as output an ordered set of chemical structure descriptions hypothesized to explain the data. Early work with HEURISTIC DENDRAL was limited to elucidating the structure of acyclic compounds because these were the only ones that Lederberg's algorithm could handle. These included saturated acyclic ethers, alcohols, thioethers, thiols, and amines. Here is one example of the power of their early program: There are 14,715,813 possible structures of N,N-dimethyl-1-octadecyl amine. Using the mass spectrum of that compound, HEURISTIC DENDRAL reduced the number to 1,284,792. Using the mass spectrum and nuclear-magnetic-resonance data, just one structure survived.[3]

The name "DENDRAL" came to describe a whole collection of programs for structure elucidation developed during the Dendral project, which continued to the end of the 1970s. Many of these programs are used by chemists today. Computer scientists and chemists working on the project were able to extend Lederberg's algorithm to handle cyclic compounds. After Lederberg persuaded Stanford chemist Carl Djerassi to join the project, performance was expanded greatly in both breadth and depth.[4]

An important innovation made during the Dendral project was a simulation of how a chemical structure would break up in a mass spectrometer. After HEURISTIC DENDRAL produced some candidate structures for a particular compound, these structures were subjected to analysis in the simulated mass spectrometer. The outputs were then compared with the actual mass spectrometer output. That structure whose simulated spectrogram was closest to the actual spectrogram was likely to be the actual structure of the compound. This process of "analysis by synthesis" came to be widely used in artificial intelligence, especially in computer vision.

From his experience during the DENDRAL years, Feigenbaum went on to champion the importance of specific knowledge about the problem domain in AI applications (as opposed to the use of general inference methods). He proposed what he called the "knowledge-is-power" hypothesis, which he later called the "knowledge principle."[5] Here is how he later described it:[6]

We must hypothesize from our experience to date that the problem solving power exhibited in an intelligent agent's performance is primarily a consequence of the specialist's knowledge employed by the agent, and only very secondarily related to the generality and power of the inference method employed. Our agents must be knowledge-rich, even if they are methods-poor.

Embedding the knowledge of experts in AI programs led to the development of many "expert systems," as we shall see later. It also led to increased concentration on specific and highly constrained problems and away from focusing on the general mechanisms of intelligence, whatever they might be.

Notes

1. The quotation taken from "Comments by Edward A. Feigenbaum" in Edward H. Shortliffe and Thomas C. Rindfleisch, "Presentation of the Morris F. Collen Award to Joshua Lederberg," *Journal of the American Medical Informatics Association*, Vol. 7, No. 3, pp. 326–332, May–June 2000. Available online at http://www.pubmedcentral.nih.gov/articlerender.fcgi?artid=61437. [197]
2. For an interesting account of the history of their collaboration, see "How DENDRAL Was Conceived and Born," by Joshua Lederberg, a paper presented at the Association for Computing Machinery (ACM) Symposium on the History of Medical Informatics at the National Library of Medicine on November 5, 1987. Later published in Bruce I. Blum and Karen Duncan (eds.), *A History of Medical Informatics*, pp. 14–44, New York: Association for Computing Machinery Press, 1990. Typescript available online at http://profiles.nlm.nih.gov/BB/A/L/Y/P/_/bbalyp.pdf. [197]

3. Robert K. Lindsay, Bruce G. Buchanan, Edward A. Feigenbaum, and Joshua Lederberg, *Applications of Artificial Intelligence for Organic Chemistry: The Dendral Project*, p. 70, New York: McGraw-Hill Book Co., 1980. **[199]**

4. For a thorough account of achievements of the Dendral project, see *ibid.* **[200]**

5. The hypothesis seems to have been implicit in Edward A. Feigenbaum, "Artificial Intelligence: Themes in the Second Decade," *Supplement to Proceedings of the IFIP 68 International Congress*, Edinburgh, August 1968. Published in A. J. H. Morrell (ed.), *Information Processing 68*, Vol. II, pp. 1008–1022, Amsterdam: North-Holland, 1969. **[200]**

6. Edward A. Feigenbaum, "The Art of Artificial Intelligence: Themes and Case Studies of Knowledge Engineering," *Proceedings of the Fifth International Joint Conference on Artificial Intelligence*, pp. 1014–1029, 1977. See also Edward A. Feigenbaum, "The Art of Artificial Intelligence: I. Themes and Case Studies of Knowledge Engineering," Stanford Heuristic Programming Project Memo HPP-77-25, August 1977, which is available online at http://infolab.stanford.edu/pub/cstr/reports/cs/tr/77/621/CS-TR-77-621.pdf. **[200]**

16

Conferences, Books, and Funding

ACCOMPANYING THE TECHNICAL PROGRESS IN ARTIFICIAL INTELLIGENCE DURING this period, new conferences and workshops were begun, textbooks were written, and financial support for basic research grew and then waned a bit.

The first large conference devoted exclusively to artificial intelligence was held in Washington, DC, in May 1969. Organized by Donald E. Walker (1928–1993) of the MITRE Corporation and Alistair Holden (1930–1999) of the University of Washington, it was called the International Joint Conference on Artificial Intelligence (IJCAI). It was sponsored by sixteen different technical societies (along with some of their subgroups) from the United States, Europe, and Japan. About 600 people attended the conference, and sixty-three papers were presented by authors from nine different countries. The papers were collected in a proceedings volume, which was made available at the conference to all of the attendees.

Because of the success of this first conference, it was decided to hold a second one in London in 1971. During the early years, organization of the conferences was rather informal, decisions about future conferences being made by a core group of some of the leaders of the field who happened to show up at organizing meetings. At the 1971 meeting in London, I left the room for a moment while people were discussing where and when to hold the next conference. When I returned, I was informed that I had been selected to be the "czar" of the next meeting – to be held at Stanford University in 1973. Later, a more formal arrangement was instituted for managing the "International Joint Conferences on Artificial Intelligence," with a President, a Board of Trustees, and a Secretariat.[1] Since the first meeting, IJCAI conferences are held biennially (on odd-numbered years) with the venue alternating (loosely) between North America and the rest of the world. As at the first conference, proceedings are distributed at the conferences. (Some of these can be obtained from various booksellers, and they are available online at the Digital Library of India Web site, http://202.41.92.139/.)

One of the oldest "special interest groups" of the Association for Computing Machinery (ACM) is SIGART (the Special Interest Group for ARTificial intelligence). It began publishing a Newsletter in 1966, which (as the SIGART Web site says) "continued in various incarnations (the SIGART Bulletin, Intelligence Magazine) until 2001." Today, SIGART supports various conferences and workshops, and it organizes meetings in which AI doctoral students can present their nearly finished work to their peers and to senior researchers for comments and critiques.

As the field began to develop its techniques and methods, graduate courses in artificial intelligence were offered at some universities. Accordingly, some of us who were teaching these courses thought it would be worthwhile to write or edit books about AI. In 1963, Edward Feigenbaum and Julian Feldman, then assistant professors at UC Berkeley, published a collection of early AI and cognitive science papers that had previously appeared in many different places. The volume was called *Computers and Thought* and was required reading for early students of AI (including me).[2] As Feigenbaum wrote in the 1995 edition, "Some of the papers are as important today for their fundamental ideas as they were in the late 1950s and early 1960s when they were written. Others are interesting as early milestones of fields that have expanded and changed dramatically."

In 1965, I published a book about neural-network and statistical methods in pattern recognition.[3] That book was followed in 1971 by a book about AI search strategies.[4] Around the same time, other texts were published by James Slagle[5] and by Bertram Raphael,[6] both former Ph.D. students of Marvin Minsky at MIT.

In 1969 Marvin Minsky and Seymour Papert published an influential book in which they proved, among other things, that some versions of Rosenblatt's percep-trons had important limitations.[7] Some have claimed that the Minsky–Papert book was the cause of a fading interest in neural-network research, but I doubt this. First, Rosenblatt himself began concentrating on other topics well before 1969,[8] and the success of heuristic programming methods caused a shift of attention (including my own) away from neural networks during the mid-1960s.

In 1965, Donald Michie at the University of Edinburgh organized the first of several invitation-only "Machine Intelligence" workshops. This first one was held in Edinburgh and was attended by American and European researchers. Attendees gave papers at the workshop, and these were all published in a book edited by N. L. Collins and Donald Michie in 1967. A second workshop was held in September 1966, also at the University of Edinburgh. Subsequent workshops were held annually in Edinburgh through 1971. Thereafter, the workshops were held every few years at various venues. Each workshop resulted in a book with the title *Machine Intelligence N*, where *N* denotes the workshop and volume number.[9] The last few volumes have been published online by the *Electronic Transactions on Artificial Intelligence*.[10] These books contain some of the most cited and important papers in the early history of the field.

These years saw the United States engaged in war in Vietnam, and Congress wanted to make sure that research supported by the U.S. Defense Department was relevant to military needs. Responding to these pressures, on November 19, 1969, Congress passed the "Mansfield Amendment" to the Defense Procurement Authorization Act of 1970 (Public Law 91-121), which required that the Defense Department restrict its support of basic research to projects "with a direct and apparent relationship to a specific military function or operation." On March 23, 1972, the Advanced Research Projects Agency was renamed the Defense Research Advanced Projects Agency (DARPA) to reflect its emphasis on projects that con-tributed to enhanced military capabilities. (The name reverted to the Advanced Research Projects Agency in 1993 and then back to the Defense Advanced Research Projects Agency in 1996.)[11]

On the other side of the Atlantic, British AI researchers experienced their own funding crisis. One of the U.K.'s main funding bodies for university research, the

Science Research Council, asked Professor James Lighthill, a famous hydrody-namicist at Cambridge University, to undertake an evaluative study of artificial intelligence research. Lighthill's report, titled "Artificial Intelligence: A General Survey," somewhat idiosyncratically divided AI research into three categories, name-ly, advanced automation, computer-based studies of the central nervous system, and the bridges in between. He called these categories A, C, and B, respectively. Although he came out in favor of continued work in categories A and C, he was quite critical of most AI basic research, including robotics and language processing, which he lumped into category B. He wrote that "In no part of the field have the discoveries made so far produced the major impact that was then [around 1960] promised." He concluded that AI's existing search techniques (which worked on toy problems) would not scale to real problems because they would be stymied by the combinatorial explosion.[12]

Lighthill's report resulted in a substantial curtailment of AI research in the United Kingdom. In particular, one of its casualties was work on FREDDY the robot and other AI work under Donald Michie at Edinburgh. Here is one of Michie's later comments about the effects of the report:[13]

Work of excellence by talented young people was stigmatised as bad science and the experiment killed in mid-trajectory. This destruction of a co-operative human mechanism and of the careful craft of many hands is elsewhere described as a mishap. But to speak plainly, it was an outrage. In some later time, when the values and methods of science have further expanded, and those of adversary politics have contracted, it will be seen as such.

DARPA's shift to shorter term applied research, together with the Lighthill report and criticisms from various onlookers, posed difficulties for basic AI research during the next few years. Nevertheless, counter to Lighthill's assessment, many AI techniques did begin to find application to real problems, launching a period of expansion in AI applications work, as we'll see in the next few chapters.

Notes

1. See http://www.ijcai.org/IJCAItrustees.php. [202]
2. Edward A. Feigenbaum and Julian Feldman, *Computers and Thought*, New York: McGraw-Hill Book Co., 1963. (The McGraw-Hill volume is now out of print; it is now available through AAAI Press/MIT Press, 1995 edition.) [203]
3. Nils J. Nilsson, *Learning Machines: Foundations of Trainable Pattern-Classifying Systems*, New York: McGraw-Hill Book Co., 1965; republished as *The Mathematical Foundations of Learning Machines*, San Francisco: Morgan Kaufmann Publishers, 1990. [203]
4. Nils J. Nilsson, *Problem-Solving Methods in Artificial Intelligence*, New York: McGraw-Hill Book Co., 1971. [203]
5. James R. Slagle, *Artificial Intelligence: The Heuristic Programming Approach*, New York: McGraw-Hill Book Co., 1971. [203]
6. Bertram Raphael, *The Thinking Computer: Mind Inside Matter*, New York: W. H. Freeman, 1976. [203]
7. Marvin Minsky and Seymour Papert, *Perceptrons: An Introduction to Computational Geo-metry*, Cambridge, MA: MIT Press, 1969. [203]
8. See Frank Rosenblatt, J. T. Farrow, and S. Rhine, "The Transfer of Learned Behavior from Trained to Untrained Rats by Means of Brain Extracts. I," *Proceedings of the National Academy of Sciences*, Vol. 55, No. 3, pp. 548–555, March 1966. [203]

9. The series maintains a Web page at http://www.cs.york.ac.uk/mlg/MI/mi.html. [203]

10. See http://www.etai.info/mi/. [203]

11. See http://www.darpa.mil/body/arpa_darpa.html. [203]

12. The text of the report, along with commentary and criticism by leading British AI researchers, was published in 1972 in James Lighthill *et al.* (eds.), *Artificial Intelligence: A Paper Symposium*, London: Science Research Council of Great Britain, 1972. [204]

13. Donald Michie, *Machine Intelligence and Related Topics: An Information Scientist's Weekend Book*, p. 220, New York: Gordon and Breach Science Publishers, 1982. [204]

Part IV

Applications and Specializations:
1970s to Early 1980s

U NTIL ABOUT THE EARLY 1970S, MOST AI RESEARCH DEALT WITH WHAT SEYMOUR Papert called "toy" problems – programs that solved puzzles or games – or the researchers pursued projects that were staged in highly controlled laboratory settings. (Of course, there were some notable exceptions – machine translation, DENDRAL, and LUNAR, for example.) However, soon after, AI efforts began a definite shift toward applications work, confronting problems of real-world importance. Inevitably, successful applications work encouraged specialization into subdisciplines such as natural language processing, expert systems, and computer vision.

One reason for the increasing interest in applications was that the power of AI methods had increased to the point where realistic applications seemed within reach. But perhaps more importantly, the sponsors of AI research in the U.S. Department of Defense (DoD) had to deal with the constraints imposed on them by the 1969 "Mansfield Amendment," which required that basic research be relevant to military needs. As one example of the increased emphasis on applications, the Information Sciences Institute (USC-ISI) was formed in 1972 specifically to pursue them. Located in Marina Del Rey, California, it is affiliated with the University of Southern California and received much of its initial support from DARPA. Other large corporations also began to explore AI's commercial potential.

Of course, theoretical and basic research continued also, and several new university groups joined the existing ones. A short list of the new ones would include those at the Universities of Toronto, Rochester, Texas, Maryland, British Columbia, California, and Washington. Other groups started as well in Europe and Asia. (In 1981, I was invited to give lectures on AI in China, which was newly recovering from its "Cultural Revolution" and beginning its program of "Opening and Reform.") But even at the universities, much of their basic research was motivated by specific applications. In this part of the book, I'll describe some of the AI applications work undertaken during the 1970s to the early 1980s.

17

Speech Recognition and Understanding Systems

17.1 Speech Processing

The NLP systems I have already described required that their English input be in text format. Yet, there are several instances in which speaking to a computer would be preferable to typing at one. People can generally speak faster than they can type (about three words per second versus about one word per second), and they can speak while they are moving about. Also, speaking does not tie up hands or eyes.

In discussing the problem of computer processing of speech, it is important to make some distinctions. One involves the difference between recognizing an isolated spoken word versus processing a continuous stream of speech. Most AI research has concentrated on the second and harder of these problems. Another distinction is between speech *recognition* and speech *understanding*.

By speech recognition is meant the process of converting an acoustic stream of speech input, as gathered by a microphone and associated electronic equipment, into a text representation of its component words. This process is difficult because many acoustic streams sound similar but are composed of quite different words. (Consider, for example, the spoken versions of "There are many ways to recognize speech," and "There are many ways to wreck a nice beach.") Speech understanding, in contrast, requires that what is spoken be *understood*. An utterance can be said to be understood if it elicits an appropriate action or response, and this might even be possible without recognizing *all* of its words.

Understanding speech is more difficult than understanding text because there is the additional problem of processing the speech waveform to extract the words being uttered. Speech, as it is captured by a microphone, is converted into an electronic signal or waveform, which can be displayed on an oscilloscope. In Fig. 17.1, I show a waveform generated by a person saying "This is a test." This diagram shows the amplitude (voltage) of the speech signal plotted against time. The sections of the waveform corresponding to the words are demarcated by the boxes at the top of the diagram. The boxes at the bottom show acoustical elements of these words, which are called "phones."

In general, phones are the sounds that correspond to vowels or consonants. English speech is thought to be composed of forty or so different phones. Special alphabets have been devised to represent phones. One is the International Phonetic Alphabet (IPA), which contains the phones of all known languages. IPA uses several special characters that do not have standard computer (ASCII) codes. Another, containing just the phones used in American English and using only standard characters, is

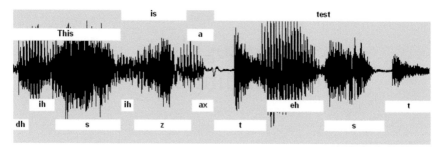

Figure 17.1. A speech waveform. (Used with permission of Gunish Rai Chawla.)

ARPAbet, which was developed during speech-processing research sponsored by DARPA. The phones boxed in Fig. 17.1 use the ARPAbet notation. The table in Fig. 17.2 shows the ARPAbet phones and sample words containing them.

Early speech recognition systems attempted first to segment the speech waveform into its constituent phones and then to assemble the phones into words. To do so,

Symbol	Example Sound	Symbol	Example Sound
Consonants		**Vowels**	
[p]	pat	[iy]	lily
[t]	tom	[ih]	miss
[k]	cat	[ey]	lazy
[b]	boy	[eh]	mess
[d]	dip	[ae]	after
[g]	garment	[aa]	pop
[m]	mat	[ao]	orchestra
[n]	nut	[uh]	wood
[ng]	sing	[ow]	lotus
[f]	five	[uw]	tulip
[v]	dove	[uh]	butter
[th]	thistle	[er]	bird
[dh]	feather	[ay]	item
[s]	sat	[aw]	flower
[z]	haze	[oy]	toil
[sh]	smash	[y uw]	few
[zh]	ambrosia	[ax]	ruffian
[ch]	chic	[ix]	lip
[jh]	page	[axr]	leather
[l]	lick	[ux]	dude
[w]	kiwi		
[r]	parse		
[y]	yew		
[h]	horse		
[q]	uh-oh (glottal stop)		
[dx]	butter		
[nx]	winter		
[el]	thistle		

Figure 17.2. Consonants and vowels in the ARPAbet phonetic alphabet.

the speech signal was first digitized, and various parameters, such as the frequency or pitch, were extracted. The ways in which the values of these parameters change in time were used to segment the waveform into units containing phones. Using dictionaries that associate the values of waveform parameters with phones and phones with words, the waveform was finally converted into text. The process sounds simple but it is actually quite complex because, among other things, the beginnings and endings of spoken words and their component phones overlap in complex patterns, and people often pronounce the same words in different ways. For example, the word "you" might be pronounced differently in "are you" [aa r y uw] and "did you" [d ih d jh uh].

Attempts to recognize speech began at Bell Laboratories as far back as the 1930s. In 1952, engineers at Bell Labs built a system for recognizing the numbers "zero" through "nine" uttered by a single speaker.[1] Other work was done in the 1950s and 1960s at RCA Laboratories, at MIT, in Japan, in England, and in the Soviet Union.[2] Work accelerated in the 1970s, some of which I'll describe next.

17.2 The Speech Understanding Study Group

Larry Roberts, who went to DARPA in late 1966 as "chief scientist" in the Information Processing Techniques Office (IPTO) and later became its director, became intrigued with the idea of building systems that could understand speech. Cordell Green, by then serving as a lieutenant in the U.S. Army, was assigned to IPTO under Roberts in early 1970 and was put in charge of funding and monitoring AI research projects. According to Green, Roberts told him "Do a feasibility study on a system that can recognize speech."[3]

So, at the end of March 1970, Green organized a meeting at Carnegie Mellon University of several of the DARPA contractors and others interested in speech processing to discuss the feasibility of speech understanding by computer. Among those attending the meeting were researchers from SDC, Lincoln Laboratory, MIT, CMU, SRI, and BBN. It was decided at the meeting to form a "study group" to assess the state of the art and to make recommendations concerning the launching of a major DARPA-supported project in speech understanding. The group was to be chaired by Allen Newell of CMU.[4]

During the March meeting, Roberts was persuaded to talk about the kind of speech-understanding system that he had in mind. According to the study group's rendition of his remarks, Roberts was thinking about a system that could accept continuous speech from many cooperative users, over a telephone, using a vocabulary of 10,000 words, with less than 10% semantic error, in a few times real time, and be demonstrable in 1973.

The study group held its first meeting at BBN on May 26 and 27, 1970. At that meeting, the group considered some specific tasks that the understanding system would be able to engage in. Among these were answering questions about data management, answering questions about the operational status of a computer, and consulting about a computer operating system.

A final meeting of the group was held at SDC in Santa Monica on July 26–28, 1970. The recommendation of the group (in brief) was to aim for a system that could accept continuous speech, from many cooperative speakers of the "general

American dialect," over a good quality microphone (not a telephone), using a selected vocabulary of 1,000 words (not 10,000 words), with a "highly artificial syntax," involving tasks such as data management or computer status (but not consulting), with less than 10% error, in a few times real time, and be demonstrable in 1976 (not 1973) with a moderate chance of success. A final report of the group was drafted after the meeting, delivered to DARPA, and eventually published in 1973.[5]

Although there had been much prior research in speech processing by computer (nicely summarized in the study group's report), not everyone was optimistic about success. One naysayer was John R. Pierce, a researcher at Bell Laboratories, where much speech-recognition work had already taken place. In 1969, Pierce wrote a letter[6] to the *Journal of the Acoustical Society of America* in which he claimed that most people working on speech recognition were acting like "mad scientists and untrustworthy engineers. The typical recognizer gets it into his head that he can solve 'the problem.'" In the same letter, though, he also wrote that

... performance would continue to be very limited unless the recognizing device *understands* what is being said with something of the facility of a native speaker (that is, better than a foreigner who is fluent in the language). If this is so, should people continue work toward speech recognition? Perhaps this is for people in the field to decide. [My italics.]

17.3 The DARPA Speech Understanding Research Program

In fact, people in the field did decide. In October 1971, Roberts established at DARPA a five-year Speech Understanding Research (SUR) program based largely on the study group's report. Its budget was about $3 million per year. CMU, Lincoln Laboratory, BBN, SDC, and SRI were contracted to build systems. Complementary research would be performed at Haskins Laboratories, the Speech Communications Research Laboratory, the Sperry Univac Speech Communications Department, and the University of California at Berkeley.

In 1976, some of these efforts resulted in systems that were demonstrated and tested against the program's goals. CMU developed two of these, HARPY and HEARSAY-II. BBN produced HWIM (Hear What I Mean). SRI and SDC formed a partnership in which SDC developed the acoustic processing components and SRI developed the parsing and semantic components. However, the SDC effort ran into difficulties with computer access, so the combined SRI/SDC system was never formally tested. I'll briefly summarize the BBN work and then describe the CMU work in more detail.[7]

17.3.1 *Work at BBN*

SPEECHLIS was the first speech understanding system developed at BBN. It was designed to answer spoken questions about the moon rocks database (the one used in BBN's earlier LUNAR system). It was rather slow and was not systematically tested.[8]

HWIM was designed to be a travel budget manager's automated assistant and was able to respond to spoken questions such as "How much is left in the speech understanding budget?"[9] In its final version, HWIM was tested on two versions, each of sixty-four different utterances by three male speakers. Thirty-one of these sentences had previously been used by the system as it was being designed, so there might have been some implicit (if unintentional) built-in extra capability for dealing with those sentences. The sentences ranged in length from three to thirteen words. HWIM was able to respond correctly to 41% of the sentences and "close" to correctly to 23% more of them. The system did not respond at all to 20% of the sentences. Although both SPEECHLIS and HWIM pioneered new and important methods in speech understanding, HWIM's performance was generally regarded as not meeting the original DARPA objectives. (Their designers claimed that the test was not indicative of HWIM's potential and that they could have done better with more time.)

17.3.2 *Work at CMU*

In 1969, Raj Reddy left Stanford to become a faculty member at Carnegie Mellon University. One of the first speech systems he and colleagues worked on at CMU was called HEARSAY (later renamed HEARSAY-I).[10] It used a number of independent computational processes to recognize spoken moves in chess from a given board position, such as "king bishop pawn moves to bishop four." It was during the early stages of this work, that DARPA formed the Speech Understanding Study Group and initiated work in speech understanding. A public demonstration of HEARSAY-I recognizing connected speech was given in June 1972.

Three different speech recognition and understanding systems were developed at CMU under the umbrella of the DARPA speech understanding research effort. These were DRAGON, HARPY, and HEARSAY-II, and they all contributed important AI ideas. Work on these systems was led by Allen Newell, Raj Reddy, James Baker, Bruce Lowerre, Lee Erman, Victor Lesser, and Rick Hayes-Roth.[11]

A. DRAGON
During the early days of CMU's speech understanding research, a Ph.D. student, James K. Baker, began work on a speech understanding system he called "DRAGON."[12] (According to Allen Newell, the name DRAGON was meant "to indicate that it was an entirely different kind of beast from the AI systems being considered in the rest of the speech effort."[13]) Like HEARSAY-I, DRAGON was designed to understand sentences about chess moves.

DRAGON introduced powerful new techniques for speech processing – elaborations of which are used in most modern speech recognition systems. It used statistical techniques to make guesses about the most probable strings of words that might have produced the observed speech signal. It was an early example of the importation of probabilistic representations and associated computational methods into AI. We'll see a good deal more of these in later chapters.

I'll try to explain the main ideas without using much mathematics. Using the notation introduced in Section 2.3.2, suppose we let x stand for a string of words and y stand for the speech waveform that is produced when x is spoken. (Actually, we'll let y be some information-preserving representation of the waveform in terms of its easily measurable properties such as the amounts of energy the waveform contains in various frequency bands. For simplicity, I'll continue to call y a waveform, even though I mean its representation, which might be different for different speech understanding systems.)

Because the same speaker may say the same words somewhat differently on different occasions, and different speakers certainly will say them differently, the word string x does not completely determine what the speech waveform y will be. That is, given any x, we can only say what the probabilities of the different y's might be. As described in Chapter 2, these probabilities are written in functional form as $p(y \mid x)$ (read as the "probability of y given x"). In principle, the actual values of $p(y \mid x)$ for some particular x, say $x = X$, could be estimated, for example, by having a number of speakers utter the word string X many different times and tabulating how frequently different speech waveforms y occur. This process would have to be repeated for many different word strings. DRAGON avoided this tedious tabulation in a way to be explained shortly.

For speech recognition, however, we want to know the probability of a word string x, given the speech signal y, so that we can select the most probable x. That is, we want $p(x \mid y)$ rather than $p(y \mid x)$. We could use Bayes's rule as before, to produce the desired probability as follows:

$$p(x \mid y) = p(y \mid x)p(x)/p(y).$$

Upon observing a particular waveform, say $y = Y$, here is how we would use the quantities in this formula to decide what word string x was most probably uttered:

1. Look up all the values of $p(Y \mid x)$ for all of the values of x we are considering. (We don't have to do this for *all* possible strings of words, but only for those allowed by the vocabulary and syntax of the specialized area appropriate to the speech understanding task – chess moves in the case of DRAGON.)
2. Multiply each of these values by $p(x)$. (The decision should be biased in favor of likely word strings.)
3. Select that x, say X, for which the product is the largest. [We can ignore dividing by $p(y)$ because its value does not affect which $p(x \mid Y)$ is largest.]

Although this process would work in principle, it is quite impractical computationally. Instead, DRAGON and other modern speech-recognition systems exploit the hierarchical structure involved in what is presumed to be the way a speech waveform is generated. There are various levels in this hierarchy that could be identified. To oversimplify a bit, at the top of the hierarchy a given semantic idea is expressed by a string of words obeying the syntactic rules of the language. The string of words, in turn, gives rise to a string of phones – the phonetic units. Finally, the phone string is expressed by a speech waveform at the bottom of the hierarchy.

At each level, we have a sequence of entities, say, $x_1, x_2, \ldots x_n$, producing a sequence of other entities, say, $y_1, y_2, \ldots, y_n$. We can diagram the process as shown in Fig. 17.3.

The DRAGON system made some simplifying assumptions. It assumed that each x_i in the sequence of x's is influenced only by its immediate precedent, x_{i-1}, and not

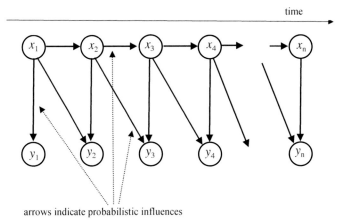

arrows indicate probabilistic influences

Figure 17.3. Two hierarchical levels in speech generation.

by any other of the x_i. This assumption is called the Markov assumption. [Andrey Andreyevich Markov (1856–1922) was a Russian mathematician. He used (what was later called) a Markov model to analyze the statistics of a sequence of 20,000 Russian letters taken from Pushkin's novel *Eugene Onegin*.[14] Markov models are used extensively in physics and engineering. Google uses the Markov assumption, for example, in its computation of page rank.] Of course, we know that each word in a sequence depends on more than just the immediately preceding word. Even so, the Markov assumption makes computations simpler and still allows good performance.

Further, it was assumed that each y_i was influenced only by x_i and x_{i-1}. All of these "influences" are probabilistic. That is, given quantities like x_3 and x_4, for example, the value of y_4 is not completely determined. One can only say what the probabilities of the values of y_4 might be; these are given by the functional expression $p(y_4 \mid x_3, x_4)$. Probability values for the y's are thus given by what is called a "probabilistic function of a Markov process." To produce estimates of these probabilities, statistics can be gathered during a "learning process" (in which a speaker utters a training set of sentences).

DRAGON combined these separate levels into a network consisting of a hierarchy of probabilistic functions of Markov processes. Entities representing segments of the speech waveform were at the bottom, entities representing phones were in the middle, and entities representing words were at the top. At each level, Bayes's rule was used to compute probabilities of the x's given the y's. Because only the speech waveform at the bottom level was actually observed, the phones and words were said to be "hidden." For this reason, the entire network employed hidden Markov models (HMMs). DRAGON was the first example of the use of HMMs in AI. They had been developed previously for other purposes.[15]

Using this network, recognition of an utterance was then achieved by finding the highest probability path through the network. Computing the probabilities for syntactically valid word sequences, given the sequence of segments of the observed speech waveform, is a problem that is similar to one I described earlier, namely, computing the confidences of strings of characters on FORTRAN coding sheets (see p. 72). Again, a method based on dynamic programming was used. As Baker wrote, "The optimum path is found by an algorithm which, in effect, explores all possible paths in parallel."[16] At the end of the process, the most probable syntactically legal string of words is identified. The mathematical operations for making these computations are too complex to explain here, but they can be performed efficiently enough to make speech recognition practical.

Although the DRAGON system was not among those that were finally tested against DARPA's speech understanding system objectives, Baker claimed that its initial results were "very promising" and that in "its first test with live speech input, the system correctly recognized every word in all nine sentences in the test."[17] DRAGON became the basis for a commercial product, "Dragon Naturally Speaking," first developed and marketed by Dragon Systems, a company founded by Baker and his wife, Janet.

B. HARPY

HARPY was a second system produced at CMU under DARPA's speech under-standing research effort. Bruce T. Lowerre designed and implemented the system as part of his Ph.D. research.[18] HARPY combined some of the ideas of HEARSAY-I and DRAGON. Like DRAGON, it searched paths through a network to recognize a spoken sentence, but it did not annotate the links between nodes in the network with transition probabilities like DRAGON did. Like HEARSAY-I, HARPY used heuristic search methods.

Versions of HARPY were developed for understanding spoken sentences about several different task areas. The main one involved being able to answer questions about, and to retrieve documents from, a database containing summaries (called "abstracts") of AI papers. Here are some examples:

"Which abstracts refer to theory of computation?"
"List those articles."
"Are any by Feigenbaum and Feldman?"
"What has McCarthy written since nineteen seventy-four?"

HARPY could handle a vocabulary of 1,011 words. Instead of using a grammar with the conventional syntactic categories such as Noun, Adjective, and so on, HARPY used what is called a "semantic grammar," one that has expanded categories such as Topic, Author, Year, and Publisher that were semantically related to its subject area, namely, data about AI papers. HARPY's grammar was limited to handle just the set of sentences about authors and papers that HARPY was supposed to be able to recognize.

The network was constructed from what were called "knowledge sources" (KSs), which consisted of information needed for the recognition process.[19] The first of these encoded syntactic knowledge about the grammar.

A second knowledge source used by HARPY described how each word in HARPY's vocabulary might be pronounced. And, because in spoken language word boundaries overlap in ways that depend on the words involved, successful recognition requires a third knowledge source dealing with such phenomena. A fourth knowledge source

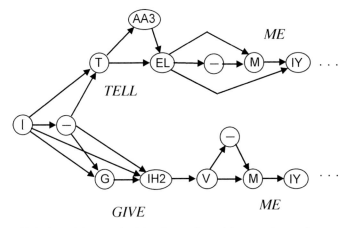

Figure 17.4. A partial network of the phones that might occur in a spoken sentence.

specified the phones involved in the pronunciation of words and transitions between words.

HARPY combined all of this knowledge into a giant network of phones representing all the possible ways that syntactically legal sentences might be spoken. Each "phone node" in the network was paired with a representation of a segment of a speech waveform, called a "spectral template," expected to be associated with that particular phone. These templates were obtained initially by having a speaker read about 700 sentences. They could be "tuned" for a new speaker by having the speaker read about 20 selected sentences during a "learning" session. A partial network of phones is shown in Fig. 17.4 to illustrate the general idea. HARPY's actual network had 15,000 nodes. The network is for those parts of the sentences that begin with "Tell me ..." and "Give me. . . ." The symbols inside the nodes represent phones, using DRAGON's notation for them. Arrows represent possible transitions from one phone to the next. Note that there are multiple paths, corresponding to different ways to pronounce the words.

To recognize the words in a spoken sentence, the observed speech waveform was first divided into variable-length segments that were guessed to correspond to the sequence of phones in the waveform. A spectral template was computed for each of these segments. The recognition process then proceeded as follows: The spectral template corresponding to the first spectral segment in the speech waveform was compared against all of the templates corresponding to the phones at the beginning of the network. In reference to Fig. 17.4, these would include comparisons against templates for –, T, G, and IH2 because they were among the nodes in the network that could be reached in one step from the start node, namely, [. (Of course, in using the complete network rather than just the partial example just illustrated, several more comparisons would be made against templates of additional phone nodes reachable in one step from the start node.) The best few matches were noted, and the paths to these nodes were designated to be the best one-step partial paths through the network. At the next stage, the spectral template of the next waveform segment was compared against the templates of all of those phone nodes reachable by extending the best one-step paths one more step. Using the values of the comparisons computed so far, a set of best two-step partial paths was identified. This process continues until the end of the network was reached. At that time the very best path found so far could be associated with the words associated with the nodes along that path. This word sequence was then produced as HARPY's recognition decision.

HARPY's method of searching for a best path through the network can be compared with the A^* heuristic search process described earlier. Whereas A^* kept the entire search "frontier" available for possible further searching, HARPY kept on its frontier only those nodes on the best few paths found so far. (The number of nodes kept on the frontier was a parameter that could be set as needed to control search.) HARPY's designers called this technique "beam search" because the nodes visited by the search process were limited to a narrow beam through the network. Because nodes not in the beam were eliminated as the process went on, it is possible that the best complete path found by HARPY might not be the overall best one in the network. (One of the eliminated nodes might be on this overall best path.) Even so, the path found usually corresponded to a correct interpretation of the spoken sentence.

At the end of the DARPA speech understanding project, HARPY was tested on 100 sentences spoken by three male and two female speakers. It was able to understand over 95% of these sentences correctly, thereby meeting DARPA's goal of less than 10% error. On average, HARPY executed about 30 million computer instructions to deal with one second of speech. Using a 0.4-million instructions per second (0.4 MIPS) machine (a DEC PDP-KA10), it would take over a minute to process a second of speech; although this is quite a bit worse than real-time performance, it achieved DARPA's goal of "a few times real time" (if we interpret "a few" somewhat accommodatingly). To put the real-time matter in perspective, today's computers process billions of instructions per second. HARPY was the only system to meet DARPA's goals.

C. HEARSAY-II

Finally, HEARSAY-II, a redesigned and improved version of HEARSAY-I, was perhaps the most ambitious of CMU's speech projects.[20] Like HARPY, HEARSAY-II was designed to answer questions about, and to retrieve documents from, a database containing abstracts of AI papers. (An earlier task considered was to retrieve wire-service news stories.) It too was limited to a vocabulary of 1,011 words and used a semantic grammar specialized to its subject area.

The first steps in HEARSAY's processing of an utterance involved segmenting the speech waveform and labeling the phones estimated to be present in each segment. HEARSAY then used a novel method of gradually building these components into syllables, the syllables into words, the words into word sequences, and finally word sequences into phrases. The phrases were then converted into appropriate routines for accessing the database of AI papers.[21]

The processing method used by HEARSAY involved a layered structure called a "Blackboard." The labels of the phones estimated to be present, along with numbers related to their probabilities of occurrence, were "written" in one of the lower layers of the Blackboard. Specialized knowledge-source routines that "knew about" how syllables were constructed from phones "read" these labels and computed guesses

blackboard   knowledge sources (KS)

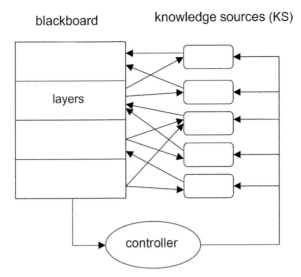

layers

controller

Figure 17.5. The Blackboard architecture.

about what syllables were in the utterance. These guesses, along with numbers measuring their confidences or likelihoods, were then written in the syllable layer of the Blackboard. Other knowledge-source routines that knew about how words were constructed from syllables read information already on the Blackboard and wrote guesses about words in the word layer of the Blackboard. And so on. HEARSAY-II had around 40 of these knowledge sources. The general idea is illustrated in Fig. 17.5.

In principle, a knowledge source could read or write information on any layer of the Blackboard that was relevant to it. Moreover, it could do so in what is called an "asynchronous" manner – not dependent on when other knowledge sources were doing their reading and writing. There were some knowledge sources that could write predictions about new words based on words already written in the word layer and on information in other layers. Knowledge sources could even write guesses about words in the word layer based on word sequences already written (with high confidence) in the sequence layer. This process of inferring what must be present in a lower layer (even though missed by initial processing) from what (from other evidence) is present in a higher layer is a theme that recurs often in later AI research. As far as I know, this extremely important AI innovation was first manifest in the HEARSAY-II system.

According to Raj Reddy,[22] one of the inventors of the Blackboard architecture (along with Victor Lesser, Lee Erman, and Frederick Hayes-Roth), Herbert Simon often used the word "blackboard" to describe the "working memory" component of the production system architecture he and Allen Newell were working with (see p. 468). A production system used IF–THEN rules (called productions), which were triggered by contents of the working memory and wrote new data in it. Reddy and team, recognizing the variety of different sources of knowledge relevant to speech processing, generalized the production system idea, extending the production rules into larger programs, renaming them "knowledge sources," and elaborated working memory into the layered Blackboard structure.

At the end of the DARPA speech understanding project, HEARSAY-II was tested on twenty-three spoken sentences, brand new to the system, having an average of seven words per sentence, and 81% of these were recognized word-for-word correctly, although 91% led to the same database query as would have a word-for-word correct sentence. HEARSAY's designers claimed that this performance "comes close to meeting the ambitious goals... established for the DARPA program in 1971." Although HEARSAY-II came close the results were not quite as good as those of HARPY.

Although the Blackboard architecture is no longer used in modern speech recognition systems, it was adopted by several other AI programs. (We'll see one of these later in the book.) According to Russell and Norvig, "Blackboard systems are the foundation of modern user interface architectures."[23]

17.3.3 *Summary and Impact of the SUR Program*

CMU's HEARSAY-II and HARPY were demonstrated at CMU on September 8, 1976, and BBN's HWIM was demonstrated at BBN on September 10. In a summary report of the projects, MIT's Dennis Klatt wrote that "it is unclear whether there are large differences in ability among [these] three systems. However, only [HARPY] was able to meet the ARPA goals."[24]

The developers of HEARSAY-II attributed HARPY's superior performance to three factors: its more thorough search of potential solutions (permitted by its precomputed network of all the sentences that might have been spoken), its more thorough built-in knowledge of transition phenomena between adjacent words, and its more thorough testing, tuning, and debugging.[25]

Some researchers and DARPA program managers, however, argued about the way in which the tests were carried out and claimed that none of the systems met the SUR program objectives. In any case, DARPA decided not to fund a proposed follow-on program. The program did show, however, that speech understanding was a reasonable technical goal and stimulated progress in speech processing technologies, notably in system organization, syntax and semantics, and acoustic processing. A National Research Council report concluded that "DARPA's funding of research on understanding speech has been extremely important. . . . the results of this research have been incorporated into the products of established companies, such as IBM and BBN, as well as start-ups such as Nuance Communications (an SRI spinoff) and Dragon Systems. . . . The leading commercial speech-recognition program on the market today, the Dragon "NaturallySpeaking" software [now sold by Nuance], traces its roots directly back to the work done at CMU between 1971 and 1975 as part of SUR. . . ."[26]

17.4 Subsequent Work in Speech Recognition

Speech recognition research was also being carried out in other laboratories besides those that were directly involved with DARPA's SUR program. For example,

Frederick Jelinek of the Speech Processing Group in IBM's Computer Sciences Department at the Thomas J. Watson Research Center in Yorktown Heights, New York, is credited with being an early proponent of the use of statistical methods (including hidden Markov models) in speech recognition.[27] The HMM approach was ultimately adopted by all the leading speech recognition companies.

In 1984, DARPA began funding speech recognition work again as part of its "Strategic Computing" program (a program that will be described in a later chapter). Participants included CMU, SRI, BBN, MIT, IBM, and Dragon Systems. Among the systems developed at CMU over the next several years, for example, were SPHINX by Kai-Fu Lee and others and JANUS, a multilingual speech recognition and translation system, by Alex Waibel and others. (These and other systems are available as open-source software from the "Speech at CMU" Web page, http://www.speech.cs.cmu.edu/. The page also has links to many other speech recognition laboratories.)

Based on their work on DRAGON at CMU, James and Janet Baker founded Dragon Systems in 1982. In 1997, Dragon introduced "Dragon NaturallySpeaking," a speech recognition program for personal computers. It had a vocabulary of 23,000 words.[28] IBM followed with ViaVoice, and other companies, including Microsoft, also have speech recognition software.

The transcription of spoken sentences to their textual equivalents is now largely a solved problem. For example, high-quality speech recognition is commonly employed today in many automated telephone response systems. However, *understanding* natural language speech (or text) to permit general dialogs with computer systems, for example, remains a long-term research problem. I'll continue my discussion of work on that problem in a later chapter.

Notes

1. K. H. Davis, R. Biddulph, and S. Balashek, "Automatic Recognition of Spoken Digits," *Journal of the Acoustical Society of America*, Vol. 24, No. 6, pp. 627–642, 1952. [211]
2. For a history of early work see B. H. Juang and Lawrence R. Rabiner, "Automatic Speech Recognition – A Brief History of the Technology Development," available online at http://www.ece.ucsb.edu/Faculty/Rabiner/ece259/Reprints/354_LALI-ASRHistory-final-10-8.pdf; or Sadaoki Furui, "50 Years of Progress in Speech and Speaker Recognition," available online at http://www.furui.cs.titech.ac.jp/publication/2005/SPCOM05.pdf. [211]
3. C. Cordell Green, "AI During IPTO's Middle Years," in Thomas C. Bartee (ed.), *Expert Systems and Artificial Intelligence: Applications and Management*, p. 240, Indianapolis: Howard W. Sams & Co., 1988. [211]
4. Other members of the group were Jeffrey Barnett of the Systems Development Corporation, James Forgie of Lincoln Laboratory, C. Cordell Green, then a lieutenant in the U.S. Army stationed at DARPA, Dennis Klatt of MIT, J. C. R. Licklider, then at MIT, John Munson of SRI, Raj Reddy of CMU, and William Woods of BBN. [211]
5. The report was published as a special issue of the journal *Artificial Intelligence*: Allen Newell *et al.*, *Speech Understanding Systems: Final Report of a Study Group*, New York: American Elsevier Publishing Co., Inc., 1973. A draft of the report is available online in the Newell collection at http://diva.library.cmu.edu/webapp/newell/item.jsp?q=box00105/fld08162/bdl0001/doc0001/. [212]

6. J. R. Pierce, "Whither Speech Recognition?," *Journal of the Acoustical Society of America*, Vol. 46, No. 4, pp. 1049–1051, Part 2, 1969. Also see a rebuttal by Arthur Samuel and Pierce's response to Samuel and to other rebuttals in *Journal of the Acoustical Society of America*, Vol. 47, No. 6, Part 2, pp. 1616–1617, 1970. [212]

7. For a description of the SRI work, see Donald E. Walker (ed.), *Understanding Spoken Language*, New York: Elsevier North-Holland, Inc., 1978. [212]

8. For more details, see William A. Woods, "Motivation and Overview of BBN SPEECHLIS: An Experimental Prototype for Speech Understanding Research," *IEEE Transactions on Acoustics, Speech, and Signal Processing*, Vol. ASSP-23, No. 1, pp. 2–9, February 1975. [212]

9. See J. Wolf and William A. Woods, "The HWIM Speech Understanding System," *Acoustics, Speech, and Signal Processing, IEEE International Conference on ICASSP '77*, Vol. 2, pp. 784–787, May 1977; also (for full details) William A. Woods *et al.*, *Speech Understanding Systems – Final Report*, BBN Report No. 3438, Vols. I–V, Bolt, Beranek, and Newman, Inc., Cambridge, MA, 1976. [212]

10. D. Raj Reddy, Lee D. Erman, and Richard B. Neely, "A Model and a System for Machine Recognition of Speech," *IEEE Transactions on Audio and Electroacoustics*, Vol. AU-21, No. 3, pp. 229–238, June 1973; and D. Raj Reddy, Lee D. Erman, R. D. Fennell, and Richard. B. Neely, "The HEARSAY Speech Understanding System: An Example of the Recognition Processes," in *Proceedings of the 3rd International Joint Conference on Artificial Intelligence*, pp. 185–183, Stanford, CA, August 1973. [213]

11. For background on the speech processing work at CMU during this period, see Lee D. Erman, "Overview of the HEARSAY Speech Understanding Research," *SIGART Newsletter*, No. 56, pp. 9–16, February 1976. [213]

12. James K. Baker, "Stochastic Modeling as a Means of Automatic Speech Recognition," doctoral dissertation, Computer Science Department, Carnegie Mellon University, Pittsburgh, PA, 1975, and James K. Baker, "The DRAGON System – An Overview," *IEEE Transactions on Acoustics, Speech, and Signal Processing*, Vol. ASSP-23, No. 1, February 1975. [213]

13. Allen Newell, "Harpy, Production Systems and Human Cognition, in Ronald A. Cole (ed.), *Perception and Production of Fluent Speech*, Hillsdale, NJ: Lawrence Erlbaum Associates, 1980. Available online as Carnegie Mellon University Technical Report CMU-CS-78-140 at http://diva.library.cmu.edu/webapp/newell/item.jsp?q=box00089/fld06145/bdl0001/doc0001/. [213]

14. For a translation see A. A. Markov, "An Example of Statistical Investigation of the Text *Eugene Onegin* Concerning the Connection of Samples in Chains," *Science in Context*, Vol. 19, No. 4, pp. 591–600, 2006. [215]

15. See L. E. Baum and J. A. Eagon, "An Inequality with Applications to Statistical Estimation for Probabilistic Functions of a Markov Process and to a Model for Ecology," *Bulletin of the American Medical Society*, Vol. 73, pp. 360–363, 1967. Baker credits Baum with introducing him to the theory of a probabilistic function of a Markov process. [215]

16. James K. Baker, "The DRAGON System – An Overview," *IEEE Transactions on Acoustics, Speech, and Signal Processing*, Vol. ASSP-23, No. 1, p. 24, February 1975. [216]

17. *Ibid*, p. 29. [216]

18. Bruce T. Lowerre, "The HARPY Speech Recognition System," doctoral dissertation, Computer Science Department, Carnegie Mellon University, Pittsburgh, PA, April 1976. [216]

19. I am basing my description of HARPY on Bruce Lowerre and Raj Reddy, "The HARPY Speech Understanding System," *Trends in Speech Recognition*, Prentice Hall. Reprinted

in A. Waibel and K. Lee (eds.), *Readings in Speech Recognition*, pp. 576–586, San Mateo, CA: Morgan Kaufmann Publishers, Inc., 1990. **[216]**

20. Lee D. Erman, Frederick Hayes-Roth, Victor R. Lesser, and D. Raj Reddy, "The HEARSAY-II Speech-Understanding System: Integrating Knowledge to Resolve Uncertainty," *Computing Surveys*, Vol. 12, No. 2, June 1980. **[218]**

21. For a detailed summary of how HEARSAY processed an example sentence, see *ibid.* **[218]**

22. Telephone conversation, August 14, 2008. **[219]**

23. Stuart Russell and Peter Norvig, *Artificial Intelligence: A Modern Approach*, second edition, p. 580, Upper Saddle River, NJ: Prentice Hall, 2003. **[220]**

24. Dennis H. Klatt, "Review of the ARPA Speech Understanding Project," *Journal of the Acoustical Society of America*, Vol. 62, No. 2, pp. 1345–1366, December 1977. **[220]**

25. Lee D. Erman, Frederick Hayes-Roth, Victor R. Lesser, and D. Raj Reddy, *op. cit.* **[220]**

26. *Funding a Revolution: Government Support for Computing Research*, Chapter 9, Committee on Innovations in Computing and Communications: Lessons from History, Computer Science and Telecommunications Board, Commission on Physical Sciences, Mathematics, and Applications, National Research Council, Washington, DC: National Academy Press, 1999. Available online at http://books.nap.edu/openbook.php?record_id=6323&page=15. **[220]**

27. See, for example, Frederick Jelinek, "Continuous Speech Recognition by Statistical Methods," *Proceedings of the IEEE*, Vol. 64, No. 4, pp. 532–556, April 1976. **[221]**

28. Dragon NaturallySpeaking is now available through Nuance. **[221]**

18

Consulting Systems

18.1 The SRI Computer-Based Consultant

As my colleagues and I at SRI cast about for ways to continue our planning and vision research we had been doing under the "Shakey the Robot" project, while satisfying DARPA's interest in militarily relevant applications, we hit upon the problem of equipment maintenance, repair, and training. We pointed out that any technology that could reduce expenditures for these items and lessen the need for utilizing scarce human experts would be extremely important to the military. Furthermore, we said, this need "cannot be satisfied merely by writing more and better manuals. A sophisticated computer system seems to us essential."

We proposed to begin work on this problem by developing an environment in which an apprentice repair person would be given advice about how to take apart and reassemble a small air compressor.[1] The advice would be generated (as needed by the apprentice) by a planning and execution system that would give suggestions about what to do next. The apprentice could ask for advice, using a predefined small vocabulary, which the system would analyze with state-of-the art speech recognition equipment, and then the system would answer, using a speech generation module. The system would also employ a machine-vision system to help keep track of progress and to observe components pointed to by the apprentice. The proposed setup is shown in Fig. 18.1.

Although the project did not last long enough to achieve all of its goals, an early version of a "Computer-Based Consultant" (CBC) system was demonstrated in which the apprentice (played by Georgia Sutherland, one of the project team members) was asked to reassemble an air compressor (a Sears Model 17209, 1/2 HP compressor) that had previously been partially taken apart. Requests and responses by both the system and the apprentice were spoken. Here is a sample of one of the interactions with the system (with my commentary in parentheses):[2]

System: Please assemble air compressor.

Apprentice: How?

(The apprentice asks for advice, and the system, using Sacerdoti's NOAH system I described previously, creates a hierarchical assembly plan.)

S: Install pump.

(The system mentions the first action in the high-level plan NOAH created.)

Figure 18.1. Proposed arrangement for helping an apprentice. (Used with permission of SRI International.)

A: OK.
(The apprentice knows how to install the pump and indicates that she does not need further advice about how to do it. At this stage of the CBC project, the system assumed, without visual checking, that the apprentice had completed this first step.)

S: Install pump brace.
(The system mentions the second action in the high-level plan.)

A: How?
(The apprentice does not know how to achieve this step and asks for advice.)

S: Connect pump brace to pump.
(The system mentions the first of the more detailed steps in the high-level action for installing the pump brace.)

A: OK.
(The apprentice knows how to achieve this step.)

S: Connect pump brace to belt-housing frame.
(The system mentions the next of the more detailed steps in the high-level action for installing the pump brace.)

This type of interaction continues until the task is completed.

The system kept track of the current state of assembly by using the procedural net created by the NOAH system (see p. 176). If the apprentice were to have asked "Why?" at any step, the system would have used the procedural net to construct an answer. The answer might have been something like "you must do x because it is one of the actions involved in doing y," or "you must do x because you must do it first in order to do the next action, z." Also, the apprentice could have asked for help in locating one of the major parts of the air compressor, and the system would have used its laser pointer to show her. Part of the procedural net computed for this example is shown in Fig. 18.2.

The CBC project also provided an opportunity for SRI's NLP group to try out some ideas they were developing about generating and understanding the sentences used in conversations. In the CBC project, the apprentice and the person giving advice are participating in a dialog about a task, namely, the task of working on an air compressor. The structure of the task, as modeled by the procedural network generated by NOAH, provided important pragmatic information useful for sentence understanding. This information was exploited in a system called TDUS (an acronym for Task Dialog Understanding System), which could engage in more complex dialogs than the spoken one just illustrated as it guided an apprentice through an assembly task.[3] TDUS integrated the NOAH planning system with a natural language understanding system (having syntactic, semantic, and pragmatic components) to allow text-based conversations with the apprentice.

I'll use an example taken from a paper about TDUS to illustrate the role that the task structure plays in sentence understanding.[4] Consider the following sentences:

Speaker 1: Why did John take the pump apart?
Speaker 2: *He did it* to fix *it*.

Interpreting the referents of the italicized words in the second sentence is aided by referring to the task context established by the first sentence. "He" refers to John, "did it" refers to the disassembly task, and the second "it" refers to the pump. TDUS makes extensive use of the shifting "context" and goals of the dialog. As the developers of TDUS wrote,[5]

As a dialog progresses, the participants continually shift their focus of attention and thus form an evolving context against which utterances are produced and interpreted. A speaker provides a hearer with clues of what to look at and how to look at it – what to focus upon, how to focus upon it, and how wide or narrow the focusing should be. We have developed a representation for discourse focusing, procedures for using it in identifying objects referred to by noun phrases, and procedures for detecting and representing shifts in focusing.

(The words "utterance," "speaker," and "hearer" are not to be taken literally. TDUS processed text-based language, not spoken language. In NLP research, these words are often used in a generalized sense to refer to sentences, sentence generators, and sentence receivers, whatever the medium.)

Focus was the main interest of Barbara J. Grosz (1948– ; Fig. 18.3), who continued work on that topic and its role in NLP as a professor at Harvard University. Besides the mechanisms for dealing with contexts, goals, and focus, TDUS contained a grammar, called DIAGRAM,[6] for recognizing many of the syntactic structures of English, means for representing and reasoning about processes and goals, and a framework for describing how different types of knowledge interact as the dialog unfolds.

A demonstration of the CBC system, like the one I described a few paragraphs ago, was given at SRI on April 23, 1975, for J. C. R. Licklider [who had returned to head IPTO in 1973]. Recollecting impressions of his visit, Licklider later said[7]

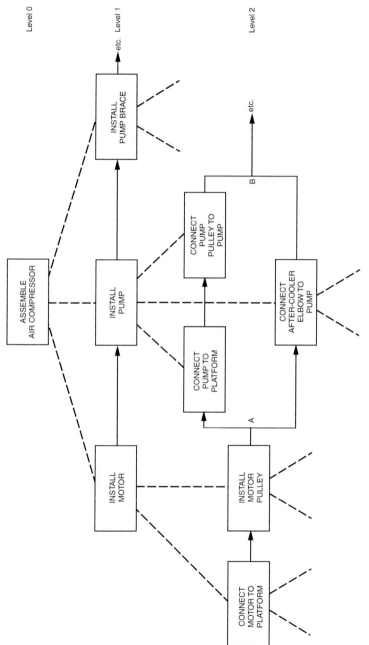

Figure 18.2. Part of a procedural net for assembling an air compressor. (Used with permission of SRI International.)

227

Figure 18.3. Barbara J. Grosz. (Photograph courtesy of photographer Tony Rinaldo.)

The second time I was in DARPA, there were very impressive AI systems dealing with maintenance of equipment. I remember SRI had a program that described how to take a pump apart and put it back together. That's not a terribly complicated device, but it was pretty impressive to see a computer that obviously understood all the parts of the pump and how they worked together.

Because of Licklider's encouragement, we were optimistic about continuing the CBC project and made plans for a system that would diagnose and give advice about repairing a military jeep engine. Unfortunately, one of DARPA IPTO's new program managers, Colonel David Russell, was not buying it. After visiting SRI a few days before Licklider's April 23 visit, Russell sent an e-mail to Licklider saying[8]

I must admit to considerable concern over the SRI program, particularly in light of the management pressures on the AI program. Looking at the projected program plan that Nils has been working on, I see a 2.2M dollar program over the next three years with the aim of developing an experimental CBC for a jeep. . . . I can't see how it can be defended as a near-term application . . .

While it may be difficult, I would suggest that you give serious thought to terminating the CBC program when it completes the air-compressor phase and redirect SRI to more Defense oriented applications or pass their work to NSF. I appreciate that this is heresy, but that is how I saw the situation.

I didn't directly discuss these comments with Nils although I did ask what he would do if the program were terminated. I may have formed a negative view based on an incorrect understanding of the program, and I didn't want to upset the SRI group without your views of the program.

Later that year, Russell replaced Licklider as Director of DARPA IPTO and terminated the CBC project. (Work on TDUS, however, continued under NSF support.) DARPA support for the SRI group was subsequently "redirected" to natural language interfaces to databases (which I'll describe later) and to "image

Figure 18.4. Bruce Buchanan (left) and Ted Shortliffe (right). (Photograph courtesy of Ed Feigenbaum.)

understanding" to aid photo interpreters. Some of us chose instead to seek non-DARPA support to work on computer-based consulting systems. Ongoing work at Stanford University on so-called expert systems encouraged us in that direction.

18.2 Expert Systems

18.2.1 MYCIN

Stanford's HEURISTIC DENDRAL project demonstrated the power of endowing computers with expert knowledge about chemistry and spectroscopy. Feigenbaum, Lederberg, and Buchanan, the senior members of the project, believed that a similar approach might work on a medical problem. In the early 1970s Buchanan began talking with Stanley Cohen, Chief of Clinical Pharmacology at Stanford's Medical School, about Cohen's computerized drug interaction warning system called MEDIPHOR. Around the same time, Edward (Ted) Shortliffe (1947– ; Fig. 18.4), a Stanford Medical School student, took a Stanford course on AI and also became an assistant on Cohen's project. Together, Shortliffe, Buchanan, and Cohen conceived the idea of building a computer program that would consult with physicians about bacterial infections and therapy. Shortliffe named the program MYCIN, a common suffix for antibacterial agents. Such a program would need to contain diagnostic and treatment knowledge of experts in infectious diseases.

The first question in developing MYCIN was how to represent expert knowledge. Shortliffe and Buchanan thought that something similar to the "IF–THEN rules" used in DENDRAL would be appropriate. When diagnosing what disease might be causing certain symptoms, as well as in prescribing therapy, physicians appear to be using a kind of IF–THEN reasoning: IF the symptoms are such-and-such, THEN the cause is likely to be so-and-so. The knowledge behind this sort of reasoning is based on experience with cases as well as on scientific knowledge about diseases. It was believed that the IF–THEN knowledge needed by the program could be obtained by interviewing the appropriate medical experts who already thought in those terms.

Interestingly, IF–THEN reasoning about medical matters has a long history. Summarizing part of a book by J. H. Breasted[9] about surgical knowledge contained in an ancient Egyptian papyrus, Robert H. Wilkins wrote "The Edwin Smith Surgical Papyrus, dating from the seventeenth century B.C., is one of the oldest of all known medical papyri."[10] (The papyrus was bought in a Luxor antique shop by Edwin Smith in 1882.) Wilkins goes on to mention several rules from the papyrus, one of which is the following:

Case Thirty

Title: Instructions concerning a sprain in a vertebra of his neck.

Examination: If thou examinest a man having a sprain in a vertebra of his neck, thou shouldst say to him: "look at thy two shoulders and thy breast." When he does so, the seeing possible to him is painful.

Diagnosis: Thou shouldst say concerning him: "One having a sprain in a vertebra of his neck. An ailment which I will treat."

Treatment: Thou shouldst bind it with fresh meat the first day. Now afterward thou shouldst treat [with] ywrw (and) honey every day until he recovers.

Two other experts who joined in the development of the nascent diagnostic and treatment system were Thomas Merigan, Chief of the Infectious Disease Division at Stanford, and Stanton Axline, a physician in that division. In their summary[11] of the history of the project, Buchanan and Shortliffe credit Axline with coming up with the name MYCIN for the program.

The team submitted a successful grant application to the National Institutes of Health in October of 1973. Shortliffe decided to combine his medical studies with work toward a Computer Science Ph.D. based on MYCIN. Since the version of LISP he wanted to use (BBN-LISP, soon to become INTERLISP) was not available at Stanford, he used the SRI AI group's PDP-10 computer.

The IF–THEN rules elicited from the medical experts usually were hedged with uncertainty. Buchanan and Shortliffe mention that "Cohen and Axline used words such as 'suggests' or 'lends credence to' in describing the effect of a set of observations on the corresponding conclusion. It seemed clear that we needed to handle probabilistic statements in our rules . . ."

After wrestling with various ways to use probabilities to qualify MYCIN's IF–THEN rules, Shortliffe finally decided on using the somewhat ad hoc notion of "certainty factors."[12]

Here, for example (in both its internal LISP form and its English translation), is one of MYCIN's rules:

```
RULE036
PREMISE: ($AND (SAME CNTXT GRAM GRAMNEG)
               (SAME CNTXTM MORPH ROD)
               (SAME CNTXT AIR ANAEROBIC))
ACTION: (CONCLUDE CNTXT IDENTITY BACTEROIDES TALLY 0.6)

IF: 1) The gram stain of the organism is gramneg, and
    2) The morphology of the organism is rod, and
    3) The aerobicity of the organism is anaerobic

THEN: There is suggestive evidence (0.6) that the identity
        of the organism is bacteroides
```

The 0.6 in this rule is meant to measure the expert's "degree of belief" in or "certainty" about the conclusion. Shortliffe thought that a degree of belief was not the same as a probability assessment because, among other things, he noted that the experts who provided Rule 036 did not necessarily think that the probability of the organism *not* being bacteroides would be 0.4. The original MYCIN system had 200 such rules. By 1978, it had almost 500.

MYCIN's rules were usually evoked in a backward-reasoning fashion. For example, a rule of the form "IF x1 and x2, THEN y" would be used if the system's overall goal was to conclude y. The use of this rule would lead to the use of rules whose "THEN" parts were either x1 or x2. At the end of a chain of rules, a physician user of the system (or a database) would be asked to supply information about the "IF" part. So, if MYCIN were trying to establish that the identity of an organism was bacteroides, RULE036 would be used and the physician (or database) would be asked if the gram stain of the organism is gramneg and so on.[13]

MYCIN was configured as a "consulting system." That is, it interacted with a physician user who supplied information about a specific patient. The use of rules and rule-chaining allowed the system to provide "explanations" for its reasoning. For example, after a query to the user evoked by Rule 036, if the user asked "Why did you ask whether the morphology of the organism is rod," the system would reply (in English) something like "because I am trying to determine whether the identity of the organism is bacteroides."

So, how did MYCIN do at its primary task of recommending therapy? Shortliffe and colleagues conducted several evaluations in which physicians were asked to compare MYCIN's recommendations with their own for several patients. Their major conclusion was that "Seventy percent of MYCIN's therapies were rated as acceptable by a majority of the evaluators." They also noted, by the way, that "75% is in fact better than the degree of agreement that could generally be achieved by Stanford faculty being assessed under the same criteria."[14]

One of MYCIN's innovations (as contrasted with DENDRAL, say) was that its reasoning process (using the rules) was quite separate from its medical knowledge

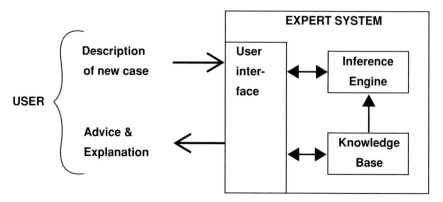

Figure 18.5. The structure of a MYCIN-style expert system.

(the rules themselves). Thus, it became common to divide the program into two parts, namely, the "inference engine" for applying rules and the "knowledge base" of rules. In principle, new rules could be added without having to change the inference engine. This division is shown in Fig. 18.5. This separation suggests that one could construct expert systems for other applications simply by replacing the medical knowledge with some other knowledge base without having to change the inference engine. William van Melle implemented a system he called EMYCIN ("E" for "empty") for doing just that.[15] A system designer along with experts in some field, X, could interact with EMYCIN to produce IF–THEN rules for field X. Using its built-in inference engine, EMYCIN could then use these rules to provide advice to a user of the system during a consultation. EMYCIN was used to build several different expert systems in fields as diverse as tax planning and mechanical structural analysis.

Researchers soon discovered that a minor variation of the certainty factors used by MYCIN and EMYCIN was equivalent to using probabilities instead. This linkage to probability theory implied consequences that neither MYCIN nor EMYCIN could escape. In particular, their reasoning was consistent with probability theory only under some rather restrictive assumptions about how rules were used. As Russell and Norvig point out, if these assumptions aren't met "certainty factors could yield disastrously incorrect degrees of belief through overcounting of evidence. As rule sets became larger, undesirable interactions between rules became more common, and practitioners found that the certainty factors of many other rules had to be 'tweaked' when more rules were added."[16] Modern methods use more sophisticated probabilistic techniques, as we shall see in a later chapter.

Even so, the success of MYCIN and the various EMYCIN programs led to the development of many more expert systems, some based on EMYCIN and some using their own specific approaches. As Allen Newell wrote in his introduction to a book by Buchanan and Shortliffe, "MYCIN is the original expert system that made it evident to all the rest of the world that a new niche had opened up. . . . MYCIN epitomized the new path that had been created. Thus, gathering together the full record of this system and the internal history of its development serves to record an important event in the history of AI."[17]

18.2.2 *PROSPECTOR*

Inspired by Shortliffe's work with MYCIN, some of us at SRI began investigating nonmedical applications of expert systems. One area we considered was "integrated pest management" in which knowledge about crops and their insect pests could be used to mitigate the effects of insect predation with minimal use of chemical insecticides. Although proposals were written and some interest was shown by scientists in the U.S. Department of Agriculture and at the Environmental Protection Agency, the idea was abandoned when the proposals went unfunded.

Peter Hart and Richard Duda eventually focused on systems for providing advice to explorationists about possible "hard-rock" mineral deposits.[18] Hart had some early discussions with John Harbaugh, a petroleum engineering professor at Stanford, and with Alan Campbell, one of Harbaugh's graduate students. (Alan Campbell was the son of the late Neal Campbell, a world-famous explorationist who had discovered what was possibly the largest lead–zinc deposit in the world. Alan spent much of his youth in mining camps.) Through Campbell, Hart and Duda met Charles Park, the former Dean of Stanford's School of Earth Sciences and an authority on hard-rock mineral deposits. Park helped Hart and Duda codify knowledge about lead–zinc deposits in the form of IF–THEN rules. Further work with Marco Einaudi, a professor in Stanford's Department of Economic Geology, led to additional rules and rule-organizing ideas. Ultimately the U.S. Geological Survey provided funding for the development of what became the PROSPECTOR expert system for consultation about mineral deposits.[19]

A large group of people participated in the design and writing of the PROSPECTOR program. Duda and Hart led the effort. I joined the project sometime after work had begun and after hearing from DARPA that the CBC project was not going to be continued. Other contributors were John Gaschnig (1950–1982), Kurt Konolige, René Reboh, John Reiter, Tore Risch, and Georgia Sutherland. MYCIN was a dominant influence on the technology being developed – "primarily through its use of rules to represent judgmental knowledge, and its inclusion of formal mechanisms for handling uncertainty."[20] Other important influences came from another medical diagnosis system, INTERNIST-1, which I'll describe shortly. These were its use of taxonomic information and its ability to handle volunteered (rather than only queried) information.

PROSPECTOR used rules to make inferences and to guide the consultation process. Two examples of these rules are

Rule 3: "Barite overlying sulfides suggests the possible presence of a massive sulfide deposit."

and

Rule 22: "Rocks with crystal-shaped cavities suggest the presence of sulfides."

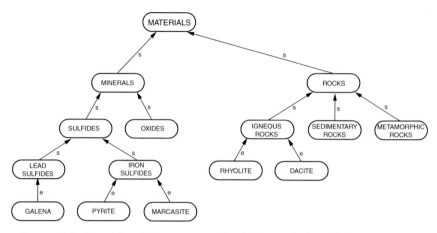

Figure 18.6. A partial geologic taxonomy. (Used with permission of SRI International.)

The rules were encoded as "partitioned semantic networks" – a format originated by Gary Hendrix (1948–) in his University of Texas Ph.D. thesis for use in representing knowledge needed by natural language processing systems.[21] Semantic networks were also used to represent the taxonomic knowledge used by PROSPECTOR. An example of such a network is shown in Fig. 18.6. The rules could be linked together in what was called an "inference network." A simplified example for reasoning about a Kuroko-type massive sulfide deposit is shown in Fig. 18.7. Note how Rule 22 helps to establish one of the premises for Rule 3. Note also that the taxonomy is used to infer the presence of sulfides when galena, sphalerite, or chalcopyrite is known to be present.

Inferences from rule premises to rule conclusions in the network depended on probabilities and Bayes's rule – not on ad hoc numbers such as "certainty factors." The geological experts were asked to quantify their uncertainty about a rule by giving the designers two numbers. One is the factor by which the odds favoring the conclusion would be increased if the premises were true. The other is the factor by which the odds favoring the conclusion would be decreased if the premises were false. Bayes's rule was used in association with these numbers to derive the probability of the conclusion given the probabilities of the premises.[22] PROSPECTOR's inference methods, even though they were an improvement over those of MYCIN, gave probabilistically valid results only for certain kinds of inference-net structures. As Glenn Shafer and Judea Pearl explain, "Probabilities could not simply tag along as numbers attached to IF–THEN rules. The results of probability calculations would be sensible only if these calculations followed principles from probability theory."[23] Modern expert systems use the more general framework of Bayesian networks, which will be described later.

The usual format for a PROSPECTOR consultation involved a session with a geologist interested in evaluating a certain site. The geologist might volunteer some information, which would evoke some of PROSPECTOR's rules. The system then calculated what additional information would be most effective in altering the

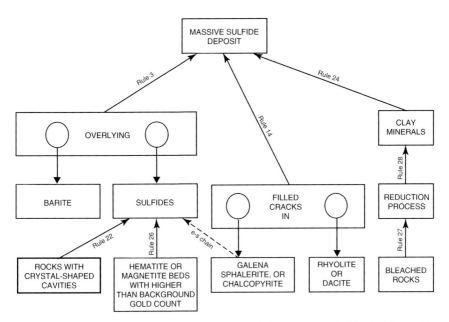

Figure 18.7. Simplified version of a PROSPECTOR inference network. (Used with permission of SRI International.)

probability of whatever it was the geologist wanted to find out. PROSPECTOR would then ask a question to elicit that information (and its probability). Throughout the process, the user could volunteer additional information at any time.

Because PROSPECTOR could use volunteered information, a run of the program need not be part of a question–and–answer consultation session. Instead, a user could input a whole set of data about "findings in the field" to PROSPECTOR, which would then draw its conclusions. These findings could be from a database or, perhaps more usefully, from a map that indicated contours of regions in which various kinds of minerals were found to be present. (Kurt Konolige of SRI joined the PROSPECTOR team around this time and wrote a program that allowed PROSPECTOR to use map data as an input.)

The most dramatic instance of PROSPECTOR's use of map data occurred when it successfully identified the location of a porphyry molybdenum deposit at Mount Tolman in the state of Washington.[24] Results of previous exploration of the Mount Tolman site were used to produce maps outlining important geological data relevant to potential molybdenum deposits. PROSPECTOR processed these maps using rules obtained primarily from Victor F. Hollister, an expert on porphyry molybdenum deposits, and Alan Campbell. The result of the processing was another map indicating the relative "favorability" of a mineral deposit. Computer displays of some of the input maps are shown in Fig. 18.8. I won't explain the geological details of what these maps depict, but they represent the kind of data thought to be important by experts such as Campbell and Hollister.

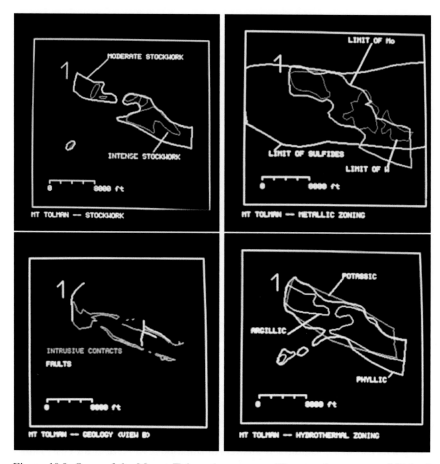

Figure 18.8. Some of the Mount Tolman input maps. (Photographs courtesy of Richard Duda.)

From data of this sort, PROSPECTOR produced favorability maps, one of which is shown in Fig. 18.9. The scale on the right of the map (when rendered in color) indicates favorability from +5 (highly favorable) through −5 (highly unfavorable). Based on previous extensive drilling in the largest of the favorable areas, a mining company had planned an open-pit mine there (outlined by the contour labeled "proposed pit").

One must be careful in evaluating this result. It is not the case that PROSPECTOR discovered an ore deposit in a site previously unexplored. As was pointed out in a letter to the editor of the journal *Artificial Intelligence*,[25]

A large mining company had already found a molybdenum ore body by drilling over 200 exploration holes in one region . . . and we knew that they intended to do further drilling for their own information.

. . .

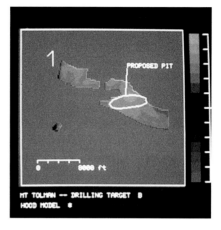

Figure 18.9. Favorability map. (Photograph courtesy of Richard Duda.)

[This further drilling] showed a remarkable congruence with PROSPECTOR's favorability map, including both verification of PROSPECTOR's prediction of a large, previously unknown region of ore-grade mineralization, and verification of PROSPECTOR's predictions for the barren areas.

. . .

Unfortunately, prolonged depressed economic conditions in the minerals industry have made this area unprofitable to mine . . . Thus, PROSPECTOR's success to date has been scientific rather than economic.

Readers interested in more details should see the *Science* article previously cited and a summarizing final report on the PROSPECTOR project.[26]

The computer code for PROSPECTOR was delivered to the U.S. Geological Survey where Richard B. McCammon developed a successor system he called PROSPECTOR II. Summarizing his system, McCammon wrote[27]

PROSPECTOR II, the successor to PROSPECTOR, was developed at the US Geological Survey. Currently, the knowledge base contains 86 deposit models and information on more than 140 mineral deposits. Within minutes, the geologist can enter the observed data for an area, select the types of deposit models to be evaluated, receive advice on those models that best match the observed data, and, for a particular model, find out which of the data can be explained, which of the data are unexplained, and which critical attributes of the model are not observed in the data.

18.2.3 *Other Expert Systems*

Several other expert systems followed the MYCIN and PROSPECTOR work. Some, like MYCIN, were for medical diagnosis and therapy.[28] Of these, I'll mention the INTERNIST-1 program by computer scientists Randolph A. Miller and Harry E. Pople and physician Jack D. Myers at the University of Pittsburgh and the CASNET (Causal-ASsociational NETwork) program by Casimir A. Kulikowski and Sholom M. Weiss of Rutgers University.

The INTERNIST-1 series of diagnosis programs contained expertise about internal medicine.[29] Part of this knowledge was represented in a kind of semantic network or taxonomy of disease states (called a *nosology* in medicine). In an article in the *New England Journal of Medicine*, Miller, Pople, and Myers state that the performance of INTERNIST-1 "on a series of 19 clinicopathological exercises (Case Records of the Massachusetts General Hospital) published in the Journal appeared qualitatively similar to that of the hospital clinicians but inferior to that of the case discussants." However, they concluded that "the present form of the program is not [yet] sufficiently reliable for clinical applications."[30] Later, much of the diagnostic knowledge assembled in INTERNIST-1 was repackaged in QMR (Quick Medical Reference), a diagnostic decision support system for internists.[31] (It has since been discontinued by its eventual purchaser First DataBank.)

CASNET also used networks.[32] In those, "inference rules" linked observations, patho–physiological states, diagnostic states, and treatment states. Their primary application was to the glaucomas, for which they had good physical models on which the inference rules could be based.

At Carnegie Mellon University, John McDermott (1942–) helped in the development of a rule-based system called XCON (for eXpert CONfigurer) to assist in the ordering and configuring of Digital Equipment Corporation's VAX computer systems. XCON grew out of an earlier system by McDermott called R1.[33] R1 and XCON were written in a special rule-processing language called OPS5, one of the OPS family of languages developed by Charles Forgy (1949–) at CMU.[34] (OPS is said to be an acronym for Official Production System.) The OPS languages used Forgy's "Rete" algorithm for efficiently stringing IF–THEN rules together.[35] XCON first went into use in 1980 in DEC's plant in Salem, New Hampshire.[36]

The problem with how to deal with uncertain information was avoided in XCON because it almost never encountered a configuration issue that it did not have enough certain knowledge to handle. By 1989, according to a paper about XCON and related configuration systems at DEC,[37] these systems had a total of about 17,500 rules. The paper went on to say that

. . . overall the net return to Digital is estimated to be in excess of $40 million per year.

The use of the configuration systems insures that complete, consistently configured systems are shipped to the customer. Incomplete orders do not get through the process. In addition, XCON generates configurations which optimize system performance, so customers consistently get the best view of our products. Before the configuration systems, we would often ship the same parts configured differently.

In addition to XCON and its DEC siblings, several expert systems were built and put in use by companies and research laboratories during the 1980s. In 1983, General Electric developed the Diesel Electric Locomotive Troubleshooting Aid (DELTA), a prototype system to assist railroad personnel in the maintenance of General Electric's diesel–electric locomotives. The developers stated that it "can diagnose multiple problems with the locomotive and can suggest repair procedures to maintenance personnel." It had 530 rules "partially representing the knowledge of a Senior Field Service Engineer."[38]

Another example is JETA (Jet Engine Troubleshooting Assistant), developed by engineers at the National Research Council in Canada. According to a paper about JETA, it "has been applied to troubleshoot the General Electric J85-CAN-15 jet engine that powers the CF–5 trainer fighters used by the Canadian Air Force."[39] Knowledge about jet engines and their possible faults and symptoms are encoded in frames. Rules are used solely for "specific control functions embedded in a frame and for asynchronous user input."

An expert system called CCH-ES for credit analysis was put in use at the Credit Clearing House (CCH) division of Dun & Bradstreet (D&B) in July 1989. It contained approximately 800 rules and could handle online transactions when CCH customers called in for service or when analysts wanted to review cases. Batch cases were run when there were updates in the relevant databases. According to a paper about the system, "Analyst agreement with CCH-ES continues to be at approximately 98.5 percent on an ongoing basis. . . . [It] has been a major success at D&B. It has provided CCH with an automated credit analyst expert system that can provide expert-level credit analysis decisions consistently and at a high-quality level. Customers have uniformly praised the system."[40]

More expert systems are described in the book *The Rise of the Expert Company*.[41] In an appendix to that book, Paul Harmon lists over 130 expert systems in use during the mid- to late 1980s, including

- *Grain Marketing Advisor* for helping farmers choose marketing or storage strategies for their grain crops,
- *ACE* for helping telephone operating companies reduce the incidence of phone cable failures,
- *IDEA* for helping technicians diagnose trouble situations in the Infotron IS4000 Local Area Network,
- *Diag 8100* for helping with the diagnosis of problems and failures in IBM 8100 computers at the Travelers Corporation,
- *Intelligent Peripheral Troubleshooter* for helping to troubleshoot Hewlett-Packard disk drives,
- *SNAP* for helping shoppers at Infomart (a Dallas computer store) assess their personal computer needs,
- *Pile Selection* for helping designers at the Kajima Construction Company select piling material to be used in the foundations of buildings,
- *ExperTAX* for helping to evaluate the application of new U.S. tax laws for clients of Coopers and Lybrand, and
- *Dipmeter Advisor* for helping in the analysis of geological formations encountered in oil-well drilling.

18.2.4 *Expert Companies*

New companies and divisions of established companies were started to develop and field these applications. The first of these was Teknowledge, organized by a group of Stanford faculty and researchers to market expert systems and to consult about expert systems. Teknowledge used EMYCIN as its basic technology. Another was Syntelligence, founded by Peter Hart and Richard Duda (along with some of the PROSPECTOR researchers) to market expert systems for insurance underwriting and loan credit analysis. At Syntelligence, expert systems were written in the

SYNTEL language, developed by René Reboh and Tore Risch and based on ideas from PROSPECTOR. After leaving CMU, Charles Forgy founded Production Systems Technologies in 1983 "to develop and market state of the art rule-based tools."[42] Among other companies formed during this period were Aion Corporation, Helix Expert System, Ltd., Exsys, Inc., Inference Corporation, and IntelliCorp.[43] Because it was not too difficult for clients who wanted expert systems to develop their own versions (which were able to run on low-cost workstations and personal computers), many of the expert systems companies ceased to exist, were bought by larger companies, or had to reorient their businesses to provide additional or related services.

After the flurry of excitement over expert systems died down a bit in the 1980s and 1990s, some developers concentrated on systems for acquiring and deploying "business rules." According to an organization called the Business Rules Group, a business rule is "a statement that defines or constrains some aspect of the business. It's intended to assert business structure, or to control or influence the behavior of the business."[44] For example, a business rule might state "when our widget inventory is below 200, notify widget production." Business rules take the form of IF–THEN statements, just like expert-system rules. In business applications, expert-system inference engines metamorphosed into business rule engines (BREs). They are used either to answer questions about business practices or to take actions such as placing orders or sending alerts.[45] Some of the people who had been involved in providing expert systems software switched to business-rule software. For example, in 2002, Charles Forgy founded RulesPower, Inc., whose business rules management systems (BRMSs) used later versions of the Rete algorithm. (In 2005, RulesPower sold some of its assets to Fair Isaac Corporation, an analytics and decision management technology company, which has since changed its name to FICO.)

Notes

1. See Nils J. Nilsson *et al.*, "Plan for a Computer-Based Consultant System," SRI AI Center, Technical Note 94, May 1974. (Available online at http://www.ai.sri.com/pubs/files/1298.pdf.) [224]

2. From Peter E. Hart, "Progress on a Computer Based Consultant," SRI AI Center Technical Note 99, p. 23, January 1975. (Available online at http://www.ai.sri.com/pubs/files/1389.pdf.) [224]

3. Ann E. Robinson, Douglas E. Appelt, Barbara J. Grosz, Gary G. Hendrix, and Jane J. Robinson, "Interpreting Natural-Language Utterances in Dialogs About Tasks," SRI AI Center Technical Note 210, March 15, 1980. (Available online at http://www.ai.sri.com/pubs/files/709.pdf.) [226]

4. *Ibid*, p. 11. [226]

5. *Ibid*, p. 11. [226]

6. Jane J. Robinson, "DIAGRAM," SRI AI Center Technical Note No. 205, 1980; available online as SRI AI Center Technical Note 205, February 1980, at http://www.ai.sri.com/pubs/files/712.pdf. [226]

7. J. C. R. Licklider, "The Early Years: Founding IPTO," in Thomas C. Bartee (ed.), *Expert Systems and Artificial Intelligence: Applications and Management*, p. 223, Indianapolis, IN: Howard W. Sams & Co., 1988. [226]

8. A copy of this e-mail is in my files. [228]

9. J. H. Breasted, *The Edwin Smith Surgical Papyrus*, two volumes, Chicago: University of Chicago Press, 1980. **[230]**

10. See http://www.neurosurgery.org/cybermuseum/pre20th/epapyrus.html for a copy of the Wilkins article. **[230]**

11. Bruce G. Buchanan and Edward H. Shortliffe (eds.), *Rule-Based Expert Systems: The MYCIN Experiments of the Stanford Heuristic Programming Project*, Reading, MA: Addison-Wesley, 1984. The book is now out of print but is available online at http://www.aaai.org/AITopics/pmwiki/pmwiki.php/AITopics/RuleBasedExpertSystems. Shortliffe's dissertation has been reprinted as a book: Edward H. Shortliffe, *Computer-Based Medical Consultations: MYCIN*, New York: Elsevier, 1976. **[230]**

12. Others too attempted to use ideas not strictly based on probability theory. Among these were Arthur Dempster and Glenn Shafer (see Glenn Shafer, *A Mathematical Theory of Evidence*, Princeton, NJ: Princeton University Press, 1976) and Lotfi Zadeh, who developed "fuzzy logic" (see, as just one of many sources, Lotfi A. Zadeh, "A Fuzzy-Algorithmic Approach to the Definition of Complex or Imprecise Concepts," *International Journal of Man-Machine Studies*, Vol. 8, pp. 249–291, 1976, available online at http://www-bisc.cs.berkeley.edu/ZadehFA-1976.pdf.) I'll mention these alternatives later in the book. **[230]**

13. For a full description of how MYCIN's rules were acquired and used see Bruce G. Buchanan and Edward H. Shortliffe, *op. cit.* **[231]**

14. Bruce G. Buchanan and Edward H. Shortliffe, *op. cit.*, Chapters 30 and 31. **[231]**

15. EMYCIN is described in Bruce G. Buchanan and Edward H. Shortliffe, *op. cit.*, Chapter 15. EMYCIN was the subject of van Melle's Ph.D. dissertation: William van Melle, "A Domain-Independent System That Aids in Constructing Knowledge-Based Consultation Programs," Stanford University Computer Science Department; see also Stanford Report Nos. STAN-CS-80-820 and HPP-80-22, 1980. **[232]**

16. Stuart Russell and Peter Norvig, *Artificial Intelligence: A Modern Approach*, second edition, p. 525, Upper Saddle River, NJ: Prentice Hall, 2003. **[232]**

17. Bruce G. Buchanan and Edward H. Shortliffe, *op. cit.* **[233]**

18. Economic geologists distinguish mineral deposits from ore deposits. An *ore* is a mineral that can be *profitably* extracted. Hard-rock minerals include copper, lead, zinc, and so on, but not hydrocarbons. **[233]**

19. PROSPECTOR was first described in Peter E. Hart, "Progress on a Computer-Based Consultant," *Proceedings of the International Joint Conference on Artificial Intelligence*, Vol. 2, pp. 831–841, 1975. **[233]**

20. Richard O. Duda *et al.*, "Semantic Network Representations in Rule-Based Inference Systems," in D. A. Waterman and Frederick Hayes-Roth (eds.), *Pattern-Directed Inference Systems*, Orlando, FL: Academic Press, Inc., 1978. Available online at http://www.ai.sri.com/pubs/files/751.pdf. **[233]**

21. Gary G. Hendrix, "Partitioned Networks for the Mathematical Modeling of Natural Language Semantics," Ph.D. thesis, University of Texas Computer Science Department, 1975. For a short paper, see Gary G. Hendrix, "Expanding the Utility of Semantic Networks Through Partitioning," *Proceedings of the Fourth International Conference on Artificial Intelligence*, pp. 115–121, 1975. This paper also appeared as SRI AI Center Technical Note 105 and is available online at http://www.ai.sri.com/pubs/files/1380.pdf. **[234]**

22. For a description of PROSPECTOR's inference methods see Richard O. Duda, Peter E. Hart, and Nils J. Nilsson, "Subjective Bayesian Methods for Rule-Based Inference Systems," in *Proceedings of the AFIPS National Computer Conference*, Vol. 45, pp. 1075–1082, 1976. Reprinted in G. Shafer and J. Pearl (eds.), *Readings in Uncertain Reasoning*,

pp. 274–281, San Francisco: Morgan Kaufmann Publishers, 1990. A version appears as SRI AI Center Technical Note 124 and is available online at http://www.ai.sri.com/pubs/files/755.pdf. **[234]**

23. Glenn Shafer and Judea Pearl (eds.), *Readings in Uncertain Reasoning*, San Francisco: Morgan Kaufmann Publishers, 1990. The book is no longer in print, but some of the chapters are available online at http://www.glennshafer.com/books/rur.html. **[234]**

24. Alan N. Campbell, Victor F. Hollister, Richard O. Duda, and Peter E. Hart, "Recognition of a Hidden Mineral Deposit by an Artificial Intelligence Program," *Science*, Vol. 217, No. 4563, pp. 927–929, September 3, 1982. **[235]**

25. Richard O. Duda, Peter E. Hart, and René Reboh, letter to the editor, *Artificial Intelligence*, Vol. 26, pp. 359–360, 1985. **[236]**

26. Richard O. Duda, "The PROSPECTOR System for Mineral Exploration," Final Report prepared for the Office of Resource Analysis, U.S. Geological Survey, Reston, VA 22090, April 1980. **[237]**

27. Richard B. McCammon, "PROSPECTOR II – An Expert System for Mineral Deposit Models," *International Journal of Rock Mechanics and Mining Sciences and Geomechanics Abstracts*, Vol. 33, No. 6, pp. 267A–267A(1), September 1996. See also Richard B. McCammon, "PROSPECTOR II," in H. J. Antonisse, J. W. Benoit, and B. G. Silverman (eds.), *Proceedings of the Annual AI Systems in Government Conference*, pp. 88–92, March 1989, Washington, DC. **[237]**

28. See Peter Szolovits (ed.), *Artificial Intelligence in Medicine*, Boulder, CO: Westview Press, 1982. Available online at http://groups.csail.mit.edu/medg/ftp/psz/AIM82/ch0.html. **[237]**

29. Harry E. Pople Jr., "Heuristic Methods for Imposing Structure on Ill-Structured Problems: The Structuring of Medical Diagnostics," Chapter 5 in Peter Szolovits (ed.), *Artificial Intelligence in Medicine*, Boulder, CO: Westview Press, 1982. Available online at http://groups.csail.mit.edu/medg/ftp/psz/AIM82/ch5.html. **[237]**

30. Randolph A. Miller *et al.*, "INTERNIST-1: An Experimental Computer-Based Diagnostic Consultant for General Internal Medicine," *New England Journal of Medicine*, Vol. 307, pp. 468–76, August 19, 1982. **[238]**

31. Randolph A. Miller *et al.*, "The INTERNIST-1/Quick Medical Reference Project – Status Report," *The Western Journal of Medicine*, Vol. 145, No. 6, pp. 816–822, 1986. Available online at http://www.pubmedcentral.nih.gov/picrender.fcgi?artid=1307155&blobtype=pdf. **[238]**

32. Casimir A. Kulikowski and Sholom M. Weiss, "Representation of Expert Knowledge for Consultation: The CASNET and EXPERT Projects," Chapter 2 in P. Szolovits (ed.), *Artificial Intelligence in Medicine*, Boulder, CO: Westview Press, 1982. Available online at http://groups.csail.mit.edu/medg/ftp/psz/AIM82/ch2.html. **[238]**

33. John McDermott, "R1: A Rule-Based Configurer of Computer Systems," *Artificial Intelligence*, Vol. 19, No. 1, pp. 39–88, 1980. **[238]**

34. Charles Forgy, "OPS5 User's Manual," Technical Report CMU-CS-81-135, Carnegie Mellon University, 1981. See also Lee Brownston *et al.*, *Programming Expert Systems in OPS5*, Reading, MA: Addison-Wesley, 1985. **[238]**

35. Charles Forgy, "Rete: A Fast Algorithm for the Many Pattern/Many Object Pattern Match Problem," *Artificial Intelligence*, Vol. 19, pp. 17–37, 1982. **[238]**

36. See http://cn.wikipedia.org/wiki/Xcon. **[238]**

37. Virginia E. Barker and Dennis E. O'Connor, "Expert Systems for Configuration at Digital: XCON and Beyond," *Communications of the ACM*, Vol. 32, No. 3, pp. 298–318, March 1989. **[238]**

38. Piero P. Bonissone and H. E. Johnson Jr., " DELTA: An Expert System for Diesel Electric Locomotive Repair," *Proceedings of the Joint Services Workshop on Artificial Intelligence in Maintenance*, Boulder, CO, October 4–6, 1983, AD-A145349, pp. 397–413, June 1984 (Defense Technical Information Center Accession Number ADA145349.) **[238]**

39. Phillippe L. Davidson *et al.*, "Intelligent Troubleshooting of Complex Machinery," *Proceedings of the Third International Conference on Industrial Engineering Applications of Artificial Intelligence Expert Systems*, pp. 16–22, Charleston, South Carolina, USA, July 16–18, 1990. See also M. Halasz *et al.*, "JETA: A Knowledge-Based Approach to Aircraft Gas Turbine Engine Maintenance," *Journal of Applied Intelligence*, Vol. 2, pp. 25–46, 1992. **[239]**

40. Roger Jambor *et al.*, "The Credit Clearing House Expert System," *IAAI-91 Proceedings*, pp. 255–269, 1991. **[239]**

41. Edward Feigenbaum, Pamela McCorduck, and H. Penny Nii, *The Rise of the Expert Company: How Visionary Companies Are Using Artificial Intelligence to Achieve Higher Productivity and Profits*, New York: Times Books, 1988. **[239]**

42. http://www.pst.com/. **[240]**

43. Harmon's appendix, just cited, lists several companies as does http://dmoz.org/Computers/Artificial_Intelligence/Companies/. **[240]**

44. From http://www.businessrulesgroup.org/defnbrg.shtml. **[240]**

45. I thank Paul Harmon, now Executive Editor of Business Process Trends (www.bptrends.com), for enlightening me about business rules. **[240]**

19

Understanding Queries and Signals

19.1 The Setting

Up until about the mid-1970s, DARPA managers were able to cushion the impact of the Mansfield Amendment (which required that Defense Department research be relevant to military needs) by describing computer research programs in a way that emphasized applications. Larry Roberts, the Director of DARPA's IPTO during the late 1960s and early 1970s, wrote[1]

The Mansfield Amendment created a particular problem during my stay at DARPA. It forced us to generate considerable paperwork and to have to defend things on a different basis. It made us have more development work compared to the research work in order to get a mix such that we could defend it. I don't think I had to drop a project in our group due to the Mansfield Amendment, however. We could always find a way to defend computer science...

The formal submissions to Congress for AI were written so that the possible impact was emphasized, not the theoretical considerations.

Cordell Green, working under Roberts at IPTO, wrote[2]

Generally speaking, anything that came along in the AI field that we thought looked good was supported...

One of my jobs was to defend the AI budget but that wasn't terribly difficult... all sorts of computer science is relevant because it will have a high impact on any large information-processing organization, and the Defense Department is certainly such an organization... all of this research should be kept alive because it had potential military relevance.

By the mid-1970s, however, the pressure to produce militarily useful systems became much more intense. DARPA, which had been generously supporting rather undirected basic AI research, started to focus instead on solving "pressing DoD problems." Although the director of DARPA's IPTO at the time, J. C. R. Licklider, was as sympathetic as ever to basic research in AI, DARPA's top management had entirely different attitudes. Licklider was having difficulties explaining his AI program to DARPA's "front office." The DARPA Director during the early 1970s, Stephen Lukasik, was (according to Licklider[3])

neither for nor against AI. He was for good management and he got the idea that maybe some of the AI stuff wasn't being very well managed.... [He] had a fixed idea that a proposal is not a proposal unless it's got milestones. I think that he believed that the more milestones, the better the proposal.... I think he was not developing a distaste for AI but a conviction that this is such an important field that the researchers have got to learn to live in a bigger, more rigid, more structured bureaucracy."

Figure 19.1. George Heilmeier. (Photograph courtesy of DARPA.)

Lukasik's view about how projects should be managed had a direct effect on DARPA-supported basic research in AI. For example, a "Quarterly Management Report" that I submitted in February 1975 describing progress on the SRI computer-based consultant caused Licklider to ask how the report might be recast to emphasize progress along certain paths in a "PERT Chart." "What I would like to have," he wrote me in a letter dated March 3, 1975, "is the PERT Chart – so that I can mark the accomplishments in red and see where you stand with respect to the overall pattern. . . . Do you have such a chart? If so, please send me a copy. If not, how about making one? It would really help us greatly here at ARPA."[4]

Of course, in basic research, although one can describe generally the problems one is trying to solve, one can't describe (ahead of time) what the solutions are going to be. In fact, as exploratory research progresses, new problems become apparent, so one can't even describe all the problems ahead of time. One can't make the kind of detailed plan for basic research that one can make for applying already developed technology to specific applications. Unfortunately, the management of DARPA was shifting from people who understood how to initiate and manage basic research to people who knew how to manage technology applications.

The shift toward shorter term, intensely managed research became more pro-nounced when George Heilmeier (Fig. 19.1) replaced Stephen Lukasik as DARPA Director in 1975. Heilmeier came from RCA, where he had headed the research group that invented the first liquid crystal display. Licklider later wrote that Heilmeier "wanted to understand AI in the way he understood liquid crystal displays . . ."[5]

One of the tasks that Heilmeier gave IPTO was to produce a "roadmap" (that is, a detailed plan) for its AI research program (and its other computer science programs too). This roadmap should summarize past accomplishments, indicate areas where existing technology could be applied to military problems, and show milestones along the way. This "guidance" from DARPA management caused great difficulties for Licklider, some of which were explained in an e-mail he sent to some leaders of

AI research in April of 1975. (I was among the recipients of his "Easter Message," e-mailed on April 2, 1975.) Here are some excerpts:

The purpose of this Easter note is to bring you up to date on a development in ARPA that concerns me greatly – and will, I think, also concern you. . . .

. . . the prevailing direction in ARPA is to do research within the specific contexts of military problems and not to do research that does not have a military 'buyer' ready to take it over as soon as the concept gets well formulated. . . .

[there are] strong pressures from the new Director, George Heilmeier, that IPTO 'redirect' the university AI efforts to work on problems that have real DoD validity . . .

. . . the situation is complicated by the fact that ARPA has been supporting basic research at a rather high level for more than ten years (has spent more than \$50 million on it), and it is natural for a new director, or even an old one, to ask, "What have we gotten out of it in terms of improvements in national defense?"

According to Licklider's Easter note, some of the things that Heilmeier thought IPTO could do for the Defense Department were the following:

- get computers to read Morse code in the presence of other code and noise,
- get computers to identify/detect key words in a stream of speech,
- solve DoD's "software problem,"
- make a real contribution to command and control, and
- do a good thing in sonar.

Even though one of the items on Heilmeier's list involved speech processing, one of the casualties of his tenure as Director of DARPA was the SUR Program. None of the systems that had been developed under the program could respond in real time, nor could they deal with large enough vocabularies. Heilmeier believed (probably with good reason) that speech understanding was still a basic research activity. Thus, he thought, it should be supported, say, by the National Science Foundation (NSF), and he rejected proposals for DARPA to continue it.

Unfortunately, most of the research areas that were on Licklider's own list (which was also mentioned in his Easter note) were not explicitly on Heilmeier's. (I can't resist mentioning one of the items on Licklider's list: "Develop a system that will guide not-sufficiently-trained maintenance men through the maintenance of complex equipment.") One of Heilmeier's items was sufficiently vague, however, to justify work both in NLP and in computer vision. That was "command and control," an activity that involves getting and presenting relevant information to commanders so that they can control military forces effectively.

DARPA program officers Floyd Hollister and Col. David Russell were able to persuade DARPA management that text-based, natural language access to large, distributed databases would be an important component of command and control systems. They argued that the technology for such access was sufficiently far along for it to be applied in what they called "command-and-control test-bed systems." After all, Bill Woods and colleagues at BBN had already demonstrated LUNAR, a natural language "front end" to databases about moon rocks. Several other researchers had also begun work on the problem of how to communicate with computers using

Figure 19.2. Gary Hendrix. (Photograph courtesy of Gary Hendrix.)

English or some other natural language. (For example, there were over forty papers on NLP presented at the Fifth IJCAI in 1977 at MIT, and the February 1977 issue of the ACM's *SIGART Newsletter* published 52 summaries of ongoing research on "Natural Language Interfaces.") In the next part of this chapter, I'll describe some of the accomplishments during this period on communicating with computers using natural language.

A second area of great importance in command and control was automating the analysis of aerial photos. Spotting targets of military interest in these photos, such as roads, bridges, and military equipment, typically required hours of effort by intelligence analysts. Because techniques being developed by researchers in computer vision might provide tools to help human analysts, DARPA had good reasons to continue funding computer vision research. In 1976, it began the "Image Understanding" (IU) program to develop the technology required for automatic and semi-automatic interpretation and analysis of military photographs and related images. Although initially conceived as a five-year program, it continued (with broader objectives) for well over twenty years. I'll summarize the image understanding work, along with other computer vision research, in a subsequent chapter.

Doing something about sonar was one of the items on Heilmeier's list. In fact, in his Easter note Licklider wrote "One of [Heilmeier's] main silver-bullet areas is underwater sound and sonar, and IPTO is in the process of 'buying in' on the HASP project (Ed Feigenbaum's AI approach)." I'll describe HASP and how DARPA "bought in" to the project toward the end of the chapter.

19.2 Natural Language Access to Computer Systems

19.2.1 LIFER

At SRI, Gary Hendrix (Fig. 19.2) had been developing a system called LIFER (an acronym for Language Interface Facility with Elliptical and Recursive Features), programmed in INTERLISP, for rapid development of natural language "front ends" to databases and other software. LIFER allowed a nontechnical user to specify a subset of a natural language (for example, English) for interacting with a database system or other software. A parser contained within LIFER could then translate sentences and requests in this language into appropriate interactions with the software. LIFER had mechanisms for handling elliptical (that is, incomplete) inputs, for correcting spelling errors, and for allowing novices to extend the language through the use of paraphrases.

An interesting feature of LIFER was that the language it could handle was defined in terms of "patterns," which used semantic concepts in the domain of application. One such pattern, for example, might be

WHAT IS THE <ATTRIBUTE> OF <PERSON>

where the words WHAT, IS, THE, and OF are actual words that might occur in an English query and <ATTRIBUTE> and <PERSON> are "wild cards" that could match any word in predefined sets. <ATTRIBUTE> might be defined to match words such as AGE, WEIGHT, HEIGHT, etc., and <PERSON> might match JOHN, SUSAN, TOM, etc. This pattern would then "recognize" a sentence such as

WHAT IS THE HEIGHT OF SUSAN

This method of defining a "grammar" is to be contrasted with the usual syntactic phrase-structure rules such as S <= NP VP. As I mentioned earlier, grammars based on concepts in the domain of application are called "semantic grammars."

LIFER used a simplified augmented transition network (like those I described in a previous chapter) to analyze an input sentence. Each pattern defined by the grammar corresponded to a possible "path" in the transition network. An input sentence was analyzed by attempting to match it with one of these paths, noting which specific instance of a wild card, such as <ATTRIBUTE>, was used in the match. Depending on the path taken and on the values of wild cards in the path, software was automatically created that was then used to make the appropriate database query or to carry out an appropriate command.[6] In 1982, Hendrix left SRI to form Symantec, a company that planned to develop and market a natural language question-answering system based on semantic grammars such as LIFER. [Perhaps natural language processing (or the intended market) was not quite ready, because Symantec was later reorganized to market computer security and anti-virus software.]

LIFER was used at SRI as the natural language component of a system called "LADDER" for accessing multiple, distributed databases.[7] LADDER (an acronym for Language Access to Distributed Data with Error Recovery) translated the English query into a hypothetical database query that assumed a very simple database organization. Using a system called IDA (an acronym for Intelligent Data Access), that hypothetical query was transformed into a series of actual database queries that took into account the actual organization of the database. It also took account of syntactic and semantic knowledge to attempt to produce very efficient queries and to detect any erroneous updates to the database content. (More research on systems similar to IDA was performed in a joint program between Stanford University and SRI, named KBMS, an acronym for Knowlege Based Management System, with support from DARPA.)

Consistent with DARPA's focus on military applications, LADDER was able to answer questions about naval ships using information about ship sizes, types, locations, and so on from various databases. Some sample interactions with an early

```
-What is the speed of the Kitty Hawk
PARSED!
((SPEED 35 KNOTS))

-Of the Ethan Allen
TRYING ELLIPSIS:  WHAT IS THE SPEED OF THE ETHAN ALLEN
((SPEED 30 KNOTS))

-Displacement
TRYING ELLIPSIS:  WHAT IS THE DISPLACEMENT OF THE ETHAN ALLEN
((STANDARD-DISPLACEMENT 6900 HUNDRED-TONS))

-length of the fastest Soviet sub
TRYING ELLIPSIS:  WHAT IS THE LENGTH OF THE FASTEST SOVIET SUB
((LENGTH 285 FEET / SPEED 30 KNOTS))

-Who onws the KIEV
     OWNS <==(assumed spelling error)
PARSED!
((COUNTRY USSR))

-who owns the JFK
TRYING ELLIPSIS:  ELLIPSIS HAS FAILED
THE PARSER DOES NOT EXPECT THE WORD "JFK" TO FOLLOW "WHO OWNS THE"
OPTIONS FOR NEXT WORD OR META-SYMBOL ARE:
<SHIP-NAME>

-Define JFK to be like Kennedy
PARSED!
  . {JFK is now a synonym for KENNEDY, which is a ship name}
  .
-REDO -2          {that is, parse WHO OWNS THE JFK}
PARSED!
((COUNTRY USA))

-? BUILT LAFAYETTE
TRYING ELLIPSIS:  ELLIPSIS HAS FAILED
  . {error message omitted}
  .
-Let "? built Lafayette" be a paraphrase of "who built the Lafayette"
PARSED!
  .
  .
-? built Lafayette
PARSED!
((BUILDER GENERAL.DYNAMICS))

-owns longest nuclear submarine
TRYING ELLIPSIS:  ? OWNS LONGEST NUCLEAR SUBMARINE
((COUNTRY USSR / LENGTH 426 FEET))
```

Figure 19.3. Sample interactions with LADDER. (Used with permission of SRI International.)

version of LADDER are shown in Fig. 19.3. Note the ability of the system to correct spelling errors, to deal with incomplete questions, and to accept paraphrases.[8]

19.2.2 CHAT-80

Between 1979 and 1982, Fernando Pereira (1952–) and David H. D. Warren (circa 1950–) developed a system called CHAT-80 at the University of Edinburgh as part of Pereira's Ph.D. dissertation there. CHAT-80 was able to answer rather complex questions, posed in English, about a database of geographical facts.

According to Pereira's dissertation,[9] work on CHAT-80 started as "an attempt to clarify and improve some previous NL work of Colmerauer." CHAT-80 was written in PROLOG, the logic-based programming language developed originally by Alain Colmerauer. In fact, the grammar used by CHAT-80 consisted of logical formulas stated in the PROLOG language. For example,

```
sentence(s(NP,VP), S0,S):- noun_phrase(NP, N, S0,S1),
verb_phrase(VP, N, S1,S)
```

is CHAT-80's way of stating that "there is a sentence between points S0 and S in a string (of words) if there is a noun phrase with number N (that is, singular or plural) between points S0 and S1, and a verb phrase with number N between points S1 and S." Grammars defined by PROLOG clauses of this kind are called *Definite Clause Grammars* (DCGs). Several clauses of this sort were used by CHAT-80 to parse English sentences. The actual parsing was done by the PROLOG program consisting of these clauses.

In CHAT-80, computation of the meaning (that is, the semantics) of an English query was guided by the syntactic structure of the query (as computed by the PROLOG program) and was expressed as a logical formula. This formula was then transformed into the individual queries of the database needed to answer the original question.[10] (For information about how to get a running version of CHAT-80, see http://www.cis.upenn.edu/~pereira/oldies.html.)

Here are a few examples (from Chapter 5 of Pereira's dissertation) of queries that CHAT-80 was able to answer:

```
Q: What is the capital of Upper Volta?
A: Ouagadougou
Q: Which country's capital is London?
A: united kingdom
Q: What is the ocean that borders African countries and that
   borders Asian countries?
A: indian ocean
Q: What are the capitals of the countries bordering the
   Baltic?
A: denmark:copenhagen; east germany:east berlin;
   finland:helsinki; poland:warsaw; soviet union:moscow;
   sweden:stockholm; west germany:bonn
Q: What is the total area of countries south of the Equator
   and not in Australasia?
A: 10,228 ksqmiles
Q: What are the continents no country in which contains more
   than two cities whose population exceeds 1 million?
A: africa, antarctica, australasia
Q: Which country bordering the Mediterranean borders a
   country that is bordered by a country whose population
   exceeds the population of India?
A: turkey
```

WORLDC

NAME	CONTINENT	CAPITAL	AREA	POP
Afghanistan	Asia	Kabul	260,000	17,450,000
Albania	Europe	Tirana	11,100	2,620,000
Algeria	Africa	Algiers	919,951	18,510,000

BCITY

NAME	COUNTRY	POP
Brussels	Belgium	1,050,787
Buenos Aires	Argentina	8,925,000
Canberra	Australia	210,600

CONT

NAME	HEMI	AREA	POP
Africa	S	11,500,000	41,200,000
Antarctica	S	5,000,000	500
Asia	N	16,990,000	2,366,000,000

PEAK

NAME	COUNTRY	HEIGHT	VOL
Anocagua	Argentina	23,080	N
Annapurna	Nepal	26,504	N
Chimborazo	Ecuador	20,702	Y

Figure 19.4. Files used in a TEAM database. (Used with permission of SRI International.)

Although these examples indicate rather impressive performance, CHAT-80s abilities were constrained by its limited vocabulary and grammar. These limitations are described in detail in Pereira's dissertation.

19.2.3 *Transportable Natural Language Query Systems*

As I have described it, CHAT-80 was implemented as a system for querying a database of geographical facts. However, since much of its design was not specific to geography, it could rather easily be modified to be able to deal with other databases. CHAT-80 was just one of several query systems that were "transportable" in the sense that they could be adapted to serve as natural language front ends to a variety of different databases. Other such systems were ASK developed at Caltech,[11] EUFID developed at SDC,[12] IRUS developed at BBN,[13] LDC-1 developed at Duke University,[14] NLP-DBAP developed at Bell Laboratories,[15] and TEAM developed at SRI.[16]

Since I know more about TEAM than I do about the others, I'll say a few things about it as representative of its class. TEAM (an acronym for Transportable English Database Access Medium) was supported by DARPA and was designed to acquire information about a database from a database administrator and to interpret and answer questions of the database that are posed in a subset of English appropriate for that database. TEAM, like many other transportable systems, was built so that the information needed to adapt it to a new database and its corresponding subject matter could be acquired from an expert on that database even though he or she might know nothing about natural language interfaces.

To illustrate the operation of TEAM, its designers used a database consisting of four "files" (or "relations") of geographic data. Partial versions of these files are shown in Fig. 19.4. I'll trace through some of the steps TEAM used to answer the query "Show each continent's highest peak."

TEAM used a subsystem called DIALOGIC[17] to convert the English query into a logical expression. Within DIALOGIC, a subsystem based on DIAMOND[18] performed syntactic analysis using the DIAGRAM grammar.[19] The highest scoring parse tree is shown in Fig. 19.5.

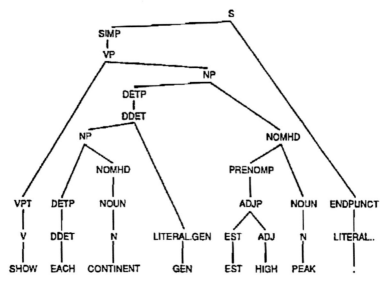

Figure 19.5. A parse tree for "Show each continent's highest peak." (Used with permission of SRI International.)

Based on this parse tree and knowledge about the concepts used in the database, a semantic analysis system converted the query into the following logical expression (here restated in an English-like form for better understandability):

```
FOR EVERY CONTINENT
    WHAT IS EACH PEAK
    SUCH THAT THE PEAK IS THE HIGHEST PEAK SUCH THAT
        THE CONTINENT IS CONTINENT OF THE PEAK?
```

TEAM then used its knowledge about the structure of the database and about how components of this logical expression are associated with relations in the database to generate the actual database query and construct an answer.

19.3 HASP/SIAP

In 1972, while Larry Roberts was still the Director of IPTO, he asked Ed Feigenbaum at Stanford to think about applying the AI ideas so successfully used in DENDRAL to the problem of identifying and tracking ships and submarines in the ocean using acoustic data from concealed hydrophone arrays.

Some of the acoustic data picked up by the hydrophone arrays come from rotating shafts and propellors and reciprocating machinery on board ships. Different ships emit sounds with their own characteristic identifying fundamental frequencies and harmonics. Human specialists who analyze this sort of surveillance data look at the sonogram displays of ocean sounds and, by matching sound spectra to stored references, attempt to identify and locate ships that might be present (if any). Making these decisions often requires using information not present in the signals themselves, information such as reports from other sensor arrays, intelligence reports, and general knowledge about the characteristics of ships and common sea lanes.

The analysis problem is complicated by several factors:[20]

The background noise from distant ships is mixed with storm-induced and biological noises. Sound paths to the arrays vary with diurnal and seasonal cycles. Arrival of sound energy over several paths may suddenly shift to no arrivals at all, or arrivals only of portions of vessel radiation. Sound from one source can appear to arrive from many directions at once. Characteristics of the receivers can also cause sound from different bearings to mix, appearing to come from a single location. Finally, the submarine targets of most interest are very quiet and secretive.

Supported by DARPA, work on this problem began in 1973 at Systems Control Technology, Inc. (SCI), a Palo Alto company with expertise in this area that could work on classified military projects. (SCI was later acquired by British Petroleum.) Feigenbaum, and his colleagues at SCI, soon realized that the "generate-and-test" strategy of DENDRAL would not work for the problem of ocean surveillance because there was no "legal move generator" that could produce candidate ship positions and their tracks given the surveillance data. However, noting that the overall analysis problem could be divided into levels similar to those used in the Blackboard architecture of HEARSAY-II (a system shown to be good at dealing with signals in noise), the team thought that something similar would work for their problem. The team developed a system called HASP (an acronym for Heuristic Adaptive Surveillance Program) based on the Blackboard model. Follow-on work that would process actual ocean data began at SCI with SIAP (an acronym for Surveillance Integration Automation Program) in 1976. I'll give a brief description of the HASP/SIAP system design and then summarize how it performed.

The top level of the Blackboard was a "situation board" – a symbolic model of the unfolding ocean situation, built and maintained by the program. It described all the ships hypothesized to be out there with a confidence level associated with each of them.

Just below the situation board level was a level containing the individual hypothesized vessels. Each vessel element had information about its class, location, current speed, course, and destination, each with a confidence weighting. Below the vessel level was a level containing hypothesized sound sources: engines, shafts, propellers and so on with their locations and confidence weightings. Spectral features abstracted from the acoustic data were at the lowest level.

The levels were linked by knowledge sources (KSs) that were capable of inferring that if certain elements were suspected to be present at one level then other elements could be inferred to be present at another level (or if they were already present at that level, their confidence could be adjusted). Just as in HEARSAY-II, the links could span multiple levels and make inferences upward, downward, or within a level. An inference caused by one KS might allow another KS to draw an additional inference, and so on in cascade, until all relevant information had been used. In this manner, new information could be assimilated and expectations concerning possible future events could be formulated.

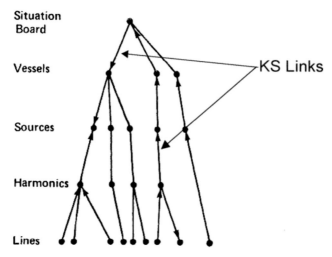

Figure 19.6. A network structure linking data at different levels. (Illustration from H. Penny Nii, Edward A. Feigenbaum, John J. Anton, and A. J. Rockmore, "Signal-to-Symbol Transformation: HASP/SIAP Case Study," *AI Magazine*, Vol. 3, No. 2, p. 26, Figure 2, © 1982, Association for the Advancement of Artificial Intelligence. Used with permission.)

One type of KS was composed of IF–THEN rules. (Other types were used also.) For example, here is an IF–THEN rule (translated into English for readability) that acted within the source level:

IF: a source was lost due to fade-out in the near-past, and a similar source started up in another frequency, and the locations of the two sources are relatively close,

THEN: they are the same source with confidence of 3.

HASP/SIAP had several kinds of knowledge sources, each represented in a way appropriate to the level(s) involved. Some KSs were based on information about the environment, such as common shipping lanes, location of arrays, and known maneuver areas. Others had information about vessels and vessel types, their speeds, component parts, acoustic characteristics, home bases, and so on. In addition to KSs dealing with knowledge appropriate to the various levels, there were "meta" KSs that had information about how to use other KSs.

The actions of the KSs in linking information at the various levels can be represented as a network, such as the one shown schematically in Fig. 19.6. At the end of an analysis session, when all KSs have had a chance to participate and the action dies down, the resulting network is called the "current best hypothesis" (CBH) about the current ocean situation. Here is a partial sample (translated into English) of how a CBH for a particular run of HASP/SIAP might be described:[21]

The class of Vessel-l, located in the vicinity of Latitude 37.3 and Longitude 123.1 at time day 2, 4 hours, 55 minutes, can be either Cherry, Iris, Tulip, or Poppy class. Two distinct acoustic sources, supported by respective harmonic sets, have been identified for Vessel-l. Source-l could be due to a shaft or propeller of vessel class Cherry or Poppy. Similar source possibilities exist for Source-5. These two sources were assimilated into Vessel-1 because of the possibility of a known mechanical ratio that exists between the two sources.

The MITRE Corporation conducted several experiments to compare the performance of HASP/SIAP against that of two expert sonar analysts. In one of these experiments, MITRE concluded that "HASP/SIAP has been shown to perform well on ocean derived data . . . For this restricted ocean scene, the program is not confused by extraneous data and gives results comparable to an expert analyst." In another experiment, it concluded that "HASP/SIAP understood the ocean scene more thoroughly than the second analyst and as well as the first analyst. . . . The program can work effectively with more than one acoustic array. SIAP classified an ocean scene over a three hour time period indicating the plausibility of SIAP efficacy in an evolving ocean situation." The third experiment led to the conclusions that "with the exception that the SIAP program obtained significantly more contacts than the human analysts, the descriptions of the ocean scene are very similar." Moreover, "SIAP can perform vessel classification in increasingly difficult ocean scenes without large increases in the use of computer resources."[22]

As mentioned earlier, the Blackboard model has been applied in several other areas as well. Examples include protein crystallographic analysis,[23] image understanding,[24] and dialog comprehension.[25] Interestingly, the Blackboard architecture has impacts beyond technology. Donald Norman, a cognitive psychologist, has said that HEARSAY-II has been a source of ideas for theoretical psychology and that it fulfills his "intuitions about the form of a general cognitive processing structure."[26] Also, as I'll mention in a later chapter, several models of the neocortex involve interacting layers resembling both the form and the mechanisms of Blackboard systems.

Notes

1. Lawrence G. Roberts, "Expanding AI Research and Founding Arpanet," in Thomas C. Bartee (ed.), *Expert Systems and Artificial Intelligence: Applications and Management*, pp. 229–230, Indianapolis, IN: Howard W. Sams & Co., 1988. **[244]**
2. C. Cordell Green, "AI During IPTO's Middle Years," *ibid*, pp. 238–240. **[244]**
3. J. C. R. Licklider, "The Early Years: Founding IPTO," *ibid*, pp. 225–226. **[244]**
4. Licklider letter in my file. **[245]**
5. J. C. R. Licklider, *op. cit.*, p. 226. **[245]**
6. For technical details about LIFER, see Gary G. Hendrix, "LIFER: A Natural Language Interface Facility," SRI AI Center Technical Note 135, December 1976 (available online at http://www.ai.sri.com/pubs/files/1414.pdf); Gary G. Hendrix, "The LIFER Manual: A Guide to Building Practical Natural Language Interfaces," SRI AI Center Technical Note 138, February 1977 (available online at http://www.ai.sri.com/pubs/files/749.pdf); and Gary G. Hendrix, "Human Engineering for Applied Natural Language Processing," *Proceedings of the 5th IJCAI*, pp. 183–191, 1977 (which also appeared as SRI AI Center Technical Note 139, available online at http://www.ai.sri.com/pubs/files/748 .pdf). **[248]**
7. Earl D. Sacerdoti, "Language Access to Distributed Data with Error Recovery," *Proceedings of the 5th IJCAI*, pp. 196–202, 1977, and reprinted as SRI AI Center Technical Note 140, February 1977 (available online at http://www.ai.sri.com/pubs/files/747.pdf); Earl D. Sacerdoti, "A LADDER User's Guide (Revised)," SRI AI Center Technical Note

163R, March 1980 (available online at http://www.ai.sri.com/pubs/files/735.pdf); and Gary G. Hendrix *et al.* "Developing a Natural Language Interface to Complex Data," *ACM Transactions on Database Systems,* Vol. 3, No. 2, pp. 105-147, June 1978 (available online as SRI AI Center Technical Note 152, August 1977, at http://www.ai.sri.com/pubs/files/741.pdf). **[248]**

8. For a more extensive interaction with a later version of LADDER, see Appendix A of Earl D. Sacerdoti, "A LADDER User's Guide (Revised)," SRI AI Center Technical Note 163R, March 1980. **[249]**

9. Fernando Pereira, "Logic for Natural Language Analysis," Ph.D. dissertation, University of Edinburgh, 1982. A slightly revised version of the dissertation was published as Technical Note 275 of the SRI AI Center and is available online at http://www.ai.sri.com/pubs/files/669.pdf. **[250]**

10. Readers interested in the details of these rather technical processes might refer to Pereira's dissertation or to David H. D. Warren and Fernando Pereira, "An Efficient Easily Adaptable System for Interpreting Natural Language Queries," *Computational Linguistics,* Vol. 8 , Nos. 3–4, pp. 110–122, July–December 1982. **[250]**

11. Bozena H. Thompson and Frederick B. Thompson, "Introducing ASK, A Simple Knowledgeable System," *Conference on Applied Natural Language Processing,* pp. 17–24, 1983. Available online at http://ucrel.lancs.ac.uk/acl/A/A83/A83-1003.pdf. **[251]**

12. Marjorie Templeton and John Burger, "Problems in Natural Language Interface to DBMS with Examples from EUFID," *Proceedings of the First Conference on Applied Natural Language Processing,* pp. 3–16, 1983. Available online at http://www.aclweb.org/anthology-new/A/A83/A83-1002.pdf. **[251]**

13. Madeleine Bates and Robert J. Bobrow, "A Transportable Natural Language Interface," *Proceedings of the 6th Annual International ACM SIGIR Conference on Research and Development in Information Retrieval,* pp. 81–86, 1983. **[251]**

14. Bruce Ballard, John C. Lusth, and Nancy L. Tinkham, "LDC-1: A Transportable, Knowledge-Based Natural Language Processor for Office Environments," *ACM Transactions on Information Systems,* Vol. 2, No. 1, pp. 1–25, January 1984. **[251]**

15. Jerrold M. Ginsparg, "A Robust Portable Natural Language Data Base Interface," *Conference on Applied Natural Language Processing,* pp. 25–30, 1983. Available online at http://ucrel.lancs.ac.uk/acl/A/A83/A83-1004.pdf. **[251]**

16. Barbara J. Grosz *et al.,* "TEAM: An Experiment in the Design of Transportable Natural-Language Interfaces," *Artificial Intelligence,* Vol. 32, No. 2, pp. 173–243, May 1987. Available online as SRI Technical Note 356R, October 20, 1986, at http://www.ai.sri.com/pubs/files/601.pdf. **[251]**

17. Barbara Grosz *et al.,* "DIALOGIC: A Core Natural-Language Processing System," *Proceedings of Ninth International Conference on Computational Linguistics,* pp. 95–100, 1982. Available online at http://www.aclweb.org/anthology-new/C/C82/C82-1015.pdf. **[251]**

18. DIAMOND was developed at SRI by William Paxton and is described in Ann E. Robinson *et al.,* "Interpreting Natural-Language Utterances in Dialogs About Tasks," AI Center Technical Note 210, SRI International, March 1980. Available online at http://www.ai.sri.com/pubs/files/709.pdf. **[251]**

19. Jane J. Robinson, "DIAGRAM: A Grammar for Dialogs," *Communications of the ACM,* Vol. 25, No. 1, pp. 27–47, January 1982. Available online as SRI AI Center Technical Note 205, February 1980, at http://www.ai.sri.com/pubs/files/712.pdf. **[251]**

20. H. Penny Nii, Edward A. Feigenbaum, John J. Anton, and A. J. Rockmore, "Signal-to-Symbol Transformation: HASP/SIAP Case Study," *AI Magazine,* Vol. 3, No. 2, pp. 23–35, 1982. **[253]**

21. From *ibid*, p. 28. **[254]**
22. From *ibid*, p. 34. **[255]**
23. Robert S. Engelmore and H. Penny Nii, "A Knowledge-Based System for the Interpretation of Protein X-Ray Crystallographic Data," Stanford Computer Science Department Technical Report CS-TR-77-589, 1977; available online at ftp://reports.stanford.edu/pub/cstr/reports/cs/tr/77/589/CS-TR-77-589.pdf. **[255]**
24. A. R. Hanson and E. M. Riseman, "VISIONS: A Computer System for Interpreting Scenes," in A. Hanson and E. Riseman (eds.), *Computer Vision Systems*, pp. 303–333, New York: Academic Press, 1978. **[255]**
25. W. C. Mann, "Design for Dialogue Comprehension," in *Proceedings of the 17th Annual Meeting of the Association of Computational Linguistics*, pp. 83–84, La Jolla, CA, August 1979; available online at http://ucrel.lancs.ac.uk/acl/P/P79/P79-1020.pdf. **[255]**
26. Donald A. Norman, "Copycat Science or Does the Mind Really Work by Table Lookup?," in R. Cole (ed.), *Perception and Production of Fluent Speech*, Chapter 12, Hillsdale, NJ: Lawrence Erlbaum Associates, Inc., 1980. **[255]**

20

Progress in Computer Vision

B EGINNING AROUND 1970 COMPUTER VISION RESEARCH GREW INTO A HIGHLY developed subspecialty of AI, joining other specialized areas such as natural language processing, robotics, knowledge representation, and reasoning (to name just a few of them). In this chapter, I'll describe some of the important advances in computer vision during this period. Some of these were made in pursuit of specific applications in several fields such as aerial reconnaissance, cartography, robotics, medicine, document analysis, and surveillance.[1]

20.1 Beyond Line-Finding

In an earlier chapter, I described some filtering techniques for enhancing image quality and for extracting edges and lines in images. But much more can be done to extract properties of a scene using specific information about the conditions under which images are obtained and general information about the properties of objects likely to be in the scene.

20.1.1 *Shape from Shading*

In what has been called a "back-to-basics" movement, researchers began investigating how information about the physics and geometry of light reflection from surfaces could be used to reveal three-dimensional properties of a scene from a single two-dimensional image. A leader in this study was Berthold K. P. Horn (1943– ; Fig. 20.1). His MIT Ph.D. dissertation derived mathematical methods for determining the shape of an object from its shading.[2] Just as humans perceive an appropriately shaded image of a circle as a sphere, a computer vision system can be made to do so also. Making it do so, using information about the reflective properties of surfaces and the geometry of the imaging process, is what Horn did.

The basic idea of Horn's technique can be explained by referring to Fig. 20.2 in which an infinitesimal piece of surface receives illumination from a light source at an angle equal to i relative to the direction that points perpendicularly away from the surface piece. Suppose a light sensor (such as a TV camera), at an angle g relative to the direction of the light source and at an angle e relative to the direction of the surface, gathers the light reflected from the surface. The amount of light gathered from this surface patch depends on these three angles, the amount of illumination, and the reflectance properties of the surface. (Horn assumed what we would call a

Figure 20.1. Berthold Horn (left) and a shaded circle (right). (Photograph courtesy of Berthold Horn.)

"matte" surface.) Because the amount of light gathered does vary in this manner, the image appears "shaded." Under certain circumstances, and with quite a bit of mathematical manipulation, the direction of the surface can be calculated if the other quantities are known. Then, by knowing the direction for many, many infinitesimal pieces of surface, the overall shape of the surface can be calculated (under the assumption that the surface is relatively smooth with no abrupt discontinuities).

Horn is now a professor of computer science and electrical engineering at MIT and continues to work on several topics related to computer vision. His thesis elicited a flurry of activity in the area of "shape from shading."[3] Several people extended the idea of shape from shading to attempt to calculate shape based on things other than shading, such as from multiple images (stereo), motion, texture, and contour. And, as we shall see in the next few pages, important work was done in extracting more than just the shape of objects.

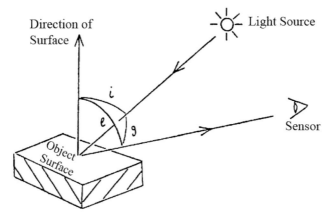

Figure 20.2. Light incident on and reflected by a small piece of a surface. (Illustration used with permission of Berthold Horn.)

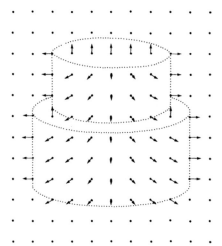

Figure 20.3. A $2\frac{1}{2}$-D sketch. (From David Marr and H. K. Nishihara, "Representation and Recognition of the Spatial Organization of Three-Dimensional Shapes," *Proceedings of the Royal Society of London*, Series B, Biological Sciences, Vol. 200, No. 1140, p. 274, February 23, 1978.)

20.1.2 *The $2\frac{1}{2}$-D Sketch*

Even though a viewer sees only a two-dimensional image of a three-dimensional scene, David Marr (augmenting Horn's ideas) observed that, nevertheless, a viewer is able to infer (and thus perceive) from image shading and other depth cues *some* of the scene's three-dimensional attributes, such as surface shapes, shapes occluding other shapes, abrupt changes between smooth surfaces, and other depth information. Marr called the representation of these attributes a "$2\frac{1}{2}$-D sketch" (because it was not *fully* three dimensional). According to Marr's theory of vision (described in his book[4]), the next step of visual processing, after producing the primal sketch (see p. 133) of blobs and edges, is to produce this $2\frac{1}{2}$-D sketch. An example sketch is shown in Fig. 20.3 in which arrows pointing perpendicularly away from surfaces are superimposed on the primal sketch of an image from which they are inferred.

Finally, according to Marr, the information in the $2\frac{1}{2}$-D sketch, along with stored information about object shapes, would be used to locate specific objects in the image and thus produce a 3-D model of the scene. I'll describe what he had to say about that process shortly.

20.1.3 *Intrinsic Images*

Two researchers at SRI, Jay Martin Tenenbaum (1943– ; Fig. 20.4) and Harry Barrow (recently relocated from Edinburgh), developed some image-processing techniques quite similar to those used in producing the $2\frac{1}{2}$-D sketch.[5] They noted that the intensity value at each pixel of an image resulted from a tangled combination of several factors, including properties of the ambient illumination and reflective and geometric properties of objects in the scene. They thought that these factors could be untangled to recover important three-dimensional information about the scene.

Barrow and Tenenbaum proposed that each of these factors (all of which influenced intensity) could be represented by imaginary images that they called "intrinsic images." These images were to consist of a grid of "pixels" overlaying a projection

Figure 20.4. Jay Martin Tenenbaum (left) and Harry Barrow (right). (Photographs courtesy of J. Martin Tenenbaum and of Harry Barrow.)

of the scene and in registration with the intensity image. One intrinsic image, for example, was an illumination image. It consisted of pixels whose values were the amounts of illumination falling on the pixels of the projected scene. These values, of course, were not known, but Barrow and Tenenbaum proposed that they could be estimated from the intensity image and from the other intrinsic images.

As examples, I show a set of such intrinsic images in Fig. 20.5. The actual image of intensity values is shown at the top. The known value of a pixel in that image depends on the unknown values of pixels in the intrinsic images below. In fact, the values of the pixels in all of the images, intrinsic and actual, are interdependent. The arrows in the figure reflect that fact. (There should also be some arrows going up.) Based on the values of pixels in some of the images, the values of others can be computed by using known physical relationships, constraints among the images, and other reasonable assumptions. These values, in turn, allow the computation of others. In essence, these computations "propagate" pixel values throughout the set of intrinsic images (much like how levels in the Blackboard architecture affect other levels). As Barrow and Tenenbaum later summarized their method, "We envisaged this recovery process as a set of interacting parallel local computations, more like solving a system of simultaneous equations by relaxation than like a feed forward sequence of stages."[6] Barrow and Tenenbaum also used some of their ideas about intrinsic images to work on the problem of interpreting line drawings as three-dimensional surfaces.[7]

Barrow and Tenenbaum intended their work to be useful not only in computer vision but also as a potential model of "precognitive" vision processes in humans. However, in a 1993 "retrospective" about their work they wrote[8]

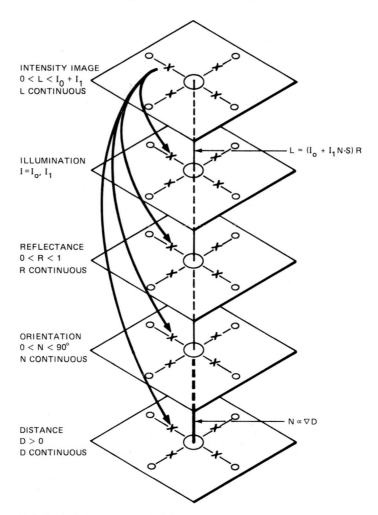

Figure 20.5. Intrinsic images. (Used with permission of Harry Barrow and Jay M. Tenenbaum.)

Despite the maturity of computational vision and the rapid developments in neural systems, we still have a long way to go before we can come close to our goal of understanding visual perception. To do so we will need to draw upon what we have learned in many fields, including neuroscience, neural networks, experimental psychology and computational vision.

20.2 Finding Objects in Scenes

20.2.1 *Reasoning about Scenes*

Even before the development of shape-from-shading and other methods for recovering depth information from scenes, a number of researchers had worked on methods for finding objects in scenes. I described many of these techniques in Section 9.3.

During the early 1970s, Thomas Garvey completed a Stanford Ph.D. thesis on a system for locating objects, such as desks, chairs, and wastebaskets, in images of office scenes.[9] As Garvey wrote in his summary,

The system uses information about the appearances of objects, about their interrelationships, and about available sensors to produce a plan for locating specified objects in images of room scenes.

In related work, Barrow and Tenenbaum developed a system, called MSYS, for reasoning about scenes "in which knowledge sources compete and cooperate until a consistent explanation of the scene emerges by consensus."[10] MSYS analyzed images of office scenes and attempted to find the most likely interpretation for the regions in an image (desk top, back of chair, floor, doorway, and so on) given a number of candidate interpretations and their probabilities. Knowing relationships between regions (such as "chair backs are usually adjacent to chair seats"), MSYS tried to find the most likely overall set of region interpretations.

An example of a scene considered by MSYS is shown in Fig. 20.6. Some of the regions in the scene have been detected and labeled with possible interpretations.

As Barrow and Tenenbaum wrote, MSYS's reasoning might proceed as follows:

Regions PIC, WBSKT, and CBACK cannot be WALL or DOOR, because their brightnesses are much less than that along the top edge of the image vertically above them, which violates [knowledge about the brightness of walls and doors]. Consequently, region PIC must be the PICTURE, WBSKT must be WASTEBASKET, and CBACK must be CHAIRBACK.

Region LWALL and RWALL must then be WALL, since they are adjacent to region PIC, and DOOR cannot be adjacent to PICTURE.

Region DR cannot be WALL because all regions labeled WALL are required to have the same brightness. Therefore, region DR must be DOOR.

20.2.2 *Using Templates and Models*

Much of the early work on object recognition was based on using object "templates" that could be matched against images. Martin A. Fischler and Robert A. Elschlager elaborated this idea by using "stretchable templates" that permitted more powerful matching techniques. They used these to find objects such as faces or particular terrain features in photographs containing such objects.[11] The process depended on having a general representation for the object being sought and then a process for matching that representation against the photograph. Their representations were based on breaking an object down into a number of primitive parts and "specifying an allowable range of spatial relations which these 'primitive parts' must satisfy for the object to be present." For the object to be present in a picture, "it is required that [the] primitives occur (or at least that some significant subset of them occurs), and also that they occur within a certain spatial relationship one to the other . . . " As Fischler and Elschlager pointed out, it is usually the case that determining whether or not some of the parts occur depends on whether or not the whole object occurs,

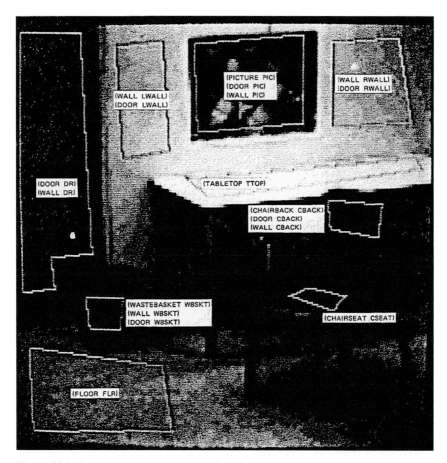

Figure 20.6. An MSYS scene with some regions detected and labeled. (Illustration used with permission of SRI International.)

and vice versa. The main contribution of their paper was the development of a dynamic-programming-style method for dealing with this circularity.

Earlier I had described David Marr's work on processes for producing a primal sketch and a $2\frac{1}{2}$-D sketch. These were the first two stages in Marr's theory of vision. He argued that these stages could uncover important shape information without specific knowledge of the shapes of objects likely to be in a scene. He had written:[12]

Most early visual processes extract information about the visible surfaces directly, without particular regard to whether they happen to be part of a horse, or a man, or a tree.... As for the question of what additional knowledge should be brought to bear, general knowledge must be enough – general knowledge embedded in the early visual processes as general constraints, together with the geometrical consequences of the fact that the surfaces co-exist in three-dimensional space.

Specific knowledge about shapes, he argued, should be utilized in a third stage. It is this stage that uses three-dimensional models of objects. He proposed using a

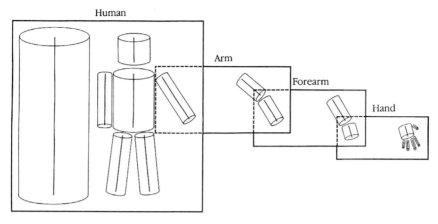

Figure 20.7. An example of one of Marr's 3-D model hierarchies. (From David Marr, *Vision*, San Francisco: W. H. Freeman and Co., p. 306, 1982.)

hierarchy of models in which a gross model is decomposed into subparts and these into subsubparts and so on. For example, the shape of a human might be modeled as in Fig. 20.7. Each box corresponds to a 3-D model and its submodel. On the left side of the box is an axis-oriented model; on the right side is how that model is represented as submodels. (Directions of the axes can be adjusted to fit matching parts of the image.)

In this third stage, comparing models of this sort with shape information and other 3-D information contained in the $2\frac{1}{2}$-D sketch helps to identify and locate objects in a scene. For Marr, vision was "the *process* of discovering from images what is present in the world and where it is."[13]

Marr was not the first to suggest the use of cylinders as models of parts of objects. In a 1971 IEEE conference paper, Thomas O. Binford (1936–) introduced the idea of "generalized cylinders" (sometimes called "generalized cones").[14] A later paper defined them as follows: "A generalized cone is defined by a planar cross section, a space curve spine, and a sweeping rule. It represents the volume swept out by the cross section [not necessarily a circular one] as it is translated along [an axis called a spine], held at some constant angle to the spine, and transformed according to the sweeping rule."[15]

Binford had several Stanford Ph.D. students who used models to help identify objects in scenes. Of these I might mention Gerald J. Agin,[16] Ramakant Nevatia,[17] and Rodney A. Brooks (1954–),[18] all of whom contributed to what came to be called "model-based vision." (Brooks later became a professor at MIT, where he worked on other topics. His subsequent work will be discussed later.)

Brooks's ACRONYM system[19] used generalized cones to model several different kinds of objects. ACRONYM used these models to help identify and locate objects in images. Some examples of the kinds of generalized cones that can be used as building blocks of models and model objects are shown in Fig. 20.8.

Other views regarding what vision is all about competed with those of Marr and others who were attempting to use vision to reconstruct entire scenes. Some,

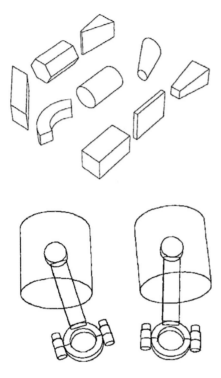

Figure 20.8. Primitive generalized cones and piston models constructed from generalized cones. (From Rodney A. Brooks, "Symbolic Reasoning among 3-D Models and 2-D Images," *Artificial Intelligence*, Vol. 17, Nos. 1–3, pp. 285–348, 1981.)

especially those involved in robotics, claimed that the purpose of vision was to perceive just what was required to guide action. Many of the vision routines in Shakey were embedded in its action programs. Professor Yiannis Aloimonos at the University of Maryland is one of the researchers advocating this "purposive" or "interactive" approach. He claims that the goal of vision is action. When vision is "considered in conjunction with action, it becomes easier." He goes on to explain that "the descriptions of space-time that the system needs to derive are not general purpose, but are purposive. This means that these descriptions are good for restricted sets of tasks, such as tasks related to navigation, manipulation and recognition."[20] In the neuroscience community, to which Marr wanted to make a contribution, there were Patricia S. Churchland, V. S. Ramachandran, and Terrence J. Sejnowski, who later wrote "What is vision for? Is a perfect internal recreation of the three-dimensional world really necessary? Biological and computational answers to these questions lead to a conception of vision quite different from pure vision [as advocated by Marr]. Interactive vision . . . includes vision with other sensory systems as partners in helping to guide actions."[21]

In any case, models still play an important role in computer vision. (However, one prominent vision researcher told me that the "residue of model-based vision is close to zero,"[22] and another told me that "most current robotic systems use vision hacks" instead of general-purpose, science-based scene-analysis methods.[23])

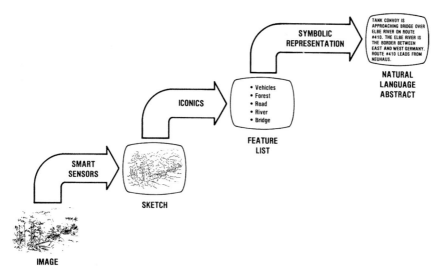

Figure 20.9. An illustration of IU goals. (Illustration used with permission of SAIC.)

20.3 DARPA's Image Understanding Program

Much of the computer vision work in the United States was being funded by DARPA, and there were concerns among vision researchers (as always) about continuing support. Tenenbaum recalls attending a DARPA meeting in 1974 where the future of computer vision research was being discussed. The program officer monitoring DARPA-supported vision work, Air Force Major David L. Carlstrom, was at the meeting and was interested in pulling together the various efforts in the field. Because DARPA had been supporting work in this area for some years, Carlstrom needed a new name that would indicate that DARPA was starting something new. Tenenbaum told me that he recommended to Carlstrom that the new initiative be called "the image understanding program."[24] (Recall that there was already an ongoing DARPA-supported effort in speech understanding, so the phrase sounded "DARPA-friendly.")

In 1976, DARPA launched its Image Understanding (IU) program. It grew to be a major effort composed of the leading research laboratories doing work in this area as well as "teams" pairing a university with a company. The individual labs participating were those at MIT, Stanford, University of Rochester, SRI, and Honeywell. The university/industry teams were USC–Hughes Research Laboratories, University of Maryland–Westinghouse, Inc., Purdue University–Honeywell, Inc., and CMU–Control Data Corporation.

Regular workshops were held to report progress. The proceedings of one held in April 1977 stated the goals of the program: "The Image Understanding Program is planned to be a five year research effort to develop the technology required for automatic and semiautomatic interpretation and analysis of military photographs and related images."[25] DARPA's ultimate goal for the IU program was well captured by the illustration on the cover of that proceedings, shown in Fig. 20.9.

As the diagram implies, military commanders would like computer vision systems to be able to analyze a photograph and to produce a written description of its important components and their relationships.

Some of the computer vision research that I have already described, such as work on the $2\frac{1}{2}$-D sketch, intrinsic images, generalized cylinders, and ACRONYM, was supported by the IU Program. But there was always some tension between DARPA's goals and those of people doing computer vision research. DARPA wanted the program to produce "field-able" systems. J. C. R. Licklider emphasized this point at a preliminary IU workshop in March 1975:[26]

At the end of the five year period the technology developed must be in a state in which it can be utilized by the DoD components to solve their specific problems without requiring a significant research effort to figure our how to apply the technology to the specific problems. For this reason, the program must result in a demonstration at the end of the five year period that an important DoD problem has been solved.

Air Force Major Larry Druffel at DARPA assumed leadership of the IU program in 1978. In November 1978, he advised "The prudent approach is to consolidate those techniques which are sufficiently mature to transfer to DoD agencies."[27] By 1979, the program's goals had expanded to include cartography and mapping. A "memorandum of understanding" (MOU) between DARPA and the Defense Mapping Agency (DMA) was concluded to support automatic mapping efforts through the development of a DARPA/DMA "testbed." In November 1979, Druffel wrote[28]

Plans are progressing for a demonstration system to evaluate the maturity of IU technology by automating mapping, charting, and geodesy functions. While focussing on specific cartographic photointerpretation functions, the system should offer the entire image exploitation community an opportunity to assess the future application of Image Understanding methodologies to their specific problem.

The "five-year" program did not end in 1981. It continued under the DARPA leadership of Navy Commander Ron Ohlander, Air Force Lt. Col. Robert L. Simpson Jr., and others until approximately 2001. In 1985 Simpson summarized some of its accomplishments:[29]

Originally conceived as a five year program in 1975 by Lt. Col. David Carlstrom, the first several years of IU established the strong base of low-level vision techniques and knowledge-based subsystems that began to differentiate computer vision from what is usually called "image processing." In the late 1970s and early 1980s, under the direction of Lt. Col. Larry Druffel, the program saw the development of model-based vision systems such as ACRONYM and demonstration of IU techniques in more meaningful concept demonstrations such as the DARPA/DMA image understanding testbed. These demonstrations and their potential for future military use warranted the continuation of the IU program beyond its initial five year lifespan. Under Cmd. Ron Ohlander, IU technology continued to mature to the point that the DARPA Strategic Computing Program could justify a major application, the autonomous land vehicle.

As Ohlander said, the IU program was extended beyond its projected five-year lifetime. It is said that even as early as 1984, DARPA had spent over $4 million on this effort.[30] One potential application was computer vision for robot-controlled military vehicles – a component of DARPA's "Strategic Computing" program. I'll describe that application and others in more detail in later chapters.

As a growing subspecialty of artificial intelligence, papers on computer vision began to appear in new journals devoted to the subject, including *Computer Vision and Image Understanding* and *IEEE Transactions on Pattern Analysis and Machine Intelligence*. The field's textbooks around this time included *Pattern Classification and Scene Analysis*[31] and two books titled *Computer Vision*.[32]

Notes

1. For an extensive list of computer vision applications see the CVonline Web site at http://homepages.inf.ed.ac.uk/rbf/CVonline/applic.htm. **[258]**
2. Berthold K. P. Horn, "Shape from Shading: A Method for Obtaining the Shape of a Smooth Opaque Object from One View," MIT Department of Electrical Engineering Ph.D. thesis, MIT Artificial Intelligence Laboratory Technical Report 232, November 1970; available online at http://people.csail.mit.edu/bkph/AIM/AITR-232-OCR-OPT.pdf. In his thesis, Horn credits Thomas Rindfleisch's 1966 work on using image brightness in studies of lunar topography. **[258]**
3. For a modern discussion of the problem, see, for example, Emmanuel Prados and Olivier Faugeras, "Shape from Shading," in N. Paragios, Y. Chen, and O. Faugeras (eds.), *Handbook of Mathematical Models in Computer Vision*, pp. 375–388, New York: Springer-Verlag, 2006; available online at http://perception.inrialpes.fr/Publications/2006/PF06a/chapter-prados-faugeras.pdf. **[259]**
4. David Marr, *Vision: A Computational Investigation into the Human Representation and Processing of Visual Information*, San Francisco: W. H. Freeman and Co., 1982. **[260]**
5. Harry G. Barrow and Jay Martin Tenenbaum, "Recovering Intrinsic Scene Characteristics from Images," in A. Hanson and E. Riseman (eds.), *Computer Vision Systems*, pp. 3–26, New York: Academic Press, 1978. Available online at http://web.mit.edu/cocosci/Papers/Barrow-Tenenbaum78.pdf and at http://www.ai.sri.com/pubs/files/737.pdf. **[260]**
6. Harry G. Barrow and Jay Martin Tenenbaum, "Retrospective on 'Interpreting Line Drawings as Three-Dimensional Surfaces,'" *Artificial Intelligence*, Vol. 59, Nos. 1–2, pp. 71–80, 1993. **[261]**
7. Harry G. Barrow and Jay Martin Tenenbaum, "Interpreting Line Drawings as Three-Dimensional Surfaces," *Artificial Intelligence*, Vol. 17, pp. 75–116, 1981. Available online at http://web.mit.edu/cocosci/Papers/Barrow-Tenenbaum81.pdf. **[261]**
8. Harry G. Barrow and Jay Martin Tenenbaum, "Retrospective on 'Interpreting Line Drawings as Three-Dimensional Surfaces,'" *Artificial Intelligence*, Vol. 59, Nos. 1–2, pp. 71–80, 1993. **[261]**
9. Thomas D. Garvey, "Perceptual Strategies for Purposive Vision," Stanford University Ph.D. thesis, published as SRI International AI Center Technical Note 117, September 1976. Abstract available online at http://www.ai.sri.com/pub_list/759. **[263]**
10. Harry G. Barrow and J. Martin Tenenbaum, "MSYS: A System for Reasoning about Scenes," SRI International AI Center Technical Note 121, April 1976. Available online at http://www.ai.sri.com/pubs/files/757.pdf. **[263]**
11. Martin A. Fischler and Robert A. Elschlager, "The Representation and Matching of Pictorial Structures," *IEEE Transactions on Computers*, Vol. C-22, No. 1, pp. 67–92, January 1973. **[263]**
12. David Marr, *op. cit.*, pp. 272–4. **[264]**
13. David Marr, *op. cit.*, pp. 23–60. **[265]**

14. Thomas O. Binford, "Visual Perception by Computer," *Proceedings of the IEEE Conference on Systems and Control*, Miami FL, December 1971. **[265]**
15. Rodney A. Brooks, "Symbolic Reasoning among 3-D Models and 2-D Images," *Artificial Intelligence*, Vol. 17, Nos. 1–3, pp. 285–348, 1981. **[265]**
16. Gerald J. Agin, "Representation and Description of Curved Objects," Stanford University Ph.D. thesis, published as Stanford Artificial Intelligence Project Memo AIM-173, October 1972. See also Gerald J. Agin and Thomas O. Binford, "Computer Descriptions of Curved Objects," *Proceedings of the Third International Joint Conference on Artificial Intelligence*, pp. 629–640, August 1973; later published as Gerald J. Agin and Thomas O. Binford, "Computer Descriptions of Curved Objects," *IEEE Transactions on Computers*, Vol. 25, No. 4, April 1976. **[265]**
17. Ramakant Nevatia, "Structured Descriptions of Complex Curved Objects for Recognition and Visual Memory," Stanford University Department of Electrical Engineering Ph.D. thesis, published as Stanford Artificial Intelligence Laboratory Memo AIM-250, October 1974. **[265]**
18. Rodney A. Brooks, "Symbolic Reasoning among 3-D Models and 2-D Images," Stanford University Computer Science Department Ph.D. thesis, 1981, published as Stanford CS Department Report STAN-CS-81-861. Also published as Rodney A. Brooks, *op. cit.*. **[265]**
19. The system was first reported in Rodney A. Brooks, Russell Greiner, and Thomas O. Binford, "The ACRONYM Model-Based Vision System," *Proceedings of the Sixth International Joint Conference on Artificial Intelligence*, pp. 105–113, Tokyo, 1979. A later revised version was reported in Brooks's *Artificial Intelligence* paper just cited. **[265]**
20. From his Web page at http://www.cfar.umd.edu/ yiannis/. **[266]**
21. Patricia S. Churchland, V. S. Ramachandran, and Terrence J. Sejnowski, "A Critique of Pure Vision," in Christof Koch and Joel L. Davis (eds.), *Large-Scale Neuronal Theories of the Brain*, pp. 23–65, Cambridge, MA: MIT Press, 1994. Available online at http://philosophy.ucsd.edu/faculty/pschurchland/papers/kochdavis94critiqueofpurevision.pdf. **[266]**
22. Martin A. Fischler, private communication, August 1, 2007. **[266]**
23. Jay Martin Tenenbaum, private communication, July 31, 2007. **[266]**
24. Private communication, July 31, 2007. **[267]**
25. Lee S. Bauman (ed.), *Proceedings: Image Understanding Workshop*, Science Applications, Inc., Report No. SAI-78-549-WA, April 1977. **[267]**
26. Quoted in the Foreword of the *Proceedings: Image Understanding Workshop*, published by Science Applications, Inc., May 1978. **[268]**
27. Quoted in the Foreword of the *Proceedings: Image Understanding Workshop*, published by Science Applications, Inc., November 1978. **[268]**
28. Quoted in the Foreword of the *Proceedings: Image Understanding Workshop*, published by Science Applications, Inc., November 1979. **[268]**
29. Quoted in the Foreword of the *Proceedings: Image Understanding Workshop*, published by Science Applications International Corporation, December 1985. **[268]**
30. Alex Roland with Philip Shiman, *Strategic Computing: DARPA and the Quest for Machine Intelligence*, p. 220, Cambridge, MA: MIT Press, 2002. **[268]**
31. Richard O. Duda and Peter E. Hart, *Pattern Classification and Scene Analysis*, New York: John Wiley and Sons, Inc., 1973. **[269]**
32. Michael Brady, *Computer Vision*, Amsterdam: North-Holland Publishing Co., 1981, and Dana H. Ballard and C. M. Brown, *Computer Vision*, New York: Prentice Hall, Inc., 1982. **[269]**

21

Boomtimes

E VEN THOUGH THE MANSFIELD AMENDMENT AND THE LIGHTHILL REPORT CAUSED difficulties for basic AI research during the 1970s, the promise of important applications sustained overall funding levels from both government and industry. Excitement, especially about expert systems, reached a peak during the mid-1980s.

I think of the decade of roughly 1975–1985 as "boomtimes" for AI. Even though the boom was followed by a period of retrenchment, its accomplishments were many and important. It saw the founding in 1980 of the American Association for Artificial Intelligence (AAAI – now called the Association for the Advancement of Artificial Intelligence), with annual conferences, workshops, and symposia. (Figure 21.1 shows a scene from one of the many trade shows during this era.) Several other national and regional AI organizations were also formed. The Arpanet, which had its beginnings at a few research sites in the late 1960s, gradually evolved into the Internet, linking computers worldwide.

Various versions of the LISP programming language coalesced into INTERLISP, which continued as the predominant language for both AI research and applications (although PROLOG was a popular competitor in Europe, Canada, and Japan). Researchers and students at MIT designed work-station-style computers, called Lisp machines, that ran LISP programs efficiently. Lisp Machines, Inc., and Symbolics were two companies that built and sold these machines. They enjoyed initial success but gradually lost out to other providers of workstations.[1]

Many other AI companies joined the expert systems companies and the Lisp machine companies. For example, in 1978 Earl Sacerdoti and Charles Rosen founded Machine Intelligence Company to market robot vision systems. In 1984, Cuthbert Hurd (1911–1996), who had earlier helped IBM develop its first computer, and David Warren founded Quintus, Inc., to market PROLOG systems. In 1984, Fritz Kunze, a graduate student at UC Berkeley, founded Franz, Inc., to market FranzLISP, a version of the LISP programming language.[2] Lavish exhibits at trade shows associated with AI conferences charged the whole field with excitement. Membership in the AAAI rose from around 5,000 shortly after the society's founding to a peak of 16,421 in 1987. (AAAI membership has since leveled off, after the boom, back to around 5,000.) Most of these new members – curious about what AI could do for them – came from industry and government agencies. Tutorials about various AI topics at both AAAI and IJCAI conferences were very well attended by people from industry wanting to learn about this newly important field.

During the early 1980s, my colleagues in several departments at SRI, especially those working on Defense Department projects, were eager to get help from the SRI

Figure 21.1. Scene from one of the AAAI trade shows during the 1980s. (Photograph from Bruce B. Buchanan, "Some Recollections about the Early Days of AAAI," *AI Magazine*, Vol. 26, No. 4, p. 14, © 2005 Association for the Advancement of Artificial Intelligence. Used with permission.)

AI Center – of which I was the director at the time. Mainly, I thought, they wanted us to "sprinkle a little AI" on their proposed projects to make them more enticing to government sponsors.

Reporting on this increasing interest in 1984, the science writer George Johnson wrote[3]

"We've built a better brain," exclaimed a brochure for [an expert system called] TIMM, The Intelligent Machine Model: "Expert systems reduce waiting time, staffing requirements and bottlenecks caused by the limited availability of experts. Also, expert systems don't get sick, resign, or take early retirement." Other companies, such as IBM, Xerox, Texas Instruments, and Digital Equipment Corporation, were more conservative in their pronouncements. But the amplified voices of their salesmen, demonstrating various wares [in the 1984 AAAI exhibit hall], sounded at times like carnival barkers, or prophets proclaiming a new age.

The boom continued with Japan's "Fifth Generation Computer Systems" project. That project in turn helped DARPA justify its "Strategic Computing Initiative." It also helped to provoke the formation of similar research efforts in Europe (such as the ALVEY Project in the United Kingdom and the European ESPRIT programme) as well as the formation of American industrial consortia for furthering advances in computer hardware. Assessments of some of AI's difficulties and achievements, compared to some of its promises, led to the end of the boom in the late 1980s – causing what some called an "AI winter." I'll be describing all of these topics in subsequent chapters.

Notes

1. By the way, the "iwhois" Web site (http://www.iwhois.com/oldest/) lists Symbolics as having the oldest registered ".com" domain name (registered on March 15, 1985.) **[271]**
2. See http://www.franz.com/about/company.history.lhtml. **[271]**
3. George Johnson, "Thinking about Thinking," *APF Reporter*, Vol. 8, No. 1, 1984. Available online at http://www.aliciapatterson.org/APF0801/Johnson/Johnson.html. **[272]**

Part V

"New-Generation" Projects

22

The Japanese Create a Stir

22.1 The Fifth-Generation Computer Systems Project

In 1982, Japan's Ministry of International Trade and Industry (MITI) launched a joint government and industry project to develop what they called "Fifth Generation Computer Systems" (FGCS). Its goal was to produce computers that could perform AI-style inferences from large data and knowledge bases and communicate with humans using natural language. As one of the reports about the project put it, "These systems are expected to have advanced capabilities of judgement based on inference and knowledge-base functions, and capabilities of flexible interaction through an intelligent interface function."[1]

The phrase "Fifth Generation" was meant to emphasize dramatic progress beyond previous "generations" of computer technology. The *first generation*, developed during and after World War II, used vacuum tubes. Around 1959, transistors replaced vacuum tubes – giving rise to the *second generation* – although the transistors, like the vacuum tubes before them, were still connected to each other and to other circuit components using copper wires. During the 1960s, transistors and other components were fabricated on single silicon wafer "chips," and the several chips comprising a computer were connected together by wires. Computers using this so-called small-scale integration (SSI) technology comprised the *third generation*. In the late 1970s, entire microprocessors could be put on a single chip using "very large-scale integration" (VLSI) technology – the *fourth generation*. The Japanese *fifth generation*, besides its sophisticated software, was to involve many parallel processors using "ultra large-scale integration" (ULSI).

MITI planned to develop a prototype machine, in the form of what computer scientists were beginning to call a "workstation," which was to consist of several processors running in parallel and accessing multiple data and knowledge bases. PROLOG, the computer programming language based on logic, was to be the "machine language" for the system because the Japanese thought it would be well suited for natural language processing, expert reasoning, and the other AI applications they had in mind. Execution of a PROLOG statement involved logical inference, so the machine's performance was to be measured in logical inferences per second (LIPS). In the early 1980s, computers were capable of performing around 100,000 LIPS. The Japanese thought they could speed that up by 1,000 times and more. Later in the project, because of difficulties of adapting PROLOG to run concurrently on many processors, a new logic-based language, GHC (for Guarded Horn Clauses), was developed that could run on multiple processing units.

Figure 22.1. Kazuhiro Fuchi (left) and Koichi Furukawa (right). (Fuchi photograph courtesy of Tohru Koyama. Furukawa photograph courtesy of Koichi Furukawa.)

For work on FGCS, MITI set up a special institute called the "Institute for New Generation Computer Technology" (ICOT). Its Research Center, headed by Mr. Kazuhiro Fuchi (1936–2006; Fig. 22.1), was to carry out the basic research needed to develop a prototype system. According to its first-year progress report,[2] the "Research Center started with forty top-level researchers from the Electrotechnical Laboratories (ETL), Nippon Telephone and Telegraph Public Corporation (NTT), and eight computer manufacturers." The project had a ten-year plan: three years of initial research, four years of building intermediate subsystems, and a final three years to complete the prototype. In 1993, the project was extended for two years to disseminate FGCS technology.

Koichi Furukawa (1942– ; Fig. 22.1), a Japanese computer scientist, was influential in ICOT's decision to use PROLOG as the base language for their fifth-generation machine. Furukawa had spent a year at SRI during the 1970s, where he learned about PROLOG from Harry Barrow and others. Furukawa was impressed with the language and brought Alain Colmerauer's interpreter for it (written in FORTRAN) back to Japan with him. He later joined ICOT, eventually becoming a Deputy Director. (He is now an emeritus professor at Keio University.)

The architecture of the planned fifth-generation system is illustrated in Fig. 22.2. Various hardware modules for dealing with the knowledge base, inference, and interface functions were to be implemented using advanced chip technology. The hardware would be controlled with corresponding software modules, and interaction with the system would be through speech, natural language, and pictures.

According to a set of slides by Mr. Shunichi Uchida summarizing the FGCS project,[3] its total ten-year budget was ¥54.2 billion or approximately (at the 1990 exchange rate) $380 million.

During this time, the project made advances in parallel processing, in computer architecture, and in developing various AI systems. Several American and European

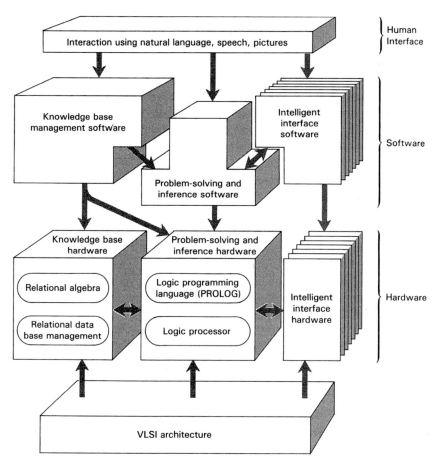

Figure 22.2. Fifth-generation system architecture. (Illustration used with permission of Edward Feigenbaum.)

visitors (especially PROLOG experts) participated in the project as ICOT visitors. Indeed, the Japanese invited international participation in the project. International conferences were held in Tokyo in 1984, 1988, and 1992.[4]

ICOT built a number of "parallel inference machines" (PIMs). The largest of these, named PIM/p, had 512 processing units.[5] (See Fig. 22.3.) Several AI systems were developed to run on these machines. Among these were MGTP (an acronym for Model Generation Theorem Prover), a parallel theorem prover;[6] MENDELS ZONE, a system for automatic program generation;[7] and HELIC-II, a legal reasoning expert system.[8]

Many observers think that most of the results of the FGCS project are now of historical interest only. The software developed did not find notable applications. Improvements in the speed and power of commercial workstations (and even of personal computers) made these superior to the PIMs. Taking full advantage of

Figure 22.3. The PIM/p parallel computer system. (Photograph from http://www.icot.or
.jp/ARCHIVE/Museum/MACHINE/pim-spec-E.html.)

the benefits of parallel processing proved difficult except for special problems susceptible to that style of computation. The development of graphical user interfaces
(GUIs) during the late 1980s and 1990s provided acceptable methods for human–
computer interaction – reducing (at least for a time) the need for AI-dependent
natural language and speech understanding systems. One legacy of the project
is the journal *New Generation Computing*, of which Koichi Furukawa was once
editor-in-chief. A "Museum" Web page for the FGCS project is maintained at
http://www.icot.or.jp/ARCHIVE/HomePage-E.html. The page contains links to
several ICOT publications, software, and other information.

A 1993 article, with contributions from several knowledgeable people, reflected
about the project.[9] Evan Tick, one of the contributors who had spent time at ICOT,
had this to say:[10]

. . . I highly respect the contribution made by the FGCS project in the academic development
of the field of symbolic processing, notably implementation and theory in logic programming,
constraint and concurrent languages, and deductive and object-oriented databases. In my
specific area of parallel logic programming languages, architectures, and implementations,
ICOT made major contributions, but perhaps the mixed schedule of advanced technology
transfer and basic research was ill advised.

This basic research also led to a strong set of successful applications, in fields as diverse as
theorem proving and biological computation. In a wider scope, the project was a success
in terms of the research it engendered in similar international projects, such as ALVEY,
ECRC, ESPRIT, INRIA, and MCC. These organizations learned from one another, and

their academic competitiveness in basic research pushed them to achieve a broader range of successes. In this sense, the computer science community is very much indebted to the "fifth-generation" effort.

Separately from what might or might not have been accomplished during the project, announcements about it in 1980 and 1981 provoked similar projects in the United States and in Europe. News about the project was spread by an early document titled "Preliminary Report on a Fifth Generation of Computers," which was circulated among a few computer science researchers in the fall of 1980. Also, an international conference to announce the FGCS project was held in Tokyo in October of 1981.[11]

22.2 Some Impacts of the Japanese Project

22.2.1 *The Microelectronics and Computer Technology Corporation*

The announcements by MITI of plans for a fifth-generation computer system and the formation of ICOT caused alarm in the United States and Europe. The American computer industry, all too aware of growing Japanese dominance in consumer electronics and in manufacturing, worried that its current world leadership in computer technology might be eroded.

William Norris, the founder of the Control Data Corporation, organized a meeting of computer industry executives in Orlando, Florida, in February 1982 to discuss the creation of a research and development consortium. Its goal would be to develop technologies that the member companies could ultimately use in their products. This meeting led in late 1982 and early 1983 to the formation of the nonprofit Microelectronics and Computer Technology Corporation (MCC) in Austin, Texas. Admiral Bobby Ray Inman, a former Director of the National Security Agency and a Deputy Director of the Central Intelligence Agency, was chosen to be its first President, Chairman, and Chief Executive Officer. Among the early joiners of the consortium were the Digital Equipment Corporation, Harris, Control Data, Sperry-Univac, RCA, NCR, Honeywell, National Semiconductor, Advanced Micro Devices, and Motorola. These were later joined by several others, including Microsoft, Boeing, GE, Lockheed, Martin Marietta, Westinghouse, 3M, Rockwell, and Kodak.

The annual budget was planned to be between $50 and $100 million – depending on the number of member companies contributing funds and research personnel. At its beginning, MCC focused on four major research areas, namely, advanced computer architectures, software technology, microelectronics packaging, and computer-aided design of VLSI circuitry. AI research was to be carried out (under the eventual direction of Woodrow Bledsoe) as part of architecture research.

Although the member companies did make use of some MCC-sponsored innovations, MCC itself began to decline after the departure of Inman in 1987. By that time, FGCS was perceived as less of a threat, and many of the member companies were having their own financial difficulties. Also, the Internet and the explosive growth and power of personal computers began to eclipse what was going on at MCC. The number of employees fell from its peak of about 400 in 1985 to 58 in June 2000, when the board voted to dissolve the consortium.[12]

22.2.2 *The Alvey Program*

In March 1982, the British government set up a committee "to advise on the scope for a collaborative research programme in information technology (IT) and to make recommendations." It was chaired by Mr. John Alvey, a senior director of British Telecommunications. In its report, issued later that year and titled "A Programme for Advanced Information Technology," the committee noted that the Japanese FGCS project was seen "as a major competitive threat" and that anticipated responses to it by the United States "would create an equal if not greater degree of competition for the UK industry."[13] The report recommended "a five-year programme to mobilise the UK's technical strengths in IT, through a Government-backed collaborative effort between industry, the academic sector and other research organisations. The goal [was to develop] a strong UK capability in the core enabling technologies, essential to Britain's future competitiveness in the world IT market." The four major technical areas identified for support were "Software Engineering, Man Machine Interfaces (MMI), Intelligent Knowledge Based Systems (IKBS) and Very Large Scale Integration (VLSI)." The recommended budget was $350 million, with the government contributing two-thirds of the cost and industry the rest.

In 1983, the UK Government accepted the committee's report and initiated the "Alvey Programme" to carry out the committee's recommendations. A new Directorate, headed by Brian Oakley, Secretary of the Science and Engineering Research Council (SERC), was set up in the Department of Trade and Industry (DTI) to coordinate the program. Sponsorship and funds were provided by DTI, the Ministry of Defence (MoD), SERC, and industry. Among its other accomplishments, the Alvey program helped revitalize AI research in Britain. According to Oakley, "If the Lighthill Report of the early 1970s was paradise lost for the AI community, the Alvey Report of the early 1980s was paradise regained."[14]

The program reached a peak level of funding of around $45 million in 1987 and went on until 1991. It is credited with energizing Britain's computer science community by expanding research and development efforts in both academia and industry. In their excellent summary of the program, published in 1990, Brian Oakley and Kenneth Owen describe Alvey's contributions in AI, parallel architecture, VLSI, integrated circuit CAD, software engineering, and speech technology.[15]

22.2.3 *ESPRIT*

In 1983, the European Economic Community (the predecessor of the European Union) launched its ESPRIT program. (ESPRIT is an acronym for European Strategic Program of Research in Information Technology.) According to Luc Steels and Brice Lepape, who wrote an article focusing on the AI aspects of ESPRIT, its goal was "to foster transnational cooperative research among industries, research organizations, and academic institutions across the European Community (EC)."[16] It was also a European response to the Japanese FGCS program.

ESPRIT was set up to support research in three major categories, namely, microelectronics, information processing systems (including software and advanced information processing), and applications (including computer-integrated manufacturing and office systems). Information processing, where most AI research was to be supported, was further divided into knowledge engineering, advanced architectures (including computer architectures for symbolic processing), and advanced system interfaces (speech, image, and multisensor applications).

It was anticipated that the ESPRIT project would go on for ten years and would be divided into two phases, ESPRIT I and ESPRIT II. (Later, a third phase was added.) The initial budget for ESPRIT I was 1.5 billion ECUs. (The euro replaced the ECU in January 1999 at one ECU = one euro.) Funds would be provided equally between the EC and the project participants. The budget for ESPRIT II was more than double that of ESPRIT I. According to Luc Steels and Brice Lepape, by 1993, the program had "more than 6,000 scientists and engineers from about 1,500 organizations working on ESPRIT projects across EC and European Free Trade Agreement countries."

Rather than being directed in a top-down manner by program managers, the projects funded by ESPRIT resulted from proposals submitted by individual investigators and organizations. The proposals were reviewed by a distributed team of experts. The program encouraged proposals that emphasized "transnational cooperative networks," industrial activities, and short-term gains. ESPRIT collaborated with Alvey in supporting some research in Britain.[17]

ESPRIT supported several AI-related projects. Among these were ones that developed various knowledge-based systems, logic programming environments, natural language parsing systems, and knowledge acquisition and machine-learning systems. As one example, I might mention the "Machine Learning Toolbox" (MLT). It was a package of machine learning techniques from which developers could select and assemble algorithms appropriate to specific kinds of tasks. Partners in its development included teams from France, the United Kingdom, Germany, Greece, and Portugal. The article by Steels and Lepape presents a thorough summary of AI efforts supported by ESPRIT.[18] ESPRIT's accomplishments helped to overcome some of industry's reluctance about AI.

While on the topic of national efforts in AI, I'll mention the German Research Center for Artificial Intelligence (DFKI, which stands for Deutsches Forschungszentrum für Künstliche Intelligenz). It was established in 1988 and continues to conduct research in all areas of AI. More information about it can be obtained from its Web page at http://www.dfki.de/web/welcome?set_language=en&cl=en.

In the United States, a DARPA program analogous to Alvey and ESPRIT got underway in the early 1980s. It was partially a response to the Japanese FGCS project, but it also owed much to the observation that the time was ripe for a major program that would take advantage of ongoing technical developments in communications technology and in computer hardware and software. I'll describe the DARPA program in the next chapter.

Notes

1. "Research Report on Fifth Generation Computer Systems Project," ICOT Progress Report, March 1983. [277]
2. *Ibid.* [278]
3. Shunichi Uchida, "FGCS Project: Knowledge Information Processing by Highly Parallel Processing," Institute for New Generation Computer Technology (ICOT), Tokyo, Japan, undated. Available online at http://www.icot.or.jp/ARCHIVE/PICS/OHP/Uchi1-FGohpE.pdf. [278]
4. ICOT Staff (eds.) *Proceedings of the International Conference on Fifth Generation Computer Systems*, June 1–5, 1992, Tokyo, Japan: IOS Press, 1992; Institute for New Generation Computer Technology (ICOT, ed.), *Proceedings of the International Conference on Fifth Generation Computer Systems*, November 28–December 2, 1988, 3 volumes, Tokyo, Japan: OHMSHA, Ltd., and Berlin: Springer-Verlag, 1988; Institute for New Generation Computer Technology (ICOT, ed.), *Proceedings of the International Conference on Fifth Generation Computer Systems*, November 6–9, 1984, Tokyo, Japan: OHMSHA, Ltd., and Amsterdam: North-Holland, 1984. [279]
5. For a Web page describing the various PIMs, see http://www.icot.or.jp/ARCHIVE/Museum/MACHINE/pim-spec-E.html. [279]
6. See, for example, Ryuzo Hasegawa, Miyuki Koshimura, and Hiroshi Fujita, "MGTP: A Parallel Theorem Prover Based on Lazy Model Generation," *Automated Deduction – CADE-11*, Lecture Notes in Computer Science, Proceedings of the 11th International Conference on Automated Deduction, Berlin/Heidelberg: Springer-Verlag, 1992. [279]
7. See, for example, Shinichi Honiden, Akihiko Ohsuga, and Naoshi Uchihira, "MENDELS ZONE: A Parallel Program Development System Based on Formal Specifications," *Information and Software Technology*, Vol. 38, No. 3, pp. 181–189, March 1996. [279]
8. See, for example, Katsumi Nitta *et al.*, "HELIC-II: Legal Reasoning System on the Parallel Inference Machine," *New Generation Computing*, Vol. 11, Nos. 3–4, pp. 423–448, July 1993. [279]
9. Kazuhiro Fuchi *et al.*, "Launching the New Era," *Communications of the ACM*, Vol. 36, No. 3, pp. 49–100, March 1993. [280]
10. *Ibid*, p. 99. [280]
11. See, for example, T. Motooka *et al.*, "Challenge for Knowledge Information Processing Systems (Preliminary Report on FGCS)," *Proceedings of the International Conference on FGCS*, JIPDEC, pp. 1–85, 1981. [281]
12. For a history of the first ten years or so of MCC, see David V. Gibson and Everett M. Rogers, *R & D Collaboration on Trial: The Microelectronics and Computer Technology Corporation*, Cambridge, MA: Harvard Business School Press, 1994. [282]
13. The committee's report, from which these quotations are taken, is available online from pointers at http://www.chilton-computing.org.uk/inf/literature/reports/alvey_report/p001.htm. [282]
14. Brian W. Oakley, "Intelligent Knowledge-Based Systems – AI in the U.K.," in Ray Kurzweil, *The Age of Intelligent Machines*, Cambridge, MA: MIT Press, 1990. Available online at http://www.kurzweilai.net/articles/art0308.html?printable=1. [282]
15. Brian Oakley and Kenneth Owen, *Alvey: Britain's Strategic Computing Initiative*, Cambridge, MA: MIT Press, 1990. [282]

16. Luc Steels and Brice Lepape, "Knowledge Engineering in ESPRIT," *IEEE Expert*, Vol. 8, No. 4, pp. 4–10, August 1993. **[283]**
17. At this writing, there are still abundant Web pages about ESPRIT. They are available from http://cordis.europa.eu/esprit/home.html. **[283]**
18. Luc Steels and Brice Lepape, *op. cit.* **[283]**

23

DARPA's Strategic Computing Program

23.1 The Strategic Computing Plan

By the early 1980s expert systems and other AI technologies, such as image and speech understanding and natural language processing, were showing great promise. Also, there was dramatic progress in communications technology, computer networks and architectures, and computer storage and processing technologies. Robert Kahn (1938– ; Fig. 23.1), who had become Director of DARPA's Information Processing Techniques Office (IPTO) in 1979, began thinking that DARPA should sponsor a major research and development program that would integrate efforts in all of these areas to create much more powerful computer systems. At the same time, there was concern that the Japanese FGCS program could threaten U.S. leadership in computer technology. With these factors as background, Kahn began planning what would come to be called the "Strategic Computing" (SC) program.

Kahn had been a professor at MIT and an engineer at BBN before he joined DARPA's IPTO as a program manager in late 1972. There he initiated and ran DARPA's internetting program, linking the Arpanet along with the Packet Radio and Packet Satellite Nets to form the first version of today's Internet. He and Vinton Cerf, then at Stanford, collaborated on the development of what was to become the basic architecture of the Internet and its "Transmission Control Protocol" (TCP). (TCP was later modularized and became TCP/IP, with IP standing for Internet Protocol.) Cerf joined DARPA in 1976 and led the internetting program until 1982. For their work, Kahn and Cerf shared the 2004 Turing Award of the Association for Computer Machinery.[1]

Kahn thought that AI, especially expert systems, could play a major role in SC. Recall that in the mid-1970s DARPA support for AI research suffered during George Heilmeier's tenure as the DARPA Director. A major casualty was the speech understanding program. The SC program could revitalize AI research, but more importantly in Kahn's view, it would help transfer promising AI techniques out of university laboratories and into actual applications. Alex Roland, who wrote a well-researched book about the history of the SC program, put it this way:[2]

Robert Kahn and the architects of SC believed in 1983 [after the expert systems boom] that AI was ripe for exploitation. It was finally moving out of the laboratory and into the real world... AI would become an essential component of SC; expert systems would be the centerpiece. [They] would allow machines to "think."

Figure 23.1. Robert E. Kahn. (Photograph courtesy of Robert E. Kahn.)

Kahn saw the SC program as a pyramid of related technologies to be developed. At the base were enabling technologies such as facilities for rapid design and implementation of the needed hardware. Above that sat hardware and software technologies, with AI being prominent. These would all come together in specific military systems, such as robot vehicles and aids for battle management. One of the (many) versions of this pyramid is shown in Fig. 23.2.

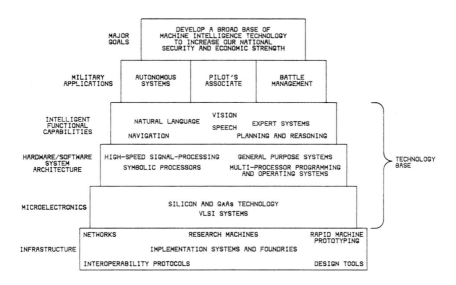

W6196DG3292

Figure 23.2. The SC program structure and goals. (Illustration used with permission of DARPA.)

The SC program would support, coordinate, and manage research and development for all of the technologies in the pyramid. It was to become a billion-dollar program – the largest computer research and development program ever undertaken by the U.S. government up to that time.

Kahn's boss was Robert Cooper, who became the DARPA Director in July 1981. Cooper was enthusiastic about Kahn's ideas for the SC program, although he differed from Kahn about research strategy and how to describe the program. As Alex Roland wrote[3]

Kahn said build the technology base and nice things will happen. Cooper said focus on a pilot's associate and the technology base will follow. One paradigm is technology push, the other technology pull. One is bubble up, the other trickle down.... The tension between them stressed SC through much of its history.

Because of its size, the SC program would have to be "sold" to those Congressional committees overseeing DARPA's budget. Cooper knew that emphasizing (indeed, promising) specific military applications was how to sell Congress. He was right as far as convincing Congress was concerned, but in the end technology pull didn't work so well.

One factor in helping to convince Congress about the need for the SC program was the Japanese FGCS program. According to Roland "Congress was more exercised by Japan's Fifth Generation program than either the Reagan administration or the computer community [including Kahn and Cooper]."[4] The publication of a book[5] about the Japanese project by Edward Feigenbaum and Pamela McCorduck had the effect of strengthening these concerns. In the preface to their book, they asked "Will we rise to [this crucial challenge]? If not, we may consign our nation to the role of the first great postindustrial agrarian society." They further warned that[6]

... our national self-interest, not to mention our economic security, does not allow us [to ignore the Japanese project]. Information processing is an $88-billion-per-year industry in the United States, and its loss would be disastrous. The default of this American industry, which has led the world for decades, would be a mortal economic wound.... The superior technology usually wins the war – whether that war is martial, entrepreneurial, or cultural.

In June 1983, Feigenbaum testified before the House Committee on Science, Space, and Technology. According to Roland he told the committee "the era of reasoning machines is inevitable.... It is the manifest destiny of computing."[7]

Kahn was persuaded to yield to Cooper's vision about how to frame the plan, and it was finally written up in October 1983.[8] Funds to support SC were approved at a level of $50 million for work to begin in fiscal year 1984. (One Congressional staff person even recommended that DARPA spend "a substantially higher amount.") During the decade from 1983 to 1993 DARPA spent just over $1 billion on SC.[9] The plan envisioned supporting two main thrusts, namely, major projects that would build specific applications and basic research to develop the "technology base" that would be needed for those applications. I will describe aspects of each of these in the following sections.

23.2 Major Projects

At the beginning of the program, three major applications were chosen. To get all three of the military services to "buy in" to the program, the plan called for a "Pilot's Associate" (for the Air Force), an aircraft carrier "Battle Management System" (for the Navy), and an "Autonomous Land Vehicle" (for the Army). However, to encourage joint service support of all of these, the plan cautioned that[10]

[i]t might, for example, prove preferable to pursue an autonomous underwater vehicle rather than a land vehicle, and a battle management system for land combat might prove more appropriate than that for the Naval application.

As Mark Stefik wrote in his excellent review and assessment of the program, "... DARPA is telling the services that the particulars of these applications can be shuffled at any time, so they had better buy the whole plan."[11] Indeed, additional applications, such as an "Autonomous Air Vehicle" for launching smart bombs behind enemy lines, were undertaken later.

23.2.1 *The Pilot's Associate*

The Pilot's Associate (PA) program, begun in February 1986, had as its goal the development of an interactive computer system that would aid a combat aircraft commander. Interaction with the system would be through a graphics user interface, voice recognition (capable of working under noisy and stressful conditions), and speech synthesis. It would prepare and revise mission plans, advise the pilot about targets, assess threats, help the pilot to take evasive action against interceptor missiles (flying the plane automatically in case it needed to maneuver so rapidly that the pilot might black out), and take over routine tasks. In addition to pilot inputs, the system would obtain information from navigational aids and several sensors. Advice and decisions would be based on several collaborating expert systems, automatic planning systems, and plan-execution systems.

Among the technical capabilities that the 1983 DARPA strategic plan predicted could be achieved by 1989 were 10,000-rule, real-time expert systems, animated displays with 10^8 polygons per second, 200-word, speaker-independent speech recognition in high-noise environments, and a speech output system capable of a 1,000-word vocabulary.[12] Of course, compact and aircraft-worthy hardware would be required also.

The program was administered by the Avionics Laboratory at Wright-Patterson Air Force Base in Dayton, Ohio (later part of the Air Force Research Laboratory).[13] After a preliminary exploratory effort (in which five contractors participated), teams led by Lockheed Aeronautical Systems (later part of Lockheed Martin Corporation) and McDonnell Douglas (later part of Boeing) were awarded contracts for work extending from 1986 through the middle of 1992. As had become standard for DARPA-managed projects, working demonstrations had to be given. According to a set of Web sites (last updated in 2004) describing the project, the Lockheed program was awarded the American Institute of Aeronautics and Astronautics (AIAA) Digital

Electronics Award ". . . in recognition of outstanding achievement in . . . advancing the state-of-the-art of artificial intelligence and decision support systems into the complex, rapidly changing world of air combat."[14] The same site also claimed the following:

Technically, by 1991, the PA was the most advanced, working, real-time intelligent system of its day and remains unsurpassed in the world. We [at Lockheed] successfully integrated 6 expert systems operating in real time in a realistic (some would say too realistic) combat simulator. The knowledge implemented in each component of this system was realistic, combat experience that was demonstrably applicable to the operation of combat aircraft today.

In spite of the successful demonstrations, the Defense Department did not follow up directly in installing the technology in fighter aircraft. As one of the Web sites just cited puts it, ". . . it was left to the PA contractors to take the technology to the marketplace."[15] One of the legacies of the Pilot's Associate program was a system that was developed for use in Army helicopters, the Rotorcraft Pilot's Associate. A possible application involving air traffic management never materialized even though "results [of NASA studies] were enough to show that PA technology could enable free flight throughout the continental and trans-oceanic air space, with enormous savings in operational costs for the airlines and the Air Traffic Control infrastructure, while also offering an extra level of safety."[16]

23.2.2 Battle Management Systems

In 1984, DARPA began funding the Fleet Command Center Battle Management Program (FCCBMP, pronounced "fik bump"). A company called Analytics was the engineering contractor for FCCBMP. It provided program management support, testing, and configuration management. In a 1990 article describing and assessing the program, Rin Saunders, an engineer at Analytics, wrote that its goal was to produce a system that would ". . . assist the commander-in-chief of the U.S. Pacific Fleet (CINCPACFLT) in planning and monitoring the operation of nearly 300 ships in the Pacific and Indian ocean regions."[17] Saunders claimed that it was the most successful of the Strategic Computing programs in bringing expert systems into operational use and had "the greatest visibility and participation within the user community."

Expert systems were planned to play a major role in FCCBMP. The DARPA strategic plan envisioned ones that could process 10,000 rules per second in highly complex contexts operating at five times real time.[18] FCCBMP consisted of two major expert systems communicating over a local area network. One of these, the "Force Requirements Expert System (FRESH)," was designed to keep track of the current positions and the readiness status of ships in the fleet and to issue alerts when there were significant changes. FRESH, developed by Texas Instruments, was supposed to be able to make suggestions about what should be done, such as proceeding with the current plan anyway, expediting repairs, or substituting other ships for unready ones.

Saunders claimed that[19]

FRESH currently provides daily alert summaries to twelve CINCPACFLT staff codes. FRESH was shown to replicate expert judgement in a trial in which FRESH and CINC-PACFLT staff were given the same nomination task to solve. CINCPACFLT staff estimate that FRESH can accomplish in one minute monitoring tasks which previous[ly] took two hours, yielding a 120-fold time savings. For the planning task of nominating a replacement for a disabled ship, the time savings is 400 to 1.

Another expert system, the "Capabilities Assessment Expert System" (CASES), used information about U.S. and enemy forces to provide estimates of how each would fare in hypothetical engagements. It was developed by BBN. According to Saunders,[20]

CASES has been used to evaluate carrier battle force operating areas; assess attack submarine employment strategies; estimate the effect of pre-D-day surveillance and early assignment of SSNs to enemy submarine attrition; and provide insights on the costs and benefits of different strike strategies relative to changes in estimated enemy capability and weather.

Both expert systems made extensive use of natural language understanding and generation abilities. They were hosted on Symbolics Lisp machines and written using commercial expert-system "shells." The battle simulations in CASES were run on an Encore parallel processor. The final prototypes for FRESH and CASES were delivered to CINCPACFLT in 1990. But when the prototype phase was complete and DARPA funding ended, the Navy decided not to continue these systems.

Saunders, now a Technical Director at Computer Sciences Corporation, has provided me with some recollections about FCCBMP. These contrast a bit with what he wrote in 1990. In e-mail notes, he wrote me that[21]

[t]he goals of FCCBMP were an overreach for the state of the art in the 1980s.
. . .
[The] Navy's decision to mothball FRESH was because there was no compelling reason to keep it. It duplicated the expert judgement of Fleet planners, in a matter of hours rather than days. But the planners were not looking to retire, and in Naval warfare, days are good enough.

Concerning CASES, the Fleet was eager to have the simulation tools. But the goal of orchestrating the simulations in an intelligent way to evaluate what-if scenarios never got off the ground.
. . .
I believe that there was a growing recognition within DARPA/ISTO that the FRESH and CASES technologies' research agendas were not best met within the vicissitudes of an operational environment. . . . There was also pressure from Congress for DARPA to divert the funding to anti-submarine warfare, which was a hot topic at the time. And relations between DARPA and Navy were always strained near the breaking point. Navy constantly fought DARPA for control of the program, both for its own sake and to redefine the program to provide greater near-term payback. In the end, everyone decided it was time to pack up and go home.

23.2.3 *Autonomous Vehicles*

The third major applications project funded under the umbrella of DARPA's SC program was the "Autonomous Land Vehicle" (ALV) project begun in August 1984. Martin Marietta (later to merge with Lockheed to become Lockheed Martin) was selected as the "project integrator" and funded at $10.6 million for a period of forty-two months.[22] SRI, Carnegie Mellon University, the University of Maryland, Hughes Research Laboratories, Advanced Decision Systems, and the Environmental Research Institute of Michigan (ERIM) provided components and research help. The U.S. Army Engineering Topographic Laboratory helped to coordinate the work. The goals of the project were in line with the Army's long-range "strategic vision" of using autonomous vehicles in logistics and supply operations, in search and rescue, and even in combat.

A great deal of information about the ALV project can be obtained from an article by Douglas W. Gage. Rather than paraphrase his summary, I'll quote it directly:[23]

The ALV was built on a Standard Manufacturing eight wheel hydrostatically-driven all-terrain vehicle capable of speeds of up to 45 mph on the highway and up to 18 mph on rough terrain. The ALV could carry six full racks of electronic equipment in dust-free air conditioned comfort, providing power from its 12-kW diesel APU. The initial sensor suite consisted of a color video camera and a laser scanner from the Environmental Research Institute of Michigan (ERIM) that returned a 64 by 256 pixel range image at 1–2 second intervals. Video and range data processing modules produced road-edge information that was used to generate a model of the scene ahead. Higher level reasoning was performed by goalseeker and navigator modules, which then passed the desired path to the pilot module that actually steered the vehicle.

A photograph of the ALV and its system configuration is shown in Fig. 23.3.

The ALV was to be the forerunner of military vehicles that could move, unguided, on roads and over rough terrain using computer vision programs to inform them about their environments and planning programs and expert systems to control their routes. They would have to avoid such hazards as other vehicles, rocks, trees, ditches, water obstacles, and steep or muddy terrain. They would also have to be able to identify landmarks and other significant objects in their immediate surroundings. They were to be entirely self-contained with all computing to be done on board.

The DARPA Strategic Computing Plan laid out some specific milestones for the ALV.[24] In 1985, there was to be a "road-following demonstration" in which the ALV was to navigate a preset route of 20 km at speeds up to 10 km/hour. By 1986, there was to be an "obstacle avoidance demonstration" using "fixed, polyhedral objects spaced no less than 100 m" apart and of a size much smaller than the road width. In 1990 and 1991, there was to be a "mixed road and open terrain demonstration" with speeds up to 90 km/hour on roads with other vehicles.

According to a report by the National Research Council assessing progress in unmanned vehicles, "the ALV made a 1 km traverse in 1985 at an average speed of 3 km/h.... This increased to 10 km/h over a 4 km traverse in 1986. In 1987, the ALV reached a top speed of 20 km/h ... and used the laser scanner to avoid obstacles placed on the road."[25] The same report continues with

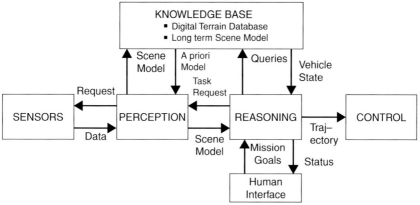

Figure 23.3. Martin Marietta's ALV (top) and its system configuration (bottom). (ALV photograph courtesy of DARPA; diagram from R. Terry Dunlay, "Obstacle Avoidance Perception Processing for the Autonomous Land Vehicle," *Proceedings of the IEEE Robotics and Automation Conference*, pp. 912–917, Los Alamitos, CA: CS Press, 1988.)

In August 1987, the ALV performed the first autonomous cross-country traverse based on sensor data. During this and subsequent trials extending for about a year, the ALV navigated around various kinds of isolated positive obstacles over traverses of several kilometers. The terrain had steep slopes (some over 15 degrees), ravines and gulleys, large scrub oaks, brushes, and rock outcrops. Some manmade obstacles were emplaced for experiments. The smallest obstacles that could be reliably detected were on the order of 2 feet to 3 feet in height. On occasion, the vehicle would approach and detect team members and maneuver to avoid them. The vehicle reached speeds of 3.5 to 5 km/hr and completed about 75 percent of the traverses.

Vision for the ALV represented the most difficult challenge. Recognizing rocks, trees, road, and ditches would stretch the state of the art of both computer vision algorithms and computer processing speeds in the 1980s. According to Roland, "DARPA estimated that the vision system for the ALV would require 10–100 billion instructions per second, compared to the rate in 1983 of only 30–40 million."[26] It has been estimated that perception for unmanned vehicles around the time of the ALV accounts for about 85% of the total computational load.[27]

Commenting on the performance of the ALV vision system, Roland wrote[28]

The vision system proved highly sensitive to environmental conditions – the quality of light, the location of the sun, shadows, and so on. The system worked differently from month to month, day to day, and even test to test. Sometimes it could accurately locate the edge of the road, sometimes not. The system reliably distinguished the pavement of the road from the dirt on the shoulders, but it was fooled by dirt that was tracked onto the roadway by heavy vehicles maneuvering around the ALV. In the fall, the sun, now lower in the sky, reflected brilliantly off the myriads of polished pebbles in the tarmac itself, producing glittering reflections that confused the vehicle. Shadows from trees presented problems, as did asphalt patches from the frequent road repairs made necessary by the harsh Colorado weather and the constant pounding of the eight-ton vehicle.

DARPA cancelled the ALV program in April 1988, but interest in autonomous vehicles continued in research labs, in industry, and in other government agencies. Among the programs supported by the Defense Department during the 1990s were DEMO-I for tele-operated vehicles and DEMO-II for autonomous vehicles. Again, Martin Marietta's Aerospace Division was chosen as the overall integration contractor. Among the co-contractors providing subsystems were CMU, Hughes Research Laboratories, Advanced Decision Systems, SRI, Teleos, JPL, and the Universities of Massachusetts and Michigan. The vehicle chosen for the demonstrations was a HMMWV (an acronym for High-Mobility Multipurpose Wheeled Vehicle, pronounced humvee). A series of demonstrations was given in the mid-1990s.[29] Carnegie Mellon University developed a number of important unmanned vehicles including the "Terragator" and a series of "Navlabs." (I'll have more to say about the Navlabs later.) Although the ALV program might not have achieved all of its goals, it can be said to have launched the era of autonomous vehicles. They are becoming more versatile and "autonomous" with each passing year.

23.3 AI Technology Base

Even though the main focus of the SC program was the suite of applications just mentioned, successful pursuit of these applications required advances in the technology on which they depended. According to Robert Cooper's view of SC, these applications would "pull" the technology of vision, robotics, expert systems, speech recognition, and natural language processing. So, in addition to the main contracts for applications, several were let for technology development. Of course, the technology developers were supposed to be closely coupled to the applications that were pulling them.

23.3.1 Computer Vision

Ron Ohlander and (later) Robert Simpson Jr. were program managers at DARPA IPTO in charge of AI research during the SC days. Continuing the work begun earlier in "image understanding," DARPA focused on four main areas of computer vision, namely, visual modeling and recognition, dynamic scene and motion analysis, vision-based obstacle avoidance and path planning, and implementation of vision algorithms using parallel computing architectures.[30]

Chuck Thorpe, Takeo Kanade, and others at CMU concentrated especially on vision systems needed by ALVs.[31] Other important computer vision research in support of Strategic Computing was done at the University of Maryland under Azriel Rosenfeld, at the University of Massachusetts under Alan Hanson and Edward Riseman, at SRI under Martin Fischler, and at industrial laboratories.

Besides applications in robotics, computer vision technology finds applications in cartography and photo interpretation. One of the early photo-reconnaissance systems was SCORPIUS (an acronym for Strategic Computing Object-Directed Reconnaissance Parallel-Processing Image-Understanding System) funded by the CIA and developed at the Hughes Research Labs. It was supposed to screen aerial and satellite photographs to detect ships, buildings, airplanes, and other objects of interest. According to SRI's Martin Fischler, the project got bogged down in infrastructure problems associated with having to use a new parallel-processing computer (the "Butterfly Multiprocessor") being developed at BBN.[32]

Later photo-reconnaissance projects, following on after the SC program, were more successful. One such project was RADIUS (an acronym for Research And Development for Image Understanding Systems) funded jointly by DARPA and the CIA. Image processing systems developed at SRI under the RADIUS project could overlay terrain texture on three-dimensional models of parts of the earth (enabling, for example, a simulated "flythrough" of Yosemite Valley). They could also be used to help locate buildings and other objects in photographs, thus aiding a human photo interpreter.[33]

23.3.2 *Speech Recognition and Natural Language Processing*

The Pilot's Associate project and the Battle Management projects depended on the ability of computer systems to understand verbal requests or commands. Speech recognition was needed by the Pilot's Associate, and both speech recognition and text understanding were needed by the Battle Management projects. Accordingly, several basic research projects were funded by DARPA to advance those technologies. Recall that DARPA discontinued its speech understanding research program in 1976, but continuing progress in the field, notably at CMU, MIT, and IBM, justified its resumption.

Texas Instruments integrated work from eight speech recognition research projects for the Pilot's Associate project. CMU integrated work from nine projects for the Battle Management projects. According to Roland, by the end of the SC program, speech recognition systems "could recognize 10,000 words of natural language spoken by anyone in an environment of moderate background noise and low stress on the speaker."[34]

Later, at CMU, Kai-Fu Lee and others developed the speaker-independent SPHINX speech recognition system under DARPA support.[35] SPHINX used HMMs (hidden Markov models) and statistical information about the likelihoods of word strings to aid recognition.

Speech recognition work continues at several industrial and university research laboratories. At CMU, to name just one example, the SPHINX project has assembled "a set of reasonably mature [open source], world-class speech components that provide a basic level of technology to anyone interested in creating speech-using applications." However, the project Web page at SourceForge[36] cautions that ". . . SPHINX is not a final product. Those with a certain level of expertise can achieve great results with the versions of SPHINX available here, but a naive user will certainly need further help. In other words, the software available here is not meant for users with no experience in speech, but for expert users." Advances in computer speed and memory have led to several high-quality, real-time, and commercially available speech recognition systems of moderate cost.

The SC program also sponsored basic research work on text understanding as part of what DARPA called "new generation systems." Seven contractors received DARPA awards in 1984.[37] BBN Laboratories, USC/Information Sciences Institute, the University of Pennsylvania, and the University of Massachusetts worked on natural language interfaces that could respond to typed queries. New York University, the Systems Development Corporation (later to become part of Unisys), and SRI International worked on understanding free-form text from military messages. BBN and USC–ISI coordinated the work on interfaces based initially on BBN's IRUS system, which later grew into JANUS.[38] New York University and SDC coordinated the work on text understanding and developed the PROTEUS and PUNDIT systems.[39]

According to Roland, the results of this work "were most promising, again exceeding the milestones laid out in the original SC plan . . . the metrics of the original plan [were] exceeded in error rate and [in] the size of vocabularies."[40] Roland goes on to elaborate:[41]

. . . BBN's IRUS system, with a vocabulary of 4,500 words and 1,200 domain concepts, received a favorable response in 1986 when it was installed in a Battle Management Program test bed. By 1987 BBN IRUS was becoming JANUS, a system designed to understand vague and confusing queries. JANUS was successfully demonstrated in the Air–Land Battle Management Program in the fall of 1987.

Meanwhile in 1986 the first version of the PROTEUS system successfully processed naval casualty reports (CASREPS) about equipment failure.

23.3.3 Expert Systems

Because expert systems appeared to be so promising in the late 1970s and early 1980s, they were slated for a prominent role in the Strategic Computing program. They were to be the reasoning agents that would give "intelligence" to the SC applications. Ronald Ohlander, the DARPA program manager for intelligent systems, sought contractors for expert systems research in 1984. Out of the fifty proposals that were submitted to DARPA, Ohlander recommended that six of them be funded. A seventh was eventually added to this list. As Roland reports, Stanford would work on new expert system architectures, BBN would work on the problem of getting the needed knowledge into expert systems, Ohio State University would work on methods for expert systems to explain their conclusions, and the University of Massachusetts and General Electric would work on techniques for reasoning with uncertain information.[42]

The other contractors were start-up companies – both founded by Edward Feigenbaum and other Stanford researchers. One, IntelliCorp (originally founded as Intelli-Genetics), had already built an EMYCIN-inspired expert system shell called KEE (an acronym for Knowledge Engineering Environment).[43] IntelliCorp proposed to extend KEE by upgrading several features, including the ability to maintain the consistency of the knowledge base as new knowledge is added or deleted, the ability to make reasonable inferences even though they might not be warranted by specific information in its knowledge base, and the ability to make plans and schedules. It would also have facilities for knowledge acquisition, user interface construction, and hierarchical descriptions of objects. IntelliCorp was awarded a DARPA contract in 1984 for $1,286,781.[44] KEE eventually evolved into a system called OPUS.[45]

The other start-up company, Teknowledge, Inc., proposed to build an expert-system toolkit called ABE to be used for building expert systems. ABE was to be brand new, and thus it was somewhat of a gamble for DARPA, but the company had plenty of AI experts either on its payroll or as consultants.[46] Teknowledge was awarded a DARPA contract for $1,813,260 to make good on its promises.[47]

Both KEE and ABE were used by the SC applications contractors, but neither provided the intelligence originally expected from expert systems. But these expectations were probably unrealistic. In their 1994 assessment of knowledge-based systems (KBSs), Frederick Hayes-Roth and Neil Jacobstein, two pioneers in expert system applications, wrote ". . . although the current generation of expert and KBS technologies had no hope of producing a robust and general human-like intelligence, many people were disappointed that it did not."[48] Even so, Hayes-Roth and Jacobstein concluded the following:[49]

KBS have been remarkably effective over the past decade of industrial experience – often delivering order-of-magnitude increases in speed, quality, or cost performance. They have penetrated every major institution from Fortune 500 companies to small entrepreneurial firms, military services, government agencies, health care, and educational institutions. KBS applications may now be found in virtually every field of human endeavor from music to medicine.

DART, an acronym for Dynamic Analysis and Replanning Tool, was a KBS whose roots can be traced to AI research during the SC program. Developed at BBN, it helped plan the movement of equipment and personnel from Europe to Saudi Arabia during the 1990 Persian Gulf War. In fact, Victor Reis, the Director of DARPA at the time, has been quoted as claiming "The DART scheduling application paid back all of DARPAs 30 years of investment in AI in a matter of a few months."[50]

23.4 Assessment

What can be said about the SC program overall? It has been criticized both by those who thought it might achieve its military goals and also by those who faulted it for not having done so. Among the former, the Computer Professionals for Social Responsibility (CPSR) had several concerns, stated in one of their newsletters:[51]

1. The SCI [Strategic Computing Initiative] promises specific new weapons systems; autonomous vehicles, such as robot tanks; a combat pilot's "associate;" and an aircraft carrier group "battle management system." Our concern is that proposals for computer research will be assessed by their relevance to these specific applications, rather than by their general scientific merit.
2. The SCI promotes the use of machine "intelligence," to control the operation of complex military systems under unpredictable circumstances. Our concern is that, particularly when the stakes are high, situations of extreme uncertainty are precisely the wrong environment for the application of artificial intelligence.
3. The SCI promotes the military application of computer technology as a solution to perceived problems in defense. Our concern is that, rather than increasing our security, past attempts to achieve superiority in new weapons technology have fueled an arms race that has no foreseeable end.

    This last concern is the gravest. In the final analysis, we believe neither that the path to national security lies in military superiority, nor that superiority can be achieved through the use of computers.

Most commentators doubt that the SC program achieved its goal of pulling new AI technology into the SC applications. Developing the kinds of capabilities envisioned by the SC applications required AI inventions, and the atmosphere needed for invention is not conducive to tightly programmed milestone demonstrations. Instead, as Roland comments, the "applications extemporized ad-hoc, off-the-shelf solutions to meet demonstration deadlines."[52] Furthermore, the showcase systems, namely, the ALVs, the Pilot's Associate, and those for battle management, were not immediately "bought" by their hoped-for military customers. Even so, these systems were the forerunners of similar ones having much higher levels of performance.

Generous SC support for the AI "technology base" nourished AI research in general even though the research did not produce results that were integrated into the SC applications. After a short diminution toward the end of the SC program, AI research has steadily prospered both at universities and in industry and continues to produce important new capabilities.

In addition to the problem of combining invention with application, the SC program suffered from institutional problems and budget reductions. There was often friction between the DARPA people and the military customers. Furthermore, many of the people who had planned the SC program, including Kahn and Cooper, had left DARPA by late 1985. In the spring of 1986, DARPA combined its Information Processing Techniques Office with its Engineering Applications Office and renamed it the Information Systems Technology Office (ISTO). A succession of ISTO directors both endured and helped cause budget fluctuations. Jacob Schwartz, who was skeptical about some AI approaches, became the ISTO director in September 1987. He promptly canceled some AI programs and failed to renew others. Then, in 1991 ISTO split into SISTO (Software and Intelligent Systems Technology Office) and CSTO (Computer Systems Technology Office), effectively ending attempts to couple basic research with applications.

The SC program gradually disappeared from view. According to Roland it was never mentioned in public documents or reports after 1989. It vanished from the DARPA budget in 1993 and was ultimately replaced by other programs including one for High Performance Computing (HPC).[53] Even though the program itself disappeared, its accomplishments, along with those of the other "new-generation" projects, were many. Progress made during the 1980s established artificial intelligence as a technology that was capable of taking on a wide variety of real-world applications. As I'll describe in a subsequent chapter, much new AI technology was invented during the 1980s and 1990s, and some of it at least was stimulated by the new-generation projects. However, before continuing with my roughly chronological history, I'll make a temporary diversion to discuss controversies that were simmering on the sidelines and within the field itself.

Notes

1. To learn more about the evolution of the Internet, see Robert E. Kahn and Vinton G. Cerf, "What Is the Internet (And What Makes It Work)" available online at http://www.cnri.reston.va.us/what_is_internet.html. [286]

2. Alex Roland (with Philip Shiman), *Strategic Computing: DARPA and the Quest for Machine Intelligence, 1983–1993*, pp. 191–192, Cambridge, MA: MIT Press, 2002. [286]

3. *Ibid*, p. 71. [288]

4. *Ibid*, p. 91. [288]

5. Edward Feigenbaum and Pamela McCorduck, *The Fifth Generation: Japan's Computer Challenge to the World*, Boston, MA: Addison-Wesley Longman Publishing Co., Inc., 1983. An article with the same title by the same authors appeared in *Creative Computing*, Vol. 10, No. 8, p. 103, August 1984, and is available online at http://www.atarimagazines.com/creative/v10n8/103_The_fifth_generation_Jap.php. [288]

6. Edward Feigenbaum and Pamela McCorduck, *op. cit.*, pp. 19–20. [288]

7. In Alex Roland, *op. cit.*, pp. 91–92. Roland cites U.S. Congress, House, Committee on Science, Space, and Technology, *Japanese Technological Advances and Possible U.S. Responses Using Research Joint Ventures. Hearings*, 98th Congress, 1st session, June, 29–30, 1983, pp. 116–143, at p. 119. [288]

8. "Strategic Computing: New-Generation Computing Technology: A Strategic Plan for Its Development and Applications to Critical Problems in Defense," Defense Advanced Research Projects Agency, Arlington, Virginia, October 28, 1983. [288]

9. Alex Roland, *op. cit.*, p. 319. [288]

10. "Strategic Computing: New-Generation Computing Technology: A Strategic Plan for its Development and Applications to Critical Problems in Defense," p. 20, Defense Advanced Research Projects Agency, Arlington, Virginia, October 28, 1983. [289]

11. Mark Stefik, "Strategic Computing at DARPA: An Overview and Assessment," *Communications of the ACM*, Vol. 28, No. 7, pp. 690–704, July 1985. [289]

12. "Strategic Computing: New-Generation Computing Technology: A Strategic Plan for Its Development and Applications to Critical Problems in Defense," Chart I.2 of Appendix I, Defense Advanced Research Projects Agency, Arlington, Virginia, October 28, 1983. [289]

13. For a description and review of the program by people from Wright-Patterson Air Force Base see Sheila B. Banks and Carl S. Lizza, "Pilot's Associate: A Cooperative, Knowledge-Based System Application," *IEEE Expert*, Vol. 6, No. 3, pp. 18–29, 1991. [289]

14. http://www.dms489.com/PA/PA_index.html. [290]

15. http://www.dms489.com/PA/PA_index.html. [290]

16. http://www.dms489.com/PA/PA_index.html. [290]

17. Rin Saunders, "The Fleet Command Center Battle Management Project: Lessons Learned," *Proceedings of the IEEE Conference on Managing Expert System Programs and Projects*, pp. 51–60, September 1990. [290]

18. "Strategic Computing: New-Generation Computing Technology: A Strategic Plan for its Development and Applications to Critical Problems in Defense," Chart I.3 of Appendix I, Defense Advanced Research Projects Agency, Arlington, Virginia, October 28, 1983. [290]

19. Rin Saunders, *op. cit.*, p. 53. [291]

20. *Ibid*, p. 53. [291]

21. E-mail correspondence of December 12, 2007. [291]

22. Alex Roland, *op. cit.*, p. 222. [292]

23. Douglas W. Gage, "UGV HISTORY 101: A Brief History of Unmanned Ground Vehicle (UGV) Development Efforts," *Unmanned Systems Magazine, Special Issue on Unmanned Ground Vehicles*, Vol. 13, No. 3, Summer 1995. [292]

24. "Strategic Computing: New-Generation Computing Technology: A Strategic Plan for Its Development and Applications to Critical Problems in Defense," Defense Advanced Research Projects Agency, Arlington, Virginia, October 28, 1983. The milestones described in this paragraph, along with many others, are taken from Chart I.1 in Appendix I. [292]

25. National Research Council Staff, *Technology Development for Army Unmanned Ground Vehicles*, pp. 152–153, Washington, DC: National Academies Press, 2003. [292]

26. Alex Roland, *op. cit.* [293]

27. National Research Council Staff, *Technology Development for Army Unmanned Ground Vehicles*, p. 148, Washington, DC: National Academies Press, 2003. [294]

28. Alex Roland *op. cit.* [294]

29. For summaries of DEMO-I and DEMO-II technology and demonstrations, see Douglas W. Gage, "UGV HISTORY 101: A Brief History of Unmanned Ground Vehicle (UGV) Development Efforts," *Unmanned Systems Magazine, Special Issue on Unmanned Ground Vehicles*, Vol. 13, No. 3, Summer 1995, and National Research Council Staff, *Technology Development for Army Unmanned Ground Vehicles*, p. 148, Washington, DC: National Academies Press, 2003. The latter book recommends Oscar Firschein and Thomas Strat (eds.), *Reconnaissance, Surveillance, and Target Acquisition for the Unmanned Ground Vehicle: Providing Surveillance "Eyes" for an Autonomous Vehicle*, San Francisco, CA: Morgan Kaufmann Publishers, 1997. [294]

30. See, for example, Robert L. Simpson Jr., "Computer Vision: An Overview," Guest Editor's Introduction, *IEEE Expert*, pp. 11–15, August 1991. [295]

31. See, for example, Takeo Kanade, Chuck Thorpe, and William Whittaker, "Autonomous Land Vehicle Project at CMU," *Proceedings of the 1986 ACM Computer Conference*, pp. 71–80, February 1986, and Yoshimasa Goto and Anthony Stentz, "Mobile Robot Navigation: The CMU System," *IEEE Expert*, pp. 44–54. 1987. (The latter paper is available online at http://www.ri.cmu.edu/pub_files/pub3/goto_y_1987_1/goto_y_1987_1.pdf.) [295]

32. Personal communication, November 15, 2007. [295]

33. See Thomas M. Strat and Oscar Firschein, *RADIUS: Image Understanding for Imagery Intelligence*, San Francisco: Morgan Kaufmann Publishers, 1997. See also the RADIUS Web site at http://www.ai.sri.com/~radius/. [295]

34. Alex Roland, *op. cit.* For this information, Roland cites Victor Zue, a speech researcher and professor at MIT. [295]

35. Kai-Fu Lee, Hsiao-Wuen Hon, and Raj Reddy, "An Overview of the SPHINX Speech Recognition System," *IEEE Transactions on Acoustics, Speech, and Signal Processing*, Vol. 38, No. 1, January 1990. Available online at http://www.ri.cmu.edu/pub_files/pub2/lee_k_f_1990_1/lee_k_f_1990_1.pdf. [295]

36. http://cmusphinx.sourceforge.net/html/cmusphinx.php. [296]

37. *Proceedings of the Workshop on Strategic Computing Natural Language*, Foreword by Robert Simpson, Morristown, NJ: Association for Computational Linguistics, 1986. [296]

38. For a brief history of the IRUS/JANUS work (as well as related work at BBN), see Ralph Weischedel, "Natural-Language Understanding at BBN," *IEEE Annals of the History of Computing*, pp. 46–55, January–March 2006. A BBN report about the project is available online a http://www.aclweb.org/anthology-new/H/H86/H86-1001.pdf. [296]

39. See the online document by Ralph Grishman and Lynette Hirschman, "PROTEUS and PUNDIT: Research in Text Understanding," available at http://www.aclweb.org/anthology-new/H/H86/H86-1002.pdf. [296]

40. Alex Roland, *op. cit.*, p. 212. [296]

41. *Ibid*, pp. 269–270. [296]

42. *Ibid*, p. 195. [297]

43. T. P. Kehler and G. D. Clemenson, "KEE – The Knowledge Engineering Environment for Industry," *Systems and Software*, Vol. 3, No. 1, pp. 212–224, January 1984. [297]

44. Alex Roland, *op. cit.* p. 198. [297]

45. Richard Fikes *et al.*, "OPUS: A New Generation Knowledge Engineering Environment," Phase 1 Final Report, IntelliCorp, Mountain View, CA, 1987. [297]

46. Lee D. Erman, Jay S. Lark, and Frederick Hayes-Roth, "ABE: An Environment for Engineering Intelligent Systems," *IEEE Transactions on Software Engineering*, Vol. 14, No. 12, pp. 1758–1770, December 1988. [297]

47. Alex Roland, *op. cit.*, p. 201. [297]

48. Frederick Hayes-Roth and Neil Jacobstein, "The State of Knowledge-Based Systems," *Communications of the ACM*, Vol. 37, No. 3, p. 36, March 1994. [297]

49. *Ibid*, p. 36. [297]

50. Sara Reese Hedberg, "DART: Revolutionizing Logistics Planning," *IEEE Intelligent Systems*, p. 81, May/June 2002. [297]

51. *The CPSR Newsletter*, Vol. 2, No. 2, Spring 1984. Also see S. M. Ornstein, B. C. Smith, and L. A. Suchman, "Strategic Computing: An Assessment," *Bulletin of the Atomic Scientists*, Vol. 40, No. 10, pp. 11–15, December 1984. [298]

52. Alex Roland, *op. cit.*, p. 243. [298]

53. *Ibid*, p. 285. [299]

Part VI

Entr'acte

24

Speed Bumps

T HERE HAVE BEEN NAYSAYERS FROM THE EARLIEST DAYS OF ARTIFICIAL INTELLI-
gence. Alan Turing anticipated (and dealt with) some of their objections in his
1950 paper. In this chapter, I'll recount some of the controversies surrounding AI –
including some not foreseen by Turing. I'll also describe some formidable technical
difficulties confronting the field. By the mid-1980s or so, these difficulties had caused
some to be rather dismissive about progress up to that time and pessimistic about
the possibility of further progress. For example, in wondering about the need for a
special issue of the journal *Dædalus* devoted to AI in 1988, the philosopher Hilary
Putnam wrote[1] "What's all the fuss about *now*? Why a whole issue of *Dædalus*? Why
don't we wait until AI achieves something and *then* have an issue?"

The attacks and expressions of disappointment from outside the field helped
precipitate what some have called an "AI winter."

24.1 Opinions from Various Onlookers

24.1.1 *The Mind Is Not a Machine*

In the introduction to his edited volume of essays titled *Minds and Machines*,[2]
the philosopher Alan Ross Anderson mentions the following two extreme opinions
regarding whether or not the mind is a machine:

(1) We might say that human beings are merely very elaborate bits of clockwork, and that our
having "minds" is simply a consequence of the fact that the clockwork is *very* elaborate, or

(2) we might say that *any* machine is merely a product of human ingenuity (in principle
nothing more than a shovel), and that though *we* have minds, we cannot impart that peculiar
feature of ours to anything except our offspring: no machine can acquire this uniquely human
characteristic.

Most AI researchers probably agree with the first of these two statements. I
certainly do (although I would not have used the word "merely"). Marvin Minsky
put this position most powerfully when he is alleged to have said "The mind is a
meat machine." However, some philosophers hold to the second view. The most
prominent of these is probably the British philosopher, John R. Lucas (1929–).

In an essay titled "Minds, Machines, and Gödel,"[3] Lucas based his argument on
Kurt Gödel's proof that there are some true statements that cannot be proved by any
mechanical system that is both consistent and able (at least) to do arithmetic. Lucas

presumes that humans (or at least some humans) can "see" these statements to be true even though machines cannot prove them. Several people have pointed to flaws in Lucas's argument,[4] and Lucas claims to have responded to at least some of them in his book *The Freedom of the Will*.[5] In a 1990 paper read to the Turing Conference at Brighton, Lucas seems to have weakened his argument a bit by saying[6]

The argument I put forward is a two-level one. I do not offer a simple knock-down proof that minds are inherently better than machines, but a schema for constructing a *dis*proof of any plausible mechanist thesis that might be proposed. . . . Essentially, therefore, the two parts of my argument are first a hard negative argument, addressed to a mechanist putting forward a particular claim, and proving to him, by means he must acknowledge to be valid, that his claim is untenable, and secondly a hand-waving positive argument, addressed to intelligent men, bystanders as well as mechanists espousing particular versions of mechanism, to the effect that some sort of argument on these lines can always be found to deal with any further version of mechanism that may be thought up.

I happen to believe that humans are subject to whatever Gödelian limitations might apply to machines, but that's because I believe humans are machines. Lucas continues to argue his point because (I think) he would like to believe they are not. In any case, the argument is somewhat sterile because it does not really limit what AI can potentially do in practice. Even Lucas admitted in his original paper that we might be capable of "constructing very, very complicated systems of, say, valves and relays," that would be "capable of doing things which we recognized as intelligent, and not just mistakes or random shots, but which we had not programmed into it. But then it would cease to be a machine." (Here, he seems to be trying to win his argument by redefining "machine.")

The engineer Mortimer Taube (1910–1965) also believed that humans were not machines. In his 1961 book *Computers and Common Sense: The Myth of Thinking Machines*,[7] he railed against efforts to get computers to reason, to translate human languages, and to learn. Many of the things he said that computers would not be able to do have, by now, been done.

24.1.2 *The Mind Is Not a Computer*

A. New Physics Is Needed
Several people have put forward the argument that, although humans may well be machines, intelligence cannot be exhibited by computers – at least not by present-day computers made of transistors and other ordinary electromagnetic components and working the way they do.

The British physicist Sir Roger Penrose (1931– ; Fig. 24.1) is persuaded by Lucas's Gödelian arguments about the limitations of computers. (Penrose is famous for work in quantum physics, relativity theory, the structure of the universe, and "Penrose tilings.") He, like Lucas, believes that computers could never be conscious, nor could they have the full range of human intelligence. But Penrose imagines that these limitations apply only to machines based on the presently known laws of physics. To escape from Gödel's limitations (as Penrose believes brains do), he

Figure 24.1. Sir Roger Penrose.

claims a new kind of physics must be invoked – one that involves something he calls "correct quantum gravity." Unfortunately, correct quantum gravity, whatever it is, remains to be discovered (or, I would rather say, invented).

Penrose puts forward these ideas (along with some very engaging material about physics) in two books: *The Emperor's New Mind*[8] and *Shadows of the Mind: A Search for the Missing Science of Consciousness*.[9] I, along with many others, am skeptical that a new physics is needed to realize all of AI's ambitions. (But, of course, we have not realized them yet.) Penrose attempts to answer some of the criticisms of his views in his article "Beyond the Doubting of a Shadow: A Reply to Commentaries on Shadows of the Mind."[10]

B. Intentionality Is Needed

The American philosopher John Searle (1932– ; Fig. 24.2) argues that computational processes, as we know them, do not have something humans *do* have – something he and some other philosophers call "intentionality." Intentionality has to do with attaching "meaning" to objects and to properties of objects. Searle's definition is as follows: "Intentionality is . . . that feature of certain mental states by which they are directed at or about objects and states of affairs in the world." For example, according to Searle, "beliefs, desires, and intentions are intentional states."[11] Thus, he would claim, although it is possible to represent the phrase "John is tall" in a computer, say as a logical expression such as "G33(K077)," there is no way for the computer to know that G33 refers to the "in-the-world" property of "tallness" nor that K077 refers to the actual John "in the world." In short, computational processes lack "aboutness"; they don't know what their symbols are about. In contrast, when humans use words, they know what those words are about.

Figure 24.2. John Searle. (Photograph courtesy of John Searle.)

Searle is famous among AI researchers and philosophers for a thought experiment he proposed about "understanding." It has come to be called "the Chinese Room" experiment.[12] Searle sets up the thought experiment by writing

Suppose that I'm locked in a room and given a large batch of Chinese writing. Suppose furthermore (as is indeed the case) that I know no Chinese, either written or spoken, and that I'm not even confident that I could recognize Chinese writing as Chinese writing distinct from, say, Japanese writing or meaningless squiggles.

To make his experiment relevant to AI work about "story understanding," Searle imagines that his room contains two batches of Chinese symbols, which, unknown to Searle, constitute a story and general background information about such stories. The room also contains rules, written in English, about how to manipulate sets of Chinese characters and how to generate Chinese characters as a result of such manipulations.

Into such a room, then, comes a third batch of Chinese symbols. As Searle puts it, he has rules in the room (written in English) that

instruct me how to give back certain Chinese symbols with certain sorts of shapes in response to certain sorts of shapes given me in the third batch. Unknown to me, the people who are giving me all of these symbols call [the first two batches a story and its background information] and they call the third batch "questions." Furthermore, they call the symbols I give them back in response to the third batch "answers to the questions," and the set of rules in English that they gave me, they call the "program." . . . Suppose also that after a while I get so good at following the instructions for manipulating the Chinese symbols and the programmers get so good at writing the programs that from the external point of view – that is, from the point of view of somebody outside the room in which I am locked – my answers to the questions are absolutely indistinguishable from those of native Chinese speakers. Nobody just looking at my answers can tell that I don't speak a word of Chinese.

Searle's question, essentially, is "Can it be said that the room (containing Searle, the rules, and the batches of Chinese symbols) 'understands' Chinese?" Searle claims the answer is "no" because all that is going on is "formal symbol manipulation" without understanding what the symbols mean. In Searle's words:

Because the formal symbol manipulations by themselves don't have any intentionality; they are quite meaningless; they aren't even *symbol* manipulations, since the symbols don't symbolize anything. In the linguistic jargon, they have only a syntax but no semantics. Such intentionality as computers appear to have is solely in the minds of those who program them and those who use them, those who send in the input and those who interpret the output.

While acknowledging that the Chinese room "simulates" understanding, he distinguishes between simulations and "the real thing." He wrote

No one supposes that computer simulations of a five-alarm fire will burn the neighborhood down or that a computer simulation of a rainstorm will leave us all drenched. Why on earth would anyone suppose that a computer simulation of understanding actually understood anything? . . . For simulation, all you need is the right input and output and a program in the middle that transforms the former into the latter. That is all the computer has for anything it does. To confuse simulation with duplication is the same mistake, whether it is pain, love, cognition, fires, or rainstorms.

Searle's Chinese Room reminds me of Herb Simon's experiment in simulating the execution of the Logic Theorist (LT) program. Recall from Section 3.2 that LT began by hand simulation, using Simon's children as the computing elements, while writing on and holding up note cards as the registers that contained the state variables of the program. Presumably, the children knew nothing about propositional logic, yet the whole assemblage, Simon, the children, and the note cards, proved a theorem. Apparently, "simulating" the proof of a theorem is pretty much the same as actually proving a theorem – just as simulating addition is the same as addition. Could it be that simulating understanding is really the same as real understanding?

There are several possible responses to Searle's arguments, and there is no shortage of responders! In his paper, Searle anticipates many potential replies, and twenty-eight actual replies were published along with Searle's original paper. Here is what I think:

Let's imagine that we can look inside Searle's brain when he is in the process of understanding a question put to him in English. There are, presumably, trillions of synapses engaged in firing and inhibiting billions of neurons in a coordinated effort to make sense of the question and to compose and deliver an answer. We would not claim that any individual synapse nor the neurons it connects is understanding English. The process of "understanding" is not a concept that is meaningful at the level of detail appropriate for analyzing the workings of neurons. Analogously, the process of proving a theorem by a computer (or by Simon's children) is not a concept that is meaningful at the level of individual transistors (or children holding note cards). In explaining phenomena, either of the brain or of computers (or of anything else), we use concepts matched to the level of explanation. The concept of "understanding" is a concept we find useful to apply to mental activities viewed at the "whole-person level," not at the nerve-cell level. Similarly, we would, I think, find it useful to say that the assemblage of room, Searle, rules, and Chinese characters understood Chinese.

But what about meaning and intentionality? If we write G33(K077) in computer memory, does it "mean" anything? Well, it depends on what else is in computer memory – especially what else in memory is linked to the symbols G33 and K077. The symbols and the links between them constitute a network, and it is the whole network that contains the meanings. Recall the question M. Ross Quillian was attempting to answer in his 1966 dissertation, namely, "What sort of representational format can permit the 'meanings' of words to be stored, so that humanlike use of these meanings is possible?" Perhaps it's worth repeating here something I wrote in Section 6.3:

According to Quillian, the meaning of a term is represented by its place in the network and how it is connected to other terms. This same idea is used in dictionaries where the meaning of a word is given by mentioning the relationship of this word to other words. The meanings of those other words are, in turn, given by their relationships to yet other words. So we can think of a dictionary as being like a large semantic network of words linked to other words.

In some cases, it is also necessary to link a network's symbols to actual objects in the world through a computer's sensory and motor facilities. Newell and Simon anticipated this need in their paper about the physical symbol system hypothesis (PSSH). That hypothesis claims that a physical symbol system (such as a computer) has the necessary and sufficient conditions for intelligent behavior. Newell and Simon wrote[13]

A physical symbol system is a machine that produces through time an evolving collection of symbol structures. Such a system exists in a world of objects wider than just these symbolic expressions themselves.

Regarding this "world of objects," a physical symbol system includes (in addition to its means for formal symbol manipulation) the ability to "designate." Here is Newell and Simon's definition: "An expression [composed of symbols] designates an object if, given the expression, the system can either *affect the object itself* or *behave in ways dependent on the object*" (my italics).

So, I believe Searle is simply confused about some basic ideas in computer science. Although it has not yet been empirically established that a computer (manipulating symbols and attached as needed to its environment) can be made to exhibit all of the aspects of intelligent behavior of which humans are capable, I don't believe that Searle's thought experiment casts doubt on the possibility.

Searle himself believes that physical systems of some sort can be intelligent and understand things. He believes that humans are one kind of such a system. He wrote as follows:

"Could a machine think?"

The answer is, obviously, yes. We are precisely such machines.

"Yes, but could an artifact, a man-made machine think?"

Assuming it is possible to produce artificially a machine with a nervous system, neurons with axons and dendrites, and all the rest of it, sufficiently like ours, again the answer to the question seems to be obviously, yes.

Yet, Searle gives us no clue as to what it is about brains, composed of neurons, that is different from computers, composed of transistors, that endows the former,

Figure 24.3. Hubert Dreyfus. (Copyright photo: Sijmen Hendriks. Used with permission from Sijmen Hendriks.)

but not the latter, with intentionality. He claims that for a machine to think it would have to have "internal causal powers" equivalent to those of brains. He does not say just what these internal causal powers might be.

C. Strong and Weak AI

Searle's paper introduced definitions for "strong AI" and "weak AI" that are useful for distinguishing between two types of AI endeavors. Strong AI is associated with the claim that an appropriately programmed computer could be a mind and could think at least as well as humans do. Achieving strong AI is the ultimate goal for many artificial intelligence researchers. Searle's article attempts to show that strong AI (using computers) is impossible. However, practitioners of weak (or "cautious") AI use programs as a tool to study the mind by formulating and testing hypotheses about it. Weak AI has also come to be associated with attempts to build programs that aid, rather than duplicate, human mental activities. Weak AI has already been (and continues to be) quite successful, whereas the quest for strong AI will no doubt go on for a rather long time.

D. "Global Processes" Are Needed

Hubert L. Dreyfus (Fig. 24.3), now a philosophy professor at UC Berkeley, began his career teaching philosophy at MIT.[14] He first encountered the AI enterprise there, and in the early 1960s he and his brother, Stuart, attended a talk by Herb Simon. Several things about AI and about what they heard in the talk rankled the brothers Dreyfus. At about that time, the RAND Corporation in Santa Monica, California, thought that having a philosopher on board along with their computer people would be a good idea. Stuart, a specialist in operations research who was working at RAND, recommended Hubert. So Hubert spent the summer of 1961 at RAND as a consultant studying AI research. Shortly after the summer, Hubert wrote a RAND paper titled "Alchemy and Artificial Intelligence," in which, among other things, he concluded that the ultimate goals of AI research were as unachievable as were those of alchemy.[15]

In his paper, Dreyfus evaluated AI progress in four areas, namely, game playing, problem solving (including theorem proving), language translation, and pattern recognition. He wrote

An overall pattern is taking shape: an early, dramatic success based on the easy performance of simple tasks, or low-quality work on complex tasks, and then diminishing returns, disenchantment, and, in some cases, pessimism.

A typical case, he claimed, was Gelernter's geometry-theorem proving machine: "No more striking example exists of an 'astonishing' early success and the equally astonishing failure to follow it up." And, answering AI's claim that progress is being made, he wrote "According to this definition [of progress], the first man to climb a tree could claim tangible progress toward flight to the moon."

One of the reasons for this stagnation, according to Dreyfus, was that AI research is based on the assumption that thinking can be analyzed as a finite set of simple determinate operations (such as the application of rules to a finite set of data). Rather, he claimed, "thinking involves global processes, which cannot be understood in terms of a sequence or even a parallel set of discrete steps." These global processes are manifest in three ways. The first is "fringe consciousness." It is what the brain uses to access the infinite "open-ended information characteristic of everyday experience." Fringe consciousness allows humans to consider details and the big picture simultaneously. Another global process is at work in human thinking when we distinguish the essential from the unessential. The third is "global context," which allows us to reduce ambiguity. A combination of these abilities permits what he calls "perspicuous grouping" – what the brain does when it recognizes complex patterns, such as human faces, for example. Dreyfus claimed that computer programs are unable to employ these global processes, which are essential for intelligent behavior.

Dreyfus stated that the brain processes information in an entirely different way than a computer does. He wrote that information in the brain is "processed globally the way a resistor analogue [a kind of analog computer] solves the problem of the minimal path through a network." Furthermore, he said that the "body plays a crucial role in making possible intelligent behavior." Several other people have emphasized the importance of "embodiment" for progress in AI, and I'll have more to say about that topic shortly.

About the future (as judged from the early 1960s), Dreyfus wrote

Only experimentation can determine the extent to which newer and faster machines, better programming languages, and clever heuristics can continue to push back the frontier. Nonetheless, the dramatic slowdown in the fields we have considered and the general failure to fulfill earlier predictions suggest the boundary may be near.

Dreyfus's comments on AI should not be taken to imply that he thought that human-level artificial intelligence by machines is impossible – he just thought (and still thinks) that it is impossible using the methods of what the philosopher John Haugeland called "good old-fashioned artificial intelligence" (GOFAI),[16] namely, the kind that uses heuristic search and discrete collections of symbolically represented facts and rules. He acknowledged that, in principle, "we could simulate intelligent behavior if we could build or simulate a device which functioned exactly like the human brain." But, he thought, such a simulation could not be realized in practice. "We do not know the equations describing the physical processes in the brain, and even if we did, the solution of the equations describing the simplest reaction would take a prohibitive amount of time." The summary of his paper concluded with "Significant developments in artificial intelligence. . . must await an entirely different sort of computer. The only existing prototype for it is the little-understood human brain."

The main ideas of his RAND paper have been presented and expanded in several of Dreyfus's books and articles.[17] Pamela McCorduck's book, *Machines Who Think*,[18] has an excellent chapter about Dreyfus, detailing his arguments and the rather contentious interactions between him and AI scientists. Because she covers that ground so well, I'll concentrate on his ideas about the need for "embodiment" as described in a couple of his recent papers.

E. "Being There" Is Needed

Dreyfus's main point, I think, is that intelligence in humans derives from their "being in the world" and not because they are guided by rules. The use of rules in AI programs (as in humans) might allow competent behavior but not expert behavior. Here are some excerpts from an address Dreyfus gave in 2005:[19]

. . . in our formal instruction we start with rules. The rules, however, seem to give way to more flexible responses as we become skilled. . . . The actual phenomenon suggests that to become experts we must switch from detached rule-following to a more involved and situation-specific way of coping.

. . .

In general, instead of relying on rules and standards to decide on or to justify her actions, the expert immediately responds to the current concrete situation.

. . .

"Expert Systems" based on the rules so-called knowledge engineers elicited from experts were at best competent. It seems that, instead of using rules they no longer remembered, as the AI researchers supposed, the experts were forced to remember rules they no longer used. Indeed, as far as anyone could tell, the experts weren't following any rules at all.

According to Dreyfus, the transition from merely competent behavior to expert behavior requires "being in the world" through having a body embedded in the world. Embodied agents, such as humans, "can dwell in the world in such a way as to avoid the infinite task of formalizing everything" (as AI programs futilely attempt to do).[20] Dreyfus's view of this need for embodiment is based on a branch of a philosophical school called "phenomenology." Dreyfus wrote me that the existential phenomenology of Martin Heidegger (1989–1976), which stresses "our practical involvement with people and things as our basic way of being," is the basis for his critique of GOFAI.[21] He argues that for AI to succeed it would need[22]

. . . a model of *our particular way of being embedded and embodied* such that what we experience is significant for us in the particular way that it is. That is, we would have to include in our program a model of a body very much like ours with our needs, desires, pleasures, pains, ways of moving, cultural background, etc.

Others arguing for embodiment point out that some of the "computations" needed by an intelligent agent could be accomplished by the dynamic interactions between parts of its body and its environment. For example, Rolf Pfeifer, Max Lungarella, and Fumiya Iida have written that "An embodied perspective, because it distributes control and processing to all aspects of the agent (its central nervous system, the material properties of its musculoskeletal system, the sensor morphology, and the interaction with the environment), provides an alternative avenue for tackling the challenges faced by robotics. The tasks performed by the controller in the classical approach are now partially taken over by morphology and materials in a process of self-organization...”[23]

But even if a body were needed, its form would seem to depend on what the associated AI system is used for. The body of the fictional HAL 9000 was the entire spacecraft that it controlled. Shakey the robot had a body that was apparently appropriate for its needs. If ever a “conversational Google” were to be developed that could engage in dialogs with users about the content of all Web pages, its “body” would be the entire Internet and the routines needed to access it.

24.1.3 *Differences Between Brains and Computers*

In addition to Dreyfus, several critics of AI have pointed out that “the brain is not a computer,” and, therefore, people who are attempting to do with computers what brains can do must necessarily fail. These critics often stress distinctions such as the following:

- Computers have perhaps hundreds of processing units whereas brains have trillions.
- Computers perform billions of operations per second whereas brains perform only thousands.
- Computers are subject to crashes whereas brains are fault tolerant.
- Computers use binary signals whereas brains work with analog ones.
- Computers do only what their programmers tell them to do whereas brains are creative.
- Computers perform serial operations whereas brains are massively parallel.
- Computers are constrained to be “logical” whereas brains can be “intuitive.”
- Computers are programmed whereas brains learn.

Aside from the fact that many of these distinctions are no longer valid,[24] comparisons depend on what is meant by “the brain” and what is meant by “a computer.” If our understanding of the brain is in terms of its component neurons, with their gazillions of axons, dendrites, and synaptic connections, and if our understanding of a computer is in terms of serial, “von Neumann–style” operation – reading, processing, and writing of bits – all accomplished by transistor circuitry, well then of course, the brain is not *that* kind of a computer.

However, we don’t understand “computation” by reference only to a low-level, von Neumann–style description. We can understand it at any one of a number of description levels. For example, computation might be understood as a very large number of concurrently active “knowledge sources” asynchronously reading from, transforming, and writing complex symbolic expressions on a “Blackboard” or as a collection of symbol-processing and neural network demons arranged in a Pandemonium-style network. Perhaps our gradually increasing understanding of how the brain operates will even lead to other useful computational models. Ideas about what “computation” can be are ever expanding, so those who would claim that the brain is not a computer will need to be more precise about just what kind of computer the brain is not. (After all, if some people, like Lucas, can restrict what

Figure 24.4. Joseph Weizenbaum. (Photograph courtesy MIT Museum.)

a machine can be, it seems only fair that others can expand the definition of what a
computer can be.)

24.1.4 *But Should We?*

Besides the criticisms of AI based on what people claim it cannot do, there are also
criticisms based on what people claim it *should not* do. Some of the "should-not"
people mention the inappropriateness of machines attempting to perform tasks that
are inherently human-centric, such as teaching, counseling, and rendering judicial
opinions. Others, such as the Computer Professionals for Social Responsibility
mentioned previously, don't want to see AI technology (or any other technology for
that matter) used in warfare or for surveillance or for tasks that require experience-
based human judgment. In addition, there are those who, like the Luddites of
19th century Britain, are concerned about machines replacing humans and thereby
causing unemployment and economic dislocation. Finally, there are those who worry
that AI and other computer technology would dehumanize people, reduce the need
for person-to-person contact, and change what it means to be human.

Joseph Weizenbaum (1923–2008; Fig. 24.4), the man who wrote the ELIZA program I mentioned in Section 2.3.3, has written and lectured about the dangers of
giving computers responsibilities that he thought ought best be left to humans. Some
say that the motivating reason for his concern was that he was surprised and shocked
by the fact that some people mistook conversations with ELIZA for conversations
with a real person. In his book *Computer Power and Human Reason: From Judgment
to Calculation*,[25] Weizenbaum argued that "there is a difference between man and
machine, and . . . there are certain tasks which computers *ought* not be made to do,
independent of whether computers *can* be made to do them.

In his book, Weizenbaum stressed the importance of the cultural milieu in which
a person grows up, lives, and works. No machine experiences (or could experience)

a human-type background, and therefore no machine should be allowed to make the kinds of decisions or give the kinds of advice that require, among other things, the compassion and wisdom engendered by such a background. He emphasizes this point by saying that inexperience with these "domains of thought and action" would also apply "to the way humans relate to one another as well as to machines and their relations to man."[26] Thus, I suppose he would think that just as it would be inappropriate for a machine to make judicial decisions, so also would it be inappropriate for a person raised in America to make judicial decisions in Japan. Moreover, he ridicules the idea that a machine could obtain the necessary background by giving it a human-like body and sensory apparatus. He wrote that "the deepest and most grandiose fantasy that motivates work on artificial intelligence . . . is nothing less than to build a machine on the model of man, a robot that is to have its childhood, to learn language as a child does, to gain its knowledge of the world by sensing the world through its own organs, and ultimately to contemplate the whole domain of human thought."[27]

Weizenbaum escaped from Nazi Germany with his family in 1936. That experience cannot but have sharpened his keen sense of social responsibility. He wrote, for example, that[28]

The very asking of the question, "What does a judge (or a psychiatrist) know that we cannot tell a computer?" is a monstrous obscenity. That it has to be put in print at all, even for the purpose of exposing its morbidity, is a sign of the madness of our times.

. . .

[The relevant issues] cannot be settled by asking questions beginning with "can." The limits of the applicability of computers are ultimately statable only in terms of oughts. What emerges as the most elementary insight is that, since we do not now have any ways of making computers wise, we ought not now to give computers tasks that demand wisdom.

Even though Weizenbaum hedges a bit on the "can" question, I believe he really believed that machines "could not" as well as "should not." For if machines really *could* make judgments with all of the "compassion and wisdom" with which humans can, why *shouldn't* they? In addition to the concern about using *any* technology for antisocial purposes (such as war), the real danger, I think, lies in the premature use of machines: thinking that they are able to perform a task before they are really competent to do so.

Another person who recoiled from the prospect of machines "taking over" is the physician, biologist, and essayist Lewis Thomas (1913–1993). In one of his celebrated columns, "Notes of a Biology-Watcher," in *The New England Journal of Medicine*, he wrote[29]

The most profoundly depressing of all ideas about the future of the human species is the concept of artificial intelligence. The ambition that human beings will ultimately cap their success as evolutionary overachievers by manufacturing computers of such complexity and ingenuity as to be smarter than they are, and that these devices will take over and run the place for human betterment or perhaps, later on, for machine betterment, strikes me as wrong in a deep sense, maybe even evil.

. . .

This is what the artificial intelligence people are talking about: a mechanical brain with the capacity to look back over the past and make accurate predictions about the future, then to lay out flawless plans for changing that future any way it feels like, and, most appalling of all, capable of feeling like doing one thing or another.

. . .

It is, in my view, an absolutely hideous prospect, and if I thought it were really something waiting ineluctably ahead of us I would spend all my days in protest.

Although there have been several other authors who have warned about the dangers of the inappropriate use of computers in general and of intelligent machines in particular, I'll mention just one more, a self-confessed "neo-Luddite." Theodore Roszak (1933–) is a prominent author and social thinker – one well worth reading in my opinion. In his book *The Cult of Information*,[30] he claimed that a growing cult, infatuated with "information" and "information processing," is having debilitating cultural effects – "especially when it comes to teaching the young." Roszak wrote that he is "an ally of all those serious students and users of information technology who hold a reasonably balanced view of what computers can and cannot, should and should not, do," but claims that "the creation of a mystique of information [has made] basic intellectual discriminations between data, knowledge, judgment, imagination, insight and wisdom impossible."[31]

Claiming that there is a "vital distinction" between information processing and thinking, he wrote[32]

Because the ability [of the computer] to store data somewhat corresponds to what we call memory in human beings, and because the ability to follow logical procedures somewhat corresponds to what we call reasoning in human beings, many members of the cult [of information] have concluded that what computers do somewhat corresponds to what we call thinking.

However, Roszak concludes, computers cannot really "think." The danger is that those who are persuaded (or duped into believing) that they can might inappropriately employ computers in tasks that require thinking and not just "data processing." I believe Roszak has a legitimate concern here – AI is not yet up to all of the tasks to which we might try to put it.

But Roszak also wrote[33]

There is no possibility that computers will ever equal or replace the mind except in those limited functional applications that do involve data processing and procedural thinking. The possibility is ruled out in principle, because the metaphysical assumptions that underlie the effort are false.

Here, I disagree. I know of no "metaphysical assumptions" of AI other than that the brain is a kind of machine and therefore we ought to be able to understand it and build something that works very much like it. Furthermore, I know of no credible evidence that that metaphysical assumption is false.

Although he does not think that computers can become minds, he worries about the additional danger that "it is possible to redefine the mind and its uses in ways that *can* be imitated by machine. Then we have a mechanical caricature which levels the activity down to a lower standard."[34]

Roszak does have at least two good things to say about AI – one a negative result and one a positive contribution. As for the negative result, he says[35]

There is an ironic but highly valuable quality to AI in all its forms. The effort to simulate or surpass human intelligence is uncovering subtleties and paradoxes about the human mind we might never have imagined. By way of heroic failures, AI is teaching us how truly strange real intelligence is.

On the positive side he comments that[36]

One field of AI, however, has made remarkable progress. . . . Often, by quizzing specialists closely about their work, computer programmers can tease out procedures, assumptions, values that can then be formally specified. The result is an Expert System, one of the few practical applications of AI. Edward Feigenbaum sees such systems as the gateway to the next era of machine intelligence; he calls it "knowledge processing," as opposed to mere *data* processing. Whatever he may mean by "knowledge," it surely represents a more complex approach to thinking than once prevailed in the field.

24.1.5 *Other Opinions*

In January 1981, to sample some opinions about AI for a talk I was planning, I wrote to some leaders in computer science and related disciplines asking them what they thought about AI's achievements, weaknesses, and prospects. I received several replies and will excerpt some comments.[37]

The computer scientist (and my colleague at Stanford) Donald Knuth wrote

I'm intrigued that AI has by now succeeded in doing essentially everything that requires "thinking" but has failed to do most of what people and animals do "without thinking" – that, somehow, is much harder! I believe the knowledge gained while building AI programs is more important than the use of the programs . . .

John R. Pierce, whom I have already mentioned in connection with both the ALPAC report on machine translation (in Section 7.2) and his negative comments about speech understanding (p. 222), wrote me a very short letter in which he stated

Concerning artificial intelligence, I believe I invented the slogan, "Artificial intelligence is real stupidity."
. . .
I resent artificial intelligence because I feel that it is unfair to computers. But then, artificial intelligence people *did* devise LISP, which is pretty good.

The letter did not elaborate either on the slogan[38] or why AI is "unfair to computers."

The Dutch computer scientist Edsger W. Dijkstra (1930–2002) was famous for many innovations in computer science, including an algorithm for finding the shortest (or least-costly) paths in graphs. He also championed what is called "structured programming," a methodology that greatly improved the efficiency of writing (and understanding) programs. In response to my letter, he wrote (most cordially and in beautiful penmanship)

To the artificial intelligentsia that argue "But we are only symbol manipulating machines, aren't we?" one can only answer "There is none so blind as them that won't see!" The analogy is so shallow that I can characterize an appeal to it only as typically medieval thinking.

In addition to concerns about AI's "overstated claims," many computer scientists thought AI to be a kind of "fringe activity" that did not adhere to rigorous scientific standards and a field that housed charlatans. I recall that when I first interviewed for a position at SRI in 1961, I was warned by one researcher there against joining research on neural networks. Such research, he claimed, was "premature," and my involvement in it could damage my reputation.

Concern for "respectability" has had, I think, a stultifying effect on some AI researchers. I hear them saying things like, "AI used to be criticized for its flossiness. Now that we have made solid progress, let us not risk losing our respectability." One result of this conservatism has been increased concentration on "weak AI" – the variety devoted to providing aids to human thought – and away from "strong AI" – the variety that attempts to mechanize human-level intelligence. This is too bad, because, although I think the goals of weak AI are important and worthy, building an artifact that mimics the abilities of the human brain would be a tremendous scientific achievement – well worth the risk and not at all an "obscenity," "evil," "hideous," nor "impossible in principle."

24.2 Problems of Scale

24.2.1 *The Combinatorial Explosion*

Because search plays such a prominent role in artificial intelligence, it is important to say something about how extremely difficult search problems can be. A typical search problem is usually cast as growing a "tree" of nodes, such as Arthur Samuel's checkers game tree shown in Section 5.4 or the sliding–tile (eight–puzzle) search tree shown in Section 5.1. For example, if each node in a search tree has three possible "child" nodes (that is, a "branching factor" of 3), the top part of the tree would look like the one in Fig. 24.5.

The "first level" of the tree has three nodes, the second has nine nodes, and so on. In the general case, for a tree with branching factor b, the dth level would have b^d nodes (that is, b multiplied by itself d times). The total number of nodes that a search process would generate if it generated a whole tree with branching factor b down to and including all of the nodes at depth level d can be calculated to be $\frac{b}{(b-1)}(b^d - 1)$. Readers who recall their high school algebra will recognize these expressions as "exponential" functions of d. Because the number of nodes in a search tree is an exponential function of its depth, search is called an exponential process.

If a program had to search a tree with branching factor of 3 to a depth level of 10 to find a goal, it would have to generate 88,572 nodes. Numbers like that were well within the range of the capabilities of computers of the 1960s and 1970s, and so they were quite capable of solving some of the simpler AI "toy problems." But more realistic problems would involve search trees of much higher branching factors, having goals at much greater depth levels. For example, to search a tree

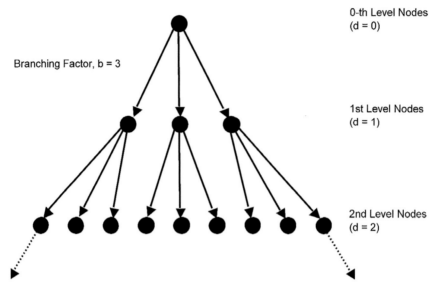

Branching Factor, b = 3

0-th Level Nodes
(d = 0)

1st Level Nodes
(d = 1)

2nd Level Nodes
(d = 2)

Figure 24.5. A search tree.

with branching factor of 10 to depth 20 (a tree corresponding to only a modestly difficult search problem) would require the generation of more than 10^{20} nodes, a quite impossible feat. (10^{20} is one followed by 20 zeros, that is, 100 billion billion.)

The difficulty of such searches has two aspects: computing time and storage space. Considering just computing time for a moment, even if we could generate a billion nodes each second (which is perhaps just barely thinkable), it would still take 100 billion seconds (over 3,000 years) to generate the tree with the branching factor and depth we have just been considering.

Regarding storage space, even personal computers these days come with lots of it – 100 gigabytes (100 billion bytes) is typical. Assuming that a single node requires about one byte, one would need the storage equivalent of around a billion such computers for even our modestly sized search tree.

The exponential nature of search means that as a problem's size increases (as measured either by the branching factor or by the depth of search trees), the computational difficulty needed to solve the problem increases drastically – creating what is called a "combinatorial explosion."

Of course, even early AI researchers knew about combinatorial explosions. That's the reason for their interest in heuristics. Unfortunately, heuristics do not change the exponential character of search – at best they reduce the branching factor. The "explosion" still happens – just not quite so rapidly. For example, reducing the branching factor from 10 to 4 and searching again to depth 20 would still require the generation of over 4^{20} or, roughly, one trillion nodes.

AI critics have focused on this problem in their pessimistic assessments of AI's achievements and prospects. For example, Sir James Lighthill (in his report that I mentioned in Chapter 16) wrote that "one rather general cause for the [AI] disappointments that have been experienced [is a] failure to recognize the implications of the 'combinatorial explosion.'" Lighthill's report did cause, as I have already mentioned, funding difficulties for AI research in Britain.

24.2.2 *Complexity Theory*

AI researchers are not the only people who are concerned about the computational difficulty of problem solving. A branch of computer science called "complexity theory" deals with how long and how much storage space different kinds of programs might take (in the worst case) to solve different kinds of problems. They ask, among other things, "How does the *size* of a problem affect the time and space required to solve it?"

Let's look at some examples. The time that it would take for a computer program to find the largest number in a list of numbers is proportional to the size of this problem, namely, the number of items in the list. (The worst case would happen if the largest item happened to be the last item in the list; a program would then have to examine each item in the list.) Such a program is said to take "linear time." Similarly, a program for finding out whether a given item is a member of a list of items would take linear time. (Again, the worst case would happen if the item happened to be the last item in the list.) In both cases, if we were to double the size, we would double the time required.

Sorting a list of names, putting them in alphabetical order for example, is a harder problem. Programs for sorting lists differ in how long they take and how complicated they are to program. Reasonably simple sorting programs take time that is proportional to the square of the number of items in the list. That is, for these programs, sorting a list that has 100 items in it would take four times as long as a list with only 50 items in it. (Multiplying the number of elements by two increases the sorting time by two squared, or four. Sorting can actually be done faster. There are programs that can sort a list in time proportional to the logarithm of the size times the size.) Programs that can (in the worst case) take time proportional to a problem's size, or the square, or the cube, or other "powers" of the size, run in what is called "polynomial time."

Problems themselves can be graded according to the complexity of the least complex programs that are able to solve them. For example, if a program exists that can solve a problem in linear time, but none could solve it faster, than that problem is said to be of "linear complexity." Finding out whether or not an item is a member of a list of items is a problem of linear complexity. We denote by P the class of problems that can be solved in polynomial time. Members of this class include calculating the greatest common divisor and determining whether or not a number is a prime number.

Unfortunately, as I have already mentioned, the search procedures used in many AI programs require running times that are exponential in the size of the problem. For example, searching a tree having branching factor of b to depth d would take time proportional to b^d. Using my previous example, we see that searching a tree with branching factor of 3 to a depth level of 10 requires the generation of 88,572 nodes. But doubling the depth to 20 would require searching not four times 88,572 nodes (which would be the case if search time was proportional to the square of the

Figure 24.6. Jacob (Jack) Schwartz. (Photograph used with permission of Diana Schwartz.)

depth) but $88,572 \times 88,572$ or almost eight-billion nodes. Exponential complexity is much, much worse than polynomial complexity!

The American computer scientist Stephen Cook (1939–) [as well as the Russian, and now American, computer scientist Leonid Levin (1948–)] made major contributions to our understanding of the complexity of problems and the programs used to solve them. In particular, Cook (and Levin independently) defined the class called the nondeterministic polynomial, or NP, class of problems. This is the class of problems for which a candidate solution can be checked (but not necessarily solved) in polynomial time. For example, a proposed sequence of moves to solve a sliding tile puzzle can be *checked* to see whether it actually solves the puzzle in polynomial time, but (as far as is known) it would require exponential time to *find* a solution. So sliding tile problems, along with many other AI problems, belong to the class NP.[39]

It is not known whether or not there might be polynomial programs for solving the problems in the class NP. If there were, NP would equal P. So far, programs for solving problems in the class NP require exponential time (in the worst case). Whether or not NP equals P is one of the most famous unsolved problems in computer science. Many people think NP does not equal P because otherwise we would have found out by now. (The Clay Mathematics Institute has offered a prize of $1,000,000 for a solution of the P versus NP question – that is, showing either that they are equal or not equal.)[40]

24.2.3 *A Sober Assessment*

These results in complexity theory caused some people to have grave doubts about the prospects for artificial intelligence. One of the most penetrating, and to my mind intelligent, assessments was written by the mathematician and computer scientist Jacob T. Schwartz (1930–2009; Fig. 24.6), whom I have already mentioned in connection with his tenure at DARPA. In his article titled "The Limits of Artificial Intelligence,"[41] Schwartz wrote that the extraordinary powers of the human brain arose from the way it used its prodigious computational and storage abilities "to organize information presented in relatively disordered form into internally organized structures on which sophisticated, coherent courses of symbolic and real-world action can be based." To rival the brain, what AI needs, and what AI has vainly been trying to achieve, Schwartz claimed, are "coherent structures capable of directly guiding some form of computer action . . . generated automatically from relatively disorganized, fragmented input." The ability to generate such "organized structures" would constitute a tremendous breakthrough because computers are "already enormously superhuman" in solving problems for which they can "accept, retain, and utilize *fully structured material*." "If the basic obstacle posed by the need to program [computers] in detail could be overcome," he wrote, "computers could ingest the information contained in all the world's libraries and use this information with superhuman effectiveness." (Nowadays, of course, besides libraries there is all the information, and misinformation, on the World Wide Web.)

The methods that AI researchers had used for automatically creating structure from fragmented input were all based on heuristic search – either searching for chains of logical deductions or for paths in trees (and more generally graphs). Logical deductions had been used (among other things) to answer questions, to provide expert advice, and to generate programs and plans. Searching for paths in graphs had been used to prove theorems in geometry, to parse sentences, and to produce plans for robots. All of these are instances of creating *structure* (to use Schwartz's term) from unstructured input. These "successes" however were all achieved on either trivially small problems or on ones whose subject matter was strictly circumscribed. Unfortunately, as Schwartz correctly claimed, all attempts to date to generate "broadly useful symbolic structures from more disorganized and fragmentary input" have invariably been defeated by the combinatorial explosion. He summarized the situation by echoing Dreyfus's charge that ". . . the history of AI research to date [consisted] always of very limited success in particular areas, followed immediately by failure to reach the broader goals at which these initial successes seem at first to hint . . ."

Schwartz's opinions about AI did have consequential effects because, as I mentioned in Section 23.4, he was the Director of the DARPA ISTO from 1987 to 1989 and presided over some cutbacks in AI research (including the cancellation of one of my own research projects in 1987). Even though he was generally dismissive of AI work, Schwartz did write that those "areas of AI to which classical scientific and algorithmic techniques apply can be expected to progress more rapidly than areas that deal with deeper problems for which only less focused approaches are available." As one example, he cited the problem of determining "whether one or more objects of known shape moving in an environment containing obstacles of other known shapes can pass from one specified position to another without colliding either with the obstacle or with each other."

Although these results from complexity theory did constitute one of the "speed bumps" in AI's rapid forward progress, AI researchers quickly recovered and found various ways around the combinatorial explosion problem. They pointed out, for example, that complexity results were based on worst-case performance, and solutions might often be found faster than in the worst case.

Figure 24.7. Richard Korf. (Photograph courtesy of Richard Korf.)

For example, I'll mention the work of Richard Korf (1956– ; Fig. 24.7), an AI researcher at the University of California at Los Angeles. Korf is well known for his work on tackling extremely difficult search problems. He often uses the sliding tile and other puzzles as laboratory "drosophila" for exploring new ideas in search.

You will recall that I used the example of a sliding tile puzzle to illustrate heuristic search processes. The one I used consisted of eight tiles in a 3×3 array; the classic version consists of fifteen tiles in a 4×4 array. One can imagine larger versions, such as twenty-four tiles in a 5×5 array. The 4×4 puzzle already presents a quite challenging problem for heuristic search. In fact, in his comments about the scaling difficulties of search processes, Jack Schwartz wrote ". . . the graph of states [of the 3×3 puzzle] consists of 9!, or 362,880 [nodes], so even for so simple a problem brute-force graph search begins to become taxing. For the corresponding 4×4 puzzle, whose state space involves 16!, or over 10^{13}, nodes, it is completely infeasible." [Actually, Schwartz was off by (an inconsequential) factor of 2 in both cases. It has been known since 1879 that if you start from any particular initial configuration, you can only reach $1/2$ of all the possible configurations.[42] Thus, for the eight-tile version, the entire state-space graph consists of two separate disconnected graphs of size $9!/2 = 181,440$.]

Yet, not only has Korf written heuristic search programs to solve instances of the 4×4 puzzle, but in an abstract of a 1996 paper he and his co-author wrote[43]

We have found the first optimal solutions to a complete set of random instances of the Twenty-Four Puzzle, the 5×5 version of the well-known sliding-tile puzzles. Our new contribution to this problem is a more powerful admissible heuristic function.

. . .

[W]e observe that as heuristic search problems are scaled up, more powerful heuristic functions become both necessary and cost-effective.

The search space for the 5×5 puzzle is about a trillion times larger than that of the 4×4 puzzle. It has about 7.756×10^{24} nodes.

Search is also made easier if one could be satisfied with "good" or approximate solutions to problems rather than insisting on the "best" solutions. In a subsequent chapter, I'll describe some rather remarkable progress on dealing with large search problems; this progress has flattened the speed bumps a bit.

Even with these ways around the complexity results, however, AI people did begin to acknowledge other shortcomings – a subject I'll turn to next.

24.3 Acknowledged Shortcomings

As AI researchers began to confront problems of practical importance, they themselves had to acknowledge several difficulties. These came up in several application areas. I'll mention just a few.

In attempting to prove nontrivial mathematical theorems, for example, theorem-proving programs quickly exhausted the space necessary to store intermediate results. But humans (well, some humans at least) are able to prove theorems. What methods are they using that computer programs are not? Mathematicians would probably say that intuition, judgment, experience, mathematical sophistication, and such are critical to their successes. So far, it has proven difficult to provide computers with these capabilities.

In game playing, although MAC HACK VI and CHESS 4.6, to name two examples, played pretty good chess, they were far from being able to beat world champions. In fact, in August 1978 at the Canadian National Exhibition in Toronto, David Levy defeated the reigning Computer Chess Champion, CHESS 4.7, from Northwestern University, thus winning the bet he made ten years before against John McCarthy and Donald Michie. As Levy put it, "I managed to beat the program fairly convincingly, by three wins to one with one game drawn (the sixth game did not need to be played) and with this match I won my bet."[44]

What accounts for championship ability? It's unlikely that chess champions look at more chess positions than computers do. However, they probably look farther ahead in the game tree along the most important branches. Their experience seems to enable them to evaluate the potential of those candidate positions that are worthy of exploration and to ignore further exploration of worthless positions. Perhaps they also think in a more strategic manner than do chess programs that consider individual chess moves.

Another game, perhaps more challenging for humans even than chess, is the game of Go – a board game that originated in China more than 4,000 years ago and is very popular in Asian countries today. In Go, two players alternate in placing black and white stones at the intersections of a 19×19 grid of two sets of lines ruled on a board. I won't describe the rules of the game here, except to say that (at least in the early stages of the game) a player is faced with the problem of deciding at which of almost 361 (19×19) positions to place a stone. Even for the most powerful search processes, searching a tree, each of whose nodes has nearly 361 immediate descendants, is out of the question. Human players must be using other strategies, and, whatever these strategies are, they are still unknown to AI researchers. Many AI researchers think that performance in Go is a better measure of AI's abilities than is performance in chess. I'll describe some recent progress later in the book.

Although expert systems reason usefully (and even with economic advantage) about specific problems in medicine, geology, chemistry, and other delimited areas, they are acknowledged to be "brittle" – that is, they break down when confronted with problems outside their area of expertise or even on problems within their area of expertise if knowledge were needed that had not been provided in their rules. They don't know what they don't know and therefore might provide wrong answers in cases where a human expert would do better. It is said that John McCarthy, in an interaction with the medical expert system MYCIN, typed in some information about a hypothetical patient, saying that he was male and also saying that he underwent amniocentesis. MYCIN accepted all of that without complaint! That male patients don't get pregnant was not considered part of the "expert knowledge" that MYCIN needed to be given.

One of the reasons why expert systems are brittle is that they lack "common sense."[45] In addition to the expert knowledge that humans might acquire through education and professional experience, they also have a lot of general knowledge. They know, for example, that only females can become pregnant, that umbrellas protect against sun and rain, that certain birds migrate, that food can be purchased in markets, and millions upon millions of other facts. Benjamin Kuipers, an AI researcher and professor at the University of Michigan (formerly at the University of Texas at Austin), defined common sense this way: "Commonsense knowledge is knowledge about the structure of the external world that is acquired and applied without concentrated effort by any normal human that allows him or her to meet the everyday demands of the physical, spatial, temporal and social environment with a reasonable degree of success."[46]

This general knowledge is acquired gradually as children grow into adults and as adults mature. For example, a child probably does not know that small tablets in little plastic bottles might be dangerous if swallowed (which is why these bottles have child-proof caps), teenagers know a lot of things that eight-year olds typically do not, and the knowledge that enables a reader of *The New Yorker*, say, to understand its reviews of books and films goes beyond what a teenager typically knows. Also, of course, people in different countries and cultures will have different common-sense knowledge.

It seems to me that the knowledge of any particular human should be thought of as an ever-growing tree whose base and lower branches comprise "common sense" and whose upper ramifications comprise the "expertise" of specialized disciplines that the person might have learned. The tree metaphor is also useful in emphasizing the point that the knowledge in the upper branches uses concepts that occur in the trunk and lower branches.

We saw in an earlier chapter that a full understanding of sentences in natural language seemed to require the common-sense information that humans have but computers still do not. The daunting prospect of endowing computers with common sense has led to two quite opposite reactions. Some see this difficulty as ruling out the possibility of AI (or at least of strong AI) for the foreseeable future. Others, though, say "Let's get on with it." (I'll be talking about the work of one of the let's-get-on-with-it people in a subsequent chapter.) Of course, it is no more to be expected that any particular AI system will understand all natural language sentences than it can be expected that any particular human will understand natural language sentences about all subjects. Humans have their limitations, and AI programs will have them too. That prospect should no more limit our attempts to produce intelligent programs than it does to educate intelligent humans.

24.4 The "AI Winter"

During the early 1980s, many AI sponsors, in government and in industry, had greatly inflated expectations of what AI could do. Undoubtedly, some of the blame for their unjustified optimism could be placed on AI researchers themselves who were motivated to make exaggerated promises. The failure to deliver systems matching these unrealistic hopes, together with the accumulating critical commentary that I have already mentioned, combined in the mid- to late 1980s to bring on what came to be called an "AI winter."

Indeed, at the 1984 AAAI National Convention several leading AI researchers warned about this possibility during a panel session titled "The 'Dark Ages' of AI – Can We Avoid Them or Survive Them?" The panel's chair, Drew McDermott of Yale University, started the session off by saying[47]

> In spite of all the commercial hustle and bustle around AI these days, there's a mood that I'm sure many of you are familiar with of deep unease among AI researchers who have been around more than the last four years or so. This unease is due to the worry that perhaps expectations about AI are too high, and that this will eventually result in disaster.
>
> . . . I think it is important that we take steps to make sure the "AI Winter" doesn't happen – by disciplining ourselves and educating the public.

But if "disciplining" and "educating" did take place, they were insufficient to prevent the worried-about downturn. During the late 1980s, membership in the AAAI gradually fell. By 1996, it had leveled off to between 4,000 and 5,000 members. Advertising in the *AI Magazine* dropped also – as did participation by government and industry in AI conference exhibits. Several AI companies closed their doors, and AI research at some of the larger computer hardware and software companies was terminated. According to Alex Roland, between 1987 and 1989, DARPA's budget for basic AI and Strategic Computing research fell from $47 million to $31 million. (Even so, according to Alex Roland, CMU's budget was increased for its speech understanding program and its autonomous vehicle program during this time.)

But the winter endured only for a season – a season not of hibernation but of renewed efforts to carry on. Several new ideas were explored, and older ones were strengthened with added powers, as I'll explain in subsequent chapters.

Notes

1. Hilary Putnam, "Much Ado about Not Very Much," *Dædalus* (Special Issue on Artificial Intelligence), pp. 269–281, Winter 1988. [305]
2. Alan Ross Anderson (ed.), *Minds and Machines*, Englewood Cliffs, NJ: Prentice-Hall, Inc., 1964. [305]

3. John R. Lucas, "Minds, Machines, and Gödel," *Philosophy*, Vol. XXXVI, pp. 112–127, 1961; reprinted in Alan Ross Anderson (ed.), *Minds and Machines*, pp. 43–59, Englewood Cliffs, NJ: Prentice-Hall, Inc., 1964; available online at http://users.ox.ac.uk/~jrlucas/Godel/mmg.html. [305]

4. Lucas himself lists some references to these in a Web site, http://users.ox.ac.uk/~jrlucas/Godel/referenc.html. [306]

5. John R. Lucas, *The Freedom of the Will*, Oxford: Oxford University Press, 1970. Lucas claims on his Web site that the book is out of print but is now available from Oxford University Press "on a one-off basis." [306]

6. Available online at http://users.ox.ac.uk/~jrlucas/Godel/brighton.html. [306]

7. Mortimer Taube, *Computers and Commonsense: The Myth of Thinking Machines*, New York: Columbia University Press, 1961. [306]

8. Roger Penrose, *The Emperor's New Mind: Concerning Computers, Minds and the Laws of Physics*, New York: Random House, Inc., 1989. [307]

9. Roger Penrose, *Shadows of the Mind: A Search for the Missing Science of Consciousness*, Oxford: Oxford University Press, 1994. [307]

10. Roger Penrose, "Beyond the Doubting of a Shadow: A Reply to Commentaries on Shadows of the Mind," *PSYCHE*, Vol. 2, p. 23, January 1996. Available online (with pointers to articles by critics) at http://psyche.cs.monash.edu.au/v2/psyche-2-23-penrose.html. [307]

11. See John R. Searle, "Minds, Brains, and Programs," *Behavioral and Brain Sciences*, Vol. 3, No. 3, pp. 417–457, 1980. Available online at http://www.bbsonline.org/documents/a/00/00/04/84/bbs00000484-00/bbs.searle2.html. [307]

12. *Ibid.* [308]

13. Allen Newell and Herbert A. Simon, "Computer Science as Empirical Inquiry: Symbols and Search," *Communications of the ACM*. Vol. 19, No. 3, pp. 113–126, March 1976. Available online at http://www.rci.rutgers.edu/~cfs/472_html/AI_SEARCH/PSS/PSSH1.html. [310]

14. For an online interview with Dreyfus about his career, see http://globetrotter.berkeley.edu/people5/Dreyfus/dreyfus-con0.html. [311]

15. Hubert L. Dreyfus, "Alchemy and Artificial Intelligence," RAND paper P-3244, The RAND Corporation, Santa Monica, CA, December 1965. Available online at http://www.rand.org/pubs/papers/2006/P3244.pdf. [311]

16. John Haugeland, *Artificial Intelligence: The Very Idea*, Cambridge, MA: MIT Press, 1985. [312]

17. See, for example, Hubert L. Dreyfus, *What Computers Can't Do: A Critique of Artificial Reason*, New York: Harper & Row, 1972 (second edition, 1979). A revised edition with the title *What Computers Still Can't Do: A Critique of Artificial Reason* was published by MIT Press, 1992. Hubert L. Dreyfus and Stuart E. Dreyfus, *Mind Over Machine: The Power of Human Intuition and Expertise in the Era of the Computer*, New York: Free Press, 1986. [313]

18. Pamela McCorduck, *Machines Who Think: A Personal Inquiry into the History and Prospects of Artificial Intelligence*, San Francisco: W. H. Freeman and Co., 1979. [313]

19. Hubert L. Dreyfus, "Overcoming the Myth of the Mental: How Philosophers Can Profit from the Phenomenology of Everyday Expertise," Presidential Address, *Proceedings and Addresses of the American Philosophical Association*, Vol. 79, No. 2, November 2005. Available online at http://socrates.berkeley.edu/~hdreyfus/pdf/Dreyfus%20APA%20Address%20%2010.22.05%20.pdf. [313]

20. Hubert L. Dreyfus, *What Computers Still Can't Do: A Critique of Artificial Reason*, p. 255, Cambridge, MA: MIT Press, 1992. [313]

21. E-mail correspondence of August 9, 2007. For Dreyfus's comments about Heidegger, see Hubert L. Dreyfus, *Being-in-the-World: A Commentary on Heidegger's Being and Time, Division I*, Cambridge, MA: MIT Press, 1991. [313]

22. Hubert L. Dreyfus, "Why Heideggerian AI Failed and How Fixing It Would Require Making It More Heideggerian," (a paper written in connection with being awarded the APA's Barwise Prize, 2006), *Philosophical Psychology*, Vol. 20, No. 2, pp. 247–248, 2007; reprinted in Michael Wheeler (ed.), *The Mechanization of Mind*, Cambridge MA: MIT Press, in press. [313]

23. Rolf Pfeifer, Max Lungarella, and Fumiya Iida, "Self-Organization, Embodiment, and Biologically Inspired Robotics," *Science*, Vol. 318, No. 5853, pp. 1088–1093, November 16, 2007. [314]

24. For example, a paper written in 2003 claimed that "Google's architecture features clusters of more than 15,000 commodity-class PCs with fault-tolerant software." Undoubtedly, Google uses many more networked computers today. See Luiz André Barroso, Jeffrey Dean, and Urs Hölzle, "Web Search for a Planet: The Google Cluster Architecture," *IEEE Micro*, March–April 2003. Available online at http://labs.google.com/papers/googlecluster-ieee.pdf. [314]

25. Joseph Weizenbaum, *Computer Power and Human Reason: From Judgment to Calculation*, San Francisco: W. H. Freeman and Co., 1976. [315]

26. *Ibid*, pp. 223–224. [316]

27. *Ibid*, pp. 202–203. [316]

28. *Ibid*, p. 227. [316]

29. Lewis Thomas, "Notes of a Biology Watcher: On Artificial Intelligence," *The New England Journal of Medicine*, Vol. 302, No. 9, pp. 506ff, February 28, 1980. [316]

30. Theodore Roszak, *The Cult of Information: A Neo-Luddite Treatise on High-Tech, Artificial Intelligence, and the True Art of Thinking*, second edition, Berkeley, CA: University of California Press, 1994. [317]

31. *Ibid*, pp. xviii–xix. [317]

32. *Ibid*, p. xiv. [317]

33. *Ibid*, p. 232. [317]

34. *Ibid*, p. 232. [317]

35. *Ibid*, p. xxiv. [318]

36. *Ibid*, p. 232. [318]

37. All responses are in my files. [318]

38. The online encyclopedia Wikipedia mentions the slogan in its entry for Pierce at http://en.wikipedia.org/wiki/John_R._Pierce. [318]

39. For a proof about sliding tile puzzles, see Daniel Ratner and Manfred Warmuth, "Finding a Shortest Solution for the N*N-extension of the 15-puzzle Is Intractable," *Journal of Symbolic Computing*, Vol. 10, pp. 111–137, 1990. [322]

40. See http://www.claymath.org/prizeproblems/index.htm. [322]

41. Jacob Schwartz, "Limits of Artificial Intelligence," in Stuart C. Shapiro and David Eckroth (eds.), *Encyclopedia of Artificial Intelligence*, Vol. 1, pp. 488–503, New York: John Wiley and Sons, Inc. 1987. [322]

42. W. W. Johnson and W. E. Story, "Notes on the 15 Puzzle," *American Journal of Mathematics*, Vol. 2, pp. 397–404, 1879. I thank Richard Korf for this citation. [324]

43. Richard E. Korf and L. A. Taylor, "Finding Optimal Solutions to the Twenty-Four Puzzle," *Proceedings of the Thirteenth National Conference on Artificial Intelligence and the Eighth Innovative Applications of Artificial Intelligence Conference*, pp. 1202–1207, Menlo Park, CA: AAAI Press and Cambridge, MA: MIT Press, August 1996. [324]

44. David Levy, *Robots Unlimited: Life in a Virtual Age*, p. 84, Wellesley, MA: A. K. Peters, Ltd., 2006. **[325]**

45. See the paper by John McCarthy, "Some Expert Systems Need Common Sense," Heinz Pagels (ed.), *Computer Culture: The Scientific, Intellectual and Social Impact of the Computer*, *Annals of the New York Academy of Sciences*, Vol. 426, November 1995. Available online at http://www-formal.stanford.edu/jmc/someneed/someneed.html. **[326]**

46. Benjamin Kuipers, "On Representing Commonsense Knowledge, in Nicholas V. Findler (ed.), *Associative Networks: The Representation and Use of Knowledge by Computers*, pp. 393–408, New York: Academic Press, 1979. Available online at ftp://ftp.cs.utexas .edu/pub/qsim/papers/Kuipers-csk-79.ps.gz. **[326]**

47. See Drew McDermott, M. Mitchell Waldrop, B. Chandrasekaran, John McDermott, and Roger Schank, "The Dark Ages of AI: A Panel Discussion at AAAI-84," *AI Magazine*, Vol. 6, No. 3, pp. 122–134, Fall 1985. **[327]**

25

Controversies and Alternative Paradigms

D IFFICULTIES SUCH AS THOSE I HAVE JUST WRITTEN ABOUT REKINDLED A
number of controversies among AI researchers themselves. Frustrated with
AI's slowdown, people with different approaches to AI eagerly stepped forward
to claim that what AI needed was more of this or that alternative to AI's reigning paradigm – the paradigm John Haugeland called "good-old-fashioned AI" or
GOFAI. GOFAI, of course, had as its primary rationale Newell and Simon's belief
that a "physical symbol system has the necessary and sufficient means for intelligent
action." But GOFAI seemed to be running out of steam during the 1980s, making
it vulnerable to challenges by AI researchers themselves – challenges that had to
be taken more seriously than those of Searle, Dreyfus, Penrose, and others outside
of the field. In this chapter, I'll describe some of these internal controversies and
mention a few of the new paradigms that emerged.

25.1 About Logic

Among the pursuers of the GOFAI approach were those who used logical representations and logical reasoning methods – ideas pioneered by John McCarthy.
These people were sometimes called "logicists." (I was among them, having co-
authored a 1987 book titled *The Logical Foundations of Artificial Intelligence*.)[1] Drew
McDermott, a professor at Yale University (who received his Ph.D. from MIT),
was one of those who began to have doubts about the role of logic in AI. This fact
was significant because McDermott himself had been a prominent logicist, but in an
influential 1987 paper he concluded that the premise that ". . . a lot of reasoning can
be analyzed as deductive or approximately deductive, is erroneous."[2]

He went on to say

Unfortunately, the more you attempt to push the logicist project, the less deduction you find.
What you find instead is that many inferences which seem so straightforward that they *must*
be deductions turn out to have nondeductive components.
. . .
Think of the last time you made a plan, and ask yourself if you could have *proven* the plan
would work. Chances are you could easily cite ten plausible circumstances under which the
plan would *not* work, but you went ahead and adopted it anyway

Several people, logicists (including me) and near-logicists, were invited to submit
"commentaries," and these were published along with McDermott's article. Have
a look if you would like to sample one of the important controversies in AI. The

Figure 25.1. Lotfi Zadeh. (Photograph courtesy of Lotfi Zadeh.)

discussions about the role of logic in artificial intelligence helped reshape AI's use of logic, and, in extended form, it still serves as the primary means for representing declarative knowledge.

25.2 Uncertainty

Another objection to the use of logical representations was based on the fact that logical sentences must be either true or false whereas so much of human knowledge is uncertain. Both MYCIN and PROSPECTOR (along with some other expert systems) were able to accommodate uncertainty – MYCIN with its "certainty factors" and PROSPECTOR with its use of probability values.

Several other ideas for dealing with uncertainty have been proposed. I'll mention two alternatives to the use of probabilities. One is the so-called Dempster–Shafer (D-S) theory for assigning degrees of belief to statements and for combining degrees of belief based on independent items of evidence.[3] D-S theory has been used extensively in problems where data from several sources need to be combined (or "fused," the term used by D-S people) to reach decisions.[4]

The other alternative to using probabilities is "fuzzy logic," invented by the computer scientist Lotfi Zadeh (1921– ; Fig. 25.1).[5] Fuzzy logic allows truth values of statements to take on any value between 1 (certainly true) and 0 (certainly false). It is based on fuzzy set theory in which set membership can take on intermediate values between "in the set" and "not in the set." That is, something can be "partially in the set." Zadeh uses, as one example, the set of tall people. Depending on one's definition of tall, John, say, who is 5 feet 10 inches (177.8 cm), might be described as being in the set "tall" to degree 0.7. Then the statement "John is tall" would have a truth value of 0.7. A truth value of 0.95, for example, might correspond to the statement "John is quite tall." Modifiers such as "slightly," "moderately," and "very" are easily converted to fuzzy truth values for the statements using them.

Here is how the truth values of combinations of statements are computed in fuzzy logic: If A and B are two statements, then the truth value of the "conjunctive" combination, (A And B), is the *smaller* of the truth values of A and of B. The truth value of the "disjunctive" combination, (A Or B), is the larger of the truth values of A and of B.

Zadeh points out that his truth values and set membership values cannot be construed as probabilities. His reasons need not concern us here; in any case, the matter is controversial. (Most statisticians claim that probability theory is the only mathematically rigorous way to deal with uncertainty.) Suffice it to say that there is an extensive literature on fuzzy logic and its several applications, especially in control systems.[6]

One oft-cited example of the use of fuzzy control is Maytag Company's "IntelliSense" dishwasher. According to a press account,[7]

Maytag Co., Newton, Iowa, has developed what it claims is the world's first "intelligent" dishwasher. At the touch of a button, the computerized machine figures out the optimum wash cycle for any load. The dishwasher's apparent ability to reason stems from fuzzy-logic control and an advanced sensor module that sits in the pump, measuring food particles, water temperature, detergent, and wash-arm rotation.

In Zadeh's view, fuzzy logic is one component of a larger effort in what he calls "soft computing" – a discipline that ". . . differs from conventional (hard) computing in that, unlike hard computing, it is tolerant of imprecision, uncertainty and partial truth. In effect, the role model for soft computing is the human mind."[8]

Contrasted with these alternatives to probability theory, the invention of Bayesian networks, to be described in a subsequent chapter, has revitalized methods based on probabilities for representing and reasoning with uncertain information.

25.3 "Kludginess"

Another controversy concerned the very nature of the mechanism (or mechanisms) underlying intelligent behavior. Opposing those who sought some unitary general principle based on search or learning or logic or massive amounts of common-sense knowledge, Marvin Minsky claimed that intelligence (at least as exhibited by the human brain) was a "kludge." (Among various dictionary definitions of "kludge" are the following: 1. A system, especially a computer system, that is constituted of poorly matched elements or of elements originally intended for other applications. 2. A clumsy or inelegant solution to a problem.) Minsky's view was that intelligence resulted from perhaps hundreds or thousands of ad hoc, special-purpose mechanisms, loosely interacting, sometimes cooperating and sometimes competing, to solve the myriad problems faced by evolving humans. In Minsky's words,[9]

The brain's functions simply aren't based on any small set of principles. Instead, they're based on hundreds or perhaps even thousands of them. In other words, I'm saying that each part of the brain is what engineers call a kludge – that is, a jury-rigged solution to a problem, accomplished by adding bits of machinery wherever needed, without any general, overall plan: the result is that the human mind – which is what the brain does – should be regarded as a collection of kludges. The evidence for this is perfectly clear: If you look at the index of any large textbook of neuroscience, you'll see that a human brain has many hundreds of parts – that is, subcomputers – that do different things. Why do our brains need so many parts? Surely, if our minds were based on only a few basic principles, we wouldn't need so much complexity.

Of course, just because the brain is a kludge does not mean that computer intelligences have to be. Nevertheless, some AI researchers favored systems consisting of collections of experimentally derived, ad hoc routines designed to solve specific problems. These people called themselves "scruffies" to distinguish themselves from the "neats" who favored programs based on theoretically based principles. (These terms were apparently first used by Roger Schank in the 1970s to contrast his approach to building natural language processing systems with the more theoretically based work of McCarthy and others.) In his keynote address at the 1981 annual meeting of the Cognitive Science Society, Robert Abelson compared the two camps by saying "The primary concern of the neat is that things should be orderly and predictable while the scruffy seeks the rough-and-tumble of life as it comes . . ."[10]

I believe that both neats and scruffies are needed in a field as immature as AI is. Scruffies are better at exploring frontiers outside the boundaries of well-established theory. Neats help codify newly gained knowledge so that it can be taught, written about, and thus remembered.

25.4 About Behavior

25.4.1 *Behavior-Based Robots*

Using an approach that harkens back to Grey Walter's "tortoises," the MIT computer scientist Rodney Brooks eschewed complex representations and reasoning processes and focused instead on what he called a "behavior-based approach to building robots that operate in the real world."

Brooks wrote that his approach drew inspiration from attempting to

[r]ecapitulate evolution, or an approximation thereof, as a design methodology, in that improvements in performance come about by incrementally adding more situation specific circuitry [or software organized like circuitry] while leaving the old circuitry in place, able to operate when the new circuitry fails to operate (most probably because the perceptual conditions do not match its preconditions for operating). Each additional collection of circuitry is referred to as a new *layer*. Each new layer produces some observable new behavior in the system interacting with its environment.[11]

Genghis, shown in Fig. 25.2, was an early example of one of Brooks's robots using layered circuitry. It was a six-legged robot about 35 cm long with a leg span of 25 cm and weighing about a kilogram. It was able to crawl over rough terrain and follow a person using its infrared sensors. (For a short movie of Genghis walking visit http://groups.csail.mit.edu/lbr/genghis/genghis-short2.mov.) Its sensors included two front "whiskers," two inclinometers (to measure pitch and roll), and six forward-looking passive infrared sensors.

Figure 25.2. Rodney Brooks (top) and his Crawling Robot, Genghis (bottom). (Photographs courtesy of Rodney Brooks.)

The on-board circuitry controlling Genghis was built by adding modules, one on top of another, incrementally. Each layer handled increasingly complex modes of walking and "subsumed" (overrided when appropriate) the layer below when the layer below was not able to handle the current situation. Brooks called this type of layered organization a "subsumption architecture." The circuitry consisted of simple computational devices called "augmented finite-state machines" (implemented by 8-bit microprocessors).[12]

Unlike earlier symbolic approaches, Brooks's approach to robotics did not use central models of the environment and programs to "plan" courses of action. He argued that "the symbol system hypothesis upon which classical AI is based is fundamentally flawed . . ."[13] Instead, Brooks wrote

. . . the specific goals of the robot are never explicitly represented [in the behavior-based approach], nor are there any plans – the goals are implicit in the coupling of actions to perceptual conditions, and apparent execution of plans unroll in real-time as one behavior alters the robot's configuration in the world in such a way that new perceptual conditions trigger the next step in a sequence of actions.[14]

In his paper "Elephants Don't Play Chess,"[15] Brooks gives examples of several other quite interesting robot systems developed in his MIT lab. The title of Brooks's paper is meant to indicate that quite complex behavior (such as the behavior of elephants for example) can be achieved with systems that (presumably) do not have the representational and reasoning powers required for intelligent activities such as playing chess. Yet, although AI scientists would certainly be pleased to be able to build machines with the intelligence of elephants, achieving AI's ultimate goals would seem to require complex representational and reasoning methods beyond what the behavior-based approaches are able to offer.

Although I think that following along the path (or paths) of the evolution of ever-more capable and intelligent animals has a lot to recommend it, I don't think we are very far along in going "from earwigs to humans" (to use the title of one of Brooks's articles) – let alone in getting up to elephants.[16]

25.4.2 Teleo-Reactive Programs

Even though it's doubtless not the whole story, coordinating behavior with ongoing perceptual input is an important part of an intelligent system. It's a part that I have been interested in ever since the days of working on intermediate-level actions for Shakey the robot. I was able to return to thinking about behavioral control during a sabbatical year in 1990 and 1991. I spent part of that year in Brooks's laboratory at MIT. There, aided by some important suggestions made by a Stanford (and soon-to-be MIT) student, Mark Torrance, I developed what I called the "teleo-reactive" (T-R) programming language. ("Teleo" comes from the Greek word *telos*, meaning "end" or "purpose.") A T-R program is an intermediate-level agent control program that robustly directs a robot toward a goal in a manner that continuously takes into account the robot's perceptions of its dynamically changing environment. Perhaps you will tolerate a slight digression into how T-R programs operate. I use it to illustrate some of the issues that arise in controlling a purpose-driven robot.

Here's an example of a T-R program, one that controls a robot kicking a soccer ball. (The program is really very simple; you can try "running it" by hand after I explain how these kinds of programs work.) This program mimics how a beginning soccer player (say a six-year old) might go about kicking a soccer ball. Not heeding what else might be going on, he or she runs to get close to the ball, faces it, and then boots it away.

```
kick(x):
1. Close(x) AND Facing(x) -> foot-swing
2. Close(x) -> face(x)
3. Facing(x) -> move-forward
4. True -> moveto(x)

face(x):
1. Facing(x) -> do-nothing
2. Left(x) -> rotate-ccw
3. True -> rotate-cw
```

```
moveto(x):
1. Close(x) -> do-nothing
2. Facing(x) -> move-forward
3. True -> face(x)
```

There are three parts to this program, a main part, namely, kick(x), and two "subprograms," namely, face(x) and moveto(x). To understand how it works, I'll first describe two important sets of components, the "perceptual routines" and the "primitive action routines." The perceptual routines determine whether or not some feature of the robot's situation is true or false. The primitive action routines control the basic motor actions of the robot and are presumed to be "built into the robot" (much like "reflexes" are built into animals).

- Perceptual Routines
  - Close(x) determines whether the robot is within "kicking distance" of x, where x can be anything at all. In programs like this, x is called a "parameter" or "variable" of the program. When the program is actually run, x will have a definite value, such as Ball, the soccer ball. But using a parameter in the program instead of a definite value permits us to use the same program for different "instances" of x.
  - Facing(x) determines whether the robot is facing x.
  - Left(x) determines whether x is somewhere (anywhere) off to the left of the direction the robot is facing. When it is true, the robot should rotate counterclockwise to be facing x.
- Primitive Action Routines
  - foot-swing is the basic action that moves the robot's "foot" forward rapidly. If a ball happens to be in the way, the ball goes sailing.
  - move-forward makes the robot move in the direction it is facing.
  - rotate-ccw makes the robot rotate (in place) in a counterclockwise direction.
  - rotate-cw makes the robot rotate (in place) in a clockwise direction.

The other action routines, namely, kick(x), face(x), and moveto(x) are not primitive but are composed of other programs. Note that the numbered lines of the T–R programs shown here consist of a part to the left of an arrow (->) and a part to the right of an arrow. The part to the left is called the "condition part" because it consists of a check to determine whether some condition is true. The part to the right is called the "action part."

My first step in explaining how T–R programs work in general is to show how kick(Ball) works in a specific situation. Let's assume that the robot is facing the ball but is not close enough to it to kick it. The robot wants to kick the ball so it activates the program kick(x) with the parameter x set to Ball. Here then is the program that the robot activates:

```
kick(Ball):
1. Close(Ball) AND Facing(Ball) -> foot-swing
2. Close(Ball) -> face(Ball)
3. Facing(Ball) -> move-forward
4. True -> moveto(Ball)
```

Note how every appearance of x in the program is now replaced by Ball because it is the ball that is to be kicked. T-R programs are interpreted by looking at the lines of the program in numeric order and identifying the first line in the program whose condition part is true. The action part of that line is then activated. In this specific case, the condition part of line 1 is not true because the robot is not close to the ball. For the same reason, the condition part of line 2 is not true either. However, the condition part of line 3 is true, so the robot activates the associated primitive action move-forward. In the meantime and while the move-forward action is proceeding (this is important!), the part of the robot system that is checking to see which is the first true line in the program is still checking (in the background, as it were). Sooner or later (if we assume the robot does not change its "heading" while it is moving forward), the condition part of line 1 will become true. Precisely at that time, line 3 is no longer the *first* line of the program whose condition part is true; line 1 is. So, line 3's action part is suspended, line 1's action part is activated, and the ball is kicked away.

Now, to illustrate the robustness of T-R programs and to explain how subprograms are activated, let's assume everything is the same as before (namely, the robot is facing the ball and is far away from the ball) but that, during the time that the robot is moving forward (because move-forward is being activated), the robot inadvertently drifts off course so that it is no longer facing the ball. At the time the robot perceives this change, line 3 of the program is no longer the first line whose condition part is true – line 4 is (because its condition, namely, True is assumed always to be true). So at that time activation of move-forward ceases, and instead moveto(Ball) is activated.

To activate moveto(Ball), the program moveto(x) is retrieved from the "program library," and its parameter, x, is replaced by Ball, and the following program is activated:

```
moveto(Ball):
1. Close(Ball) -> do-nothing
2. Facing(Ball) -> move-forward
3. True -> face(Ball)
```

The first line of this program whose condition part is true is line 3 – resulting in activating face(Ball), another subprogram. If we assume that the robot's drift off its heading resulted in the ball being to its left, activation of face(Ball) will cause the robot to rotate in a counterclockwise direction. Sooner or later, the robot will be facing the ball again. Now, an interesting thing happens. The subprogram moveto(Ball), with all of its condition-checking apparatus, is still running in the background. Its line 2 is now the first line in the program whose condition part is true (instead of its line 3 as before). So, the face(Ball) program ceases operation and the move-forward primitive program is activated. If nothing further untoward happens, line 1 of kick(x) will be the first line in that program whose condition part is true [moveto(Ball) will be suspended], and foot-swing will be activated. (Whew! It's easier for the circuitry that controls all of this to function automatically than it is for us to think about it.) If you aren't exhausted, you might want to consider some of the other ways that these programs might be activated.

Figure 25.3. David Rumelhart (left) and James McClelland (right). (Rumelhart photograph courtesy of Donald Rumelhart. McClelland photograph courtesy of James McClelland.)

25.5 Brain-Style Computation

25.5.1 *Neural Networks*

Because apparently the brain does what it does by massive parallel computations implemented by networks of interconnected neurons, some people began anew to explore the possibilities of neural networks. During the late 1970s a group at the University of California at San Diego (UCSD) headed by cognitive psychologists David E. Rumelhart (1942–) and James L. McClelland (1948–) (Fig. 25.3) began a study of networks that they called "parallel distributed processing" (PDP) systems. The group came to be known as the PDP group.

The PDP group held that mental processes in the brain were the result of inter-actions among elementary neural units connected in networks. These units excite and inhibit each other in parallel. This view of computation is quite at odds with the serial computations performed by most symbol processing approaches and with Newell and Simon's physical symbol system hypothesis. Thus, rather than storing information as lists in localized data structures, PDP systems distributed infor-mation throughout the connections among the units. Furthermore, PDP neural networks were not limited to feed-forward, layered arrangements. Harking back to Rosenblatt's original view of general perceptrons, some of the PDP systems allowed what were called "recurrent" connections – ones that were parts of loops through the various units. As Rumelhart later pointed out, "The common theme to all these efforts has been an interest in looking at the brain as a model of a parallel computa-tional device very different from that of a traditional serial computer."[17]

PDP work gained prominence with the publication of two volumes by McClelland, Rumelhart, and the PDP Research Group.[18] An important chapter in Volume One, titled "Learning Internal Representations by Error Propagation" by Rumelhart, Geoffrey E. Hinton, and Ronald J. Williams, introduced a new technique, called "back propagation," for adjusting network weights. It led to many new applications, which I'll describe in a subsequent chapter.

The physicist John J. Hopfield (1933–) invented another type of neural network.[19] Each neural element in a Hopfield network is connected to all of the others. The weights on these connections are symmetrical; that is, the weight connecting unit i to unit j has the same value as the weight connecting unit j to unit i. The operation of the network is a dynamical process; that is, the values of the units at each time step depend on the values at the just-preceding time step. The collection of unit values are related to what physicists call an "energy function," and (regardless of the initial state of the network) these values tend to converge to values that correspond to a locally minimal energy state. These are called the "stable states" of the network and can be thought of as the set of memories stored by the net. Hopfield nets have been used as associative memories and for some simple computations. (For a demonstration of a Hopfield net solving a ten-city "traveling salesman" problem, visit http://to-campos.planetaclix.pt/neural/hope.html.) A "Boltzmann machine" is an elaboration of the Hopfield net in which unit values at each time step depend randomly on the unit values at the just-preceding time step.

Much of the neural network research during this period came to be called "connectionist" or "brain-style" computation, to contrast it with GOFAI. Another person active in this movement was Jerome A. Feldman, who in 1974 moved from Stanford to the University of Rochester to set up the Department of Computer Science there as well as to pursue connectionist-oriented research.[20]

25.5.2 Dynamical Processes

Some researchers believe that dynamical processes, similar to those exhibited by Hopfield and Boltzmann networks (and including those described by sets of differential or difference equations), underlie much of the computation performed by the brain. For example, in an article in *The MIT Encyclopedia of Cognitive Science*, Tim van Gelder wrote[21]

A dynamical system for current purposes is a set of quantitative variables changing continually, concurrently, and interdependently over quantitative time in accordance with dynamical laws described by some set of equations. Hand in hand with this first commitment goes the belief that dynamics provides the right tools for understanding cognitive processes.
. . .
A central insight of dynamical systems theory is that behavior can be understood geometrically, that is, as a matter of position and change of position in a space of possible overall states of the system. The behavior can then be described in terms of attractors, transients, stability, coupling, bifurcations, chaos, and so forth – features largely invisible from a classical perspective.

However, in the same article van Gelder wrote "Currently, many aspects of cognition – e.g., story comprehension – are well beyond the reach of dynamical treatment."

The University of Indiana computer scientist Randall Beer (1961–) is more optimistic. In an article titled "Dynamical Approaches to Cognitive Science," Beer wrote that "dynamical approaches are beginning to engage substantive empirical questions in cognitive science."[22] He gives three examples, one of which is a simulated agent whose horizontal motion is controlled by a dynamical system implemented by a fourteen-neuron, continuous-time recurrent neural network. The agent's task is to discriminate between two differently shaped falling objects – avoiding one shape (by moving out of its path) and engaging the other (by moving into its path). He terms this behavior "minimally cognitive," which he defines as "the simplest behavior that begins to raise questions of cognitive interest." To my knowledge, dynamical systems have not yet been used in tasks requiring more than these minimally cognitive behaviors.

A feature stressed by Beer and others is the importance of the interaction between the network and its environment. Indeed, the environment itself provides an important component of most dynamical systems. Exploiting properties of the environment to make the overall system simpler has been carried to an extreme by Mark W. Tilden, who did some of his work at the Los Alamos National Laboratory. For example, Tilden's walking robots don't use computers at all but are able to walk by exploiting the resistive input from their motors as they amble over rough terrain.[23]

25.6 Simulating Evolution

In Chapter 2, I discussed attempts to create intelligent artifacts by using the evolutionary processes of random generation and selective survival. Of these, John Holland's genetic algorithms (GAs) seemed to offer the most promise. GAs attempt to evolve strings of symbols that encode a solution to some particular problem. Much of the early work in GA used binary-valued symbols (0's and 1's), although other symbols can be used also.

The traveling salesman problem is often used to illustrate the use of GAs. In that problem, we have a list of cities that must be visited, and we must find a tour that starts at one city, visits all of the others just once, and returns to the starting city. The problem is to find an ordering of the cities that minimizes the total distance traveled. To encode the solution, the names of the cities can be used as the symbols. If, for example, there are fourteen cities named by the letters A, B, ..., N, and if we must start and end at city C, then the symbol string (C, F, N, K, B, L, M, H, D, A, E, G, I, J, C) would represent a tour that starts with C, visits F next, and so on. In keeping with evolutionary terminology, the total distance traversed by this tour is related to the *fitness* of this string. We want shorter tours to have greater fitness, so let us set the fitness of a tour to minus its distance traveled. The GA process attempts to evolve a a string having maximal fitness.

The evolutionary process starts by assembling a large population of random strings. In our traveling-salesman-problem example, they would all start and end with C but have all of the other names just once in each string. Populations of these strings are subjected to two different processes – analogous to some of what happens in biological evolution. First, some of the strings undergo random mutations in which the values of some of their components are changed. An example of a mutation of a traveling-salesman string might be to interchange two symbols selected randomly within the string.

parent one

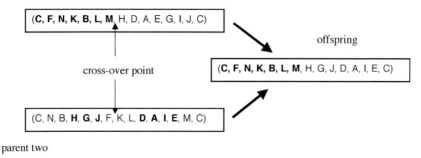

Figure 25.4. A cross-over operation.

Second, pairs of strings within a population that have relatively high fitness are selected to participate in an operation called "cross-over," which generates an "offspring" string. Different kinds of cross-over operations are used in GAs. For the traveling-salesman example, the operation must preserve the "legality" of the offspring string; that is, it must correspond to a tour that visits the other cities just once. One way to do this is to repeat in the offspring string the first k symbols of one of the parents and then scan the symbols in the other parent to fill out the offspring string with symbols not already appearing there. The value of k is selected randomly.

The illustration in Fig. 25.4 shows how this style of cross-over operates.

At each stage of the evolutionary process, the current generation of strings gives rise to a new generation. The new generation contains some of the strings from the old one (preferring strings with high fitness), the mutated strings, and the new strings resulting from cross-over operations. Interestingly, succeeding generations eventually contain strings that are better and better at solving the problem at hand (for some kinds of problems).

GAs have been applied to various combinatorial optimization problems in computer science, engineering, economics, chemistry, and other fields. The online encyclopedia Wikipedia has some excellent material on GAs, including pointers to tutorials, at http://en.wikipedia.org/wiki/Genetic_algorithm.[24]

We can think of a genetic algorithm as a search process attempting to locate high points in a "fitness landscape." Each possible GA string can be thought of as a "place" in a contour map, with the fitness of that string being the elevation at that place. Initially, "paratroopers" are dropped randomly over the landscape, and these report their elevations. Some of them move slight distances from their current positions (corresponding to the mutations), and some pairs rocket to a position somewhere in between their current positions (corresponding to cross-over). Then the process repeats. The fitness landscape may have several peaks, with some higher than others, and it may have several plateaus. After several generations, a GA process may succeed only in finding the location of minor peaks, or it may have difficulty getting off a large plateau. But occasionally it may find the highest peak in the landscape. AI has used what mathematicians call hill-climbing (or gradient ascent) procedures, but before GAs these techniques usually involved only one "climber." GAs, along with other

Figure 25.5. John Koza. (Photograph courtesy of John Koza.)

evolutionary algorithms, allow several climbers to search simultaneously, resulting in what is called "parallel search."

One of John Holland's students, John Koza (1943– ; Fig. 25.5), developed a somewhat different evolutionary procedure called Genetic Programming (GP). GP evolves LISP programs rather than strings. The process starts with a random collection of programs containing some basic LISP functions and constants thought to be important for solving the task at hand. Again, random mutations and cross-over are used to produce new generations of programs. (Later versions of GP have added biologically inspired operations analogous to inversion, gene duplication, and gene deletion.) Various techniques can be used for the mutation part, including replacing parts of a program with randomly selected new program components. In cross-over, two "parent programs" with relatively high fitness are selected. Randomly selected parts of each program are then interchanged to produce two new programs for the next generation of programs.

Koza has employed GP to produce programs that have created new kinds of electrical filters, optical lenses, antennas, and control circuitry, among other things. Many of these programs are, as he says, "competitive with human performance." He claims that because the main goal of AI is to produce programs that are capable of intelligent behavior, one should use a program synthesis technique able to produce such programs directly and that GP is (so far) the best such synthesis technique. As he puts it, "Virtually all problems in artificial intelligence, machine learning, adaptive systems, and automated learning can be recast as a search for a computer program. Genetic programming provides a way to successfully conduct the search for a computer program in the space of computer programs."[25]

Since 1999, Koza has been using a 1,000-Pentium "Beowulf-Style Cluster Computer" for his GP work.[26] He and co-authors have written several books and papers on GP.[27]

There is a Special Interest Group for Genetic and Evolutionary Computation (SIGEVO) of the Association for Computing Machinery (ACM). It sponsors conferences dealing with various aspects of evolutionary computation including GAs and GPs.[28] A compelling narrated video demonstration of the power of simulated evolution, presented at the 1991 SIGGRAPH conference, can be viewed at http://www.archive.org/details/sims_evolved_virtual_creatures_1994. As described by the Web site, "A population of several hundred creatures is created within a supercomputer, and each creature is tested for [its] ability to perform a given task, such [as] the ability to swim in a simulated water environment."[29]

25.7 Scaling Back AI's Goals

During the AI winter, many AI researchers began to focus on more modest and achievable goals than on those of previous years. One heard fewer brave predictions about what AI could *ultimately* achieve. Increasingly, effort was devoted to what AI could (at the time) *actually* achieve. The result was more work on limited or "weak" AI and less on "strong AI." The emphasis was on using AI to help humans rather than to replace them.

Companies and government agencies with funds to support research looked to computer technologies generally (rather than to AI specifically) to help solve their problems. Research funds were directed at improving database systems, user interfaces, graphics, computer networks, data mining, computer games, information retrieval, computer vision, and word-processing and spreadsheet programs, to name just a few areas. The AI technologies of search and inference, expert systems, speech recognition, and natural language processing were used, when appropriate, as components of large, integrated systems. AI researchers began to be satisfied with adding bits of intelligence here and there to these systems to make them more useful and appealing.

Notes

1. Michael Genesereth and Nils Nilsson, *Logical Foundations of Artificial Intelligence*, San Francisco: Morgan Kaufmann Publishers, 1987. [331]
2. Drew McDermott, "A Critique of Pure Reason," *Computational Intelligence*, Vol. 3, No. 3, pp. 151–160, August 1987. [331]
3. For a brief online summary with citations to longer articles, see Glenn Shafer, "Dempster–Shafer Theory," 2002; available at http://www.glennshafer.com/assets/downloads/articles/article48.pdf. [332]
4. See, for example, David L. Hall and Sonya A. H. McMullen, *Mathematical Techniques in Multisensor Data Fusion*, Norwood, MA: Artech House, Inc., 2004. [332]
5. Zadeh's original article is Lotfi Zadeh, "Fuzzy Sets," *Information and Control*, Vol. 8, pp. 338–353, 1965; available online at http://www-bisc.cs.berkeley.edu/Zadeh-1965.pdf. For a summary, see E. Cox, "Fuzzy Fundamentals," *IEEE Spectrum*, Vol. 29, No. 10, pp. 58–61, 1992. The Association for the Advancement of Artificial Intelligence (AAAI) maintains a fuzzy logic Web page (with lots of pointers to tutorials, papers, and applications) at http://www.aaai.org/AITopics/html/fuzzy.html. [332]
6. See, for example, Kevin M. Passino and Stephen Yurkovich, *Fuzzy Control*, Menlo Park, CA: Addison Wesley Longman, 1998. (The book is no longer in print but can be downloaded from http://www.ece.osu.edu/~passino/FCbook.pdf.) [333]
7. See *Machine Design*, March 1995. [333]
8. See The Berkeley Initiative in Soft Computing Web site at http://www-bisc.cs.berkeley.edu/. [333]

9. Marvin Minsky, "Smart Machines," Chapter 8 of John Brockman, *The Third Culture: Beyond The Scientific Revolution*, New York: Simon & Schuster, 1995. Available online at http://edge.org/documents/ThirdCulture/p-Ch.8.html. The whole book is available at http://www.edge.org/documents/ThirdCulture/d-Contents.html. [333]

10. The quotation is taken from Wendy G. Lehnert, "Cognition, Computers, and Car Bombs: How Yale Prepared Me for the 1990s," in Roger Schank and Ellen Langer (eds.), *Beliefs, Reasoning, and Decision Making: Psycho-Logic in Honor of Bob Abelson*, pp. 143–173, Hillsdale, NJ: Lawrence Erlbaum Associates, 1994. [334]

11. Rodney A. Brooks, "From Earwigs to Humans," *Proceedings IIAS The Third Brain and Mind International Symposium on Concept Formation, Thinking and Their Development*, pp. 59–66, Kyoto, Japan, May 1996. Available online at http://people.csail.mit.edu/brooks/papers/ascona.pdf. [334]

12. For a description of how Genghis works, see Rodney A. Brooks, "A Robot That Walks: Emergent Behavior from a Carefully Evolved Network," *Neural Computation*, Vol. 1, No. 2, pp. 253–262, Summer 1989. Also in *Proceedings of the IEEE International Conference on Robotics and Automation*, pp. 292–296, Scottsdale, AZ, May 1989. Available online as an MIT AI Lab Memo (No. 1091) at http://people.csail.mit.edu/brooks/papers/AIM-1091.pdf. [335]

13. Rodney A. Brooks, "Elephants Don't Play Chess," *Robotics and Autonomous Systems*, Vol. 6, pp. 3–15, 1990. Also in Pattie Maes (ed), *Designing Autonomous Agents: Theory and Practice from Biology to Engineering and Back*, pp. 3–15, Cambridge, MA: MIT Press, 1990. Available online at http://people.csail.mit.edu/brooks/papers/elephants.pdf. [335]

14. Rodney A. Brooks, *op. cit.* [335]

15. Rodney A. Brooks, *op. cit.* [336]

16. See Brooks's Web pages for pointers to others of his publications: http://people.csail.mit.edu/brooks/. [336]

17. David E. Rumelhart, "Brain Style Computation: Learning and Generalization," in Steven E. Zornetzer, Joel L. Davis, and Clifford Lau (eds.), *An Introduction to Neural and Electronic Networks*, San Diego: Academic Press, 1990. [339]

18. James L. McClelland, David E. Rumelhart, and the PDP Research Group, *Parallel Distributed Processing, Explorations in the Microstructure of Cognition, Volume 1: Foundations*, Cambridge, MA: MIT Press, 1986, and James L. McClelland, David E. Rumelhart, and the PDP Research Group, *Parallel Distributed Processing, Explorations in the Microstructure of Cognition, Vol. 2: Psychological and Biological Models*, Cambridge, MA: MIT Press, 1986. [339]

19. John J. Hopfield, "Neural Networks and Physical Systems with Emergent Collective Computational Abilities," *Proceedings of the National Academy of Science*, Vol. 79, No. 8, pp. 2554–2558, 1982. Available online from http://www.pubmedcentral.nih.gov/articlerender.fcgi?artid=346238. [340]

20. See, for example, Jerome A. Feldman *et al.*, "Computing with Structured Connectionist Networks," *Communications of the ACM*, Vol. 31, No. 2, pp. 170–187, February 1988. [340]

21. T. J. van Gelder, "Dynamic Approaches to Cognition" in R. Wilson and F. Keil (eds.), *The MIT Encyclopedia of Cognitive Sciences*, pp. 244–246, Cambridge MA: MIT Press, 1999. Available online at http://sites.google.com/site/timvangelder/publications-1/dynamic-approaches-to-cognition/MITDyn.pdf?attredirects=0. [340]

22. Randall D. Beer, "Dynamical Approaches to Cognitive Science," *Trends in Cognitive Sciences*, Vol. 4, No. 3, March 2000; available online at http://mypage.iu.edu/~rdbeer/Papers/TICS.pdf. For a longer paper, see Randall D. Beer, "A Dynamical Systems

Perspective on Agent-Environment Interaction," *Artificial Intelligence*, Special Volume on Computational Research on Interaction and Agency, Part 1, Vol. 72, Nos. 1–2, pp. 173–215, 1995; available online at http://mypage.iu.edu/~rdbeer/Papers/AIJ95.pdf. Beer's Web pages (http://mypage.iu.edu/~rdbeer/) provide many additional citations. [341]

23. For more about these kinds of simple robots, visit the Wikipedia site http://en.wikipedia.org/wiki/BEAM_robotics. [341]

24. See also Melanie Mitchell, *An Introduction to Genetic Algorithms*, Cambridge, MA: MIT Press, 1996. [342]

25. The quotation is from Koza's homepage at http://www.genetic-programming.com/johnkoza.html. [343]

26. See Forest H. Bennett *et al.*, "Building a Parallel Computer System for $18,000 That Performs a Half Peta-flop per Day," in Wolfgang Banzhaf *et al.* (eds.), *GECCO-99: Proceedings of the Genetic and Evolutionary Computation Conference*, pp. 1484–1490, San Francisco, CA: Morgan Kaufmann Publishers, 1999. [343]

27. See, for example, John R. Koza, *Genetic Programming: On the Programming of Computers by Means of Natural Selection*, Cambridge, MA: MIT Press, 1992; John R. Koza, *Genetic Programming II: Automatic Discovery of Reusable Programs*, Cambridge, MA: MIT Press, 1994; John R. Koza, Forrest H Bennett III, David Andre, and Martin A. Keane, *Genetic Programming III: Darwinian Invention and Problem Solving*, San Francisco: Morgan Kaufmann Publishers, 1999; and John R. Koza, Martin A. Keane, Matthew J. Streeter, William Mydlowec, Jessen Yu, and Guido Lanza, *Genetic Programming IV: Routine Human-Competitive Machine Intelligence*, Norwell, MA: Kluwer Academic Publishers, 2003. [343]

28. Visit the SIGEVO Web site at http://www.sigevo.org/index.html. [343]

29. I thank Mykel Kochenderfer for telling me about this video. [344]

Part VII

The Growing Armamentarium: From the 1980s Onward

T HROUGHOUT THE 1980S, WHILE AI WAS ENJOYING INCREASED POPULARITY AND commercial successes and then suffering funding cuts and a wintry season, its basic research workers produced a significant number of powerful new technical tools and sharpened others. New results unfolded in all of its subfields, including reasoning and representation, machine learning, natural language processing, and computer vision. This work, technically and mathematically deeper than before and strengthened by new connections with statistics and control engineering, helped vitiate some of the criticisms hurled at earlier AI systems and greatly enhanced AI's abilities.

26

Reasoning and Representation

26.1 Nonmonotonic or Defeasible Reasoning

Those AI researchers called logicists, who favor the use of logical languages for representing knowledge and the use of logical methods for reasoning, acknowledge one problem with ordinary logic; namely, it is *monotonic*. By that they mean that the set of logical conclusions that can be drawn from a set of logical statements does not decrease as more statements are added to the set. If one could prove a statement from a given knowledge base, one could still prove that same statement (with the very same proof!) when more knowledge is added.

Yet, much human reasoning does not seem to work that way – a fact well noticed (and celebrated) by AI's critics. Often, we jump to a conclusion using the facts we happen to have, together with reasonable assumptions, and then have to retract that conclusion when we learn some new fact that contradicts the assumptions. That style of reasoning is called *nonmonotonic* or *defeasible* (meaning "capable of being made or declared null and void") because new facts might require taking back something concluded before.

One can even find examples of nonmonotonic reasoning in children's stories. In *That's Good! That's Bad!*, by Margery Cuyler,[1] a little boy floats high into the sky holding on to a balloon his parents bought him at the zoo. "Wow! Oh, that's good," the story goes. The balloon breaks on a branch of a tall, prickly tree. "Pop! Oh, that's bad," the story continues. The boy falls into a muddy river and climbs up onto a hippopotamus and rides to shore. "Oh, that's good." The story goes on like that – changing back and forth about whether the balloon ride is turning out "good" or "bad."

There were already some methods used in AI (and elsewhere in computer science) for defeasible reasoning. For example, in the problem-solving language PLANNER proposed by Carl Hewitt, if a goal, say G, could not be achieved by a program then Not G could be asserted (under the assumption that G was a statement that the program was trying to establish). Such reasoning was defeasible because if additional statements were later added to the program or to its knowledge base, then establishing G might become possible. Similarly, in the PROLOG programming language, if a statement could not be proved by a program, then it was inferred to be false. Inferring that something is false if it cannot be proved true is called "negation as failure."

The SRI planning system, STRIPS, was also a type of nonmonotonic reasoning system. Assumptions about things "staying the same" after actions were performed were

349

certainly just that – assumptions. Conclusions drawn after making such assumptions might be defeated after adding new information whose implications might negate those assumptions.

Another method for defeasible reasoning was being used in the database world. Databases are used for encoding a wide variety of information. For example, a company might have a database about its employees. One can query such a database to find out an employee's salary, the department he or she works in, and so on. Suppose we attempt to find out from one of these employee databases information about a person, say Jack Smith, whose name is not found in the database. We might reasonably conclude then that Mr. Smith is not an employee of that company, and that's what some database systems would do. That conclusion would be based on the assumption that the database names *all* of that company's employees – an instance of the so-called closed-world assumption (CWA). Of course, Jack Smith may later join the company, and then his name would be added to the database. At that time we would have to take back the conclusion that Jack Smith is not one of the company's employees; this is another example of defeasible reasoning.

You may recall that, way back in 1964, Bertram Raphael's question-answering system, SIR, included a style of defeasible reasoning he called the "exception princi-ple." In SIR, general information about all the elements of a set applied to particular elements – but only in the absence of more specific information about those particu-lar elements. Several AI knowledge representation schemes represent some of their knowledge in "taxonomic hierarchies," somewhat like the one Raphael used, and use the exception principle, which is now often called "cancellation of inheritance," for defeasible reasoning.

In Fig. 26.1, I show a taxonomic hierarchy of some office machines. A program using this hierarchy would conclude that the energy source of a laser printer, for example, is a wall outlet because that property is inherited from the general class "office machines." However, more specific information about the energy source for robots would force the conclusion that the energy source for R2D2, for example, is a battery, overriding the inheritance of properties of the general class of office machines.

During the 1980s some of the most creative AI researchers became fascinated with the problem of defeasible reasoning and made several new proposals for how to do it. Their proposals were accompanied by a good deal of theoretical analyses comparing and contrasting the different approaches and how some of them could be considered either as specializations or as generalizations of the others.

The Canadian AI researcher Raymond Reiter (1939–2002) proposed one of the new methods.[2] In its simplest form, it uses special inference rules that permit drawing a conclusion from a knowledge base if some specified condition is satisfied and if that conclusion is not contradicted by what could ordinarily be deduced from that knowledge base. Reiter's special inference rules are called *default rules*, and his system that uses them is called *default logic*. As an example of its use, suppose we have a knowledge base used by a robot that specifies which rooms in an office building may be entered by the robot. We might have a rule that says that for rooms on the second floor, if it is impossible to prove that the robot may not enter a room there, then one can conclude that the robot may enter that room. Again,

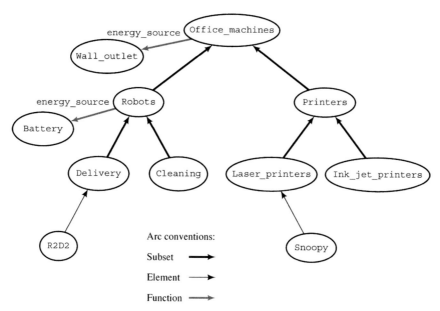

Figure 26.1. A hierarchy of office machines. (From Nils J. Nilsson, *Artificial Intelligence: A New Synthesis*, p. 311, San Francisco: Morgan Kaufmann Publishers, 1998.)

the reasoning is defeasible, because someone may later add to the knowledge base a fact that permits the deduction that some room on the second floor may not be entered.

John McCarthy, the originator of the proposal that knowledge should be encoded as logical statements, was also worried about the problem of nonmonotonicity. To deal with the problem, he proposed a method called *circumscription*.[3] Circumscription is rather difficult to explain without using a lot of logical jargon. In principle, a version of it called "predicate circumscription" (just one of several versions of circumspection[4]) involves limiting (thus "circumscribing") the set of entities that make predicates true to just those that can be proved to be true. For example, if we have a knowledge base that contains statements such as Tall(John) and Tall(Frank), plus a lot of other facts, we can circumscribe (if we wish) the predicate Tall. Doing so allows us to conclude ¬Tall(Susy) if Tall(Susy) is not logically implied by the knowledge base.

One of the motivations for McCarthy's interest in nonmonotonic reasoning was the possibility that it would be a key to solving the frame problem (see p. 169). Recall that the frame problem concerns the difficulty of how to represent which things change and which things stay the same when an action is taken (say by a robot). One approach is to make the assumption that if a predicate describing some state of the world is not mentioned by a description of an action (including the action's preconditions and effects) then that predicate is not changed by the action. This assumption is nonmonotonic because later (or more detailed) information may imply that a nonmentioned predicate is indeed changed. Some early attempts to solve the frame problem using nonmonotonic reasoning ran into various technical difficulties (which are too technical to bother about here), but work continued. A recent paper claimed that "the Frame Problem as it was originally formulated has been solved with Shanahan's and Thielscher's approaches and that at least the logical chapter of the Frame Problem has been closed." (The two people mentioned are Murray Shanahan of Imperial College, London, and Michael Thielscher of the Dresden University of Technology.)[5]

It might not have escaped your attention that the many proposals for nonmonotonic reasoning are rather similar, but there are many subtle technical differences. There are even other proposals that I have not mentioned, including auto-epistemic logics, nonmonotonic logics, abductive reasoning, truth-maintenance systems, and methods based on probability theory.[6] This profusion of defeasible reasoning methods can probably be attributed to the creativity and mathematical sophistication of many of the AI researchers involved and their keen abilities to spot and to attempt to escape the limitations of each others' proposals.

26.2 Qualitative Reasoning

Many of you have probably taken courses in physics, either in high school or in college or in both. The job of physics is to build theories of the physical world, and these theories are usually formulated using mathematics. For example, the formula $F = Ma$, relates the force, F, acting on an object to the object's mass, M, and its acceleration, a. Many mathematical formulas describing physical processes are more complex. For example, the following "wave equation" can be used to calculate the velocity of a water wave:

$$v = \sqrt{\frac{g\lambda}{2\pi} \tanh \left[2\pi \frac{h}{\lambda} \right]}.$$

Engineers could use it, for example, to predict when the crest of a wave would pass by a certain point.

We humans are also able to predict, with useful accuracies, the future course of many of the physical processes we commonly experience. For example, when people play in ocean waves at the beach, they are usually able to predict when a wave crest will arrive so that they can jump up in time. Do our brains use anything like the equation just shown to make that prediction? Probably not. Instead, prediction routines for guiding skilled actions are learned by repeated experiences and are part of what psychologists call "procedural knowledge."

In addition to acting automatically and effectively using procedural knowledge embedded in our various motor skills, we can also make declarative statements predicting what will happen in certain situations. For example, a surfer looking out at incoming waves can tell a friend "Take the next wave; it's going to be a big one."[7] Apparently we have some facility for representing and using "qualitative knowledge" about physical processes – knowledge that is neither part of our procedural "muscle memory" nor represented in our brains by complex mathematical formulas. I could give several examples. How do we know that when we knock over a glass of water on a table the water will eventually come to the edge of the table and spill off? How do we know that if we stack heavy boxes on top of light, fragile boxes, the fragile boxes might collapse? How do we know that if we drive to our destination a little bit faster, we'll get there a little bit sooner?

Several AI researchers have worked on systems having the ability to represent and to reason with qualitative knowledge. Scott Fahlman (1948–) wrote such a program for his master's thesis while a student at MIT. Called BUILD, the program was able to plan how to stack toy blocks by taking into account various forces acting on the blocks, such as gravity and friction.[8] It did this in a more-or-less qualitative way rather than by using exact mathematical models. Thus, BUILD can be said to be one of the first AI attempts to do qualitative reasoning about physics.

Soon after, another MIT student, Johan de Kleer (1951–), wrote a program called NEWTON for his master's thesis that included a component able to do qualitative reasoning. NEWTON, de Kleer claimed, "understands and solves problems in a mechanics mini-world of objects moving on surfaces."[9] NEWTON used its qualitative knowledge about physics to produce approximate problem solutions, which it then used to plan and carry out subsequent quantitative calculations. Most physics teachers will tell you that qualitative reasoning about "the physics" of a problem is essential before plunging into the mathematics.

In doing qualitative reasoning, NEWTON used a process called "envisioning" for "generating a progression of scenes encoded in a symbolic description which describe what could happen." It used descriptions of six basic actions appropriate to the kinds of problems NEWTON could solve. One of these descriptions, for example, was for FLY. It encoded the knowledge that "[i]f the object is moving on top of a surface which is concave away from the motion, the object might fly off." de Kleer's main contribution was to show how qualitative calculations and quantitative reasoning can be combined in a computer program.

In 1979 Pat Hayes published "The Naive Physics Manifesto."[10] A revised version appeared in 1985.[11] He proposed that the artificial intelligence research community begin "the construction of a formalization of a sizable portion of common-sense knowledge about the everyday physical world: about objects, shape, space, movement, substances (solids and liquids), time, etc." These topics had long presented particularly difficult representational and reasoning challenges for AI. Encoding our everyday knowledge about these subjects so that computers can reason about them is at the heart of qualitative physics, which Hayes called "naive physics."

His manifestos presented some general ideas about how to represent "clusters" of common-sense knowledge about the physical world. As one example, he proposed the notion of "histories" for representing events, instead of states and functions of states as he and John McCarthy had earlier advocated. He defined a history as "a piece of spacetime with natural boundaries, both temporal and spatial." For example, "the event of putting four blocks together in a square is the beginning of the history of a platform, and the end of that history is when and where they are separated from one another."

Hayes said, in effect, that we should not be "too hasty" about writing naive physics programs – preferring instead to delay implementations until more foundational work had been done on the representations themselves. He had already sketched out some of this work on liquids.[12]

```
Printers
```

```
  subset_of: Office_machines
```

```
  superset_of: {Laser_printers,
                Ink_jet_printers}

  energy_source: Wall_outlet
```

Figure 26.2. A frame. (Adapted from Nils J. Nilsson, *Artificial Intelligence: A New Synthesis*, p. 313, San Francisco: Morgan Kaufmann Publishers, 1998.)

```
  creator: John_Jones
```

```
  date: 16_Aug_91
```

These initial explorations in qualitative reasoning soon led to a rapidly growing subfield of AI with many applications, especially in diagnosing faults based on qualitative models of equipment. (I'll mention one example, diagnosing faults in spacecraft equipment, in Part 8.) Prominent groups were formed by Professor Kenneth D. Forbus (1955–) at Northwestern University[13] and by Benjamin Kuipers (1949–) at the University of Texas at Austin. (Kuipers has now relocated to the University of Michigan).[14] Special issues of journals and edited volumes and books devoted to the subject have appeared.[15]

I'll conclude this chapter on Reasoning and Representation by turning next to new developments in the use of semantic networks for knowledge representation.

26.3 Semantic Networks

In my earlier discussion of defeasible reasoning, I showed a semantic network representing a taxonomic hierarchy of office machines. Taxonomic networks are widely used in AI and in computer science to represent what are called "ontologies." In AI, an ontology consists of a set of concepts and relationships among those concepts. (In philosophy, it means the study of being or existence.) AI systems for reasoning with these networks would commonly have mechanisms for property inheritance using exception principles.

Although we understand taxonomic networks best by thinking about them in the form of trees, a collection of special data structures is used when encoding them for computers. These structures are often called "frames," following Minsky's original use of the word. For example, one of the frames for the office machines network might be represented as in Fig. 26.2.

Typically there would be a frame for each class of individuals or entities in a taxonomy as well as for each of the entities themselves. Frames for classes would name the superclass to which it belonged and the subclasses belonging to it. It would also specify properties of the entities belonging to the class. It is also common for a frame to have "meta-information," such as the date the frame was created.

26.3.1 *Description Logics*

Earlier in AI's history there was controversy about whether knowledge should be represented by data structures such as semantic networks (encoded, say, as frames) or by

Figure 26.3. Ronald Brachman (left) and Hector Levesque (right). (Courtesy of Ronald Brachman and of Hector Levesque.)

sets of logical statements. Gradually the controversy moderated because researchers came to accept the idea that semantic networks could be thought of as a special way of representing certain kinds of logical statements, thereby permitting some deductions to be made directly from the network. Two of the researchers who helped to establish this view were Ronald J. Brachman (1949–) and Hector J. Levesque (1951–) (Fig. 26.3). (Each of them has also done related foundational work in knowledge representation and reasoning generally.[16])

Brachman did his Ph.D. work[17] at Harvard under Bill Woods. (Besides his work in natural language processing, Woods had also written about the relationship between semantic networks and logic.[18]) Expanding on the ideas in his thesis, Brachman, along with other colleagues at BBN (including Woods) and at USC-ISI, developed a frame-based knowledge representation system called KL-ONE,[19] which became the basis for what came to be called *description logics.*

Levesque did all of his college work (B.S., M.S., and Ph.D.) at the University of Toronto. After receiving his Ph.D. degree in 1981, he joined Brachman at the Fairchild Laboratory for Artificial Intelligence Research in Palo Alto, a group founded by Peter Hart after Hart left SRI. There, Brachman and Levesque, together with Richard Fikes (then at Xerox PARC), developed the KRYPTON representation and reasoning system.[20] KRYPTON was a hybrid system – meaning it represented knowledge both by logical formulas and by a semantic network.

Although semantic networks make it easy to reason about individuals and their properties in a hierarchy, it is difficult for them to represent statements containing negations and disjunctions. As the KRYPTON paper states, "... a statement such as 'either Elsie or Bessie is the cow standing in Farmer Jones's field' cannot be made in

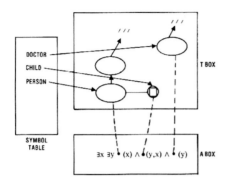

Figure 26.4. Parts of a KRYPTON T Box and A Box. (Adapted from Ronald J. Brachman, Richard E. Fikes, and Hector J. Levesque, "KRYPTON: A Functional Approach to Knowledge Representation, *IEEE Computer*, Vol. 16, No. 10, p. 71, October 1983.)

a typical assertional frame system." KRYPTON's solution is to use a combination of both types of representations:

> ... we have split the [reasoning] operations into two separate kinds, yielding two main components for our representation system: a terminological [that is, network-based] one, or *T Box*, and an assertional [that is, logic-based] one, or *A Box*. The T Box allows us to establish taxonomies of structured terms and answer questions about analytical relationships among these terms; the A Box allows us to build descriptive theories of domains of interest and to answer questions about those domains.[21]

The diagram from the KRYPTON paper shown in Fig. 26.4 illustrates the structure of the system. As the authors wrote, it consists of "a T Box of structured terms organized taxonomically, an A Box of (roughly) first-order sentences whose predicates come from the T Box, and a symbol table maintaining the names of the T Box terms so that a user can refer to them." The T Box in the diagram represents (among other things) that a child is a person. The A Box states that there exists a doctor who has a child.

KRYPTON was the forerunner of several description-logic systems, including CLASSIC, developed by Brachman and colleagues after he moved to AT&T Bell Laboratories.[22] In addition to their use in AI reasoning systems, description logics are used in ontology languages for the semantic Web, for example DAML-ONT[23] and OWL.[24]

26.3.2 *WordNet*

WordNet is a large "conceptual" dictionary of English words, organized somewhat like a semantic network and inspired by psycholinguistic and computational theories of human lexical memory.[25] Its development was begun at Princeton University in the 1980s under the direction of Professor George A. Miller (the same George Miller whom I mentioned earlier and who wrote "The Magical Number Seven, Plus or Minus Two"). In a 1990 paper, Miller and his colleagues had this to say about the beginnings of the project:[26]

> In 1985 a group of psychologists and linguists at Princeton University undertook to develop a lexical database along lines suggested by [earlier psycholinguistic] investigations. The initial idea was to provide an aid to use in searching dictionaries conceptually, rather than merely

alphabetically – it was to be used in close conjunction with an on-line dictionary of the conventional type. As the work proceeded, however, it demanded a more ambitious formulation of its own principles and goals. WordNet is the result. Inasmuch as it instantiates hypotheses based on results of psycholinguistic research, WordNet can be said to be a dictionary based on psycholinguistic principles.

WordNet groups its words into collections called "synsets." Each synset contains a group of synonymous words, that is, words with more-or-less the same meaning. I'll use WordNet's online search facility (at http://wordnetweb.princeton.edu/perl/webwn) to provide some examples of synsets and relations among them. The word "computer," for example, is in two different synsets. One of these synsets contains, besides "computer," the synonyms "computing machine," "computing device," "data processor," "electronic computer," and "information processing system." The other synset contains the synonyms for the older use of the word "computer" (when it referred to humans doing the computing), namely, "calculator," "reckoner," "figurer," and "estimator." A synset may also be accompanied by a short definition, called a "gloss," which provides a meaning for the words in the synset. For the first synset, the gloss is "a machine for performing calculations automatically." For the second, the gloss is "an expert at calculation (or at operating calculating machines)." Sometimes, the gloss also contains an example sentence to illustrate typical usage.

Synsets are connected to other synsets using relations similar to those used in semantic networks. One such relation is called a "hypernym," corresponding (roughly) to "is a kind of." For example, the hypernym of our synset containing "computer" and "computing device," etc. is the synset containing the word "machine" (and possibly other words too) having the gloss "any mechanical or electrical device that transmits or modifies energy to perform or assist in the performance of human tasks." A "hyponym," corresponding (roughly) to "is a general case of," is the opposite of a hypernym. The "computer" synset just mentioned has several hyponyms, among them are ones containing the words "digital computer" and any of its synonyms (a computer that represents information by numerical digits), "number cruncher" and any of its synonyms (a computer capable of performing a large number of mathematical operations per second), "Turing machine" and any of its synonyms (a hypothetical computer with an infinitely long memory tape), and others.

There are other relations also. For synsets containing nouns there is a relation called a "meronym," corresponding to "has as parts." The synset containing "computer" and "computing device," has several meronyms, among them are ones containing the words "chip" and its synonyms (all with the gloss "electronic equipment consisting of a small crystal of a silicon semiconductor fabricated to carry out a number of electronic functions in an integrated circuit"), "monitor" and its synonyms (all with the gloss "display produced by a device that takes signals and displays them on a television screen or a computer monitor"), and several others. A "holonym" is the opposite of a meronym.

Each synset also mentions the part of speech of the words it contains: noun, verb, adjective, or adverb. The relations among synsets differ somewhat depending on the part of speech. For example, verb synsets have a relation called "entailment." For example, one of the synsets for the verb "walk" (use one's feet to advance; advance by steps) entails the synset containing the verb "step" (shift or move by taking a step).[27]

According to its Web site (as of this writing), WordNet contains 155,287 words and 117,659 synsets. It is being maintained and expanded at Princeton and is freely and publicly available for download. Besides its use as an online dictionary and thesaurus, it is being used to support automatic text analysis, in natural language processing applications, as a knowledge base for question answering, and in semantic Web applications. Similar "wordnets" have been created in dozens of other languages.

WordNet's use as an ontology in a taxonomic knowledge base depends on the hypernym/hyponym relationships among the noun synsets and on WordNet's use of an inheritance mechanism to infer properties of objects represented by synsets from the properties of their ancestors. For example, one chain (from specific to general) in such a hierarchy is the following:

$$\text{workstation} \rightarrow \text{digitalcomputer} \rightarrow \text{computer} \rightarrow \text{machine}$$
$$\rightarrow \text{device} \rightarrow \text{instrumentality} \rightarrow \text{artifact} \rightarrow \ldots$$

Of course, there are side branches along this chain (which you can explore using WordNet's online search facility).

Some modifications may be needed when using WordNet as an ontology, however, because, according to Wikipedia, ". . . it contains hundreds of basic semantic inconsistencies such as (i) the existence of common specializations for exclusive categories and (ii) redundancies in the specialization hierarchy," among other things.[28]

In a related effort, Karin Kipper Schuler has created "VerbNet."[29] According to a Web page about it,[30] VerbNet "is the largest on-line verb lexicon currently available for English. It is a hierarchical domain–independent, broad–coverage verb lexicon with mappings to other lexical resources such as WordNet, Xtag, and FrameNet."

26.3.3 Cyc

In 1984, realizing that a large amount of common-sense knowledge would be needed for many AI applications, especially for natural language understanding, Stanford professor Douglas Lenat (1950–), who had previously done work on automating the discovery of mathematical concepts and heuristics,[31] decided to undertake the immense task of providing computers with common-sense knowledge. (See Fig. 26.5.) The first step, he thought, would be to "prime the pump with the millions of everyday terms, concepts, facts, and rules of thumb" that comprise common sense. As he later described it, the project began this way:[32]

In the fall of 1984, Admiral Bobby Ray Inman convinced me that if I was serious about taking that first step, I needed to leave academia and come to his newly formed MCC (Microelectronics and Computer Consortium) in Austin, Texas, and assemble a team to do it. The idea was that over the next decade dozens of individuals would create a program, Cyc, with common sense. We would "prime the knowledge pump" by handcrafting and spoon-feeding Cyc with a couple of million important facts and rules of thumb.

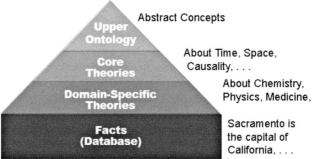

Figure 26.5. Douglas Lenat (top) and the structure of the Cyc knowledge base (bottom). (Photograph courtesy of Douglas Lenat.)

The name "Cyc" (pronounced like "psych") comes from three letters in the middle of the word "encyclopedia." The idea was that if Cyc had enough knowledge to understand articles in an encyclopedia, it would be able to read all kinds of material and acquire additional knowledge on its own – a "second step" toward smart computers. (The "third step" would be to conceive of and perform experiments to gain more knowledge, that is, knowledge beyond what humans already know.)

To understand encyclopedia articles, humans must already know quite a bit about the world. As Lenat put it:[33]

If we take any sentence from an encyclopedia article and think about what the writer assumes the reader already knows about the world, we will have something worth telling Cyc. Alternatively, we can take a paragraph and look at the "leaps" from one sentence to the next and think about what the writer assumes the reader will infer "between" the sentences. [Consider, for example, the sentences] "Napoleon died on St. Helena. Wellington was greatly saddened." The author expects the reader to infer that Wellington heard about Napoleon's death, that Wellington outlived Napoleon, and so on.

Just how much knowledge would Cyc need to have to understand articles in an encyclopedia? Lenat recently told me that he originally thought Cyc would need "a couple million general assertions, such as 'mammals have hair' (plus a vastly larger number of specific facts, such as what the capital of California is)." Now he believes that "the number is more like 200 million."[34]

Lenat and his team of programmers and "knowledge enterers" worked away on Cyc, entering knowledge by hand, for about ten years at MCC. Several reports, a number of papers, and a book were written describing the project and its goals.[35] In 1994, partly because of difficulties at MCC, Lenat founded Cycorp in Austin, Texas, "to research, develop, and commercialize Artificial Intelligence." Work on Cyc continues there under Lenat and his staff.

The language Cyc uses for representing knowledge is called CycL, an extension of the first-order predicate calculus. The object classes that Cyc knows about are arranged in a taxonomic hierarchy (such as the one shown in Fig. 26.5), which permits object classes to inherit the properties of object classes higher in the hierarchy. In Cyc's hierarchy, for example, an "event class" such as "turning on a light switch" is a subclass of a "temporal-thing," which is a subclass of an "individual," which is a subclass of the most general class in Cyc, namely, a "thing." Cyc uses "rules" (stated in its logical language) to describe relationships among objects. For example, an English version of one of its rules is "For all events A and B, A causes B implies A precedes B."

Cyc's knowledge base (KB) is divided into thousands of "micro-theories" – collections of concepts and facts about some circumscribed area. For example, one micro-theory contains knowledge about European geography. Others are devoted to expert knowledge about "chemistry, biology, military organizations, diseases, and weapon systems." Each micro-theory is consistent, although the entire Cyc knowledge base, taken as a whole, might have contradictions. Cyc's KB contains over five-million general assertions.[36] Most of these capture common-sense knowledge about "the objects and events of everyday human life, such as buying and selling, kinship relations, household appliances, eating, office buildings, vehicles, time, and space." In addition, the KB contains grammatical and lexical knowledge needed for natural language processing.

Cyc uses an "inference engine" to conclude new facts from other existing facts and rules in its KB. Two main inference methods are used. One is the inference rule called resolution, which I mentioned in Section 11.1. To reason efficiently with resolution, Cyc has developed some proprietary heuristics and restricts the scope of its search processes by its use of micro-theories. The other inference method is property inheritance, as is commonly used in semantic network representations. "Cyc also over 1,000 special-purpose inferencing modules for handling specific classes of inference. One such module handles reasoning concerning collection membership/disjointness. Others handle equality reasoning, temporal reasoning, and mathematical reasoning . . . CycL uses a form of circumscription . . . and can make use of the closed world assumption where appropriate."[37]

Cycorp is working on several applications, including intelligent search and information retrieval from the World Wide Web and natural language understanding. Its Web site claims that it "is now a working technology with applications to many real-world business problems."

Yet, there are several criticisms of Cyc. It gets stumped on some reasoning problems that humans find easy. Its vast knowledge base makes some of its reasoning impractically slow (and it will undoubtedly get even slower as more knowledge is added). It does not have satisfactory solutions for certain representation problems that AI researchers are still struggling to solve – such as how to represent substances. Also, because most of the work on Cyc is done in a private setting, it is not generally available for peer evaluation.

Although Cyc has pretensions of having enough knowledge to understand natural language, it cannot yet automatically (that is, without interaction by the user) adequately translate typical English questions into CycL. To query Cyc, one must either use the cumbersome CycL language or work in an interactive fashion. Lenat described to me a working example of such interaction employed at the Cleveland Clinic where medical researchers use Cyc to get information from patient databases.[38] The researcher types in his or her query in English. "Cyc parses what it can, recognizing some portions of the query, and presents the user with a set of partial query 'fragments' that are like fill-in-the-blank templates." Cyc then uses its specialized knowledge about medicine plus its common-sense knowledge to figure out how to paraphrase the query for the user to check. On getting user agreement about what the user asked, it uses its knowledge about how the database is organized to generate database queries to retrieve the desired information.

There are two versions of Cyc available for download. One is called Research-Cyc and is available to the research community (for research-only purposes) under a ResearchCyc license.[39] Besides the Cyc Inference Engine, it contains "nearly 3,000,000 assertions (facts and rules), using 26,000+ relations, that interrelate, constrain, and, in effect, (partially) define the concepts." Another, called OpenCyc, is a publicly available open source version of the Cyc technology.[40] It contains "hundreds of thousands of terms, along with millions of assertions relating the terms to each other. . . ." One can also examine the concept hierarchy in OpenCyc using an online browser.[41]

No one knows exactly how humans organize and use their common-sense (and expert) knowledge. Whether the facts and relations already amassed (and yet to be gathered) by the Cyc project will be adequate in amount and organization to permit human-level reasoning has yet to be demonstrated. Yet, I applaud the effort and wish the project well. Certainly, I think something at least as ambitious as Cyc will be required. (Another attempt to gather common-sense knowledge is that of the "Commonsense Computing Initiative" at the MIT Media Lab. The work there is described at http://xnet.media.mit.edu/.)

It's possible that Cyc might get to the point where (with some human help) it will be able to gather more of the required knowledge directly from the Internet. Lenat mentions[42] a game called "FACTory," designed to help gather knowledge from humans who play the game. You can play it at http://game.cyc.com/game.html. In the game, Cyc generates natural language statements it has gathered from English sentences it has found on the Web. It presents these statements to ten randomly chosen players of the game. If enough of them answer that the statement is "true," Cyc adds that fact to its KB (and the players get points in the game). I tried the game, and Cyc asked me whether or not "All spaghetti marinara includes some garlic." I answered "true," and Cyc said that I agreed with 66% of the other players and that it now (therefore) believes the sentence is "true."

Notes

1. Margery Cuyler, *That's Good! That's Bad!*, New York: Henry Holt and Co., 1991. **[349]**
2. Raymond Reiter, "A Logic for Default Reasoning," *Artificial Intelligence*, Vol. 13, pp. 81–132, 1980. **[350]**
3. John McCarthy, "Circumscription – A Form of Non-monotonic Reasoning," *Artificial Intelligence*, Vol. 13, pp. 27–39, 1980. There are several papers about circumscription by Vladimir Lifschitz, for example, "On the Satisfiability of Circumscription," *Artificial Intelligence*, Volume 28, No. 1, pp. 17–27, 1986. **[351]**
4. See, for example, John McCarthy, "Applications of Circumscription to Formalizing Common Sense Knowledge," *Artificial Intelligence*, Vol. 28, No. 1, pp. 89–116, 1986. **[351]**
5. For people who are interested in the history of the problem, the major players, and the technical details of its alleged solution, see M. Kamermans and Tijn Schmits, "The History of the Frame Problem," available online from http://student.science.uva.nl/~tschmits/Bachelorproject/index.html, 2004. (The paper has a nice chart summarizing this history, which is available separately at http://student.science.uva.nl/~tschmits/Bachelorproject/poster_HotFP.PNG.) See also Murray Shanahan, *Solving the Frame Problem: A Mathematical Investigation of the Common Sense Law of Inertia*, Cambridge, MA: MIT Press, 1997. **[352]**
6. See, for example, papers in collections by Matt Ginsberg (ed.), *Readings in Nonmonotonic Reasoning*, Los Altos, CA: Morgan Kauffman Publishers, 1987, and D. Gabbay, C. Hogger, and J. Robinson (eds.), *Handbook of Logic in Artificial Intelligence and Logic Programming*, Vol. 3, Oxford and New York: Oxford University Press, 1994. **[352]**
7. I found the wave equation on a Web site belonging to a manufacturer of surfing products: http://www.waveequation.com/wave_equation_data.html. **[352]**
8. Scott E. Fahlman, "A Planning System for Robot Construction Tasks," *Artificial Intelligence*, Vol. 5, No. 1, pp. 1–49, 1974. The thesis is available online as an MIT AI Laboratory Technical Report No. 283 with the same title and dated May 1973 at http://dspace.mit.edu/bitstream/handle/1721.1/6918/AITR-283.pdf?sequence=2. **[353]**
9. Johan de Kleer, "Qualitative and Quantitative Knowledge in Classical Mechanics," Artificial Intelligence Laboratory, Technical Report 352, December 1975. Available online at http://dspace.mit.edu/bitstream/handle/1721.1/6912/AITR-352.pdf?sequence=2. (Some of his ideas were described in his master's thesis proposal. See http://www2.parc.com/spl/members/dekleer/Publications/QualitativeandQuantitativeKnowledgeinClassicalMechanics.pdf.) **[353]**
10. Patrick J. Hayes,"The Naive Physics Manifesto," in D. Michie (ed.), *Expert Systems in the Micro-Electronic Age*, pp. 242–270, Edinburgh: Edinburgh University Press, 1979. **[353]**
11. Patrick J. Hayes, "The Second Naive Physics Manifesto," in Jerry R. Hobbs and Robert C. Moore (eds.), *Formal Theories of the Commonsense World*, pp. 1–36, Norwood, NJ: Ablex Publishing Corporation, 1985. **[353]**
12. Patrick J. Hayes, "Naive Physics 1: Ontology for Liquids," in Jerry R. Hobbs and Robert C. Moore (eds.), *Formal Theories of the Commonsense World*, pp. 71–107, Norwood, NJ: Ablex Publishing Corporation, 1985, An early version appeared as *Memo 35* of the Institut pour les Études Semantiques et Cognitives, Université de Genève, 1978. **[353]**
13. The group's Web page is at http://www.qrg.northwestern.edu/. **[354]**
14. The Web page for the Texas group is at http://www.cs.utexas.edu/~qr/. **[354]**
15. See, for example, *Artificial Intelligence*, Vol. 51, Nos. 1–3, October 1991; *IEEE Expert: Intelligent Systems and Their Applications*, Vol. 12, No. 3, May/June 1997; the

introductory article by Yumi Iwasaki, "Real World Applications of Qualitative Reasoning: Introduction to the Special Issue," *AI Magazine*, Vol. 24, No. 4, pp. 16–21, Winter 2003 (a preprint of which is available online at http://ksl-web.stanford.edu/people/iwasaki/my-intro.ps); Benjamin J. Kuipers, *Qualitative Reasoning: Modeling and Simulation with Incomplete Knowledge*, Cambridge, MA: MIT Press, 1994; and Daniel S. Weld and Johan de Kleer, *Readings in Qualitative Reasoning about Physical Systems*, San Francisco: Morgan Kaufmann Publishers, 1990. [354]

16. See Ronald J. Brachman and Hector J. Levesque, *Knowledge Representation and Reasoning*, San Francisco: Morgan Kaufmann Publishers, 2004. [355]

17. Ronald J. Brachman, "A Structural Paradigm for Representing Knowledge," Ph.D. dissertation, Division of Engineering and Applied Physics, Harvard University, Cambridge, MA, 1977. [355]

18. William A. Woods, "What's in a Link: Foundations for Semantic Networks," in Daniel Bobrow and Allan Collins (eds.), *Representation and Understanding: Studies in Cognitive Science*, pp. 35–82, New York: Academic Press, 1975. [355]

19. Ronald J. Brachman and James G. Schmolze, "An Overview of the KL-ONE Knowledge Representation System," *Cognitive Science: A Multidisciplinary Journal*, Vol. 9, No. 2, pp. 171–216, 1985. [355]

20. Ronald J. Brachman, Richard E. Fikes, and Hector J. Levesque, "KRYPTON: A Functional Approach to Knowledge Representation," *IEEE Computer*, Vol. 16, No. 10, pp. 67–73, October 1983. Reprinted in Ronald J. Brachman and Hector J. Levesque (eds.), *Readings in Knowledge Representation*, pp. 411–429, San Francisco: Morgan Kaufmann Publishers, 1985. [355]

21. *Ibid*, pp. 68–69. [356]

22. For a Web site with much information and resources about description logics, see http://dl.kr.org/. [356]

23. Deborah L. McGuinness, Richard Fikes, Lynn Andrea Stein, and James Hendler, "DAML-ONT: An Ontology Language for the Semantic Web," in Dieter Fensel, Jim Hendler, Henry Lieberman, and Wolfgang Wahlster (eds.), *The Semantic Web: Why, What, and How*, Cambridge, MA: MIT Press, 2002; available online at http://www.ksl.stanford.edu/people/dlm/papers/daml-ont-semantic-web.htm. [356]

24. Deborah L. McGuinness and Frank van Harmelen, "OWL Web Ontology Language Overview," W3C Recommendation, February 10, 2004; available online at http://www.w3.org/TR/owl-features/. [356]

25. Christine Fellbaum (ed.), *WordNet: An Electronic Lexical Database*, Cambridge, MA: MIT Press, 1998. See also the WordNet Web site at http://wordnet.princeton.edu/ and the Wikipedia article at http://en.wikipedia.org/wiki/WordNet. [356]

26. George A. Miller *et al.*, "Introduction to WordNet: An On-line Lexical Database," *International Journal of Lexicography*, Vol. 3, No. 4, pp. 235–244, 1990. [356]

27. The reader interested in details about WordNet might refer to the WordNet Web site and to the set of five papers appearing in *International Journal of Lexicography*, Vol. 3, No. 4, 1990. [358]

28. http://en.wikipedia.org/wiki/WordNet. [358]

29. Karin Kipper Schuler, "VerbNet: A Broad-Coverage, Comprehensive Verb Lexicon," University of Pennsylvania Ph.D. dissertation, 2005. Online version available from http://repository.upenn.edu/dissertations/AAI3179808/. [358]

30. http://verbs.colorado.edu/~mpalmer/projects/verbnet.html. [358]

31. Douglas B. Lenat, "AM: Discovery in Mathematics as Heuristic Search," in Randall Davis and Douglas B. Lenat (eds.), *Knowledge-Based Systems in Artificial Intelligence*, pp. 1–225, New York: McGraw-Hill, 1982; Douglas B. Lenat, "Eurisko: A Program

Which Learns New Heuristics and Domain Concepts," *Artificial Intelligence*, Vol. 21, Nos. 1–2, 61–98, 1983. **[358]**

32. From an article by Lenat in David G. Stork (ed.), *Hal's Legacy: 2001's Computer as Dream and Reality*, Cambridge, MA: MIT Press, 1998. The article is available online at http://www.cyc.com/cyc/technology/halslegacy.html. **[358]**

33. *Ibid.* **[359]**

34. E-mail communication, January 24, 2008. **[360]**

35. The main paper is Douglas B. Lenat *et al.*, "Cyc: Toward Programs with Common Sense," *Communications of the ACM*, Vol. 33, No. 8, pp. 30–49, August 1990. The first five years of the Cyc project is described in Douglas B. Lenat and R. V. Guha, *Building Large Knowledge-Based Systems*, Reading, MA: Addison-Wesley, 1990. **[360]**

36. January 13, 2009, e-mail from Doug Lenat. **[360]**

37. The reader who is interested in more details about how Cyc represents knowledge and how Cyc reasons can view a set of tutorial slides available online at http://www.opencyc .org/releases/doc/tut/index_html?tree-e=eJyLLWTUCOVxhAJnIwPbQiYE38 Ux2baQOVUPALHZCUs#AAAAAAAADAc=. **[360]**

38. E-mail communication, January 25, 2008. **[361]**

39. See http://researchcyc.cyc.com/. **[361]**

40. See http://opencyc.org/. **[361]**

41. http://www.cycfoundation.org/concepts. **[361]**

42. E-mail communication, January 24, 2008. **[361]**

27

Other Approaches to Reasoning and Representation

27.1 Solving Constraint Satisfaction Problems

In addition to reasoning methods based on logic or semantic networks, several other techniques have been explored. In this section, I'll describe a class of problems called constraint satisfaction problems (or assignment problems) and methods for solving them. In these problems, we have a set of objects that must be assigned values that satisfy a set of constraints. We have already seen one example of an assignment problem – that of assigning labels to lines in an image. In that problem, the constraint is that each line in the image can be assigned one and only one label.

Constraints can be expressed in the form of database relations, logical formulas, equations, or inequalities. Thus, constraint satisfaction problems arise naturally in many settings including scheduling, simulation, computer vision, and robotics. (A spreadsheet is a simple constraint satisfaction system, for example.) Fortunately, there are some general-purpose solution methods for these problems that are independent of the application. I'll illustrate one such method with a small example.

Consider the problem of placing four queens on a 4×4 chessboard in such a way that no queen can capture any other. In the Four-Queens problem, we have four objects, c_1, c_2, c_3, and c_4, representing the columns 1 through 4, respectively, in which a queen might be placed. Each of these objects can have one of four values, 1, 2, 3, or 4, corresponding to the row numbers. So, for example, when c_3 has value 2, a queen is placed in the second row of the third column. The Four-Queens problem constrains the values of these variables. For example, if c_1 has value 1, c_2 cannot have value 1 or 2; c_3 cannot have value 1 or 3; and c_4 cannot have value 1 or 4. Constraints are represented as a graph called a *constraint graph*. Each node in this graph is labeled by an object name together with a set of all of the values for that object. A pair of nodes is connected by an arc (an edge that has a direction) if the possible values of the object at the tail of the arc are constrained by any of the values of the object at the head of the arc. I show an example of such a graph for the Four-Queens problem in Fig. 27.1. In this problem, each object constrains all of the others, so all of the nodes have arcs to all of the other nodes. (To make this figure less cluttered, I represent two different arcs by a single line with arrow heads at each end.)

We start by assigning a value to one of the objects. This assignment is a "trial" value and the beginning of a search process. If it does not work out, we'll have to backtrack and try another value. Suppose we begin by assigning value 2 to object c_1 (corresponding to placing a queen in column 1, row 2). Now we iteratively examine all of the arcs in Fig. 27.1 and eliminate any value of an object at the tail of an arc

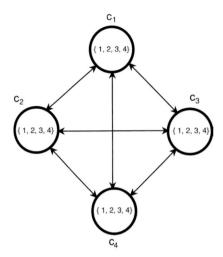

Figure 27.1. A constraint graph for the Four-Queens problem. (From Nils J. Nilsson, *Artificial Intelligence: A New Synthesis*, p. 185, San Francisco: Morgan Kaufmann Publishers, 1998.)

that is inconsistent (according to the constraints) with *all* of the values at the head of the arc. This process, called constraint propagation, halts when no more values can be eliminated. The first few steps of the process might be as follows:

1. First, look at the arc from c_2 to c_1: We can eliminate $c_2 = 1$, $c_2 = 2$, and $c_2 = 3$ because each of those values is inconsistent with the values (there being only one) of c_1.
2. Next, look at the arc from c_3 to c_1: We can eliminate $c_3 = 2$ and $c_3 = 4$.
3. Next, look at the arc from c_4 to c_1: We can eliminate $c_4 = 2$.

Eliminating some of the values, as we just did, now renders even more values susceptible to elimination. Revisiting the arcs to check again for consistency will reveal which ones. Value elimination can be said to "propagate" over the constraint graph. Continuing the propagation process eliminates all but one value of a variable for each node. At this point, all of the arcs are consistent and no more values can be eliminated. The graph shown in Fig. 27.2 shows how the process might go, starting with the values remaining after performing the three steps listed. In this case, constraint propagation has solved the problem (given that we started with $c_1 = 2$, a lucky guess). The placement of the four queens is shown in Fig. 27.3.

This process for dealing with constraint satisfaction problems is based on AC-3 (short for Arc Consistency Algorithm No. 3), an algorithm proposed by Alan K. Mackworth (1945– ; Fig. 27.4), a professor at the University of British Columbia.[1] Mackworth has continued work on constraint problems and their applications in robotics and agent control. (He also proposed and built the first soccer-playing robots.)

Various extensions and improvements to AC-3 have been proposed. These are well described in a book by Rina Dechter[2] (who has made substantial contributions to the field herself) and in Chapter Five of the text by Russell and Norvig.[3] Vipin Kumar's article surveys the entire field.[4] Commercial companies, such as

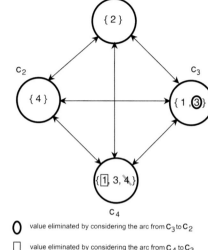

Figure 27.2. A constraint graph illustrating constraint propagation. (From Nils J. Nilsson, *Artificial Intelligence: A New Synthesis*, p. 187, San Francisco: Morgan Kaufmann Publishers, 1998.)

Figure 27.3. A solution to the Four-Queens problem.

Figure 27.4. Alan Mackworth. (Photograph courtesy of Alan Mackworth.)

ILOG (being acquired by IBM), routinely use constraint programming languages for applications involving scheduling and simulation.

The Four-Queens example I used to illustrate constraint propagation happened to find a solution without searching (because I started it with the selection of $c_1 = 2$). But, if I had selected $c_1 = 1$ initially instead, constraint propagation would have eliminated *all* of the values in all of the nodes – indicating that there is no solution to the Four-Queens problem with a queen in column 1, row 1. (You are invited to check that out.) Making that selection, and finding out that there is then no solution, would have required a higher level search process to backtrack to try another value. Also, it is possible that a trial selection followed by constraint propagation would have left unresolved the values of some of the objects. In that case, a selection would have to be made for a value of one of these objects followed by more constraint propagation, possible backtracking, and so on. Thus solving constraint satisfaction problems typically requires search, and several backtracking procedures have been proposed and used.

27.2 Solving Problems Using Propositional Logic

An important special case of logical knowledge representation and reasoning is the case in which none of the logical formulas contains variables. Although this case could not have formulas such as $(\forall x)[\text{Man}(x) \supset \text{Mortal}(x)]$, it could have formulas such as $[\text{Man}(\text{Socrates}) \supset \text{Mortal}(\text{Socrates})]$ and $[\text{Man}(\text{Plato}) \supset \text{Mortal}(\text{Plato})]$ and so on. Because there are no variables, this special case is essentially the same as propositional logic. That's because expressions such as Man(Socrates) and Mortal(Socrates), whenever they occur in the knowledge base, could be replaced by propositions, such as P014 and Q234, which have no internal structure and are thus completely unrelated. The disadvantage of limiting ourselves to propositional logic is that we would have to have a possibly very large number of formulas to cover *all* of the entities that we want to talk about – instead of using just single formulas with variables covering them all. The compensating advantage however is that extremely potent methods have been developed for reasoning with very large numbers of propositional formulas.

I'll illustrate how these methods work using a simple logical puzzle. Suppose that among the invitees to a dinner party are three rather troublesome individuals, Ann, Bill, and Charlie. A friend who is aware of the social dynamics among these people informs the hostess that at least one of these guests will definitely attend, but that if Ann attends, Bill will not, and if Bill attends, Charlie will not, and if Charlie attends, Ann will not. Based on that information, can the hostess figure out who might attend?

If she were a logician, she could convert her friend's information into the following set of formulas in propositional logic (where A stands for "Ann is coming," and so on):

$$A \vee B \vee C,$$
$$\neg A \vee \neg B,$$
$$\neg B \vee \neg C,$$
$$\neg C \vee \neg A.$$

Recall from my previous use of logical formulas that "¬" stands for "not" and that "∨" stands for "or." Formulas like these that consist of propositions (or their negations) connected by "or" signs are called "clauses." The individual propositions themselves are called "variables" because their truth values are yet to be assigned.

To solve her problem, our hostess must figure out how to assign truth values (T or F) to the three propositions A, B, and C such that all of the clauses have value T (because they come from statements presumed to be true). If a clause has value T, a logician would say that it is "satisfied." For example, if A has value T, meaning Ann is coming, the first clause would be satisfied (no matter what the values of B and C).

Logicians and computer scientists have figured out ways to tackle the problem of whether or not there is an assignment of truth values to the variables in a set of clauses such that all of the clauses are satisfied and what those values might be. The difficulty is that the problem of determining satisfiability, called the "SAT problem," is NP-complete, which implies that, in the worst case, the time taken by all known algorithms for solving SAT problems grows exponentially with the size of the problem.

Of course the problem our hostess faces is not a large problem, and she would have no difficulty solving it simply by trying out the (only) eight possible ways of assigning truth values to A, B, and C to discover which of these eight (if any) satisfies all of her clauses. But many computational problems encoded as sets of clauses might involve hundreds of thousands of clauses containing thousands of variables. Such problems would be intractable for a trial-and-error method. Fortunately, more efficient methods have been developed that are able to solve very large problems indeed. In fact, Bart Selman, one of the inventors of some of these more efficient methods, says ". . . current solvers can solve instances with one million or more variables and several million clauses." Furthermore, he claims that this is not "just a result of faster hardware . . . it's really 95% the result of better algorithms. We're still dealing with an NP-complete problem and an exponential search space. So, hardware improvements without algorithmic ideas don't have too much impact."[5]

There are two main types of methods for solving SAT problems. One class consists of what are called systematic methods, and the other class consists of what are called local search methods. In fact, some of the best solvers use techniques from both of these two methods. I'll describe the basic ideas in the next section.

27.2.1 *Systematic Methods*

Most of the systematic methods are based on a procedure called the DPLL algorithm and its various enhancements.[6] (The DPLL algorithm is derived from an earlier algorithm, the DP algorithm, proposed by Martin Davis and Hilary Putnam.[7]) The DPLL algorithm works by searching a tree of the possible ways to assign truth values to variables. At each node of the search tree a variable is assigned a value of T along one branch and a value of F along another branch. These assignments convert the set of clauses at a node to new sets at the two successor nodes by the following simplification process:

1. In each clause replace the variable just assigned by either a T or an F depending on the branch taken.

2. Eliminate those clauses that contain a T or a ¬F. (These clauses are already satisfied by this assignment.)
3. Eliminate any ¬T's or F's from any clauses in which they appear. (For the set of clauses to be satisfiable, at least one of the remaining variables in these clauses must have value T.)
4. For any clause that contains just a single variable, set that variable to the value that will satisfy that clause and continue to simplify if possible.

DPLL terminates when either one or the other of the following conditions occurs:

i. If the set of clauses arrived at is empty, DPLL finishes, having determined that the original set of clauses is satisfiable and that the truth values that have been assigned so far satisfy these clauses.
ii. If any of the clauses arrived at along a branch of the tree is empty (that is, there are no more variables left to try to satisfy it), then DPLL has determined that the original set of clauses is unsatisfiable by the truth values that have been assigned so far along that branch. In that case search continues along another branch of the tree if there are still variables with unassigned truth values. If not, DPLL finishes having determined that the original set of clauses is not satisfiable.

As an example, let's look at the tree that would be associated with my "who-is-coming-to-dinner" problem. I show in Fig. 27.5 part of the search tree that would be produced by assigning truth values (in the order A, B, and C) and simplifying.

One interesting thing to note from this example is that, depending on how the search is ordered, DPLL can (and usually does) terminate before all of the branches of the search tree have been explored. Chances for rapid termination are improved by performing a depth-first (rather than a breadth-first) search. DPLL achieves its high efficiency and speed by using what computer scientists call a "recursive backtracking search." Further improvements to DPLL have resulted in much faster and powerful global methods for solving SAT problems. These improvements involve making backtracking more "intelligent," by using what are called "clause-learning" mechanisms, and taking advantage of some strategies used by the local search methods.[8] A Web site for one of these programs, called zChaff, claims "We have success stories of using zChaff to solve problems with more than one million variables and 10 million clauses. (Of course, it can't solve every such problem!)"[9]

27.2.2 Local Search Methods

Local search methods work by performing a hill-climbing search, making a sequence of one-at-a-time modifications to a set of randomly chosen initial truth values for all of the clauses. For SAT problems, each possible set of truth values corresponds to a location in a landscape, and the number of clauses satisfied (for that set of truth values) corresponds to the height or elevation of the corresponding location. A highest location in the landscape (of which there may be more than one) corresponds to the maximum number of clauses that can be satisfied (which would be all of them if the set of clauses is satisfiable).

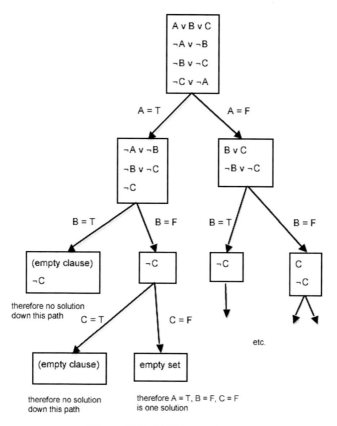

Figure 27.5. A DPLL search tree.

In 1992, Bart Selman (1959– ; Fig. 27.6), Hector Levesque, and David Mitchell (1957– ; Fig. 27.6) introduced a method for attacking SAT problems called GSAT.[10] (The "G" stands for greedy, and we'll see why in a moment.) GSAT and its various extensions, such as WALKSAT, have been applied successfully to problems with as many as 200,000 variables. GSAT conducts a local hill-climbing search over the landscape of truth values.

In outline form, here is how it works. It starts with a random assignment of truth values and evaluates how many clauses this assignment satisfies. If it satisfies all of them, the process terminates with a solution. Otherwise, it flips the truth value of each of the propositions one at a time in turn. It selects that flip that results in the largest ("greediest") increase in the number of clauses satisfied, and local search continues from the new set of truth values (with the flipped value).

It is often the case that no single flip can increase the number of clauses satisfied. Even so, there are usually flips that at least maintain this number. In that case, GSAT selects one of them (randomly) and takes the corresponding step on the "plateau" that it has reached, hoping that it can later resume its climb uphill. Or it might be that all possible steps taken in the landscape would be downhill. (One paper[11] describing these local techniques states that such a result "almost never occur[s].")

Figure 27.6. Bart Selman (left) and David G. Mitchell (right). (Photographs courtesy of Bart Selman and of David Mitchell.)

In that rare case, GSAT has certainly traversed as high as it can go and has reached a "local maximum." In some applications, an assignment of truth values that does not satisfy all of the clauses might be useful and acceptable, but if it is not, GSAT can be "restarted" with a different set of random truth assignments with the hope that a greater local maximum might be obtained in the new traverse. In any case, GSAT places limits on the number of flips that it tries so that it does not wander endlessly on a plateau. Because the SAT problem in general is NP-complete, it is possible to find problems for which the local methods (or any methods) would take an exponential amount of time, but the GSAT authors claim that such problems "appear to be extremely rare, and do not occur naturally in the applications we have examined."[12]

Here is how GSAT might work on our "who-is-coming-to-dinner" problem, whose clauses are repeated here:

$$A \lor B \lor C,$$
$$\neg A \lor \neg B,$$
$$\neg B \lor \neg C,$$
$$\neg C \lor \neg A.$$

It selects a random set of truth values, say T for A, T for B, and T for C. This set satisfies only one clause, namely, $A \lor B \lor C$. If GSAT were to flip any one of the truth values (from T to F), three clauses would be satisfied – all big steps "uphill." Suppose GSAT decides to flip the value of A, resulting in the the first, the second, and the last clause being satisfied. Flipping either the value of B or C results in all four clauses being satisfied – each a step uphill to a solution. Suppose it decides to flip the value of B. In that case GSAT would have found one solution, namely, F for A, F for B, and T for C. (The logically inclined reader will have noted that there are actually three solutions, corresponding to either of the three invitees being the sole attendee among them. Of course, the hostess would not be able to decide among these three, but at least she would know how many places to set at her table.)

It is not surprising that GSAT found a solution for this small problem. In fact, for large randomly generated problems, when the number of variables (the A's, B's, and C's) is much smaller than the number of clauses, there are likely to be many satisfying truth assignments, and GSAT (as well as other methods) would be likely to find a solution. However, when the number of variables is much greater than the number of clauses, it is likely that there are no solutions at all.[13]

One important extension to GSAT is WALKSAT (sometimes called WSAT) in which instead of always flipping the truth value of that proposition leading to the largest increase in the number of clauses satisfied, sometimes a random choice is made. This addition of a small amount of randomness helps to avoid getting stuck on local maxima of the landscape.[14]

In comparing global versus local search methods, Bart Selman claims "Local search methods are still competitive in many domains but... because the DPLL methods are less sensitive to problem encodings, they are used more often nowadays to solve structured problems [such as hardware and software verification]." However, he says that "the use of randomization and restarts in DPLL ... [brings some of] the nonsystematic aspect[s] of local search to DPLL."[15]

27.2.3 *Applications of SAT Solvers*

Several important problems can be encoded as SAT problems. For example, Henry Kautz and Bart Selman showed that generating a plan of actions can be expressed as a SAT problem.[16] SATPLAN[17] and Blackbox[18] are two systems that encode planning tasks as SAT problems and then use SAT solvers to produce plans. SATPLAN starts with specially devised logical formulas describing effects of actions, and Blackbox starts with STRIPS planning rules. (You will recall the STRIPS automatic planning system, which I described in Section 12.1.3.) According to Bart Selman, SAT solvers working on logistics planning problems, for example, can produce optimal plans of around 500 steps in a few minutes.[19] Recent versions of SAT-based planning systems have won first-place prizes in the biennial International Planning Competitions.[20]

Efficient SAT solvers have also been applied to problems in the verification of programs and digital circuitry[21] and in genomics. A closely related topic involves what are called "Binary Decision Diagrams" (BDDs) used in the verification of logical circuit designs.[22]

27.3 Representing Text as Vectors

In previous chapters, I described question-answering systems in which a question is converted into a computationally manageable form (perhaps into a logical formula), which is then used to query a computer database (perhaps a knowledge base of logical formulas). Probably the most familiar examples of question answering today take place using World Wide Web search engines. An AI person of the logicist persuasion might hope that ultimately the text in Web pages could be represented as logical formulas and that a query could be represented as a logical formula to be answered (proved) from formulas in one (or more) of those Web pages. There are some beginning attempts[23] to answer English-language queries in this manner, but most Web search engines use simpler and more efficient techniques. I'll give a rough idea of how some of them work. They convert the text in both documents and queries to *vectors* and compare a query vector against competing document vectors. First, I'll say a few things about vectors, and then I'll describe how text can be represented as a vector. (You will recall my earlier discussions of the use of vectors in pattern recognition.)

In mathematics, a vector is a quantity having magnitude and direction. In three-dimensional space, for example, one portrays a vector as an arrow drawn from the origin of that space to a point in that space. The arrow points in the vector's direction, and the length of the arrow is the vector's magnitude. Because the point determines the vector (there being only one way to draw an arrow from the origin to a point), the words "point" and "vector" are often used synonymously. Any ordered list of numbers can be thought of as the coordinates of a point and thus as the components of a vector. For example, the list $(7, 4, 3, 20)$ is a vector, one in a four-dimensional space. One can have vectors of many dimensions; the vectors used to represent documents can have thousands of dimensions. The length of a vector is the square root of the sum of the squares of all of the components of the vector. (For two-dimensional vectors, this calculation is just an application of Pythagoras's theorem, namely, the square of the length of the hypotenuse of a right triangle is the sum of the squares of its sides.) For example, the length of the vector $(7, 4, 3, 20)$ is 21.77.

One can measure the similarity between two vectors either by calculating the distance between their endpoints (perhaps adjusted to take into account their lengths) or by the "smallness" of the angle between their two directions – the smaller that angle, the more similar are the vectors. For the angle method, one performs the following similarity computation: Multiply each component of one of the vectors by the corresponding component of the other vector and then add together all of these products. Then, divide that sum by the product of the lengths of each vector. This final number, which we will call S for similarity, can be at most 1 when the two vectors are exactly aligned (that is, pointing in the same direction). It is 0 when the two vectors are perpendicular to each other, and it is negative when they point in opposite directions. So, the more similar the vectors, the closer to 1 is their S calculation. (Readers familiar with trigonometry will recognize this calculation as the cosine of the angle between the two vectors.)

As an example, the value of S for the vectors $(7, 4, 3, 20)$ and $(7, 0, 2, 15)$ can be calculated to be $(49 + 6 + 300)/(21.77 \times 16.67) = 0.978$, a value that indicates that these two vectors are quite similar.

How can we convert text to a vector? People who have been involved in computer retrieval of documents (so-called information retrieval) have come up with a method.[24] First, an ordered list of terms (words or phrases) is chosen for the set of documents to be represented by vectors. If the documents are about artificial intelligence, there could be several hundred terms that would be appropriate, including "search," "heuristic," "computer vision," and so on. If the documents are all in English and could be about anything, there might be hundreds of thousands of terms (essentially all of the words in the English language). Usually, the terms chosen are word stems, so that "computing," "computers," and "computed" would all be covered by the term "compute." (One has to be careful about this kind of conflation, called "stemming," to avoid substituting "flow" for "flower" and such.) Also, because words such as "and," "if," and "therefore" and so on are seldom relevant to the content of a document, these words are not used as terms.

Next, in the process of representing a document as a vector, all of the occurrences of each of these terms in the document are counted. A list of these occurrence numbers is then assembled (in the same order as the list of terms), and this list is the vector representation of the document. So, for example, if the term "search" does not occur at all in a document being represented, if the term "heuristic" occurs seven times, and the term "computer vision" occurs three times, then the list would be, say,

$$(0, 0, 0, \underline{0}, 0, \underline{7}, 0, 0, \underline{3}, 0, 0, \ldots),$$

where the underlined numbers are the number of times the terms I just mentioned occur in that document. Of course, there might be many, many 0's because many of the terms in the chosen list of terms might not occur at all in the document, and there might be many more nonzero numbers corresponding to the numbers of times other terms occur in that document.

Now, suppose we are interested in the question "What heuristics are used in computer vision?" and pose this query to an Internet search engine. If we assume that some kind of preprocessing is used on the query (and on the documents) to change words to their "stems," the vector representation of our query would be

$$(0, 0, 0, 0, 0, \underline{1}, 0, 0, \underline{1}, 0, 0, \ldots).$$

The similarity S between our query and the document we just considered would be 10 divided by the product of the lengths of the two vectors. This value would be compared with the similarity values against other documents to determine which documents are the most similar and therefore should be retrieved in response to our query.

This all sounds pretty simple, but, although the basic idea is simple, several elaborations are needed (and have been added) to make document retrieval and Internet retrieval of Web sites based on this idea practical and useful. First, the count for a term in a document is usually adjusted to take into account the length of the text in that document. Because longer documents might contain relatively more occurrences of a given term, the count for a term is computed as a percentage of the total number of all the terms in the document. Second, because a given term may be quite common among all the documents being searched (and thus not very useful for discrimination), the count is diminished by a factor that depends on the overall frequency of that term among these documents. More sophisticated retrieval programs also use various statistical methods to compute the probability of a document's relevance to a query. An innovation invented by Google ranks Web sites according to an estimate related to their popularity or "centrality." Increasingly, "machine learning" methods (some of which will be described in a subsequent chapter) are also being used to improve the performance of retrieval systems, and,

Figure 27.7. Thomas K. Landauer. (Photograph courtesy of Libby Landauer.)

of course, efficiency requires appropriate indexing schemes and the use of many thousands of computers.

27.4 Latent Semantic Analysis

Some researchers have suggested that representing text as vectors captures the "meaning" of the text. How can that be when the vector representations are computed only from how often various terms occur in documents and not at all from the order in which those terms occur? (After all, the meaning of "Dog bites man" is quite different from that of "Man bites dog.") Thomas K. Landauer (1932– ; Fig. 27.7) and colleagues, first in his Cognitive Science Research Group at Bell Communications Research (a descendent of Bell Laboratories) in the mid-1980s, and later at the University of Colorado, have proposed a vector-based scheme for capturing meaning, which they call Latent Semantic Analysis (LSA). I think I can explain the basic idea without using all of the mathematics that a full description would require.

Here, in a scaled-down example, is basically how the LSA method works. Let's say we have a rather long document or other text material about a certain topic. We divide the material into sections, called "passages," of around 100 or so terms each. Supposing that the vocabulary of the material is captured by 1,000 terms (which could consist of individual words or word combinations), then each of these passages is represented by a 1,000-dimensional vector. (The term counts used in constructing these vectors are adjusted by methods similar to those I have already explained.) Let's suppose we have 100 such vectors.

It is difficult (impossible really) to visualize a 1,000-dimensional space in which our vectors are embedded, but perhaps one can at least imagine that some lower dimensional "subspace" would contain all or most of the vectors. It might help

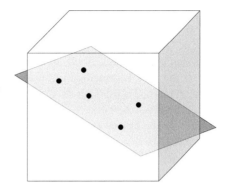

Figure 27.8. A two-dimensional subspace within a three-dimensional space.

to consider a three-dimensional example as shown in Fig. 27.8. In the diagram, I show five points that happen to lie on a plane (a two-dimensional space) within a three-dimensional space. The two-dimensional space is a subspace of a three-dimensional space. In that two-dimensional space, the five points can be represented by two-dimensional vectors instead of three-dimensional ones.

Using various complex mathematical techniques, it is possible to construct a lower dimensional space that adequately "contains" the 100 vectors (perhaps, say, a 50-dimensional space). LSA uses methods based on a technique called "Singular Value Decomposition" (SVD), the details of which need not concern us here. Of course, the representation of these vectors in 50 dimensions will be different than it was in 1,000 dimensions. Many of the terms associated with dimensions in the larger space get conflated into new components in the smaller space. Moreover, according to Landauer and colleagues, it is this very conflation that allows extraction of the latent overall meaning from the separate passages of the document. As they put it in explaining an example of the process, ". . . if we were to change the entry in any one cell of the original, the values in the reconstruction with reduced dimensions might be changed everywhere; this is the mathematical sense in which LSA performs inference or induction."[25]

Transforming vectors into ones with fewer components essentially links together many of the terms occurring (and not occurring) in the original passages from which the vectors were derived. This linking together can be thought of as creating a higher level "concept" based on the associated terms. Expressing a text document in terms of these concepts (that is, in terms of the vectors of reduced dimension) has extracted, according to the LSA people, the essential "meaning" of the document. The reduced-dimension vectors can link together terms from different sections of a text if they occur in passages having a similar meaning even though they never occur in the same passage.

The LSA process allows the computation of the similarity between any two passages in the document, say by computing the size of the angle between the two corresponding reduced-dimension vectors. Along with the process of representing passages by vectors of reduced dimension, the LSA method also produces a representation of each term in the entire set of terms by a vector having the same reduced dimension. By using that representation, the similarity between two terms can also be computed, as well as the similarity between a term and a passage. Finally, a document itself can be represented as a vector consisting of the average of its passage vectors. Once so represented, the similarity between documents can be computed. This step is used in one of the applications of LSA called "Latent Semantic Indexing" (LSI). The LSI method is reported to offer some improvement over standard retrieval methods (although the point is still controversial).[26]

LSA has been used in several settings, including grading essays written by college-entrance-exam test-takers, helping students learn writing skills, helping to diagnose schizophrenia from patient verbalizations, and creating key-word summaries of documents.[27] In addition, it has been used to mimic some human abilities, such as scoring as well as average test-takers on the synonym portion of TOEFL (the ETS TEst of English as a Foreign Language) and achieving a passing score on a multiple-choice exam using the vectors from an LSA analysis of an introductory psychology textbook.[28]

A reader might object that an LSA system for grading essays could be foiled by someone who wrote a large number of appropriate words in random order without expressing any coherent thoughts at all. Landauer counters this objection by saying that it would be hard "to get the good words without writing a good essay.... We've tried to write bad essays and get good grades and we can sometimes do it if we know the material really well. The easiest way to cheat this system is to study hard, know the material and write a good essay."[29]

In 1998, Landauer and colleagues formed Knowledge Analysis Technologies (KAT) to develop educational applications of LSA. KAT was acquired by Pearson Education in 2004 and markets LSA-based educational products as Pearson Knowledge Technologies (PKT).

Some researchers have pointed out that the main power of the LSA methods is in vector dimensionality reduction and that there are several other methods (some of which are simpler than that used in LSA) for reducing dimensionality. In fact, in one of their early papers about LSA, Landauer and Susan Dumais describe an LSA analog based on a neural network.[30]

A probabilistic extension to Latent Semantic Indexing has been proposed and tested by Thomas Hofmann.[31] A more general probabilistic model has been developed by David Blei, Andrew Ng, and Michael Jordan.[32] Probabilistic models of all sorts began to play a very prominent role in artificial intelligence beginning in the late 1980s. It is to that subject that I turn next.

Notes

1. Alan K. Mackworth, "Consistency in Networks of Relations," *Artificial Intelligence*, Vol. 8, No. 1, pp. 99–118, 1977. **[366]**
2. Rina Dechter, *Constraint Processing*, San Francisco: Morgan Kaufmann Publishers, 2003. **[366]**
3. Stuart Russell and Peter Norvig, *Artificial Intelligence: A Modern Approach*, second edition, Upper Saddle River, NJ: Prentice Hall, 2003. **[366]**
4. Vipin Kumar, "Algorithms for Constraint-Satisfaction Problems: A Survey," *AI Magazine*, pp. 32–44, Spring 1992. Available online at http://www.cs.cinvestav.mx/ ~constraint/papers/kumar-survey.pdf. **[366]**

5. E-mail communication, April 8, 2008. [369]
6. The algorithm is named for Martin Davis, Hilary Putnam, George Logemann, and Donald W. Loveland. See Martin Davis, George Logemann, and Donald Loveland, "A Machine Program for Theorem-Proving," *Communications of the ACM*, Vol. 5, No. 7, pp. 394–397, 1962. [369]
7. Martin Davis and Hilary Putnam, "A Computing Procedure for Quantification Theory," *Journal of the ACM*, Vol. 7, No. 3, pp. 201–215, 1960. [369]
8. See, for example, Matthew Moskewicz *et al.*, "Chaff: Engineering an Efficient SAT Solver," *Proceedings of the 38th Design Automation Conference (DAC'01)*, 2001 (available online at http://www.princeton.edu/~chaff/publication/DAC2001v56.pdf), and Niklas Eén and Niklas Dörensson, "An Extensible SAT-Solver," *Theory and Applications of Satisfiability Testing*, Lecture Notes in Computer Science, Berlin and Heidelberg: Springer-Verlag, 2004 (available online at http://een.se/niklas/Satzoo/An_Extensible_SAT-solver.ps.gz). [370]
9. See http://www.princeton.edu/~chaff/zchaff.html. A Web site for another efficient SAT solver, MiniSat, is at http://minisat.se/Main.html. [370]
10. Bart Selman, Hector Levesque, and David Mitchell, "A New Method for Solving Hard Satisfiability Problems," *Proceedings of the Tenth National Conference on Artificial Intelligence*, pp. 440–446, Menlo Park, CA: AAAI Press, 1992. Available online at http://www.cs.sfu.ca/~mitchell/papers/ai92-gsat.ps. [371]
11. Bart Selman, Henry Kautz, and Bram Cohen, "Local Search Strategies for Satisfiability Testing," in David S. Johnson and Michael A. Trick (eds.), *Cliques, Coloring, and Satisfiability: Second DIMACS Implementation Challenge, October 11–13, 1993* (*DIMACS Series in Discrete Mathematics and Theoretical Computer Science*, Vol. 26, Providence, RI: AMS, 1996.) A version of the paper is available online at http://www.cs.rochester.edu/u/kautz/papers/dimacs93.ps. Also see a Web page about local search methods at http://www.cs.rochester.edu/u/kautz/walksat/. [371]
12. Bart Selman, Hector Levesque, and David Mitchell, *op. cit.* [372]
13. Bart Selman, Hector Levesque, and David Mitchell, *op. cit.* [373]
14. See Bart Selman, Henry Kautz, and Bram Cohen, *op. cit.*. [373]
15. Bart Selman, e-mail of April 8, 2008. [373]
16. Henry Kautz and Bart Selman, "Planning as Satisfiability," *Proceedings of the 10th European Conference on Artificial Intelligence*, pp. 359–363, New York: John Wiley and Sons, Inc., 1992 (available online at http://www.cs.rochester.edu/u/papers/satplan.ps), and Henry Kautz and Bart Selman, "Pushing the Envelope: Planning, Propositional Logic, and Stochastic Search," *Proceedings of the 13th National Conference on Artificial Intelligence (AAAI-96)*, pp. 1194–1201, Menlo Park, CA: AAAI Press, 1996 (available online at https://eprints.kfupm.edu.sa/58089/1/58089.pdf). [373]
17. Henry Kautz, Bart Selman, and Joerg Hoffmann, "SATPLAN: Planning as Satisfiability," *Abstracts of the 5th International Planning Competition*, 2006 (available online at http://www.cs.rochester.edu/u/kautz/papers/kautz-satplan06.pdf). See http://www.cs.rochester.edu/u/kautz/walksat/ for information about and downloads of SATPLAN programs. [373]
18. Henry A. Kautz and Bart Selman, "Unifying SAT-Based and Graph-Based Planning," *Proceedings of the Sixteenth International Joint Conference on Artificial Intelligence*, pp. 318–325, San Francisco: Morgan Kaufmann Publishers, 1999. Available online at http://www.cs.rochester.edu/u/kautz/satplan/blackbox/ijcai99blackbox.ps. See http://www.cs.rochester.edu/u/kautz/satplan/blackbox/ for information about and downloads of Blackbox programs. [373]
19. Bart Selman E-mail of April 8, 2008. [373]

20. See http://zeus.ing.unibs.it/ipc-5/ for information about the International Planning Competitions. [373]

21. See, for example, Armin Biere *et al.*, "Bounded Model Checking," *Advances in Computers*, Vol. 58, San Diego: Academic Press, 2003. One of the co-authors of this paper, Edmund M. Clarke, a computer science professor at Carnegie Mellon University, was a co-recipient of the 2007 ACM Turing Award for his work in this field. [373]

22. See Randy E. Bryant, "Graph-Based Algorithms for Boolean Function Manipulation," *IEEE Transactions on Computers*, Vol. C-35, No. 8, pp. 677–691, August 1986. Available online at http://www.cs.cmu.edu/~bryant/pubdir/ieeetc86.pdf. [373]

23. See, for example, http://www.powerset.com/. [374]

24. The paper in which this method was first presented is Gerard Salton, A. Wong, and C. S. Yang, "A Vector Space Model for Automatic Indexing," *Communications of the ACM*, Vol. 18, No. 11, pp. 613–620, November 1975. For some quibbles about this topic see http://www.ideals.uiuc.edu/bitstream/2142/1697/2/Dubin748764.pdf. [374]

25. Thomas K Landauer, Peter W. Foltz, and Darrell Laham, "Introduction to Latent Semantic Analysis," *Discourse Processes*, Vol. 25, pp. 25–284, 1998. Available online at lsa.colorado.edu/papers/dp1.LSAintro.pdf. [377]

26. Susan T. Dumais, "Latent Semantic Indexing (LSI) and TREC-2," in D. Harman (ed.), *The Second Text Retrieval Conference (TREC2)*, National Institute of Standards and Technology Special Publication 500-215, pp. 105–116, 1994. A copy is available online at trec.nist.gov/pubs/trec2/papers/txt/10.txt. [378]

27. Thomas Landauer, e-mail communication, January 30, 2008. [378]

28. For more information about these applications, see the LSA Web site at http://lsa.colorado.edu/ and the various papers cited there. [378]

29. From a press release available online at http://lsa.colorado.edu/essay_press.html. [378]

30. Thomas K Landauer and Susan T. Dumais, "Solution to Plato's Problem: The Latent Semantic Analysis Theory of Acquisition, Induction and Representation of Knowledge," *Psychological Review*, Vol. 104, No. 2, pp. 211–240, 1997. An online version, dated 1977, is available at http://lsi.research.telcordia.com/lsi/papers/PSYCHREV96.html. [378]

31. Thomas Hofmann, "Probabilistic Latent Semantic Indexing," *Proceedings of the Twenty-Second Annual International SIGIR Conference on Research and Development in Information Retrieval*, 1999. Available online at http://www.cs.brown.edu/~th/papers/Hofmann-SIGIR99.pdf. [378]

32. David M. Blei, Andrew Y. Ng, and Michael I. Jordan, "Latent Dirichlet Allocation," *Journal of Machine Learning Research*, Vol. 3, pp. 993–1022, 2003. Available online at http://www.cs.princeton.edu/~blei/papers/BleiNgJordan2003.pdf. [378]

Bayesian Networks

28.1 Representing Probabilities in Networks

Much human reasoning is about propositions and quantities that are uncertain. Our beliefs about many things are provisional (that is, subject to change) and qualified (that is, having various levels of confidence). AI systems, too, need to be able to deal with uncertain information. An AI agent's facts, statements, and rules should most appropriately be thought of as provisional and qualified. After all, some of its information is provided by humans and some originates from sensors with limited precision and reliability. Yet, much of the early work in AI ignored the uncertain nature of knowledge. In fact, Marvin Minsky observed that his edited volume of early AI papers contained "no explicit use of probabilistic notions."[1]

Most AI researchers nowadays, however, acknowledge that much of the knowledge needed by machines needs to be qualified by probability values and that reasoning with this knowledge can therefore most appropriately be done with the tools of probability theory. But just as is the case with logical reasoning, probabilistic reasoning is subject to AI's old nemesis, the combinatorial explosion. Suppose, for example, that an agent's knowledge consists of a set of propositions. Because of possible interdependencies among the propositions, accurate probabilistic reasoning depends on knowing more than just the probability of each of those propositions individually. Instead, probability values for various combinations of the propositions taken together, called "joint probabilities," are usually required; this leads, in the general case, to impractically large representations and intractable computations.

Earlier AI systems that could deal with uncertainty, such as MYCIN and PROSPECTOR, made simplifying assumptions to ease these representational and computational difficulties. However, because these systems failed to take into account important interdependencies among their beliefs, they often gave inappropriate results owing to such things as overcounting of evidence. During the 1980s some powerful new methods were invented (and imported from other fields) that were better able to deal with dependencies. These methods greatly simplified both the representational and the computational problems. They involve representing uncertain beliefs and their dependencies in a graphical form, called a "probabilistic graphical model." I'll describe the most important version of such models in this chapter.

First, to illustrate some of the difficulties involved in reasoning about uncertain beliefs and how we might deal with them, let's look at an example involving various propositions about an automobile engine. Here are some of the things we might say about an engine and its components:

P1: The starter motor is ok.
P2: The starter motor cranks the engine when the starter switch is turned on.
P3: The fuel system is ok.
P4: The car starts when the starter switch is turned on.

These propositions are quite obviously related. For one thing, P4 depends on the other three – the sad observation that P4 is false would certainly change our confidences about the other three. Moreover, it would not take an auto mechanic to know that P1 and P2 are related.

A full account of the dependencies involved here requires a listing of *all* of the possibilities for things being ok and not ok, and there are sixteen such possibilities. If we denote the opposite of a proposition by putting a negation sign ($\neg$) in front of it, then $\neg$P1 denotes "The starter motor is not ok." Using this notation, the sixteen possibilities are

$$P1, P2, P3, P4,$$

$$P1, P2, P3, \neg P4,$$

$$P1, P2, \neg P3, P4,$$

$$P1, P2, \neg P3, \neg P4,$$

$$P1, \neg P2, P3, P4,$$

$$P1, \neg P2, P3, \neg P4,$$

$$P1, \neg P2, \neg P3, P4,$$

$$P1, \neg P2, \neg P3, \neg P4,$$

$$\neg P1, P2, P3, P4,$$

$$\neg P1, P2, P3, \neg P4,$$

$$\neg P1, P2, \neg P3, P4,$$

$$\neg P1, P2, \neg P3, \neg P4,$$

$$\neg P1, \neg P2, P3, P4,$$

$$\neg P1, \neg P2, P3, \neg P4,$$

$$\neg P1, \neg P2, \neg P3, P4,$$

Figure 28.1. Judea Pearl. (Photograph courtesy of Judea Pearl.)

and

$$\neg P1, \neg P2, \neg P3, \neg P4.$$

An expert who knows about engines and their expected reliabilities would, presumably, be able to assign probability values to each of these sixteen "states" in which an engine system might find itself. For example, the expert might specify that the overall joint probability that everything is ok, denoted by $p(P1, P2, P3, P4)$, is 0.999. He or she would have to specify sixteen such numbers. (Actually, only fifteen would be needed because the sixteen would have to sum to one. These are the only possible states and one of them must be the case.) Knowing these joint probabilities would enable a person (possessing patience and skills in probability theory) to calculate certain other probabilities, such as the probability that the car starts given only, say, that the fuel system is definitely ok.

Specifying the fifteen numbers for this small example does not seem too arduous, but for a more realistic problem, say one with thirty different propositions, one would have to specify $2^{30} - 1 = 1,073,741,823$ numbers. Moreover, if there are also quantities that might take on several values (in addition to propositions, which are binary-valued), the number of possibilities expands even further.

Of course, I have assumed here the worst case, namely, the case in which all four propositions might depend in complex ways on each other. At the other extreme is the case in which the propositions are completely independent of each other. Then, each of the sixteen probabilities could be computed by formulas such as

$$p(P1, P2, P3, P4) = p(P1)p(P2)p(P3)p(P4)$$

(with $\neg$ signs put in as required), and we would need only to specify probabilities for each of the four propositions individually.

My example about automobile engines is actually somewhat in between these two extremes. So also are many much larger and more realistic problems. This "in-betweenness" is the key to making probabilistic reasoning more tractable. Although there was previous recognition and exploitation of this fact by statisticians, it was Judea Pearl (1936– ; Fig. 28.1) who developed some of the main representational and computational methods.

Pearl, a professor of computer science at the University of California at Los Angeles, was puzzled by the contrast between, on the one hand, the ease with which humans reason and make inferences based on uncertain information and, on the other

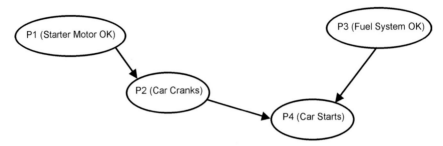

Figure 28.2. A network representation.

hand, the computational difficulties of duplicating those abilities using probability calculations. As he later put it, he started with the following conjectures:[2]

1. The consistent agreement between plausible reasoning [by humans] and probability calculus could not be coincidental but strongly suggests that human intuition invokes some crude form of probabilistic computation.
2. In light of the speed and effectiveness of human reasoning, the computational difficulties that plagued earlier probabilistic systems could not be very fundamental and should be overcome by making the right choice of simplifying assumptions which humans store in their head.

Pearl's key insight was that beliefs about propositions and other quantities could often be regarded as "direct causes" of other beliefs and that these causal linkages could be represented in graphical structures that encode simplifying assumptions about relationships among probabilities.

To be sure, Pearl was not the first to suggest using graphical structures to encode probabilistic information. He himself mentions earlier work.[3] Russell and Norvig[4] wrote that work by the British statistician I. J. Good "could be regarded as a forerunner of modern Bayesian networks...."[5] And physicists point to closely related work by Hans A. Bethe.[6]

For our automobile engine problem, the sort of graph that Pearl might use is as shown in Fig. 28.2. Each proposition of interest is represented by a "node" in the graph. The arrows show the direct influences among the various propositions and also indicate certain probabilistic independencies among them. For example, the probability of P4 (the car starts when the starter switch is turned on) does not depend at all on the probability of P1 (the starter motor is ok) if we already know (are given) P2 (the starter motor cranks the engine when the starter switch is turned on) and P3 (the fuel system is ok). Knowing P1 does not tell us anything new about P4 if we already know P2 and P3. In the language of probability theory, the probability of P4 is *conditionally independent* of P1, given P4's parents, namely, P2 and P3. In real-world reasoning tasks there are many such conditional independencies, which can be revealed by these kinds of causally derived graphs. Taking account of them greatly reduces the complexity of probabilistic reasoning.

For our automobile engine example, instead of the fifteen probabilities that would be needed in the general case, now we need only eight. These are as follows: the probabilities of P4 given P2 and P3 for the four different states of P2 and P3,

$$p(\text{P4} \mid \text{P2}, \text{P3}),$$
$$p(\text{P4} \mid \text{P2}, \neg\text{P3}),$$
$$p(\text{P4} \mid \neg\text{P2}, \text{P3}),$$
$$p(\text{P4} \mid \neg\text{P2}, \neg\text{P3});$$

the probability of P2 given P1 for the two different states of P1, namely, $p(\text{P2} \mid \text{P1})$ and $p(\text{P2} \mid \neg\text{P1})$; and the probabilities of P1 and P3, namely, $p(\text{P1})$ and $p(\text{P3})$. Each of these sets of probability values is stored in what is called a "conditional probability table" (CPT) associated with its corresponding node in the network. (The CPT of a node with no parents is just the unconditional probability for that node.)

By using a result from probability theory all sixteen joint probabilities (required for accurate probabilistic reasoning) can be computed from these eight. We aren't actually getting something for nothing here. Instead, we are exploiting the added knowledge provided by the conditional independencies made evident by the network.

Because Bayes's rule plays a prominent role in computing probabilities of the various nodes given the probabilities of others, Pearl coined the phrase "Bayesian belief networks" (usually simplified to Bayesian networks or belief networks) for these sorts of graphs.[7] It has proven rather easy to construct large Bayesian networks by carefully noting which propositions directly influence ("cause") others. Networks thus constructed are what graph theorists call "directed acyclic graphs" (DAGs): "directed" because arrows point from cause nodes to caused nodes and "acyclic" because following the arrows outward from a node never leads back to that same node.

One might ask, where do the probability values in the CPTs come from? For some networks, perhaps an expert familiar with how certain propositions affect others might be able to make guesses about probabilities. Such guesses are called "subjective probabilities," based as they are on an expert's subjective notions about cause and effect. However, by far the most useful method for populating the CPTs with values is to estimate them from a large database of actual cases. I'll explain how that is done in the next section.

By whatever means they are obtained, the CPTs (together with the structure of the network) are used in computations about how the probabilities of some nodes in the network are affected by the probabilities of others. These computations are called "probabilistic inference." Various practical computational methods have been devised – even for the rather large networks needed for realistic problems.

Without going through any actual computations, I'll use the small engine network to illustrate three main styles of probabilistic inference in Bayesian networks. For example, if all we knew for certain was that the starter motor was ok [that is, $p(\text{P1}) = 1$)], we could compute the probability that the car will start. "Migrating" known probability values downward in the network (in the direction of the arrows) is usually called "causality reasoning." Conversely, if we knew that the car would not start [that is, $p(\text{P4}) = 0$], we could compute the probabilities of the starter motor being ok and of the fuel system being ok. Migrating probability values upward in the network (against the direction of the arrows) is usually called "evidential" or

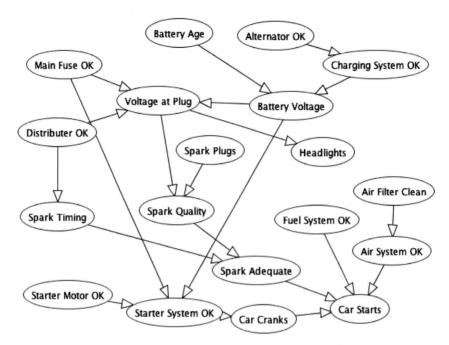

Figure 28.3. A Bayesian network from an interactive Web site. (Used with permission of Alan Mackworth and David Poole.)

"diagnostic" reasoning. It is what physicians (and other trouble-shooters) do when they have a symptom and attempt to infer the probabilities of causes.

There is another important reasoning style also, and that is called "explaining away." Here is an example: Suppose we know that the car does not start and we have computed probability values for the fuel system being the problem (that is, not ok) and for the starter motor being the problem. Then, later, we find out that actually the starter motor has, in fact, failed. Taking that additional information into account, we would find that the probability of the fuel system being the problem would decrease. The starter motor problem "explains" the fact that the car would not start, so we have less reason to suspect the fuel system. The fact that the starter motor does not start "explains away" the possible fuel system problem. The strategy of explaining away is commonly used by people in medicine, law, science, and everyday reasoning. For example, a defense attorney might cite evidence that some other person (not his client) was identified on a bank's TV monitoring system, thus explaining away his client's involvement in a bank robbery.

I can illustrate the explaining-away effect with actual inference calculations performed on the somewhat larger network about engines shown in Fig. 28.3.[8] After observing that the car does not start, the probability that the starter motor is the problem is computed to be 0.023 (by using the network's conditional probability tables, which are not shown in the diagram), and the probability that the fuel system is the problem is computed to be 0.283. But upon additionally observing that the starter motor has failed, the probability that the fuel system is the cause of the problem drops by more than half to 0.1.

If we wanted to build a Bayesian network about an automobile engine that was more realistic and useful, we would have to mention many more components and subsystems. Such a network might contain hundreds of nodes along with their associated conditional probability tables. Even though conditional independencies would reduce the number of individual probabilities that need to be specified, still their number can be so large that exact probabilistic inferences would still be computationally intractable – assuming that values for these probabilities could even be gathered. Fortunately, various simplifications are possible that permit further reductions in the number of probabilities needed. With them, computations for approximate, but still useful, inference in large networks become practicable. It is worth mentioning that some of these simplifications and approximate computational methods involve rather complex mathematical tools, many of them stemming from adjacent fields such as statistics and control engineering.[9] These kinds of Bayesian network calculations provide another instance of how problems previously thought to be computationally intractable have yielded to technical advances.

In Fig. 28.4, I show an example of a rather large Bayesian network.[10] The network represents knowledge about hepatobiliary disease (of the liver, gall bladder, and related organs) and was developed as a tool to use with medical students. This network was derived in part from the knowledge base of INTERNIST-1 (see p. 237). It has 448 nodes and 908 arrows. If full conditional probability tables were used, 133,931,430 probabilities would have to be specified. The network's developers were able to reduce this number to 8,254 values using various simplifications.

Bayesian networks containing hundreds of nodes have been used for applications in biology, medicine, document classification, image processing, law, error-correction decoding, and many other fields.[11] Many of these networks are derived automatically from large data sets, a topic I'll discuss in the next section.

28.2 Automatic Construction of Bayesian Networks

One of the reasons why Bayesian networks have become so important is that they can be automatically constructed from large databases. That is, they can be "learned," and the learned versions can be used to reason about the subject area in question. Two of the pioneers in the development of these learning methods were Greg Cooper and Edward Herskovits.[12] The subject continues to be an active research area, and there are several others who have made significant contributions.[13]

Here, in general terms, is how the process works. To learn a network involves learning the structure of the network, that is, the disposition of its nodes and links, as well as the network's CPTs. First, I'll explain how the CPTs for a known structure can be learned and next how the structure itself can be learned, even though the two processes are actually interlinked. Let's consider again the four-node Bayesian network for the automobile engine. How might we learn the CPT for the node P4 (that is, Car Starts) – the one whose parents are P2 (that is, Car Cranks) and

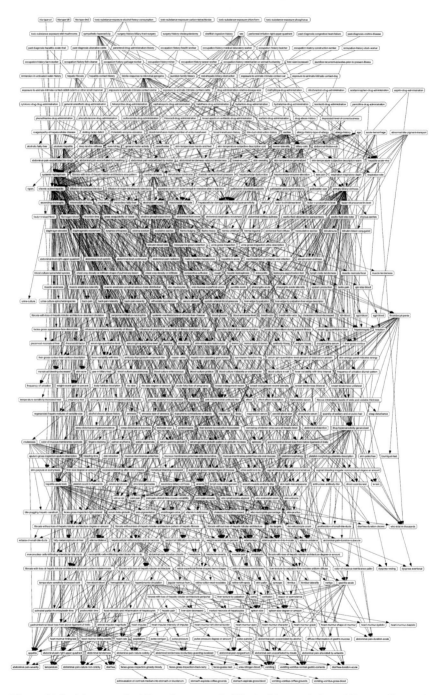

Figure 28.4. A large medical Bayesian network. (Used with permission of Gregory Provan.)

P3 (that is, `Fuel System OK`)? Using my abbreviations for those propositions, that CPT is composed of the following conditional probabilities:

$$p(P4 \mid P2, P3),$$
$$p(P4 \mid P2, \neg P3),$$
$$p(P4 \mid \neg P2, P3),$$

and

$$p(P4 \mid \neg P2, \neg P3).$$

If we had a large collection of samples of situations in which the car sometimes starts and sometimes did not, in which the car sometimes cranks and sometimes did not, and in which the fuel system sometimes was ok and sometimes was not, we could use them to tabulate what are called "sample statistics." For example, we could note the number of times in these samples that the car did start when the car did not crank and the fuel system was ok and divide that number by the total number of times that the car did not crank and the fuel system was ok. That fraction could be used as an estimate of $p(P4 \mid \neg P2, P3)$. We could make similar estimates of the other three probabilities and similar estimates for the probabilities in the other CPTs in the network. With a sufficiently large collection of samples, these estimates would be reasonably reliable: The greater the number of samples, the better the estimates.

Compilation of the sample statistics (sometimes augmented by some additional computations, which I won't go into here) provides a means for estimating the CPTs of a network with *known* structure. Now, how could we learn the structure of an unknown network? The method involves the following sequence of steps:

1. Start with some basic candidate structure, such as one that has no connections between nodes, and use the data collection to estimate its CPTs. (Recall that the CPT of a node with no parents is just the unconditional probability for that node. It can be estimated by the fraction of times its associated proposition is true in the data set.)
2. Calculate a "goodness measure" for this network. One of the proposed measures is based on how well the network, with its calculated CPTs, could be used to transmit (that is, regenerate) the original data collection.
3. Begin a "hill-climbing" search process by evaluating "nearby" networks that differ from the previous one by small changes (which might involve adding an arc, deleting one that is already there, and swapping nodes). To evaluate the changed networks, their CPTs and goodnesses are calculated. Settle on that changed network with the best improvement in goodness.
4. Continue the hill-climbing process until no more improvements can be made (or until some predefined stopping criterion is met).

Although this process appears to be quite tedious (and it is), computers can execute this hill-climbing process reasonably efficiently, and some rather complex networks have been learned.

As an example, consider the networks in Fig. 28.5. Three networks are shown. The first is a network encoding relationships among 37 variables for a problem

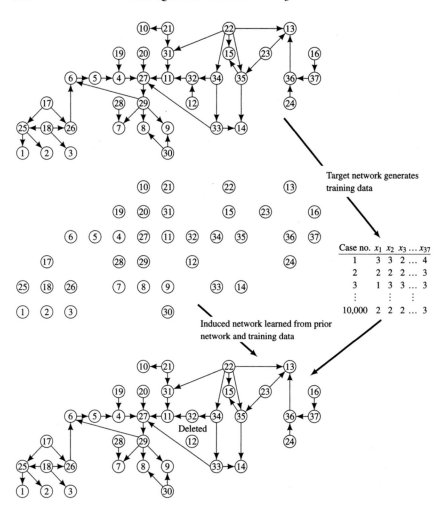

Figure 28.5. Learning a Bayesian network. (From Nils J. Nilsson, *Artificial Intelligence: A New Synthesis*, p. 350, San Francisco: Morgan Kaufmann Publishers, 1998.)

involving an alarm system used in ventilator management in a hospital intensive-care unit. This known network was used to generate a size-10,000 training set of random values for the 37 nodes. By using this random sample, and starting with the second network (the one without any dependencies and thus no links between nodes), the third network was learned (in about five hours on a SUN SPARCstation 20) using methods similar to those just described.[14] Note the very close similarity in structure – only one arc is missing.

Sometimes network structure can be simplified substantially by adding nodes to the network that represent attributes that do not occur in the data set. Network learning methods have been extended to be able to learn to install "hidden nodes" that represent these invented attributes. Attributes invented from the data are often

Figure 28.6. Daphne Koller. (Photograph courtesy of Daphne Koller.)

useful for deepening our understanding of the phenomena that gave rise to the data.

28.3 Probabilistic Relational Models

An important elaboration of Bayesian networks, called "Probabilistic Relational Models" (PRMs),[15] has been developed by Stanford professor Daphne Koller (1968– ; Fig. 28.6), together with her students Avi Pfeffer and Lise Getoor and a collaborator, Nir Friedman (a former Stanford student and now a professor at Hebrew University). PRMs integrate probability with predicate calculus. [Some earlier work on combining these two representational forms was done by several researchers, notably by David Poole (1958–) at the University of British Columbia.][16] PRMs exploit the fact that some nodes in a network might share the same attributes except for the values of variables internal to those attributes (much like the fact that in the predicate calculus the same predicate may be written with different values for its internal variables).

For example, a network showing that a person's blood type and chromosomal information depends on chromosomes inherited from his or her parents would have repeated subnetworks. I show an example in Fig. 28.7. In this case, a single "template" is used to make different subnetworks whose attribute variables are instantiated to different individuals. Using PRMs makes the design of Bayesian networks much more efficient than would be the process of having to design each (only slightly different) subnetwork separately. Koller says she was motivated to think about PRMs in a conversation with a student who was having to convert a Bayesian network modeling a three-lane freeway to one modeling a four-lane freeway. She recalls saying "... but that's just adding one more lane, surely you can reuse some of the structure."[17]

The structure and CPTs of a PRM can either be specified by a designer or learned from data.[18] An added benefit of PRMs is that objects resulting from instantiating template variables can be linked in the resulting Bayesian network (as some are in the diagram); relationships among these objects can be specified by hand or learned.

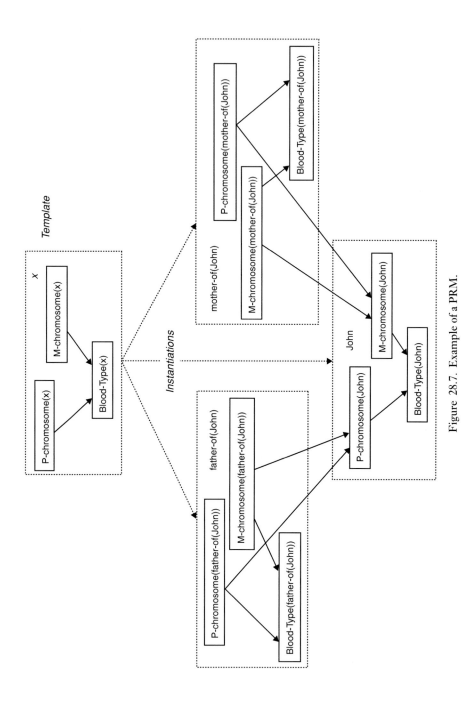

Figure 28.7. Example of a PRM.

392

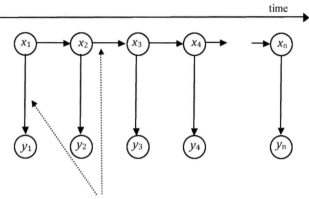

arrows indicate probabilistic influences, which are
specified by conditional probability tables

Figure 28.8. A hidden Markov model.

As with any Bayesian network, probabilistic inference procedures can be used to answer queries about the probabilities of some nodes given those of others.

PRMs and related structures have been used in a variety of applications, including one for recovering regulatory networks from gene expression data.[19]

As regards Bayesian networks in general, there are by now many, many applications – too many to list here. To give a flavor of their variety, I'll mention their use in genomic studies,[20] in automobile traffic forecasting and routing,[21] in modeling disease outbreaks,[22] and in guessing at a computer user's next actions to enable the Windows operating system to "prefetch" application data into memory before it is demanded.[23] There are also companies that sell knowledge-capturing and reasoning systems based on Bayesian networks.[24]

One thing that all of these applications has taught us is the importance of massive amounts of data, which according to Peter Norvig, the co-author of the leading AI textbook and Director of Research at Google, has turned out to be the major theme of modern AI.[25] In fact, Peter told me that Google is the world's biggest AI system. I asked him why, and he simply replied "data, data, data," and Google has more of it than anybody."[26]

28.4 Temporal Bayesian Networks

The examples of Bayesian networks illustrated in the last sections, along with larger ones used in many applications, are what one might call "static." That is, the propositions and quantities represented by the nodes and CPTs are timeless in the sense that they deal with the same moment in time (or all moments in time). Yet, I have already described a probabilistic network that does involve quantities at different times, namely, hidden Markov models. In Section 17.3.2, I explained how HMMs were used in speech recognition. One common form of an HMM is shown in Fig. 28.8.

This diagram is meant to show how a time sequence of entities, $x_1, x_2, \ldots x_n$, causes a time sequence of other entities, $y_1, y_2, \ldots, y_n$. The influence of each x_i on subsequent x's and on the y's is governed by probabilities. One can easily see that this network is a Bayesian network, even though the quantities involved occur in a temporal sequence. This particular HMM is called a *first-order* Markov process because each state depends only the immediately preceding state. In higher order processes, each state is influenced by more than one preceding state.

In an HMM network, each x_i is a "state variable," and the y_i are "observable variables." It is presumed that the values of the states are unknown (that is, "hidden") but that the observables can be measured and thus known. Each state causes an associated observable and the next state. We presume that we know the conditional probability tables of the network, that is, the probabilities of the observables and the next state given the value of a state. Given the value of one or more observables, we can calculate updated probabilities of states using any of the methods for computing probabilities in a Bayesian network.

Here is an example. Suppose aircraft weather conditions at a remote airport are either foggy or not. A sensor at the airport records the weather and a transmitter broadcasts a signal every five minutes. This signal, as it is received by an airplane attempting to land at the airport, might occasionally be in error. So, the states, that is, the x's in the HMM modeling this process, can have values of 1 or 0, with a value of 1 indicating fog. The signals received by the aircraft, the y's in the HMM, also have values of 1 or 0, with a value of 1 indicating fog is observed. But the observations might be in error. To be concrete, let us suppose the probability that the next state has the same value as that of the present state is 75% (fog tends to persist) and the probability that an observable is in error is 5%. These probabilities allow the construction of Bayesian network conditional probability tables. (The example can be made more realistic by allowing each state to reflect degrees of fogginess and to depend on states in addition to the single preceding state.)

The pilot of an aircraft must make a decision about attempting to land or not based on the sequence of y's received. For example, he or she might want to know the probability that the landing strip is foggy right now based on a sequence of previous observations up to and including the present one. In HMM parlance, the operation that computes this probability is called "filtering." Alternatively, the pilot might want to compute the probability that the landing strip will be foggy 10 minutes from now based on these observations. This operation is called "prediction." Although it would not be of much use to the pilot, he or she might be curious about the probability that the landing strip was foggy 10 minutes ago based on a sequence of observations up to and including the present. This operation is called "smoothing."

In my discussion of speech recognition in Section 17.3.2, I mentioned that the HMM states correspond to single words and that the observations correspond to waveform segments. In that application we want to compute the most likely sequence of words given all of the observations of waveforms up to the present.

All of these computations – filtering, prediction, smoothing, and most-likely-state sequence – can be performed using Bayesian network inference procedures. There are several specialized versions, some of which originated in fields outside of AI. These depend on the application and on the particulars of the networks involved.

Of these, I might mention (but won't try to explain here) the forward-backward algorithm, the Viterbi algorithm, and Kalman filtering. The mathematically brave reader can find clear explanations in Russell and Norvig's excellent textbook.[27] The fact that full explanations involve rather complex mathematics testifies again to the great increase in AI's technical depth that began in the 1980s.

HMMs, including my foggy/not-foggy example, have only a single state variable at each instant of time. It is possible to construct networks in which there are more state variables at every time instant – all of which affect each other, the observations, and subsequent state variables. These are typically called "dynamic Bayesian networks" (DBNs) and were first explored in AI by Thomas Dean (1950–) and Keiji Kanazawa.[28] Additional state and observation variables make exact computations intractable, but several practical approximate methods, such as "particle filtering" (which I'll describe in more detail later) have been developed. And, just as with ordinary Bayesian networks, DBNs can be learned from databases containing information about temporal processes. They have been used in several applications, primarily those involving perception. One such is the processing of movies in which probabilistic frame-to-frame dependencies can be exploited for recognizing and tracking moving objects. Another is in the certification of collision avoidance systems for manned and unmanned aircraft.[29]

Although this chapter has been about Bayesian networks, they are just one type of an important general class called "probabilistic graphical models." Markov random fields, often called Markov networks, are another member of that class in which the links between nodes are nondirectional. They were originally developed to deal with problems in statistical physics, and they now find applications in many areas including image processing, sensory perception, and brain modeling. Boltzmann machines, which were mentioned in Section 25.5.1, are instances of Markov random fields. There are also ways to interpret other neural networks as instances of probabilistic graphical models.[30]

Notes

1. Marvin Minsky (ed.), "Introduction," *Semantic Information Processing*, p. 14, Cambridge, MA: MIT Press, 1968. **[381]**

2. Judea Pearl, "Two Journeys into Human Reasoning," in Paul Cohen and Clayton Morrison (eds.), *Artificial Intelligence: The First Century*, (to appear). Online version available at http://ftp.cs.ucla.edu/pub/stat_ser/r331.pdf. **[384]**

3. See p. 131ff of Pearl's foundational book about such representations: Judea Pearl, *Probabilistic Reasoning Systems: Networks of Plausible Inference*, San Francisco: Morgan Kaufmann Publishers, 1988. **[384]**

4. Stuart Russell and Peter Norvig, *Artificial Intelligence: A Modern Approach*, second edition, p. 528, Upper Saddle River, NJ: Prentice Hall, 2003 **[384]**

5. They cite I. J. Good, "A Causal Calculus (I)," *The British Journal for the Philosophy of Science*, Vol. XI, No. 44, pp. 305–318, 1961. **[384]**

6. Hans A. Bethe, "Statistical Theory of Superlattices," *Proceedings of the Royal Society of London*, Series A, Vol. 150, No. 871, pp. 552–575, 1935. **[384]**

7. Judea Pearl, "Fusion, Propagation, and Structuring in Belief Networks," *Artificial Intelligence*, Vol. 29, pp. 241–288, 1986. **[385]**

8. This network is the subject of an interactive demonstration available as one of the online resources for the textbook by David Poole, Alan Mackworth, and Randy Goebel, *Computational Intelligence: A Logical Approach*, New York: Oxford University Press, 1998. See the applet available from http://aispace.org/bayes/. One can add and delete nodes, change the conditional probability tables, and query the values of probabilities after making observations about the performance of components. [386]

9. For a description of some of these techniques, see Stuart Russell and Peter Norvig, *op. cit.* [387]

10. Malcolm Pradhan *et al.*, "Knowledge Engineering for Large Belief Networks," *Proceedings of the 10th Annual Conference on Uncertainty in Artificial Intelligence (UAI-94)*, pp. 484–490, San Francisco: Morgan Kaufmann Publishers, 1994. Compressed PostScript version available online at ftp://ftp.ksl.stanford.edu/pub/KSL_Reports/KSL-94-47.ps.gz. [387]

11. See, for example, Olivier Pourret (ed.), Patrick Naïm (co-ed.), and Bruce Marcot (co-ed.), *Bayesian Networks: A Practical Guide to Applications*, New York: John Wiley and Sons, Inc., 2008. [387]

12. Greg F. Cooper and Edward Herskovits, "A Bayesian Method for the Induction of Probabilistic Networks from Data," *Machine Learning*, Vol. 9, pp. 309–347, 1992. Available online at http://www.genetics.ucla.edu/labs/sabatti/Stat180/bayesNet.pdf and at http://bmir.stanford.edu/file_asset/index.php/610/SMI-91-0355.pdf. [387]

13. See, for example, the tutorial by David Heckerman and his publications, all available from his Web site at http://research.microsoft.com/~heckerman/, and the edited volume by Michael Jordan (ed.), *Learning in Graphical Models*, Cambridge, MA: MIT Press, 1998. [387]

14. For details, see Peter Spirtes and Christopher Meek, "Learning Bayesian Networks with Discrete Variables from Data," *Proceedings of the First International Conference on Knowledge Discovery and Data Mining*, pp. 294–299, San Francisco: Morgan Kaufmann Publishers, 1995. [390]

15. Daphne Koller and Avi Pfeffer, "Probabilistic Frame-Based Systems," *Proceedings of the Fifteenth National Conference on Artificial Intelligence*, pp. 580–587, Menlo Park, CA: AAAI Press, 1998. [391]

16. David Poole, "Representing Diagnostic Knowledge for Probabilistic Horn Abduction," *Proceedings of the Twelfth International Joint Conference on Artificial Intelligence*, pp. 1129–1135, Sydney, Australia, August 1991. Reprinted in W. Hamscher, L. Console, and J. de Kleer (eds.), *Readings in Model-based Diagnosis*, San Francisco: Morgan Kaufmann Publishers, 1992. Available online at http://www.cs.ubc.ca/spider/poole/papers/ijcai91.pdf. [391]

17. E-mail from Daphne Koller, July 27, 2008. [391]

18. Nir Friedman *et al.*, "Learning Probabilistic Relational Models," *Proceedings of the International Joint Conference on Artificial Intelligence*, pp. 1300–1309, 1999; available online at http://www.cs.huji.ac.il/~nirf/Papers/FGKP1.pdf. [391]

19. Eran Segal *et al.*, "Module Networks: Identifying Regulatory Modules and Their Condition-Specific Regulators from Gene Expression Data," *Nature Genetics*, Vol. 34, pp. 166–176, 2003. Available online at http://www.wisdom.weizmann.ac.il/~eran/ModuleNetworks.pdf. [393]

20. Nir Friedman, "Inferring Cellular Networks Using Probabilistic Graphical Models," *Science*, Vol. 303, No. 5659, pp. 799–805, February 6, 2004. [393]

21. Microsoft uses a program called ClearFlow, based on Bayesian networks, in its driving direction Web site, http://maps.live.com/. See Eric Horvitz *et al.*, "Prediction, Expectation, and Surprise: Methods, Designs, and Study of a Deployed Traffic

Forecasting Service," *Proceedings Twenty-First Conference on Uncertainty in Artificial Intelligence*, UAI-2005, pp. 275–283, Edinburgh, Scotland, July 2005; available online at http://research.microsoft.com/en-us/um/people/horvitz/horvitz_traffic_uai2005.pdf. Also, Cyril Furtlehner, Jean-Marc Lasgouttes, and Arnaud De La Fortelle, "Belief Propagation and Bethe Approximation for Traffic Prediction," Rapport de Recherche 6144, INRIA, March 2007; available online at http://www-rocq.inria.fr/~lasgoutt/publications/RR-6144.pdf. **[393]**

22. Gregory F. Cooper *et al.*, "Bayesian Biosurveillance of Disease Outbreaks," *Proceedings of the Twentieth Conference on Uncertainty in Artificial Intelligence*, pp. 94–103, ACM International Conference Proceeding Series; Vol. 70, 2004; available online at http://www.dbmi.pitt.edu/panda/papers/UAI2004.pdf. **[393]**

23. Eric Horvitz, "Continual Computation Policies for Utility-Directed Prefetching," *Proceedings of the Seventh ACM Conference on Information and Knowledge Management (CIKM 98)*, pp. 175–184, New York: ACM Press, 1998. **[393]**

24. One such is Hugin Expert. See http://www.hugin.com/info/. **[393]**

25. Peter Norvig, private communication, November 12, 2007. **[393]**

26. Peter Norvig, private communication, November 21, 2008. **[393]**

27. Stuart Russell and Peter Norvig, *op. cit.* **[395]**

28. Thomas Dean and Keiji Kanazawa, "A Model for Reasoning about Persistence and Causation," *Computational Intelligence*, Vol. 5, pp. 142–150, 1989. **[395]**

29. Mykel J. Kochenderfer *et al.*, "A Bayesian Approach to Aircraft Encounter Modeling," *Proceedings of the AIAA Guidance, Navigation and Control Conference*, Honolulu, Hawaii, 18–21 August 2008. **[395]**

30. For more about graphical models, see the book by Daphne Koller and Nir Friedman, *Structured Probabilistic Models: Principles and Techniques*, Cambridge, MA: MIT Press, 2009; also helpful is Kevin Murphy's Web page, "A Brief Introduction to Graphical Models and Bayesian Networks at http://people.cs.ubc.ca/~murphyk/Bayes/bnintro.html. **[395]**

29

Machine Learning

A UTOMATED DATA-GATHERING TECHNIQUES, TOGETHER WITH INEXPENSIVE MASS-memory storage apparatus, have allowed the acquisition and retention of prodigious amounts of data. Point-of-sale customer purchases, temperature and pressure readings (along with other weather data), news feeds, financial transactions of all sorts, Web pages, and Web interaction records are just a few of numerous examples. But the great volume of raw data calls for efficient "data-mining" techniques for classifying, quantifying, and extracting useful information. Machine learning methods are playing an increasingly important role in data analysis because they can deal with massive amounts of data. In fact, the more data the better.

Most machine learning methods construct hypotheses from data. So (to use a classic example), if a large set of data contains several instances of swans being white and no instances of swans being of other colors, then a machine learning algorithm might make the inference that "all swans are white." Such an inference is "inductive" rather than "deductive." Deductive inferences follow necessarily and logically from their premises, whereas inductive ones are hypotheses, which are always subject to falsification by additional data. (There may still be an undiscovered island of black swans.) Still, inductive inferences, based on large amounts of data, are extremely useful. Indeed, science itself is based on inductive inferences.

Whereas before about 1980 machine learning (represented mainly by neural network methods) was regarded by some as on the fringes of AI, machine learning has lately become much more central in modern AI. I have already described one example, namely, the use of Bayesian networks that are automatically constructed from data. Other developments, beginning around the 1980s, made machine learning one of the most prominent branches of AI. I'll describe some of this work in this chapter.

29.1 Memory-Based Learning

The usual AI approach to dealing with large quantities of data is to reduce the amount of it in some way. For example, a neural network is able to represent what is important about a large amount of training data by the network's structure and weight values. Similarly, learning a Bayesian network from data condenses these data into the network's node structure and its conditional probability tables.

However, our growing abilities to store large amounts of data in rapid-access computer memories and to compute with these data has enabled techniques that store and use *all* of the data as they are needed – without any prior condensation whatsoever. That is, these techniques do not attempt to reduce the amount of data *before* it is actually used for some task. All of the necessary reduction, for example to a decision, is performed at the time a decision must be made. I'll describe some of these *memory-based* learning methods next.

In Section 4.3, I mentioned "nearest-neighbor" methods for classifying a point in a multidimensional space. The "k-nearest-neighbor rule," for example, assigns a data point to the same category as that of the majority of the k stored data points that are closest to it. A similar technique can be used to associate a numerical value (or set of values) to a data point. For example, the average of the stored values associated with the k nearest neighbors can be assigned to the new point. This version of the rule can be used in control or estimation applications. The k-nearest-neighbor rule is a prototypical example of memory-based learning, and it evokes several questions about possible extensions.

First, to apply the nearest-neighbor rule (as I have presented it so far), each datum must be a list of numbers – a point or vector in a multidimensional space. So, one question is "How to represent the data so that something like the nearest-neighbor method can be applied?" Second, how is "distance" to be measured between data points? When the data are represented by points in a multidimensional space, ordinary Euclidean distance is the natural choice. Even in that case, however, it is usual to "scale" the dimensions so that undue weight is not given to those dimensions for which the data are more "spread out." If the data are not represented as points in a space, some other way of measuring data "closeness" has to be employed. Several methods have been proposed depending on the form of the data.

Third, among the k closest data points, should closer ones influence the outcome more than distant ones? The basic k-nearest-neighbor method can be extended by weighting the importance of data points in a manner depending on their closeness. Usually, something called a "kernel" is used that gives gradually diminishing weight to data points that are farther and farther away.

Fourth, what should be the value of k? How many nearby neighbors are we going to use in making our decision about a new piece of data? Well, with the right kind of kernel, *all* of the data points can be considered. The ones that are farthest away would simply have zero or negligible influence on the decision. The question about what value of k to use is now replaced by a question about how far away the influence of the kernel should extend.

Lastly, after all of the weighted neighbors are taken into account, how do we make a decision or assign a numerical value or values? Should it be the same as that associated with a majority vote of the neighbors or perhaps with some "average" of the weighted neighbors? Various versions of what are called statistical regression methods can be implemented depending on this choice.[1]

Andrew W. Moore (1965– ; Fig. 29.1) and Christopher G. Atkeson (1959– ; Fig. 29.1) are among the pioneers in the development of extensions to k-nearest-neighbor rules and the application of these extensions to several important problems in data mining and in robot control.

Experiments in applying these ideas to control problems are described in several papers. One paper[2] mentions the control of a robotic device for playing a juggling game called "devil-sticking." A memory-based system was developed to learn how to keep the stick in play. Figure 29.2 shows a schematic of a human doing the

Figure 29.1. Andrew Moore (left) and Chris Atkeson (right). (Photographs courtesy of Andrew Moore and of Christopher Atkeson.)

juggling. The robotic setup is also shown with some of the sensory and control parameters.

Besides applications in robotics and control, memory-based learning methods have also been used in other areas including data mining and natural language processing.[3]

29.2 Case-Based Reasoning

A subfield of AI, called "Case-Based Reasoning" (CBR), can be viewed as a generalized kind of memory-based learning. In CBR a stored library of "cases" is used to help in the analysis, interpretation, and solution of new cases. In medicine, for example, the diagnostic and therapeutic records for patients constitute a library of cases; when a new case is presented, similar cases can be retrieved from the library to help guide diagnosis and therapy. In law, previous legal precedents are used in interpretations of and decisions about new cases (following the legal practice of *stare decisis*, which mandates that cases are to be decided based on the precedents set by previous cases).

Cases that are similar to a new case can be thought of as its "neighbors" in a generalized "space" of cases. To retrieve close neighbors, the idea of closeness in this space must be based on some measure of similarity. One of the pioneers in case-based reasoning, Janet Kolodner (1954– ; Fig. 29.3), a professor of computing and cognitive science at the Georgia Institute of Technology, describes the process as follows:[4]

Good cases [for retrieval] are those that have the potential to make relevant predictions about the new case. Retrieval is done by using features of the new case as indexes into the case

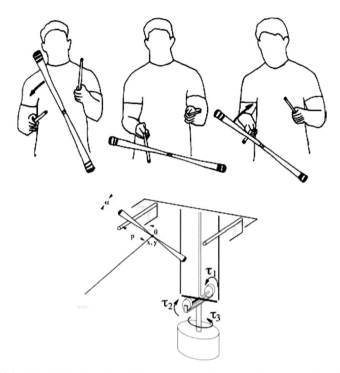

Figure 29.2. "Devil Stick" as played by a human and by a robotic memory-based learning system. (Illustrations from Christopher G. Atkeson, Andrew W. Moore, and Stefan Schall, "Locally Weighted Learning for Control," *Artificial Intelligence Review*, Vol. 11, pp. 75–113, 1997. Available online at http://www.cs.cmu.edu/~cga/papers/air1.ps.gz.)

library. Cases labeled by subsets of those features or by features that can be derived from those features are recalled.

[We then select from among these] the most promising case or cases to reason with.... Sometimes it is appropriate to choose one best case; sometimes a small set is needed.

When the retrieved case (or cases) is adapted to apply to a new case it might then (if it is successful) be revised so that the parts that might be useful for future problem solving can be retained in the ever-growing case library.

Case-based reasoning has roots in Roger Schank's model of dynamic memory (see p. 158). Early work was done by two of Schank's Ph.D. students, Janet Kolodner and Michael Lebowitz.[5] Another important source of ideas for CBR comes from Minsky's ideas about frames. Edwina Rissland (1947– ; Fig. 29.3), a professor at the University of Massachusetts at Amherst and another pioneer in CBR, writes[6] that her CBR work is a direct outgrowth of her "work on 'constrained example generation,'... which modeled the construction of new (counter) examples by modification of existing past 'close' examples (represented as frames) retrieved from a network of examples."[7] Rissland and her students have made important contributions to the use of CBR in the law.[8] She wrote me that the CBR process is sometimes summarized by the four "R's," Retrieve, Reuse, Revise, and Retain.[9]

Figure 29.3. Janet Kolodner (left) and Edwina Rissland (right). (Photographs courtesy of Janet Kolodner and of Edwina Rissland.)

According to a Web page maintained by the Artificial Intelligence Applications Institute at the University of Edinburgh, "Case-based Reasoning is one of the most successful applied AI technologies of recent years. Commercial and industrial applications can be developed rapidly, and existing corporate databases can be used as knowledge sources. Helpdesks and diagnostic systems are the most common applications."[10]

29.3 Decision Trees

Next on my list of new developments in machine learning is the automatic construction of structures called "decision trees" from large databases. Decision trees consist of sequences of tests for determining a category or a numerical value to assign to a data record. Decision trees are particularly well suited for use with non-numeric as well as numeric data. For example, a personnel database might include information about an employee's department, say, marketing, manufacturing, or accounting. In database parlance, data items like these are called "categorical" (to distinguish them from numerical data). In this section, I'll describe these structures, learning methods for automatically constructing them, and some of their applications.

29.3.1 *Data Mining and Decision Trees*

Data mining is the process of extracting useful information from large databases. For example, consider a database about peoples' credit card behavior. It might include payment records, average purchase amounts, late fee charges, average balances, and so on. Appropriate data-mining methods might reveal, among other things, that people with high late fee charges, high average purchases, and other identified features tended to have high average balances.

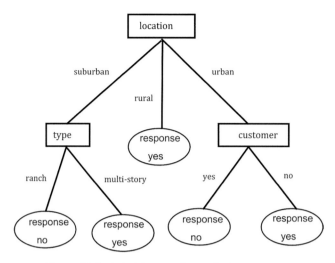

Figure 29.4. A decision tree for predicting responses.

One important data-mining method uses data to construct decision trees. Let's consider a very simple database to illustrate how decision trees work. Suppose a company, say Wal-Mart, maintains a database in which it stores information about households to which it had previously mailed discount coupons for some of its products. Suppose the database has information about the location of the household (urban, suburban, or rural), the type of house (either ranch or multistory), whether or not the household is a previous Wal-Mart customer, and whether or not the household responded to any of its previous coupon mailings. (Obviously, this is just a made-up illustrative example; I don't actually know anything about Wal-Mart's real databases.)

A tabular representation of such a database would look like this:

Household	Location	Type	Customer	Response
3014	suburban	ranch	yes	no
3015	rural	multistory	no	yes
. . .	. . .	. . .	. . .	. . .
5489	urban	ranch	yes	no

Each row in the table is called a "record." The items at the top of each column are called "attributes," and the items in a column are called the "values" of the corresponding attribute.

Analysis of this database, by methods I'll be explaining later, might reveal that the decision tree shown in Fig. 29.4 captured information about which households responded to the coupon mailing and which did not. The tests on attribute values are at the interior nodes of the tree (in boxes), and the results (whether or not there was a response) are at the tips (or leaves) of the tree (in ovals). Such a tree might be useful for making predictions about expected responses prior to sending out another mailing.

Methods have been developed to construct (that is, learn) decision trees like this one (and much larger ones too) automatically from large databases. I'll describe some of the history and how the major methods work.

29.3.2 *Constructing Decision Trees*

A. EPAM

Probably the earliest system for constructing decision trees was developed in the late 1950s by Edward Feigenbaum as part of his Ph.D. dissertation under Herbert Simon at Carnegie Mellon University (then called Carnegie Institute of Technology).[11] His system was called EPAM, an acronym for Elementary Perceiver and Memorizer. The goal of the research was to "explain and predict the phenomenon of [human] verbal learning." A standard psychological experiment for testing this ability involved showing people pairs of nonsense syllables, such as DAX-JIR and PIB-JUX. The first member of a pair was called a "stimulus" and the second a "response." After seeing a number of such pairs repeatedly, the subject is then shown a random stimulus and tested on his or her ability to generate the correct response.

Pairs like these were shown to EPAM during its "learning phase." Learning consisted in growing what Feigenbaum called a "discrimination net" for storing associations between stimuli and responses. The net was what we would now call a decision tree with tests on features of the letters at the internal nodes and responses stored at the tips or leaves of the tree. In EPAM's "testing phase," a nonsense stimulus syllable was filtered through the tests down the tree until a leaf was reached where (one hopes) the correct response was stored. A sample EPAM discrimination net is shown in Fig. 29.5. The round nodes are tests, and the boxed nodes are responses.

Not only did EPAM successfully model the performance of humans in this "paired-associate" learning task, it also modeled forgetting. Feigenbaum claimed that "As far as we know, [EPAM] is the first concrete demonstration of this type of forgetting in a learning machine."[12] EPAM was written in Carnegie's list-processing language, IPL-V. In fact, the list-processing features of languages such as IPL-V were required to write programs that could *grow* decision trees. Thus, it is not surprising that EPAM was the first such program.

Feigenbaum's program is still regarded as a major contribution both to theories of human intelligence and to AI research. Simon, Feigenbaum, and others continued work on EPAM programs, culminating in EPAM-VI, coded in IPL-V and running on a PC.[13]

B. CLS

The next significant work on learning decision trees was done at Yale University around 1960. There, psychologist Carl I. Hovland and his Ph.D. student Earl B. (Buz) Hunt developed a computer model of human concept learning.[14] After Hovland succumbed to cancer in 1961, Hunt continued work on concept learning and collaborated with Janet Marin and Philip Stone in developing a series of decision-tree learning programs called CLS, an acronym for Concept Learning System.[15] Hunt and his colleagues acknowledged the related prior work on EPAM.

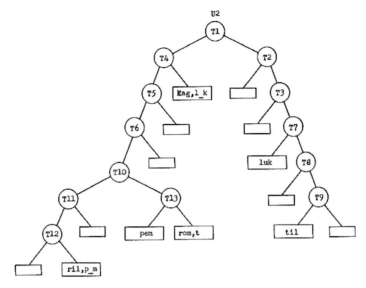

Figure 29.5. An EPAM discrimination net. (From Edward A. Feigenbaum, "An Information Processing Theory of Verbal Learning," Ph.D. dissertation, Carnegie Institute of Technology, p. 99, 1959, published as Report P-1817 by The RAND Corporation, Santa Monica, CA, October 9, 1959. Used with permission of Edward Feigenbaum.)

For AI purposes at least, the CLS systems were soon eclipsed by other decision-tree learning systems, namely, ID3, CART, and related programs. I'll describe how ID3 works as a way of explaining the main ideas behind these programs.

C. ID3

J. Ross Quinlan (1943– ; Fig. 29.6) developed ID3,[16] an acronym for Iterative Dichotomizer, in the late 1970s while he was on sabbatical leave (from the University of Sydney) at Stanford. (The name derived from the fact that the program constructed decision trees by iteratively dividing sets of data records until they could be classified into one of two distinct categories. Later versions allowed classification into more than two categories, but the "D" persisted in the name.) Quinlan had previously been a Ph.D. student (the first, actually) in the Computer Science Department at the University of Washington, working under Earl Hunt. Quinlan explained the genesis of ID3 in an e-mail note to me:[17]

I sat in on a course given by Donald Michie [also visiting Stanford at that time] and became intrigued with a task he proposed, namely, learning a rule for deciding the result of a simple chess endgame. ID3 started out as a recoding of Buz's [that is, Earl B. Hunt's] CLS, but I changed some of the innards (such as the criterion for splitting a set of cases) and incorporated the iterative approach that allowed ID3 to handle the then-enormous set of 29,000 training cases.

Here, in brief, is how ID3 would proceed to construct a decision tree for predicting the value of the response attribute using my fictitious Wal-Mart database. First, ID3 would look for that single attribute to use as the "best" test in distinguishing between

Figure 29.6. J. Ross Quinlan. (Photograph courtesy of Ross Quinlan.)

those data records having the value yes for the response attribute from those having the value no. (I will have more to say about how "best" is defined momentarily.) No single test separates the data perfectly, but let us suppose that location does better than the others. After all, in this example *all* of the data records having value rural for the attribute location have the value yes for the response attribute, and none of those have the value no. Let's assume that the preponderance (but not all) of the data records having the value suburban have the value yes for the response attribute and that the preponderance (but again not all) of the data records having the value urban have the value no for the response attribute. Thus, the location attribute does a pretty good (but imperfect) job of separating data records with respect to the response attribute. A test for the value of the location attribute would thus be used as the first test in the decision tree being constructed.

So far then, we would have split the database into three subsets, two of which have data records with mixed values for the response attribute. ID3 would then apply the same splitting technique to each of these two mixed-value subsets, finding for each one of them the best next feature to use as a test. In this simple and rather nonrealistic example, the two tests that would be used, namely, type and customer, would each produce "pure" splits (that is, ones with no mixed values), and we would end up with the decision tree already shown in Fig. 29.4.

If the splits were not pure or not otherwise acceptable, however, ID3 would have gone on selecting tests on the resulting subsets of databases until the splits did give either pure or acceptable results.

The choice of which attribute to test on is critical in producing useful decision trees. In his original ID3 program,[18] Quinlan used a measure related to the "accuracy" of the resulting split in determining which attribute to use for testing. In later work, he used a measure called "information gain,"[19] whose precise definition I won't go into here except to say that it is that attribute whose values convey the most "information" about the categorization being sought. Quinlan used Claude Shannon's definition for measuring the amount of information.[20] Still later, he used a normalized measure of information gain in order not to bias in favor of tests with many outcomes.[21]

In my discussion of expert systems in Section 18.2, I mentioned that they were based on IF–THEN rules. Interest in symbolically based machine learning by Quinlan and others was mainly directed at learning these sorts of rules from data. It is quite easy to construct rules from a decision tree by tracing down the tests to generate the "IF" part and using what lies at the tips for the "THEN" part. For example, in the Wal-Mart database example, we could derive the following rules from the decision tree:

    IF (location = suburban) and (type = ranch), THEN (response = no)
    IF (location = suburban) and (type = multi-story), THEN (response = yes)
    IF (location = rural), THEN (response = yes)
    IF (location = urban) and (customer = yes), THEN (response = no)
    IF (location = urban) and (customer = no), THEN (response = yes)

In Quinlan's work at Stanford, ID3 was able to generate rather large decision trees, and thus rule sets, for predicting whether certain endgame chess positions would end in a loss for black. For a problem of this type suggested by Donald Michie, ID3 used twenty-five attributes (involving features of the positions of pieces on the board) and a database of 29,236 different piece arrangements to construct a tree with 393 nodes whose predictions were 99.74% correct.[22]

One problem that must be avoided in constructing decision trees is that of "overfitting," that is, selecting tests based on so little data that the test results don't capture meaningful relationships in the data as a whole. No matter how large the original database, if a succession of tests eventually produces a subset that is still not pure but has been reduced to too few data records, any attempt to split that subset would overfit the data and thus not be useful. For that reason, decision-tree learning techniques typically halt tree construction just before data subsets would have too few records but would still give acceptable results.

D. C4.5, CART, and Successors

Quinlan continued his work on decision-tree-constructing systems, improving their power and applicability. He told me that "ID3 was pretty simple – about 600 lines of PASCAL."[23] His system C4.5 (which had about 9,000 lines of C) could work with databases whose attributes had continuous numerical values in addition to categorical ones. It could even deal with databases some of whose records had missing values for some of their attributes. Finally, it had methods for improving overall performance by pruning away some parts of the tree and for simplifying IF–THEN rules derived from trees.[24] A commercial company Quinlan founded in 1983 markets an improved version of C4.5 called C5.0 (along with a Windows version called See5).[25] Donald Michie also founded a company,[26] which independently developed a commercial version of ID3 called ACLS.

One of the significant developments in machine learning during this period was a fruitful collaboration between AI people and statisticians who were doing foundational as well as applied research on classification, estimation, and prediction. Each group has learned from the other, and machine learning is much richer for it. Although several people were involved in this collaboration, I might mention in

particular the Stanford statistician Jerome Friedman (1939–), who began working
with some Stanford AI Ph.D. students in the 1990s. Following his earlier work on
decision-tree construction,[27] Friedman, in collaboration with Leo Breiman, Richard
Olshen, and Charles Stone, had helped develop a system called CART, an acronym
for Classification and Regression Trees.[28] CART shares many features with C4.5
(and, in fact, C4.5 used CART's techniques for dealing with numeric attributes). At
the time of this writing, the latest version, CART 5, is available from a commercial
company.[29]

   Systems for learning decision trees have been applied to a wide variety of data-
mining problems.

E. Inductive Logic Programming

Expressed in the language of propositional logic, the IF–THEN rules produced
from decision trees have the form $P1 \wedge P2 \wedge \ldots PN \rightarrow Q$. The P's and Q's are
propositions with no internal structure. Earlier, I spoke of the predicate calculus in
which propositions, called predicates, had internal arguments. In that language,
one could have much more expressive rules such as $\forall(x, y, z)[\mathtt{Father}(x, y) \wedge$
$\mathtt{Sibling}(z, y) \rightarrow \mathtt{Father}(x, z)]$, for example. Several techniques have been developed to learn these types of "relational" rules from databases and from other
"background knowledge." (I mentioned a related topic before, namely, learning
"probabilistic relational models," which are versions of Bayesian networks that
permitted predicates with variables.) One of the early systems for learning relational rules was developed by Quinlan and called FOIL.[30] Because the rules learned
have the same form as do statements in the computer language PROLOG (a language based on logic), the field devoted to learning these rules is called "Inductive
Logic Programming" (ILP). Although ILP methods involve logical apparatus too
complex for me to try to explain here, some of them bear a close relationship to
decision-tree construction.[31] There are several applications of ILP, including learning relational rules for drug activity, for protein secondary structure, and for finite-
element mesh design. These are all examples of what can be called "relational data
mining."[32]

29.4 Neural Networks

During the 1960s, neural net researchers employed various methods for changing a
network's adjustable weights so that the entire network made appropriate output
responses to a set of "training" inputs. For example, Frank Rosenblatt at Cornell
adjusted weight values in the final layer of what he called the three-layer alpha-
perceptron. Bill Ridgway (one of Bernard Widrow's Stanford students) adjusted
weights in the first layer of what he called a MADALINE. We had a similar scheme
for adjusting weights in the first layer of the MINOS II and MINOS III neural
network machines at SRI. Others used various statistical techniques to set weight
values. But what stymied us all was how to change weights in more than one layer of
multilayer networks. (I recall Charles Rosen, the leader of our group, sitting in his
office with yellow quadrille tablets hand-simulating his ever-inventive schemes for
making weight changes; none seemed to work out.)

29.4.1 *The Backprop Algorithm*

That problem was solved in the mid-1980s by the invention of a technique called "back propagation" (backprop for short) introduced by David Rumelhart, Geoffrey E. Hinton, and Ronald J. Williams.[33] The basic idea behind backprop is simple, but the mathematics (which I'll skip) is rather complicated. In response to an error in the network's output, backprop makes small adjustments in all of the weights so as to reduce that error. It can be regarded as a hill-climbing (or rather hill-descending) method – searching for low values of error over the landscape of weights. But rather than actually trying out all possible small weight changes and deciding on that set of them that corresponds to the steepest descent downhill, backprop uses calculus to precompute the best set of weight changes.

Readers who remember a bit of college (or perhaps high school) calculus will have no trouble recalling that it can be used to calculate the slope of a curve or surface. The error in the output of a neural network can be thought of as a function of the network's weights, that is, a surface in "weight space." This function can be written down and "differentiated" (an operation in calculus) with respect to the weights to yield the set of weight changes that will take us downhill in the steepest direction. The problem with implementing this idea in a straightforward fashion for neural networks lies in the fact that these networks have "thresholds," whose effect is to populate the error surface with abrupt "cliffs." (The outputs of a network with thresholds can change from a 1 to a 0 or from a 0 to a 1 with infinitesimally small changes in some of the weight values.) Calculus operations require smoothly changing surfaces and are frustrated by cliffs.

Rumelhart and colleagues dealt with this problem by replacing the thresholds with components whose outputs can only change smoothly, even though they change quite steeply enough for the network to do approximately the same thing as a network with thresholds. With these replacements, calculus can be used to propagate the error function backward (from output to input) through the network to calculate the best set of changes to the weight values in all of the network's layers. Although this process of zeroing in on acceptable weight values is slow, it has been used with impressive results for many neural-network learning problems.

Why didn't *me* think of that? Actually, some people apparently did think of a similar idea before Rumelhart and his colleagues did. The earliest was probably Arthur E. Bryson Jr. and Y. C. Ho who used iterative gradient methods for solving Euler–Lagrange equations.[34] Paul Werbos, in his Harvard Ph.D. thesis, also proposed back-propagating errors to train multilayer neural networks.[35]

As with all local search techniques, backprop might get stuck on one of the local minima of the error surface. Of course, the learning process can be repeated, starting with different initial values of the weights, to attempt to find a lower (or perhaps the lowest) error value. In any case, the backprop method still is, as Laveen Kanal wrote in 1993, "probably the most widely used general procedure for training neural networks for pattern classification."[36]

Neural network learning methods have been applied in a variety of areas including aircraft control, credit card fraud detection, vending machine currency recognition, and data mining. I'll describe a couple of other applications next.

Figure 29.7. Terrance Sejnowski (top) and the neural network used in NETtalk (bottom). (Photograph and illustration courtesy of Terrance Sejnowski.)

29.4.2 *NETtalk*

One very interesting application of the backprop learning method was developed by Terrence J. Sejnowski (1947–) and Charles Rosenberg (1961–). They taught a neural network to talk![37] In one of their experiments, their system, called NETtalk, learned to "read" text that was transcribed from informal, continuous speech of a six-year-old child and produced acoustic output (that sounded remarkably like that of a child). (You can listen to an audio demo at http://www.cnl.salk.edu/ ParallelNetsPronounce/.) The network structure is shown in Fig. 29.7.

The network had 203 input units designed to encode a string of seven letters. Text was streamed through these seven units letter by letter. There were 80 "hidden units" that were connected to the inputs by adjustable weights. It was hoped that the hidden units would "form internal representations that were appropriate for solving the mapping problem of letters to phonemes." There were 26 output units that were supposed to produce coded versions of phonemes, the basic units of speech sounds. The output units were connected to the hidden units by additional adjustable weights. (Altogether, there were 18,629 adjustable weights.) Finally, the phonemic codes were fed to a commercial speech synthesizer to produce audible output.

The network was trained by comparing, at every time step, the phonemic code at the output units against what that code should have been for the text input at that time step. Backprop was used to modify the weights in a way that tended to reduce this error. The authors claim that "it proved possible to train a network with a seven letter window in a few days." (Remember that computers were much slower in 1987.) They concluded that "overall, the intelligibility of the speech was quite good" and that "the more words the network learns, the better it is at generalizing and correctly pronouncing new words." After training on a corpus of 1,024 words, the network "was tested [without further training] on a 439 word continuation from the same speaker. The performance was 78%, which indicates that much of the learning was transferred to novel words even after a small sample of English words." In addition to the specific network shown in Fig. 29.7, experiments were also done on networks with more hidden units and with two layers of hidden units. In general, the larger networks performed better.

29.4.3 *ALVINN*

Another neural network application, this one for steering a van, was developed by Dean Pomerleau, a Ph.D. student at Carnegie Mellon University.[38] The system, which included the van, a TV camera for looking at the road ahead, and interface apparatus, was called ALVINN, an acronym for Autonomous Land Vehicle in a Neural Network. ALVINN used the CMU Navlab vehicle, which was built on a commercial van chassis with hydraulic drive and electric steering. According to a CMU paper, "Computers can steer and drive the van by electric and hydraulic servos, or a human driver can take control to drive to a test site or to override the computer."[39] A picture of Navlab is shown in Fig. 29.8.

The input to ALVINN's neural network was a low–resolution 30×32 array of gray-scale image intensity values produced by a video camera mounted on top of the van. Each of these 960 inputs was connected to each of four hidden units through adjustable weights. The hidden units, in turn, were connected to a left–to–right line of 30 output units through adjustable weights. The output units controlled the van's steering mechanism as follows:[40]

The centermost output unit represents the "travel straight ahead" condition, while units to the left and right of center represent successively sharper left and right turns. The units on the extreme left and right of the output vector represent turns with a 20 m radius to the left and right respectively, and the units in between represent turns which decrease linearly in their curvature down to the "straight ahead" middle unit . . .

The steering direction dictated by the network is taken to be the center of mass of the "hill" of activation surrounding the output unit with the highest activation level. Using the center

Figure 29.8. CMU's Navlab vehicle used by ALVINN. (Photograph courtesy of Carnegie Mellon University.)

of mass of activation instead of the most active output unit when determining the direction to steer permits finer steering corrections, thus improving ALVINN's driving accuracy.

Figure 29.9 shows the arrangement of the network and a typical low-resolution road image as presented to the network.

There were various versions of ALVINN. In one, training of the network was "on-the-fly," meaning that the network was trained in real time as the van was steered by a human driver along various roads and paths. The desired steering angle was the

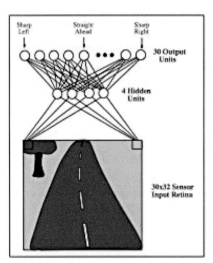
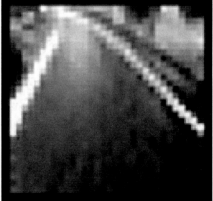

Figure 29.9. The ALVINN network (left) and a typical road image (right). (From Dean A. Pomerleau, "Neural Network Vision for Robot Driving," Michael Arbib (ed.), *The Handbook of Brain Theory and Neural Networks*, Cambridge, MA: MIT Press, 1995. A version of this paper is available online at http://www.ri.cmu.edu/pub_files/pub2/pomerleau_dean_1995_1/pomerleau_dean_1995_1.pdf.)

one selected by the driver, and the network weights were adjusted by backprop to attempt to mimic the driver's performance. One problem with this method was that the network was never exposed to possible "going-off-the-road" images. Simulations of what such images would look like (labeled by what the steering angle should be in those cases) were added to the training set.

In summarizing a typical test of ALVINN's performance, Pomerleau wrote[41]

Over three runs, with the network driving at 5 miles per hour along the 100 meter test section of road, the average position of the vehicle was 1.6 cm right of center, with a standard deviation of 7.2 cm. Under human control, the average position of the vehicle was 4.0 cm right of center, with a standard deviation of 5.47 cm.

Carnegie Mellon's Robotics Institute continued (and still continues) to work on autonomous vehicles, although the neural-network approach to image-guided steering was replaced by more robust computer-vision algorithms. Their 1995 visual perception system RALPH (an acronym for Rapidly Adapting Lateral Position Handler) used special image-processing routines to determine road boundary curvature. According to Pomerleau,[42] "RALPH has been able to locate the road and steer autonomously on a wide variety of road types under many different conditions. RALPH has driven our Navlab 5 testbed vehicle over 3000 miles on roads ranging from single lane bike paths, to rural highways, to interstate freeways."

In the summer of 1995, one of their specially outfitted vehicles, a 1990 Pontiac Trans Sport (Navlab 5) donated by Delco Electronics, steered autonomously (using RALPH) for 2,797 of the 2,849 miles from Pittsburgh, PA to San Diego, CA. (Only the steering was autonomous – Pomerleau and Ph.D. student Todd Jochem handled the throttle and brake.) The average speed was above 60 miles per hour.[43]

29.5 Unsupervised Learning

The decision tree and neural network learning methods described so far in this chapter are examples of "supervised learning," a type of learning in which one attempts to learn to classify data from a large sample of training data whose classifications are known. The "supervision" that directs learning in these systems involves informing the system about the classification of *each* datum in the training set. Yet, it is sometimes possible to construct useful classifications of data based just on the data alone. Techniques for doing so fall under the heading of "unsupervised learning."

Recall that in Section 4.3 I showed a diagram (Fig. 4.11) in which data to be classified were represented by points in a two-dimensional "feature space." The coordinates of the points corresponded to the values of two numerically valued features, f_1 and f_2, of the data. In Fig. 4.11, the category of each point was indicated by small squares for points belonging to one category and small circles for points belong to another category. Because the points were thus labeled, they could be used as training examples for a supervised learning procedure.

But suppose we have a set of unlabeled sample points, such as those shown in Fig. 29.10. Can anything be learned from data of that sort? By visual inspection, we see that the points seem to be arranged in three clusters. Perhaps each cluster contains points that could be thought to belong to the same category. So, if we could

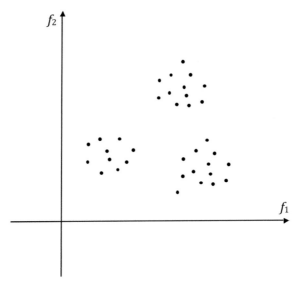

Figure 29.10. Unlabeled points in a feature space.

automatically process data samples to identify clusters and the boundaries between them, we would have a method of unsupervised learning.

AI researchers have used several methods for identifying clusters of training samples. A popular one, and one that is easy to explain, is the so-called k-means method. It works by repeating over and over the following steps:

1. Install, perhaps at random locations, some number, say k, of "cluster seekers" in the space of samples.
2. For each of these cluster seekers, group together those training samples that are closer to it than to any other cluster seekers.
3. Compute the centroid (the "center of gravity") of each of these groups of samples.
4. Move each of the cluster seekers to the centroid of its corresponding group.
5. Repeat these steps until none of the cluster seekers needs to be moved again.

At the end of this process, the cluster seekers will all be at the centroids of groups of training samples that can be considered to be clusters or separate categories of data. Now to classify some new data point not in the training set, we simply compute to which cluster seeker it is closest. The process depends, of course, on being able to guess the number of clusters, k. Methods for doing so generally involve adjusting the number of them so that points within clusters are closer together than the distances between clusters.

Statisticians and others have developed several methods for clustering data, including variations related to the k-means method. One prominent technique, AutoClass, was developed by Peter Cheeseman and colleagues at NASA.[44] According-ing to a Web site about AutoClass,[45]

AutoClass takes a database of cases described by a combination of real and discrete valued attributes, and automatically finds the natural classes in that data. It does not need to be told how many classes are present or what they look like – it extracts this information from the data itself. The classes are described probabilistically, so that an object can have partial membership in the different classes, and the class definitions can overlap.

AutoClass is famous for having discovered a new class of infrared stars. It has also discovered new classes of proteins, introns, and other patterns in DNA/protein sequence data.

There are even techniques that can be applied to non-numeric data. Statisticians group all of these methods (numeric and non-numeric) under the general heading of "cluster analysis." A good overview can be found in the online Electronic Text-book *StatSoft* at http://www.statsoft.com/textbook/stcluan.html. The textbook by Duda, Hart, and Stork has a thorough discussion of unsupervised learning (as well as other topics in data classification).[46]

29.6 Reinforcement Learning

29.6.1 *Learning Optimal Policies*

There is another style of learning that lies somewhat in between the supervised and unsupervised varieties. An example would be learning which of several possible actions a robot, say, should execute at every stage in an ongoing sequence of experiences given only what final result of all of its actions. An extreme case would be learning to play excellent chess given only information about a win or a loss at the end of play. No system has yet been built that can learn to play chess that way, but it is possible for a program to learn to play backgammon that way and to learn to perform other interesting tasks, such as controlling the flight of helicopters. Borrowing terms from psychological learning theory, we can call the win or loss information (or in general the good-result or bad-result information) a "reward" or a "reinforcement," and this style of learning is called "reinforcement learning" or (sometimes) "trial-and-error learning."

Reinforcement learning has a long and varied history. The psychologist Edward L. Thorndike (1874–1949) studied this style of learning in animals.[47] In their book *Reinforcement Learning: An Introduction*,[48] Richard S. Sutton (1957– ; Fig. 29.11) and Andrew G. Barto (1948– ; Fig. 29.11), two of the field's pioneers, mention some additional historical milestones, including Arthur Samuel's method for learning evaluation functions in checkers, the use of Richard Bellman's dynamic programming techniques in optimal control, John Andreae's trial-and-error learning system STeLLA,[49] Donald Michie's learning systems for tic-tac-toc (MENACE[50]) and pole-balancing (BOXES[51]), and A. Harry Klopf's work on "hedonistic neurons."[52] Reinforcement learning is another one of those subdisciplines of AI that has become highly technical and multibranched. I'll attempt a gentle and nonmathematical description of how it works.

In its simplest setting, reinforcement learning is about learning how to traverse a collection of states, going from one state to another and so on, to reach a state in

Figure 29.11. Andrew Barto (left) and Richard Sutton (right). (Photographs courtesy of Andrew Barto and of Richard Sutton.)

which a reward is obtained. The problem is much like one that a rat faces in learning how to run a maze (or one that a robot faces in learning how to carry out a task). In fact, let us use a maze example to describe some of the aspects of reinforcement learning. A typical maze is shown in Fig. 29.12.

The rat's problem is to go from its starting position to the cheese at the goal position. The gray dots in the figure are meant to depict situations that the rat might find itself in and recognize. In reinforcement learning terminology, these situations are called "states." At each state, the rat can select from among, say, four actions, namely, turn left, turn right, go forward, or go back. Depending on the state, only some of the actions are possible – one cannot go forward when up against a dead end for example. Each possible action takes the rat from one state to an adjacent one in the maze. The collection of states and the actions that link them can be thought of as a graph, similar to those I discussed when I talked about search methods.

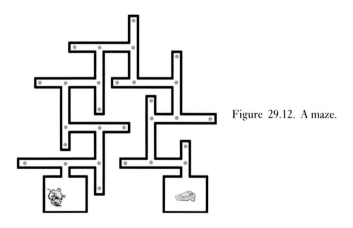

Figure 29.12. A maze.

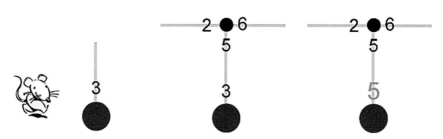

Figure 29.13. Initial stages of the Q-learning process.

So as not to stray too far from what is known about real rats running mazes, let us switch now to describe how a fictional "robotic rat" might learn how to run this maze. The main problem for the robot is that it starts out by not having a map of the maze nor having any idea about the effects of its actions. That is, for any given state that it finds itself in, it does not know which next states would result for the various actions it could take in that state. For if it did have such a map, say one represented by a graph, it could search the graph (using a method like A*) to find a path to the goal node. One way to proceed would be to attempt to learn a graph of states and their connections by trial-and-error methods and then to use graph-searching methods to figure out how to navigate the maze.

An alternative, and the one used by most reinforcement learning methods, involves naming all of the states that the robot encounters as it wanders randomly in search of the goal. (We assume that eventually it does reach the goal.) In reinforcement learning terminology, a "policy" for running the maze associates some single action with each named state. A best or "optimal policy" would associate with each state that action that would lead to a shortest (or otherwise least costly) path through the maze. Reinforcement learning is about learning the best policy, or, at least, good policies.

One method for learning a policy involves associating a "valuation" number with every possible action at each state and then adjusting these numbers (based on experience) until they point the way toward the goal. This method is called "Q-learning" and was originally suggested by Christopher Watkins (1959–) in his Cambridge University Ph.D. thesis.[53] The robot begins its learning process by assigning a name to the state in which it begins and by assigning randomly selected valuation numbers to every action it can take in that state. The learning process will expand this table by assigning names and valuation numbers to all of the actions it can take in every *new* state encountered. (We assume that the robot remembers, in its table, the names of all the states it has already visited in its learning process and can distinguish these from new states.) The robot's initial state, with a randomly selected valuation number assigned to its only action possible, is shown in the left-hand sketch of Fig. 29.13. At every stage of the learning process, the robot takes that action having the highest valuation number. Because there is only one action in the robot's initial state, it takes that action, finds itself in a new state, and assigns random valuation numbers to the actions possible in that new state. This step is shown in the middle sketch of Fig. 29.13. Now comes the key step in learning. Because the robot

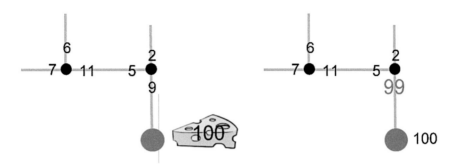

Figure 29.14. Stages leading to the goal.

now "knows" that it can reach a new state having actions whose highest valuation number is 6, it updates the valuation number, namely, 3, of the action leading to that state by adjusting it to a number more consistent with being able now to take an action that it imagines is worth 6. To account for the "cost" of its just-completed action, the adjustment of 3 does not go all the way to 6 but just to 5, say. The result is shown in the right-hand sketch of Fig. 29.13 in which the adjusted valuation is shown a bit larger than the other numbers and shaded.

This process continues. In each state, take that action whose valuation number is largest and then adjust that valuation number by making its value closer to the value of the action with the highest valuation number in the state just entered. And, even though the process starts with randomly selected valuation numbers, eventually the trial-and-error process will stumble into the goal state where a high "reward" will be obtained. At that stage, the action just taken, which led to that reward, has its valuation number raised to the same value (or maybe just a little bit less) than the value of the reward. I illustrate this step in Fig. 29.14. The sketch on the left of the figure shows some of the states and action valuations at the time the robot takes the action that achieves the goal. In the sketch on the right of the figure, I show the adjusted valuation (shaded) for that goal-achieving action. Now, for the first time, an action valuation is based on getting a reward rather than being set randomly. If the robot ever finds itself in the state adjacent to the goal state again, it will certainly take the same action. More importantly, when it reaches this penultimate state in a subsequent experience, it will propagate this reward-based value backward.

I illustrate how backward propagation works in Fig. 29.15. Suppose, in the sketch on the left, the robot finds itself in the state marked by an arrow. From that state, it takes that action with the largest valuation, which leads it to a state adjacent to the goal. The action with the largest valuation leading out of that state has a valuation of 99, so the valuation of the action just taken is changed from 11 to 98, as shown in the sketch on the right. Increasing the valuations of actions in states close to the goal by backward propagation, in effect, makes those states intrinsically "rewarding" just as if they were goal states themselves.

The astute reader may complain that I have cleverly set the "random" valuation numbers to values that would lead to the goal once the robot gets to states close to

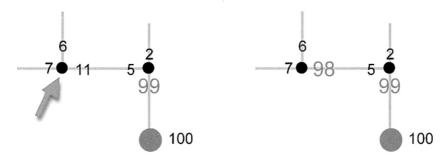

Figure 29.15. Backward propagation of goal-achieving action valuations.

the goal. What if these values were such, as they most probably would be, that, upon getting close, the robot wanders away from the nearly achieved goal? If the valuation numbers are adjusted as I prescribed, always taking into account the cost of a move, a little thought will convince one that eventually the numbers will be such as to force the robot toward the goal, with all other avenues eventually being closed off.

With continued experience, the valuations of actions involved in achieving the goal gradually propagate backward from the goal. Eventually, after much trial-and-error experience (and with some "reasonable" assumptions), the values will converge to those that implement an optimal policy, that is, one that always gets the robot to the goal in the most efficient manner.

Most versions of reinforcement learning have the following elaborations:

- Rewards might be given at more than one of the states. That is, there is not necessarily a single goal state but many states that might contribute to reward. Rewards are represented by numerical values, which could be positive (true "rewards"), zero, or negative ("punishments").
- Rather than attempting to find a policy that corresponds to an optimal path to a single goal state, one tries to learn policies that maximize the amount of reward expected over time. Usually in learning a policy, rewards that are anticipated in the distant future are "discounted," that is, they don't count as much as rewards expected more immediately.
- Any given action taken at a state might not always lead to the same state. One could attempt to learn the probabilities that certain actions taken in a state lead to which other states, and some reinforcement learning methods, such as "prioritized sweeping,"[54] do that. The Q-learning process avoids the need to learn these probabilities explicitly because, whatever they are, they (along with rewards) appropriately affect the values that the learning process assigns to state–action pairs.
- As a further complication, it might be that the robot has only imperfect knowledge of what state it is in because its sensory apparatus is not sufficiently accurate or informative. In that case, the actual state that the robot is in is said to be "hidden" from it, which adds additional complications to the problem of learning an optimal policy.

With these elaborations, the problem becomes one of what is called a "Markov Decision Process" (MDP). With imperfect state knowledge, it is called a "Partially-Observable Markov Decision Process" (POMDP). MDPs and POMDPs have been well studied by people in control theory as well as in AI.[55]

I can use the robot maze example to mention several things that are important in the use of reinforcement learning in practical applications. First, I assumed that the robot's random exploration eventually would land it in the goal state. In complex problems, the chance of randomly achieving a goal (or other rewards) might be slim to none. Breaking the problem down into a hierarchy of subproblems in which rewards are more easily obtained is sometimes used to speed up learning. Additionally, "shaping" strategies can be used in which the robot is first placed in a situation sufficiently close to the goal that random exploration will find the goal. Then, after some actions close to the goal have been assigned goal-relevant evaluations, the starting situations can be gradually moved farther and farther from the goal. Alternatively, hints might be given, perhaps in the form of intermediate rewards given to let the robot know that it is doing well so far. Strategies such as these are used in teaching skills to humans and animals.

Another problem concerns the tradeoff between "exploiting" an already learned policy versus "exploring" to find better policies. It is often the case that a set of action valuations obtained early in the learning process might not be the best set possible. To learn a better set, the robot must be encouraged in some way to strike out randomly away from a known policy to lock on to a better one. Finally, many problems might have "state spaces" so large that the entire set of all of the states and their actions and valuations cannot be explicitly listed in a table like the one I assumed for the robot maze problem. In that case, the valuations of actions that can be taken in a state must be computed rather than stored. I'll show an example of how that might be done in the next few pages.

29.6.2 *TD-GAMMON*

One of the most impressive demonstrations of the power of machine-learning methods is the TD-GAMMON system developed by Gerald Tesauro at IBM.[56] Versions of TD-GAMMON learned to play excellent backgammon after playing against themselves during millions of games. TD-GAMMON used a combination of neural net learning and a type of reinforcement learning called "temporal difference learning" (which explains the prefix TD).

TD-GAMMON's neural network consisted of three layers. In one version there were 198 input units, 40 hidden units, and 4 output units. Each of the output units could have an output value between 0 and 1. (Instead of threshold units, the network had the kinds of components I talked about earlier, namely, those whose outputs changed smoothly, but still abruptly, between 0 and 1.) Each of the outputs was charged with the task of estimating a probability of a particular outcome of the game. The four possible outcomes considered were white wins, white gammons, black wins, or black gammons. The input units were coded to represent the configuration of pieces on the board. The values of the four outputs were combined to yield a number giving the estimated "value" of a board position from white's point of view.

I'll describe how the network learned in a moment. First, here is how the network was used to select a move. (I'm assuming here that the reader has some familiarity with backgammon, but my description should make sense even for those who do not.) At each stage of play, the dice are thrown, and the program considers all of the possible moves that it might make given that throw of the dice. The network computes the value of each possible resulting board, and the program selects the move producing the board with the best value (which is the highest value when it is white's move and the lowest value when it is black's move).

Now, here's how the network learns: For each board position encountered during actual play, the network's weights are adjusted, using backprop, so that the value computed for that board position is closer to the value computed for the temporally next board position (and thus we see why the term "temporal difference" arises). The network starts with randomly selected weight values, so the moves early in the learning process, as well as the weight adjustments, are random. But eventually, even randomly selected moves result in a win for one of the players. After a win occurs, the four probability values are then known for sure – one of them is "1," and the rest are "0." The network's weights can then be adjusted so that the value of the penultimate board is made closer to the value of this final, winning board position. As in all reinforcement learning procedures, values are gradually propagated backward from the end of the game toward the starting position. After millions of games, the network weights take on values that result in expert play. In commenting on a version of TD-GAMMON that uses search in addition to learning, Sutton and Barto wrote[57]

TD-GAMMON 3.0 appears to be at, or very near, the playing strength of the best human players in the world. It may already be the world champion. These programs have also already changed the way the best human players play the game. For example, TD-GAMMON learned to play certain opening positions differently than was the convention among the best human players. Based on TD-GAMMON's success and further analysis, the best human players now play these positions as TD-GAMMON does.

29.6.3 *Other Applications*

There are probably hundreds of important applications of reinforcement learning methods. A typical, as well as dramatic, example is the work of Andrew Ng (1976–) and his group at Stanford on learning to perform aerobatic helicopter maneuvers.[58] Some photographs of a model helicopter that has learned to "roll" are shown in Fig. 29.16. Other applications have been in elevator dispatching, job–shop scheduling, managing power consumption, and four-legged walking robots.

As a final comment about reinforcement learning, it is interesting to observe that part of the technology of machine learning, a part whose name was borrowed from psychology, now pays back its debt by providing a theoretical framework for how animal brains learn at the neurophysiological level. In an article in *The Journal of Neuroscience*, Christopher H. Donahue and Hyojung Seo wrote[59]

To make effective decisions while navigating uncertain environments, animals must develop the ability to accurately predict the consequences of their actions. Reinforcement learning has emerged as a key theoretical paradigm for understanding how animals accomplish this feat . . .

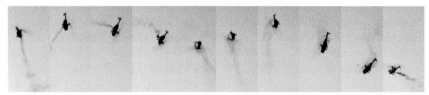

Figure 29.16. Andrew Ng (top) and his model helicopter during a roll maneuver (bottom). (Photographs courtesy of Andrew Ng.)

In addition to successfully predicting the animal's choice behavior, the reinforcement learning model has been successfully used to elucidate the function of the basal ganglia in goal-directed behavior. Dopaminergic neurons in the ventral tegmental area and the substantia nigra have been shown to encode a reward-prediction error, which is used to improve the outcomes of an animal's future choices. Another study in monkeys engaged in a free-choice task showed that the activity of striatal neurons is correlated with action values, which were estimated by integrating the previous outcome history associated with each action.

29.7 Enhancements

Many of the machine learning methods I have mentioned can be enhanced in various ways. Some of these are based on work by statisticians and others by people working on what is called "computational learning theory." One technique, called "bagging" (an acronym for bootstrap aggregating) is due to Professor Leo Breiman of the University of California, Berkeley.[60] For classification problems, bagging works by combining the outputs of a number, say m, of separate classifiers. Each classifier is trained by using a different subset of the original training set. These subsets are obtained from the original by randomly selecting (with replacement) some of its examples. (Statisticians call these samples "bootstrap samples.") After each of the m classifiers is trained, final classification is made by a majority vote. The technique can be applied independently of the kind of individual classifier used – neural network, decision tree, nearest-neighbor, or what have you. Bagging can also be used for the problem of associating a number (rather than a category) with an example. In that case, outputs are averaged rather than participating in a vote. The voting and averaging operations help avoid overfitting the data and thus yield better performance than would have been obtained with one classifier trained on all of the data. [One wonders how the performance of the 1960s MADALINE neural network (see p. 69) might have been improved had each of its threshold units been trained on bootstrap samples.]

A related idea, called "boosting," was proposed by Robert E. Schapire.[61] Although there are many versions, here in outline is how it works. Using any of the supervised machine learning methods, a classifier is trained on the original training set in which each sample is equally "weighted." (The ith sample's weight, say w_i, can be set, for example, by including that sample w_i times in the training set.) Then a new training set is constructed in which those samples that were misclassified have their "weights" increased, and those samples that were correctly classified have their weights decreased. Using this new training set, another classifier is trained. (That one will, presumably, work harder on the earlier misclassified samples.) This process is repeated until we have some number, say m, of classifiers. Now, each of the classifiers votes on the categorization of new samples. Their votes are weighted by how well they performed on the original training set. Votes of the more reliable classifiers count more than do those of less reliable classifiers. Even when the original classifiers are "weak" (that is, not very reliable at all), the overall accuracy of the combined set of m classifiers can be quite good, thus "boosting" the results.

Several ways of doing boosting have been proposed. One of the popular ones, due to Yoav Freund and Robert Schapire, is called "Adaboost."[62] It is also possible to combine bagging and boosting.[63]

Finally, I'll mention "Support Vector Machines" (SVMs). A complete description of them would involve more mathematics than we want to get into here, but I can give a rough-and-ready idea of how they work by using a geometric example. On the left-hand side of Fig. 29.17 I show the same points that I used in Fig. 4.11 to illustrate a separating boundary in feature space. The points indicated by small squares correspond to samples in one category, and the points indicated by small circles correspond to samples in another category.

As a reminder, the points in the diagrams have coordinates equal to the features, f_1 and f_2, computed from items (such as speech sounds, images, or other data) that we want to classify. It happens in this case that there exists many straight-line (that is, linear) boundaries that would separate the points in the two categories perfectly. Therefore an attempt to train a neural element to classify the points (considered as "training samples") would be successful. If we used the standard error–correction procedure for training, we would certainly get *some* linear boundary, but with SVMs we ask more of the boundary than that it merely separate the training samples. We want it to be such that the distances (called the "margin") from it to the closest points of opposite categories are as large as possible. Such a linear boundary is shown on the right-hand side of Fig. 29.17. The parallel dashed lines on either side go through these closest points, which are called "support vectors." Boundaries with margins as large as possible are desirable because they are better at classifying new points not in the training set. That is, they have better "generalizing" properties.

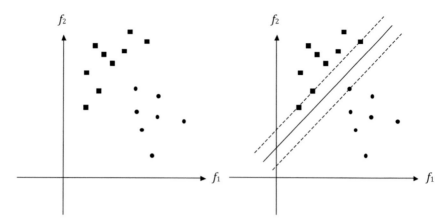

Figure 29.17. Points and a linear separating boundary in a two-dimensional space.

Our early work on pattern recognition (of the supervised learning variety) at SRI included some experiments in which we attempted to find separating boundaries that were insulated away from the training samples. One of the methods for doing so involved including training samples derived from the original ones by adding small amounts of "noise" to them. The idea was that the error-correction training procedure applied to this augmented set would be forced away from the original samples. A more elegant method was proposed by H. Glucksman, in which error-correction training continued until some minimum allowed distance between training samples and separating boundaries was achieved.[64] To ensure margins as large as possible, however, requires some complex optimization procedures. (Mathematically inclined readers can refer to an online tutorial by Tristan Fletcher at http://www.tristanfletcher.co.uk/SVMExplained.pdf or to a textbook by Nello Cristianini and John Shawe-Taylor about SVMs.[65])

Now, you might ask, how does one get feature spaces that are linearly separable? One way is to use something like Rosenblatt's alpha-perceptron. Recall that the elements in the alpha-perceptron's first layer of threshold elements, say N of them, each received its own input from a random collection of data measurements (such as pixels or speech waveform values). The binary outputs of these "association units" (as these first-layer elements were called) were then features like those I used in the two-dimensional example. They determined points in an N-dimensional feature space, which (Rosenblatt hoped) was linearly separable. Often, in Rosenblatt's work, they were.

The people working with SVMs use a different method for defining features. Their method ensures that the resulting feature space is linearly separable (or, at least, nearly so). Their features involve the use of what they call "kernels," and machines using such features are called "kernel machines." Again, the mathematics is too complex to be described here, but the interested reader can look at the book by Nello Cristianini and John Shawe-Taylor. As that book points out, the history of the mathematics leading up to kernel machines and SVMs goes as far back as the beginning of the twentieth century and has involved people in optimization theory, statistics, and computational learning theory.

SVMs and kernel machines are superb examples of how work in several disciplines, using highly technical mathematical apparatus, has contributed to powerful new techniques in artificial intelligence. Important venues for describing new work in machine learning are the Neural Information Processing Systems (NIPS) Conferences sponsored annually by the Neural Information Processing Systems Foundation.[66]

After hearing about all of the methods for machine learning described in this chapter, you might reasonably ask, which method is best? Should one use the nearest-neighbor method, a decision tree, a neural network, or something else? Researchers have asked that question also, and there have been "bake-offs" in which different methods have competed on various standard problems, such as character recognition. One such competition, organized by the European Community ESPRIT project StatLog, is described in a book edited by Donald Michie, D. J. Spiegelhalter, and C. C. Taylor.[67] Another comparison of several methods was reported in the AI text by Russell and Norvig.[68] Some methods work better for some problems than for others, but often these differences are only marginal, and most people in the field agree that having lots and lots of data is, in the end, more important than the particular machine learning algorithm used. That is, spend time gathering more data rather than tuning a particular method.[69]

Notes

1. For a nice review, see the online tutorial put together by Andrew H. Moore, one of the pioneers of memory-based learning, at http://www.autonlab.org/tutorials/mbl08.pdf. [399]
2. Christopher G. Atkeson, Andrew W. Moore, and Stefan Schall, "Locally Weighted Learning for Control," *Artificial Intelligence Review*, Vol. 11, pp. 75–113, 1997; available online at http://www.cs.cmu.edu/~cga/papers/air1.ps.gz. See also Stefan Schaal and Christopher G. Atkeson, "Robot Juggling: An Implementation of Memory-based Learning," *IEEE Control Systems Magazine*, Vol. 14, No. 1, pp. 57–71, February 1994; available online at http://www-clmc.usc.edu/publications/S/schaal-CSM1994.pdf. [399]
3. Walter Daelemans and Antal van den Bosch, *Memory-Based Language Processing*, Cambridge: Cambridge University Press, 2005. [400]
4. Janet Kolodner, *Case-Based Reasoning*, pp. 18–19, San Francisco: Morgan Kaufmann Publishers, 1993. [400]
5. See Janet Kolodner, "Reconstructive Memory: A Computer Model," *Cognitive Science*, Vol. 7, No. 4, pp. 281–328, 1983, and Michael Lebowitz, "Memory-Based Parsing," *Artificial Intelligence*, Vol. 21, pp. 363–404, 1983. [401]
6. Edwina L. Rissland, unpublished notes. [401]
7. Edwina L. Rissland, "Example Generation," *Proceedings Third National Conference of the Canadian Society for Computational Studies of Intelligence*, pp. 280–288, Victoria, BC, 1980. [401]
8. See, for example, Edwina L. Rissland, "Examples in the Legal Domain: Hypotheticals in Contract Law," *Proceedings Fourth Annual Cognitive Science Conference*, pp. 96–99, University of Michigan, Ann Arbor, 1982. [401]
9. E-mail of February 17, 2009. [401]

10. http://www.aiai.ed.ac.uk/technology/casebasedreasoning.html. **[402]**

11. Feigenbaum told me about another tree-construction system developed independently (and for different purposes) around 1959 by Edward Fredkin. See Edward Fredkin, "Trie Memory," *Communications of the ACM*, Vol. 3, No. 9, pp. 490–499, September 1960. **[404]**

12. Edward A. Feigenbaum, "The Simulation of Verbal Learning Behavior," *Proceedings of the Western Joint Computer Conference*, Vol. 19, pp. 121–132, 1961. Reprinted in Edward A. Feigenbaum and Julian Feldman (eds.), *Computers and Thought*, New York: McGraw-Hill, 1963. **[404]**

13. See, for example, Edward A. Feigenbaum and Herbert Simon, "EPAM-like Models of Recognition and Learning," *Cognitive Science*, Vol. 8, No. 4, pp. 305–336, 1984; Howard B. Richman, J. J. Staszewski, and Herbert A. Simon, "Simulation of Expert Memory Using EPAM-IV," *Psychological Review*, Vol. 102, No. 2, pp. 305–330, 1995; and Howard B. Richman, Herbert A. Simon, and Edward A. Feigenbaum, "Simulations of Paired Associate Learning Using EPAM-VI," Complex Information Processing Working Paper #553, Department of Psychology, Carnegie Mellon University, March 7, 2002. The latter paper is available online at http://www.pahomeschoolers.com/epam/cip553.pdf. **[404]**

14. Carl I. Hovland and Earl B. Hunt, "Programming a Model of Human Concept Formulation," *Proceedings of the Western Joint Computer Conference*, pp. 145–155, May 9–11, 1961. Reprinted in Edward A. Feigenbaum and Julian Feldman (eds.), *Computers and Thought*, pp. 310–325, New York: McGraw-Hill, 1963. **[404]**

15. Earl B. Hunt, Janet Marin, and Philip J. Stone, *Experiments in Induction*, New York: Academic Press, 1966. **[404]**

16. For Quinlan's descriptions of ID3, see J. Ross Quinlan, "Discovering Rules by Induction from Large Collections of Examples," in Donald Michie (ed.), *Expert Systems in the Micro Electronic Age*, pp. 168–201, Edinburgh: Edinburgh University Press, 1979, and J. Ross Quinlan, "Induction of Decision Trees," *Machine Learning*, Vol. 1, pp. 81–106, 1986. Available online at http://www.cs.toronto.edu/~roweis/csc2515-2006/readings/quinlan.pdf. **[405]**

17. From an e-mail from Quinlan to me dated March 18, 2008. **[405]**

18. That is, the one described in J. Ross Quinlan, *op. cit.* **[406]**

19. See, for example, J. Ross Quinlan, "Learning Efficient Classification Procedures and Their Application to Chess End Games," Ryszard S. Michalski, Jaime G. Carbonell, and Tom M. Mitchell (eds), *Machine Learning: An Artificial Intelligence Approach*, pp. 463–482, San Francisco: Morgan Kaufmann Publishers, 1983. (By the way, the very title of that volume indicates, I think, that the editors wanted to contrast the approach used in the volume's papers with neural network approaches to machine learning.) **[406]**

20. The classic paper is Claude E. Shannon, "A Mathematical Theory of Communication," *Bell System Technical Journal*, Vol. 27, pp. 379–423 and 623–656, July and October 1948. Available online at http://cm.bell-labs.com/cm/ms/what/shannonday/shannon1948.pdf. **[406]**

21. See, for example, J. Ross Quinlan, "Decision Trees and Multi-Valued Attributes," in Jean E. Hayes, Donald Michie, and J. Richards (Eds.), *Machine Intelligence 11*, pp. 305–318, Oxford: Oxford University Press, 1988. All of these measures are described in J. Ross Quinlan, *C4.5: Programs for Machine Learning*, San Francisco: Morgan Kaufmann Publishers, 1993. **[406]**

22. J. Ross Quinlan, "Discovering Rules by Induction from Large Collections of Examples," in Donald Michie (ed.), *Expert Systems in the Micro Electronic Age*, pp. 168–201, Edinburgh: Edinburgh University Press, 1979. **[407]**

23. E-mail communication, March 18, 2008. **[407]**

24. See J. Ross Quinlan, *C4.5: Programs for Machine Learning*, San Francisco: Morgan Kaufmann Publishers, 1993. **[407]**

25. A complete version of C4.5 can be downloaded free of charge from Ross Quinlan's homepage, http://www.rulequest.com/Personal/. Scaled-down versions of C5.0 and See5 can be downloaded free of charge from http://www.rulequest.com/download.html. **[407]**

26. Intelligent Terminals, Ltd. **[407]**

27. See, for example, Jerome H. Friedman, "A Recursive Partitioning Decision Rule for Nonparametric Classification," *IEEE Transactions on Computers*, Vol. 26, No. 4, pp. 404–408, 1977. **[408]**

28. See Leo Breiman, Jerome H. Friedman, Richard A. Olshen, and Charles J. Stone, *Classification and Regression Trees*, Pacific Grove, CA: Wadsworth, 1984. **[408]**

29. CART 5 is available from Salford Systems. See http://www.salford-systems.com/1112.php. **[408]**

30. J. Ross Quinlan, "Learning Logical Definitions from Relations," *Machine Learning*, Vol. 5, pp. 239–266, 1990. **[408]**

31. The interested reader who is comfortable with logic theory might consult Stephen Muggleton and Luc De Raedt, "Inductive Logic Programming, Theory and Methods," *Journal of Logic Programming*, Vols. 19–20, pp. 629–679, 1994, and Nada Lavrac and Saso Dzeroski, *Inductive Logic Programming: Techniques and Applications*, New York: Ellis Horwood, 1994 (available online at http://www-ai.ijs.si/SasoDzeroski/ILPBook/). See also Claude Sammut, "The Origins of Inductive Logic Programming: A Prehistoric Tale," in Stephen Muggleton (ed.), *Proceedings of the Third International Workshop on Inductive Logic Programming*, pp. 127–147, Bled, Slovenia, 1993. **[408]**

32. See Saso Dzeroski and Nada Lavrac (eds.), *Relational Data Mining*, Berlin: Springer-Verlag, 2001. **[408]**

33. David Rumelhart, Geoffrey E. Hinton, and Ronald J. Williams, in James L. McClelland, David E. Rumelhart, and the PDP Research Group (eds.), *Parallel Distributed Processing: Explorations in the Microstructure of Cognition, Vol. 1: Foundations*, pp. 318–362, Cambridge, MA: MIT Press, 1986. See also David Rumelhart, Geoffrey E. Hinton, and Ronald J. Williams, "Learning Representations by Back-Propagating Errors," *Nature*, Vol. 323, Letters, pp. 533–536, October 9, 1986. **[409]**

34. Arthur E. Bryson Jr. and Y. C. Ho, *Applied Optimal Control: Optimization, Estimation, and Control*, Waltham, MA: Blaisdell, 1969. **[409]**

35. Paul Werbos, "Beyond Regression: New Tools for Prediction and Analysis in the Behavioral Sciences," Ph.D. thesis, Harvard University, Cambridge, MA, 1974. Laveen Kanal, on the occasion of his acceptance of the 1992 King-Sun Fu award of the International Association for Pattern Recognition (IAPR), recalls a 1975 conversation with Werbos. See Laveen N. Kanal, "On Pattern, Categories, and Alternate Realities," *Pattern Recognition Letters*, Vol. 14, pp. 241–255, 1993. Available online at http://www.lnk.com/prl14.pdf. **[409]**

36. Laveen N. Kanal, "On Pattern, Categories, and Alternate Realities," *Pattern Recognition Letters*, Vol. 14, pp. 241–255, 1993. Available online at http://www.lnk.com/prl14.pdf. **[409]**

37. Terrence J. Sejnowski and Charles R. Rosenberg, "Parallel Networks That Learn to Pronounce English Text," *Complex Systems*, Vol. 1, pp. 145–168, 1987. Available online at http://www.cnl.salk.edu/ParallelNetsPronounce/ParallelNetsPronounce-TJSejnowski.pdf. **[410]**

38. An early paper was Dean Pomerleau, "ALVINN: An Autonomous Land Vehicle in a Neural Network," *Advances in Neural Information Processing Systems*, Vol. 1,

pp. 305–313, San Francisco: Morgan Kaufmann Publishers, 1989. Pomerleau's thesis was "Neural Network Perception for Mobile Robot Guidance," Carnegie Mellon University, February 1992. **[411]**

39. Charles Thorpe *et al.*, "Vision and Navigation for the Carnegie Mellon Navlab," *IEEE Transactions on Pattern Analysis and Machine Intelligence*, Vol. 10, No. 3, pp. 362–373, May 1988. **[411]**

40. Dean A. Pomerleau, "Neural Network Vision for Robot Driving," in Michael Arbib (ed.), *The Handbook of Brain Theory and Neural Networks*, Cambridge, MA: MIT Press, 1995. A version of this paper is available online at http://www.ri.cmu.edu/pub_files/pub2/pomerleau_dean_1995_1/pomerleau_dean_1995_1.pdf. **[411]**

41. *Ibid.* **[413]**

42. Dean Pomerleau, "RALPH: Rapidly Adapting Lateral Position Handler," *Proceedings of the IEEE Symposium on Intelligent Vehicles*, pp. 506–511, September 1995. Available online at http://www.ri.cmu.edu/pub_files/pub2/pomerleau_dean_1995_2/pomerleau_dean_1995_2.pdf. **[413]**

43. The "No Hands Across America" homepage is at http://www.cs.cmu.edu/afs/cs/usr/tjochem/www/nhaa/nhaa_home_page.html. There are pointers on that site to the trip's journal and photos. For more recent work, see the NavLab's homepage at http://www.ri.cmu.edu/labs/lab_28.html. **[413]**

44. Peter Cheeseman *et al.*, "AutoClass: A Bayesian Classification System," *Proceedings of the Fifth International Conference on Machine Learning*, pp. 54–64, San Francisco: Morgan Kaufmann Publishers, 1988. See also Peter Cheeseman and J. Stutz, "Bayesian Classification (AutoClass): Theory and Results," in Usama M. Fayyad *et al.* (eds.), *Advances in Knowledge Discovery and Data Mining*, Menlo Park, CA: AAAI Press and Cambridge, MA: MIT Press, 1996. Available online at http://ti.arc.nasa.gov/m/project/autoclass/kdd-95.ps. **[414]**

45. http://ti.arc.nasa.gov/project/autoclass/. **[414]**

46. Richard O. Duda, Peter E. Hart, and David G. Stork, *Pattern Classification*, New York: John Wiley and Sons, Inc., 2001. **[415]**

47. Edward L. Thorndike, *Animal Intelligence*, New York: The Macmillan Co., 1911. **[415]**

48. Richard S. Sutton and Andrew G. Barto, *Reinforcement Learning: An Introduction*, Section 1.6, Cambridge, MA: MIT Press, 1998; available online at http://www.cs.ualberta.ca/~sutton/book/ebook/the-book.html. **[415]**

49. John H. Andreae, "STeLLA: A Scheme for a Learning Machine," *Proceedings of the 2nd IFAC Congress*, 1963. Published in *Automation and Remote Control*, London: Butterworths, 1964. **[415]**

50. Donald Michie, "Experiments on the Mechanisation of Game Learning: 1. Characterization of the Model and its Parameters," *Computer Journal*, Vol. 1, pp. 232–263, 1963. **[415]**

51. Donald Michie and R. Chambers, "BOXES: An Experiment in Adaptive Control," in E. Dale and Donald Michie (eds.), *Machine Intelligence 2*, pp. 137–152, Edinburgh: Oliver and Boyd, 1968. **[415]**

52. A. Harry Klopf, *The Hedonistic Neuron: A Theory of Memory, Learning, and Intelligence*, Washington, DC: Hemisphere, 1982. **[415]**

53. Christopher J. C. H. Watkins, "Learning from Delayed Rewards," Ph.D. thesis, Cambridge University, Cambridge, England, 1989. **[417]**

54. Andrew Moore and Christopher G. Atkeson, "Prioritized Sweeping: Reinforcement Learning with Less Data and Less Real Time," *Machine Learning*, Vol. 13, October 1993. Online version available at http://www.ri.cmu.edu/pub_files/pub1/moore_andrew_1993_1/moore_andrew_1993_1.pdf. **[419]**

55. For more information, see, for example, the following: Richard S. Sutton and Andrew G. Barto, *Reinforcement Learning: An Introduction*, Cambridge, MA: MIT Press, 1998 (an html version of the book is available online at http://www.cs.ualberta.ca/~sutton/book/ebook/the-book.html.), and Leslie P. Kaelbling, Michael L. Littman, and Andrew W. Moore, "Reinforcement Learning: A Survey," *Journal of Artificial Intelligence Research*, Vol. 4, pp. 237–285, 1996. A Web page with lots of pointers to papers and demonstrations is at http://rlai.cs.ualberta.ca/RLAI/rlai.html. [420]

56. Gerald Tesauro, "Temporal Difference Learning and TD-GAMMON," *Communications of the ACM*, Vol. 38, No. 3, March 1995. An html version of the paper is available online at http://www.research.ibm.com/massive/tdl.html. [420]

57. The quotation is taken from the html version of their book on reinforcement learning at http://www.cs.ualberta.ca/~sutton/book/11/node2.html. [421]

58. Pieter Abbeel *et al.*, "An Application of Reinforcement Learning to Aerobatic Helicopter Flight," in Bernhard Scholkopf, John Platt, and Thomas Hofmann (eds.), *Advances in Neural Information Processing Systems 19: Proceedings of the 2006 Conference*, pp. 1–8, Cambridge, MA: MIT Press, 2007. A pdf version is available at http://www.cs.stanford.edu/~ang/papers/nips06-aerobatichelicopter.pdf. Videos are available at http://www.cs.stanford.edu/group/helicopter See the roll video at http://www.cs.stanford.edu/group/helicopter/video/rolls_080130_web960.mp4. [421]

59. Chrisopher H. Donahue and Hyojung Seo, "Attaching Values to Actions: Action and Outcome Encoding in the Primate Caudate Nucleus," *The Journal of Neuroscience*, Vol. 28, No. 18, pp. 4579–4580, April 30, 2008. The authors refer to Sutton and Barto's book as well as to the earlier paper by Wolfram Schultz, Peter Dayan, and P. Read Montague, "A Neural Substrate of Prediction and Reward," *Science*, Vol. 275, No. 5306, pp. 1593–1599, March 14, 1997. [421]

60. Leo Breiman, "Bagging Predictors," Department of Statistics Technical Report No. 421, University of California, Berkeley, September 1994. Available online at http://salford-systems.com/doc/BAGGING_PREDICTORS.pdf; and Leo Breiman, "Bagging Predictors," *Machine Learning*, Vol. 24, No. 2, pp. 123–140, 1996. [422]

61. Robert E. Schapire, "The Strength of Weak Learnability," *Machine Learning*, Vol. 5, pp. 197–227, 1990. Available online at http://www.cs.princeton.edu/~schapire/papers/strengthofweak.pdf. [423]

62. Yoav Freund and Robert E. Schapire, "A Decision-Theoretic Generalization of On-Line Learning and an Application to Boosting," *Journal of Computer and System Sciences*, Vol. 55, No. 1, pp. 119–139, 1997. Compressed PostScript version available online at http://www.cs.princeton.edu/~schapire/papers/FreundSc95.ps.Z. [423]

63. See S. B. Kotsiantis and P. E. Pintelas. "Combining Bagging and Boosting," *International Journal of Computational Intelligence*, Vol. 1, No. 4, pp. 324–333, 2004. Available online at http://www.math.upatras.gr/~esdlab/en/members/kotsiantis/ijci paper kotsiantis.pdf. [423]

64. H. Glucksman, "On the Improvement of a Linear Separation by Extending the Adaptive Process with a Stricter Condition," *IEEE Transactions on Electronic Computers*, Vol. EC-15, No. 6, pp. 941–944, 1966. [424]

65. Nello Cristianini and John Shawe-Taylor, *An Introduction to Support Vector Machines: And Other Kernel-based Learning Methods*, Cambridge, UK: Cambridge University Press, 2000. [424]

66. See http://nips.cc/. [425]

67. Donald Michie, D.J. Spiegelhalter, and C.C. Taylor (eds.), *Machine Learning, Neural and Statistical Classification*, Chichester: Ellis Horwood, 1994. The book is now out of print but is available online from http://www.maths.leeds.ac.uk/~charles/statlog/. [425]

68. Stuart Russell and Peter Norvig, *Artificial Intelligence: A Modern Approach*, second edition, pp. 752–754, Upper Saddle River, NJ: Prentice Hall, 2003. **[425]**
69. For additional perspective on comparing different algorithms, see David J. Hand, "Classifier Technology and the Illusion of Progress," *Statistical Science*, Vol. 21, No. 1, pp. 1–15, 2006. Available online at http://arxiv.org/pdf/math.ST/0606441. **[425]**

30

Natural Languages and Natural Scenes

I N SOME OF THE JUST-PRECEDING CHAPTERS, WE HAVE SEEN THE IMPORTANT ROLE
of data and of machine learning techniques for distilling and using these data. If
one single theme has lately begun to unite the several disparate approaches to AI,
ranging from logical representations and reasoning in Cyc to decision and estimation
by neural networks, it is their dependence on massive amounts of data. Moving
beyond toy problems and simple puzzles into real-world problems requires real-
world data. In this chapter, I'll explore how the latest systems for natural language
processing and computer vision exploit data that are representative of the inputs
they must deal with.

30.1 Natural Language Processing

The growing need for systems able to deal with written and spoken languages,
together with new technical advances, large databases, and increased computational
power, has led to improved systems for performing such tasks as summarizing
pieces of text, answering queries, and translating languages. In this section, I'll
describe some of the technical developments in NLP during the past two or three
decades. Impressive as they are though, they have not yet allowed us to realize Terry
Winograd's hope back in 1971 that "We will talk to [computer systems] just as
we talk to a research assistant, librarian, or secretary, and they will carry out our
commands and provide us with the information we ask for." Many people say that
the problem of realizing such systems is "AI complete," in the sense that they must
be *generally* as intelligent as humans, being able to reason and to solve problems as
well as humans do those things. In any case, it is probable that such systems, when
we finally do have them, will employ some or all of the technology I'll be describing
here.

30.1.1 *Grammars and Parsing Algorithms*

Earlier I described some of the basic ideas of linguistic theory. For example, I
mentioned that sentences can be analyzed in terms of their syntactic structure
using context-free grammars (CFGs). I also mentioned more complex grammars
such as definite clause grammars (DCGs), systemic grammars, transition network
grammars, and DIAGRAM. Systems that use grammars for analyzing natural language
sentences must use parsing algorithms to search among candidate "parse trees" to
find one or more that fits an input sentence. For realistic grammars that "accept"

those word strings we think of as legal sentences and reject those strings we take to be nonsentences, it is often the case that there are many possible parses, each conveying a different meaning. Choosing one "best" parse tree from among all of these then depends on semantic and pragmatic analyses, which take into account the context in which the sentence occurs and common-sense world knowledge.

As a humorous example of how one can get into trouble by failing to take into account common-sense knowledge, Daniel Jurafsky and James Martin quote a sentence from the 1930 movie *Animal Crackers*: Groucho Marx says "One morning I shot an elephant in my pajamas. How he got into my pajamas I don't know."[1]

Work on natural language processing continues to explore new and more complex grammars, parsing algorithms, and semantic processing techniques. The newer grammars are able to deal more efficiently with larger subsets of English, and many of them can handle languages other than English. Some examples are lexical functional grammars (LFGs),[2] tree adjoining grammars (TAGs),[3] dependency grammars, head-driven phrase structure grammars (HPSGs),[4] government and binding,[5] and categorical grammars.[6]

Many improvements have been made to parsing algorithms also. When used with realistic grammars, breadth-first search (either with a bottom-up or top-down method) quickly exhausts storage space. Backtracking depth-first search, although more economical of memory, risks having to do much of the search over if the search runs into trouble and must unwind back to earlier parts of a sentence. To avoid having to reparse parts of a sentence after unwinding, parsers have been invented that employ charts and other constructs in which to store, for possible reuse, already computed parses of segments of sentences. Martin Kay developed the first chart parser.[7] Other parsers that use chart-like structures are the Earley parser (invented by Jay Earley)[8] and the Cocke–Younger–Kasami (CYK) algorithm.[9] Modern parsers use one version or another of dynamic programming, a technique I mentioned previously. It permits saving of intermediate results. I list these examples of grammars and parsers, without attempting descriptions (which are quite technical), just to illustrate the breadth and depth of activity in these aspects of NLP.[10]

Natural language processing research and applications have benefitted greatly by having large text files. Such files contain millions of sentences and exist in many languages. They include newspaper articles, literary texts, and other materials. Large files of sentences are called corpora (the plural of corpus, meaning body). One of the NLP Web sites at Stanford, http://nlp.stanford.edu/links/statnlp.html, provides examples. Other corpora can be found at the "Linguistic Data Consortium" Web page at http://www.ldc.upenn.edu/. Sentences from these files can be parsed and annotated by humans, sometimes aided by parsing algorithms, and the parses can be stored along with their associated sentences in structures called "tree banks." Prominent examples are those developed at the University of Pennsylvania, called the "Penn Treebanks."[11] The Penn Treebank Project maintains a Web site at http://www.cis.upenn.edu/~treebank/. Tree banks, with their annotations, can be used to induce more powerful grammars covering the sentences in them. As usual, the larger the tree bank, the better the induced grammar. Statistically based machine learning techniques are used in this process, and that brings me to my next topic.

30.1.2 *Statistical NLP*

A. Context-Free Rules with Probabilities

As I mentioned earlier, a grammar is supposed to be able to distinguish between sentences that are acceptable in a language and those that are not. But as Christopher Manning and Hinrich Schütze point out, "It is just not possible to provide an exact and complete characterization of well-formed utterances that cleanly divides them from all other sequences of words, which are regarded as ill-formed utterances. This is because people are always stretching and bending the 'rules' to meet their communicative needs."[12] This fact was recognized quite early in the study of language. In his 1921 book, the linguist and anthropologist Edward Sapir wrote "Unfortunately, or luckily, no language is tyrannically consistent. All grammars leak."[13] Sapir meant, of course, that any grammar, no matter how complex, will accept some sentences that people find unacceptable and reject some that people find acceptable.

Eugene Charniak, one of the first AI researchers who recognized this difficulty, proposed that syntactic analyses should be qualified by probabilities. Some sentences are "probably" ok, and some are probably not, and there are all gradations in between.[14] An immediate advantage of such an approach is that the probability of a parse can be used to choose among alternative parses for ambiguous sentences. Consider, for example, two alternative ways to read the Groucho-like sentence "John shot elephants in pajamas":

- John (while in pajamas) shot elephants.
- John shot elephants (which were in pajamas).

Each of these interpretations of the sentence has a different parse tree. Is there a way to consider one of them more probable than the other?

In 1969, the automata theorist Taylor L. Booth proposed a variation on context-free grammars that assigned probabilities to the rules used to define a grammar.[15] Such grammars are called "Probabilistic Context-Free Grammars" (PCFGs). I'll use the following very simple (and quite incomplete) grammar just to illustrate the idea:[16]

S → NP VP (1.0)	NP → NP PP (0.4)
PP → P NP (1.0)	NP → *John* (0.1)
VP → VP NP (0.7)	NP → *pajamas* (0.18)
VP → VP PP (0.3)	NP → *shot* (0.04)
P → *in* (1.0)	NP → *elephants* (0.18)
V → *shot* (1.0)	NP → *uniforms* (0.1)

The number in parentheses following a rule represents the probability of that rule. Thus, according to this grammar for example, the probability is 0.18 that a noun phrase in a sentence is the word "elephants." Because a noun phrase has to be *something*, the sum of all of the noun phrase probabilities is 1.0.

B. Probabilities of Parse Trees

Assuming that the probabilities of these rules are independent (a wildly inappropriate assumption for realistic grammars), we can calculate the probability of a parse tree

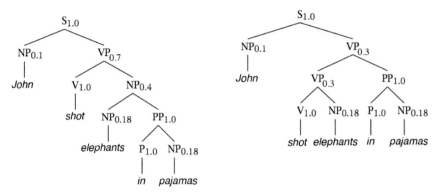

Figure 30.1. Two parse trees for "John shot elephants in pajamas."

by taking the product of the probabilities of all of the rules used in the tree. Two parse trees for this sentence are shown in Fig. 30.1. The one on the right, in which it is John who is in pajamas while shooting, would seem to be the more appropriate one in most settings other than, perhaps, cartoons.

The numbers subscripting each grammar term in the trees are the probabilities of the corresponding rules. The parse tree on the left has probability

$$\text{Prob}_{\text{left}} = 1.0 \times 0.1 \times 0.7 \times 1.0 \times 0.4 \times 0.18 \times 1.0 \times 1.0 \times 0.18 = 0.0009072.$$

The parse tree on the right has probability

$$\text{Prob}_{\text{right}} = 1.0 \times 0.1 \times 0.3 \times 0.7 \times 1.0 \times 0.18 \times 1.0 \times 1.0 \times 0.18 = 0.0006804.$$

The one on the left would therefore be preferred. (Well, I would not want to be talking about actually shooting elephants. I had in mind cartoon elephants that were wearing pajamas.)

Another important aspect of PCFGs is that they can be used to predict the overall probability of a sentence. That is, how likely is it that a sentence like "John shot elephants in pajamas" would occur? We can compute that probability simply by adding the probabilities of all of the possible parses of that sentence. In this case, we just add two probabilities to obtain 0.0015876. The probabilities in this example are contrived for illustrative purposes only and should not be taken seriously. More realistic probability values would be based on a much larger grammar and corpus of sentences, which brings me to my next topic.

C. Learning PCFGs

How does one obtain values for the probabilities of the rules in a PCFG? In particular, how does one obtain values that appropriately model actual sentences? An annotated tree bank provides a way to get values appropriate for the sentences in the tree bank because each of its sentences has an associated parse tree. The parse trees use rules all of the form $l \rightarrow r$, where l is the left-hand side of the rule (such as VP) and r is the right-hand side of the rule (such as VP NP). To obtain a probability value for a rule $l \rightarrow r$, we count how many times that very rule occurs in the tree bank and divide that count by the number of times *l* occurs. The PCFG so obtained can then be used to parse new sentences.

A PCFG can also be generated without having a tree bank if one has an ordinary (nonprobabilistic) context-free parser that can be applied to a corpus of sentences. But unlike a tree bank, it is likely that each sentence in the corpus will have multiple parses, with some having many. When counting the occurrences of rules how can we avoid overweighting the rules in those sentences with lots of parses? Here's a method that seems to work well:

1. Convert the original CGF into a PCGF with equal rule probabilities.
2. Parse the sentences with this PCFG, computing a probability for each ambiguous parse.
3. Count the rules in each parse for each sentence, and weight the count by the probability of that parse.
4. Use these weighted counts to compute new probabilities for the rules and thus a new PCFG.
5. Repeat this process until the rule probabilities cease to change (which will happen eventually).

This procedure is a version of an algorithm often used in machine learning, called the Expectation Maximization (EM) algorithm.

To account for non-context-free aspects of sentence structure and for detailed information about specific words, practical applications typically use PCFGs that have been augmented in various ways. Several parsers for versions of PCFGs have been developed. I can't resist mentioning one based on the A* search algorithm. In presenting it, Dan Klein and Christopher D. Manning wrote[17]

On average-length Penn treebank sentences, our most detailed estimate [for use as the heuristic function] reduces the total number of edges processed [using A* search] to less than 3% of that required by exhaustive parsing, and a simpler estimate, which requires less than a minute of precomputation, reduces the work to less than 5%.

Several other statistically based methods for analyzing sentences have been developed. I'll mention just a few of these.[18] Rens Bod and colleagues at the University of Amsterdam have been developing a technique they call "Data–Oriented Parsing" (DOP), which is based on the idea that "human language perception and production work with representations of *concrete* language experiences, rather than with *abstract* grammatical rules."[19] Statistical methods have also enhanced Lexical Functional Grammars (LFGs), both by using DOP ideas[20] and by the work of Josef van Genabith and his group at Dublin City University on learning LFG grammars from annotated tree-bank data.[21] Finally, Ron Kaplan and his group at a commercial natural language query company, Powerset (now part of Microsoft), are trying to learn how to assign probability orderings to the multiple parse trees of a sentence that are produced by a parser using a handwritten (rather than a learned) grammar.

Other uses of statistics in natural language processing include using data about how frequently certain combinations of words occur in various text sources. Such combinations are called "*n*-grams." For example, a two-word sequence such as "just now" is a 2-gram, and a five-word sequence such as "put it on the shelf" is a 5-gram.

Using the slogan "that there's no data like more data," Google has analyzed a corpus of one-trillion words from public Web pages, for example, to publish "the counts for all 1,176,470,663 five-word sequences that appear at least 40 times."[22]

Summarizing the impact of the use of statistical methods in NLP Manning and Schütze wrote "Indeed, much of the recent enthusiasm for statistical methods in natural language processing derives from people seeing the prospect of statistical methods providing practical solutions to real problems that have eluded solution using traditional NLP methods." They even mention some possible new names for the field, such as "Language Technology" or "Language Engineering" instead of NLP.[23]

30.2 Computer Vision

In this section I'll discuss a few representative samples of recent work in computer vision, much of which builds on the fundamental image-processing techniques I described in previous chapters. In fact this debt to previous work is acknowledged by most researchers, as in the following excerpt from a recent paper:[24]

It is interesting to note that a lot of what are considered modern ideas in computer vision – region and boundary descriptors, superpixels, combining bottom–up and top–down processing, Bayesian formulation, feature selection, etc. – were well-known three decades ago!... However, it seems that the early pioneers were simply ahead of their time. They had no choice but to rely on heuristics because they lacked the large amounts of data and the computational resources to learn the relationships governing the structure of our visual world. The advancement of learning methods in the last decade brings renewed hope for a complete scene understanding solution.

Now we have the needed data and computational resources. Besides these, computer vision has benefitted from contributions from several other fields, including optics, mathematics, computer graphics, electrical engineering, physics, neuroscience, and statistics. All of these disciplines continue to provide ideas and techniques, but one in particular has begun to dominate, namely, machine learning.

Some people distinguish between "computer vision" and "machine vision," – confining computer vision mainly to robotics and using machine vision to include that application and many others as well. Because we'll ultimately want robots to be involved in most of these applications, I don't think the distinction is very useful, so I'll continue to refer to the whole field as computer vision.

Another distinction is between what is called "scene analysis vision" on the one hand and "purposive (or active) vision" on the other. The scene analysis approach guided much vision research since its earliest days. This view held that the goal of computer vision was to transform a two-dimensional image into a description of a three-dimensional scene. For example, the vision system for the MIT "Copy Demo" constructed a three-dimensional model of an arrangement of toy blocks. (See Fig. 10.1.) In contrast, some researchers pointed out that the purpose of vision was to provide just and only that specific information needed for motor control. We can see that approach followed in the various vision routines used by Shakey, for example.

Rather than construct a complete model of its visual world, Shakey used vision to give it information needed to guide motor actions and to make plans. This kind of "purposive vision" is usually less demanding of computational resources than a complete scene analysis would be.

People who study the visual processes of animals (including humans) have also argued about these two approaches. David Marr, who was interested in modeling human visual processes, advocated the scene analysis approach. However, the people who analyzed visual perception in the frog (see p. 126), noted that its visual system was organized more purposively, to catch insects for example. The computational neurobiologist Terrence Sejnowski (the same Sejnowski who worked on NETtalk) and colleagues describe biological and psychological evidence that human vision is purposive, not scene reconstructive, the latter of which they call "pure vision." They wrote[25]

What is vision for? Is a perfect internal recreation of the three-dimensional world really necessary? Biological and computational answers to these questions lead to a conception of vision quite different from pure vision. Interactive vision, as outlined [in this paper], includes vision with other sensory systems as partners in helping to guide actions.

As I look at many of the computer vision systems produced in the past twenty years or so, I see both kinds. There are systems that are proficient at guiding autonomous vehicles along roads – paying attention only to the road and to other vehicles on the road without analyzing or even being aware of houses along the way that, although they might be in the scene, are irrelevant to the driving task. There are also systems that analyze photographs to construct three-dimensional models of the buildings and other objects in them. In addition, there are systems that have aspects of both approaches, as I will discuss in the next section.

30.2.1 *Recovering Surface and Depth Information*

Derek Hoiem, Alexei Efros, and Martial Hebert at the Robotics Institute of Carnegie Mellon University developed a program that was able to classify segments of a single image as belonging to surfaces of various types and orientations.[26] Although these classifications do not constitute a three-dimensional model of the scene that gave rise to the image, they do give information about important physical properties of the scene, somewhat like David Marr's $2\frac{1}{2}$-D sketch does. Such information that might be useful for a robot having to navigate and recognize objects in the scene, for example.

Their work used images of outdoor subjects such as "forests, cities, roads, beaches, lakes, etc." taken under a variety of conditions "(snowy, sunny, cloudy, twilight)." Two examples are shown in Fig. 30.2.

Their program classified regions of an image into one of three major surface categories: "support," "vertical," or "sky." As the authors define these categories, "Support surfaces are roughly parallel to the ground and could potentially support a solid object. Examples include road surfaces, lawns, dirt paths, lakes, and table tops. Vertical surfaces are solid surfaces that are too steep to support an object, such as walls, cliffs, the curb sides, people, trees, or cows. The sky is simply the image

Figure 30.2. Typical outdoor images. (Images courtesy of Derek Hoiem.)

region corresponding to the open air and clouds." To justify this classification, the authors point out that in 300 images that they collected using Google image search, "over 97% of the pixels belong to horizontal (support), nearly vertical surfaces, or the sky" (as established by human inspection of the images).

The program further classified each vertical surface into one of the following subclasses: "planar surfaces facing to the 'left,' 'center,' or 'right' of the viewer, and nonplanar surfaces that are either 'porous' or 'solid.' Planar surfaces include building walls, cliff faces, and other vertical surfaces that are roughly planar. Porous surfaces are those which do not have a solid continuous surface. Tree leaves, shrubs, telephone wires, and chain link fences are all examples of porous surfaces. Solid surfaces are nonplanar vertical surfaces that do have a solid continuous surface, including automobiles, people, beach balls, and tree trunks."

Their program learned to make these classifications (and subclassifications) by using a training set of the 300 Google images. Groups of adjacent pixels in each of the training images in this set were assembled into nearly uniform regions, called "superpixels," on the basis of similarity of color and intensity. Then each superpixel was (tediously!) manually assigned a classification and subclassification. Superpixels were further grouped into larger regions called segments, which inherited classifications from their constituent superpixels. From here on the mathematics gets more complex than I want to describe here (or than you would care to read), but in essence the learning process constructed a decision tree that could adequately match the hand-classified regions in the training set images. The trained decision tree could then be used to classify the regions of any images. The nodes of the decision tree were based on pixel and segment features involving location, color, texture, and perspective, all of which could be computed using previously invented techniques (some of which I have described in previous chapters).

Although not entirely representative of overall results, the images in Fig. 30.3 give an indication of how well their program performed. In the images in Fig. 30.3, green indicates a support surface, red indicates a vertical surface, and blue indicates sky. The subclasses for vertical surfaces are indicated by left arrows for left-facing planes, up arrows for center-facing planes, and right arrows for right-facing planes, "O" for porous surfaces, and "X" for solid surfaces.

Stanford professor Andrew Ng and his students have gone farther, extracting actual depth information and scene-structure information from monocular images.

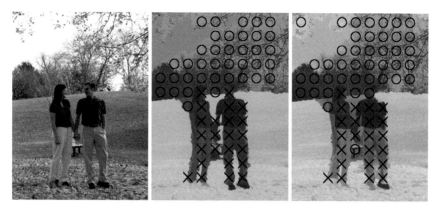

Figure 30.3. Original image (left), hand-labeled image (center), and system's output (right). (Images courtesy of Derek Hoiem.)

"Ground truth" depth information for a set of training images is first gathered by a three-dimensional laser scanner. A learning algorithm attempts to match its estimates of depth against ground-truth depth using several image features.[27] These include texture variations, texture gradients, color, and occlusion information. Because depth information about close objects is captured at larger scales than that of distant objects, features are extracted at multiple image scales. The learning process trains a hierarchical, multiscale Markov random field network to represent the relationships between the depth of an image patch and the depths of neighboring patches. Figure 30.4 is a condensed illustration of two of the three levels of such a network. (Again, the details of how the system learns from examples are more complex than I can explain here.)[28]

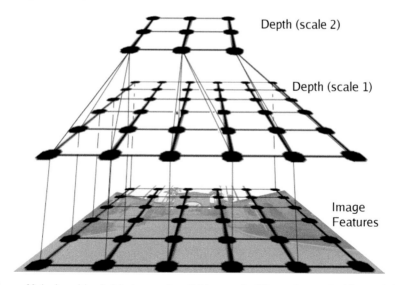

Figure 30.4. A multiscale Markov random field network. (Illustration used with permission of Andrew Ng.)

Figure 30.5. Typical images (left) and predicted depth maps (right). (Photographs courtesy of Andrew Ng and Ashutosh Saxena.)

Figure 30.5 shows some images downloaded from the Internet together with associated "depth maps" (with different depths indicated by different colors) predicted by their system.

Ashutosh Saxena and Andrew Ng continue to perfect these techniques. They have a Web site, http://make3d.stanford.edu/, at which you can use YouTube or other software to "fly around" three-dimensional models constructed by their system from various monocular images. (These fly-around demonstrations are an impressive illustration of just how far computer vision, based on large numbers of images and statistical methods, has progressed.) Also from this Web site, you can upload your own photographs to have them converted to three-dimensional versions.[29]

30.2.2 *Tracking Moving Objects*

If vision systems are to work on natural scenes in the real world, one of the things they will have to deal with is moving objects. Several researchers have worked on the problem of tracking objects visually, with some of the earliest work dating back to the late 1970s. One example, which I'll use to explain some of the methods

Figure 30.6. Michael Isard (left) and Andrew Blake (right). (Photographs courtesy of Michael Isard and of Andrew Blake.)

employed, is the work of Michael Isard (1971– ; Fig. 30.6) and Andrew Blake (1956– : Fig. 30.6) at the University of Oxford. They have developed an algorithm, called CONDENSATION (for Conditional Density Propagation), for tracking moving objects.[30] The algorithm is able "to track outlines and features of foreground objects, modeled as curves, as they move in *substantial* clutter, and to do it at, or close to, video frame-rate."

Here, in brief overview, is how their system works on one of their several examples – a movie of a leaf on a bush blowing in the wind against a background of similar leaves. It starts with a beginning frame of the movie in which the particular leaf of interest is outlined by a hand-drawn curve as in the left-hand part of Fig. 30.7. Tracking the outline of the leaf as it moves requires knowledge about the leaf's dynamics. That is, given its position and shape in the image at one instant of time, what position and shape is it likely to have at the next instant of time? And at subsequent instants of time? We can't know for sure, but we can use dynamic Bayesian networks (DBNs), suitably modified to use continuous probability distributions instead of probability distributions over discrete variables, to make estimates. The required probabilities are estimated by a learning process, and these are gradually refined by observing the leaf as it actually moves. However, to observe it, we have to track it, and that requires knowing the probabilities – a "chicken-and-egg" problem that Isard and Blake have been able to work through.

Figure 30.7. Tracking a leaf in the wind. (From the initial still frame and from a frame one-half second later of the movie at http://homepages.inf.ed.ac.uk/rbf/CVonline/LOCAL_COPIES/ISARD1/images/leafmv.mpg. Used with permission of Michael Isard and Andrew Blake.)

 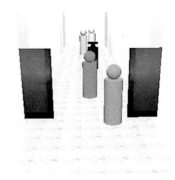

Figure 30.8. Tracking multiple people. (From the movie. Used with Permission of Dieter Fox.)

As time marches on, the probabilities about the leaf's position and shape in the image diffuse, causing more and more uncertainty about the outline of the leaf. But we do make observations – taking in a new image at every time instant. These observations, being imprecise themselves, also provide probabilities (using Bayes's rule) about the the leaf's position and shape. These latter probabilities help to sharpen the diffusing ones about the leaf's dynamics – to the point that rather precise estimates can be made. For example, at twenty-five time steps later (0.5 s), the system guesses at the outline shown in the right-hand side of Fig. 30.7. (You can see the movie with the leaf being tracked at http://homepages.inf.ed.ac.uk/rbf/ CVonline/LOCAL_COPIES/ISARD1/images/leafmv.mpg.)

Isard and Blake use an array of complex technology to achieve all of this. One problem is how to represent probability functions for the leaf's dynamics and how to move this representation forward from one time step to another. They have adopted a technique called "particle filtering," which represents the probability of an outlining curve by a large set of weighted samples, called particles, of outlines. At each time step the group of particles is brought forward to the next time step and the whole lot is rerepresented as a probability function. Particle filtering is used exensively for image processing and other perception problems.

I have used the Isard–Blake work to illustrate object tracking, but there are many other projects. Dieter Fox and colleagues, at the University of Washington Robotics and State Estimation Lab, have used particle filtering in many applications. At one of their Web sites, http://www.cs.washington.edu/ai/Mobile_Robotics/mcl/, you can see "particle filters in action." A particularly impressive demonstration available there is a movie of simultaneous tracking of a changing number of people using a *moving* robot's laser range finders.[31] A typical screen shot is shown in Fig. 30.8. The image on the left (not used by the robot; it's just for us) shows the actual locations of the people and the robot. The image on the right shows the computed locations of the people and the robot, represented by graphical objects. This application uses an extension to particle filtering, which the authors call "sample-based joint probabilistic data association filters."[32]

A group headed by Ernst D. Dickmanns (1936–) at the Institut für Systemdynamik und Flugmechanik at the Universität der Bundeswehr in Munich, Germany, has been working on vision and control systems for driverless automobiles since the late 1970s. Their dynamic vision systems are able to detect and track adjacent vehicles using spatio-temporal models of object motion, what they call a "4-D" approach.[33] They are perhaps the first group to use Kalman filtering for visual object tracking. In fact, their work has been called "the first significant real world application of computer vision."[34]

Installed in various Mercedes-Benz vehicles, their vision and control systems have been able to drive autonomously for long distances, changing lanes and overtaking slower vehicles. In 1995, their VaMP vehicle (a Mercedes-Benz 500 SEL) drove the 1,758-km trip from Munich to Odense, Denmark, and back at speeds exceeding 175 km/hour. About 95% of the trip was driven fully autonomously with a total of 400 lane-change maneuvers. Some additional details about their autonomous vehicle and vision projects can be found in Dickmann's book about "Dynamic Vision."[35]

Space does not permit describing several other object-tracking projects, but I'll mention just two more. Jitendra Malik heads a vision group at the University of California, Berkeley, where object-tracking research (along with other vision work) has been done.[36] In the Vision Group at the University of Leeds in the United Kingdom work has been done on tracking soccer players and automobiles, for example.[37] Other work at Leeds has as its goal improving object-tracking accuracy by reasoning about "fundamental constraints on the spatio-temporal continuity of objects."[38]

30.2.3 *Hierarchical Models*

I believe that one of the potentially most promising developments in computer vision (and maybe even for all of AI) involves hierarchical models. There are different versions of these models, and different ways to construct them, but if we stand far enough back from the details, they have similar structures and features. First, the raw pixels are aggregated spatially (and in some systems temporally) to form higher level groupings. These groupings might constitute small edges, or corners, or other primitive components appropriate for the kinds of images being processed. At the next level of the hierarchy, the first-level groupings are aggregated again into somewhat higher level components, and so on until, say, recognizable objects in the image are represented at the highest level.

Many of the ideas used in these systems harken back to certain features of earlier systems (such as Pandemonium, the Neocognitron,[39] Blackboard architectures, speech recognition systems, and PDP recurrent networks), but many of the newer systems combine and extend these features in ways that no individual earlier system did. Specifically, let me mention the following:

1. The aggregations at the various levels are *learned* using massive data sets – not predesigned by hand. And, in some systems, the learning is "unsupervised" – relying on the continuity of an object's appearance within a temporal stream of images to provide information about object identities.
2. Occurrences of aggregations at each level are qualified by probabilities with probabilistic graphical models (such as Markov random fields) providing the main representational and computational mechanisms.

Figure 30.9. Tai Sing Lee (top left), David Mumford (top right), and their layers of visual processing (bottom). (Photographs courtesy of Tai Sing Lee and of David Mumford. Diagram adapted from Tai Sing Lee and David Mumford, "Hierarchical Inference in the Visual Cortex," *Journal of the Optical Society of America*, A, Vol. 20, No. 7, July 2003.)

3. The probabilities of aggregations at one level can affect not only the probabilities of aggregations at higher levels but also the probabilities of aggregations at the same and at lower levels. That is, unlike as in Pandemonium and in feed-forward neural networks, in these newer systems there are "backward" connections from higher levels to lower levels. These backward connections allow the systems to make predictions about what was probably in the scene even though it might have been obscured or absent in the image.

Several researchers have been involved in the development of hierarchical models. Some are motivated mainly by attempts to model the storage and inference mechanisms in the visual cortex of humans and primates. Even so, their models are nonetheless quite interesting to AI people, combining, as they do, insights and evidence from neuroscience with quite elaborate computational apparatus – including hierarchical graphical models and statistical sampling techniques. Others use hierarchical models and advanced computational methods, without particular concern for their biological plausibility, to build more powerful computer vision systems.

To begin, I'll describe the proposal by Tai Sing Lee (1961–) and David Mumford (1937–) that the hierarchy of processing layers of the visual cortex can be modeled as in Fig. 30.9.[40]

In the Lee–Mumford model (based partly on the pattern theory work by Ulf Grenander[41]), "bottom-up" visual observations coming in from the left are integrated with "top-down" hypotheses formed at the right. In the diagram, think of x_0 as standing for a representation of the image as an array of pixels. Think of x_1 as a more abstract representation of the image, say in terms of features such as short line segments. As we move one step to the right, the computations produce a yet more abstract representation, x_2, which then serves as a hypothesis about x_1. The formulas in the boxes (which I won't attempt to explain here), and the arrows connecting them, are meant to show that at every level the probability of a representation, x_i, is dependent both on x_{i-1} (regarded as input) and on x_{i+1} (regarded as a hypothesis about x_i).

Lee and Mumford describe this feed-forward–feedback process as follows:

The feedforward input drives the generation of the hypotheses, and the feedback from higher inference areas provides the priors to shape the inference at the earlier levels. Neither the feedforward messages nor the feedback messages are static: As the interpretation of an image proceeds, new high-level interpretations emerge that feed back new priors, and as low-level interpretations are refined, the feedforward message is modified. Such hierarchical Bayesian inference can proceed concurrently across multiple areas . . . [with] successive cortical areas in the visual hierarchy [constraining] one another's inference in small loops rapidly and continuously as the interpretation evolved. One might hope that such a system, as a whole, would converge rapidly to a consistent interpretation of the visual scene incorporating all low-level and high-level sources of information; but there are problems . . .

One of the "problems" is that because none of the levels can be completely sure of its interpretation there might be multiple high-probability global interpretations. Lee and Mumford suggest a remedy based on other ongoing AI work, namely, "not to jump to a conclusion" at any level but to allow several high-probability interpretations to "stay alive" until one overall interpretation for the whole chain emerges as the most probable. (You might recall that two of Barrow and Tenenbaum's systems, namely, MSYS and the one that used intrinsic images, attempted to do just that back in the 1970s.) To implement their idea, Lee and Mumford suggest using particle filtering, which, as I have already mentioned, uses a weighted set of samples to represent the probability distribution over interpretations at each level. Using these distributions, which are to be learned from experience, and the formulas linking the levels, the system can settle on a most probable interpretation at each level.

Although Lee and Mumford suggest implementational ideas for their probability calculations, such as the use of Markov random fields, they did not implement their model. As they explain,

We have not offered a simulation to accompany our proposal, partly because many details remain to be worked out and partly because the choice of model is still quite unconstrained and any specific simulation provides only weak support for a high-level hypothesis like ours.

They do, however, cite neurophysiological and psychophysical evidence support- ing their model. They use the illustration in Fig. 30.10 to help explain how models like theirs might work to improve processing of visual images. The brightly illumi- nated part of the image suggests that the image might be of a face. That hypothesis, in turn, makes lower level processing of the image more sensitive to the occurrence of a faint edge of the face – allowing its detection. (Humans might say, "Oh yes, now I see that edge.")

Geoffrey E. Hinton (1947–), Simon Osindero (1977–), and Yee-Whye Teh (1977–) devised (rather complex) unsupervised learning strategies for another

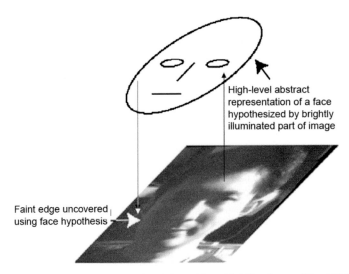

Figure 30.10. Seeing a face more clearly. (Adapted from Tai Sing Lee and David Mumford, "Hierarchical Inference in the Visual Cortex," *Journal of the Optical Society of America*, A, Vol. 20, No. 7, July 2003.)

hierarchical model called a "deep belief network."[42] They conducted experiments with the version shown in Fig. 30.11. The overall structure is a layered neural network, with the top level consisting of 2,000 units each with bidirectional connections to the units in the level below. Training of the network proceeds from the bottom in steps, level by level. As each level is trained, its weights are "frozen," and its results are used as inputs for training the next higher level, and so on. This so-called greedy method of training results in a good hierarchical model of the distribution of the images seen.

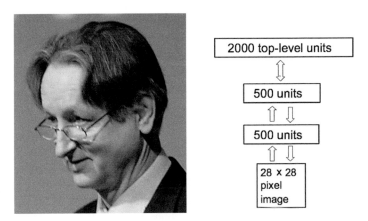

Figure 30.11. Geoffrey Hinton (left) and the deep belief network (right). (Photograph from http://www.scholarpedia.org/article/Image:Geoffnew3.jpg. Network diagram and photograph used with permission of Geoffrey Hinton.)

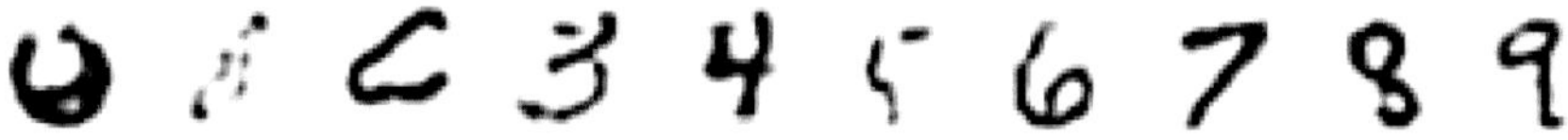

Figure 30.12. Some images generated by the trained network. (Used with permission of Geoffrey Hinton.)

The authors also describe experiments in which ten decision units are added to the top of the previously trained hierarchical network. The decision units are then trained to discriminate among handwritten digits, each presented as a 28×28 pixel image. A large, standard database of digits was used for training and another large one for testing. Results surpassed those of more conventional techniques. To see what the top level of the trained network "has in mind," the downward-directed arrows are used to generate images at the bottom level based on label encodings entered at the top level. Some examples of these generated images are shown in Fig. 30.12.

Jeff Hawkins (1957–), the designer of the original Palm Pilot, has suggested that the neocortex is a hierarchical temporal memory whose layers (from bottom to top) store increasingly abstract representations of sensory input sequences and whose function (from top to bottom) is to make increasingly detailed predictions of future experience.[43] He proposes that the visual cortex learns in unsupervised fashion by being subjected to sequences of images in time. Because we see images as they occur continuously in time, there are bound to be stretches in which each image is of the same object moving across our visual field – albeit appearing at different translations, scales, and orientations. This sameness provides an implicit labeling that is exploited in learning representations at all levels of the hierarchy. Furthermore, Hawkins claims, the hierarchical memory and its learning procedures are used not only for visual input but for other sensory modalities as well. At the highest levels of the hierarchy these separate modalities combine to give an integrated model of our sensory world based on vision, touch, and hearing – a model we use to make predictions about what might be happening next.

Based on these ideas, he and Dileep George (1977–), a Stanford Ph.D. student, developed a network model they call a "Hierarchical Temporal Memory" (HTM)." In his dissertation,[44] George implemented a version of this model illustrated in Fig. 30.13. The bottom level is a 32×32 array of pixels on which a sequence of images is presented. Level 1 consists of an 8×8 array of network nodes, with each node receiving inputs from a 4×4 patch of input image pixels. For example, node "a" receives inputs from its "receptive field," namely, the pixel patch marked "A," and node "b" receives inputs from the pixel patch marked "B." Level 2 is a 4×4 array of nodes, with each node receiving inputs from a 2×2 set of level 1 nodes. This sort of set up continues up to the single node at level 3. That node is meant to recognize the class labels or categories of input images.

The nodes in each layer are trained to recognize commonly occurring sequences in its receptive field in the layer below. For example, the level 1 node marked "a" in Fig. 30.13 is trained to represent the probabilities of frequently occurring sequences of pixel groups in its receptive field, "A." One such high-probability sequence, for example, might be small corners moving to the right. The nodes in level 2 are,

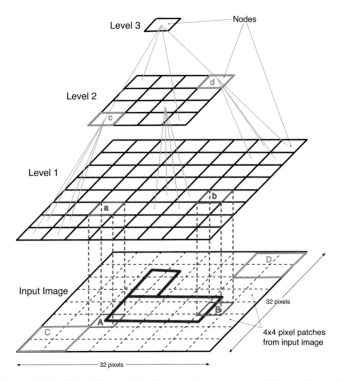

Figure 30.13. The HTM model. (Used with permission of Dileep George.)

in turn, trained to represent the probabilities of frequently occurring sequences of the high-probability sequences in their receptive fields in level 1, and so on. Training involves presenting movies as input images and proceeds level by level up the hierarchy. After training, the probabilities of the sequences represented at each level are conditioned by feedback from above. For example, if a movie is presented in which a small corner is moving from left to right in the pixel patch marked "A," and if such a small corner moved in this way frequently during training, then node "a" in level 1 would predict that it will continue its motion.

As we proceed up the hierarchy of levels, each node receives inputs, albeit indirectly, from larger and larger segments of the image. Finally, the node at the top (level 3 in the diagram) represents a probability distribution over the categories of images that the network has seen. When the network is operating in "recognition mode" (after training), the top node identifies the most probable category of the image on the retina. The network was able to learn to recognize a variety of simple images used by George in his dissertation work. George is continuing his work at Numenta, a company founded by Hawkins for the purpose of developing these kinds of networks.

Although the models described so far have been developed for perception tasks, they could, with some elaboration, serve as foundations for general architectural schemes for intelligent agents. (See the next chapter.) To do so, the elaborations would have to include, among other things, provisions for them to plan and execute actions guided by their existing provisions for perception. Of course, if these models are at all relevant to how the neocortex might work (as their proponents claim they are), then they would need to be able to do more of what the neocortex does, including planning and executing actions. In any case, the cortical models research provides an avenue for collaboration between AI researchers and neuroscientists. As Thomas Dean, who has built probabilistic models of the neocortex, points out, "The availability of cortex-scale models will facilitate not only our understanding of the brain but enable researchers to combine lessons learned from biology with state-of-the-art machine-learning techniques to design hybrid systems that combine the best of biological and traditional computing approaches."[45]

Space does not permit me to describe the work of several other prominent vision researchers who have developed hierarchical models, but I'll briefly mention just a few more; the interested reader can look at their Web sites.

Tomaso Poggio and colleagues at the McGovern Institute for Brain Research at MIT apply mathematical and statistical learning mechanisms to help model how the brain learns to recognize visual objects.[46] One of their application areas has been face recognition.[47]

Yann LeCun at the Computational and Biological Learning Laboratory at the Courant Institute of Mathematical Sciences, New York University, studies what he calls "deep architectures," namely, ones "composed of multiple layers of train-able nonlinear modules." One emphasis of his group is on "energy-based models" (EBMs), which are graphical models in which a concept related to physical energy is associated with the variables (instead of the usual probabilities).[48]

30.2.4 *Image Grammars*

Because of the successful use of grammars and syntactic analyses in natural language processing, it is not surprising that there would be attempts to use similar ideas for processing pictures and images. In fact, Russell Kirsch is quoted in an interview as saying "by 1957 I was intrigued by what the linguists were able to do with grammar on computers. . . . So I asked what seemed to me to be sort of an obvious question: Could you do the same thing with pictures?"[49] Kirsch and his wife, Joan, did go on to develop a grammar for analyzing (and producing) pictures.[50] According to the interview just mentioned they used their grammar in a computer program that could "create lines and patterns in the style of [the artist Richard Diebenkorn]. When finished, the Kirsches showed their generated image to the artist himself, who agreed it looked strikingly similar to something he would be likely to paint. In fact, the computer simulation was almost identical to one that Diebenkorn had already painted."

Other work on "picture grammars" has been done by Professor Azriel Rosenfeld and his group at the University of Maryland."[51]

Song-Chun Zhu (1969–), who directs the UCLA Center for Image and Vision Science, has applied a variety of statistical and physics-based techniques to vision problems. He and colleagues have developed "stochastic grammars of images," which

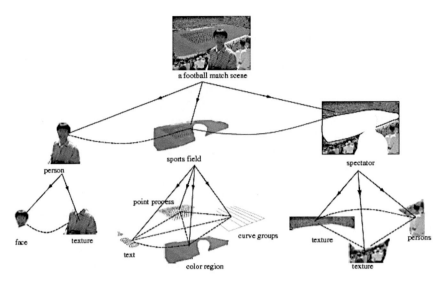

Figure 30.14. Parsing an image. (From Song-Chun Zhu and David Mumford, "A Stochastic Grammar of Images," *Foundations and Trends in Computer Graphics and Vision*, Vol. 2, No. 4, pp. 259–362, 2006.)

can be used to decompose images into their component parts.[52] (The decomposition method realizes some of the ideas described in Section 30.2.3 in the work by Lee and Mumford.) Figure 30.14 shows an example of decomposing an image, represented as a parse tree.

Work on computer vision has made amazing progress in the past several years and is an important part of many applications, including[53] detecting events (such as traffic violations), medical imaging, tracking objects (such as faces, pedestrians, and vehicles), visual prostheses, finding objects in photographs, inventory control in warehouses, robot vehicle navigation and mapping, character and handwriting recognition, danger warning systems, process control, circuit board inspection, grading fruits and vegetables, topographic mapping, forest surveys, recognizing and identifying faces in a crowd, Internet image search, image compression, and agricultural crop inspection.

Readers who would like to learn more will find a wealth of material in textbooks, in computer vision publications, and on the Internet. A recommended text is *Computer Vision – A Modern Approach.*[54] A recommended Web site is the "On–Line Compendium of Computer Vision" maintained by Robert B. Fisher at the University of Edinburgh at http://homepages.inf.ed.ac.uk/rbf/CVonline/. It is full of links to interesting material.

After seeing all of the new AI technical apparatus described in this part of my history of the field, you might be wondering how it can all be put together to control agents that can reason, plan, perceive, act, and communicate in an intelligent manner. Researchers have come up with several ways to integrate component technologies in what they call "architectures." I'll be describing some of them in the next chapter.

Notes

1. Quoted in Daniel Jurafsky and James H. Martin, *Speech and Language Processing: An Introduction to Natural Language Processing, Computational Linguistics, and Speech Recognition*, second edition, p. 432, Upper Saddle River, NJ: Pearson Prentice Hall, 2008. [432]

2. Ronald M. Kaplan and Joan Bresnan, "Lexical-Functional Grammar: A Formal System for Grammatical Representation," in Joan Bresnan (ed.), *The Mental Representation of Grammatical Relations*, pp. 173–281, Cambridge, MA: MIT Press, 1982. [432]

3. Aravind K. Joshi, L. S. Levy, and M. Takahashi, "Tree Adjunct Grammars," *Journal Computer Systems Science*, Vol. 10, No. 1, 1975. [432]

4. Carl Pollard and Ivan A. Sag, *Head-Driven Phrase Structure Grammar*, Chicago: University of Chicago Press, 1994. [432]

5. Noam Chomsky, "Some Concepts and Consequences of the Theory of Government and Binding," *Linguistic Inquiry Monograph 6*, Cambridge, MA: MIT Press, 1982. [432]

6. Mark Steedman, "Categorial Grammar (Tutorial Overview)," *Lingua*, Vol. 90, pp. 221–258, 1993. [432]

7. See Martin Kay, "The MIND System," in Randall Rustin (ed.), *Natural Language Processing*, pp. 155–188, New York: Algorithmics Press, 1973. [432]

8. Jay Earley, "An Efficient Context-Free Parsing Algorithm," *Communications of the Association for Computing Machinery*, Vol. 13, No. 2, pp. 94–102, 1970. [432]

9. See John Cocke and Jacob T. Schwartz, "Programming Languages and Their Compilers: Preliminary Notes," Technical Report, Courant Institute of Mathematical Sciences, New York University, 1970; Tadao Kasami, "An Efficient Recognition and Syntax-Analysis Algorithm for Context-Free Languages," Scientific Report AFCRL-65-758, Air Force Cambridge Research Lab, Bedford, MA, 1965; and Daniel H. Younger, "Recognition and Parsing of Context-Free Languages in Time n^3," *Information and Control*, Vol. 10, No. 2, pp. 189–208, 1967. [432]

10. The reader wanting to dig deeper can consult a textbook on NLP such as Daniel Jurafsky and James H. Martin, *op. cit.* [432]

11. Mitchell P. Marcus, Beatrice Santorini, and Mary Ann Marcinkiewicz, "Building a Large Annotated Corpus of English: The Penn Treebank," *Computational Linguistics*, Vol. 19, pp. 313–330, 1993. Compressed PostScript file available online at ftp://ftp.cis.upenn.edu/pub/treebank/doc/cl93.ps.gz. [432]

12. Christopher D. Manning and Hinrich Schütze, *Foundations of Statistical Natural Language Processing*, Cambridge, MA: MIT Press, 1999. [433]

13. Edward Sapir, *Language: An Introduction to the Study of Speech*, Chapter II, The Elements of Speech, New York: Harcourt Brace, 1921. [433]

14. Eugene Charniak, *Statistical Language Learning*, Cambridge, MA: MIT Press, 1993. [433]

15. Taylor L. Booth, "Probabilistic Representation of Formal Languages," *Tenth Annual IEEE Symposium on Switching and Automata Theory*, pp 74–81, 1969. [433]

16. The grammar is an adaptation of one from Chapter 11 of the Manning and Schütze book with accompanying slides available online at nlp.stanford.edu/fsnlp/pcfg/fsnlp-pcfg-slides.pdf. As Manning and Schütze point out, the NP rules are a bit unusual because the grammar is in what is called "Chomsky Normal Form." [433]

17. Dan Klein and Christopher D. Manning, "A* Parsing: Fast Exact Viterbi Parse Selection," *Proceedings of the 2003 Conference of the North American Chapter of the Association*

for Computational Linguistics on Human Language Technology – Vol. 1, pp. 40–47, Morristown, NJ: Association for Computational Linguistics, 2003. **[435]**

18. Ronald Kaplan mentioned these to me in an e-mail dated June 9, 2008. **[435]**

19. Rens Bod, 1 "Data Oriented Parsing (DOP)," *Proceedings COLING '92*, Nantes, France, 1992. See also the Data-Oriented Web page at staff.science.uva.nl/~rens/dop.html. **[435]**

20. Rens Bod *et al.*, "A Data-Oriented Approach to Lexical-Functional Grammar," in Jan Landsbergen (ed.), *Computational Linguistics in the Netherlands 1996*, Eindhoven, The Netherlands, 1996. **[435]**

21. Anette Frank *et al.*, "From Treebank Resources to LFG F-Structures: Automatic F-Structure Annotation of Treebank Trees and CFGs extracted from Treebanks," in Anne Abeille (ed.), *Treebanks: Building and Using Syntactically Annotated Corpora*, Dordrecht/Boston/London: Kluwer Academic Publishers, 2003. **[435]**

22. See http://googleresearch.blogspot.com/2006/08/all-our-n-gram-are-belong-to-you.html. **[436]**

23. Christopher D. Manning and Hinrich Schütze, *op. cit.*, p. 7. **[436]**

24. Derek Hoiem, Alexei Efros, and Martial Hebert, "Recovering Surface Layout from an Image," *International Journal of Computer Vision*, Vol. 75, No. 1, pp. 151–172, 2007. Available online at http://www.ri.cmu.edu/pubs/pub_5818.html. **[436]**

25. Patricia S. Churchland, V. S. Ramachandran, and Terrence J. Sejnowski, "A Critique of Pure Vision," in Christof Koch and Joel L. Davis (eds.), *Large-Scale Neuronal Theories of the Brain*, pp. 23–60, Cambridge, MA: MIT Press, 1994. Available online at http://papers.cnl.salk.edu/PDFs/ACritiqueofPureVision1994-2933.pdf. **[437]**

26. Derek Hoiem, Alexei Efros, and Martial Hebert, *op. cit.* **[437]**

27. I base my description on one of their many papers: Ashutosh Saxena, Sung H. Chung, and Andrew Y. Ng, "3-D Depth Reconstruction from a Single Still Image," *International Journal of Computer Vision (IJCV)*, August 2007. Available online at http://ai.stanford.edu/~asaxena/learningdepth/saxena_ijcv07_learningdepth.pdf. **[439]**

28. Readers interested in these details can refer to Saxena *et al.*, *ibid.* **[439]**

29. Their computer code and image data are available at http://make3d.stanford.edu/code.html. **[440]**

30. See Michael Isard and Andrew Blake, "CONDENSATION: Conditional Density Propagation for Visual Tracking," *International Journal of Computer Vision*, Vol. 29, pp. 5–28, 1998. Available online at http://www.cs.cmu.edu/~efros/courses/AP06/Papers/isard-blake-98.pdf. Also see a homepage for the algorithm, with pointers to examples and papers, at http://homepages.inf.ed.ac.uk/rbf/CVonline/LOCAL_COPIES/ISARD1/condensation.html. **[441]**

31. See http://www.cs.washington.edu/ai/Mobile_Robotics/mcl/animations/floor3D.avi. **[442]**

32. Dirk Schulz, Wolfram Burgard, Dieter Fox, and Armin B. Cremers, "People Tracking with a Mobile Robot Using Sample-based Joint Probabilistic Data Association Filters," *The International Journal of Robotics Research (IJRR)*, Vol. 22, No. 2, pp. 99–116, 2003. **[442]**

33. See Ernst D. Dickmanns, "Dynamic Vision-Based Intelligence," *AI Magazine*, Vol. 25, No. 2, pp. 10–30, 2004. Available online at http://www.aaai.org/ojs/index.php/aimagazine/article/viewFile/1758/1656. **[443]**

34. The quote is from an e-mail from Sebastian Thrun, June 27, 2008. **[443]**

35. Ernst D. Dickmanns, *Dynamic Vision for Perception and Control of Motion*, Berlin: Springer-Verlag, 2007. **[443]**

36. See http://www.eecs.berkeley.edu/Research/Projects/CS/vision/vision_group.html. [443]

37. See http://www.comp.leeds.ac.uk/vision/behaviour.html. [443]

38. See http://www.comp.leeds.ac.uk/vision/cogvis/continuity.html and Brandon Bennett *et al.*, "Enhanced Tracking and Recognition of Moving Objects by Reasoning about Spatio-Temporal Continuity," *Image and Vision Computing*, Vol. 26, No. 1, pp. 67–81, January 2008. Available online at http://www.comp.leeds.ac.uk/qsr/pub/Bennett08imavis.pdf. [443]

39. K. Fukushima, "Neocognitron: A Self-organizing Neural Network Model for a Mechanism of Pattern Recognition Unaffected by Shift in Position," *Biological Cybernetics*, Vol. 36, No. 4, pp. 93–202, 1980. [443]

40. Tai Sing Lee and David Mumford, "Hierarchical Inference in the Visual Cortex," *Journal of the Optical Society of America A*, Vol. 20, No. 7, July 2003. [444]

41. Ulf Grenander, *General Pattern Theory*, Oxford: Oxford University Press, 1993. [444]

42. Geoffrey E. Hinton, Simon Osindero, and Yee-Whye Teh, "A Fast Learning Algorithm for Deep Belief Nets," *Neural Computation*, Vol. 18, No. 7, pp. 1527–1554, July 2006. Available online at http://www.cs.utoronto.ca/~hinton/absps/ncfast.pdf. [446]

43. Jeff Hawkins with Sandra Blakeslee, *On Intelligence*, New York: Times Books, 2004. [447]

44. Dileep George, "How the Brain Might Work: A Hierarchical and Temporal Model for Learning and Recognition," Ph.D. dissertation, Department of Electrical Engineering, Stanford University, June 2008. Available online at http://www.numenta.com/for-developers/education/DileepThesis.pdf. [447]

45. Dean, formerly a computer science professor at Brown University, now is a scientist at Google. His Web page at Brown is http://www.cs.brown.edu/research/projects/cortex.html. [449]

46. See, for example, Thomas Serre, Aude Oliva, and Tomaso Poggio, "A Feedforward Architecture Accounts for Rapid Categorization," *Proceedings of the National Academy of Sciences (PNAS)*, Vol. 104, No. 15, pp. 6424–6429, 2007. Available online at http://cbcl.mit.edu/projects/cbcl/publications/ps/serre-PNAS-4-07.pdf. [449]

47. See, for example, R. Brunelli, and Tomaso Poggio, "Face Recognition: Features Versus Templates," *IEEE PAMI*, Vol. 15, pp. 1042–1052, 1993. Available online at http://cbcl.mit.edu/people/poggio/journals/brunelli-poggio-IEEE-PAMI-1993.pdf. [449]

48. See Yann LeCun *et al.*, "A Tutorial on Energy-Based Learning," in G. Bakir *et al.* (eds.), *Predicting Structured Data*, Cambridge, MA: MIT Press, 2006. Available online at http://yann.lecun.com/exdb/publis/pdf/lecun-06.pdf. [449]

49. From an interview titled "Russell Kirsch: The Language of Shapes," by Kennedy Smith, *Portland's Daily Journal of Commerce*, July 28, 2006. Available at http://www.mel.nist.gov/msid/shape.pdf. [449]

50. Russell Kirsch and Joan Kirsch, "The Structure of Paintings: Formal Grammar and Design," *Environment and Planning B: Planning and Design*, Vol. 13, pp. 163–176, 1986. Available online at http://www.nist.gov/msidlibrary/doc/kirsch_1986_structure.pdf. [449]

51. Azriel Rosenfeld, "Isotonic Grammars, Parallel Grammars, and Picture Grammars," in Bernard Meltzer and Donald Michie (eds.), *Machine Intelligence 6*, pp. 281–294, Edinburgh: Edinburgh University Press, 1971. [449]

52. Song-Chun Zhu and David Mumford, "A Stochastic Grammar of Images," *Foundations and Trends in Computer Graphics and Vision*, Vol. 2, No. 4, pp. 259–362, 2006. Available online at http://www.stat.ucla.edu/~sczhu/papers/Reprint_Grammar.pdf. [450]

53. David Lowe, a professor in the Computer Science Department of the University of British Columbia, maintains a Web site of companies selling computer vision products: http://www.cs.ubc.ca/spider/lowe/vision.html. **[450]**

54. David Forsythe and Jean Ponce, *Computer Vision – A Modern Approach*, New York: Prentice Hall, 2002. An online version of complete draft chapters is available at http://decsai.ugr.es/mia/complementario/tl/book3chaps.html. **[450]**

31

Intelligent System Architectures

COMPUTER SCIENTISTS HAVE DEVELOPED VARIOUS WAYS TO PUT TOGETHER LARGE programs consisting of many specialist subprograms. The traditional framework that controls the running of most programs involves having a main program that runs through its instructions step by step, retrieving from and storing data in memory, executing various operations on such data, and taking other allowed actions. Some of the instructions in the main program might be to "call" a subprogram, handing control over to it. The subprograms, in turn, can call other subprograms, and so on. After a subprogram finishes doing what it has been called to do, overall control returns to the program that called it, which might then call another subprogram, and so on until control finally returns to the main program. Eventually, the main program can finally quit running, having accomplished all that it was supposed to do, or it can continue running (in principle, forever) because, like a program that makes airline reservations on demand for all who use it, its work is never done. This scheme is the so-called von Neumann architecture.

There are many elaborations on this general idea. "Interrupts" can be included in programs and subprograms. These are ever watchful for special conditions within the computer system itself or in the environment – conditions, which if met, would call for control to be transferred immediately to programs that are able to handle such conditions. Computer operating systems, for example, depend on interrupts to be responsive to user inputs and to other things going on with the computer hardware.

The earliest AI programs ran on computers that used the von Neumann architecture, and thus it was natural for the architecture of the programs (that is, the way they themselves were organized) to adhere to the von Neumann style of the computer's operation. They did so even though, underneath and over time, lower level programs that actually controlled the computer gradually became more complex in ways that the programmers did not need to notice. For example, one innovation important for running programs written in LISP, involved making more efficient use of valuable computer storage resources. So-called garbage collection routines scanned computer memory from time to time to find list structures that would not ever be used again. The memory used to store these structures could then be reclaimed to be used to store new list structures. Program writers could ignore this aspect of lower level computer software architecture and could go on writing their von Neumann–style, sequentially running programs as if they had lots of available memory.

In contrast with the von Neumann idea of executing instructions one after another in sequence, one can conceive of an architecture in which many instructions are executed simultaneously. One can accomplish such "parallelism," either by actually

455

having several hardware processors to which programs are farmed out for execution or by the *simulation* of parallel operation on the simpler von Neumann architecture in which the programs are actually being executed in sequence but the programmers, for all they know, think of them as running simultaneously. For example, in the nonsymbolic world of neural networks, one could imagine groups of neural elements operating simultaneously, even though simulations of these networks have to consider each neural element in turn sequentially. In Pandemonium, the demons (some implemented by neural elements perhaps and some implemented by programs) could conceivably run in parallel, but Selfridge's programs had to simulate such parallelism. Simulation of parallelism can also be accomplished by a "time-sharing" system, in which the user (or several different users) can imagine that their programs are all running simultaneously.

A modern computer "operating system," such as UNIX, Windows, or Mac OS, is a very complex aggregation of programs whose organization (that is, whose architecture) must be very carefully designed. They exploit both actual parallel hardware (as in so-called multicore systems) and time-sharing, so that users can run their e-mail programs, for example, simultaneously (for all they know) with their spreadsheet programs.

In this chapter, I'm going to describe some of the ways researchers have organized their programs to achieve intelligent behavior. Some of them were inspired mainly by engineering and computational considerations and some by cognitive science in its attempt to model psychological data. Some were even influenced by ideas about how various brain regions function. Parallel operation is assumed in many of these architectures, even though it is often of the simulated variety.

31.1 Computational Architectures

31.1.1 *Three-Layer Architectures*

I have already described how the components of one AI system, Shakey, were organized into high-, intermediate-, and low-level groups – a "three-layer" architecture. In Fig. 31.1, I show how Shakey's programs and data can be grouped into levels. Interaction among programs in these levels is illustrated by connecting lines. All of Shakey's perceptual and basic motor programs were embedded in the low-level actions, whereas the intermediate-level actions combined the low-level ones in various ways to perform certain common tasks. The high level was in charge of planning and overall execution of plans.

Three-layered architectures, such as the one used by Shakey, were (and still are) used in several other robot systems. As Erann Gat, a researcher who has used these architectures at the Jet Propulsion Laboratory, points out in his survey paper,[1]

The three-layer architecture arises from the empirical observation that effective algorithms for controlling mobile robots tend to fall into three distinct categories: 1) reactive control algorithms which map sensors directly onto actuators with little or no internal state, 2) algorithms for governing routine sequences of activity which rely extensively on internal state but perform no search, and 3) time-consuming (relative to the rate of change of the environment) search-based algorithms such as planners.

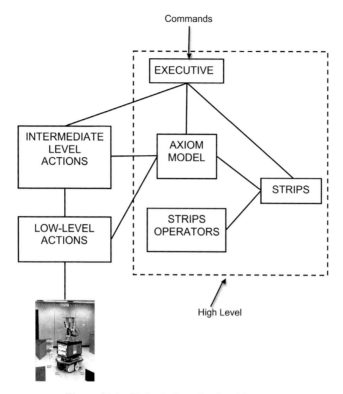

Figure 31.1. Shakey's three-level architecture.

Several of the three-layer architectures described by Gat are based on R. James Firby's three-layer scheme using "Reactive Action Packages" (RAPs).[2] RAPs are quite similar to teleo-reactive programs in that they group together and describe all known ways to carry out a task in different situations.[3]

A modern example of a three-layered architecture is the one used by the German driverless "seeing passenger car," VaMoRs-P, described by Ernst D. Dickmanns and colleagues.[4] One of the architecture diagrams for their system is shown in Fig. 31.2.

31.1.2 *Multilayered Architectures*

As an alternative to the three-layered schemes, all of which involved a planning level, Rodney Brooks and others proposed architectures that controlled robot actions in a way that reacted directly to changes in the environment (as sensed) without the need for planning. Originally called "subsumption architectures," these were later called "behavior-based" because they were composed of specifically programmed robot behaviors.[5] One type of behavior-based architecture is illustrated in Fig. 31.3.

The different behaviors, for example "wander," "avoid obstacles," and "explore," are arranged in levels, each responsive to its own set of environmental stimuli and each able to control the robot depending on the sensed situation. This close coupling

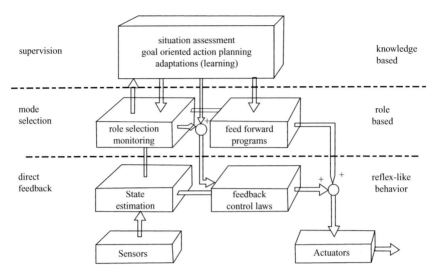

Figure 31.2. A three-layered architecture for a driverless automobile. (Used with permission of Ernst D. Dickmanns.)

and interaction with what is going on in the environment causes what some have called "emergent behavior." As Maja Matarić and François Michaud put it,[6]

> For example, a robot that flocks with other robots may not have a specific *flocking* behavior; instead, its interaction with the environment and other robots may result in flocking, although its only behaviors may be *avoid-collisions, stay-close-to-the-group,* and *keep-going.*

James Albus (1935– ; Fig. 31.4), at the National Institute of Standards and Technology (formerly the National Bureau of Standards), developed what he called a "reference model architecture." The architecture consists of multiple layers of "real-time control systems" (RCSs) developed earlier at NIST as components of a "theory of intelligence."[7] (Albus claims that his RCS model was originally inspired

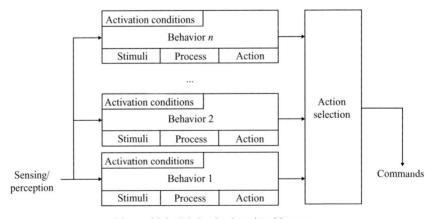

Figure 31.3. A behavior–based architecture.

Figure 31.4. James Albus. (Photograph courtesy of James Albus.)

by a model of the cerebellum that he and David Marr devised.[8]) Each RCS "partitions the control problem into four basic elements: behavior generation (or task decomposition), world modeling, sensory processing, and (in more recent versions) value judgment. It clusters these elements into computational nodes that have responsibility for specific subsystems, and arranges these nodes in hierarchical layers such that each layer has characteristic functionality and timing."[9]

A layered structure of RCSs, called NASREM (for NASA/NBS Standard Reference Model), was proposed (but not implemented as far as I know) as the architecture for a flight tele-robotic servicer on the space station. It is illustrated in Fig. 31.5. In each layer, the RCS units have sensory processing (SP) components, world modeling (WM) components, and task decomposition (TD) components. The lowest layer RCS is essentially a servo controller; as one moves up the hierarchy, the RCSs handle increasingly strategic tasks. Albus and his team at NIST developed a variety of architectures using layered RCSs.

Inspired by Albus's architecture, I developed one I called the "triple-tower architecture" illustrated in Fig. 31.6.[10] The lowest level of the central Model Tower receives inputs through sensors directly from the environment and stores them as primitive perceptual predicates. Programs (represented as rules) in the Perception Tower rerepresent these primitive predicates as more abstract ones – adding them to the Model Tower. This process of creating higher and higher level abstractions proceeds in stair-step fashion up the Perception and Model Towers. In the Action Tower, the lowest level action routines are simple reflexes, evoked by predicates in the Model Tower corresponding to the primitive predicates. More complex actions are evoked by more abstract predicates appropriate for those actions. High-level actions call other actions until the process bottoms out at the primitive actions that actually affect the environment. The actions in the Action Tower were all to be

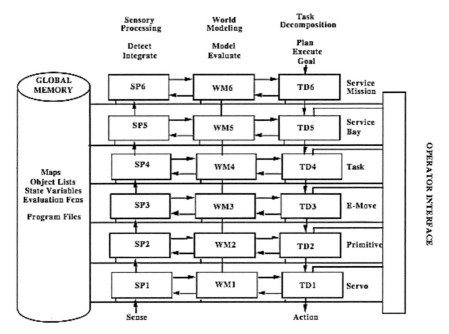

Figure 31.5. The NASREM architecture. [From Figure 2 of James S. Albus, "A Reference Model Architecture for Intelligent Systems Design," in P. J. Antsaklis and K. M. Passino (eds.), *An Introduction to Intelligent and Autonomous Control*, Chapter 2, pp. 27–56, Dordrecht: Kluwer Academic Publishers, 1993.]

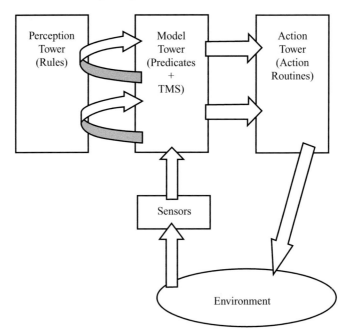

Figure 31.6. Triple-tower architecture.

programmed using my teleo-reactive language (see p. 336). The perceived effects of these actions, in turn, change the values of predicates in the Model Tower, evoking, perhaps, different actions. To model faithfully ongoing environmental changes, a truth-maintenance system (TMS) is included as part of the model tower. The TMS continuously deletes predicates and values from the Model Tower that are no longer derivable (through the perceptual rules) from the then-present components of the Model Tower. The only implementation of this architecture that I know of was to control a block-stacking simulated robot.[11]

I have already described the Blackboard architecture, devised at Carnegie Mellon University for its HEARSAY-II speech understanding system (see p. 218). It was also used in the HASP/SIAP system for ocean surveillance (see p. 253). As I quoted Russell and Norvig earlier, "Blackboard systems are the foundation of modern user interface architectures." They are also used in several computer applications, including, for example, an automatic genome annotation system for predicting gene locations and structures.[12]

To review what I said earlier, a Blackboard is a layered memory structure in which programs, called "knowledge sources" (KSs) can read data from and write data into the various layers. (See Fig. 17.5.) Typically, a KS might look for and then read some data from one or more layers, do some computations using that data, and then write results of those computations into one or more layers. A controller decides which KS, of those which see data upon which they can act, should be active. In some applications, several KSs can be active at once. The result of all of this is a very dynamic process in which the data on the Blackboard are constantly evolving, eventually producing desired information, such as the prediction of a gene location, recognition of a sentence, or interpretation of ocean sonar signals. Because information at one layer of the Blackboard can cause, through the KSs, other information to appear at any other level, the Blackboard architecture foreshadowed the upward and downward propagation of probabilities in the cortical models I described earlier.

31.1.3 *The BDI Architecture*

Michael Georgeff (1946– ; Fig. 31.7) and others have proposed agent architectures based on the philosophical concepts of *beliefs*, *desires*, and *intentions*.[13] These are the so-called BDI architectures. An agent's beliefs represent its knowledge about its environment (including itself and other agents), usually expressed in some kind of logical language, such as the first-order predicate calculus. (The word "belief" is used instead of "knowledge" because an agent's beliefs are subject to change and might not accurately model its environment.) An agent's desires represent the agent's goals – situations that it wants to achieve. An agent's intentions represent those desires that the agent has actually chosen to begin to achieve. That is, it has begun executing a plan to achieve them. BDI architectures, as distinct from behavior-based, reactive ones for example, explicitly represent beliefs, desires, and intentions as actual data structures.

Stated in such general terms, some of the architectural schemes I have already mentioned can be thought of as BDI architectures. Shakey, for example, had beliefs

Figure 31.7. Michael Georgeff. (Photograph courtesy of Michael Georgeff.)

(its world model), at any time it was given a desire (its goal), and its executive system sometimes was in the process of executing a plan (its intention) to achieve that goal. Georgeff and colleagues, however, proposed a specific version of a BDI architecture, which they called a Procedural Reasoning System (PRS).[14] I illustrate it in Fig. 31.8.

Here, in brief, is how the architecture works. (For more detail, see the Georgeff and Ingrand paper.)

- The database consists of the agent's current beliefs about its environment (including itself) and its subject area. Some beliefs are installed initially by the designer and some are obtained by the agent through its perceptual apparatus and by its inference mechanisms. In PRS, beliefs are represented by expressions in first-order predicate calculus.

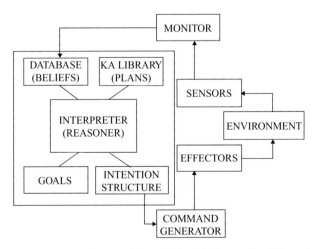

Figure 31.8. PRS, a BDI architecture. (From Michael P. Georgeff and François F. Ingrand, "Decision-Making in an Embedded Reasoning System," *Proceedings of the Eleventh International Joint Conference on Artificial Intelligence*, pp. 972–978, August, 1989.)

- Goals (the agent's desires) are conditions to be achieved and can refer both to the external world and to internal states of the agent.
- The KA library of plans contains what are called "Knowledge Areas" (KAs). Each KA is a specific procedure specifying a plan for accomplishing a task, such as picking up an object. A KA consists of a body, which describes the steps of the procedure, and an invocation condition, which specifies under what situations the KA can be usefully applied. "Primitive" KAs have no bodies but refer to actions directly performable by the system. There are also "metalevel" KAs that can choose among multiple applicable KAs, modify and manipulate intentions, and compute the amount of reasoning to be devoted to a problem, given real-time constraints.
- The intention structure contains tasks that the system has chosen to execute. An intention is expressed as a main KA along with all the sub-KAs that are used to execute the main KA.
- The interpreter runs the system. It maintains the other components of the system and chooses an intention from the intention structure (a KA) for execution. One feature of PRS is that the execution of a KA may be interrupted by certain perceived situations (such as emergencies), giving it the ability to react rapidly to unanticipated changes in the environment.

There have been several applications of the PRS-style architecture, including handling malfunctions of the space shuttle[15] and control of an autonomous robot.[16]

Along with the specific architectural ideas I have just described, there have been many other general suggestions for how to organize intelligent systems, some of which have resulted in running programs (or at least programming languages in which one could write running programs). There have been several proposals for systems capable of what is called "meta-level reasoning," that is, reasoning about how to reason. Of these, I'll mention Brian Smith's 3-LISP system[17] and Richard Weyhrauch's FOL system,[18] both of which were capable of "reflecting" on their own processes. Meta-level reasoning systems have also been proposed by Pat Hayes,[19] Michael Genesereth,[20] and Stuart Russell and Eric Wefald.[21]

Important considerations in the meta-level problem of deciding how best to solve a base-level problem involve estimates of the expected costs and benefits of different solution methods. Eric Horvitz (1958–) pioneered the application of "decision theory to control the solution of difficult problems given limitations and uncertainty in reasoning resources."[22] The use of probabilistic methods and decision theory in meta-level reasoning has since become an important part of AI research. The journal *Artificial Intelligence* devoted a special issue to the topic in 2001.[23]

Marvin Minsky's ideas about a "Society of Mind"[24] are also suggestive about potential designs for intelligent systems even though they were not sufficiently specific for immediate implementation. Such a "society" would be composed of a large number of simple "agents," none of which was powerful or complete enough to be an intelligent entity itself, but a "mind" would presumably emerge from their joint behaviors and interactions. In a similar vein, William Kornfeld and Carl Hewitt suggested that an intelligent system ought to be organized in a manner similar to a "scientific community," exploiting individual and parallel research, publication, and criticism.[25]

31.1.4 *Architectures for Groups of Agents*

It is to be expected that intelligent agents will exist in environments containing other intelligent agents, both humans and machines. Many of these agents will collaborate or compete in the performance of their tasks. Agent-to-agent communication strategies and multiagent architectures have become important AI topics.

I have already paid some attention to interactions between AI systems and humans. These interactions use restricted versions of natural language or some other kind of user interface apparatus. Indeed, the world is full of computers communicating with other computers over networks using specially designed protocols. What I want to talk about here is how AI methods are used to enable more flexible and effective communication among AI agents than would be possible with fixed communication and organizational protocols. AI agents should be able to plan their communications to other agents along with planning their other actions. Moreover, they must be able to interpret communications from other agents along with interpreting other perceptual data. To do so they must take into account the expected actions, knowledge, and goals of other agents.

Some of the early work in what is now called "multiagent systems" (previously, "distributed AI") was done by Victor Lesser (1944–) at the University of Massachusetts and Lee Erman (1944–) at Carnegie Mellon University. They had adapted Blackboard architecture ideas from HEARSAY-II to develop a system they called DISTRIBUTED HEARSAY-II. It was a combination of several distributed Blackboards, each with its own KSs, communicating among themselves to process noisy signals arising from a number of distributed sources.[26] Lesser and Erman envisioned applications in several areas including "sensor networks (composed of low-power radar, acoustic, or optical detectors, seismometers, hydrophones, etc.), network (automotive) traffic control, inventory control (for example, car rentals), power network grids, and tasks using mobile robots." As they pointed out, "an architecture that locates processing capability at the sensor sites and requires only limited communication among the processors is especially advantageous and is, perhaps, the only way to meet the demands of real-time response, limited communication bandwidth, and reliability."

Lesser and colleagues continue work on multiagent systems at the MAS Lab at the University of Massachusetts in Amherst. Building on the DISTRIBUTED HEARSAY-II work, they developed the "Distributed Vehicle Monitoring Testbed" (DVMT).[27] Research with the testbed focused on tracking vehicle motion using a distributed sensor network and was a resource for testing methods of cooperative distributed problem solving. The DVMT work was followed by a number of other multiagent systems projects.[28]

During the late 1970s and into the 1980s several ideas were developed for coordinating the activities of multiple agents. One of these was the Contract Net system developed by Reid Smith.[29] It was based on a protocol and a "negotiation process" for "problem-solving communication and control for nodes in a distributed problem

Figure 31.9. Manuela Veloso (top) and soccer-playing Aibo robots (bottom). (Photographs courtesy of Manuela Veloso.)

solver." An early application involved a distributed sensor network in which the locations and types of sensors were not known until after sensor deployment.[30]

Another important system was the "Multi-Agent Computing Environment" (MACE) developed by Les Gasser and colleagues at the University of Southern California.[31] The paper about MACE describes it as follows:

MACE ... is an instrumented testbed for building a wide range of experimental Distributed Artificial Intelligence systems. ... MACE computational units (called "agents") run in parallel, and communicate via messages. They provide optional facilities for knowledge representation (world knowledge, models of other agents, their goals and plans, their roles and capabilities, etc.) and reasoning capabilities.

An interesting application for multiagent systems research involves cooperative (and competitive) robots. Professor Manuela Veloso (1957– ; Fig. 31.9) at Carnegie Mellon University is one of the major researchers working in this area. She has, in addition to her work on "research on intelligent robots that Cooperate, Observe, Reason, Act, and Learn,"[32] been active in the RoboCup matches of soccer-playing robots. Typically in these matches each robot has its own sensing and processing capabilities. Each needs to take into account the actions of other players and what they might do.

RoboCup is "an international joint project . . . to foster AI and intelligent robotics research by providing a standard problem where [a] wide range of technologies can be integrated and examined."[33] Its ultimate goal is to "develop a team of fully autonomous humanoid robots that [by 2050] can win against the human world champion team in soccer." Some of you will be around then to see.

When the environment includes other agents with whom an agent must cooperate or compete, it is important for that agent to have models of those other agents as part of its environmental model. These models should include information about what other agents believe and how those beliefs might be modified. To deal with matters like these, researchers began to consider problems such as how an agent A should represent for itself that agent B knows some fact P and under what circumstances agent A should tell some fact, P, to agent B. One major difficulty was how to distinguish between A knowing that B knows (P $\vee$ Q) and A knowing either that B knows P or that B knows Q. Another was how agent A can reason about telling agent B a fact about some object, say OB, when A does not know the name that B uses for OB. Yet another concerned what A could assume about the conclusions that B might reach by B's own reasoning processes. Various solutions were proposed. The most prominent among them involved what is called "epistemic logic" (logic of belief).[34]

An agent that has knowledge about what another agent knows and what it might conclude is in a position to attempt to add to, correct, or learn from that other agent's knowledge. Adjusting and learning from another agent's knowledge is key to cooperation among agents and requires communication from the sender to the receiver and understanding and possible compliance by the receiver. Researchers noted that there were several types of communication actions. They are usually called "speech acts" even when communication is by means other than speech. Many of these types had been classified earlier by John Searle following the work of John L. Austin.[35] Chief among these for use by multiple agents are "assertives" for transmitting facts from one agent to another, "directives" for requesting or commanding the receiver to take some action, and "commissives" for promising that the sender is committing to some action.

Once communication between agents is regarded in terms of actions, one can think about generating plans using these actions. Philip R. Cohen (1950–) at BBN and C. Raymond Perrault (1949–) at the University of Toronto were among those who did just that.[36] They dealt in particular with the speech acts REQUEST and INFORM (based on the earlier "assertives" and "directives") and proposed conditions under which those acts could be executed and what their effects would be. Conditions and effects were stated in terms of logical expressions occurring in (or derivable from) the knowledge bases of the sender and receiver. (Both the sender and receiver were assumed to have knowledge about the knowledge of each other and that they could reason with that knowledge.) A planning system, somewhat like STRIPS, could then generate plans consisting of instances of those speech acts that would achieve desired effects.

Cohen's and Perrault's speech acts formed the basis of KQML, an acronym for Knowledge Query Manipulation Language. KQML was developed under DARPA support under its "knowledge sharing initiative."[37] It defines various communicative actions that can take place between agents, such as ask-if, inform, tell, and reply.

KQML uses KIF (Knowledge Interchange Format), a language based on first-order predicate calculus, for expressing the content of a message.[38] So, when agent A wants to send a message to agent B, it encodes the content of the message in KIF and then wraps it in the appropriate KQML communicative action. For example, here is a typical KQML/KIF dialog:[39]

A to *B*: (ask-if (> (size chip1) (size chip2)))
B to *A*: (reply true)
B to *A*: (inform (= (size chip1) 20))
B to *A*: (inform (= (size chip2) 18))

Motivated by projects such as KQML and KIF, the Foundation for Intelligent Physical Agents (FIPA) was formed in Switzerland in 1996. FIPA is now one of the standards committees of the IEEE Computer Society. Its standards are "intended to promote the interoperation of heterogeneous agents and the services they can represent." They deal with "Agent Communication Language" (ACL) messages and provide for "message exchange interaction protocols, speech act theory-based communicative acts, and content language representations."[40]

There are now several systems and languages for implementing multiagent systems. For example, the open source Jason interpreter for the logic-based language AgentSpeak provides a platform for users to build complex multiagent systems.[41]

Although much work on multiagent systems has concentrated on applications in which the several agents cooperate to solve some overall problem, it is also the case that agents can be self-interested, which can lead to competition among them. Opposing teams of soccer-playing robots are one example. Other examples are agents that engage in commerce such as buying and selling (presumably acting for humans). These aspects of multiagent research involve negotiations and auctions. There is a well-known framework, namely, game theory, for dealing with situations in which an agent's success in making choices depends on the choices of other agents. Game theory was introduced into multiagent systems research by Jeff Rosenschein (1957–) and Michael Genesereth (1948–) in their paper "Deals among Rational Agents."[42] Now, multiagent systems comprise a major subtopic of AI, and speech-act theory and game theory are among its important theoretical underpinnings.[43]

31.2 Cognitive Architectures

31.2.1 *Production Systems*

Allen Newell and Herb Simon were among the first to be interested in computational models of human problem solving. I have already described GPS, the General Problem Solver (see p. 87), which can be considered one of the first architectures for cognitive processes. I'll describe a few other so-called cognitive architectures in this section. As the developers of one family of these architectures later put it,[44]

[A cognitive architecture is] the fixed base of tightly-coupled mechanisms underlying intelligent behavior. [Such an] architecture then forms the basis for wide-ranging investigations into basic intelligent capabilities – such as problem solving, planning, learning, knowledge representation, natural language, perception, and robotics – as well as applications in areas such as expert systems and psychological modeling.

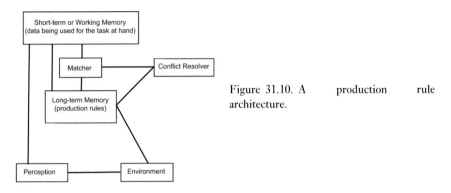

Figure 31.10. A   production   rule architecture.

Following their work on GPS, Newell and Simon focused on "production systems," models that used IF–THEN rules, called productions. I first talked about rules of this kind when I described expert systems in Section 18.2. There, the rules were used mainly for inference, either forward to produce inferred statements or backward to produce subgoals. Newell and Simon were interested in the use of these rules for producing actions. The IF part was, as usual, a condition, and the THEN part was an action, which was executed if the condition was satisfied in a model. (My teleo-teactive programs described in Section 25.4.2 also used these action-producing rules.) Newell and Simon conceived of an architecture consisting of two kinds of memory structures. One, a "long-term memory," consists of the production rules. The other, a short-term or "working memory," holds the dynamic information about the task being worked on. The long-term memory persists over time and might contain thousands of rules. The working memory contains the data to be tested by the condition parts of the rules. When the condition part of a rule matches data in the working memory, that rule "fires"; that is, its action part is executed. Execution may result in writing or erasing (or both) some data in the working memory or taking some action in the external environment. When data in the working memory are changed, different rules are fired, which change the data again, and so on.

Figure 31.10 shows a simple version of this production-rule architecture. In case more than one rule's condition part matches data in the working memory (which would be usual), the "Conflict Resolver" chooses which one (or ones, in case of parallel operation) should fire. In this version of the architecture, which produces actions in the external environment, a "Perception" system is able to write data into the Short-term Memory to represent any salient features of the environment's current state.

Newell and Simon did extensive experimental work with human subjects performing problem-solving tasks – showing that their performance could be well modeled by the operation of versions of this architectural scheme. Their book, *Human Problem Solving*, is an account of much of this work.[45] Mostly, they considered their production-system architecture a contribution to the scientific study of human cognition, not a proposal for how to structure AI systems. In commenting on their book, Newell later wrote "The aim was to make the case that *psychology* was being done, not something that could be pigeon-holed as associated with computers."[46] However,

Figure 31.11. John Anderson. (Photograph courtesy of John Anderson.)

others did associate production systems with computers, most notably through the use of the OPS5 computer language.

Later proposals for cognitive architectures, namely, ACT-R and SOAR, were influenced by the production system model and were used both as models of problem solving and as architectures for AI systems. I'll describe those systems next.

31.2.2 ACT-R

John R. Anderson (Fig. 31.11) and others have been developing a series of cognitive architectures called ACT (Adaptive Control of Thought) at Carnegie Mellon University.[47] (As I mentioned in Section 11.4, when Anderson was a student at Stanford, he and Gordon Bower developed a theory of human associative memory, HAM, which can be regarded as a precursor to his ACT work.) The latest in this series of models is ACT-R ("R" standing for rational). According to its Web site,[48]

ACT-R is a cognitive architecture: a theory for simulating and understanding human cognition. Researchers working on ACT-R strive to understand how people organize knowledge and produce intelligent behavior. As the research continues, ACT-R evolves ever closer into a system which can perform the full range of human cognitive tasks: capturing in great detail the way we perceive, think about, and act on the world.

The basic idea of the ACT-R architecture is illustrated in Fig. 31.12. There are three main components: modules, buffers, and a pattern matcher. The Motor Module can act on the Environment through motor routines or on the ACT-R Buffers. Besides the Visual Module, which is illustrated, there may be other perceptual modules for audition, touch, and so on.

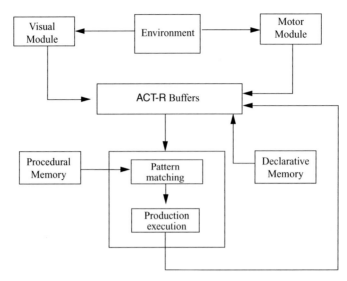

Figure 31.12. The basic ACT-R architecture. (Used with permission of John Anderson.)

There are two types of memory modules in ACT-R. Declarative Memory consists of facts, such as "Washington, DC is the capital of the United States, France is a country in Europe, or $2 + 3 = 5$." Declarative knowledge is represented in ACT-R by units called chunks. Procedural Memory consists of production rules representing "knowledge about how we do things: for instance, knowledge about how to type the letter 'Q' on a keyboard, about how to drive, or about how to perform addition."[49] Often we are unable to verbalize our knowledge about how we do certain things: We just do them; thus knowledge about them is considered procedural, not declarative.

Buffers in ACT-R serve as interfaces between modules. "The contents of the buffers at a given moment in time represent the state of ACT-R at that moment . . . The pattern matcher searches for a production that matches the current state of the buffers. Only one such production can be executed at a given moment. That production, when executed, can modify the buffers and thus change the state of the system. Thus, in ACT-R cognition unfolds as a succession of production firings."

According to one of the ACT-R Web sites,[50]

ACT-R is a *hybrid cognitive architecture*. Its *symbolic* structure is a production system; the *subsymbolic structure* is represented by a set of massively parallel processes that can be summarized by a number of mathematical equations. The subsymbolic equations control many of the symbolic processes. For instance, if several productions match the state of the buffers, a subsymbolic utility equation estimates the relative cost and benefit associated with each production and decides to select for execution the production with the highest utility. Similarly, whether (or how fast) a fact can be retrieved from declarative memory depends on subsymbolic retrieval equations, which take into account the context and the history of usage of that fact. Subsymbolic mechanisms are also responsible for most learning processes in ACT-R.

Figure 31.13. John Laird (left) and Paul Rosenbloom (right). (Photographs courtesy of John Laird and of Paul Rosenbloom.)

ACT-R models have been used to explain and simulate a wide variety of cognitive behaviors in humans, including learning, language processing, perception, problem solving, and decision making. There are hundreds (if not thousands) of papers describing this work.[51] Applications of ACT-R cover a wide range of topics from, for example, "predicting the effects of cellular-phone dialing on driver performance" to intelligent tutoring systems. In applications more directly related to AI, Greg Trafton and Alan C. Schultz at the Navy Center for Applied Research in Artificial Intelligence (NCARAI) have been building an "embedded cognitive robot" using a version of ACT-R they call ACT-R/E. It includes "visual and auditory modules" and "motor and spatial modules" for perception and action.[52]

In addition to its role in explaining psychological processes, functional magnetic resonance imaging (fMRI) studies have been used to associate components of the ACT-R architecture with brain regions that are active in complex tasks.[53]

ACT-R software, together with reference materials and tutorials, is available from http://act-r.psy.cmu.edu/actr6/.

31.2.3 SOAR

In the early 1980s, John Laird (1954– ; Fig. 31.13), Allen Newell, and Paul Rosenbloom (1954– ; Fig. 31.13) began development of a series of cognitive architectures called SOAR (which originally, it is said, was an acronym for State, Operator And Result). SOAR's developers said that their "ultimate goal for the SOAR architecture is that it serve as a basis for both human and artificial cognition."[54] Like ACT, SOAR evolved from Newell and Simon's work on GPS and production systems and included ideas involving problem spaces, heuristic search, cognitive skill acquisition, and learning. Laird and Rosenbloom were Ph.D. students of Newell's and completed dissertations on aspects of SOAR.[55] The SOAR architecture and its applications are described in books and in several hundred articles[56] and on the SOAR Web sites accessible from http://sitemaker.umich.edu/soar/home.

There have been a series of SOAR architectures, SOAR1 (in 1982) through SOAR9 (2008), each with improvements on its predecessor.[57] Some of the latest versions of the SOAR software can be downloaded from http://sitemaker.umich.edu/soar/soar_software_downloads. Understanding exactly how these various versions of SOAR work can best be gained by tracing through some of the examples in articles and papers about SOAR. I'll limit my brief account here to mentioning some of the main ideas.

SOAR is something like a programming language having a fixed set of routines. Different kinds of tasks can be "programmed" in SOAR using these routines. Examples range from AI's favorite "toy" problems (such as the eight-puzzle) to "real-world" applications (such as configuring computer systems and robot control). SOAR solves each task given to it by creating and solving a hierarchy of subtasks. Each task (including the main one and each of the subtasks) is posed as the goal of finding a desired state in a "problem space" consisting of a set of operators that apply to a current state to produce a new state.

To set up a problem space, SOAR needs to know its current state and what operators can be applied to that state. If it does not know these things directly, say from prior experience, it sets up a subsidiary problem space whose goal is to discover them (and so on). Once SOAR has defined a problem space, it must select an operator to apply to the current state in that space. If it does not already know which operator to apply, it sets up a subsidiary problem space whose goal is to find out. As stated in the volume of SOAR papers, "SOAR's mechanisms form a tightly coupled hierarchy of layers – memory, decision, and goal – in which each layer forms the inner loop of the layer above it. These layers increase progressively in both complexity and time scale from the bottom to the top of the hierarchy."

Setting up subsidiary problem spaces is called "universal subgoaling," which can result in a deep tree of subgoals and problem spaces. When these involve control decisions (such as which operator to apply), SOAR can be said to be "reflecting" on its own problem-solving behavior. The process of universal subgoaling can invoke a variety of so-called weak methods, such as hill climbing, means–ends analysis, and heuristic search, depending on the knowledge SOAR has previously learned about the kind of task it is working on.

A production system, with the usual long-term and short-term memory structures, is used to set up problem spaces. The long-term memory (LTM) stores information that is independent of the current situation. The short-term or working memory (WM) holds information that is most relevant to the current situation. SOAR learns by caching results of its problem-solving experiences, both as productions in its LTM and as general facts in WM about previous situations that might be useful in future situations. Assembling learning sequences of previously experienced problem-solving traces is called "chunking," a term sometimes used to describe analogous learning in humans.

Relationships between these memory structures (for a recent version of SOAR) are shown in Fig. 31.14.

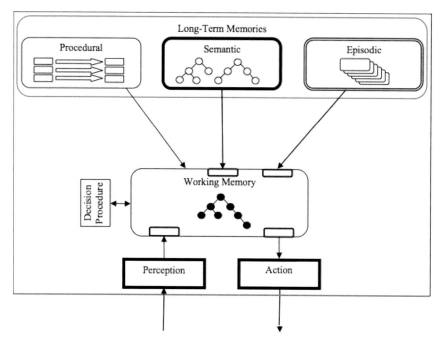

Figure 31.14. Memory structures in SOAR. (Illustration used with permission of John Laird and Paul Rosenbloom.)

There are three kinds of LTM structures, namely, procedural, semantic, and episodic. Here is how one of the SOAR papers describes them:[58]

Procedural knowledge is about how and when to do things – how to ride a bike, how to solve an algebra problem, or how to read a recipe and use it to bake a cake. Semantic knowledge consists of facts about the world – things you believe to be true in general – things you "know," such as bicycles have two wheels, a baseball game has nine innings, and an inning has three outs. Episodic knowledge consists of things you "remember" – specific situations you've experienced, such as the time you fell off your bicycle and scraped your elbow. LTM is not directly available, but must be "searched" to find what is relevant to the current situation.

To say this a little more intuitively, it is useful to think about LTM as containing what can be relevant to many different situations but must be explicitly retrieved, and WM as containing what the model thinks is relevant to the particular situation it is currently in. One of the key distinctions between WM and LTM is that knowledge in working memory can be used to retrieve other knowledge from LTM, whereas LTM must first be retrieved into WM. Knowledge moves from LTM to WM by both automatic and deliberate retrieval of relevant LTM structures.

The SOAR architecture (in its various versions) has been used by researchers all over the world for a variety of tasks. The intention of the people working on SOAR is to enable it to[59]

• work on the full range of tasks expected of an intelligent agent, from highly routine to extremely difficult, open-ended problems,

- represent and use appropriate forms of knowledge, such as procedural, declarative, episodic, and possibly iconic,
- employ the full range of problem-solving methods,
- interact with the outside world, and
- learn about all aspects of the tasks and its performance on them.

This is a tall order so stay tuned. One interesting SOAR application area has been in programming automated agents as stand-ins for humans in simulated training exercises. For example, TacAir-SOAR simulates the intelligent behavior of a tactical fighter pilot.[60] In 1998, Laird founded SOAR Technology, an Ann Arbor (Michigan) company specializing in creating autonomous AI entities using the SOAR architecture.

ACT-R and SOAR are probably the most prominent cognitive architectures, but there are others also. The field is well surveyed in a paper by Pat Langley, John Laird, and Seth Rogers.[61]

Notes

1. Erann Gat, "On Three-Layer Architectures," in David Kortenkamp, R. Peter Bonnasso, and Robin Murphy (eds.), pp. 195–210, Cambridge, MA: MIT Press, 1998. Available online at http://www.flownet.com/ron/papers/tla.pdf. [456]

2. R. James Firby, "Adaptive Execution in Dynamic Domains," Ph.D. dissertation, Yale University, Computer Science Department Technical Report No. 672, 1989. For a summary, see R. James Firby, "An Investigation into Reactive Planning in Complex Domains," *Proceedings of AAAI-87*, pp. 202–206, 1987. [457]

3. Several other architectures for controlling robots, including three-layered ones, are described in Bruno Siciliano and Oussama Khatib (eds.), *Springer Handbook of Robotics*, Berlin and Heidelberg: Springer-Verlag, 2008. [457]

4. Ernst D. Dickmanns *et al.*, "The Seeing Passenger Car 'VaMoRs-P,'" *Proceedings of the IEEE 1994 Symposium on Intelligent Vehicles*, pp. 68–73, 24–26 October 1994. [457]

5. For a review, see Chapter 38 of Bruno Siciliano and Oussama Khatib (eds.), *op. cit.* [457]

6. *Ibid*, p. 895. [458]

7. See James S. Albus, "Outline for a Theory of Intelligence," *IEEE Transactions on Systems, Man, and Cybernetics*, Vol. 21, No. 3, May/June 1991. [458]

8. See James S. Albus, "A New Approach to Manipulator Control: The Cerebellar Model Articulation Controller (CMAC)," *Journal of Dynamic Systems, Measurement and Control*, Vol. 97, American Society of Mechanical Engineers, pp. 220–227, September 1975; a version is available online at http://www4.cs.umanitoba.ca/~jacky/Robotics/Papers/Albus-ANewApproachForManipulatorControlCMACS.pdf. [459]

9. James S. Albus, "A Reference Model Architecture for Intelligent Systems Design," in P. J. Antsaklis and K. M. Passino (eds.), *An Introduction to Intelligent and Autonomous Control*, Chapter 2, pp. 27–56, Dordrecht: Kluwer Academic Publishers, 1993. [459]

10. Nils J. Nilsson, "Teleo-Reactive Programs and the Triple-Tower Architecture," *Electronic Transactions on Artificial Intelligence*, Vol. 5, Section B, pp. 99–110, 2001. PostScript version available online at http://www.ep.liu.se/ej/etai/2001/006/. [459]

11. *Ibid.* [461]

12. See Stéphane Descorps-Declère *et al.*, "Genepi: A Blackboard Framework for Genome Annotation," *BMC Bioinformatics*, Vol. 7, pp. 450ff, October 12, 2006. Available online at http://www.biomedcentral.com/1471-2105/7/450. [461]

13. For a philosophical treatment of these ideas see Michael E. Bratman, *Intention, Plans, and Practical Reason*, Stanford CA: CSLI Publications, 1999. **[461]**

14. There are several papers and reports about PRS. One is Michael P. Georgeff and François F. Ingrand, "Decision-Making in an Embedded Reasoning System," *Proceedings of the Eleventh International Joint Conference on Artificial Intelligence*, pp. 972–978, August 1989. Available online at http://www.agent.ai/download.php?ctag=download&docID=147 and at http://www.ai.sri.com/pubs/files/493.pdf. **[462]**

15. Michael P. Georgeff and Amy L. Lansky, "A System for Reasoning in Dynamic Domains: Fault Diagnosis on the Space Shuttle," SRI AI Center Technical Note 375, 1986. Available online at http://www.ai.sri.com/pubs/files/584.pdf. **[463]**

16. Michael P. Georgeff and Amy L. Lansky, "Reactive Reasoning and Planning: An Experiment with a Mobile Robot," *Proceedings of the Sixth National Conference on Artificial Intelligence*, 1987. A longer version is Michael P. Georgeff, Amy L. Lansky, and Marcel J. Schoppers, "Reasoning and Planning In Dynamic Domains: An Experiment with A Mobile Robot," Technical Note 380, AI Center, SRI International, April 1987. Available online at http://www.ai.sri.com/pubs/files/579.pdf. **[463]**

17. Brian Cantwell Smith, "Reflection and Semantics in a Procedural Language," MIT Ph.D. dissertation and MIT Laboratory of Computer Science Technical Report 272, 1982. Available online at http://publications.csail.mit.edu/lcs/pubs/pdf/MIT-LCS-TR-272.pdf. **[463]**

18. Richard Weyhrauch, "Prolegomena to a Theory of Formal Reasoning," *Artificial Intelligence*, Vol. 13, Nos. 1 and 2, pp. 133–176, April 1980. Available also as Stanford Computer Science Department Technical Report CS-TR-78-687, 1978, at http://www-db.stanford.edu/TR/CS-TR-78-687.html. **[463]**

19. Patrick J. Hayes, "Computation and Deduction," *Proceedings of the Second Mathematical Foundations of Computer Science Symposium*, Czechoslavak Academy of Sciences, pp. 105–118, 1973. **[463]**

20. Michael R. Genesereth, "An Overview of Meta-Level Architecture," *Proceedings of the Third National Conference on Artificial Intelligence*, pp. 119–124, Los Altos, CA: Morgan Kaufmann Publishers, 1983. **[463]**

21. Stuart Russell and Eric H. Wefald, *Do the Right Thing: Studies in Limited Rationality*, Cambridge, MA: MIT Press, 1991. **[463]**

22. Eric J. Horvitz, "Reasoning about Beliefs and Actions under Computational Resource Constraints," *Proceedings of the Third Workshop on Uncertainty in Artificial Intelligence*, pp. 429–444, Seattle WA, July 1987. An online version is available at ftp://ftp.research.microsoft.com/pub/ejh/u87.ps. **[463]**

23. *Artificial Intelligence*, Vol. 126, Nos. 1–2 (Special Issue on Computational Tradeoffs under Bounded Resources), February 2001. **[463]**

24. Marvin Minsky, *The Society of Mind*, New York: Simon and Schuster, 1988. **[463]**

25. William Kornfeld and Carl Hewitt, "The Scientific Community Metaphor," *IEEE Transactions on Systems, Man, and Cybernetics*, Vol. SMC-11, No. 1, pp. 24–33, 1981. Available online as MIT AI Laboratory Memo No. 641, January 1981, at http://dspace.mit.edu/bitstream/1721.1/5693/2/AIM-641.pdf. **[464]**

26. Victor R. Lesser and Lee D. Erman, "Distributed Interpretation: A Model and Experiment," *IEEE Transactions on Computers*, Vol. C-29, No. 12, pp. 1144–1163, December 1980. Available online at ftp://mas.cs.umass.edu/pub/lesser/LesserIEEE1980.pdf. **[464]**

27. Victor R. Lesser and Daniel Corkill, "The Distributed Vehicle Monitoring Testbed: A Tool for Investigating Distributed Problem Solving Networks," *AI Magazine*, Vol. 4, No. 3, pp. 15–33, 1983. **[464]**

28. See the Lab's Web site at http://mas.cs.umass.edu/ and a history of the Lab's work at ftp://mas.cs.umass.edu/pub/LabHistory_Web-Article.pdf. [464]

29. Reid G. Smith, "The Contract Net Protocol: High Level Communication and Control in a Distributed Problem Solver," *IEEE Transactions on Computers*, Vol. C-29, No. 12, pp. 1104–1113, December 1980. [464]

30. See also Randy Davis and Reid G. Smith, "Negotiation as a Metaphor for Distributed Problem Solving," *Artificial Intelligence*, Vol. 20, No. 1, pp. 63–109, 1983. [465]

31. Les Gasser, Carl Braganza, and Nava Herman, "MACE: A Flexible Testbed for Distributed AI Research," in Michael N. Huhns (ed.), *Distributed Artificial Intelligence*, pp. 119–152, London: Pitman Publishers, 1987. Available online at http://www.isrl .uiuc.edu/%7Egasser/papers/gasser-braganza-herman-mace-a-flexible-testbed-for-dai-research-1987.pdf. [465]

32. See the CORAL Web site at http://www.cs.cmu.edu/~coral/main/. [465]

33. See http://www.robocup.org/. [465]

34. Mathematically brave readers might consult, for example, Robert C. Moore, "Reasoning about Knowledge and Action," *Proceedings of IJCAI-77*, Vol. 1, pp. 223–227, 1977. An expanded version is Robert C. Moore, "A Formal Theory of Knowledge and Action," SRI AI Center Technical Note 320, February 1984, available online at http://www.ai.sri.com/pubs/files/632.pdf. Also see Kurt Konolige, "A Deduction Model of Belief and Its Logics," SRI AI Center Technical Note 326, August 1984, available online at http://www.ai.sri.com/pubs/files/626.pdf. [466]

35. John L. Austin, *How to Do Things with Words*, New York: Oxford University Press, 1962; John Searle, *Speech Acts*, New York: Cambridge University Press. 1969. [466]

36. Philip R. Cohen and C. Raymond Perrault, "Elements of a Plan Based Theory of Speech Acts," *Cognitive Science*, Vol. 3, No. 3, pp. 177–212, 1979. Available online at http://www.cs.huji.ac.il/~imas/readings/cohen79.pdf. [466]

37. KQML is described in Tim Finin *et al.*, "KQML as an Agent Communication Language," in Jeff Bradshaw (ed.), *Software Agents*, Cambridge, MA: MIT Press, 1997, available online at http://www.cs.umbc.edu/kqml/papers/kqmlacl.pdf. The DARPA knowledge sharing initiative is described in Robert Neches *et al.*, "Enabling Technology for Knowledge Sharing," *AI Magazine*, Vol. 12, No. 3, pp. 16–36, 1991. [466]

38. See http://www-ksl.stanford.edu/knowledge-sharing/kif/. [466]

39. This example is taken from one of Michael Wooldridge's lecture slides on multiagent systems, accessible from http://www.csc.liv.ac.uk/~mjw/pubs/imas/. [467]

40. See the FIPA Web page at http://www.fipa.org/. [467]

41. Rafael H. Bordini, Jomi Fred Hübner, and Michael Wooldridge, *Programming Multi-Agent Systems in AgentSpeak Using Jason*, New York: John Wiley and Sons, Inc., 2007. A Jason Web site is at http://jason.sourceforge.net/JasonWebSite/Jason%20Home.php. [467]

42. Jeffrey S. Rosenschein and Michael R. Genesereth, "Deals among Rational Agents," *Proceedings of the Ninth International Joint Conference on Artificial Intelligence*, pp. 91–99, 1985. Available online at http://dli.iiit.ac.in/ijcai/IJCAI-85-VOL1/PDF/017.pdf. [467]

43. See, for example, Michael Wooldridge, *An Introduction to MultiAgent Systems*, Chichester, England: John Wiley and Sons, Inc., 2002; Yoav Shoham and Kevin Leyton-Brown, *Multiagent Systems: Algorithmic, Game Theoretic, and Logical Foundations*, New York: Cambridge University Press, 2008: and Tim Finin's "Agents 101," a Web page to learn about agents at http://agents.umbc.edu/. [467]

44. Paul S. Rosenbloom, John E. Laird, and Allen Newell (eds.), *The SOAR Papers: Research on Integrated Intelligence*, Chapter 1, Cambridge, MA: MIT Press, 1993. [467]

45. Allen Newell and Herbert A. Simon, *Human Problem Solving*, Englewood Cliffs, NJ: Prentice-Hall, 1972. **[468]**

46. Allen Newell, "This Week's Citation Classic," *Current Contents*, No. 34, p. 167, August 25, 1980. Available online at http://www.garfield.library.upenn.edu/classics1980/A1980KD04600001.pdf. **[468]**

47. A recent description can be found in John R. Anderson *et al.*, "An Integrated Theory of the Mind," *Psychological Review*, Vol. 111, No. 4, pp. 1036–1060, 2004; available online from http://act-r.psy.cmu.edu/publications/pubinfo.php?id=526. See also John R. Anderson, *How Can the Human Mind Occur in the Physical Universe*, New York: Oxford University Press, 2007. **[469]**

48. http://act-r.psy.cmu.edu/. **[469]**

49. The quotation is from http://act-r.psy.cmu.edu/about/. **[470]**

50. http://act-r.psy.cmu.edu/about/. **[470]**

51. For a list, see http://act-r.psy.cmu.edu/publications/index.php. **[471]**

52. See J. Greg Trafton *et al.*, "Integrating Vision and Audition within a Cognitive Architecture to Track Conversations," *Proceedings of the 3rd ACM/IEEE International Conference on Human Robot Interaction*, pp. 201–208, 2008. Available online at http://www.nrl.navy.mil/aic/iss/aas/documents/trafton.hri08.pdf. **[471]**

53. See John R. Anderson, *et al.*, "A Central Circuit of the Mind," *Trends in Cognitive Science*, Vol. 12, No. 4, pp. 136–143, 2008 (available online from http://act-r.psy.cmu.edu/publications/pubinfo.php?id=800), and John R. Anderson *et al.*, "An Integrated Theory of the Mind," *Psychological Review*, Vol. 111, No. 4, pp. 1036–1060, 2004 (available online from http://act-r.psy.cmu.edu/publications/pubinfo.php?id=526). **[471]**

54. Paul S. Rosenbloom, John E. Laird, and Allen Newell (eds.), *op. cit.* **[471]**

55. John E. Laird, "Universal Subgoaling," Ph.D. thesis, Computer Science Department, Carnegie Mellon University, Pittsburgh, PA, 1983; Paul S. Rosenbloom, "The Chunking of Goal Hierarchies: A Model of Practice and Stimulus–Response Compatibility," Ph.D. thesis (also Technical Report No. 83–148), Computer Science Department, Carnegie Mellon University, Pittsburgh, PA, 1983. **[472]**

56. Sixty-eight articles (along with an extensive bibliography) are collected in a two-volume book: Paul S. Rosenbloom, John E. Laird, and Allen Newell (eds.), *op. cit.* (An introductory chapter of the book is available online at http://www.isi.edu/soar/papers/soar-papers-book/intromosaic.ps.) The primary paper on SOAR is John E. Laird, Allen Newell, and Paul S. Rosenbloom, "SOAR: An Architecture for General Intelligence," *Artificial Intelligence*, Vol. 33, pp. 1–64, 1987. **[472]**

57. SOAR9 is described in John E. Laird, "Extending The SOAR Cognitive Architecture," *Proceedings of the Artificial General Intelligence Conference*, Memphis, TN, March 2008, Amsterdam: IOS Press; available online at http://ai.eecs.umich.edu/people/laird/papers/Laird-GAIC.pdf. **[472]**

58. Jill Fain Lehman, John Laird, and Paul Rosenbloom, "A Gentle Introduction to SOAR: An Architecture for Human Cognition: 2006 Update"; available online at http://ai.eecs.umich.edu/soar/sitemaker/docs/misc/GentleIntroduction-2006.pdf. **[473]**

59. From the SOAR Web site, http://sitemaker.umich.edu/soar/home. **[473]**

60. R. M. Jones *et al.*, "Automated Intelligent Pilots for Combat Flight Simulation," *AI Magazine*, Vol. 20, No. 1, pp. 27–41, 1999. **[474]**

61. Pat Langley, John E. Laird, and Seth Rogers, "Cognitive Architectures: Research Issues and Challenges," 2006; available online at http://cll.stanford.edu/~langley/papers/final.arch.pdf. **[474]**

Part VIII

Modern AI: Today
and Tomorrow

A I TECHNOLOGY HAS MATURED MARKEDLY IN THE PAST COUPLE OF DECADES AND now includes an impressive array of powerful computational tools. These can be deployed with great effectiveness because of the increasing power of relatively inexpensive computers, the availability of large databases, and the growth of the World Wide Web. Today's AI programs are capable of approximating many human cognitive abilities, automating some of them completely, and even bettering what humans can do in others. Because AI is now capable of contributing to the solution of many real-world problems, many graduates who have specialized in AI studies go to work for companies and start-ups instead of pursuing academic AI research. Google and Microsoft, just to name two examples, have hired many of these graduates.

Just as other branches of engineering gradually develop a number of subspecialties, so has AI. For example, the July 2009 International Joint Conference on Artificial Intelligence (IJCAI) had papers in the following "theme" areas: Agent-based and Multi-agent Systems; Constraint, Satisfiability, and Search; Knowledge Representation, Reasoning, and Logic; Machine Learning; Multidisciplinary Topics and Applications; Natural-Language Processing; Planning and Scheduling; Robotics and Vision; Uncertainty in AI; and Web and Knowledge-based Information Systems. (Note that many of the theme areas combine two or more broad topics, and the topics themselves are further articulated in the call for papers.[1]) Of course, many of these subspecialties draw on each other so the field as a whole stays connected.

Even though more accomplished historians than I have wisely avoided writing accounts that get too close to the present (and predicting the future is even more hazardous), in this final part of the book I'll attempt a look at how the quest for AI is faring and speculate about the future. Because the past several years have seen an explosion of new AI technology and applications, I'll have space for just a limited number of what I take to be representative examples of what AI programs are doing now and might yet do.

32

Extraordinary Achievements

S OME OF AI'S RECENT ACHIEVEMENTS STAND AS EXTRAORDINARY MILESTONES OF its progress, and others have insinuated themselves almost invisibly into our daily routines. In between these extremes, AI programs have become important tools in science and commerce. These three categories provide a useful way of organizing the state of AI today. First, I'll look at some of the headline-making systems appearing just before and just after the beginning of the twenty-first century, beginning with AI game-playing programs.

32.1 Games

Although getting computers to excel at games, such as chess and checkers, is thought by some to be a somewhat frivolous diversion from more serious work, computer game-playing has served as a laboratory for exploring new AI techniques – especially in heuristic search and in learning. In a previous chapter, for example, I explained how reinforcement learning methods were used to develop a championship-level backgammon program. From the earliest days of AI, people worked on programs to play chess and checkers, and now, mainly by using massive amounts of heuristically guided computation, computers are able to play these and other games better than humans can.

32.1.1 *Chess*

The big news in 1997 was the defeat of the world chess champion, Garry Kasparov, by IBM's "Deep Blue" chess-playing computer. (See Fig. 32.1.) The first time Kasparov played Deep Blue, in February 1996, Deep Blue won the first game but lost the match. But on May 11, 1997, a hardware-enhanced 1997 version (unofficially nicknamed "Deeper Blue") won a six-game match (under regular chess tournament time controls) by two wins to one with three draws. (For a Computer History Museum movie, *Endgame: Challenging the Chess Masters*, visit http://www.youtube .com/watch?v=5hRNlfAUeEE. For records of the play of the games in the 1997 match, see http://www.research.ibm.com/deepblue/watch/html/c.shtml.)

The 1997 Deep Blue was a combination of special-purpose hardware and software running on an IBM RS/6000 SP2 supercomputer. Some of its features included improvements "in response to specific problems observed in the 1996 Kasparov games..."[2]

Figure 32.1. Garry Kasparov playing chess against Deep Blue in game two of a six-game rematch. (Photograph used with permission of AP/Wide World Photos. ©)

After his defeat, Kasparov was quoted in the *New York Times* as saying "I was not in the mood of playing at all."[3] The *Times* article goes on to say "that after Game 5 on Saturday, he had become so dispirited that he felt the match was already over. Asked why, he said: 'I'm a human being. When I see something that is well beyond my understanding, I'm afraid.'" Several Web sites mention that, after his loss, Kasparov said that he sometimes saw deep intelligence and creativity in the machine's moves. But his statement was meant to imply that human chess players must have intervened during the second game of the match. Kasparov wanted a rematch, but IBM dismantled the machine, and there was none.

Kasparov did have his defenders however. The *Times* article just mentioned quotes Lev Albert, a former U.S. champion, as saying "This was a show. If they [IBM] want to prove it was more than a show, let them play anyone but Garry. If it would play against, say, Grandmaster Boris Gulko, who is not even among the top 50, I am willing to bet $10,000 the computer would lose."[4]

Deep Blue's history began with the chess program "Deep Thought" developed by Ph.D. student Feng-Hsiung Hsu at Carnegie Mellon University. According to IBM's Web site about Deep Blue (http://www.research.ibm.com/deepblue/), the "IBM Deep Blue project began when Hsu and Murray Campbell [Hsu's classmate at Carnegie Mellon] joined IBM Research in 1989" and began work on parallel processing systems. The version of Deep Blue that won the match against Kasparov was a computer containing 256 "chess processors," which, in combination, could examine about 200 million chess positions per second. (For comparison, note that back in the 1970s, Northwestern University's CHESS 3.0 could evaluate only about 100 positions per second.)

Deep Blue evaluated a chess position using both a "fast" evaluation function and a "slow" one. The values of some 8,000 features used in these functions were computed by special hardware. According to a Deep Blue paper,[5]

This [use of both fast and slow functions] is a standard technique to skip computing an expensive full evaluation when an approximation is good enough. The fast evaluation, which computes a score for a chess position in a single clock cycle, contains all the easily computed major evaluation terms with high values. The most significant part of the fast evaluation is the "piece placement" value, i.e., the sum of the basic piece values with square-based location adjustments. Positional features that can be computed quickly, such as "pawn can run," are also part of the fast evaluation. The slow evaluation scans the chess board one column at a time, computing values for chess concepts such as square control, pins, x-rays, king safety, pawn structure, passed pawns, ray control, outposts, pawn majority, rook on the 7th, blockade, restraint, color complex, trapped pieces, development, and so on. The features recognized in both the slow and fast evaluation functions have programmable weights, allowing their relative importance to be easily adjusted.

Heuristic search (guided by Deep Blue's evaluation functions) permitted search to a depth of between six and sixteen ply to a maximum of forty ply in some situations. In addition to search, Deep Blue could draw on standard "book moves" containing over 4,000 positions. Its play could also be influenced by a database of 700,000 grandmaster games. It also used endgame databases that included "all chess positions with five or fewer pieces on the board, as well as selected positions with six pieces that included a pair of blocked pawns."

Because Deep Blue won by using what some computer science people call "brute-force" methods, can it be said that its victory was an "AI achievement?" Here is IBM's opinion of the matter:[6]

Does Deep Blue use artificial intelligence? The short answer is "no." Earlier computer designs that tried to mimic human thinking weren't very good at it. No formula exists for intuition. . . . Deep Blue relies more on computational power and a simpler search and evaluation function.

The long answer is [also] "no." "Artificial Intelligence" is more successful in science fiction than it is here on earth, and you don't have to be Isaac Asimov to know why it's hard to design a machine to mimic a process we don't understand very well to begin with. How we think is a question without an answer. Deep Blue could never be a HAL-9000 if it tried. Nor would it occur to Deep Blue to "try."

Among the differences that IBM lists between how Kasparov and Deep Blue each approached the problem of playing chess are the following:[7]

- Deep Blue can examine and evaluate up to 200,000,000 chess positions per second; Garry Kasparov can examine and evaluate up to three chess positions per second.
- Deep Blue has a small amount of chess knowledge and an enormous amount of calculation ability; Garry Kasparov has a large amount of chess knowledge and a somewhat smaller amount of calculation ability.
- Garry Kasparov uses his tremendous sense of feeling and intuition to play world champion–calibre chess; Deep Blue is a machine that is incapable of feeling or intuition.

- Garry Kasparov is able to learn and adapt very quickly from his own successes and mistakes; Deep Blue, as it stands today, is not a "learning system." It is therefore not capable of utilizing artificial intelligence to either learn from its opponent or "think" about the current position of the chessboard.
- Any changes in the way Deep Blue plays chess must be performed by the members of the development team between games; Garry Kasparov can alter the way he plays at any time before, during, and/or after each game.

But I have a broader view of AI. Although Deep Blue relied mainly on brute-force methods rather than on rule-based reasoning (for example), it did use heuristic search, one of AI's foundational techniques. The differences between Kasparov and Deep Blue simply indicate how much better chess programs would fare if they employed human-chess-playing knowledge and skills (once these become known well enough to program) and machine learning methods in addition to brute force.

John McCarthy has expressed similar views. In a recent article,[8] he wrote

However, it is a measure of our limited understanding of the principles of artificial intelligence (AI) that this [championship] level of play requires many millions of times as much computing as a human chess player does.

... Champion-level play is possible with enormously less computation than Deep Blue and its recent competitors use.

McCarthy goes on to recommend that computer chess tournaments "should admit programs only with severe limits on computation. This would concentrate attention on scientific advances."

Matches between computers and humans, as well as between computers, continue to be played. In a match staged between November 25 and December 5, 2006, in Bonn, Germany, World Champion Vladimir Kramnik played a match with Deep Fritz, a chess program developed by Frans Morsch and Mathias Feist in Germany. Of the six games in the match, Deep Fritz won two games, and four ended in draws. Kramnik is quoted as saying "Deep Fritz 8 [an inexpensive version] is stronger than Deep Blue." The latest version is Deep Fritz 11. (Deep Fritz 8 can be purchased from http://www.chesscentral.com/software/deep-fritz-8.htm.)

Several Web sites are devoted to computer chess programs and their matches.

32.1.2 *Checkers*

In September 2007, Professor Jonathan Schaeffer (1957– ; Fig. 32.2) and his team at the University of Alberta in Edmonton, Canada, published an article with the title "Checkers is Solved" – announcing that "Perfect play by both sides leads to a draw."[9] Schaeffer and colleagues have been working to solve checkers since 1989. They claim that computations to do so have been running almost continuously since then. The finally completed proof that checkers leads to a draw "consists of an explicit strategy that never loses – the program can achieve at least a draw against any opponent, playing either the black or white pieces." The checkers team credits their result to "advanced AI algorithms and improved hardware (faster processors, larger memories, and larger disks)..." It's not surprising that the effort required

Figure 32.2. Jonathan Schaeffer. (Photograph courtesy of Jonathan Schaeffer.)

eighteen years of skilled effort and massive amounts of computation: There are 500,995,484,682,338,672,639 different positions in the game of checkers!

Along the way to the proof, the team developed a constantly improving, excellent checkers program named "CHINOOK." (Chinook is the name of a warm winter wind from the west coming downslope from the Canadian Rocky Mountains onto the Great Plains.) In 1992's first man–machine world chess championship, checkers champion Marion Tinsley beat CHINOOK four wins to two, with thirty-three draws.[10]

A rematch with a much-improved CHINOOK was held at the Computer Museum in Boston in 1994. According to the CHINOOK team,[11] "CHINOOK 1994 searched better and deeper [than CHINOOK 1992], evaluated positions better, had access to more and better quality endgame databases, and had access to 12 times as much (and better quality) opening knowledge." The first six games of the rematch were drawn. Before game seven could be played, Tinsley resigned the match, citing health reasons. According to the rules, CHINOOK was declared the Man–Machine World Champion. (Soon after, Tinsley was diagnosed with pancreatic cancer.) The match organizers arranged for play to continue in Boston by having Grand Master Don Lafferty play a challenge match against CHINOOK. CHINOOK retained its title because the match ended with one game for each and eighteen draws. Tinsley's health improved sufficiently for him to ask for a rematch to reclaim his title, but he died in 1995 before it could take place.

The proof that one can always be guaranteed at least a draw in checkers involves a prodigious amount of computation and very large databases. The proof team wrote that "checkers represents the most computationally challenging game solved to date." I'll give a general idea of the structure of the proof. Figure 32.3 is a schematic diagram showing the relationship between the number of pieces still on the board and the number of ways these pieces can be configured in checkers positions. (The vertical axis is the number of pieces; the horizontal axis is the logarithm of the number of positions.) The shaded area at the bottom of the diagram represents all of

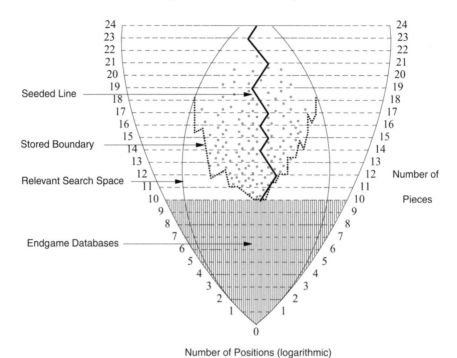

Figure 32.3. Schematic for the checkers proof. (Illustration used with permission of Jonathan Schaeffer.)

the ways that ten or fewer pieces can be configured. There are 39,271,258,813,439 such positions, and Schaeffer and his team have calculated and stored in the endgame database whether these positions result in a win, a loss, or a draw for each player. The small open circles in the diagram represent positions (with more than ten pieces) for which a value (win, loss, or draw) has been established. Optimum play involves using heuristic search to find a line of play guaranteed to get from the starting position to a position in the shaded area from which at least a draw can be guaranteed. An example path is shown by the solid line marked "seeded" in the diagram. (Other features of this diagram are explained in the paper announcing the proof.) You can inspect how the proof evaluates various positions by visiting the CHINOOK Web pages at http://www.cs.ualberta.ca/~chinook/. You can also play against CHINOOK from these Web pages.

I believe the checkers result is a superb AI achievement. As the authors put it in the conclusion of their paper,

The checkers computation pushes the boundary of what can be achieved by search-intensive algorithms. It provides compelling evidence of the power of limited-knowledge approaches to artificial intelligence. Deep search implicitly uncovers knowledge. Furthermore, search algorithms are well poised to take advantage of the increase in on-chip parallelism that multicore computing will soon offer. Search-intensive approaches to AI will play an increasingly important role in the evolution of the field.

So, it appears that intensive search methods have resurfaced to challenge the "in-the-knowledge-is-the-power" doctrine, which I mentioned on page 200. It should be noted though how much personal effort also was required for this achievement. Jonathan Schaeffer's wife, Stephanie, has been quoted as saying "Its been 18 years!... obsessive-compulsive behavior... not normal... Get a life, Jonathan."[12]

But what about chess with its much, much larger search space – at least 10^{40} positions. Checkers has *only* 500×10^{18} positions, about the square root of that of chess. The authors think that solving chess anytime soon is unlikely. They wrote, "Given the effort required to solve checkers, chess will remain unsolved for a long time, barring the invention of new technology."[13]

32.1.3 *Other Games*

There are several other games that computers are now very good at. One example that has attracted a lot of attention is the game of poker. The University of Alberta maintains a Web page at http://www.cs.ualberta.ca/~pokert/index.html devoted to the AAAI's Computer Poker Competition. For example, the 2008 competition had nine entrants for both "Heads-Up Texas Hold'em Limit" and "Heads-Up Texas Hold'em No Limit" and six for "6-Player Texas Hold'em Limit."[14] You can play against some of the Unversity of Alberta's poker-playing programs at http://poker.cs.ualberta.ca/.

Matt Ginsberg (1955–) developed a program called GIB, an acronym for Goren in a Box (or Ginsberg's Intelligent Bridgeplayer), for playing bridge.[15] At any stage of play, GIB knows the cards in its own hand, in the dummy's hand, and the cards played so far. It then assigns the remaining cards randomly to the opponents and calculates the best card to play based on that random assignment. It goes through this process thousands of times before actually playing a card. Based on the statistics gathered by this "Monte Carlo" approach, it selects what it considers to be the best card to play.

In a *New York Times* article of March 14, 2008, the bridge columnist Phillip Alder analyzed a game in which two humans (each with a GIB partner) played against each other. In summarizing GIB's play, Alder said "These robots, as such programs are sometimes called, are quirky. Occasionally they bid and play well, but often they make strange decisions."[16] You can play bridge (with or against GIB) at http://www.bridgebase.com/, and there is a GIB Web site, from which you can purchase a copy of GIB, at http://www.gibware.com/. Ginsberg has ceased work on GIB, and there are probably stronger programs around. Commenting on bridge, Jonathan Schaeffer wrote me that "The bottleneck in achieving strong play continues to be bidding. Bidding conventions are human-designed conventions, and it is difficult to capture all the rules that human players have developed to play using this 'bidding language.'"[17]

Probably one of the hardest games for computers is the game of Go. In 2008, a program named MoGo Titan,[18] developed by INRIA France and Maastricht University in the Netherlands, beat a professional Go player in a game in which the computer, the Dutch supercomputer Huygens, was given a handicap of nine stones. Computer Go programs continue to improve. The best of them now use Monte

Carlo methods to make move selections. The Web page at http://www.computer-go
.info/h-c/index.html lists results of human–computer Go games.

Finally of course, there is Scrabble®, a game especially suited for computers with
their abilities to access large dictionaries and conduct massive searches. Scrabble
programs now routinely beat expert humans.[19]

Much more could be written about computer game-playing. Many programs are
available for purchase or download. You can select your favorite games and match
your own abilities against what AI has achieved! The International Computer Games
Association (ICGA) maintains a Web site that provides information about all kinds
of computer game-playing tournaments.[20] But let us turn now from what some
consider to be a frivolous (albeit challenging) pursuit to talk about the possibly more
exciting subject of robots.

32.2 Robot Systems

Robots are everywhere! They have gone to Mars, to the ocean depths, and even into
volcanoes. There are agricultural robots, factory robots, surgical robots, and warehouse robots. The business of building robots is thriving, especially in Pittsburgh,
Pennsylvania, the home of Carnegie Mellon University and its Robotics Institute.
According to a July 16, 2008, article in *The Christian Science Monitor*, "Today there
are more than 30 robotics companies in Pittsburgh."[21] Some of today's "robots" are
actually just remote-controlled mechanical devices operated by humans, but more
and more of them have become autonomous and capable of acting intelligently on
their own. I'll describe some examples.

32.2.1 *Remote Agent in Deep Space 1*

On October 24, 1998, NASA launched Deep Space 1 (DS1), a spacecraft whose
mission was to evaluate the space-worthiness of twelve advanced technologies. One
of these technologies was "Remote Agent" (RA), a robotic system for planning and
executing spacecraft actions.[22] An artist's rendering of DS1 approaching Comet
19P/Borrelly is shown in Fig. 32.4.

Although not quite up to all of the capabilities of HAL 9000 (the intelligent system
controlling the spacecraft in the novel and film *2001: A Space Odyssey*), the Remote
Agent was a major AI achievement. It was so named because it served as an intelligent
agent on DS1, intermediate between the operators back on earth and the sensors and
effectors on board. One of the NASA reports about the project states that[23]

... one of the most unique characteristics of RA, and a main difference with traditional
spacecraft commanding, is that ground operators can communicate with RA using goals (e.g.,
"During the next week take pictures of the following asteroids and thrust 90% of the time")
rather than with detailed sequences of timed commands. RA determines a plan of action that
achieves those goals and carries out that plan by issuing commands to the spacecraft.

RA was developed by engineers at the Jet Propulsion Laboratory in Pasadena and
at the Ames Research Center in Mountain View, California. It consists of three
major tightly integrated subsystems. A Planner and Scheduler uses heuristic search

Figure 32.4. Artist's rendering of DS1 approaching a comet.

to produce plans for accomplishing mission goals; an Executive system carries out the activities specified by these plans; and a Mode Identification and Recovery System monitors the status of the spacecraft and attempts to discover, diagnose, and correct faults. The system architecture is shown in Fig. 32.5.

RA's Smart Executive (EXEC) issues commands to the Real-Time Execution system, which controls the spacecraft and its components. These commands involve turning on and off the ion propulsion system, orienting the spacecraft, positioning the

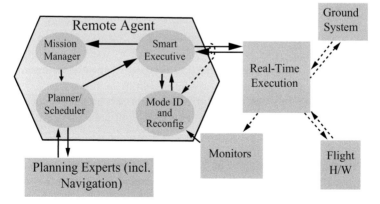

Figure 32.5. Remote agent architecture. (Used with permission of P. Pandurang Nayak.)

camera, and so on. RA's Mode ID system receives information about the status of the spacecraft through a set of sensory Monitors. Based on mission goals and anticipated spacecraft state provided by EXEC, the Mission Manager (MM) formulates a planning problem for the Planner/Scheduler (PS). PS, in turn, constructs a plan consisting of a time schedule of actions for execution by the EXEC. Planning Experts participate in the planning process for dealing with specialized tasks, such as navigation. EXEC decomposes the schedule of high-level activities composed by the PS into commands to motors, valves, and other effectors and monitors the execution of these commands. If some task cannot be achieved, EXEC may either attempt an alternative command or may ask the Mode ID and Recovery system for an analysis and repair of the problem. If neither of these courses of action work out, EXEC aborts its current plan, puts the spacecraft into a "safe state," and requests a new plan from MM. All the while, the Mode Identification system observes EXEC issuing commands, receives data about events taking place from the sensory Monitors, and uses its models of the spacecraft's components to deduce their states, which are communicated to EXEC.

RA was subjected to thorough testing and evaluation before NASA allowed it to fly on DS1. The space-tested version was called RAX (the added "X" signifying experiments). RAX was given control of the spacecraft for periods between May 17 and May 21, 1999. (It first ran from May 17, 1999, 5 am PST to May 19, 1999, 7 pm PST. It ran again from May 21, 1999, 7:15 am PST to 1:30 pm PST.) In these experiments, a "RAX Manager" (part of the DS1 flight software) supervised RAX's control of the spacecraft. As a final report about RAX notes "The ability to tightly control RAX activity through the RAX manager was an important factor in convincing the DS1 project that ground controllers could easily recover control of the spacecraft from RAX."[24] While RAX was in control, it could issue commands to the Ion Propulsion System (IPS), which was also being tested during the DS1 mission, to a Miniature Integrated Camera and Spectrometer, to an Autonomous Navigation system, to the spacecraft Attitude Control System, and to a series of power switches. As described in the final report, "The main scenario goals were to execute an IPS thrust arc, acquire optical navigation images as requested by the autonomous navigator, and respond to several simulated faults. The faults included minor ones that could be responded to without disrupting the current plan and more serious ones that required generating a new plan to achieve the remaining goals." The report concludes, "In spite of a couple of bugs that occurred during the flight experiment, RA successfully demonstrated 100% of its flight validation objectives."[25]

Figure 32.6 is a diagram of telemetry data showing what RAX was up to during several hours of its final test run. It was captured from an interactive Web applet, which you can access and run from http://ti.arc.nasa.gov/project/remote-agent/. (The Web site also has details about RA and RAX, with pointers to papers, press releases, and other material.)

As an interesting aside, the RA software was programmed in LISP Works, a LISP product originally marketed by The Harlequin Group, Ltd. As far as I know, RAX was the first instance of LISP programs running in space. MIT professor Brian C. Williams, one of the RA developers while he worked at NASA, continues related work on planning, execution, and model-based reasoning in his "Model-based

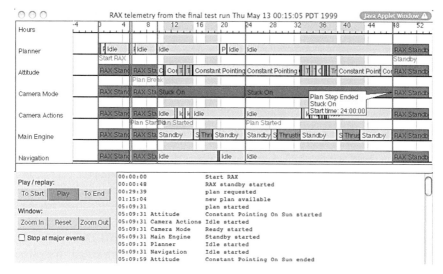

Figure 32.6. Illustration of RAX activities. (Illustration courtesy of Mark Shirley at NASA.)

Embedded and Robotic Systems" group at MIT.[26] He wrote me that "the remote agent architecture has been extensively emulated and deployed on a wide range of robotic systems, including earth orbiters, air vehicles, boats, submersibles, and ground vehicles."[27]

32.2.2 Driverless Automobiles

Perhaps driving an automobile under a wide range of conditions is even more challenging than controlling a spacecraft. The pace of dealing with the many controls on a spacecraft is leisurely compared with the rapid planning and reaction required to negotiate traffic skillfully. Thus, we might expect that the perception and action computations needed for driving to be quite different from those of the Remote Agent.

Humans drive cars, more or less well, on sunny and stormy days, at night, on city streets, on high-speed motorways, and on and off desert roads. Yes, there are crashes. In the United States there were 28,933 people who died and 2,221,000 people who were injured in passenger-car accidents in 2007.[28] But that represents only slightly over one person killed per 100 million vehicle miles traveled.

There is a long history of attempting to get AI systems to drive vehicles as well as humans do. DARPA began work on this problem in the mid-1980s with its ALV project of the Strategic Computing Program (see Chapter 23). Carnegie Mellon University had continuing programs on driverless vehicles, notably the ALVINN, RALPH, and Navlab systems (see Section 29.4.3). The most impressive early work was probably that of Ernst Dickmanns and his team at the Universität der Bundeswehr in Munich. Supported in part by the European EUREKA Prometheus driverless-automobile project, Dickmanns's VaMP vehicle (a Mercedes-Benz 500 SEL) drove from Munich to Odense, Denmark, and back in 1995 (95% of the way autonomously), using computer vision and radar.[29] Other driverless-vehicle projects have been undertaken in Japan (Tsukuba Mechanical Engineering Lab), in the Netherlands (2getthere), and in Italy (the ARGO Project).

DARPA returned to tackle the driverless car problem by announcing a "Grand Challenge" on July 30, 2002. The challenge (a competition for U.S.-based teams only) was to demonstrate a vehicle that could drive autonomously on and off roads in the desert from Barstow, California, to Primm, Nevada, on March 13, 2004. The team that most quickly completed the 142-mile course in less than the ten-hour time limit would receive a cash prize of $1,000,000. As the DARPA commemorative Web site for the challenge notes, "Competitors' entries must be unmanned, autonomous ground vehicles, and cannot be remotely driven. Boundaries define the course, and vehicles that go outside of them will be disqualified. Each vehicle will be trailed on the course by a manned control vehicle equipped with an emergency stop system to prevent collisions and other unsafe situations."[30]

The motivation for the challenge was a mandate by the FY2001 Defense Authorization Act (H.R. 4205/P.L. 106–398 of October 30, 2001), which stated "It shall be a goal of the Armed Forces to achieve the fielding of unmanned, remotely controlled technology such that – (1) by 2010, one-third of the aircraft in the operational deep strike force aircraft fleet are unmanned; and (2) by 2015, one-third of the operational ground combat vehicles are unmanned."

Out of 106 teams that originally applied to compete in the challenge, fifteen driverless vehicles left the starting line in Barstow, California. There were teams from large and small companies, from universities, and from specially assembled groups of individual innovators.[31] Each team was given a CD with the coordinates of some 2000 "waypoints" to help them chart their way along the course using their GPS systems. Navigating around obstacles, staying on roads, and avoiding drop-offs was up to the sensory and planning mechanisms on board.

None of the vehicles completed the course.[32] Eight failed before traveling a mile and others crashed soon after starting. (For a short film, see http://www.youtube.com/watch?v=wTDG5gjwPGo.) The farthest any vehicle traveled was just under seven and a half miles. According to DARPA's final data, as reported by CNN, "Vehicle 22 Red Team (Carnegie Mellon): At mile 7.4, on switchbacks in a mountainous section, vehicle [which was named "Sandstorm"] went off course, got caught on a berm and rubber on the front wheels caught fire, which was quickly extinguished. Vehicle was command-disabled."[33] Commenting on the results, Tom Strat, the deputy program manager of the Grand Challenge, said[34]

Some of the vehicles were able to follow the GPS waypoints very accurately; but were not able to sense obstacles ahead, and we had some collisions at the qualification rounds . . . Other vehicles were very good at sensing obstacles, but had difficulty following waypoints or were scared of their own shadow, hallucinating obstacles when they weren't there.

Although the 2004 Grand Challenge hardly displayed any "extraordinary achievements," it was, perhaps, a necessary precursor to sequels that did. Three months after the 2004 event, DARPA announced "a second Grand Challenge for Autonomous Robotic Ground Vehicles" to be held on October 8, 2005, with a prize this time of $2 million.[35] Twenty-three finalists competed in the 2005 event, and all but one

Figure 32.7. Stanley on Beer Bottle Pass followed by a DARPA chase vehicle. (Photograph courtesy of DARPA.)

of them went farther than Sandstorm did in the 2004 event. Five of the vehicles completed the course – a 132-mile desert route starting and ending in Primm, Nevada:

1. Stanley (a modified 2004 Volkswagen Touareg R5 TDI; Fig. 32.7) entered by "The Stanford Racing Team" from Stanford University. Stanley came in first in six hours and fifty-four minutes.
2. Sandstorm (a modified 1986 AM General M998 HMMWV; Fig. 32.8) entered by "The Red Team" from Carnegie Mellon University. Sandstorm (which was upgraded from the 2004 version) came in second in seven hours and five minutes.
3. H1ghlander (a modified 1999 AM General H1 Hummer Sport Utility Truck) entered by "The Red Team Too" also from Carnegie Mellon University. H1ghlander came in third in seven hours and fourteen minutes. (As a "cultural note," a Web page for the film *Déjà Vu* states "The Humvee time machine is a real-life robot H1ghlander built by Carnegie Mellon's Red Team for the 2005 DARPA Grand Challenge."[36])
4. Kat-5 (a modified 2005 Ford Escape Hybrid) entered by "Team Gray" from the Gray Insurance Company of Metairie, Louisiana (a suburb of New Orleans). Kat-5 came in fourth in seven hours and thirty minutes. (Development of Kat-5 was hampered by two hurricanes, notably Katrina – which hit New Orleans in late August of 2005. Paul Trepagnier, one of the team members, wrote me that "Most of us had lost our homes right before the Grand Challenge. [The name, Kat-5,] was not made in honor of Katrina, as some people have incorrectly stated, but rather it was more of an act of defiance. You gave us your best, and we are still standing. You can knock us down, but we'll persevere and come back stronger than before. It was also a pun on Cat-5 cabling."[37])

Figure 32.8. Sandstorm on Beer Bottle Pass. (Photograph courtesy of DARPA.)

5. TerraMax (a modified tactical cargo hauler) entered by "Team TerraMax" from the Oshkosh Truck Corporation. TerraMax came in fifth (after being paused overnight) in a total running time of twelve hours and fifty-one minutes, which was over the ten-hour limit.

In some respects the 2005 course was easier than the one in 2004. The roads were somewhat wider and had fewer curves. The most harrowing stretch, with steep drop-offs, was over Beer Bottle Pass. A false move there would send a vehicle tumbling down the mountainside. Figure 32.7 shows Stanley navigating a stretch of that section. H1ghlander had the best time for a good part of the race but a problem developed just past the 100-mile mark, and Stanley passed it to gain the lead, the victory, and the $2 million. (Videos of the CMU and Stanford entrants can be found from sites at http://www.redteamracing.org/ and http://robots.stanford .edu/talks/stanley/RaceDay.wmv. A PBS *NOVA* program about the race can be found at http://www.pbs.org/wgbh/nova/darpa/.)

The entrants in the 2005 Grand Challenge used ranging and optical sensors that, together with computer vision technology, enabled them to avoid obstacles and to distinguish drivable from undrivable terrain. They could also construct plans to control speed and driving direction even though the perceptual information on which these plans were based was uncertain. Space does not permit a description of all of the vehicles, but I'll describe some of the technology used by Stanley, the winner.[38]

Stanley was outfitted with a six-processor computing platform provided by Intel, a suite of sensors, and a drive-by-wire control system connected to the computers. The sensors included five laser range-finding units, a video camera, a GPS system, and gyroscopes and accelerometers.[39] Stanford professor Sebastian Thrun (1967– ; Fig. 32.9) was the overall supervisor of the project, and Stanford senior research

Figure 32.9. Sebastian Thrun (left) and Michael Montemerlo (right). (Photo courtesy of John Markoff.)

engineer Michael Montemerlo (1975– ; Fig. 32.9) headed up the software design group. They decided early on that autonomous navigation was primarily a software problem, and designing the software and its architecture was critical to success. Methods were developed, and existing methods extended, to deal with the problems of long-range terrain perception, real-time collision avoidance, and stable vehicle control on slippery and rugged terrain. In particular, three important software innovations played a major role in Stanley's performance.

One of these innovations was the development of a probabilistic terrain analysis (PTA) algorithm. It used probabilistic techniques to integrate range measurements over time from a single-scan laser. It then employed efficient statistical tests to distinguish drivable from nondrivable terrain. During the Grand Challenge, the PTA algorithm was able to accommodate severe errors in sensing and to identify obstacles with nearly 100% accuracy at speeds of up to 35 mph.[40]

Another innovation was in computer vision. First, a nearby patch of surface identified to be drivable by the PTA algorithm was located in the visual field. This patch was then used as a sample of what drivable surfaces look like and used as training data for the computer vision algorithm. As a paper describing the technique states, "The vision algorithm then classifies the entire field of view of the camera [extending beyond that of the laser scanner], and extracts a drivability map with a range of up to 70 m. The combined sensors [laser plus computer vision] are integrated into a driving strategy, which allows for very robust, long range sensing."[41] It is worth noting that Stanley's vision system was not the kind (as advocated by David Marr,

The Quest for Artificial Intelligence

for example) that thoroughly analyzed a scene to determine the kinds and locations of objects in it. Instead it used special-purpose routines whose only job was to help Stanley decide where it was safe to drive.

Finally, a supervised learning system was developed for online speed control. Speed control was critical in Stanley's achievement of the fastest finishing time. The vehicle needed to drive slowly on risky terrain but then speed up on safe terrain. Using supervised learning matched to human driving over both risky and safe terrain, the system was able to learn to choose driving speeds that traded off risk and speed.[42]

In January 2006 Stanley was judged to be the "Best Robot of All Time" by *Wired*.[43] (Shakey was judged to be the fifth best robot, behind the Martian robots Spirit and Opportunity and two fictional ones.) Stanley currently resides at the Smithsonian National Museum of American History.

DARPA sponsored another autonomous driving event on November 3, 2007. Called an "Urban Challenge," it was held near Victorville, California, at what was once the site of George Air Force Base. Entrants had to be capable of visiting a set of "check points" within six hours along a sixty-mile course through a mock city environment. Successful completion required the performance of complex maneuvers, such as merging, passing, parking, and negotiating intersections, in the presence of other traffic and obeying all California driving regulations. In all, over fifty vehicles, both manned and autonomous, were navigating the city streets simultaneously during the final event. (Pictures and videos of the event are available at http://www.darpa.mil/grandchallenge/gallery.asp.)[44]

Through a series of qualifying procedures and actual vehicle testing, DARPA narrowed the field down first from eighty-nine original applicants to thirty-five teams from twenty-two states and finally to eleven teams. Six of these successfully finished the course on race day. DARPA announced the following finishers and completion times:

1. Boss (a 2007 Chevy Tahoe) entered by Tartan Racing from Carnegie Mellon University. (See Fig. 32.10.) Boss took first place, and a prize of $2 million, with a time of 4:10:20 (for an average speed of approximately 14 mph).
2. Junior (a 2006 Volkswagen Passat Wagon) entered by the Stanford Racing Team from Stanford University. Junior took second place, and a prize of $1 million, with a time of 4:29:28.
3. Odin (a 2005 Ford Hybrid Escape) entered by Team Victor Tango from Virginia Tech. Odin took third place, and a prize of $500,000, with a time of 4:36:38.
4. Talos (a Land Rover LR3) entered by Team MIT from the Massachusetts Institute of Technology. Talos took fourth place with a time of approximately six hours.

(Note that the times mentioned here were adjusted to account for periods during the event when the vehicles were paused due to no fault of their own.) Two other teams also finished the course, one from a combination of the University of Pennsylvania and Lehigh University and one from Cornell University.

The Urban Challenge made new and strong demands on perception and planning technology. Consider, for example, some of the things the vehicles had to do: follow rules of the road, detect and track other vehicles at long ranges, find a spot and

Figure 32.10. Tartan Racing team leader William (Red) Whittaker and Boss pose with first place trophy. (Photograph courtesy of Carnegie Mellon University.)

park in a parking lot, obey intersection precedence rules, follow vehicles at a safe distance, and react to dynamic conditions such as blocked roads or broken-down vehicles. All of the finishers accomplished these feats, and interested readers can refer to papers and Web sites of the entrants to learn details about how they did so. Here is a summary description from Boss's Web site:[45]

Boss uses perception, planning and behavioral software to reason about traffic and take appropriate actions while proceeding safely to a destination.

Boss is equipped with more than a dozen lasers, cameras and radars to view the world. High-level route planning determines the best path through a road network. Motion planning requires consideration of the static and dynamic obstacles detected by perception, as well as lane and road boundary information, parking lot boundaries, stop lines, speed limits, and similar requirements. Boss handles surprises such as other vehicles running a stop sign or making sudden stops or turns. Defensive driving skills allow Boss to avoid crashes.

Based on the success of vehicles in the various DARPA Challenges, the automobile industry is expanding its interest in driverless vehicles. (At least it was before the 2008–2009 financial problems.) In November 2007, Volkswagen of America announced that it was donating $2 million to Stanford University to construct a building to house the Volkswagen Automotive Innovation Lab (VAIL) and $750,000 a year for five years for research on automotive technology. Dr. Burkhard Huhnke, executive director of the Electronics Research Laboratory, Volkswagen of America, said "The VAIL will be a solid foundation on which Volkswagen researchers and Stanford scientists will be able to find new ways to explore automotive technology. The work done at VAIL will help to further develop the future of mobility and autonomous driving that we started with our partnership on the DARPA Grand Challenge vehicles, Stanley and Junior."[46]

In June 2008, General Motors announced a program to supply Carnegie Mellon University $1 million annually for five years (and possibly beyond) for research on autonomous driving technology. Alan Taub, GM's executive director of research and development, told a news conference, "We at General Motors believe that autonomous driving is feasible to begin to enter the marketplace in the next decade and clearly by 2020."[47] You might wonder what effect GM's recent bankruptcy has had on this pledge. I am told by William H. Swisher, Director of Corporate Relations at CMU, that $1 million has in fact been granted but that "it is unknown if they will complete the 5 year agreement."[48]

Sebastian Thrun tells me that he expects his research vehicles "will be driving [autonomously] from San Francisco to Los Angeles routinely . . . [by] around June 2010."[49] He also predicts that "By 2030, half of our highway miles will be driven autonomously without human input."[50] He doubts, however, that driverless cars will appear in showrooms anytime soon. He cites various societal and legal problems such as updating vehicle codes, determining accident liability, and the human desire to be in control. Instead, he thinks that for the next few years the main benefits stemming from driverless automobile research will be automated aids to human drivers. These will allow more efficient use of highways and will markedly reduce traffic injuries and fatalities. Examples of some of these aids are all-around collision warning systems, radar-based cruise control, lane-change warning devices, electronic stability control, satellite global positioning systems, and digital maps.

Just as AI technology will soon be helping us drive automobiles, bits and pieces of AI are already in everyday use all around us, which leads me to my next topic.

Notes

1. See http://ijcai-09.org/fcfp.html. [479]
2. Murray Campbell *et al.*, "Deep Blue," available online at http://sjeng.org/ftp/deepblue.pdf. [481]
3. Bruce Webber, "Swift and Slashing, Computer Topples Kasparov," *New York Times*, May 12, 1997. [482]
4. http://www.nytimes.com/library/cyber/week/051297weber.html. [482]
5. Murray Campbell *et al.*, "Deep Blue," available online at http://sjeng.org/ftp/deepblue.pdf. [483]
6. http://www.research.ibm.com/deepblue/meet/html/d.3.3a.shtml#ai. [483]
7. http://www.research.ibm.com/deepblue/meet/html/d.2.shtml. [483]
8. John McCarthy, "AI as Sport," book review, *Science*, Vol. 276, No. 5318, pp. 1518–1519, June 6, 1997. [484]
9. Jonathan Schaeffer *et al.*, "Checkers is Solved," *Science*, pp. 1518–1522, Vol. 317, September 14, 2007. [484]
10. Jonathan Schaeffer. "Man versus Machine: The Silicon Graphics World Checkers Championship," TR 92-19, Department of Computing Science, University of Alberta, 1992. Available online at http://www.cs.ualberta.ca/~jonathan/Papers/Papers/TR92-19.ps. Also see Jonathan Schaeffer *et al.*, "Man versus Machine for the World Checkers Championship," *AI Magazine*, Vol. 14, No. 2, pp. 28–35, 1993. [485]
11. Jonathan Schaeffer *et al.*, "CHINOOK: The Man–Machine World Checkers Champion," *AI Magazine*, Vol. 17, No. 1, pp. 21–29, 1996. [485]

12. From one of Jonathan Schaeffer's slides about CHINOOK at http://www.cs.ualberta.ca/~chinook/news/ChinookTalk.pdf. [487]

13. For more on Schaeffer and checkers, see Jonathan Schaeffer, *One Jump Ahead: Computer Perfection at Checkers*, second edition, New York: Springer-Verlag, 2008. [487]

14. See http://www.cs.ualberta.ca/~pokert/2008/results/ for the results. [487]

15. Matthew L. Ginsberg, "GIB: Imperfect Information in a Computationally Challenging Game," *Journal of Artificial Intelligence Research*, Vol. 14, pp. 303–358, 2001. Available online at http://www.cs.cmu.edu/afs/cs/project/jair/pub/volume14/ginsberg01a.pdf. [487]

16. Phillip Alder, "BRIDGE; A Case Study of the Mysteries of the Robot Thought Process," *New York Times*, April 14, 2008. [487]

17. E-mail of February 14, 2009. [487]

18. See http://www.nwo.nl/nwohome.nsf/pages/NWOA_7HHBNS. [487]

19. See Brian Sheppard, "World-Championship-Caliber Scrabble," *Artificial Intelligence*, Vol. 134, Nos. 1–2, pp. 241–275, January 2002. [488]

20. http://www.icga.org/. [488]

21. Tom A. Peter, "Pittsburgh Is Robot Country," *The Christian Science Monitor*, July 16, 2008. [488]

22. Nicola Muscettola *et al.*, "Remote Agent: To Boldly Go Where No AI System Has Gone Before," *Artificial Intelligence*, Vol. 103, pp. 5–47, 1998. Available online at http://groups.csail.mit.edu/mers/papers/aij98.pdf. [488]

23. Available online at http://nmp-techval-reports.jpl.nasa.gov/DS1/Remote_Integrated_Report.pdf. [488]

24. Douglas E. Bernard *et al.*, "Remote Agent Experiment DS1 Technology Validation Report," Jet Propulsion Laboratory, California Institute of Technology and NASA Ames Research Center, Moffett Field. Available online at http://nmp-techval-reports.jpl.nasa.gov/DS1/Remote_Integrated_Report.pdf. [490]

25. For a full description of the "bugs," see P. Pandurang Nayak *et al.*, "Validating the DS1 Remote Agent Experiment," Artificial Intelligence, Robotics and Automation in Space, *Proceedings of the Fifth International Symposium, ISAIRAS '99*, held June 1–3, 1999, in ESTEC, Noordwijk, the Netherlands, M. Perry (ed.), ESA SP-440, Paris: European Space Agency, pp. 349–356, 1999. Available online at http://citeseerx.ist.psu.edu/viewdoc/download?doi=10.1.1.30.2688&rep=rep1&type=pdf. [490]

26. mers.csail.mit.edu. [491]

27. E-mail of January 25, 2009. [491]

28. These data are from "Traffic Safety Facts," available online at http://www-nrd.nhtsa.dot.gov/Pubs/811017.PDF. [491]

29. See http://ijcai.org/Past%20Proceedings/IJCAI-97-VOL2/PDF/117.pdf. [492]

30. http://www.darpa.mil/grandchallenge04/program.pdf. [492]

31. See http://www.darpa.mil/grandchallenge04/program.pdf for descriptions. [492]

32. To see how they fared, visit http://www.msnbc.msn.com/id/4517001/. [492]

33. See http://www.cnn.com/2004/TECH/ptech/03/14/darpa.race/index.html. [492]

34. This quotation is taken from a CNN report written by Marsha Walton at http://www.cnn.com/2004/TECH/ptech/03/14/darpa.race/index.html. [492]

35. See http://www.darpa.mil/grandchallenge05/InitialPressRelease.pdf. [492]

36. See http://www.imdb.com/title/tt0453467/trivia. [493]

37. E-mail communication of December 1, 2008. [493]

38. Readers who are interested in digging deeper might consult various papers available on the Web, for example one describing Sandstorm at http://www.darpa.mil/

grandchallenge05/TechPapers/RedTeam.pdf and one describing H1ghlander at http://www.darpa.mil/grandchallenge05/TechPapers/RedTeamToo.pdf. [494]

39. For an overview paper describing Stanley, see Sebastian Thrun *et al.*, "Stanley: The Robot That Won The DARPA Grand Challenge," *Journal of Field Robotics*, Vol. 23, No. 9, pp. 661–692, June 2006. Available online at http://robots.stanford.edu/papers/thrun.stanley05.pdf. [494]

40. For more information, see Sebastian Thrun, Michael Montemerlo, and Andrei Aron, "Probabilistic Terrain Analysis for High-Speed Desert Driving, in G. Sukhatme *et al.* (eds.), *Proceedings of the Robotics Science and Systems Conference, II*, Philadelphia, PA, 2006. Available online at http://robots.stanford.edu/papers/thrun.mapping-Stanley.pdf. [495]

41. Hendrik Dahlkamp *et al.*, "Self-supervised Monocular Road Detection in Desert Terrain," in G. Sukhatme *et al.* (eds.), *Proceedings of the Robotics Science and Systems Conference, II*, Philadelphia, PA, 2006. Available online at http://robots.stanford.edu/papers/dahlkamp.adaptvision06.pdf. [495]

42. For more information, see David Stavens, Gabriel Hoffmann, and Sebastian Thrun, "Online Speed Adaptation Using Supervised Learning for High-Speed, Off-Road Autonomous Driving," *Proceedings of the International Joint Conference on Artificial Intelligence*. pp. 2218–2224, 2007. Available online at http://robots.stanford.edu/papers/stavens_hoffmann_thrun_ijcai07.pdf. [496]

43. See http://www.wired.com/wired/archive/14.01/robots.html?pg=1&topic=robots&topic_set=. [496]

44. The official DARPA Web site for the event is at http://www.darpa.mil/GRANDCHALLENGE/index.asp. [496]

45. http://www.tartanracing.org/tech.html. [497]

46. See http://www.vw.com/vwbuzz/browse/en/us/detail/Volkswagen_to_contribute_5_75_million_to_Stanford_University/180. [497]

47. Reported by the Associated Press. See http://www.mercurynews.com/nationworld/ci_9664682. [498]

48. E-mail of June 21, 2009. [498]

49. E-mail of October 17, 2008. [498]

50. E-mail of January 14, 2009. [498]

33

Ubiquitous Artificial Intelligence

IN TODAY'S WORLD, THE MAGIC OF AI IS EVERYWHERE – MAYBE IT'S NOT "FULL AI" but there are significant parts. Allen Newell foresaw these bits and pieces as part of an "enchanted land." In an address given in 1976, he called computers the "technology of enchantment." He noted two ingredients that made it so:[1]

First, it is the technology of how to apply knowledge to action to achieve goals. . . . That is what algorithms and programs are all about – frozen action to be thawed when needed.

The second ingredient is the miniaturization of the physical systems that have this ability for intelligent action.

Thus, computer technology differs from all other technologies precisely in providing the capability for an enchanted world:

For brakes that know how to stop on wet pavement
For instruments that can converse with their users
For bridges that watch out for the safety of those who cross them
For streetlights that care about those who stand under them – who know the way, so no one need get lost
For little boxes that make out your income tax for you

In short, computer technology offers the possibility of incorporating intelligent behavior in all the nooks and crannies of our world. With it, we could build an enchanted land.

Let's see some examples of how AI is already inhabiting the "nooks and crannies of our world." I'll start with our houses and some of the things in and around them.

33.1 AI at Home

Homes and their contents are becoming more intelligent. Here is a partial list of what you might find today (or sometime soon) on a tour of a modern house:

- thermostats for heat and air-conditioning systems that anticipate temperature changes and the needs of occupants, communicate with other home devices, and take appropriate actions in advance;
- microwave ovens that read barcodes on packages to determine how long to cook an item;
- smart running shoes with a computer chip that senses the runner's size and stride length and directs on-going changes in the heal cushioning via a miniature screw and cable system;

- washing machines that automatically adjust to different conditions to wash clothes better;
- refrigerators that automatically inventory their contents and inform owners of needed items;
- cameras with computer vision systems to identify faces and to control focusing, exposure, and framing;
- hearing aids that adapt to ambient sound levels and block out "cocktail party" chatter;
- robotic pet "animals" and toys that interact with people;
- floor-washing and vacuum-cleaning robots; and
- caretaker robots for the elderly or infirm.

This list will continue to grow. Some AI researchers talk about a field called "ambient intelligence," where the "broad idea is to enrich a space (such as a room, house, building, bus station, or a critical area in a hospital) with sensors tied to intelligent software, so that the people using the space can benefit from a responsive, even wise environment."[2] The components in an environment permeated by ambient intelligence are also being networked so that they can communicate with each other and so that people can communicate with them using ordinary speech. Vlingo, Nuance, and Yap are three companies that sell products for mobile phones (such as the iPhone) that translate voice into text. Vlingo, for example, claims on its Web site that if you say "pizza places in Pittsburgh" to your phone, it then "figures out what you want, finds it and shows you how to get there. No tapping, no thumbs, just good old speaking."[3] Presumably similar technology could enable one to command and query one's smart appliances by talking to them.

33.2 Advanced Driver Assistance Systems

Perhaps the landscape with the most places into which computers and artificial intelligence have crept is the modern passenger automobile. Today's cars can have as many as fifty microprocessors controlling, such things as automatic transmissions, fuel injection systems, antilock brakes, airbags, security systems, and cruise control systems to name just a few. And, although not yet completely autonomous, more and more automobiles are beginning to be equipped with safety features called "advanced driver assistance systems" (ADAS).

Here is a list of just a few of the ADAS features that are either available now or are being planned by several automobile manufacturers:

- adaptive cruise control (ACC) for providing more intelligent control of speed, enabling the vehicle to slow down or speed up depending on traffic conditions as perceived by radar or laser sensors;
- intelligent speed adaptation (ISA) for monitoring local speed limits, slowing the vehicle down (or warning the driver) when it enters zones with speed limits;
- lane control systems for monitoring the presence of vehicles or obstructions in adjacent lanes and for monitoring when a driver drifts into an adjacent lane or off the roadway;
- automatic parking systems for assisting a driver when executing a parallel parking maneuver;

- traffic sign recognition systems;
- driver drowsiness detection systems; and
- intelligent tire pressure control systems.

Although not all automobile computers employ AI technology, the most ambitious of the ADAS features use computer vision, planning methods, probabilistic inference, and machine learning. The motivation for using ADAS is the desire to eliminate automobile injuries and fatalities. In 1997, for example, the Swedish parliament passed a "Road Traffic Safety Bill" whose goal, "Vision Zero," is that "no one will be killed or seriously injured when moving within the road transport system."[4]

33.3 Route Finding in Maps

While we are on the subject of automobiles, one of the things drivers often need to know is how to get from one place to another. Many automobiles have devices that "talk" you to your destination using on-board GPS systems, map databases, and speech synthesis. Map databases can be thought of as graphs consisting of place "nodes" and connecting road "links." So whether the navigation advice is provided ahead of time by your home computer (using Google Maps, for example) or by an on-board navigation system, it is generated by a process of searching a graph to find a path from some node, A, to some other node, B.

You will recall that the most commonly used graph-searching procedure is A*, a heuristic search method that takes into account both the distance traveled so far and an estimate of the distance to the goal (see p. 168.) Is A* used in route-finding programs? Well, Google, for example, will only say that it uses "state-of-the-art hierarchical graph algorithms to compute shortest paths in routing networks in a matter of milliseconds."[5] Most likely these algorithms, and similar ones used by other route-finders, use heuristic techniques similar to those used by A* but specialized to the case of searching two-dimensional maps. For example, the searches are hierarchically organized. That is, for trips to a distant goal, large-scale maps with just the major roads and highways are searched. Then, to get from a starting position to a major road on the way to the goal, a more detailed map with less-traveled roads is used. Hierarchical search may result in slightly suboptimal, but nevertheless quite acceptable, paths. In addition, when responding to billions of queries, some of the computations that would have to be repeated for each query can be shared among them instead.

Most route-finding programs can (and do) take into account criteria other than distance, such as estimated travel times. For example, Microsoft's ClearFlow program, which uses Bayesian networks informed by traffic-monitoring sensors to estimate traffic densities, can base route recommendations either on shortest time, shortest distance, or current traffic conditions. (Try it out at http://maps.live.com/.)

33.4 You Might Also Like . . .

When I log on to Amazon.com's Web site, it responds "Hello, Nils J. Nilsson. We have recommendations for you." It then lists some items that it guesses I might like including the book *Portuguese Irregular Verbs* by Alexander McCall Smith (recommended because I had previously purchased another book by the same author) and the video *Lipstick Jungle* with Brooke Shields because I had previously downloaded the video *BBC Shakespeare: Othello*(?!). It then lets me make some changes. When I say that I am not interested in *Lipstick Jungle* it wonders whether or not I might be interested in the video *How I Met Your Mother*. Perhaps I have not ordered enough videos to give it a better idea of what I might be interested in.

Amazon's recommendations are based on what is called social or collaborative filtering. A database of preferences (for books, movies, or whatever) is maintained for every user. If user B's preferences correlate sufficiently with those of user A, a collaborative filtering system would recommend some of B's purchases (not already bought by user A) to user A. Rather straightforward machine learning techniques are used to find preference correlations among users. Several other sites, including iTunes, TiVo, and Netflix, base their recommendations on collaborative filtering.

Another type of recommending system uses what is called content-based filtering, in which a user's preferences for books, movies, documents, or whatever are analyzed to find similarities with other *items* of the same kind (instead of with other users having the same preferences). The most similar items are then recommended. For documents, for example, comparisons might be made using the vector representations I discussed in Section 27.3. Content-based filtering is widely used for blocking unwanted e-mail (such as spam) and Web sites (such as pornography). It's also used for personalized Web searches – for example in customizing news feeds to gather news about particular topics. Recommendation systems that combine collaborative and content-based methods have also been developed. Interested readers might want to see a special issue of the journal *AI Communications* on "Recommender Systems."[6]

33.5 Computer Games

In addition to the use of AI techniques for playing games such as chess and checkers, AI is beginning to be used in the kinds of computer games in which human users interact with artificial characters in a simulated world. Although the emphasis in these games has been on rich and realistic graphics, the use of AI techniques can make them even more appealing and challenging. Developers and aficionados of these games use the term "Game AI" to distinguish the kinds of AI in computer games from what they call academic or "R&D AI." They point out that in many games all that is required is the illusion or appearance of intelligence – much like the ELIZA program appears to be able to carry on a conversation but does not really know what it is talking about.

Nevertheless, computer games are rich with possibilities for the use of AI. In the usual setting, a human player interacts with and competes with artificial agents in the game; these agents are called nonplayer characters (NPCs). Among other tasks, the NPCs have to be able to navigate from place A in their world to place B without bumping into obstacles or other NPCs, and thus many games use A*. But also, the NPCs should be able to perceive their simulated environment, make and execute plans, and learn – just like robots in real environments do. The more intelligently they can do those things, the more realistic they will appear to the human player (and purchaser) of the game. I'll mention two representative examples of games with these abilities.[7]

The game *Black and White 2*, developed by Lionhead Studios and marketed by Electronic Arts, uses a combination of neural nets and decision trees. According to a Web site for the game, the NPCs (evil and benevolent deities) "can learn strategies, master new abilities and skills, [and] lead armies into battle.... Every choice you make will have an impact. Each action and inaction prompts obvious changes to buildings, flora and fauna, all morphing to reflect your personality."[8]

The game *F.E.A.R.* (*First Encounter Assault Recon*) by Jeff Orkin and Monolith Productions uses A* to plan sequences of NPC actions in addition to its usual role in path finding.[9]

Black and White and *F.E.A.R.* were rated numbers 1 and 2, respectively, of the "Top 10 Most Influential AI Games," by http://AIGameDev.com, a Web site about the use of AI in games. There are several Web sites and conferences devoted to AI in games.[10]

Some AI researchers have advocated using computer games as a convenient arena for developing new ideas for intelligent agents. For example, University of Michigan professor John Laird has written, "[because] research in robotics requires solving many difficult problems related to low-level sensing and acting in the real world that are far removed from the cognitive aspects of intelligence, . . . computer games provide us with a source of cheap, reliable, and flexible technology for developing our own virtual environments for research."[11]

The bits and pieces of AI just discussed, whether in the home, in the automobile, or in computer games, are usually of the "reactive" or "behavior-based" variety. Conditions are sensed, and actions are taken depending on what is sensed. Building systems that are able to react appropriately to the situation at hand has been an important strand of AI research. AI agents that inhabit dynamic environments, whether simulated or real, must also be able to decide when to react and when to deliberate. Albert Lewis, when he was a cornerback of the Oakland Raiders Football team, had this to say about when to react and when to think:[12]

When you think on the field, you've automatically lost that down. The time you should be thinking is during the course of the week in practice. That's when the light should go on. When you get in the game, it's all about reacting to what you see.

One can imagine that the simulated football players (the NPCs) in games like *Madden NFL 09* will use increasingly complex reactive strategies aided, when appropriate, by higher level reasoning.

Notes

1. For a published version of his address, see Allen Newell, "Fairy Tales," *AI Magazine*, Vol. 13 No. 4, 1992. Available online at http://www.aaai.org/ojs/index.php/aimagazine/article/download/1020/938. [501]
2. See the article by Juan Carlos Augusto and Daniel Shapiro, "The First Workshop on Artificial Intelligence Techniques for Ambient Intelligence (AITAmI '06)," *AI Magazine*, Vol. 28, No. 1, pp. 86–87, Spring 2007. Also see http://www.infj.ulst.ac.uk/~jcaug/aitami07.htm. [502]

3. See http://www.vlingo.com/. **[502]**

4. Swedish Ministry of Transport and Communications, 1997. **[503]**

5. E-mail from Peter Norvig, Director of Research at Google, Inc., September 9, 2008. **[503]**

6. *AI Communications*, Special Issue on Recommender Systems, Dietmar Jannach, Markus Zanker, and Joseph Konstan (guest eds.), Vol. 21, Nos. 2–3, 2008. **[504]**

7. I thank John Laird for mentioning these games to me (e-mail of September 10, 2008). **[505]**

8. http://www.lionhead.com/bw2/Default.aspx. **[505]**

9. See Jeff Orkin, "Three States and a Plan: The A.I. of F.E.A.R."; available online at http://web.media.mit.edu/~jorkin/gdc2006_orkin_jeff_fear.doc. **[505]**

10. See, for example, http://www.gameai.com/, http://www.igda.org/ai/, http://www.aiwisdom.com/bygame.html, and http://aigamedev.com/. **[505]**

11. John E. Laird, "Research in Human-Level AI Using Computer Games," *Communications of the ACM*, Vol. 45, No. 1, pp. 32–35, 2002. **[505]**

12. As quoted by Sam Farmer in the *San Jose Mercury News*, page 1D, August 30, 1996. **[505]**

34

Smart Tools

I N BETWEEN THE HEADLINE-MAKING, MILESTONE AI ACHIEVEMENTS AND THE smaller bits of computational intelligence that we find everywhere are impressive AI programs that are used by physicians, scientists, engineers, and business people to help them in (and sometimes automate) their workaday tasks. I call these the "smart tools" of AI. Sometimes these are stand-alone systems, but more often they are integrated into a larger computational framework or into hardware devices. Some work only when called upon to help solve some particular problem, such as disease diagnosis. Some are constantly active, such as online stock-trading systems. I'll not be able to mention all of them since there are far too many, and some are known only to their corporate and government users. But a few examples will serve to illustrate their utility and variety.

34.1 In Medicine

Let's start with how AI is being used in medical clinical practice. Beginning as early as the 1980s, AI technology has been an important part of medical systems and devices. In March 2000, a monthly magazine titled *Medical Device & Diagnostic Industry* published an article claiming that "the medical device industry is seeing an emergence of computer-based intelligent decision support systems (DSSs) and expert systems, the current success of which reflects a maturation of artificial intelligence (AI) technology."[1] It mentioned several AI-infused devices, including the "Agilent Acute Cardiac Ischemia Time-Insensitive Predictive Instrument . . . , an intelligent electro-cardiagram (ECG) device that predicts the probability of acute cardiac ischemia (ACI), a common form of heart attack," and the General Electric "MAC 5000 Resting Test System, [incorporating] the Marquette 12SL ECG analysis program, an integrated DSS that uses newly developed digital processing methods and diagnostic program algorithms to interpret and classify ECG waveforms."

A September 2005 online review[2] in *Clinical Window* (which is sponsored by GE Healthcare) of ECG devices by Dr. Paul Kligfield, Division of Cardiology at Cornell University, stated that "digital electrocardiographs of all major manufacturers now are capable of providing automated diagnostic statements that can help the physician." However, he also mentioned cases where these statements could "mislead the physician." In evaluating a particular device, Dr. Kligfield stated that in 3,954 patients without pacemakers, 7.8% of the cardiac rhythm interpretations required revision by the combined opinion of two expert cardiologists.

OpenClinical[3] maintains a family of Web sites listing a number of decision support systems in current use. Among these are Athena DSS (for hypertension management), Gideon (for infectious diseases), Iliad (for internal medicine), TherapyEdge HIV (for HIV patient management), and several others. Some of the systems listed trace their ancestry back to MYCIN, INTERNIST-1, PUFF, and diagnostic systems based on Bayesian networks. More details about these and other systems can be gleaned from the OpenClinical Web pages. Another source of information is the Elsevier journal *Artificial Intelligence in Medicine*.

I'll describe a couple of representative examples. ATHENA DSS is a system for providing advice to physicians about managing hypertension in a manner consistent with guidelines defined by the U.S. Institute of Medicine. It was developed jointly by Stanford Medical Informatics, the Veterans Administration Palo Alto Health Care System, and the Stanford Center for Primary Care and Outcomes Research. ATHENA processes a patient's clinical data against hypertension management knowledge in its knowledge base and generates patient-specific recommendations for management during a clinical visit. It is in use and undergoing continuing evaluation and upgrading at several Veterans Administration medical centers. A new version, called ATHENA-HTN, is being evaluated. ATHENA's technology stems from previous medical rule-based systems developed at Stanford. According to Mark Musen, Head of the Stanford Biomedical Informatics Division, "ATHENA uses the EON task-specific architecture for assisting protocol-based medical care that grew out of my dissertation work in the late 1980s, which grew out of ONCOCIN [a program for helping to manage oncology protocols], which grew out of MYCIN . . . ."[4]

Another system, Gideon, is a program to help physicians diagnose and treat country-specific diseases. Gideon makes its diagnoses based on a large database of diseases, symptoms, signs and laboratory findings, and countries. Bayesian analysis is used in the computation of the probability of a disease given data about a patient. The original version of Gideon was developed by Stephen A. Berger, M.D., at the Tel Aviv Sourasky Medical Center and Uri Blackman at the University of Tel Aviv. Blackman is now CEO of Gideon Informatics, Inc., in Los Angeles.[5] There is a version of the program that can be accessed on mobile phones or PDAs.

According to the Gideon Web site,[6]

Gideon is made up of four modules: Diagnosis, Epidemiology, Therapy and Microbiology. The constantly updated database includes 337 diseases, 224 countries, 1,147 microbial taxa and 306 antibacterial (-fungal, -parasitic, -viral) agents and vaccines. Gideon's world wide data sources essentially include the entire world's literature and adhere to the standards of Evidence Based Medicine. Over 10,000 notes outline the status of specific infections within each country. Also featured are over 20,000 images, graphs, interactive maps and references.

. . .

In a blinded multicenter field trial of 495 patients, the correct diagnosis was displayed in over 94% of cases, and was listed first in over 75%.

A reviewer in the *Journal of the American Medical Association* wrote "Gideon: The Global Infectious Disease and Epidemiology Network is a superbly designed expert system created to help physicians diagnose any infectious disease (337 recognized) in any country of the world (224 included). . . . This diagnostic system is remarkable for its ease of use, breadth of scope, and depth of information. It is as practical a program as one could hope for."[7]

Notwithstanding the success of diagnostic systems, such as Gideon, most of the applications of AI in medicine involve DSSs, which can be used by physicians for reference. As Thomas Rindfleisch, an expert in medical informatics says, "The name DSS is significant in that doctors always need be in charge of final patient-related decisions to avoid FDA regulation of the software." Rindfleisch also mentions that for DSSs to be useful for most physicians, they have to be integrated with electronic medical and health record systems (so that doctors don't have to type in all the needed background information about a patient).[8] However, a survey of 2,758 American physicians (taken in late 2007 and early 2008) found that only 17% of them had access to electronic record systems.[9]

34.2 For Scheduling

Intelligent scheduling software is another area where AI techniques are being used. One example is the AURORA™ system marketed by Stottler Henke Associates, Inc., a company specializing in applying "artificial intelligence and other advanced software technologies to solve problems that defy solution using traditional approaches." AURORA is being used by the Boeing Company to help schedule and manage the building of the Boeing Dreamliner™. Stottler Henke says that "once AURORA has created a schedule, it displays it in a series of graphical images that allow the user to see the scheduled activities, resource allocations and the temporal relationships among the activities."[10]

TEMPORIS™, developed by United Space Alliance, LLC, is an intelligent space-flight mission management and planning tool for use by the crew on board future space missions. TEMPORIS will help crews schedule all aspects of their in-flight lives, including routine daily activities, spacecraft housekeeping, and conducting on-board experiments. But producing acceptable schedules requires "volumes of spaceflight constraints, flight rules, dependencies, sequences, medical guidelines and safety requirements." According to a company press release, these can now be "efficiently embedded into TEMPORIS's intelligence. To illustrate: It currently takes 50 mission planners working 24/7 for two weeks to schedule one day's worth of activities on the International Space Station. TEMPORIS reduces that 2-week job to a few moments with the click of a computer mouse."[11] Stottler Henke's AURORA software is an integral part of TEMPORIS.

34.3 For Automated Trading

AI data mining, text processing, and decision methods are used in the analysis of real-time trading data and news feeds to make automatic buy-and-sell decisions on stocks, commodities, and currencies. Up-to-the-minute news sources in digital form are readily available. The Reuters "NewsScope Archive"[12] and the Dow Jones

"Elementized News Feed"[13] are among news feeds that are used for automated trading and analysis. Reuters, for example, claims to provide[14]

customers seeking to develop news-based programmatic trading strategies with a comprehensive, machine-readable archive of Reuters global news. Events are presented exactly as they broke to the markets, with each release of information timestamped to the millisecond and tagged with an array of metadata fields for easy machine consumption.

According to an article in the *New York Times* about automated trading,[15] Professor Andrew Lo, the Director of the MIT Laboratory for Financial Engineering, and colleagues discovered that there was a correlation between how often certain words, such as "anxiety," "depression," and "bankrupt," appeared in news stories and future values of the S&P stock index. These correlations, among other things, can be used by stock trading algorithms to initiate stock trades.

Vhayu Technologies Corporation, one of the firms offering algorithmic trading services, claims that "8 of the top 10 global financial institutions use one of its products," namely, Vhayu Velocity^{TM}, "to identify opportunities in milliseconds."[16] Another firm, Streambase Systems, says that with one of its products "leading trading organizations track critical market conditions across multiple markets and instantaneously execute sophisticated strategies to capture short-lived trading opportunities."[17] Of course, with such instant feedback there is the potential that news of a sell order might trigger other sell orders, and so on, leading to swift downdrafts in the market (and vice versa).

34.4 In Business Practices

Business Rule Management Systems (BRMSs) are descendants of the rule-based expert systems of the 1980s. Examples are Fair Isaac's "BLAZE ADVISOR 6.1," ILOG's "JRules 6.0," and Information Builders's "WebFOCUS." Business rules express information about how a business operates – its policies and constraints. All companies have such rules. As Fair Isaac puts it, these are usually expressed "in conversation, written text and software – as 'If, then' statements [such as] 'If the loan applicant does not have a sufficient credit history, then pull a report from a debit bureau.'" In BRMSs, these rules are usually encoded in English-like, computer-readable syntax. Unlike rules used in some expert systems, they are not annotated with probabilities or certainty factors but are definite statements of business practice. Because the information expressed by business rules changes from time to time, it is important that the rules be maintained to reflect current policies.

Rule engines are used to perform both forward and backward inference over a network of rules. A descendant of the Rete algorithm, which was mentioned on page 238, is used by the inference engine in BLAZE ADVISOR, for example. Conclusions are used to communicate policy, late-breaking business opportunities, and needs for action among staff and other parties. In some cases, conclusions evoke automatic actions such as ordering, sending e-mails, and so on. For example, Information Builders advertises that with their suite of event management solutions, "the automated process itself is able to make predetermined decisions and take specific courses of action based on thresholds contained within the business intelligence content that is fed to it."[18] An article about WebFocus gives an example: "[An order arriving] can trigger a series of responses and decisions – e.g. based on WebFOCUS analytics embedded in the process, the physical size of the order can be determined. If it is too big for the warehouse space available, WebFOCUS analytics can trigger a change in the process that ships the order to a different warehouse that has the required space, and then alerts warehouse employees that a larger than expected order will be arriving."[19]

34.5 In Translating Languages

Several commercial natural language translation systems now exist. IBM's speech-to-speech translator (MASTOR) can (according to its Web site) translate free-form English speech into Mandarin speech (and vice versa).[20] BBN Technologies has developed a number of speech processing systems. One is their "Broadcast Monitoring System," which (according to its Web site) "creates a continuous searchable archive of international television broadcasts." As explained on the site, "The system automatically transcribes the real-time audio stream and translates it into English. Both the transcript and translation are searchable and synchronized to the video, providing powerful capabilities for effective retrieval and precise playback of the video based on its speech content. With this revolutionary system, users can sift through vast collections of news content in other languages quickly and efficiently."[21] SRI International's IraqComm translation system can transform spoken English into translated spoken colloquial Iraqi Arabic (and vice versa). Currently (according to its Web site) it is "tailored to translate spoken interactions on topics on force protection, security, and basic medical services, and can be customized to include other topics as needed."[22]

34.6 For Automating Invention

John Koza, the inventor of Genetic Programming (GP), a search method based on simulating the processes of evolution, claims that GP is itself an "invention machine." (He also claims that GP more-or-less subsumes AI because AI's goal is to produce intelligent programs and GP does just that.) For example, Koza and colleagues used GP to evolve (after thirty-one generations) an optimal antenna system.[23] They have also evolved (sometimes after hundreds of generations) designs for optical lenses. As one of their papers states, "One of the genetically evolved lens systems infringed a previously issued patent, whereas the others were noninfringing novel designs that duplicated (or improved upon) the performance specifications contained in the patents."[24] Other evolved designs include those for electrical circuits, controllers, mechanical systems, and other devices.[25] The goal of the group is to produce what they call "human-competitive designs," that is, ones whose specifications meet or exceed those of the best human designers. With expected increases in computer power, I believe that the use of GP and GP-like search methods will likely produce several interesting new inventions.

34.7 For Recognizing Faces

People are quite good at recognizing familiar faces whether "live" or in photographs. They can often do this regardless of pose, scale, facial expression, or lighting conditions. (Interestingly, they don't do very well if the photograph of a face is presented upside down.) Computers are getting better, so much so in fact that I might have included computer face recognition in the chapter on Ubiquitous Artificial Intelligence. Although not quite ubiquitous yet, face-recognizing systems are becoming more common at airports, banks, and places where personal identity must be verified or established. According to some people who worry about privacy, the practice is too common.

Work on face recognition by computer has continued from its early days. How far has it progressed? A 2007 National Institute of Standards and Technology report on face-recognition tests claimed (among other things), "The results show that, at low false alarm rates for humans, seven automatic face recognition algorithms were comparable to or better than humans at recognizing faces taken under different lighting conditions. Furthermore, three of the seven algorithms were comparable to or better than humans for the full range of false alarm rates measured."[26] The best methods use machine learning algorithms working on very large data sets.[27]

A variety of different algorithms have been developed. Some are based on well-known pattern-recognition techniques that sample features from a face image and then compare these features against those of a large library of identified faces to find the closest match. Some algorithms use Bayesian techniques and HMMs. Many of the methods use mathematical techniques to project a high-dimensional vector representation of a face image into a vector in a lower dimensional subspace. One method uses lower dimensional spaces whose coordinates consist of a set of reduced images, called *eigenfaces*, which have the property that they can be combined to give good approximations to any of the faces in the database (much like a set of individual audio tones of different frequencies can be combined to approximate arbitrary sounds). For a Web page with information about face recognition with links to research papers, books, algorithms, and vendors, see http://www.face-rec.org/.

New approaches continue to be developed. One method purports to show that "image averaging" (that is, merging different images of the same face to form a single image) "greatly improves performance of [the commercially available FaceVACS] automatic face-recognition system."[28] An article in *Wired* reports on a method developed by researchers at the University of California, Berkeley, and the University of Illinois at Urbana-Champaign. According to that article, Shankar Sastry, the Dean of UC Berkeley's College of Engineering, noted that this new method "renders years of research in the field obsolete."[29]

There are already several commercial companies selling face-recognition and face-locating software and equipment. For example, Oki Electric Industry Co., Ltd., sells a product called FSE (Face Sensing Engine). It boasts many applications including controlling access to information in camera–equipped cell phones and other devices, sorting photographs based on recognizing faces, and locating faces in a camera's field of view. The German company Cognitec Systems GmbH markets the FaceVACS system previously mentioned.[30]

Before closing this section on smart tools, I should mention that there are several other areas in which AI tools are enhancing human productivity. For example, I could have mentioned tools for aiding (and automating) the processes of movie animation, for computer program writing and debugging, for industrial process control, for circuit and program verification, and for enhancing and searching the semantic Web. Tools powered by AI techniques will be increasingly used to aid and amplify (and sometimes to substitute for) human cognitive, motor, and perceptual abilities. Just wait!

As I hope the past few chapters have demonstrated, some parts of the quest for artificial intelligence have been quite successful. AI has become more and more a part of all of our lives as well as of those of specialists. But the main goal of the quest (for some of us at least) still remains, namely, endowing artifacts with full human (as well as superhuman) capabilities for language, perception, reasoning, and learning. So, let's look next at where the quest might lead us.

Notes

1. Ralph J. Begley *et al.*, "Adding Artificial Intelligence to Medical Devices," *Medical Device & Diagnostic Industry*, pp. 150ff, March 2000. Available online at http://www.devicelink.com/mddi/archive/00/03/014.html. [507]
2. See http://www.clinicalwindow.net/cw_issue_20_article1.htm. [507]
3. See http://www.openclinical.org/aisinpracticeDSS.html. OpenClinical is a nonprofit organization created and maintained as a public service with support from Cancer Research UK under the overall supervision of an international technical advisory board. [508]
4. E-mail communication on September 25, 2008. [508]
5. See Stephen A. Berger and Uri Blackman, "A Computer Program for Diagnosing and Teaching Geographic Medicine," *Journal of Travel Medicine*, Vol. 2, No. 3, pp. 199–203. Available online at http://www.gideononline.com/reviews/JTM1995.pdf. [508]
6. http://www.gideononline.com/index.htm. [508]
7. Vincent J. Felitti, MD, Reviewer, *Journal of the American Medical Association*, Vol. 293, pp. 1674–1675, 2005. [509]
8. Thomas Rindfleisch, e-mail of November 20, 2008. [509]
9. Catherine M. DesRoches *et al.*, "Electronic Health Records in Ambulatory Care – A National Survey of Physicians," *The New England Journal of Medicine*, Vol. 359, No. 1, pp. 50–60, July 3, 2008. [509]
10. See http://www.stottlerhenke.com/news/pr_aurora_boeing.htm. [509]
11. See http://www.unitedspacealliance.com/news/press/2006/060404.pdf. [509]
12. See http://about.reuters.com/productinfo/newsscopearchive/. [509]
13. See http://www.djnewswires.com/us/djenf.htm. [510]
14. http://about.reuters.com/productinfo/newsscopearchive/. [510]
15. Tim Arango, "I Got the News Instantaneously, Oh Boy," *New York Times*, p. WK3, September 14, 2008. Available online at http://www.nytimes.com/2008/09/14/weekinreview/14arango.html?partner=rssnyt&emc=rss. [510]
16. See http://www.vhayu.com/. [510]
17. See http://www.streambase.com/algorithmic-trading.htm. [510]
18. From http://www.informationbuilders.com/products/webfocus/intelligent_processes.html. [511]

19. From *Expert Systems*, Vol. 23, No. 4, p. 245, September 2006. [511]
20. See http://domino.research.ibm.com/comm/research.nsf/pages/r.uit.innovation
    .html. [511]
21. See http://www.bbn.com/products_and_services/bbn_broadcast_monitoring_system/.
    [511]
22. See http://www.iraqcomm.com/. [511]
23. John R. Koza *et al.*, "Automated Synthesis of a Fixed-Length Loaded Symmetric Dipole
    Antenna Whose Gain Exceeds That of a Commercial Antenna and Matches the Theo-
    retical Maximum," *Proceedings of the 9th Annual Conference on Genetic and Evolutionary
    Computation*, pp. 2074–2081, New York: Association for Computing Machinery, 2007.
    [511]
24. John R. Koza, Sameer H. Al-Sakrana, and Lee W. Jones, "Automated *ab Initio* Synthesis
    of Complete Designs of Four Patented Optical Lens Systems by Means of Genetic Pro-
    gramming," *AIEDAM: Artificial Intelligence for Engineering, Design, and Manufacturing*,
    Vol. 22, pp. 249–273, Cambridge: Cambridge University Press, 2008. [511]
25. See John R. Koza, Sameer H. Al-Sakran, and Lee W. Jones, "Multi-Domain Observations
    Concerning the Use of Genetic Programming to Automatically Synthesize Human-
    Competitive Designs for Analog Circuits, Optical Lens Systems, Controllers, Antennas,
    Mechanical Systems, and Quantum Computing Circuits," in Rick Riolo, Terence Soule
    and Bill Worzel (eds.), *Genetic Programming Theory and Practice IV*, pp. 131–147, New
    York: Springer-Verlag, 2007. [511]
26. P. Jonathon Phillips *et al.*, "FRVT 2006 and ICE 2006 Large-Scale Results,"
    NISTIR 7408, March 2007. Available online at http://www.frvt.org/FRVT2006/docs/
    FRVT2006andICE2006LargeScaleReport.pdf. [512]
27. Some of the data sets used by researchers are itemized at http://www.face-rec.org/
    databases/. See also Ralph Gross, "Face Databases," in Stan Z. Li and Anil K. Jain
    (eds.), *Handbook of Face Recognition*, New York: Springer-Verlag, 2005. Available at
    http://www.ri.cmu.edu/pub_files/pub4/gross_ralph_2005_1/gross_ralph_2005_1.pdf.
    [512]
28. R. Jenkins and A. M. Burton, "100% Accuracy in Automatic Face Recognition," *Science*,
    Vol. 319, p. 435, January 25, 2008. [512]
29. Bryan Gardiner, "Engineers Test Highly Accurate Face Recognition," *Wired*, March
    24, 2008. Available at http://www.wired.com/science/discoveries/news/2008/03/
    new_face_recognition. [512]
30. http://www.cognitec-systems.de/index.html. [512]

35

The Quest Continues

W HERE WILL THE AI ADVENTURE LEAD NEXT? WE CAN GET SOME IDEA OF THE immediate future simply by extrapolating present trends. Probably there will be some new milestone achievements. Undoubtedly, pieces of AI technology will become ever more common in our homes, automobiles, and activities, and the specialists' smart tools will become ever smarter and more numerous.

But predicting beyond where AI's present momentum will take us is problematic. Let's look at how some previous predictions have fared. Simon's 1957 prediction of a computer chess champion within ten years was markedly overoptimistic. In 1973, SRI engineers led by Oscar Firschein iteratively queried several AI "experts" about when certain "products" would be realized. The medians and ranges of predicted dates were reported back to them, they were given a chance to modify their predictions, and so on until the results settled down. (This process of making predictions is called a *Delphi method*.[1]) The following table shows a few of the final predictions:[2]

Product	Median prototype date	Median commercial date
Automatic medical diagnostician	1976	1980
Robot servant capable of performing all household tasks	2000	2010
Voice-operated typewriter	1985	1992
Automatic high-quality language translator of text	1987	1995
Robot chauffeur for driving on city streets and country highways	1992	2000

The "robot servant" and the "robot chauffeur" still seem quite a ways off, but the others were perhaps only somewhat too optimistic. (Well, the year 2000 seemed a long way off back in 1973.)

Against this background of prediction successes and failures, I hesitate to make any that do not seem rather obvious. Except, I will predict that *someday* we'll have human-made artifacts with levels of intelligence (in all of its manifestations) equalling and exceeding that of humans. I make that prediction because I believe that we humans are machines (for what else could we be?) and that *eventually* we'll be able to build machines that can do whatever we can do because there will be economic as well as scientific reasons for doing so.

515

I'll have more to say about "human-level artificial intelligence" later, but let's first look at some of the research projects underway in AI laboratories during the early part of this century to see whether they give us any insights about the future.

35.1 In the Labs

There are now probably hundreds of laboratories – industrial, government, and academic – that carry on research in artificial intelligence. I could not possibly describe even a small part of what is going on in them, and, in any case, projects come and go. Just as a historian cedes accounts of current events to newspapers and other media, I recommend that readers wanting to stay current on AI research visit the Web sites maintained by the individual AI laboratories, AI societies, government agencies that support AI research, and specialized conferences and workshops.[3] To give some of the flavor of the breadth of current research, I'll mention a few projects ongoing during the first few years of this century. Of course, these are research projects so it's possible, but not certain, that some of them will leave their marks on the future.

35.1.1 *Specialized Systems*

Building smart tools for work in specialized areas is still a big part of AI research. However, work on these tools is increasingly less AI-centric and is merging with the disciplines upon whose technologies these efforts depend – such as statistics, control engineering, image processing, and linguistics, among others. Of course the new techniques invented and used in building even the most specialized niche systems might, in fact, be broadly applicable in other areas of interest to AI.

A. Content-Based Image Retrieval

Present-day image and video search engines that respond to queries composed of words, such as "motorcycles," do so by looking for Web sites that contain the text "motorcycle" along with some image or video file (say in jpeg, quicktime, or some other appropriate format). Unfortunately, the image or video file in some of the sites retrieved by these methods might not even contain a motorcycle. Research is underway to base image and video search more on the content of images rather than on the content of associated text alone.

One such project has been undertaken by researchers at Oxford University and at Microsoft Corporation.[4] Using images from a public Web site (Flickr), a "query" consists of outlining (with a rectangle) that part of an image that contains a sought-for object. That part of the image is then converted into a vector representation that preserves key features of the image of the object. Vector representations of images in a large image database are analyzed to form "clusters" of similar vectors. The idea is that each cluster is associated with images of similar objects. The vector representation of the query is then matched against the image database vectors to find clusters of the most similar images. These can then be ranked, and the high-ranking images, with object regions outlined, are returned as answers to the query. Some examples of query images and response images are shown in Fig. 35.1. The query

Figure 35.1. Searching for objects in images. (From James Philbin *et al.*, "Object Retrieval with Large Vocabularies and Fast Spatial Matching," *Proceedings of the IEEE Conference on Computer Vision and Pattern Recognition (CVPR)*, 2007.)

image, with the query region outlined, is on the left, and seven returned images (with target regions outlined) are on the right. Of course, as with any search process, there will be false positives returned also, but in these examples the false positives appeared later in the list than the response images shown.

The authors evaluate their work as follows:

The system returns photos from the corpus that contain a query object, despite substantial differences in lighting, perspective, image quality and occluders between the query and retrieved images.

We view this as a step towards the ultimate goal of building a Web-scale retrieval system that will scale to billions of images. We have therefore concentrated on algorithms which are scalable, and which we believe are straightforward to distribute over a cluster of computers.

They acknowledge that further work is needed to find "efficient ways to include spatial information in the index [which is computed before images are queried], and move some of the burden of spatial matching from the ranking stage to the filtering stage."

Other projects involve content-based video retrieval. When users submit a video to YouTube, for example, they also submit "tag" words to help describe it. Example tag words that might be used are beach, hiking, soccer, cats, concerts, and so on. Tagging takes effort, so some researchers are attempting to automate that process using statistical machine learning methods. From a database of already tagged videos, a group of German researchers has developed a prototype system that extracts image information for use in suggesting tag words for other videos.[5] Systems such as theirs might ultimately be used for tagging large corpora of videos. Once tagged, these corpora could be more easily searched.

Along these lines, two different companies, VideoSurf and Digitalsmiths, have announced products that allow versions of content-based searching. VideoSurf's Web site (http://www.videosurf.com/about) claims that "using a unique combination of new computer vision and fast computation methods, VideoSurf has taught computers to 'see' inside videos to find content in a fast, efficient, and scalable way."

B. Meaning-Based Web Search

Next, I'll mention an AI project at a commercial company, Powerset. Powerset began as a San Francisco start-up developing an Internet search engine that uses natural language understanding techniques. (The company was acquired by Microsoft in 2008.) Powerset claims to be able to find "articles related to the meaning of your query. And sometimes direct answers."

The query can be a statement or a question posed in ordinary natural language. A grammar and semantic processor are then used to parse the query – converting it to a representation that expresses the meaning of the original sentence. Their prototype version is limited to searching Wikipedia articles, which have also been processed to extract meanings. A matching procedure is then used to return those articles whose meanings are most related to the query.

The developers think that their technology will scale beyond Wikipedia to be able to deal with more of the Web. The natural language processing technology used by Powerset is based on the Lexical Functional Grammar originally developed by Joan Bresnan and Ronald Kaplan. Kaplan, formerly a researcher at PARC (Palo Alto Research Center) is now an employee of Powerset. Here is an example of a Powerset search using their Web site.[6] I typed the query "What technology has powerset licensed?" It answered "The company has licensed natural language technology from PARC, the former Xerox Palo Alto Research Center . . . ," and referred me to the Wikipedia page from which it lifted its answer, namely, "Powerset (company)," which is at http://en.wikipedia.org/wiki/PowerSet. If techniques for meaning-based search scale up, as the Powerset people hope, the quality of Internet search would be dramatically improved.

C. Legged Robots

Marc Raibert did research at Caltech on walking, running, and hopping robots. He continued related research as a professor at CMU and later at MIT. In 1992, he started a company called Boston Dynamics, which according to its Web site "specializes in robotics and human simulation." One of their prototype products is called BigDog (Fig. 35.2), a four-legged walking robot, about the size of a Great Dane, claimed to be the "most advanced quadruped robot on earth." BigDog is extremely stable. It can walk, run, and climb on rough terrain. It is said to be able to carry a 340-pound load. It is powered by a gasoline engine driving a hydraulic actuation system. BigDog's suite of sensors includes a laser gyroscope, a stereo vision system, devices for sensing joint positions and forces, as well as internal things such as engine temperature and so on. Overall control is provided by an on-board computer. A movie of its operation shows it walking through a forest, climbing a hill, recovering from a strong kick to its side and negotiating an icy parking lot – all without falling. (Well, at least it didn't fall in the movie I saw. The movie is available at http://www.bostondynamics.com/dist/BigDog.wmv.) The BigDog project is being supported by DARPA.

According to a paper about BigDog,[7] the team is continuing to work on such problems as getting BigDog to right itself if it does happen to fall over and giving it more ability to navigate by itself. (It now relies mostly on a human operator to guide it.)

There are hundreds of more projects going on in the labs where "smart tools" are being developed for hundreds of professions. The variety is amazing. People are

Figure 35.2. Marc Raibert (left) and BigDog (right). (Photographs courtesy of Boston Dynamics © 2008.)

working on automating the process of movie animation,[8] computational genomics,[9] robotic surgery, business intelligence,[10] and much more. Most of these are what I would call "niche" systems, focused on performing specific, rather than generic, tasks. In the next section, I'll mention some laboratory work aimed either at building general-purpose systems or at developing technology that might be applicable in a wide range of settings.

35.1.2 *Broadly Applicable Systems*

A. Robotics

Ever since the days of Shakey the robot, AI researchers have used robots as platforms for developing AI systems that integrate many aspects of intelligent behavior and, therefore, aim for a kind of general utility. Work on general-purpose robot systems has gone in and out of style, and robotics researchers sometimes had to focus instead on special tasks, as might arise in industrial automation, for example. Reacting to some of my proposals in the 1970s and 1980s for work on general-purpose robots, potential sponsors would sometimes ask "Just exactly what is your robot going to do?" My answer that they were supposed to be "general purpose" seldom satisfied sponsors with specific problems to solve. Now, however, there does seem to be a return to working on robots that are able to do a lot of things – decathlon robots instead of high-hurdle robots or pole-vaulting robots.

One example is the work headed by Stanford professor Andrew Ng with a robot named STAIR, an acronym for STanford AI Robot. STAIR is designed to be a kind of "general factotum," that is, a robot that can do a lot of things including navigating

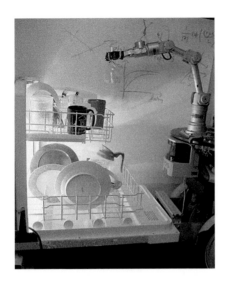

Figure 35.3. STAIR unloading a dish-washer at the Stanford AI Lab. (Photo-graph courtesy of Andrew Ng and Ashutosh Saxena.)

home and office environments, picking up and interacting with objects and tools, and intelligently conversing with and helping people in these environments. (See Fig. 35.3.) According to its Web page,[11] STAIR integrates "methods drawn from all areas of AI, including machine learning, vision, navigation, manipulation, planning, reasoning, and speech/natural language processing. This is in distinct contrast to the 30-year trend of working on fragmented AI subfields, and will be a vehicle for driving research towards true integrated AI."

STAIR even learns how to pick up objects it has never seen before. Using machine learning methods, STAIR's perceptual system was trained on a database of a thou-sand or more pictures of each of a number of common objects as they might be seen in a home or office. Each image was labeled with the appropriate grasping position for that particular object. The objects included a stapler (2,001 exam-ple pictures), a coffee mug (2,001 example pictures), a cereal bowl (1,001 exam-ple pictures), and several other items. The training pictures showed the objects under different lighting conditions, from different camera positions, and in differ-ent orientations. (To ease the task of collecting and labeling training data, synthetic computer-graphics images were used.) After training, STAIR could predict the best grasping point for several novel objects and develop a plan to guide the arm and grasper. The system was tested on a large set of novel objects, examples of which it had not seen before. These included "rolls of duct tape, markers, a translucent box, jugs, knifecutters, cellphones, pens, keys, screwdrivers, staplers, toothbrushes, a thick coil of wire, [and] a strangely shaped power horn." On average, STAIR successfully picked up these objects 87.8% of the time. (To be counted as suc-cessful, "the robot had to grasp the object, lift it up by about 1 ft, and hold it for 30 seconds."[12])

Videos of STAIR performing various tasks, such as opening a door, fetching a stapler from inside an office, and unloading a dishwasher can be seen from the team's multimedia Web page at http://stair.stanford.edu/multimedia.php.

Figure 35.4. HERB (top left), DOMO (top right), and SMARTPAL V (bottom). (HERB photograph used with permission of Siddhartha Srinivasa; DOMO photograph used with permission of Aaron Edsinger; SmartPal photograph used with permission of Yaskawa Electric.)

Ng and his colleagues and students envision robots that would be able to perform tasks such as the following:

• fetch or deliver items around the home or office,
• tidy up a room, including picking up and throwing away trash and using the dishwasher,
• prepare meals using a normal kitchen, and
• use tools to assemble a bookshelf.

Ultimately, they say, robots will "*revolutionize* home and office automation and [will] have important applications ranging from home assistants to elderly care."

Ng is not alone in pursuing this kind of robotics research. A team consisting of researchers at Intel Research in Pittsburgh and at the Robotics Institute at Carnegie Mellon University are developing a robot called HERB, an acronym for Home Exploring Robotic Butler. (See Fig. 35.4.) It consists of a laser range finder, Segway

RMP mobile base, WAM arm, Barrett Hand, and two video cameras. According to a paper describing HERB, it can search for objects, learn to navigate in cluttered dynamic indoor environments, recognize objects using vision, and manipulate doors and other constrained objects.[13] A video showing HERB performing tasks is available at http://pittsburgh.intel-research.net/~ssrin10/HERB09/HERB.wmv.

Another example is DOMO (Fig. 35.4.), a behavior-based, multiarticulator robot developed by MIT Ph.D. student Aaron Edsinger for accomplishing "useful manipulation tasks in human environments."[14]

Yaskawa Electric Corporation in Japan has developed a service robot they call SMARTPAL V for work around the home and office.[15] (See Fig. 35.4.) Other Japanese companies are developing home robots also. Helping this trend toward general-purpose robots are competitions sponsored by AAAI, IJCAI, and other groups.[16]

In previous chapters, I described more specialized robot systems designed for specific tasks, such as soccer-playing and autonomous automobile-driving. Even these, however, are integrated systems that advance AI perception, learning, planning, and plan-execution techniques that will be broadly useful.

B. Intelligent Assistants

Now let's move away from robots to consider disembodied "agents" that help people in ways that do not require mobility. Instead they help with databases, communication, Internet access, and task performance. I'll mention a couple of projects that are representative of those seeking to develop such agents.[17]

DARPA's "PAL Program" has been a source of support for some of this work. PAL is an acronym for Personalized Assistant that Learns. According to the program's Web site,[18]

The mission of the PAL program is to radically improve the way computers support humans by enabling systems that are cognitive, i.e., computer systems that can reason, learn from experience, be told what to do, explain what they are doing, reflect on their experience, and respond robustly to surprise.
. . .
This is the first broad-based research program in cognitive systems since the Strategic Computing Initiative funded by DARPA in the 1980s. Since then, there have been significant developments in the technologies needed to enable cognitive systems, such as machine learning, reasoning, perception, and, multimodal interaction. Improvements in processors, memory, sensors and networking have also dramatically changed the context of cognitive systems research. It is now time to encourage the various areas to come together again by focusing on by [sic] a common application problem: a Personalized Assistant that Learns.

One of the systems being developed under the general umbrella of the PAL Program is CALO, an acronym for Cognitive Assistant that Learns and Organizes.[19] CALO is being managed by SRI International and includes over thirty participants from American universities and companies. The project brings together experts in machine learning, natural language processing, knowledge representation, human–computer interaction, flexible planning, and behavioral studies. The CALO software learns by interacting with and being advised by its users and is meant to help users

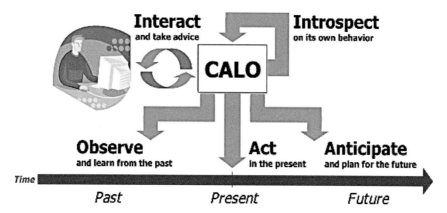

Figure 35.5. CALO's functions. (Used with permission of Karen Myers and Thomas Garvey.)

with military decision-making tasks. (The name, CALO, was inspired by the Latin word "calonis," which means "soldier's servant.")

The ways in which CALO is supposed to learn and help are depicted in Fig. 35.5. Two of the components worked on under the CALO project are the following:

- Organize and Prepare Information (OPI) organizes user's information to improve decision making and situational awareness. (A video about OPI is available at http://caloproject.sri.com/videos/OrganizeInformation.mov.)
- Project Execution Assistant (PEXA) performs delegated tasks, anticipates needs and opportunities, and manages user's time and commitments.[20] (A video is available at http://caloproject.sri.com/videos/TaskMgtMov2.mov.)

Many of the individual components of the overall CALO system represent important contributions to intelligent systems research generally. One such is the Marginal Probability Architecture developed by Professor Thomas Dietterich and Xinlong Bao at Oregon State University.[21] It uses "Markov Logic,"[22] a representation combining first-order logic and probabilistic graphical models, to integrate multiple learning components into the CALO system.

Another component of CALO is its user interface and knowledge repository, called IRIS (an acronym for Integrate. Relate. Infer. Share). A version of IRIS has been released as an open source application. According to its Web site,[23] "IRIS is a semantic desktop application framework that enables users to create a 'personal map' across their office-related information objects. IRIS includes a machine-learning platform to help automate this process. It provides 'dashboard' views, contextual navigation, and relationship-based structure across an extensible suite of office applications, including a calendar, Web and file browser, e-mail client, and instant messaging client." You can download this version of IRIS from the Web site.

Now let us move across the Atlantic where another intelligent assistant project is ongoing. Yorick Wilks (1939–), a professor in the Computer Science Department at the University of Sheffield in the United Kingdom, is the coordinator of a project called "COMPANIONS." It is being sponsored by the European Commission and includes participants from Europe and the United States. According to its Web site,[24] the project

aims to change the way we think about the relationships of people to computers and the Internet by developing a virtual conversational "Companion."

This will be an agent or "presence" that stays with the user for long periods of time, developing a relationship and "knowing" its owner's preferences and wishes. It will communicate with the user primarily by using and understanding speech, but also using other technologies such as touch screens and sensors.

Video demonstrations of two prototype systems can be seen on YouTube. One COMPANION engages in a conversation with a user about "Health and Fitness." The other one shows photographs to a senior from her digital album and discusses them with her. (See http://www.youtube.com/watch?v=KQSiigSEYhU and http://www.youtube.com/watch?v=s33_UcGyFSE.)

Versatile conversational agents may well serve a useful role for some people as occasional surrogates for human interaction. But one should bear in mind warnings, such as those voiced by Theodore Roszak and others, about their misuse and overuse. Aaron Sloman of the University of Birmingham's School of Computer Science in the United Kingdom has written a thoughtful position paper about some of the difficulties of building digital companions.[25]

C. Learning by Reading

All AI researchers agree that both common-sense knowledge and specialized knowledge is the key to intelligence. Various approaches have been pursued to gather and organize that knowledge in a form exploitable by computer programs. Projects like Cyc attempt to do so by hand-coding millions of small pieces of knowledge as logical sentences. Machine learning research has shown that statistical methods can be used to "mine" large databases for knowledge.

A third approach is to build programs that can read (and understand) natural language text. After all, as the proponents of that approach claim, the world is full of knowledge – in books, in news feeds, and on the Web. (Of course, it is full of a lot of nonsense also, but smart programs may ultimately be able to highlight the trustworthy parts.) As we have already seen, computer understanding of natural language text requires both general common-sense knowledge and background knowledge about the subject matter of the text. Thus, "Learning by Reading" (LbR), as this third approach is called, draws on the technologies of knowledge representation and reasoning as well as on natural language processing.

One of the earliest attempts to extract knowledge from the Web was by a group led by Professor Tom M. Mitchell (1951–) at Carnegie Mellon University. In a 1999 paper they proposed "to automatically create a *computer understandable* knowledge base whose content mirrors that of the World Wide Web."[26] Subsequently, DARPA funded a two-year study called "Project Möbius" to determine the feasibility of learning by reading. The project final report, describing the construction and evaluation of a prototype LbR system, concluded that "Learning by Reading produced statistically significant improvements in the problem solving abilities [i.e., question answering] of the target knowledge, and that, with a major research effort,

substantial progress could be made in the general application of LbR."[27] At the time
of this writing, and based on the conclusions of the Project Möbius report, it appears
that DARPA will soon be supporting more LbR research.[28]

Several researchers are now involved in working on learning by reading and related
problems. (A sampling of work being done in this field can be obtained by looking
at the schedule of talks given at a March 2007 AAAI Spring Symposium available
online at http://www.cs.washington.edu/homes/pjallen/aaaiss07/schedule.htm.)
One group is led by Professor Oren Etzioni (1964–), Director of the University of
Washington's Turing Center.[29] The Center's "KnowItAll Project"[30] has developed
a search program called "TextRunner." Among other things, it attempts to extract
logical relations from text so that they can be used to populate (or add to) a computer-
accessible knowledge base. In one of Etzioni's examples, TextRunner extracts the
list "(Ebay, Founded-by, Pierre-Omidyar)" from the sentence "EBay was
originally founded by Pierre Omidyar." This list is a way of writing a logical relation
having the predicate Founded-by and arguments Ebay and Pierre-Omidyar. As
I have already mentioned, sets of logical relations are used in most of the schemes
for representing declarative knowledge. According to its Web page,[31] "TextRunner
searches hundreds of millions of assertions extracted from 500 million high-quality
Web pages." The TextRunner Web page includes a facility that lets you query its
database of assertions to produce answers along with their Web page sources.[32]

35.2 Toward Human-Level Artificial Intelligence

35.2.1 *Eye on the Prize*

In a 1995 article titled "Eye on the Prize" I argued that AI researchers ought to be
putting more effort into developing generally intelligent systems in addition to their
work on the kinds of smart tools I mentioned in the previous chapter. I suggested
that AI ought to focus on building what I called "habile" systems – ones that could
learn to use smart tools, just as humans are able to learn to use them. More generally,
it has always seemed to me that AI's grand goal – the "prize" we are questing
for – should be to develop artifacts that can do most of the things that humans
can do – specifically those things that are thought to require "intelligence." These
systems would have what some AI researchers have called "Human Level Artificial
Intelligence" (HLAI).

HLAI was the goal of the founders and of many other early AI researchers. John
McCarthy claims that the "first scientific discussion of human level machine intelligence was apparently by Alan Turing" in his lecture to the London Mathematical
Society on Febuary 20, 1947.[33] Turing made the mechanization of human-level intelligence an explicit goal in his 1950 "Computing Machinery and Intelligence" paper.
Later, in the proposal for the 1956 Dartmouth Summer Study, John McCarthy
wrote "The study is to proceed on the basis of the conjecture that every aspect of
learning or any other feature of intelligence can in principle be so precisely described
that a machine can be made to simulate it."

Newell and Simon's "General Problem Solver" (GPS) was aimed specifically at
HLAI, and they continued to work on the problems both of understanding and

mechanizing intelligent behavior. In a 1957 talk, Simon said that "that there are now in the world machines that think, that learn and that create. Moreover, their ability to do these things is going to increase rapidly until – in a visible future – the range of problems they can handle will be coextensive with the range to which the human mind has been applied." In his 1961 paper "Steps Toward Artificial Intelligence" Marvin Minsky wrote "We are on the threshold of an era that will be strongly influenced, and quite possibly dominated, by intelligent problem-solving machines." In a 2003 paper, Edward Feigenbaum concluded "Computational Intelligence is the manifest destiny of computer science, the goal, the destination, the final frontier. More than any other field of science, our computer science concepts and methods are central to the quest to unravel and understand one of the grandest mysteries of our existence, the nature of intelligence. Generations of computer scientists to come must be inspired by the challenges and grand challenges of this great quest."[34]

Some people have pointed out that HLAI necessarily implies superhuman-level intelligence. Back in 1965 the English statistician (and co-worker of Alan Turing) I. J. Good wrote[35]

Let an ultraintelligent machine be defined as a machine that can far surpass all the intellectual activities of any man however clever. Since the design of machines is one of these intellectual activities, an ultraintelligent machine could design even better machines; there would then unquestionably be an "intelligence explosion," and the intelligence of man would be left far behind. Thus the first ultraintelligent machine is the last invention that man need ever make, provided that the machine is docile enough to tell us how to keep it under control.

In 1987 Jack Schwartz, the sometime critic of AI, wrote[36]

If artificial intelligences can be created at all, there is little reason to believe that initial successes could not lead swiftly to the construction of artificial superintelligences able to explore significant mathematical, scientific, or engineering alternatives at a rate far exceeding human ability, or to generate plans and take action on them with equally overwhelming speed. Since man's near-monopoly of all higher forms of intelligence has been one of the most basic facts of human existence throughout the past history of this planet, such developments would clearly create a new economics, a new sociology, and a new history.

The idea of machines becoming more and more intelligent inspired Vernor Vinge (1944–), a mathematician, computer scientist, and science fiction writer, to predict that a computer superintelligence would emerge by 2030. He called this event a "singularity," that is, a point in time when the rate of technological progress becomes unimaginably rapid. In an essay about the singularity, he wrote "When greater-than-human intelligence drives progress, that progress will be much more rapid. In fact, there seems no reason why progress itself would not involve the creation of still more intelligent entities – on a still-shorter time scale."[37] He foresaw the day when "Large computer networks (and their associated users) may 'wake up' as a superhumanly intelligent entity."

The inventor and AI researcher Ray Kurzweil (1948–) has popularized the idea of the singularity in his book *The Singularity is Near*.[38] Based largely on the idea that the *rate* of technological progress increases exponentially (and will continue to do so), Kurzweil makes a number of predictions about what technology will produce in various decades starting with 2010 and leading up to "The Singularity" in 2045 and beyond. Some of his predictions seem rather outlandish, and the whole idea of a singularity has provoked much derision, but I'll leave it to you to judge for yourself. (Here is one sample prediction: By 2045, "machines enter into a 'runaway reaction' of self-improvement cycles, with each new generation of A.I.s appearing faster and faster. From this point onwards, technological advancement is explosive, under the control of the machines, and thus cannot be accurately predicted.") The Web page http://singularity.com/themovie/ says that a movie version of "The Singularity is Near" (featuring Kurzweil as well as other futurists and computer scientists) will appear in late 2009. Several commentators about the singularity have written articles for the June 2008 special issue of *IEEE Spectrum*. Its Web site has pointers to the articles and to auxiliary material.[39]

In 2004, The Singularity Institute for Artificial Intelligence (SIAI)[40] was formed "to confront this urgent challenge, both the opportunity and the risk." Its Director of Research, Ben Goertzel, is also chair of an organization called the "Artificial General Intelligence Research Institute" (AGIRI) whose "mission is to foster the creation of powerful and ethically positive Artificial General Intelligence."[41] AGIRI sponsors conferences and workshops and manages some open source projects. AGIRI uses the term "artificial general intelligence" (AGI) somewhat in the same sense that I have been using HLAI. According to one of its Web sites, "the term is used to stress the 'general' nature of the desired capabilities of the systems being researched – as compared to the bulk of mainstream Artificial Intelligence (AI) work, which focuses on systems with very specialized 'intelligent' capabilities."

I'll conclude this chapter and the book by talking about HLAI, what it might be, some arguments for and against it, the possible consequences of it, and proposed methods for achieving it.

35.2.2 *Controversies*

HLAI (and beyond) is still the goal of many AI researchers even though we may still be a long way from achieving it – whatever it is. In fact, there is controversy about just what HLAI might be. Will we have achieved it when we have programs that can pass various tests, such as the Turing test? Pat Hayes and Ken Ford of the Institute for Human and Machine Cognition in Pensacola, Florida, are among those who argue, on various practical and methodological grounds, against using the Turing test as a measure of AI's progress.[42]

Other tests have been proposed that could be taken as helping to define HLAI. For example, in a 2005 paper, I suggested one, which I called the "employment test." In that paper, I wrote that to pass the test "programs must be able to perform the jobs ordinarily performed by humans. Progress toward human-level AI could then be measured by the fraction of these jobs that can be acceptably performed by machines." I had in mind all kinds of jobs that humans get paid to perform – from skilled and unskilled labor to managerial and office work.[43] For me, achieving HLAI implies (at least) knowing how to build artifacts that can do what we now pay humans to do.

Hayes and Ford reject the very idea of HLAI as a goal for AI research.[44] For one thing, they point to the fact that AI programs can already outperform humans in many areas. So, achieving HLAI may in some ways be too modest a goal. Furthermore, just as airplanes fly without mimicking birds, AI need not attempt to mimic humans. Observing that "there is no shortage of humans, and we already have well-proven ways of making more of them," they conclude that "human cognition is not in short supply" – implying, I suppose, that there is no need to automate the full range of human cognitive abilities.

Yes, even though we already have AI systems that can do some things better than humans can do them, there are still many, many human cognitive skills that we don't yet know how to automate. I believe there are two reasons why AI researchers will continue to strive to automate these skills. One is economic: The prospect of someday being able to employ AI systems rather than more expensive humans (no matter how many humans there might be) will sustain a strong and irresistible urge to build artifacts that can do what we now pay humans to do. The other reason is scientific: In their attempts to understand how the human brain works, people will continue to build computational models of its many functions. Thus, I think achieving some version of HLAI will continue to be AI's long-term goal.

Even though HLAI may be hard to define, there is money riding on a prediction that we'll achieve something like it. In 2002, Mitchell Kapor bet $20,000 that "By 2029 no computer – or 'machine intelligence' – will have passed the Turing Test." Kapor is the designer of Lotus 1-2-3, the founder of Lotus Development Corporation, and the co-founder of the Electronic Frontier Foundation. The Long Now Foundation posted this bet on its "Long Bets" Web page at http://www.longbets. org/. Ray Kurzweil accepted it. Both Kapor and Kurzweil gave arguments for their positions, and these along with detailed terms of the bet can be found at http://www .longbets.org/1#terms.

35.2.3 *How Do We Get It?*

Assuming that HLAI remains one of AI's goals, how do we achieve it? Can the technical tools that have been developed so far be utilized and combined in the right way to produce human-level intelligence? Will continuing research on machine learning, neural networks, graphical models, simulated evolution, knowledge representation, reasoning, heuristic search, natural language processing, behavioral mechanisms, and perception (especially vision) lead inexorably toward the goal? Or is something completely different needed as well?

John McCarthy mentions two approaches toward achieving HLAI. One is to attempt to simulate how the human intellect works, but, as he wrote, "Understanding the human brain well enough to imitate its function . . . requires theoretical and experimental success in psychology and neurophysiology." The other is to write programs that mimic human intelligent behavior, which is what AI researchers have largely been trying to do. McCarthy says that "It isn't a question of deciding between them, because each should eventually succeed; it is more a race."[45]

But should the racers aim immediately for the goal or pursue it in stages? I think the latter. In his 1961 paper "Steps Toward Artificial Intelligence," Marvin Minsky presciently wrote "It is my conviction that no scheme for learning, or for pattern-recognition, can have very general utility unless there are provisions for recursive, or at least hierarchical use of previous results." He might well have included, besides learning and pattern recognition, other aspects of intelligence as well. He went on to say[46]

We cannot expect a learning system to come to handle very hard problems without preparing it with a reasonably graded sequence of problems of growing difficulty. The first problem must be one that can be solved in reasonable time with the initial resources. The next must be capable of solution in reasonable time by using reasonably simple and accessible combinations of methods developed in the first, and so on. The only alternatives to this use of an adequate "training sequence" are 1) advanced resources, given initially, or 2) the fantastic exploratory processes found perhaps only in the history of organic evolution.

I think Minsky was exactly right. We've been trying the alternatives of "advanced resources, given initially," and simulating "organic evolution." These approaches have produced smart tools and other useful programs but not HLAI yet. What about working on a "graded sequence of problems of growing difficulty"? This strategy has been suggested and deserves serious consideration.

In his 1950 paper, Alan Turing suggested that "Instead of trying to produce a programme to simulate the adult mind, why not rather try to produce one which simulates the child's? If this were then subjected to an appropriate course of education one would obtain the adult brain . . . ." The "appropriate course of education" would then correspond to Minsky's "graded sequence of problems."

The staged approach is also reflected in a list of AI capabilities that Rodney Brooks would like to see implemented. He suggested they might have been "the foundation for the emergence, through an evolutionary process, of higher levels of intelligence in human beings." Here is his list:[47]

- the object-recognition capabilities of a 2-year-old child,
- the language capabilities of a 4-year-old child,
- the manual dexterity of a 6-year-old child, and
- the social understanding of an 8-year-old child.

Brooks points out that computer systems don't yet have these capabilities. I believe that working toward them would constitute important, and perhaps necessary, steps toward HLAI. With them, AI could implement Turing's strategy of educating machines in the same way as we educate people. But achieving these abilities will be very hard.

I think that Brooks had in mind achieving them by attempting to mimic human behavior – in this case the behavior of human children – the second of the approaches that McCarthy suggested.

As regards the other approach, namely, "understanding the human brain well enough to imitate its function," there has been work on that problem too. Several computer scientists are attempting to use concepts familiar to AI people to explain the brain. I have already mentioned the hierarchical models of the cortex proposed by Mumford, Hinton, Hawkins, Dean, and their various colleagues. Building on features of primitive sensory inputs from an array of pixels, for example, and ascending through ever-more-abstract percepts, these models are able to learn to classify images independently of size, translation, and orientation. Yet, to my knowledge, no work has yet been done to use these models for more than perception. Can they learn to understand, to reason, to plan, and to select actions? Looked at from the point of view of my "triple-tower architecture" (see p. 459), they have tackled the problem of how the brain might implement the perception and model towers but they have not yet tried to do anything with the action tower. Could one of these cortical models control a robot, for example?

Dharmendra Modha (1969–), manager of cognitive computing at IBM's Almaden Research Center in San Jose, California,[48] is among those pursuing a more "bottom-up" approach. In 2007, Modha's team carried out an historic experiment in which they constructed a computer simulation of a rat-scale model of the cortex (with 55 million spiking neurons and 448 billion synapses with spike-timing-dependent plasticity) that could function in near real-time using a BlueGene supercomputer with 32,768 processors and 8 TB of main memory. Modha is the principal investigator of a DARPA project to develop "Systems of Neuromorphic Adaptive Plastic Scalable Electronics" (SyNAPSE), or, in plain English, a project whose goal is to build a machine that mimics the actions of about 100 million neurons. That's twice the number of neurons in a rat brain but only about 0.25% of the number in a human brain. One can hope that the top-down and bottom-up approaches will meet in the middle somewhere.

Many of the laboratory efforts I mentioned earlier in this chapter are what I would call "HLAI-friendly"; that is, they are likely to develop the technology that will be needed by HLAI systems. One of them, the STAIR project, is working directly toward a challenge problem I posed back in 1996, namely,[49]

... to produce a robot factotum and errand-runner for a typical office building – an office building that is not specially equipped to accommodate robots.... The robot must be able to perform (or learn to perform with instruction and training – but without explicit post-factory computer programming) any task that a human might "reasonably" expect to be able to perform given its [the robot's] effector/sensor suite.
...
The second part of the challenge is that the robot must stay on-the-job and functioning for a year without being sent back to the factory for reprogramming.
...
I do not think that it will be feasible for the robot's builders to send it to its office building with a suite of programs that anticipate all of the tasks that could be given. I think the robot will need to be able to plan and to learn how to perform some tasks that the building occupants (who know only about its sensors and effectors) might expect it to be able to perform but that its programmers did not happen to anticipate.

Independently of the various concerns about the appropriateness of (and even the definition of) HLAI as a goal, I think we'll indeed achieve it. I won't predict when except that it will probably be sometime in this century. But what if we do? That's a topic I turn to next.

35.2.4 *Some Possible Consequences of HLAI*

Suppose that someday superintelligent machines become part of our society, to help us, to entertain us, and to do much of our work for us. They are likely to take various forms – humanoid and other varieties of robots, "presences" on the World Wide

Web, software on our home and laptop computers, and, possibly, special implants to aid our own intellectual functioning. Will we by then have constructed a social order that will preclude these machines fighting us and each other? Can we even define what it would mean for them to serve only socially acceptable goals?

These are concerns that have engaged both computer scientists and humanists. In 1987, Jack Schwartz wrote that many humanist thinkers

> ... express the amorphous unease of a much broader public. The fear is that the whole fabric of human society, which at times seems terrifyingly fragile, may be torn apart by enormously rapid technological changes set in motion by AI research as it begins to yield its major fruits. For example, it is possible to imagine that would-be dictators, small centrally placed oligarchies, or predatory nations could exploit this technology to establish a power over society resting on robot armies and police forces independent of extensive human participation and entirely indifferent to all traditional human or humane considerations. Even setting this nightmare aside, one can fear a variety of more subtle deleterious impacts, for example, rapid collapse of human society into a self-destructive pure hedonism once all pressures, and perhaps even reasons or opportunities, for work and striving are undermined by the presence of unchallengeably omnicompetent mechanisms. Certainly man's remaining sense of his own uniqueness may be further impaired, and he may come to seem in his own eyes little more than a primitive animal, capable only of fleeting enjoyments.[50]

To confront these fears, Stephen M. Omohundro (1959–), an AI researcher, founded Self-Aware Systems, an organization "devoted to bringing wisdom into emerging technologies."[51] He thinks "we must be very careful" about developing AI systems. That's because they will have, by design, various goals and drives. Among these are the goals to be self-improving and rational. They will attempt to accomplish these goals and the goals given to them by humans in the most effective manner possible. To be maximally effective they will have drives to preserve themselves and to acquire resources. These characteristics remind us of HAL 9000, the robot on the spaceship in the book and movie *2001: A Space Odyssey*. Omohundro wants to make sure that we build "wisdom," and not just intelligence, into our technologies. By that he means building in "human values, such as caring about human rights and property rights and having compassion for other entities." He thinks it "absolutely critical that we build these in at the beginning, otherwise we'll get systems that are very powerful, but which do not support our values."[52] I think Omohundro brings up valid concerns, but to put his version of wisdom into AI systems we'll first have to agree on just what we mean by "human values." That will be tough given that our different opinions about values often lead to wars.

After many years working on mobile robotics, Professor Ronald Arkin (1949–) of the Georgia Institute of Technology has devoted attention to the problem of ethical issues surrounding the use of military robots. His book *Governing Lethal Behavior in Autonomous Robots* explores how to program an "artificial conscience" in robots.[53] He maintains that such robots might behave more ethically in the battlefield than humans currently can. Of course many people believe that even *being* on a battlefield is unethical – for humans or robots.

The possibility of HLAI brings up many other interesting questions. Will they have "rights"? Can they own property? Could they be participants in civil or criminal judicial proceedings? Would they be able to create literature, music, and art? Will they have emotions or be capable of feeling pain or joy? Will they be conscious? Would humans become emotionally attached to some versions of them (and vice versa)? These are all fascinating questions, and many people have written about them.

Whether or not society accords intelligent artifacts rights and other legal powers will be up to us humans. After all, we have decided that several nonhumans (such as corporations) can have certain rights and obligations, and some humans (such as children) will not have certain rights. We'll have to make similar decisions about intelligent artifacts.

What about creativity? Here's an example. Professor emeritus David Cope at the University of California at Santa Cruz has developed a set of programs he calls "Experiments in Musical Intelligence."[54] These programs analyze the style of a musical composer and then use special "recombination" procedures to create entirely new compositions in that same style. Cope has used his software to produce works in the style of hundreds of composers. From one of Cope's Web sites you can download any of 5,000 MIDI files of different computer-created Bach-style chorales.[55] For those more inclined to listen to ragtime (in the style of Scott Joplin) check out ftp://arts.ucsc.edu/pub/cope/joplin.mp3. Cope argues that "recombinancy appears everywhere as a natural evolutionary and creative process."[56] Some version of it might well be the basis of all creativity, whether in literature, in art, or in music.

Marvin Minsky, drawing on his many years of research in artificial intelligence, has written an excellent book about emotions and other mental phenomena.[57] In its Introduction, Minsky claims that "Each of our major 'emotional states' results from turning certain [parts of the brain] on while turning certain others off – and thus changing some ways that our brains behave." The book describes what some of these brain parts, which he calls "resources," do and how overlapping clusters of them get turned on and off – resulting not only in various emotional states but in "the processes that we call 'thinking.'"

Minsky's book has a chapter about consciousness. He argues that consciousness "is a suitcase word, which we each fill up with far more stuff than could possibly have just one common cause." He argues that being "conscious" of something involves dozens of mental activities; such collections are different in different circumstances. Furthermore, neuroscience does not yet have a proper scientific view of just how all of these mental activities actually work. Minsky agrees with the philosopher Aaron Sloman, whom he quotes as writing[58]

The whole idea [of consciousness] is based on a fundamental misconception that just because there is a noun "consciousness" there is some "thing" like magnetism or electricity or pressure or temperature, and that it's worth looking for correlates of that thing.

. . .

There will not be one thing to be correlated but a very large collection of very different things.

Someday, I believe, AI researchers aided by (and aiding) neuroscience, will know enough about how brain "resources" work that they will be able to build artifacts that will convincingly argue that they are conscious. When that day comes I would have to assent to their claim, just as I assent to yours.

However, we have not done it yet, so the argument remains open. Computer scientist and Yale professor David Gelernter (1955–) argues that "... it is hugely unlikely, though not impossible, that a conscious mind will ever be built out of software." Nevertheless, he thinks that "an *unconscious* simulated intelligence certainly could be built out of software – and might be useful." [Might be?!] "Unfortunately, AI, cognitive science, and philosophy of mind are nowhere near knowing how to build one." He thinks that AI needs to refocus its efforts toward what he calls "the mechanisms (or algorithms) of thought ... " Until that time, he laments "AI is lost in the woods."[59]

Lost? I don't think so. Do we have long way to go? Probably, but we won't know until we get there. And until we do, we'll hear various calls to "refocus" both from within and from outside the field. In any case, we should continue to pursue many different approaches, guided by our best judgments. It's like heuristic search for a goal that we'll recognize when we achieve it.

As we work toward that goal, some of the consequences of HLAI will emerge gradually. For one thing, we'll become more and more dependent on smart machines. Just as we have become dependent on the automobile and other inventions of the past century and a half, it is already the case that our society depends in many ways on the Internet, sophisticated trading and auction programs, spreadsheet programs, weather forecasting models, and a host of other computer-related technologies. Furthermore, unlike as is the case with the automobile and the radio, fewer and fewer people understand these new technologies, putting us already in the precarious position of having to trust them.

As more and more "jobs" are performed by inexpensive hardware–software combinations, people who used to get paid for those jobs will have to find others or risk being jobless. That does not mean that the total gross domestic product will shrink; in fact it will probably rise. Society will need to find ways to let its members enjoy a just share of the wealth that machines create. In a thoughtful article[60] about these matters, the economist Robin Hanson likens the effects of machines substituting for human workers to an inexorably rising sea level ...

... with the tasks that are "most human" [those in which humans have an economic advantage over machines] on the higher ground. Here you find chores best done by humans, like gourmet cooking or elite hairdressing. Then there is a "shore" consisting of tasks that humans and machines are equally able to perform and, beyond them an "ocean" of tasks best done by machines. When machines get cheaper or smarter or both, the water level rises, as it were, and the shore moves inland.

This sea change has two effects. First, machines will substitute for humans by taking over newly "flooded" tasks. Second, doing machine tasks better complements human tasks, raising the value of doing them well.

Hanson believes that it is possible that the "machine ocean" might ultimately inundate all of "Task-Land" and that consequently "wages would fall so far that most humans would not, through their labor alone, be able to live on them, though they might work for other reasons." (Of course, automation may create new and higher peaks in Task-Land, slowing the effects of the rising ocean.) Nevertheless, he imagines that any small part of the greatly expanded wealth created by the machines should "allow humans to live comfortably...."

35.3 Summing Up

On that optimistic note, I come to the end of my story about the quest for artificial intelligence – a quest that is not yet complete. AI has explored a variety of paths, and in doing so it has achieved several successes and has assembled many powerful computational tools. One way to summarize the ideas and achievements I have talked about is to divide them into four main categories, namely, *complete AI systems* (ones that do things), *architectures* (organizational principles for AI systems), *processes* (routines that actually do the work), and *representations* (structures that are created, modified, and accessed by *processes*). Without trying to be complete, I'll mention some of what I think have been AI's major accomplishments in each of these categories.

- *Complete AI systems*: LT, Heuristic DENDRAL, Shakey, expert systems (such as MYCIN and PROSPECTOR), MSYS, speech recognition systems (such as HARPY, DRAGON, and HEARSAY II), Genghis, driverless automobiles (the whole class of them), Deep Blue, and other game-playing machines, RAX, and CALO.
- *Architectures*: Pandemonium, production systems, three-level architectures, Blackboard architectures, BDI architectures (such as PRS), behavior-based architectures, SOAR, ACT-R, and cortical models.
- *Processes*: edge- and region-finding filters (including Laplacian of Gaussian), spreading activation, parsing, resolution, A^* and its progeny, beam search, the Rete algorithm, STRIPS and other planning systems, case-based reasoning, clustering (such as k-means and AutoClass), constraint propagation, Bayes's rule, genetic algorithms and genetic programming, GSAT and DPLL-based methods, knowledge sources (such as those used in blackboards and for computing intrinsic images), backprop, circumscription, latent semantic analysis, Q-learning and prioritized sweeping, particle filtering, kernel computations (for support vector machines), and expectation maximization (EM).
- *Representations*: state (problem) spaces, vectors, logical expressions (including IF–THEN rules), semantic networks, programs (as data structures), blackboards, graphical models (including Bayesian networks and HMMs), grammars, neural networks, decision trees, scripts, frames, and augmented transition networks.

[The *processes* and *representations* they work on are usually intimately linked. For example, GSAT works on sets of propositions (in the form of clauses), Blackboard knowledge sources respond to and modify Blackboard items, and genetic programming operates on LISP-program representations.]

Several disciplines have contributed to AI's successes. As I wrote at the beginning of this book, the early AI pioneers used many clues about how to proceed – clues from mathematics and logic, from neuroscience, from linguistics, from statistics and probability theory, from control engineering, from psychology, and from computer science. Indeed, the substantial progress made in the quest for AI to date is due to the use of ideas from all of those disciplines. No overarching theory of AI has yet emerged, nor is one likely to in my opinion.

The quest will continue. What combinations of AI's methods, buttressed by AI's supporting disciplines, will be used in the intelligent systems of the future? No one really knows, so we'll have to keep all of them active on AI's "search frontier." Some of the ones developed early in the quest (and now perhaps forgotten) might with better technology be useful. Researchers who want to pursue the quest should be familiar with the full variety of AI's methods, its contributing disciplines, and (yes) its history.

Future writers will doubtless continue to tell the story of the quest. One of them, someday, will be able to report that some two and half millennia after Aristotle's musings, we now do have tools that perform our tasks, "either at our bidding or [themselves] perceiving the need . . ."

Notes

1. See, for example, http://www.iit.edu/~it/delphi.html. **[515]**
2. Excerpted from Oscar Firschein *et al.*, "Forecasting and Assessing the Impact of Artificial Intelligence on Society," *Proceedings of the IJCAI*, pp. 105–120, 1973. **[515]**
3. Good places to start would be sites maintained by the Association for the Advancement of Artificial Intelligence (AAAI), accessible from http://www.aaai.org/home.html; the European Coordinating Committee for Artificial Intelligence (ECCAI), accessible from http://www.eccai.org/; the Japanese Society for Artificial Intelligence (JSAI), accessible from http://www.ai-gakkai.or.jp/jsai/english.html (English version); the Chinese Artificial Intelligence Society, accessible from http://caai.cn/; DARPA's Information Processing Techniques Office, accessible from http://www.darpa.mil/ipto/; the German Center for Artificial Intelligence (DFKI), accessible from http://www.dfki .de/web/welcome?set_language=en&cl=en; and INRIA, accessible from http://www .inria.fr/index.en. **[516]**
4. See James Philbin *et al.*, "Object Retrieval with Large Vocabularies and Fast Spatial Matching," *Proceedings of the IEEE Conference on Computer Vision and Pattern Recognition (CVPR)*, 2007. Available online at http://www.robots.ox.ac.uk/~vgg/publications/ papers/philbin07.pdf. **[516]**
5. See Adrian Ulges *et al.*, "Content-based Video Tagging for Online Video Portals," *Third MUSCLE/ImageCLEF Workshop on Image and Video Retrieval Evaluation*, 2007. Available online at http://demo.iupr.org/videotagging/youtube.pdf. Also visit http://demo.iupr.org/videotagging/tagging-description.html to see a demonstration of the system. **[517]**
6. http://www.powerset.com/. **[518]**
7. Marc Raibert *et al.*, "BigDog, the Rough-Terrain Quaduped Robot," *Proceedings of the 17th World Congress of The International Federation of Automatic Control*, Seoul, Korea, July 6–11, 2008. Available online at http://www.nt.ntnu.no/users/skoge/prost/ proceedings/ifac2008/data/papers/4278.pdf. **[518]**
8. See, for example, http://graphics.cs.cmu.edu/projects/behavior_planning/. **[519]**
9. See, for example, http://www.psrg.csail.mit.edu/. **[519]**
10. See, for example, http://www.dfki.de/pas/f2w.cgi?ltp/musing-e. **[519]**
11. http://stair.stanford.edu/index.php. **[520]**
12. See, Ashutosh Saxena, Justin Driemeyer, and Andrew Y. Ng, "Robotic Grasping of Novel Objects Using Vision," *International Journal of Robotics Research (IJRR)*, Vol. 27, No. 2, pp. 157–173, February 2008. Available online at http://ai.stanford .edu/~asaxena/learninggrasp/IJRR_saxena_etal_roboticgraspingofnovelobjects .pdf. **[520]**
13. Siddhartha Srinvasa *et al.*, "HERB: A Home Exploring Robotic Butler"; available online at http://pittsburgh.intel-research.net/~ssrin10/HERB09/HERB09.pdf. **[522]**

14. See the DOMO Web page at http://people.csail.mit.edu/edsinger/domo.htm. Edsinger's 2007 Ph.D. dissertation, "Robot Manipulation in Human Environments," can be downloaded from that page. [522]
15. See http://www.yaskawa.co.jp/en/newsrelease/2007/04.htm. [522]
16. For a list of these see the "Robot Competition FAQ" at http://robots.net/rcfaq.html. [522]
17. More projects are described in a special issue on "Mixed-Initiative Assistants" of the *AI Magazine*, Vol. 28, No. 2, Summer 2007. [522]
18. http://www.darpa.mil/ipto/programs/pal/pal.asp. A DARPA brochure about PAL is available at http://caloproject.sri.com/PALbrochure.pdf, and a video is available at http://www.darpa.mil/ipto/programs/pal/docs/PAL.wmv. [522]
19. For more information, see http://caloproject.sri.com/. The first three years of the CALO project ended in earlty 2009. It is anticipated that another three-year project will follow to transfer the technology to actual applications. [522]
20. For a technical description of PEXA, see Karen Myers *et al.*, "An Intelligent Personal Assistant for Task and Time Management," *AI Magazine*, Vol. 28, No. 2, pp. 47–61, Summer 2007. [523]
21. Thomas G. Dietterich and Xinlong Bao, "Integrating Multiple Learning Components through Markov Logic," *Proceedings of the Twenty-Third AAAI Conference on Artificial Intelligence*, pp. 622–627, 2008. A preprint is available at http://web.engr.oregonstate.edu/~tgd/publications/aaai08-ilr.pdf. [523]
22. Matthew Richardson and Pedro Domingos, "Markov Logic Networks," *Machine Learning*, Vol. 62, pp. 107–136, 2006. Available online at http://www.cs.washington.edu/homes/pedrod/papers/mlj05.pdf. [523]
23. http://www.openiris.org/. [523]
24. http://www.companions-project.org/. [524]
25. Aaron Sloman, "Requirements for Digital Companions: It's Harder Than You Think," Position Paper for Workshop on Artificial Companions in Society: Perspectives on the Present and Future, Organised by the Companions Project, Oxford Internet Institute, October 25–26, 2007. Available online at http://www.cs.bham.ac.uk/research/projects/cogaff/sloman-oii-2007.pdf. [524]
26. Mark Craven *et al.*, "Learning to Construct Knowledge Bases from the World Wide Web," *Artificial Intelligence*, Vol. 118, No. 1, pp. 69–113, April 2000. A preprint is available at http://www.cs.cmu.edu/afs/cs.cmu.edu/project/theo-11/www/wwkb/overview-aij99.ps.gz. [524]
27. Noah S. Friedland *et al.*, "Project Möbius: A study on the Feasibility of Learning by Reading"; available online at http://www.noahfriedland.com/uploads/Moebius_Final_Report.pdf. [525]
28. See, for example, http://www.darpa.mil/ipto/solicit/baa/RFI-08-11.pdf. [525]
29. http://turing.cs.washington.edu/index.htm. [525]
30. See http://www.cs.washington.edu/research/knowitall/. [525]
31. http://www.cs.washington.edu/research/textrunner/. [525]
32. For technical details about TextRunner, see Michele Banko and Oren Etzioni, "The Trade-offs between Open and Traditional Relation Extraction," *Proceedings of ACL-08: Human Language Technologies*, pp. 28–36, Association for Computational Linguistics, June 2008. Available online at http://www.aclweb.org/anthology-new/P/P08/P08-1004.pdf. [525]
33. John McCarthy, "From Here to Human-Level AI," *Artificial Intelligence*, Vol. 171, No. 18, pp. 1174–1182, December 2007. Preprint available online at http://www-formal.stanford.edu/jmc/human/human.html. [525]

34. Edward A. Feigenbaum, "Some Challenges and Grand Challenges for Computational Intelligence," *Journal of the ACM*, Vol. 50, No. 1, pp. 32–40, January 2003. **[526]**
35. Irving J. Good, "Speculations Concerning the First Ultraintelligent Machine," in Franz L. Alt and Morris Rubinoff (eds.), *Advances in Computing*, Vol. 6, pp. 31–88, 1965. **[526]**
36. Jacob Schwartz, "Limits of Artificial Intelligence," in Stuart C. Shapiro and David Eckroth (eds.), *Encyclopedia of Artificial Intelligence*, Vol. 1, pp. 488–503, New York: John Wiley and Sons, Inc., 1987. **[526]**
37. Vernor Vinge, "The Coming Technological Singularity: How to Survive in the Post-Human Era"; available online at http://www-rohan.sdsu.edu/faculty/vinge/misc/singularity.html. The original version of this essay was presented at the VISION-21 Symposium sponsored by NASA Lewis Research Center and the Ohio Aerospace Institute, March 30–31, 1993. A slightly changed version appeared in the Winter 1993 issue of *Whole Earth Review*. That version (with some annotations by the author) is available online at http://wholeearth.com/ArticleBin/111-3.pdf. **[526]**
38. Ray Kurzweil, *The Singularity Is Near: When Humans Transcend Biology*, New York: Viking Press, 2005. **[526]**
39. See http://spectrum.ieee.org/singularity. **[527]**
40. See http://singinst.org/. **[527]**
41. http://www.agiri.org/wiki/Artificial_General_Intelligence_Research_Institute. **[527]**
42. Patrick Hayes and Kenneth Ford, "Turing Test Considered Harmful," *Proceedings of IJCAI-95*, Vol. 1, pp. 972–997, 1995. Available online at http://dli.iiit.ac.in/ijcai/IJCAI-95-VOL%201/pdf/125.pdf. **[527]**
43. Nils J. Nilsson, "Human-Level Artificial Intelligence? Be Serious!," *AI Magazine*, Vol. 26, No. 4, pp. 68–75, Winter 2005. Available online at http://ai.stanford.edu/~nilsson/OnlinePubs-Nils/General Essays/AIMag26-04-HLAI.pdf. **[527]**
44. See, for example, Kenneth Ford and Patrick Hayes, "On Computational Wings: Rethinking the Goals of Artificial Intelligence," *Scientific American Presents*, Vol. 9, No. 4, pp. 78–83, 1998. **[527]**
45. The quotations are from John McCarthy, *op. cit.* **[528]**
46. Marvin Minsky, "Steps toward Artificial Intelligence," *Proceedings of the IRE*, Vol. 49, No. 1, pp. 8–30, January 1961. Online version available at http://web.media.mit.edu/~minsky/papers/steps.html. **[529]**
47. Rodney Brooks, "I, Rodney Brooks, Am a Robot," *IEEE Spectrum*, Vol. 45, No. 6, pp. 62–67, June 2008. Available online at http://spectrum.ieee.org/jun08/6307. **[529]**
48. http://www.almaden.ibm.com/cs/people/dmodha/. **[530]**
49. Bart Selman *et al.*, "Challenge Problems for Artificial Intelligence," *Proceedings of AAAI-96*, Thirteenth National Conference on Artificial Intelligence, pp. 1340–1345, Menlo Park, CA: AAAI Press, 1996. Available online at ftp://ftp.research.microsoft.com/pub/ejh/selman.ps. **[530]**
50. Jacob Schwartz, *op. cit.* **[531]**
51. http://selfawaresystems.com/. **[531]**
52. Stephen M. Omohundro, "Self-Improving AI and the Future of Computation," lecture given at Stanford on November 1, 2007; transcript available at http://selfawaresystems.com/2007/11/01/standford-computer-systems-colloquium-self-improving-ai-and-the-future-of-computing/. **[531]**
53. Ronald C. Arkin, *Governing Lethal Behavior in Autonomous Robots*, Boca Raton, FL: CRC Press, 2008. **[531]**
54. See http://arts.ucsc.edu/faculty/cope/experiments.htm. **[532]**
55. Visit http://arts.ucsc.edu/faculty/cope/5000.html. **[532]**
56. The quotation is from http://arts.ucsc.edu/faculty/cope/experiments.htm. **[532]**

57. Marvin Minsky, *The Emotion Machine: Commonsense Thinking, Artificial Intelligence, and the Future of the Human Mind*, New York: Simon and Schuster, 2006. A draft is available from Minsky's homepage at http://web.media.mit.edu/~minsky/. **[532]**
58. For the note from which the quotation comes, see http://www.cs.bham.ac.uk/~axs/misc/consciousness/consciousness.june.18.96.txt. **[532]**
59. David Gelernter, "Artificial Intelligence Is Lost in the Woods," *Technology Review*, MIT, July/August 2007; available online at http://www.technologyreview.com/Infotech/18867/?a=f. **[533]**
60. Robin Hanson, "Economics of the Singularity," *IEEE Spectrum*, Vol. 45, No. 6, pp. 45–50, June 2008. Available online at http://spectrum.ieee.org/jun08/6274. **[533]**

Index

Printed in the United States
by Baker & Taylor Publisher Services